Technology and Values in American Civilization

AMERICAN STUDIES INFORMATION GUIDE SERIES

Series Editor: Donald Koster, Professor of English Emeritus, Adelphi University, Garden City, New York

Also in this series:

AFRO-AMERICAN LITERATURE AND CULTURE SINCE WORLD WAR II—*Edited by Charles D. Peavy*

AMERICAN ARCHITECTURE AND ART—*Edited by David M. Sokol*

AMERICAN LANGUAGE AND LITERATURE—*Edited by Donald Koster**

AMERICAN POPULAR CULTURE—*Edited by Larry Landrum**

THE AMERICAN PRESIDENCY—*Edited by Kenneth E. Davison**

AMERICAN RELIGION AND PHILOSOPHY—*Edited by Ernest R. Sandeen and Frederick Hale*

AMERICAN STUDIES—*Edited by David W. Marcell**

EDUCATION IN AMERICA—*Edited by Richard G. Durnin**

HISTORY OF THE UNITED STATES OF AMERICA—*Edited by Ernest Cassara*

JEWISH WRITERS OF NORTH AMERICA—*Edited by Ira Bruce Nadel**

THE RELATIONSHIP OF PAINTING AND LITERATURE—*Edited by Eugene L. Huddleston and Douglas A. Noverr*

SOCIOLOGY OF AMERICA—*Edited by Charles Mark*

WOMAN IN AMERICA—*Edited by Virginia R. Terris*

*in preparation

The above series is part of the

GALE INFORMATION GUIDE LIBRARY

The Library consists of a number of separate series of guides covering major areas in the social sciences, humanities, and current affairs.

General Editor: Paul Wasserman, Professor and former Dean, School of Library and Information Services, University of Maryland

Managing Editor: Denise Allard Adzigian, Gale Research Company

Technology and Values in American Civilization

A GUIDE TO INFORMATION SOURCES

Volume 9 in the American Studies Information Guide Series

Stephen H. Cutcliffe

*Administrative Assistant
Lehigh Science, Technology, and Society Program
Lehigh University
Bethlehem, Pennsylvania*

Judith A. Mistichelli

*Reference Librarian
Library of Congress*

Christine M. Roysdon

*Head Librarian, Reference Division
Linderman Library
Lehigh University
Bethlehem, Pennsylvania*

Gale Research Company
Book Tower, Detroit, Michigan 48226

85- 91

Library of Congress Cataloging in Publication Data

Cutcliffe, Stephen H
    Technology and values in American civilization.

    (American studies information guide series ; v. 9)
    (Gale information guide library)
    Includes indexes.
    1. Technology and civilization—Bibliography.
2. Technology—Social aspects—United States—Bibliog-
raphy.   3. United States—Civilization—Bibliography.
I. Mistichelli, Judith, joint author.   II. Roysdon,
Christine, joint author.   III. Title.   IV. Series.
Z5579.C87   [HM221]   016.306'4   80-23728
ISBN 0-8103-1475-4

To Ed and Steve

VITAE

Stephen Cutcliffe, graduate of Bates College, received his Ph.D. in American history from Lehigh University. He presently serves as administrative assistant in the Lehigh Science, Technology, and Society Program, where he edits SCIENCE TECHNOLOGY AND SOCIETY (formerly HUMANITIES PERSPECTIVES ON TECHNOLOGY), a national newsletter devoted to curriculum interests in the STS field.

Judith Mistichelli is a reference librarian at the Library of Congress and was formerly senior reference librarian for the social sciences and humanities at Lehigh University. She is a graduate of Wilkes College, received an M.S.L.S. from Syracuse University, and is presently pursuing graduate studies in English literature at Lehigh University. She has published several bibliographic guides, journal articles and reviews, and is coauthor of BEYOND TECHNICS: HUMANISTIC INTERACTIONS WITH TECHNOLOGY; A BASIC COLLECTION GUIDE, and the forthcoming JULES VERNE; A GUIDE TO SCIENCE FICTION.

Christine Roysdon is head librarian, reference division, Linderman Library, Lehigh University. A graduate of the University of Arizona, she holds an M.A. in anthropology from Kent State University and an M.S.L.S. from Syracuse University. Coauthor of AMERICAN ENGINEERS OF THE NINETEENTH CENTURY: A BIOGRAPHICAL INDEX and BEYOND TECHNICS, she has also published reviews, articles, and bibliographies.

CONTENTS

Contents

Contents

Contents

FOREWORD

As one who has lived long enough to be acutely aware of the changes in the
quality of life on planet Earth brought about by technological achievements, I
have quite naturally shared an interest in them and a growing concern with
the impact they have had, and will continue to have, on human values. Increasingly, however, I have felt it to be an almost hopeless task to thrash
one's way through the jungle of published materials on the interaction between
man and technology. What I have been looking for, I suppose, is a thoroughly
reliable guide to lead me to and through this mass of information and opinion.
In TECHNOLOGY AND HUMAN VALUES IN AMERICAN CIVILIZATION I
believe that I have found such a guide.

In consequence, it is a pleasure for me to express publicly my gratitude and
admiration to Stephen H. Cutcliffe, Judith A. Mistichelli, and Christine
Roysdon for the magnificent job that they have done. Although necessarily
selective, their guide is notable for the scope of its materials and for the pain-
staking, thorough, and balanced judgment revealed in the annotations. It is my
profound conviction that, considering its remarkable currency, it will be an
indispensable research tool in the field for years to come.

Donald N. Koster
Series Editor

ACKNOWLEDGMENTS

The acknowledgments page of any work is that one place where authors have a chance to thank those who contribute in so many ways to the final worth of a book, but whose names cannot appear on the title page. Unfortunately readers frequently look at such acknowledgments with a jaundiced eye, if they do not overlook them entirely. However, those whose names appear below will know what they have contributed and the sincerity of our appreciation of their aid.

Special thanks go to Professors Edward J. Gallagher and Steven L. Goldman, past and present directors, respectively, of the Lehigh University Science, Technology and Society Program for their constant, good-natured support and encouragement during the three years of this project. Equally important to the volume's compilation has been the assistance rendered by the library staffs of Lehigh University, Princeton University, the University of Pennsylvania, and Temple University. Special recognition must be accorded the staff of the Lehigh Interlibrary Loan Office--William Fincke, Pat Ward, Nancy Simmers, and students Laura Mihatov and Cindy Tatko--without whose help in obtaining countless books and journals such a work could not have been completed. Dorene Hari, Leslie Ramsey, and Angelo Spinosa also deserve thanks for their yeoman work in ferreting out titles, tracking down call numbers, and retrieving volumes. We would also like to thank Professors Roy Eckardt, John Ellis, and Roger Simon, all of Lehigh, for their advice with respect to various sections. Perhaps only another typist can truly understand the agony through which we put Mary Jo Carlen, Betty Miller, Sophie Chayka, Valerie VanBilliard and Eloise Miller in transforming the henscratching we like to call handwriting into the volume's present form. To them go our profound admiration and appreciation. Finally, we would all like to thank Doug Roysdon for his patience and humor.

INTRODUCTION

The view of technology as an intrinsically human activity has been increasingly recognized and voiced in recent decades. Professionals in diverse fields, including engineering, the sciences, medicine, law, business, and teaching, find that an awareness and comprehension of the social and environmental impacts of new as well as existing technologies are necessary to their pursuits. Invention proceeds in the "post-industrial age" at a pace well beyond an individual's capacity to grasp its implications. A guide to materials documenting not only the manner in which American values have molded attitudes toward technology, but also technology's effect on the formation of values will assist in the development of a many-faceted perspective on the role of technology in American culture.

Those investigating the interaction between technology and man are faced with a burgeoning output of research and comment which appears in a wide range of journals, monographs, and other materials. Scholars lament the existing gaps in specific areas, yet the aggregate sum of relevant publications is staggering. The diffuse nature of the field transcends the developed expertise of most inquirers. Our educational system of academic and professional specialty leaves scholars at a distinct disadvantage when approaching such cross-disciplinary study or attempting a holistic understanding of our society.

The present guide to information relating technology and values in America is designed with a threefold purpose: to provide a basis for undertaking investigations of the scholarship in various disciplines which impinges on the effects of advancing technology on civilization; to steer the user, through selectivity and annotations, to the most significant statements resulting from considerations of technology from the perspectives of social or humanistic values; and to furnish an extensive initial source for the researcher in need of information or commentary on specific topics in the field.

The guide has been developed to assist not only teachers, researchers, and students on the collegiate level, but also participants in and administrators of programs integrating technology, science, and society, as well as professionals and managers involved with confrontations between technology and man.

Introduction

The breadth of the topic, and the immense number of potential entries, required that we be highly selective, both in terms of quality and of subject. Scholarly materials received preference over popular selections, though influential works of the latter category are well represented. Technology, rather than science, is the object of concern, so that works that treat only the history of science, science policy, or philosophy of science, to name three areas, have not been included. Among works treating the technological enterprise, only those were sought in which human values are discussed, explicitly or implicitly. In the sections concerned with history, however, the reader will note a larger number of works that treat technological facts and processes with less emphasis on social implications. The inclusion of such works reflects the authors' belief that a grounding in the history of American invention and industrialization is prerequisite to an understanding of technology's impact on American civilization.

Though technology has been instrumental in forging an international culture, this compilation focuses on literature treating American concerns. Seminal works of such thinkers as Jacques Ellul and Martin Heidegger appear by virtue of their enormous influence on American writers. However, such areas as the international arms race or American technology transfer to developing countries do not fall within the volume's purview.

Although the authors are in substantial agreement with Jacques Ellul's identification of "technique as an organizing principle in all human affairs," to address all literature appropriate to such a definition of technology would clearly be an impossible task. Therefore, we have restricted our scope to those works which discuss man's confrontation with the tangible aspects of technology--machines, assembly lines, communication devices--rather than the bureaucracies and behavioral science methodologies that must also be considered "technique." Thus, the section on behavior control focuses on the implications of monitoring and control hardware as well as psychosurgery, rather than on literature on brainwashing. The section on the response of labor to industrialization encompasses a wide spectrum of literature, but the topic of unionization receives limited coverage.

Finally, it was decided that space limitations required a concentration on civilian technology, to the exclusion of the substantial literature dealing solely with war, military technology, and the arms race.

The authors have striven to maintain a neutral or impartial stance toward technology. Attempts have been made to provide a balance of statements expressing various viewpoints for both specific issues and general attitudes. Documentation of the changes in attitude toward technology over the course of American industrialization and technological development is also provided through the inclusion of publications spanning the period from the late nineteenth century to the present. The necessary emphasis on materials produced in the last two decades results from the mushrooming of considerations of the value implications of technology during that era. It must be recognized that the original faith in rationality and utilitarianism has waned in recent times. Questioning of technology's impact on man and his habitat, futuristic views, and sensitive statements of doubt, all of which have recently received credence, dominate the contemporary literature.

Several interdisciplinary bibliographies served as initial sources for basic monographs and journal articles. While all resources appear under appropriate sections within the body of the text, chief among them are Eugene Ferguson's A BIBLIOGRAPHY OF THE HISTORY OF TECHNOLOGY; Carl Mitcham and Robert Mackey's BIBLIOGRAPHY OF THE PHILOSOPHY OF TECHNOLOGY; annual subject bibliographies in the journals TECHNOLOGY AND CULTURE, AMERICAN QUARTERLY, CLIO, and ISIS; the annual compilation produced by the American Association for the Advancement of Science, SCIENCE FOR SOCIETY; and the current checklist provided in the Harvard journal SCIENCE, TECHNOLOGY AND HUMAN VALUES. Of the major indexing and abstracting services consulted, the most fruitful were AMERICA: HISTORY AND LIFE, SOCIAL SCIENCES INDEX, SOCIOLOGICAL ABSTRACTS, HUMANITIES INDEX, PHILOSOPHER'S INDEX, and ENERGY ABSTRACTS FOR POLICY ANALYSIS.

Many annual or book-length bibliographies and newsletters devoted to specific interest areas or disciplines were utilized, such as those concerned with biomedical ethics, communications, environment, energy, business ethics, planning, and futures studies. The interdisciplinary nature of the topic, however, dictated considerable use of bibliographies appearing in books and journal articles, as well as the constant scanning of recent issues of numerous journals regularly or occasionally publishing material relating technology and values.

The library collections of the following institutions were extensively searched and materials examined: Lehigh University, Princeton University, Temple University, the University of Pennsylvania, and the Library of Congress.

Materials chosen for citation and annotation herein include monographic publications, journal articles, bibliographies, symposia proceedings, government publications, as well as major journals and newsletters in the field, and indexing-abstracting services. They range in date from the latter half of the nineteenth century through late 1978 with scattered coverage of publications appearing early in 1979.

The diverse experience and scholarship of the three authors furthered the goal of a balanced and integrated treatment of the topic. Subject expertise in American history, anthropology, and literature, aided by familiarity with library sources in science and technology, as well as public policy and the humanities was merged and shared as a result of a mutual professional commitment to Lehigh University's Science, Technology, and Society Program (formerly the Humanities Perspectives on Technology Program).

Introduction

ORGANIZATION AND USE

The organization of such a complex and interdisciplinary field as that of technology studies, even when limited to works dealing with values, is difficult to say the least. Although it should be obvious to readers with even a slight familiarity with the included works that many of them could have been placed under more than one heading, some users no doubt will argue with our arrangement at some point; however, we have attempted to develop an organizational logic.

Believing neither a chronological nor a traditional academic disciplinary arrangement totally satisfactory to our interdisciplinary needs, we settled on a combination of the two. Given this combination, the guide as a whole and each section within it moves from the general to the specific. We have included bibliographies at the head of some sections, but only when directly applicable. Many of the books included in the guide have their own bibliographies, which are very useful for the scholar seeking additional sources. Part 1 of the guide includes those general titles which cover a multiplicity of disciplines, time periods, and points of view. This is the only section which is arranged by type of publication--book, article, symposium, anthology. All others combine such works, moving as noted from the general and historical to the specific and recent.

Central to the understanding of technology's impact upon society and its values is the historical background for and development of that context. Before one can have a sociological, ethical, or religious perspective on technology, and before a reflection in art or literature can develop, the technology itself must be established and grasped. Hence, we have begun with historical sections which provide the necessary background for understanding the technological origins of many of the value questions.

To make the best use of this guide, the reader may take advantage not only of the extensive table of contents, but also of the three indexes. In addition to author and short-title indexes, there is an extensive subject index, which not only indicates inclusive reference numbers for the major subject areas as delineated in the table of contents but also titles in other sections which touch upon the subject matter in question. This index has also eliminated the need for cross-referencing within annotations except where directly alluding to other titles included in the guide. All three indexes refer to item numbers rather than page numbers.

The last section of the guide, part 22, includes two lists of journals which will be useful to scholars delving further into specific topics. The first, which is annotated, contains periodicals which regularly publish articles in the area of technology studies, and the second, journals which occasionally publish such pieces. Finally, we have provided a brief list of indexing-abstracting services.

Part 1

GENERAL

A. BIBLIOGRAPHIES

1   Cohen, Hennig, ed. ARTICLES IN AMERICAN STUDIES, 1954-68: A
     CUMULATION OF ANNUAL BIBLIOGRAPHIES FROM AMERICAN QUAR-
     TERLY. 2 vols. Ann Arbor, Mich.: Pierian Press, 1972. 898 p.

     While this cumulation of the interdisciplinary bibliographies ap-
     pearing in AMERICAN QUARTERLY (no. 2303) simply reprints the
     yearly lists in chronological order, each annual bibliography is di-
     vided into subject areas such as art and architecture, econom-
     ics, history, literature, mass culture, science, and technology.
     Journal articles dealing with all aspects of American culture
     are indexed. The entries include brief annotations. There is
     an index to personal names mentioned in titles and annotations.

2   Dasbach, Joseph M. SCIENCE FOR SOCIETY: A BIBLIOGRAPHY.
     6th ed. Washington, D.C.: American Association for the Advancement
     of Science, 1976. x, 104 p.

     Covering periodical articles spanning one year and books span-
     ning four, the bibliography "focuses on ideas having to do with
     the interrelationships of humankind, the environment, science
     and technology." Categories include: general; bibliographies;
     aging and death; conflict; energy; environmental manipulation;
     ethics, values, responsibility, and science; health care; natural
     resources; pollution; population; technology and humankind;
     and transportation. Sparsely annotated.

3   Davenport, William H. "Resource Letter TLA-1 on Technology, Litera-
     ture, and Art Since World War II." AMERICAN JOURNAL OF PHYSICS
     38 (April 1970): 407-14.

     Over one hundred books and articles are annotated. Publica-
     tions selected give physics students a perspective on how sci-
     ence and technology are viewed by artists and writers. Inter-
     disciplinary considerations ranging from engineering design to

changes in attitudes, reactions, and vision caused by the dominance of technology are chosen. An annotated list of fiction titles is appended.

4   Goldberg, Maxwell H. NEEDLES, BURRS AND BIBLIOGRAPHIES: STUDY RESOURCES IN TECHNOLOGICAL CHANGE, HUMAN VALUES AND THE HUMANITIES. University Park: Center for Continuing Liberal Education, Pennsylvania State University, 1969. v, 200 p.

Part 1 encompasses literature on social and economic change, the "two cultures," and science and human values. Part 2 includes entries on computers, automation, and leisure; education; the humanities; and futurism. Not annotated.

5   Harrison, Annette. BIBLIOGRAPHY ON AUTOMATION AND TECH-NOLOGICAL CHANGE AND STUDIES OF THE FUTURE. Santa Monica, Calif.: Rand Corp., 1968. 34 p.

Entries (about 350) center on automation and employment, computers, education, and technology as related to human welfare. Appendix of futures-oriented organizations.

6   Kowalski, Gregory S. TECHNOLOGY AND SOCIAL CHANGE BIBLI-OGRAPHY. Exchange Bibliography no. 1200. Monticello, III.: Council of Planning Librarians, 1977. 31 p.

7   La Follette, Marcel Chotkowski. THE CITIZEN AND SCIENCE ALMA-NAC AND ANNOTATED BIBLIOGRAPHY. Bloomington: Poynter Center in American Institutions, Indiana University, 1977. 149 p.

The bibliography covers selected references pertaining to the public role of American science. Emphasis is on recently published materials and on science rather than technology. Useful list of periodicals.

8   Marien, Michael. SOCIETAL DIRECTIONS AND ALTERNATIVES: A CRITICAL GUIDE TO THE LITERATURE. LaFayette, N.Y.: Information for Policy Design, 1976. viii, 400 p.

Covering over a thousand items, primarily books, this broad and highly personal guide offers two lists. "Directions" surveys the literature on the "technological, affluent, service society," as viewed by both optimists and pessimists. "Alternatives" comprises literature on ecology, world order, government and economic reform, wealth redistribution, and spatial alternatives. A rating system and extensive indexes add to the compilation's usefulness.

9   Mistichelli, Judith, and Roysdon, Christine. BEYOND TECHNICS:

HUMANISTIC INTERACTIONS WITH TECHNOLOGY. A BASIC COLLECTION GUIDE. Bethlehem, Pa.: Humanities Perspectives on Technology, Lehigh University, 1978. v, 63 p.

Annotated guide to the one hundred books which provide the most significant statements resulting from considerations of technology from humanistic points of view. Overviews, anthologies, and historical and case studies are chosen, plus interactive studies of technology with art, fiction, science fiction, poetry, social impact, technology assessment, philosophy, and ethics. Major interdisciplinary journals are described.

10   Sharma, Prakash C. A SELECTED BIBLIOGRAPHY OF STUDIES IN SOCIAL CHANGE AND TECHNOLOGY. Exchange Bibliography no. 553. Monticello, Ill.: Council of Planning Librarians, 1974. 25 p.

11   Taviss, Irene. TECHNOLOGY AND THE INDIVIDUAL. Research Review no. 6. Cambridge, Mass.: Harvard University Program on Technology and Society, 1970. v, 62 p.

Long abstracts and bibliographic essay enhance the usefulness of the review. Part 1 is concerned with "Technology, Social Structure and the Individual" and describes important works on work and leisure, and family and the state. The second part, "Technology, Culture and the Individual," summarizes significant writings on values, psychological and social change.

12   TECHNOLOGY AND VALUES. Research Review no. 3. Cambridge, Mass.: Harvard University Program on Technology and Society, 1969. v, 55 p.

A bibliographic essay ties together publications abstracted in the subsequent four sections. Sections cover the interaction of technology and values; values problems in a technological society; social planning and the role of the social sciences; and economic, political, and religious values.

B. BOOKS

13   Aron, Raymond. PROGRESS AND DISILLUSION: THE DIALECTICS OF MODERN SOCIETY. New York: Frederick A. Praeger, 1968. xviii, 230 p.

Aron's study of the relationships in modern industrial societies between individuals and institutions stresses the contradiction between the reality and the ideal. The first part contrasts the hierarchical organization of industrial society to its egalitarian ideals; the second part compares the ideal of individuality with the realities of alienation and conformism dictated

by the "pitiless mechanism of production and economic growth."
Concluding chapters assess the outlook for a planetary society.

14   Bell, Daniel. THE COMING OF POST-INDUSTRIAL SOCIETY: A
      VENTURE IN SOCIAL FORECASTING. New York: Basic Books, 1973.
      xiii, 507 p. Illus.

      The resultant transformations in society caused by the change
      from a goods-producing culture to an information or knowledge
      culture are considered. The economic shift from manufactur-
      ing to service places science industries in a central position,
      gives rise to a technical elite, and creates tension between
      populism and elitism. A "meritocracy" is necessary to deal
      with the assessment of the effects of technological innovation.
      A final section explores questions facing the postindustrial
      society in the next decades.

15   Benthall, Jonathan. THE BODY ELECTRIC: PATTERNS OF WESTERN
      INDUSTRIAL CULTURE. London: Thames and Hudson, 1976. 224 p.
      Illus., bibliog.

      Literature, art, and architecture clarify the contradictory
      nature of man's response to technology. Wells, Verne and
      the futurist painters exemplified a romanticization of man's
      technical capacity. In opposition is the "recoil to the body"
      espoused by Blake, Rimbaud, dance, and avant-garde theater.
      An understanding of both positions can lead to the "liberating
      technology" evident in the works of Whitman, Wright, Bellow,
      and the cult of the motorbike.

16   Borsodi, Ralph. THIS UGLY CIVILIZATION. New York: Simon and
      Schuster, 1929. 468 p. Bibliog.

      One of the original American dropouts, Borsodi decries the
      uniformity and artificiality of factory-based life, calling for
      a return to domestic production, crafts, natural experiences,
      and natural pleasures. Above all, he says, "this civilization
      is ugly because of the subtle hypocrisy with which it persuades
      people to engage in factory production of creature comforts
      while improving conditions which destroy the capacity for
      enjoying them."

17   Boulding, Kenneth E. THE MEANING OF THE TWENTIETH CENTURY:
      THE GREAT TRANSITION. New York: Harper and Row, 1964. xvi,
      199 p.

      The twentieth century, Boulding believes, represents the middle
      era of a great transition of mankind. The basis of this is the
      scientific revolution, which is transforming the image of society
      from folk to scientific. Boulding warns of three traps which

must be avoided if the transition is to be completed: war, overpopulation, and entropy. The last pitfall can be avoided through the achievement of a stable, closed-cycle, high-level technology.

18   Braden, William. THE AGE OF AQUARIUS: TECHNOLOGY AND THE CULTURAL REVOLUTION. Chicago: Quadrangle Books, 1970. 306 p.

Through a colorful and provocative assemblage collected from reading and interviewing, Braden analyzes the "nebulous movement referred to as the 'cultural revolution,'" a humanist rejection of technology. Technology is credited with a major role in the creation of Yippies, drug addicts, black revolutionaries, and other figures of the time.

19   Brady, Robert A. ORGANIZATION, AUTOMATION, AND SOCIETY: THE SCIENTIFIC REVOLUTION IN INDUSTRY. Publications of the Institute of Business and Economic Research. Berkeley and Los Angeles: University of California Press, 1961. xv, 481 p.

The interplay between science, technology, and organization in contemporary industrial societies is analyzed. Based on the assumption that there is a need for flexibility in science and technology to ensure the continuance of human life and culture, this study seeks answers regarding how best "to organize the productive resources of an economy."

20   Bronowski, Jacob. THE IDENTITY OF MAN. Garden City, N.Y.: Doubleday, 1965. xii, 153 p.

In four essays, Bronowski discourses on a fundamental question of modern man: is he a person or is he but a machine? The first essay establishes man as part of nature, while the second describes the machinery of the natural world. The last two essays distinguish between the many-valued knowledge of the self and the single-valued knowledge of science. Knowledge of the self, gained through experience and the arts, teaches one how to be; science teaches one how to act.

21   Brzezinski, Zbigniew. BETWEEN TWO AGES: AMERICA'S ROLE IN THE TECHNETRONIC ERA. New York: Viking Press, 1970. xvii, 334 p.

A future "technetronic society" is foreseen, one shaped culturally, psychologically, socially, and economically by technology and linked fully by electronic media. Rather than a video utopia, Brzezinski envisions a tyranny of effective exploiters of the media over an atomized, easily swayed population. America occupies an ambivalent role as perpetrator of revolution, but principal preserver of the international status quo. To curb abuses, Brzezinski calls for a strengthening of pluralism and citizen participation.

22   Calder, Nigel. TECHNOPOLIS: SOCIAL CONTROL AND USES OF SCIENCE. New York: Simon and Schuster, 1970. 376 p. Bibliog.

In a knowledgeably written and popular book, Calder describes the current state and future capabilities of physics, biology, chemistry, oceanography, and engineering. His concern is for who or what is to control an increasingly influential scientific and bureaucratic elite and to what extent control can be achieved without sacrificing freedom in research. He calls for increased citizen participation in current science policymaking.

23   Callahan, Daniel [J.]. THE TYRANNY OF SURVIVAL: ON A SCIENCE OF TECHNOLOGICAL LIMITS. New York: Macmillan, 1973. xv, 284 p. Bibliog.

Drawing upon ideas on the dynamic of personality and culture expressed in Sigmund Freud's CIVILIZATION AND ITS DISCONTENTS (1930) and Philip Rieff's THE TRIUMPH OF THE THERAPEUTIC (1966), Callahan looks at some problems of technological society, particularly population control and genetic engineering. He concludes that the combination of an ethic of autocratic individualism and technological hubris must give way to a public morality and a science of technological limits.

24   Davenport, William H. THE ONE CULTURE. New York: Pergamon Press, 1970. xiv, 182 p. Bibliog.

By presenting an overview of the major studies which discuss the relationships between science, technology and the humanities, Davenport reveals the state-of-the-art of the merger of the two cultures. An update of C.P. Snow's seminal work is followed by a look at literature and art since Hiroshima. It also includes discussion of programs in the humanities, the history of technology at schools of engineering, and possible approaches to rapprochement.

25   Dorf, Richard C. TECHNOLOGY, SOCIETY AND MAN. San Francisco: Boyd and Fraser, 1974. iv, 428 p. Illus.

This well-researched textbook covers technological history and the relation of technology to economics, trade, and agriculture. The question of a technological imperative, particularly as it relates to the problem of automation and safety, is discussed. A concluding section reviews critical problems of the age and the technological future.

26   Dubos, Rene. REASON AWAKE: SCIENCE FOR MAN. New York:
      Columbia University Press, 1970. 280 p. Bibliog.

      The theme of these essays by a "despairing optimist" is the
      penetration of science into all areas of human life. Not
      concurring with dystopians or antitechnologists, Dubos con-
      tends that the present age is technological, but not because
      of the presence of machines. Man has come to perceive his
      life as governed by technological imperatives rather than by
      his own chosen values. Scientists and citizens alike must
      adopt an active role in determining technology's future course.

27   Dumont, Rene. UTOPIA OR ELSE. New York: Universe Books, 1975.
      180 p. Bibliog.

      The author confesses that "almost all my life I've felt thor-
      oughly revolted by something." He is revolted not only by
      the gravity of the world's population and resource problems,
      but also by the facile optimism of some futurists. Dumont
      predicts that the greed of rich nations "snatching the proteins
      from the mouths of poor children" will lead to conflict be-
      tween the haves and have-nots. He concludes with proposals
      for wealth distribution and population control.

28   Ellul, Jacques. THE BETRAYAL OF THE WEST. Tranlated by
      Matthew J. O'Connell. New York: Seabury Press, 1978. ix, 207 p.

      Almost ironically, Ellul, well-known for his critiques of the
      effect of technology upon society, defends Western civiliza-
      tion, noting its important legacies of freedom, equality, and
      individualism. "The end of the West today would mean the
      end of any possible civilization." Still pessimistic.

29   _____. THE TECHNOLOGICAL SOCIETY. Translated by John Wilkin-
      son. New York: Alfred A. Knopf, 1964. xxxvi, 449 p. Bibliog.

      The author presents his case for the growing pervasiveness of
      "technique" as an organizing principle of all human activities.
      Technique is defined as the "totality of methods rationally
      arrived at and having absolute efficiency in every field of
      human endeavor." The history of mechanization is interpreted
      as a process in which technique has permeated not only
      economic activities but government and social life as well.

30   Ferkiss, Victor C. TECHNOLOGICAL MAN: THE MYTH AND THE
      REALITY. New York: George Braziller, 1969. ix, 336 p. Bibliog.

      Technological change, which has transformed human society
      into a "seamless web" of interrelationships, necessitates changes
      if man is to survive. With almost unlimited power to change
      himself and the world, man is on the verge of an evolutionary

breakthrough. The new man, though not ecologically or psychologically altered, will have a systems mentality, with a
consciousness capable of controlling all interacting elements
in a social system. This outlook will be based on a philosophy of naturalism, holism, and immanentism.

31   Flanders, Ralph E. TAMING OUR MACHINES: THE ATTAINMENT
      OF HUMAN VALUES IN A MECHANIZED SOCIETY. New York:
      Richard R. Smith, 1931. 244 p.

      The two objects of this loosely written book are to "discover
      whether the machine be evil or no" and to discover future
      benefits of the machine. After a quick survey of the ma-
      chine age, Flanders optimistically concludes that engineers
      will find solutions to remaining problems, such as the danger
      of resource exhaustion. Flanders is more concerned about the
      immediacies of Depression employment problems.

32   Fromm, Erich. THE REVOLUTION OF HOPE: TOWARD A HUMANIZED
      TECHNOLOGY. New York: Harper and Row, 1968. xviii, 162 p.

      Fromm attributes a growing hopelessness in the world to mecha-
      nization, which has rendered man a passive appendage to the
      machine and has deprived him of privacy and personal con-
      tact. He concludes that technology must be humanized
      through participatory institutions and the encouragement of
      free, spontaneous expression.

33   Goodman, Paul. NEW REFORMATION: NOTES OF A NEOLITHIC
      CONSERVATIVE. New York: Random House, 1970. xiii, 208 p.

      Scientific technology has become a mass faith that we will
      not relinquish freely, but it is so tarnished that we are ripe
      for a New Reformation. According to the new faith, science
      and technology will become "prudent, ecological and decen-
      tralized"; education must become a personal experience. In
      "Notes of a Neolithic Conservative," Goodman sways from the
      subject to declare his alienation from his former allies, em-
      bittered youths.

34   Grant, George. TECHNOLOGY AND EMPIRE. Toronto: House of
      Anansi, 1969. 143 p.

      For this Canadian, technology appears to be the tentacle of
      a grasping American empire. In this loosely woven collection
      of essays, Grant's dislike for technology stems from a concern
      for preserving local heterogeneity and cultural heritage. Lib-
      eral education has failed in that it no longer offers alternative
      definitions to cultural excellence or human purpose to the
      technological imperative that dominated the past century.

35   Hamilton, David. TECHNOLOGY, MAN AND THE ENVIRONMENT.
      New York: Charles Scribner's Sons, 1973. 357 p. Illus., bibliog.

      Now that man has achieved unprecedented control over the
      environment, learning to live with technology has become his
      primary task. Hamilton's book is mainly a catalog of the past
      century's technical achievements in energy, materials, produc-
      tion, transport, food, and other areas. Written in a highly
      readable style for nonspecialists, urges constant vigilance to
      the social implications of new technologies.

36   Hardy, John T. SCIENCE, TECHNOLOGY AND THE ENVIRONMENT.
      Philadelphia: W.B. Saunders Co., 1975. x, 329 p. Illus.

      Convinced that the general public must be well informed about
      science and technology so that they can participate in its di-
      rection and control, Hardy presents the science behind crucial
      contemporary problems. This course for college freshmen and
      sophomores who are nonscience majors aims at an aesthetic
      appreciation of scientific knowledge and an awareness of the
      dangers of misapplied technology. Social issues confronted
      are the expanding universe, cybernetics, automation, compu-
      ters, electronic communication, brain manipulation, biomedical
      technologies, technology of warfare, pollution of the environ-
      ment, population resources, and the molding of the future by
      technology.

37   Harrington, Michael. THE ACCIDENTAL CENTURY. New York: Mac-
      millan, 1965. 322 p.

      Harrington analyzes the technological transformation of the
      Western world in the twentieth century. Contemporary society
      has become decadent and is floundering for loss of goals be-
      cause the control of technology is in private hands for private
      use. "Realities outstrip their vision." The author's only hope
      is through a new "socialist ideal" which is truly democratic.

38   Heilbroner, Robert L. AN INQUIRY INTO THE HUMAN PROSPECT.
      New York: W.W. Norton and Co., 1974. 150 p.

      The pressures which put the survival of our world in jeopardy
      are Heilbroner's concerns. The three major issues are popula-
      tion growth, the spread of "obliterative weapons," and the
      abuse of the environment. The book comprises three broad
      chapters: external challenges, socioeconomic capabilities,
      and politics. The author sees catastrophe in which the only
      hope is to face the future as a challenge with the willingness
      to abandon cherished values. For most of the world, "iron
      governments of a military-socialist cast must be faced."

39   Hellman, Hal. TECHNOPHOBIA: GETTING OUT OF THE TECHNOL-

OGY TRAP. New York: M. Evans and Co., 1976. xvi, 307 p. Bibliog.

A science writer tries to dissuade the reader of "technophobia" in this wide-ranging volume. He stresses that these are rational and irrational fears regarding technology and its interrelationships with man. Although somewhat glibly debunking "technophobia" as unfounded and unrealistic, Hellman does assert the dangers of a "blind, uncomprehending reverence for science and technology."

40 Herber, Lewis [Bookchin, Murray]. POST-SCARCITY ANARCHISM. Berkeley, Calif.: Ramparts Press, 1971. 288 p.

In a collection of essays written between 1965 and 1968, some of which were published in the periodical ANARCHOS, Bookchin makes suggestions for the nongovernance of a "post-scarcity society," which he predicts will be the "fulfillment of the social and cultural potentialities latent in a technology of abundance." Essays call for a union of ecological-utopian and libertarian-anarchistic ideals.

41 Jünger, Friedrich G. THE FAILURE OF TECHNOLOGY: PERFECTION WITHOUT PURPOSE. Hinsdale, Ill.: H. Regnery Co., 1949. x, 186 p.

In a highly pessimistic and negative work, Jünger asserts that technology has had a devastating effect on the spiritual and intellectual life of man. The wealth promised by early advocates of industrialization has been realized by only a few entrepreneurs. Socialism is not an alternative to economic dominance by a few capitalists but an ultimate surrender to a technical mode of organization. Even such seemingly harmless pursuits as photography and mechanized sports are viewed as further evidence of the permeation of technique.

42 Jungk, Robert. TOMORROW IS ALREADY HERE: SCENES FROM A MAN-MADE WORLD. London: Hart-Davis, 1954. 241 p.

In a loosely written travelogue, Jungk critically recalls technological developments observed on a trip through the United States. His stops include Alamagordo, a western airfield, a Princeton "thinktank," and New York skyscrapers. Observations exhibit skepticism about the worth of relentless progress, particularly if it entails the loss of privacy and a heightening need for material satisfaction.

43 Kouwenhoven, John A. THE BEER CAN BY THE HIGHWAY: ESSAYS ON WHAT'S "AMERICAN" ABOUT AMERICA. Garden City, N.Y.: Doubleday, 1961. 255 p. Illus.

In these revisions of speeches and previously published essays, Kouwenhoven finds technology, democracy, and mobility to be the foundations of our culture. He discusses how divergent liberal and technical education can serve each other by attempting to instill such values as adaptability, mobility, and the disdain of absolutes. Our buildings demonstrate the effects of specialization since too much has been done by engineers and industrial designers instead of by the architect, who can synthesize needs. A concern for process causes the essential American pattern of infinitely repeatable units evident from the assembly line to comic strips. Our advertising and litter tell of the paradox of waste and abundance.

44 _____. MADE IN AMERICA: THE ARTS IN MODERN AMERICAN CIVILIZATION. Newton Centre, Mass.: C.T. Branford, 1948. Reprint. Garden City, N.Y.: Doubleday, 1962. xix, 259 p. Illus., bibliog.

The American tradition in art developed from a conflict of European taste with the functional patterns of both settlement-builders on the frontier and technological design. The "vernacular," the forms produced by people dealing with an unprecedented environment, emerged the victor. What was originally purely functional frequently evolved into a unique "democratic-technical" beauty. The author traces this process with attention to specific implements and to prairie construction, railroads, bridges, architecture, literature, painting, jazz, and the cinema.

45 Krutch, Joseph Wood. . . . AND EVEN IF YOU DO. . .ESSAYS ON MAN, MANNERS, AND MACHINES. New York: William Morrow and Co., 1967. ix, 342 p.

In this compilation of essays which originally appeared in journals such as AMERICAN SCHOLAR, HARPER'S, PLAYBOY, and SATURDAY REVIEW, Krutch voices a disenchantment with modern man which is leavened by hope. The essays are grouped into five sections, the most relevant of which are "Men and Machines," "Manners and Morals," and "The Two Cultures." He discusses moon shots, invention, man as machine, "the sloburbs," the value of the humanities, literature in an age of science, and modernism.

46 Kuhns, William. THE POST-INDUSTRIAL PROPHETS. New York: Weybright and Talley, 1971. 280 p. Bibliog.

A comparative discussion of three traditions of contemporary thought on the machine is presented. Mumford, Ellul, and Giedion are identified as most prominent among those who have taken a look at technology's effect on human existence.

A second tradition is found in the media-centered theory of change espoused by Innis and McLuhan. Buckminster Fuller and other technological optimists form Kuhns's third tradition. A critical comparison of the three stances enables the author to map a rather broad philosophical ground.

47   Landers, Richard R. MAN'S PLACE IN THE DYBOSPHERE. Englewood Cliffs, N.J.: Prentice-Hall, 1966. 266 p. Bibliog.

Landers depicts a world of harmonious man-machine symbiosis. The "dybosphere" is a realm of artificially created things which behave in a lifelike manner. From current developments in space technology, bioengineering, and computer technology, the author projects the evolution of such a world, in which men--or partially mechanized cyborgs--cheerfully play second fiddle.

48   Marcuse, Herbert. ONE-DIMENSIONAL MAN. Boston: Beacon Press, 1964. xvii, 260 p.

Until recently, Marcuse believes, social progress depended on a tension between the "what is" and the "what might be." Through the diffusion of modern conveniences and the amelioration of working conditions, modern technology has eased traditional class tensions, joining worker and capitalist into a "welfare and warfare" state of sufficient harmony to resist change.

49   Mesthene, Emmanuel G. TECHNOLOGICAL CHANGE: THE IMPACT OF MAN AND SOCIETY. Cambridge, Mass.: Harvard University Press, 1970. ix, 127 p. Bibliog.

The author takes umbrage with three prevailing views of technology: that it is a blessing, a curse, or no longer worthy of intense study because the worst of its effects have passed. Mesthene, in contrast, views technology as a force that continuously generates new opportunities; however, the choice of a particular technological path closes other avenues. Therefore, technology is a "neutral" force that can be used for benefit or harm.

50   Muller, Herbert J. THE CHILDREN OF FRANKENSTEIN: A PRIMER ON MODERN TECHNOLOGY AND HUMAN VALUES. Bloomington: Indiana University Press, 1970. xiii, 431 p. Bibliog.

Defining modern technology as the "elaborate development of standardized, efficient means to practical ends," Muller explores its economic, social, and cultural consequences. Unlike Jacques Ellul and antimachine Luddites, Muller appreciates material and cultural goods which have resulted from technology and have contributed to the "good life." But many of man's innate drives, such as natural curiosity, the aesthetic sense and the desire for self-realization have been stifled by machine culture. Yet the author believes that it is "technically possible" for man to control the Frankenstein monster, and to "employ it for saner, more civilized purposes than he does right now."

51 Parkman, Ralph. THE CYBERNETIC SOCIETY. New York: Pergamon Press, 1972. 396 p. Bibliog.

Man's relation to technology is treated. The history of technology from the British industrial revolution to the development of the computer is surveyed. Chapters treat cybernetics, technology and government, and technology's relations with the arts, education, and the future. Useful bibliographies close each chapter.

52 Piel, Gerard. THE ACCELERATION OF HISTORY. New York: Alfred A. Knopf, 1972. 369 p.

A collection of essays on the interactions of science, technology and society. A basic theme in each is Piel's belief that "each man has personal responsibility for his role in the civilization of high technology." His explanation for America's failure to employ its technology for more productive purposes is the "acceleration of history" in which our technological knowledge is exponentially accumulative and hence difficult to accommodate into tradition, institutions, and value sets.

53 Pyle, James L. CHEMISTRY AND THE TECHNOLOGICAL BACKLASH. Englewood Cliffs, N.J.: Prentice-Hall, 1974. xiii, 354 p. Illus.

Chemists have played a large part in creating modern technological benefits and deficits. This text for students of chemistry is intended to infuse a sensitivity to social problems into chemists' academic training. The book covers the chemical aspects of the problems of energy, pollution, wastes, food, and drugs, emphasizing ethical considerations.

54 Ramo, Simon. CENTURY OF MISMATCH. New York: David McKay Co., 1970. xiii, 204 p.

Technology is not uncontrollable, but society must be reorganized to take full advantage of its benefits. Two contrasting scenarios for the future are outlined: a totalitarian dystopia based on the use of technology for enslavement; and the preferred alternative, a laissez-faire cybernetic utopia, the "electronic supermarket."

55 Reich, Charles A. THE GREENING OF AMERICA: HOW THE YOUTH

REVOLUTION IS TRYING TO MAKE AMERICA LIVABLE. New York: Random House, 1977. 399 p.

In a book whose impact has faded with the demise of the counterculture, Reich interprets the youth revolt as a coming to terms with the technological revolution and its undesirable consequences. Consciousness I, the original American Dream, became mired in robber barons, business chicanery, and excessive individualism. Consciousness II, the Corporate State, which emerged from the chaos of the Depression, must now give way, Reich avers, to the open, egalitarian, generous, responsible, and antirational ideals of the countercultural Consciousness III.

56   Rogers, Everett, and Shoemaker, F. Floyd. COMMUNICATION OF INNOVATIONS: A CROSS-CULTURAL APPROACH. 1962. 2d ed. New York: Free Press of Glencoe, 1971. xix, 476 p. Illus., bibliog.

Research published in some fifteen hundred sources, from various social science fields, was reviewed and synthesized to form the basis of this book. Various diffusion processes-- innovation, adoption, communication, etc.--are described from the literature, then distilled to a number of generalizations. A lengthy bibliography supplements the volume. The first edition of this volume was published under the title DIFFUSION OF INNOVATIONS.

57   Rose, John. TECHNOLOGICAL INJURY: THE EFFECT OF TECHNOLOGICAL ADVANCES ON ENVIRONMENT, LIFE AND SOCIETY. London: Gordon and Breach Science Publishers, 1973. 224 p. Illus., bibliog.

Fifteen chapters by experts in a number of fields discuss various dangers facing society. The first half addresses dangers to the environment posed by pollution, wastes, and pesticides. The second half assesses dangers to the individual posed by drugs, genetic manipulation, computers, transport, noise, stress, and leisure. Authors are mostly British; scope is broad.

58   Roszak, Theodore. THE MAKING OF A COUNTER-CULTURE: REFLECTIONS ON THE TECHNOCRATIC SOCIETY AND ITS YOUTHFUL OPPOSITION. Garden City, N.Y.: Doubleday, 1969. 318 p.

Despite their admittedly underdeveloped radical background, the American young, asserts Roszak, have been first to engage in the principal struggle of the day against the "technocracy," a society controlled by the technological elite. Though intellectually weak, with an eclectic taste for mysticism and "mind-bending" experiences, the counterculture deserves to win its battle against a fatally Apollonian culture. For, Roszak concludes, "we must insist that a culture which negates or subordinates or degrades visionary experience commits the sin of diminishing our existence."

59   . PERSON/PLANET: THE CREATIVE DISINTEGRATION OF IN-
DUSTRIAL SOCIETY. Garden City, N.Y.: Anchor Press, Doubleday,
1978. xii, 346 p. Bibliog.

A number of trends--from the growth of special-issue movements
for women, Indians, homosexuals, and others, to the reawaken-
ed interest in mysticism and spiritualism--suggest to Roszak the
beginnings of a revolt against massification. "We live in a
time when the very private experience of having a personal
identity to discover, a personal identity to fulfill has become
a subversive political force of major proportions." From an
acute vision of the self and a personalist ethos may evolve
heightened respect for nature and human relationships, accompanied by disenchantment with the oversized political and
technological structures that now threaten to engulf the individual.

60   . WHERE THE WASTELAND ENDS: POLITICS AND TRANS-
CENDENCE IN POST-INDUSTRIAL SOCIETY. Garden City, N.Y.:
Doubleday, 1972. xxxiv, 492 p.

Concerned about the encroaching artificial environment of technological society, Roszak fears that soon the world's remaining wilderness will be usurped for vacation playgrounds. Technology retains its capacity to inflict spiritual harm through such techniques
as mind control and terror-therapy. The growth of such techniques
and the spread of the artificial environment promise a gradual impoverishment of symbolism, mystery, and poetry, all incongruent
with rationalist-reductionist thought. Only in religious revivals
and homesteading movements does the author take heart.

61 Schwartz, Eugene. OVERSKILL: THE DECLINE OF TECHNOLOGY IN
MODERN CIVILIZATION. Chicago: Quadrangle Books, 1971. x,
338 p. Bibliog.

Schwartz's thesis is that "the crises that threaten human survival
are inherent in science and technology and are not amenable
to rectification by more science and technology." In a rather
popular exposition he traces the rise of science through the past
three centuries to its current status as a "faith." Global ill-
nesses--food, population, energy, waste--cannot be healed by
this faith. Eight "alternative principles" to save mankind are
offered.

62 Snow, C[harles].P[ercy]. THE TWO CULTURES: AND A SECOND LOOK.
Cambridge: Cambridge University Press, 1964. 107 p.

Snow's voicing, in 1959, of the unwillingness and inability to

communicate between literary intellectuals and scientists
served as a major catalyst to the programs of the last two decades which have broken through the barriers of "mutual in-
comprehension." In isolation, technologists and scientists become immured in what is predictable while artists remain
unaware of the forces changing the world. The meeting of the
two cultures, even if it is a clash, would spark imaginations
and creative chances. For Snow the answer is more interdisciplinary education.

63   Spengler, Oswald. MAN AND TECHNICS. New York: Alfred A.
       Knopf, 1932. 104 p.

       Man the toolmaker is presented as a tragic figure, who from
       inward spiritual necessity has developed his arts and is power-
       less to alter the development of machine-techniques. With
       each new invention man departs further from nature, Spengler
       laments, becoming more her enemy. That schism is the es-
       sence of man's tragedy, for nature will emerge victorious.

64   Susskind, Charles. UNDERSTANDING TECHNOLOGY. Baltimore:
       Johns Hopkins University Press, 1973. x, 163 p. Illus.

       A very brief survey of highlights in the development of modern
       technology sets the stage for more probing questions regarding
       its social impact, ethical dimensions, and future challenges.
       Susskind gainsays the pessimists, seeing no reason why society
       cannot revive itself through responsive human action. Some-
       what disjointed, but suggestive.

65   Taviss, Irene. OUR TOOL-MAKING SOCIETY. Englewood Cliffs,
       N.J.: Prentice-Hall, 1972. 145 p. Bibliog.

       Technology in American civilization is assessed. Taviss sum-
       marizes the theories of many major writers in the field con-
       cerning government decision making, values, freedom, social
       problems, and the city. Some essays have appeared else-
       where.

66   Thompson, William Irwin. AT THE EDGE OF HISTORY. New York:
       Harper and Row, 1971. xi, 252 p.

       An intriguing combination of history, anthropology, and fu-
       turology. It is Thompson's contention that "Western Civiliza-
       tion is drawing to a close in an age of apocalyptic turmoil
       in which the old species, collectivizing mankind with ma-
       chines, and the new species, unifying it in consciousness,
       are in collusion with one another to end what we know as
       human nature." At this precipitious edge only the mythic
       and the occult, not history, can help us.

67   Thring, Meredith. MACHINES--MASTERS OR SLAVES OF MAN?
      Stevenage [Engl.]: Peter Peregrinus, 1974. 115 p.

      To date, this engineer argues, we have constructed not a
      creative technology, but a cheap technology, whose purpose
      is to produce things profitably and quickly. If human factors
      are given more importance, engineers can as easily construct
      a technology-based utopia with machine slaves that will free
      humans to devote their lives to creative efforts. Specific
      technical innovations in energy and transport that would fa-
      cilitate this life of leisure are described.

68   Watkins, Bruce O., and Meador, Roy. TECHNOLOGY AND HUMAN
      VALUES: COLLISION AND SOLUTION. Ann Arbor, Mich.: Ann
      Arbor Science, 1977. ix, 174 p.

      An engineer who confesses frequent disagreement with arts-
      oriented colleagues and a technical writer have collaborated
      to produce this update on the clash of the "two cultures."
      A review of problems of war, hunger, and energy is presented,
      in which the culpability of the technologist is minimized.
      Brief summaries of the ideas of critics (e.g., Roszak, Marcuse,
      Ellul) and advocates (e.g., Bronowski, Kranzberg, Fuller)
      follow. For engineers, the tenets of major schools of ethical
      philosophy are presented.

69   Wells, H[erbert].G[eorge]. THE FUTURE IN AMERICA: A SEARCH
      AFTER REALITIES. New York: Harper and Brothers, 1906. Reprint.
      New York: Arno Press, 1974. 259 p. Illus.

      The inevitability and invincibility of material progress is seen
      as the dominant force directing the future of America. Wells
      relates his impressions of urban symbols of commerce: sky-
      scrapers, transportation systems, the Brooklyn Bridge. Mechani-
      cal wonders, such as the dynamos of the Niagara Falls Power
      Company, are carefully noticed: "These are altogether noble
      masses of machinery, huge black slumbering monsters, great
      sleeping tops that engender irresistible forces in their sleep."
      Undirected growth resulting in disorder is Wells's primary
      impression of the machine culture.

70   Winner, Langdon. AUTONOMOUS TECHNOLOGY: TECHNICS OUT-
      OF-CONTROL AS A THEME IN POLITICAL THOUGHT. Cambridge:
      M.I.T. Press, 1977. x, 386 p.

      The notion that there is an ordered, sequential "march of
      progress" is challenged. Technological change, Winner coun-
      ters, is better conceived as a "variety of currents of innova-
      tion moving in a number of directions toward highly uncertain
      destinations." Because contemporary technology cannot be

fully comprehended, it cannot be controlled. Despite its confusing countenance, however, technology has become a model
for society. The complex rational nature of the technological
effort has required a complete restructuring of the work,
political, and social environment in accordance with technological, not social, goals and desires.

71   Yablonski, Lewis. ROBOPATHS. Baltimore: Penguin Books, 1972.
xiv, 204 p.

Yablonski's "robopaths" are people who exhibit robot-like behavior and activities. Molded by the dehumanizing forces of
media and bureaucracy, robopaths manifest a fact-orientation,
conformity, hostility, ritualism and alienation. Yablonski
praises the spontaneous youth culture as a proper antidote to
robopathology.

C. ANTHOLOGIES AND EDITED WORKS

72   Bereano, Philip L., ed. TECHNOLOGY AS A SOCIAL AND POLITICAL
PHENOMENON. New York: John Wiley and Sons, 1976. viii, 544 p.

In assembling this anthology, the editor focuses on general and
theoretical concepts, organized into clusters of materials emphasizing a theme. Selections include introductions to books,
such as Murray Bookchin's POST-SCARCITY ANARCHISM
(no. 40), and Herbert Marcuse's ONE-DIMENSIONAL MAN
(no. 48), widely reprinted articles (e.g., John McDermott's
"Technology, the Opiate of the Intellectuals," no. 138), and
a selection of shorter, vehement pieces.

73   Boyko, Hugo, ed. SCIENCE AND THE FUTURE OF MANKIND. Den
Haag, Holland: Junk, 1961. viii, 380 p. Illus., maps.

Twenty-one scientists and humanists explore the human problems that have emerged in the wake of scientific and technological development. Given particular attention are food
supply, natural resources, genetics, and the scientific impact
on civilization as a whole.

74   Burke, John G., ed. THE NEW TECHNOLOGY AND HUMAN
VALUES. 2d ed., rev. Belmont, Calif.: Wadsworth Publishing Co.,
1972. ix, 266 p.

The interaction between basic science and applied science is
what Burke refers to as the "new technology." Due to its
wide-ranging scope and imaginative inclusions, this anthology
has become a standard text. Chapters cover basic issues involving technology's relation to values, the environment, the

individual, government, and the future of man. The concluding chapter looks at means of achieving control over technology. The brief selections have been drawn from scholarly
journals, government reports and popular magazines. Introductions
by the editor integrate each section.

75   Clarke, Robin, ed. NOTES FOR THE FUTURE: AN ALTERNATIVE
      HISTORY OF THE PAST DECADE. New York: Universe Books, 1976.
      238 p.

      It is hoped that those utilizing this critical "history" will not
      be condemned to repeat it. Clarke has assembled some well-
      known papers and portions of books that are highly critical
      of contemporary technology and its misuses. Emphasis is on
      ecological and resources issues, with alternative technology
      espoused as an answer. Selections include well-known pieces
      by Georg Borgstrom, Garrett Hardin, E.F. Schumacher,
      Theodore Roszak, Robin Clarke, and Murray Bookchin.

76   Cooper, Chester L., ed. GROWTH IN AMERICA. Westport, Conn.:
      Greenwood Press, 1976. 262 p.

      Produced by outside scholars for use in a series of conferences
      sponsored by the Woodrow Wilson International Center for
      Scholars, these essays address the American growth experience.
      Aspects of growth that have given rise to contemporary con-
      cern are emphasized. Eugene B. Skolnikoff writes on the
      difficulty of governing complexity. John Holdren expresses
      skepticism about the efficacy of technological "fixes" in over-
      coming complexities posed by the environment. To provide
      a historical perspective, growth's portrayal in art, literature,
      and historical documents is surveyed, with accompanying il-
      lustrative plates. Concluding papers assess the impact of
      growth on the American future.

77   Douglas, Jack D., ed. FREEDOM AND TYRANNY: SOCIAL PROB-
      LEMS IN A TECHNOLOGICAL SOCIETY. New York: Alfred A.
      Knopf, 1970. xii, 289 p.

      The centralization, size, and specialization that characterize
      contemporary technology form, in Douglas's view, an imminent
      threat to traditional freedoms. Excerpts from Herbert Marcuse
      and Jacques Ellul suggest that this tyranny is secret and yet
      omnipresent. Specific forms of technological tyranny are
      identified by other authors included in the anthology. The
      worst form is the dominance of expertise.

78   _____. THE TECHNOLOGICAL THREAT. Englewood Cliffs, N.J.:
      Prentice-Hall, 1971. vi, 185 p.

      Perceiving technology to be the ultimate challenge to freedom and individualism, Douglas proposes to expose the nature of the technological transformation. A number of widely anthologized articles provide documentation. These include one by Daniel Bell on post-industrial society, by Robert Nisbet on ethical decision making, by Norbert Wiener on automation effects, by Carl Rogers and B.F. Skinner on behavior control, and by Edward T. Chase on politics and technology.

79 Fishwick, Marshall W., ed. AMERICAN STUDIES IN TRANSITION. Philadelphia: University of Pennsylvania Press, 1964. 329 p.

Essays which explore the complexity of American culture are grouped into three categories: discussions of modes of understanding America, methods of teaching, and the impact of American studies abroad. Included are John Kouwenhoven's argument that our preoccupation with words has neglected things, Brooke Hindle's consideration of the teaching of the history of science and technology as a way to bridge the two cultures, the role of communication in social synthesis by John Hague, and Lawrence Chisholm's analysis of expanded human possibilities.

80 Gleison, Patrick, ed. AMERICA CHANGING. Columbus, Ohio: Charles E. Merrill Publishing Co., 1968. viii, 431 p.

This collection of essays treating the social questions of the sixties is composed of widely reprinted papers by well-known figures. The second part, on the city, includes pieces by Daniel Bell, Susanne Langer, Marshall McLuhan, and Dorothy Lee. The sixth part, on man and machines, encompasses noted essays by Lewis Mumford, Oscar Handlin, Hannah Arendt, and others.

81 Knelman, Fred H., ed. NINETEEN EIGHTY FOUR AND ALL THAT: MODERN SCIENCE, SOCIAL CHANGE AND HUMAN VALUES. Belmont, Calif.: Wadsworth Publishing Co., 1971. xiv, 314 p.

This reader in the sociology of science addresses a number of key concerns relating to the control of technology's impact on government, values and social structure. Opening papers by William Ogburn, Jacques Ellul, Derek de Solla Price, and Alvin Weinberg offer widely varying viewpoints on the nature of technological change. Specific threats posed by pollution, genetic manipulation, new chemicals, nuclear energy, and information technology are discussed in subsequent sections. Robert Jungk, Barry Commonor, and Aldous Huxley are among those assessing the gravity of the crisis for values.

82 Kostelanetz, Richard, ed. BEYOND LEFT AND RIGHT: RADICAL THOUGHT FOR OUR TIMES. New York: William Morrow and Co., 1968. xli, 436 p. Bibliog.

Billed as "an anthology of innovative ideas," this collection
concentrates on the "threats and opportunities implicit in new
technologies--the primary sources of social change--as well
as the basic problems and possibilities." Kostelanetz contends
that only thinking that transcends such old and outmoded po-
larities as "right" and "left" can confront and shape the future. Contributors to the book span the political and intellectual spectrum: Herman Kahn, Kenneth Boulding, Robert Theobold, Marshall McLuhan, Zbigniew Brzezinski, Paul Goodman,
Daniel Bell, and others.

83 _____. THE EDGE OF ADAPTATION: MAN AND THE EMERGING
SOCIETY. Englewood Cliffs, N.J.: Prentice-Hall, 1973. xii, 180 p.

Described as less optimistic in tone than the previous collection, this anthology evinces the editor's desire for a return to
the ebullient sixties. Essays by Buckminster Fuller and John
Diebold describe promising technological advances. Other
authors discuss the need for planning and the threat posed by
such societal and behavioral trends as family disintegration
and drug abuse. An optimistic piece by Herman Kahn is
placed between Hasan Ozebekhan's lament over the triumph of
technology and Murray Bookchin's paean to vanishing spontaneity.

84 _____. SOCIAL SPECULATIONS: VISIONS FOR OUR TIME. New
York: William Morrow and Co., 1971. 306 p. Bibliog.

In a sequel to BEYOND LEFT AND RIGHT (no. 82), Kostelanetz
attempts to assemble "images of human possibility" that envision
the rapidly approaching future. A strong futurist component
is provided by Isaac Asimov, Herman Kahn, and Robert
Deutsch. The futures of automation, communication, and
transport technologies are projected by John Pierce and J.C.
Licklide. Other sections speculate on the future of government and the metropolis.

85 Krohn, Wolfgang; Layton, Edwin T., Jr.; and Weingart, Peter, eds.
THE DYNAMICS OF SCIENCE AND TECHNOLOGY: SOCIAL VALUES,
TECHNICAL NORMS AND SCIENTIFIC CRITERIA IN THE DEVELOP-
MENT OF KNOWLEDGE. Boston: D. Reidel Publishing Co., 1978.
xi, 293 p.

Interrelations of science and technology are studied from the
viewpoints of history, sociology, economics, and philosophy.
Part 1 reconsiders the "conceptual distance." In the second
part, three historical case studies look at the interaction of
science and technology in the development of the turbine,
the radio, and combustion technology. The social history of
nineteenth-century education and the appearance of the European assembly line are featured in the third part. Concluding
papers deal with a perceived "scientification of technology."

86   Kwiat, Joseph J., and Turpie, Mary C., eds. STUDIES IN AMERICAN
      CULTURE: DOMINANT IDEAS AND IMAGES. Minneapolis: University
      of Minnesota Press, 1960. viii, 233 p.

      With prestigious contributors from the field of American studies,
      articles chosen for this book of readings present outstanding
      interdisciplinary views. The following studies are among those
      included: John Ward, "The Meaning of Lindbergh's Flight";
      David Weimer, "The Man with the Hoe and the Good Ma-
      chine"; Bernard Bowron, Leo Marx, and Arnold Rose, "Litera-
      ture and Covert Culture"; J.C. Levenson, "Henry Adams and
      the Culture of Science"; and David Noble, "Dreiser and
      Veblen and the Literature of Cultural Change."

87   Lauda, Donald P., and Ryan, Ronald D., eds. ADVANCING TECHNOL-
      OGY: ITS IMPACT ON SOCIETY. Dubuque, Iowa: William C. Brown
      Publishers, 1971. xvii, 536 p.

      A balanced selection of materials by prominent authors, re-
      printed from books, journals, addresses, and popular sources
      composes this anthology. Part 1, a chronology of technology,
      assesses its role as a prime mover in history, and features work
      by Jacques Ellul, Melvin Kranzberg, and Carroll Pursell.
      Part 2 turns to the world of work, covering the issues of auto-
      mation, leisure, and women's entry into the work force. Au-
      thors include Ben Seligman, Sebastian de Grazia, and Robert
      Theobold. The problem of technological change and projections
      for the future are themes for the last two parts.

88   Lawless, Edward W., ed. TECHNOLOGY AND SOCIAL SHOCK.
      New Brunswick, N.J.: Rutgers University Press, 1977. xli, 616 p.
      Illus., bibliog.

      As a means of illustrating the effect of technology on contempo-
      rary lives and institutions, the author presents a representative
      series of case studies, made up of episodes of public alarm or
      "social shock" over specific technology-related developments.
      Forty-five studies touch on such diverse problems as artificial
      insemination, fluoridation, DDT, and taconite in Lake Superior.
      Each case history includes background material, a historical
      synopsis, and the disposition. Theoretical and methodological
      appendixes supplement.

89   Levine, George, and Thomas, Owen, eds. THE SCIENTIST VS. THE
      HUMANIST. New York: W.W. Norton and Co., 1963. viii, 184 p.
      Bibliog.

      Designed for a course in English composition, the readings in
      this volume span the seventeenth to the twentieth centuries.
      The selections focus on the values in the sciences and the
      humanities and the benefits to be derived from their combina-

tion. Readings, gleaned from scholarly and popular journals, include classic statements by C.P. Snow, Herbert Muller, Matthew Arnold, Thomas Huxley, Robert Oppenheimer, H.M. Jones, and P.W. Bridgman. Fiction and poetry by Jonathan Swift, Charles Dickens, Walt Whitman, and Isaac Asimov round out the volume. Questions for discussion and writing are provided.

90   Lewis, W. David, and Griessman, B. Eugene, eds. THE SOUTHERN MYSTIQUE: THE IMPACT OF TECHNOLOGY ON HUMAN VALUES IN A CHANGING REGION. University: University of Alabama Press, 1977. xx, 131 p.

Opening this volume is a reconsideration of the North-South differential as it has been affected by Southern industrialization. Lewis and Melvin Kranzberg review direct impacts of technological change, while other authors measure more indirect effects on race relations and education. Griessman offers a tentative answer to the question "Will the South Rise Again or Just Roll Over?"

91   Moore, Wilbert E[llis], ed. TECHNOLOGY AND SOCIAL CHANGE. Chicago: Quadrangle Books, 1972. vii, 236 p.

Twenty-one articles previously published in the NEW YORK TIMES MAGAZINE and prefaced by a lengthy introduction furnish a balanced overview of the technology-society interface. The first part considers consequences of technological change, including brief essays by William F. Ogburn, Kenneth Keniston, Eric Hoffer, and Richard Kostelanetz. The second part focuses on the process of change, while in the third, authors debate the sort of change desirable for the future. Brooks Atkinson supplies a defense of materialism; Herbert J. Gan calls for an "equality revolution." Jacob Bronowski contends that "1984 may be a good year."

92   Olsen, Fred A., ed. TECHNOLOGY: A REIGN OF BENEVOLENCE AND DESTRUCTION. New York: Mss. Information, 1974. 250 p. Illus., bibliog.

Man's association with technology and the contemporary issues created by technology are examined in this anthology. The essays are grouped in four sections: historical perspectives, disordered technology, ordered technology, and future perspectives. Classic statements, such as Garrett Hardin's "Tragedy of the Commons," are joined by discussions of the effects of technology on women's work, the progress of invention, pro and con thoughts on DDT, technology and the Jesus movement, and the culture of machine living. Among the contributors are René Dubos, Max Lerner, E.J. Mishan, and Herbert J. Muller.

93   Rochlin, Gene I., ed. SCIENTIFIC TECHNOLOGY AND SOCIAL
CHANGE: READINGS FROM SCIENTIFIC AMERICAN. San Francisco:
W.H. Freeman and Co., 1974. 403 p.

Thirty-one articles previously published in the magazine and
written by physical and biological scientists, historians, and
social scientists illuminate changes stimulated by physics and
physics-based technology. The first section chronicles the
origins of technology from the first wheeled vehicle to the
bicycle. The next two parts examine the relationship between
science and technology beginning in the nineteenth century,
from the steam engine to such "soft" developments as information technology. The last two parts focus on energy, culminating in an examination of waste-heat effects, described as the
"ultimate waste."

94   Spiegel-Rosing, Ina, and Price, Derek de Solla, eds. SCIENCE,
TECHNOLOGY AND SOCIETY: A CROSS-DISCIPLINARY PERSPECTIVE.
Beverly Hills, Calif.: Sage Publications, 1977. 607 p. Bibliog.

The first part of this impressive collection looks at the "contextual values of science and technology." Editor Spiegel-
Rosing provides an overview of recent studies. Social studies
of science and technology from differing perspectives are
found in the second section. Science policy studies, brought
together in the third, include essays by Sanford A. Lakoff,
Dorothy Nelkin, and Harvey M. Sapolsky. The bibliographies
at the end of each review article enhance the usefulness of a
rich, scholarly compendium.

95   "Technology and the Future of Man." HUMANITIES 14 (February 1978):
1-138.

Potential changes generated by technology in values, attitudes,
and the surroundings effecting man are explored in this special
issue. The wide range of topics includes the control of technologies of violence (Victor Ferkiss), the meaning of technology (Charles Sabatino), an integration of the spiritual and
artistic with the practical (Andrée Bindewald), technology
assessment (Lynton Caldwell), the effect of the media on communication skills (Ann Davis), technological variables and work
performance (James Russell and Albert Mehrabian), and merging
of technological phenomena in the human condition (Roger
Evered). A partially annotated, selective bibliography covering the past ten years is provided.

96   Teich, Albert H., ed. TECHNOLOGY AND MAN'S FUTURE. 2d ed.
New York: St. Martin's Press, 1977. xi, 375 p.

Scientific, philosophical, empirical, and policy-oriented perspectives on the relation of technology to society are furnished.

The first section features the views of such scientists as Alvin
Weinberg and Christopher Freeman, reflecting the assumptions
that science and technology will eventually provide solutions
to technical problems. The writings of several contemporary
philosophers--including Herbert Marcuse, Jacques Ellul, and
Marshall McLuhan--provide a spectrum of views from "apocalyptic to utopian" in the second part. Concluding papers on
technology assessment encompass statements by Harvey Brooks
and Raymond Bowers, Joseph Coates, the U.S. Office of
Technology Assessment, and Langdon Winner.

97   Truitt, Willis H., and Solomons, T.W. Graham, eds. SCIENCE,
      TECHNOLOGY AND FREEDOM. Boston: Houghton Mifflin, 1974.
      xii, 272 p.

      This collection of readings addresses the rise of science and
      technology to its current dominant societal position, and the
      political, ethical, cultural, and environmental implications
      of that dominance. Chapter 1 provides a general background
      to the important issues, featuring papers by Jacques Ellul,
      C.P. Snow, Jacob Bernal, and Paul Goodman. The historical
      and philosophical rise of science and technology is chronicled
      in the second chapter by authors including Dirk Struik,
      Thomas S. Kuhn, and Stephen E. Toulmin. Social questions
      of work and leisure are taken up by D.N. Michael, David
      Riesman, and others. Concluding papers, authored by Aldous
      Huxley, Barry Commoner, and René Dubos address environmen-
      tal concerns. Recommended supplementary readings close
      each chapter.

98   Walker, Charles R[umford], ed. TECHNOLOGY, INDUSTRY AND
      MAN: THE AGE OF ACCELERATION. New York: McGraw-Hill,
      1968. 362 p. Bibliog.

      An overall view of the impact of the technological revolution
      on the recent life and work of man is supplied. Each chapter
      includes an introduction by the editor and a bibliography.
      Chapters cover the history of industrialization; studies of man
      in the factory; man-machine problems; automation; new tech-
      nologies in management, labor, and government; and the
      knowledge revolution. Among the well-known sociologists
      and historians contributing are Charles Singer, Lewis Mumford,
      William F. Whyte, Robert Merton, and Floyd Mann.

D. SYMPOSIA AND CONFERENCES

99   Albertson, Peter, and Barnett, Margery, eds. "Environment and Society
      in Transition." ANNALS OF THE NEW YORK ACADEMY OF SCI-
      ENCES 184 (June 1971): 1-699.

The papers and working group discussions of the International Joint Conference on Environment and Society in Transition, 1970, are compiled. This transnational and interdisciplinary undertaking focuses on the social consequences and policy implications of scientific knowledge. Participants provide a review of significant relevant developments in science fields and speculate on the future. Papers include "Social Implications of the Computer," "Psychological Adaptation in a World of Programmed Machines," "From Economic to Socioeconomic Development," and "The Environmental Consequences of Man's Quest for Food."

100   Blanpied, William A., and Weisman-Dermer, Wendy, eds. PROCEEDINGS OF THE AAAS INTERDISCIPLINARY WORKSHOP ON THE INTERRELATIONS BETWEEN SCIENCE AND TECHNOLOGY, AND ETHICS AND VALUES. Washington, D.C.: American Association for the Advancement of Science, 1975. 116 p.

Scholars from a variety of disciplines in the humanities, social sciences, natural sciences, and engineering exchanged thoughts on differing disciplinary perceptions and methodologies. Papers include Thomas Nagel's comparison of ethical versus other values, Daniel Callahan on bioethics, William Davenport on literature and science, and George Baralla on energy and civilization. Included are brief summaries of working group discussions on freedom, values basic to industrial civilization, hallucinogenics, and national energy priorities.

101   Charlesworth, James C., and Eggers, Alfred J., eds. HARMONIZING TECHNOLOGICAL DEVELOPMENTS AND SOCIAL PHILOSOPHY IN AMERICA. Monograph no. 11. Philadelphia: American Academy of Political and Social Science, 1970. viii, 247 p.

The outgrowth of a 1970 conference, this collection of papers addresses five key areas relating technology and society: the relationship between social policy and technology development; technological developments with especial social impact (the automobile, electronics, etc.); likely future technologies; appropriate education for technologists; and directions for technology policy.

102   Dorr, Harold M., ed. "Social Implications of Modern Science." ANNALS OF THE AMERICAN ACADEMY OF POLITICAL AND SOCIAL SCIENCE 249 (January 1947): 1-176.

An important postwar conference presents a thoughtful overview of rapidly growing American science and technology in its social context. Arthur Compton surmises the social implications of the atomic crusade, while Howard A. Meyerhof takes a dour look at the world's diminishing natural resources. In addition to William F. Ogburn's paper, "How Technology Changes Society," the volume offers an early warning of technology's potential threat to personal security by William Haber.

103   Eckman, Philip K., ed. TECHNOLOGY AND SOCIAL PROGRESS-- SYNERGISM OR CONFLICT? AAS Science and Technology Series, vol. 18. Tarzana, Calif.: distributed by the American Astronautical Society, 1969. xi, 158 p.

The purpose of the sixth AAS Goddard Memorial Symposium was to examine the effect of technology on human progress, focusing particularly on the contribution of the space program. Brief papers, written by military officials, government officials, journalists, and aerospace researchers, project a basically optimistic, high-technology outlook.

104   Edge, David O., and Wolfe, James N., eds. MEANING AND CONTROL: ESSAYS IN SOCIAL ASPECTS OF SCIENCE AND TECHNOLOGY. London: Tavistock, 1973. x, 274 p. Bibliog.

Twelve papers presented to an international meeting sponsored by the University of Edinburgh explore the social meaning and challenge to society of the emergence of science and technology. Featured are D.C. Bloor on philosophy and science, David O. Edge on technological metaphor, and William Armytage on technocrats. Others ponder the role of technology in industry, education, and government in the United Kingdom and the United States.

105   Ginzberg, Eli, ed. TECHNOLOGY AND SOCIAL CHANGE; EDITED FOR THE COLUMBIA UNIVERSITY SEMINAR ON TECHNOLOGY AND SOCIAL CHANGE. New York: Columbia University Press, 1964. viii, 155 p.

Representing academia, industry, and government, contributors explore the implications of technological innovation for society and its work. Charles R. DeCarlo's general observations on values and Daniel Bell's insights into post-industrial society are followed by Earl D. Johnson's analysis of the employment problems of scientific and technical personnel. Deciding that an increasingly complex technology is inevitable, William O. Baker concludes that it is society's lot to accommodate. Ginzburg closes with a summary discussion.

106   Hoselitz, Bert F., and Moore, Wilbert [Ellis]., eds. INDUSTRIALIZATION AND SOCIETY. Chicago: UNESCO, 1963. 437 p.

Originally prepared for the North American Conference on the Social Implications of Industrialization and Technological

Change, twenty four papers of international authorship survey research concepts and findings. "Social implications" are broadly construed to include such areas as entrepreneurship and innovation, consumption and savings, and government and public administration. Surveyed as well are more typical sociological concerns such as urbanization, population, the family, and education. An extended summary by Wilbert E. Moore closes the volume.

107　Mooney, Michael, and Stuber, Florian, eds. SMALL COMFORTS FOR HARD TIMES: HUMANISTS IN PUBLIC POLICY. New York: Columbia University Press, 1977. xv, 402 p.

Of numerous noteworthy papers in this volume, most germane are those contained in the third section, "Technology and the Ideal of Human Progress." Discussions of physical and ethical survival in an age of scarcity, of reuse of neomorts and re-vivification of cities demonstrate that technology has truly emerged as a life-or-death matter. Several authors surmise that technology, if properly controlled, can heighten health, well-being, and the aesthetic environment.

108　Morse, Dean, and Warner, Aaron W., eds. TECHNOLOGICAL INNO-VATION AND SOCIETY. New York: Columbia University Press, 1966. 214 p.

In its third year of convening, the Columbia Seminar on Technology and Social Change turned to consideration of technological innovation and its social impact. The first part of the book, authored by scientists, presents an optimistic view of the social progress promised by innovation. The second part, by social scientists, more cautious in tone, emphasizes the gap between the technologically feasible and the culturally possible.

109　Pickett, William Beatty, ed. TECHNOLOGY AT THE TURNING POINT. San Francisco: San Francisco Press, 1977. iv, 75 p.

Six papers presented at the Rose-Hulman Bicentennial Conference on American Technology--Past, Present, and Future are included in this brief volume. Authors and titles are: Thomas P. Hughes, "Edison's Method"; Ruth Cowan, "Women and Technology in American Life"; Melvin Kranzberg, "Technology the Liberator"; Paul Horwitz, "Public Funds and Private Technology"; Joseph Weizenbaum, "Computers and Hope"; and Victor Ferkiss, "The Future of American Technology." The "turning point" generally reflected in all papers is the changing perception which no longer regards technology with unbounded optimism, but rather recognizes its threat to life and liberty at the same time it benefits humankind.

110   Rasmussen, John P., ed. THE NEW AMERICAN REVOLUTION: THE
       DAWNING OF THE TECHNETRONIC ERA. New York: John Wiley
       and Sons, 1972. viii, 250 p. Bibliog.

       Essays represent a wide range of issues, problems, and opinions
       concerning the relationship between technology and rapid social
       change. Sections cover the idea of post-industrial society;
       the reign of automation; megalopolis; technology's children;
       technology and the global environment; the question of control;
       and the future. The youth culture and urban problems are
       accorded broader treatment than in similarly themed anthologies.

111   Snow, Robert [E.], and Wright, David [E.], eds. "Technology in
       American Culture." AMERICAN EXAMINER 5 (April 1978): 1-65.

       The ubiquity of technology has stimulated a flood of scholarly
       literature that is "both fascinating and badly fragmented."
       This special issue proposes to provide an introduction to these
       ideas through three essays, which "share in common an appre-
       ciation for the ambivalence and paradox with which technol-
       ogy is treated in the American experience." David Wright
       supplies a review essay plus an outline of his own theory.
       John Conroy restudies Hawthorne's "Ethan Brand," noting
       the technological elements that enhance the aesthetically
       rich narrative. Jack Colldewich's analysis of the motives of
       "phone phreaks" studies contradictory motives--from Luddite
       to technological aggrandizement--for this peculiar and wide-
       spread activity.

112   Staley, Eugene, ed. CREATING AN INDUSTRIAL CIVILIZATION: A
       REPORT ON THE CORNING CONFERENCE. New York: Harper and
       Brothers, 1952. xvi, 368 p.

       Held in May 1951, a conference attended by nearly one-
       hundred industrial representatives and academics focused on
       human values in industrial civilization. Specific areas dis-
       cussed include leisure, sense of community, and "confidence
       in life." Among the "rapporteurs" were John Kouwenhoven,
       Reuel Denney, and David Riesman. Includes a collection of
       background papers on the topics covered.

113   Steg, Leo, ed. "Should We Limit Science and Technology?" JOUR-
       NAL OF THE FRANKLIN INSTITUTE 300 (August 1975): 89-167.

       Participants at the first Franklin Conference (October 1974)
       confronted three questions, the first being the limits to science
       and growth, discussed by, among others, Gerard Piel and
       J. W. Forrester. The social responsibility of scientists and
       engineers served as the second topic, while in "Implications,"

the final section, the potential power of society to influence technology's direction was assessed by Gerald Feinberg, Albert Rosenfield, Cheryl Fox, and Leo Steg.

114   Stover, Carl F., ed. THE TECHNOLOGICAL ORDER: PROCEEDINGS OF THE ENCYCLOPEDIA BRITANNICA CONFERENCE. Detroit: Wayne State University Press, 1963. xii, 280 p. Also published in TECHNOLOGY AND CULTURE 3 (Fall 1962): 381-658.

Includes the partial proceedings of a 1962 conference by the same name. Major themes are "Ideas of Technology"; "The Technical Act"; "Nature, Science, and Technology"; and "Technology in Focus--The Emerging Nation." Contributors include Jacques Ellul, W. Norris Clarke, Walter Ong, Lynn White, Jr., Ritchie Calder, Melvin Kranzberg, Warren Preece, Robert Theobold, Ralph W. Tyler, and Aldous Huxley.

115   TECHNOLOGY AND THE FRONTIERS OF KNOWLEDGE: THE FRANK NELSON DOUBLEDAY LECTURES 1972-73. New York: Doubleday, 1975. ix, 134 p.

The five lecturers chosen by the Smithsonian Institution explore the import of modern technology for the expansion of knowledge. Saul Bellow, in "Literature in the Age of Technology," discusses the meaning literary artists find in the modern age. Technology's role in forming knowledge about society is considered by Daniel Bell in "Technology, Nature and Society." Historian Edmundo O'Gorman looks at the ways American technology has shaped views of the past. Sir Peter Medawar examines the impact of technology on evolution. Arthur C. Clarke links technology and knowledge as entities dependent on each other.

116   Thrall, Charles A., and Starr, Jerrold, eds. TECHNOLOGY, POWER AND SOCIAL CHANGE. Lexington, Mass.: Lexington Books, 1972. viii, 169 p.

Papers from a conference held at the University of Pennsylvania in 1971 confront the nature of technology and its relation to man, the values it implies, and the question of scarcity versus abundance in the technological future. A symposium on bureaucracy features the views of Victor Ferkiss and Murray Bookchin. Considerable space is allotted to technology and the countercultures.

117   Warner, Aaron W.; Morse, Dean; and Cooney, Thomas E., eds. THE ENVIRONMENT OF CHANGE. New York: Columbia University Press, 1969. xv, 186 p.

Papers are presented from two conferences sponsored by TIME

magazine, organized by the Steering Committee of the Columbia University Seminar on Technology and Social Change.
The scientific revolution and its aftermath is the subject of
papers by I.I. Rabi, Jacob Bronowski, and David Sidersley.
Eli Ginsberg discusses changes in employment patterns and
social values brought about by technology. Loren Eiseley
questions the assumption that the only good life is one lived
in a technical society.

E. JOURNAL ARTICLES

118 Bell, Daniel. "Modernity and Mass Society: On the Varieties of
Cultural Experience." STUDIES IN PUBLIC COMMUNICATION 4
(Autumn 1962): 3-34.

Mass culture, the product of an egalitarian, anonymous society,
is an achievement but subject to numerous criticisms. Chief
among these is the lack of encouragement given creativity and
serious art, indicative of a society that champions mediocrity
and cultural pretense. The primary aesthetic, according to
Bell, has become the organization of space.

119 _____. "Technology, Nature and Society; the Vicissitudes of Three
World Views and the Confusion of Realms." AMERICAN SCHOLAR 42
(Summer 1973): 385-404.

Bell affirms the view that what uniquely distinguishes the contemporary world is the growing power of technology. But to
view man as homo faber only is inadequate; he is also homo
pictor, a symbol producer. Bell concludes that civilization
has three distinct dimensions: culture, polity, and society,
each evolving according to its own "historical rhythm."

120 Boas, George. "In Defense of Machines." HARPER'S MAGAZINE
June 1932, pp. 93-99.

In a diatribe against romanticism, Boas argues that machines
are not the cause of either happiness or unhappiness--that
they are indifferent to inner life. Far from being dehumanizing, machines have encouraged the exhibition and fulfillment
of individual differences. Noting that older machines are
treated with familiar reverence, the author interprets contemporary hatred of machines as a fear of innovations.

121 Bottomore, Tom B. "Machines without a Cause." NEW YORK REVIEW
OF BOOKS 17 (4 November 1971): 12-19.

The mistrust of science and technology can no longer be
viewed as a lack of understanding between "two cultures" or

the cry of peevish conservatives. Bottomore finds a concern about the relations between technology and society in the work of Emmanuel Mesthene, Radovan Richta, Dennis Gabor, Anthony Oettinger, and Eugene Schwartz, scholars of widely variant values, academic viewpoints, and political persuasions.

122 Bronowski, Jacob. "Technology and Culture in Evolution." AMERICAN SCHOLAR 41 (Summer 1972): 197-211.

In our rush to safeguard the environment, we must avoid stabilizing it, succumbing to the fallacy that future human life must necessarily be similar to that of the present. The trouble with technology is not that it is "unnatural," for it is indeed part of man's evolutionary milieu. Rather the problem is that mankind, fulfilling an ethic of plenty, has been overindulgent with limited resources. Bronowski calls upon intellectuals to "stand fast to knowledge" against faddish antitechnologists and "anti-knowledge" crusaders.

123 Brooks, Harvey. "Technology: Hope or Catastrophe?" TECHNOLOGY IN SOCIETY 1 (Spring 1979): 3-18.

In the past decade, technological pessimism has spread from humanist ranks to those of scientists. Critical of deeply pessimistic thinkers and skeptical about the logic of alternative technology, Brooks offers a model for the future that is "relatively-optimistic." The persistence of recent problems is attributed partly to societal whims and fancies that have resulted in a failure to achieve difficult solutions. The food, environmental, and energy "crises" have attracted intense but only very brief public notice.

124 Brzezinski, Zbigniew. "America in the Technetronic Age: New Questions for Our Time." ENCOUNTER 30 (January 1968): 16-26. Reprinted in ATLANTIC COMMUNITY QUARTERLY 6 (Summer 1968): 175-82.

In ushering in the technetronic revolution, America is anticipating the future of the rest of the world. An unpromising portrait of the future society is painted by Brzezinski. Drugged, atomized masses will seek amusement obsessively in an artificial world, run by an overworked, overeducated elite. However, he reassures, citizens will experience a minimum of social conflict or physical pain.

125 Catton, William R., Jr. "Environmental Optimism: Cargo Cults in Modern Society." CORNELL JOURNAL OF SOCIAL RELATIONS 10 (Spring 1975): 63-72. Reprinted from SOCIOLOGICAL FOCUS 8 (January 1975): 27-35.

The open spaces of the Americas led European immigrants to

believe that they were settling in a land of infinite carrying capacity. Americans must now recognize two facts: that the world's resources and space are finite, and that human activities and institutions based on the assumption of limitlessness must also change. The author outlines a typology of current adaptations to these two statements. One response, the belief that technological progress can stave off the need for change, is compared to the "cargo cults" created by equally unrealistic primitive Pacific Islanders.

126   Crowe, Michael J. "A New Age in Science and Technology?" RE-VIEW OF POLITICS 34 (October 1972): 172-84.

Many observers feel that we are, in some sense, entering a "revolutionary" period of man. Ten statements of the type generally presented as evidence for the dawn of a "new age" are critiqued. In place of these, the author suggests an alternative group of criteria for a new age, while warning of the dangers of "presenticentrism" in overestimating the extent of future change.

127   Dubos, René. "Civilizing Technology." In ESSAYS IN HONOR OF DAVID LYALL PATRICK, [by] René Jules Dubos, Germaine Bree, Louis B. Wright, pp. 3-17. Tucson: University of Arizona, 1971.

The image of technology as protector and as a power to which man must conform began to be dispelled early in the twentieth century. Quantitative growth will be brought to an end by decreasing population, energy use, and technological production. The coming steady state will offer a closed system with challenging possibilities for creative change. A merger of the holistic point of view of the humanities and the fractionate outlook of the sciences could lead to man's greater understanding of reality and his place in the cosmos.

128   _____. "Science and Man's Nature." DAEDALUS 94 (Winter 1965): 223-44.

In Western countries technology transforms the external world, while medicine manipulates the body, and social institutions attempt to ease adaptation. Yet the fundamental nature of man--his cyclic body rhythms, his flight-or-fight responses-- has not changed. Dubos fears that the artificial environment created by technology will reduce the evolutionary adaptability of man.

129   Eiseley, Loren. "The Illusion of the Two Cultures." AMERICAN SCHOLAR 33 (Summer 1964): 387-99.

Narrow professionalism, in both the sciences and the humanities, has resulted in the institutionalization of method and a puritanical disdain of imagination. Man the tool-user has become convinced he is useful only as a tool. However, from the cave man who wasted some time embellishing an implement to the very great scientists like Leonardo, Einstein, and Newton, all display an emotional hunger and wonder that unites knowledge with dream. The "two cultures" is an illusion; man has two dependent sides, the artistic and the practical.

130   Gilkey, Langdon [B.]. "Robert L. Heilbroner's Vision of History." ZYGON 10 (September 1975): 215-33.

An extended analysis of Heilbroner's AN INQUIRY INTO THE HUMAN PROSPECT (no. 38) as related to the structure, philosophy, and theology of history. Heilbroner's view of the future is pessimistic because of the self-destructive nature of science, technology, and industrialism, which Gilkey compares to the orthodox theological interpretation of man based on original sin. However, he disputes Heilbroner's fated future, saying there is freedom because no historical factor "operates other than through human beings."

131   Griffiths, Dorothy. "Science and Technology: Liberation or Oppression?" IMPACT OF SCIENCE ON SOCIETY 25 (October-December 1975): 295-306.

The dream of a Baconian science--the relief from hunger, disease and drudgery through scientific efforts--has not been realized. We have been diverted from these goals, Griffiths says, at two levels. At the material level, military, not human, applications have prevailed. Intellectually, science has dictated an orthodox, limited mode of consciousness. She concludes that "only when the contradiction of interests between rulers and ruled is resolved in socialist society can a science be developed 'for the people.'"

132   Hassan, Ihab. "Beyond Arcadians and Technophiles: New Convergences in Culture?" MASSACHUSETTS REVIEW 17 (Spring 1976): 7-18.

Certain affinities shared by scientists, technologists, and artists are being recognized and discussed today. Scientists are venturing into "shadier realms" of myth and mystical experience with inquiries into altered and expanded consciousness. Art and literature produce functional fusions of art and technology while technology assessment creates new values. The reliance on dream, however, for mythos and logos, is the most powerful convergence.

133   Heald, Morrell. "Technology in American Culture." STETSON UNIVERSITY BULLETIN 62 (October 1962): 1-18.

While all the resources of scientific and technological knowledge and ingenuity are at our command, Americans have not
developed a satisfactory quality of civilization. At the root
of the problem is an inability to envision the "framework and
ends of a democratic society in full mastery of the dynamic
forces of science and technology." Heald demonstrates that
we have turned to the agrarian ideal as a source of criticism
of industrial society, and we assure ourselves that mass media
has led to standardization, commercialization, and apathy.
The mass leisure achieved through technology is laced with
fear. The consequences of technology for society are being
recognized by scientists and engineers who look for understanding to the humanist. What holds us back is an insistence
on judging changes by preindustrial standards.

134   Kouwenhoven, John A. "What's American about America?" HARPER'S
MAGAZINE, July 1956, pp. 25-33.

To discover a distinctly American trait, Kouwenhoven looks
at such typically American "artifacts" as skyscrapers, the
gridiron town plan, jazz, the Constitution, Twain's and
Whitman's writings, comic strips, soap operas, assembly-line
production, and chewing gum. Common to all is a structural
principle based on simple, infinitely repeatable units. What
is important is process, not climax or resolution. Motion is
essential, but no end is demanded by symmetry or proportion.
With such diverse entities as chewing gum, Huck Finn, and
science, the preoccupation is with process not final outcome.

135   LaPorte, Todd [R.]., and Metlay, Daniel. "Public Attitudes toward
Present and Future Technologies: Satisfactions and Apprehensions."
SOCIAL STUDIES OF SCIENCE 5 (November 1975): 373-98.

Results of a study of public attitudes toward technology reveal
that the public perceives a strong association between technology and social change. Technology is seen as beneficial in
solving such day-to-day problems as transportation and energy
but as aggravating or not alleviating the problems of war,
privacy loss, and inflation.

136   Lerner, Max. "Big Technology and Neutral Technicians." AMERICAN
QUARTERLY 4 (Summer 1952): 99-109.

Americans have shown an affinity for the machine, whose development was spurred by American invention, "know-how,"
and scientific management. Ironically, the success of industrial civilization has resulted in a cutting away of Americans
from their machines, as ever-greater numbers work in service
and other nonmechanical occupations. Interest has been trans-
ferred from the making of goods to the consumption of goods.

137   Lindbergh, Charles. "A Letter from Lindbergh." LIFE, 4 July 1969,
        pp. 60A-61.

>   Written on the eve of the Apollo 8 moonshot, Lindbergh
>   eloquently expresses his motivation toward adventure. Intui-
>   tion, not rationality, led to his transatlantic flight; but as the
>   art of flying became a science, he lost interest in aviation.
>   He "revolted" from the technological advances that upset the
>   balance between intellect and senses. Working in biomedicine,
>   the mechanics of life soon became less interesting than its
>   mystical qualities. Working during the war for the Air Force,
>   the destruction of the environment appalled him. Decades
>   spent with science and technology directed his mind to areas
>   beyond their reach--to the essence of life. "I have turned
>   my attention from technological progress to life, from civili-
>   zation to the wild."

138   McDermott, John. "Technology, the Opiate of the Intellectuals."
        NEW YORK REVIEW OF BOOKS 13 (31 July 1969): 25-35.

>   If religion was formerly the opiate of the masses, technology
>   serves that function for the educated today. McDermott is
>   particularly critical of the widespread optimistic beliefs that
>   technology is self-correcting, and that it will inevitably func-
>   tion to the good of mankind and should thus be left to grow
>   unrestricted. This doctrine of "laissez-innover" has been used
>   to justify numerous technically rational but fundamentally
>   irrational activities, most notably the conflict in Vietnam.
>   Technology must be recognized as an institutional, highly
>   political system.

139   Mesthene, Emmanuel G. "Technology and Humanistic Values." COM-
        PUTERS AND THE HUMANITIES 4 (September 1969): 1-10.

>   Technology is tools and techniques, from machines to computer
>   programs and planning. The humanities, in contrast, deal
>   with the "expressive, moral, and contemplative aspects of liv-
>   ing." Technology confronts the humanities with the challenge
>   of enabling us to see the import of tools for man. The failure
>   of the arts is due to their falling victim to the "seductiveness
>   of fine tools." Enamored of analytic devices and processes,
>   the humanities have not focused on the relationships of means
>   to ends.

140   Mumford, Lewis. "The Rise of Caliban." VIRGINIA QUARTERLY RE-
        VIEW 30 (Summer 1954): 321-41.

>   The union of the automaton and the id which has led to the
>   dominance of science and technics is personified in the figure
>   of Shakespeare's "fawning brute," Caliban. The detached
>   scientific intelligence is equipped with "neither a brake nor a

steering wheel." While technology is mastered, we are as
incapable of dealing with the rest of our lives as was the
primitive id. The scientist will serve any kind of tyranny for
the sake of research freedom. Like Faust, he has sold his
soul and has turned his thinking self into an automaton.

141   Nichols, William. "Skeptics and Believers: The Science-Humanities
       Debate." AMERICAN SCHOLAR 45 (Summer 1976): 377-86.

       The tone evident in exchanges regarding the "two cultures"
       debate reveals why most of the discourse has been unheeded.
       The controversial arguments of Carlyle-Walker; Abse, Milgram,
       and Baumrind; Snow-Leavis; Huxley-Arnold are examined.
       Nichols demonstrates that the "believers" in science and tech-
       nology are rational, cool, in control, and sanctimonious.
       However, the "skeptics" are shrill, angry, and passionate.
       If the skeptic argues from a position that rejects accepted
       patterns of contemporary science, the scientific community
       rules out debate. Skeptics must move beyond rage to complex
       debate.

142   Silberman, Charles E. "Is Technology Taking Over?" FORTUNE,
       February 1966, pp. 112-15, 217-22.

       Man as victim of technology has become a persistent theme of
       contemporary thought. The alternatives from which men
       choose seem increasingly determined by technology. The
       author discusses two contrasting views: Jacques Ellul's con-
       cept of "technique" and Marshall McLuhan's optimistically
       conceived global village.

143   Simpson, Richard L. "Beyond Rational Bureaucracy: Changing Values
       and Social Integration in Post-Industrial Society." SOCIAL FORCES
       51 (September 1972): 1-6.

       Rational values and their bureaucratic manifestations have of
       late suffered great criticism in the United States. Activist
       groups representing beauty, environmental purity, and social
       equality have received much public attention. Their values
       have been gradually institutionalized by besieged institutions,
       resulting in a more responsive and responsible society.

144   Sklair, Leslie. "The Revolt against the Machine: Some 20th-Century
       Criticisms of Scientific Progress." CAHIERS D'HISTOIRE MONDIALE
       12, no. 3 (1970): 479-89.

       A brief analysis of several critics of the machine and techno-
       logical progress, most of whom are European, including W.R.
       Inge, L.P. Jocks, Josiah Stamp, Gina Lombroso, Georges
       Friedmann, Simon Kuznets, Alfred Sauvy, Friedrich Georg

Juenger, Gabriel Marcel, and Jacques Ellul. Sklair suggests that this opposition arises from a variety of sources and concludes that twentieth century opposition to science and technology may be more widespread than generally believed.

145   Sypher, Wylie. "The Poem as Defense." AMERICAN SCHOLAR 37 (Winter 1967-68): 85-93.

The technological frame of mind applies method to everything and to predict results. The unexpected is thus ruled out. Technology has spread from industry into life, so that human behavior is subject to an "obsessive use of techniques." The artist, however, denies the repeatable. Art yields recognitions which are unexpected and unique and sanctions the "single intense perception." Sypher pleads for educational and critical methods that are not programmatic.

146   Taviss, Irene. "Notes and Queries: A Survey of Popular Attitudes toward Technology." TECHNOLOGY AND CULTURE 13 (October 1972): 606-21.

The results of a pilot survey undertaken in 1970 by the Harvard University Program on Technology and Society are summarized. The sample suggested that people view technology as generally beneficial, evincing little desire to return to nature. Antitechnology sentiments are inversely related to the technology information level of the respondent.

147   Thayer, Lee. "On the Functions of Incompetence." PERSPECTIVES IN BIOLOGY AND MEDICINE 18 (Spring 1975): 332-44.

In the Industrial Revolution society achieved a new power through the invention of mass production and mutual interdependence in the manufacturing process. The advance was made at a cost of radically improverishing man's competence. The industrial economy supports only those who function predictably, in a specialized position and who are, to Thayer's mind, incompetent.

148   Traschen, Isodore. "Modern Literature and Science." COLLEGE ENGLISH 25 (January 1964): 248-55.

Modern man is alienated from the universe and himself because of his "objectification by science and his thingification by technology and bureaucracy." To alter this state we must believe in our "naive" (in comparison to the sophistication of science) sensation of things. While we use the reality of the scientific view, we live in the "illusory human reality." Art is a representation of the naive world; it expresses the human situation in colors and designs that appeal to our senses. In

this way it is a "rescue" from the scientific world view.
Science and technology have replaced our old myths. Spirituality, if measured by devotional energies, now resides in the
applied sciences.

149   Winner, Langdon. "On Criticizing Technology." PUBLIC POLICY 20
       (Winter 1972): 35-59.

       The frequency with which technology is mentioned as a social
       problem is one of the primary features of contemporary society.
       Yet the present main-line university establishment, Winner
       surmises, does not consider "unbalanced" criticisms of technology or suggestions of the need for major social and political
       change. Thus they subtly reinforce the belief in the autonomy
       of technology.

Part 2

HISTORICAL OVERVIEW

A. BIBLIOGRAPHIES

150   Bell, Whitfield J., Jr. EARLY AMERICAN SCIENCE: NEEDS AND OPPORTUNITIES FOR STUDY. Needs and Opportunities for Study Series. Williamsburg, Va.: Institute for Early American History and Culture, 1955. ix, 85 p.

> Similar to Brooke Hindle's TECHNOLOGY IN EARLY AMERICA (no. 154). A brief bibliographical survey of needs and opportunities, somewhat dated but still valuable, is followed by four bibliographical sections on the general history of science, American science to 1820, periodicals, and fifty selected American scientists, of which the last section is the most extensive.

151   Besterman, Theodore. TECHNOLOGY, INCLUDING PATENTS: A BIBLIOGRAPHY OF BIBLIOGRAPHIES. 2 vols. Totowa, N.J.: Rowman and Littlefield, 1971. xiv, 681 p.

> A listing of bibliographical titles extracted from the author's broader A WORLD BIBLIOGRAPHY OF BIBLIOGRAPHIES is arranged under the following categories: technology, inventions and patents, aeronautics, automation, engineering, mechanical engineering, metal and metallurgy, mineralogy and mining, motor-cars and motoring, photography, radio, water, and special subjects. While the bibliography is unannotated, each citation does list the number of items included. World coverage.

152   Ferguson, Eugene S. BIBLIOGRAPHY OF THE HISTORY OF TECHNOLOGY. History of Technology Monograph Series, vol. 5. Cambridge: M.I.T. Press and the Society for the History of Technology, 1968. xx, 347 p.

> The basic bibliographical guide to the history of technology. Approximately two-thirds of the volume covers various types of

resource guides, while the remainder includes monographs and articles in particular subject fields. Ferguson captures the essence of each work in pithy one and two sentence annotations.

153   Goodwin, Jack. "Current Bibliography in the History of Technology." TECHNOLOGY AND CULTURE, 1964-- . Annual.

An ongoing bibliography generally published each year in the journal's April issue. The first installment appeared in the winter 1964 issue and included books and articles published during the 1962 calendar year. A similar schedule has been maintained with previously unlisted titles included as unearthed. Items are arranged both chronologically and topically and often include very brief annotations. International in scope--a basic source.

154   Hindle, Brooke. TECHNOLOGY IN EARLY AMERICA: NEEDS AND OPPORTUNITIES FOR STUDY. Needs and Opportunities for Study Series. Institute of Early American History and Culture. Chapel Hill: University of North Carolina Press, 1966. xix, 145 p.

As an outgrowth of a conference sponsored by the Institute of Early American History and Culture and the Eleutherian Mills-Hagley Foundation, the author combines an interpretive essay with an excellent bibliography on needs and opportunities in American technological history prior to 1850. Hindle calls for an awareness of technology's central role in this period, in particular, through a detailed understanding of its innermost workings. Contains a directory of artifact collections.

155   Miller, Genevieve. BIBLIOGRAPHY OF THE HISTORY OF MEDICINE IN THE UNITED STATES AND CANADA, 1939-1960. Baltimore: Johns Hopkins Press, 1964. xvi, 428 p.

A reissue under one cover of the bibliography published annually in the BULLETIN OF THE HISTORY OF MEDICINE since 1940. Entries are not annotated and are divided into the following categories: biography, dentistry, diseases, general, hospitals, journals, libraries-museums, local history and societies, medical education, medical science and specialities, military medicine, nursing, pharmacy, primitive medicine, professional history, and public health and social medicine.

156   National Library of Medicine. BIBLIOGRAPHY OF THE HISTORY OF MEDICINE, 1964-1977. 13 vols. Bethesda, Md.: U.S. Department of Health, Education, and Welfare, 1965-78.

Extensive annual volumes covering material published during the previous year, with cumulative volumes appearing every five years. Includes non-English language material. The majority of titles are scientific and medical in nature, but several subsections deal with technology in medicine.

157 Neu, John. "Critical Bibliography of the History of Science and its Cultural Influences." Philadelphia: ISIS, 1913-- . Annual.

An ongoing bibliography of recent titles now published annually as a separate number of ISIS, the History of Science Society's journal, although in earlier years, it appeared more frequently. Most works included are science-oriented, but there is a separate technology section.

158 Rider, K.J. HISTORY OF SCIENCE AND TECHNOLOGY: A SELECT BIBLIOGRAPHY FOR STUDENTS. 2d ed. London: Library Association, 1970. 75 p.

A short introductory guide to 353 titles, the bibliography is meant for the student new to the field, but is useful for all. Emphasis is on Britain, but a great deal of American material is included.

159 Sarton, George. A GUIDE TO THE HISTORY OF SCIENCE. New York: Ronald Press, 1952. xix, 316 p.

Sarton, the founder of the discipline of the history of science, viewed technology as part of his field and, thus, this volume lists many items of technological interest. Includes three introductory essays on "the purpose and meaning of the history of science." International scope.

160 Weimer, David R. BIBLIOGRAPHY OF AMERICAN CULTURE 1493-1875. Ann Arbor, Mich.: University Microfilms, 1957. xvi, 228 p.

A basic collection of Americana is selected with the purpose of promoting interdisciplinary study in colleges and universities. All 5,000 books and pamphlets appearing in the bibliography are available as a microfilm series. All of the publications first appeared prior to 1876. Relevant subject classifications are art and architecture, utopian and reform movements, literature, philosophy, psychology and religion, the city, social science theories, economics, commerce and industry, transportation and communication, science, medicine, engineering, technology, and invention.

161 Weiss, John H. TECHNOLOGY AND SOCIAL HISTORY. Research Review no. 8. Cambridge, Mass.: Harvard University Program on Technology and Society, 1971. v, 93 p.

This volume covers the historical relationship between technological and social change. An integrative essay introduces fifty-seven titles which are divided into four major categories: general, technology and economic growth, agencies of diffusion and resistance, and studies of the roles of single technologies. Lengthy annotations include numerous quotations. Most titles were published during the 1960s and are included in the present compilation.

162   Whitehill, Walter Muir. THE ARTS IN EARLY AMERICAN HISTORY: NEEDS AND OPPORTUNITIES FOR STUDY. Needs and Opportunities for Study Series. Institute of Early American History and Culture. Chapel Hill: University of North Carolina Press, 1965. xv, 170 p.

An annotated not primarily concerned with technology--the index does not even include the word--or its relationship to early American arts, there is enough of value in the lengthy annotated bibliography to make this volume worth looking at for the scholar interested in crafts and artisans prior to 1826. Includes entries under architecture, crafts, furniture, silver, pottery, glass, lighting devices, and textiles.

B. GENERAL WORKS RELATING TECHNOLOGY TO SOCIETY AND VALUES

163   Allen, Frederick Lewis. THE BIG CHANGE: AMERICA TRANSFORMS ITSELF, 1900-1950. New York: Harper and Brothers, 1952. xi, 308 p. Bibliog.

An optimistic survey of the first half of the twentieth century which emphasizes the "democratization of our economic system, or the adjustment of capitalism to democratic ends." Something of a cold war product but written in the style that made the author's earlier history of the 1920s, ONLY YESTERDAY (1931), so refreshing. Contains some interesting material on technological developments.

164   Armytage, W.H.G. THE RISE OF THE TECHNOCRATS: A SOCIAL HISTORY. Toronto: University of Toronto Press, 1965. vii, 448 p.

A social history of the rise of science and technology and the resultant attitudes surrounding them during the past four hundred years. Although this book has received mixed reviews, e.g. Edwin Layton, TECHNOLOGY AND CULTURE, 7 (Fall 1966): 532-34, and covers much more than just the American scene, there is much elusive information contained herein.

165   Beard, Charles A., ed. A CENTURY OF PROGRESS. New York: Harper and Brothers, 1933. ix, 452 p.

The central theme of these fifteen essays, compiled under the auspices of the 1933 Chicago Century of Progress Exposition, is that of American progress during the previous hundred years. Of particular interest are the chapters on "Invention as a Social Manifestation" by Waldemar Kaempffert, "Industry" by Henry Ford and Samuel Crowther, "Transportation and Communication" by Edward Hungerford, "Agriculture" by Frank O. Lowden, "Labor" by William Green, and Beard's introductory piece on "The Idea of Progress."

166   Boorstin, Daniel J[oseph]. THE AMERICANS: THE DEMOCRATIC EXPERIENCE. New York: Random House, 1973. xiv, 717 p. Bibliog.

The final volume of Boorstin's trilogy of American history considers the democratization of things. Through examination of specific items developed during the past century, the author reveals how change produced by new products has moved society toward standardization and homogenization.

167   _____. THE REPUBLIC OF TECHNOLOGY: REFLECTIONS ON OUR FUTURE COMMUNITY. New York: Harper and Row, 1978. xv, 105 p.

Boorstin presents brief explanations of America's relationship with technology in seven somewhat unconnected essays, most of which have been previously published. The book is offered in the belief that the converging powers of technology have reduced differences among the nations of the world and that America, the "Republic of Technology," has had and will continue to serve a central role. Specific topics include political technology and the Constitution, the machine, immigration, and education.

168   Buchanan, Angus [Robert]. "Technology and History." SOCIAL STUDIES OF SCIENCE 5 (November 1975): 489-99.

An essay review which laments the "notable dearth of speculative literature" about the history of technology. However, Buchanan suggests Arnold Pacey's THE MAZE OF INGENUITY (1974) may provide a starting point for the missing conceptual framework by arguing that technological development is socially determined. Nothing radically new for those intimately versed in the field, but useful for those who are not.

169   Cochran, Thomas Childs. BUSINESS IN AMERICAN LIFE: A HISTORY. New York: McGraw-Hill, 1972. xi, 402 p. Bibliog.

In a wide-ranging social and economic history of American life with many references to the impact of technology upon business, Cochran emphasizes "role playing as the central process involved in social change," and relates the manner in which business institutions reacted to new environments and innovations.

170 _____ . SOCIAL CHANGE IN AMERICA: THE TWENTIETH CENTURY. New York: Harper and Row, 1972. 178 p. Bibliog.

The author argues for a behavioral science approach to explain social change based on the theory of role playing. Chapters 5 and 6 deal with the impact of technological change, in particular mass media, electricity, and the automobile.

171 Drucker, Peter F. THE AGE OF DISCONTINUITY: GUIDELINES TO OUR CHANGING SOCIETY. New York: Harper and Row, 1968. xiii, 402 p.

The existing structure, meaning, and values of today's society are examined for the opportunities and priorities of tomorrow's civilization. In contrast to the technical and economic continuity of the first half of the twentieth century, the second half has brought major "discontinuities" in terms of new technologies, a worldwide economy, and a community of knowledge which raise important questions of responsibility for those in political and economic power.

172 _____ . THE NEW SOCIETY: THE ANATOMY OF THE INDUSTRIAL ORDER. New York: Harper and Brothers, 1950. ix, 356 p.

A discussion of the effects of mass production, which analyzes the principles and problems of the economics, management, worker, and organization within the "Industrial Order." The author hopes the United States can serve as a model for the "free" social and political institutions necessary to industrialized society. Obviously written in the early Cold War era.

173 _____ . "The Technological Revolution; Notes on the Relationship of Technology, Science, and Culture." TECHNOLOGY AND CULTURE 2 (Fall 1961): 342-51.

To the question, "What brought about the explosive change in the human condition these last two hundred years," Drucker answers, not science, but "a fundamental change in the concept of technology," involving the systematic collection, organization, and application of knowledge. The unanswered question is what caused this basic change in attitudes, beliefs, and values. An early article noting the importance of technology in contrast to traditional emphasis on science.

174 _____ . TECHNOLOGY, MANAGEMENT AND SOCIETY: ESSAYS BY PETER F. DRUCKER. New York: Harper and Row, 1970. x, 209 p.

These previously published essays deal with aspects of the "material civilization," by which Drucker means man and his tools, materials, and organizations. Five essays deal with the

impact of technology on man and his culture from early irrigation projects to the present. The remainder considers management as a central social function and as part of the enterprise.
Within these contexts, specific tools, such as the computer and
planning are discussed.

175   . "Work and Tools." TECHNOLOGY AND CULTURE 1 (Winter
1960): 28-37.

Technology is about work, that is, about "human action on
physical objects." Only through a historical study of work
can the development of the tools and processes of technology
be understood. Scientific management, which dealt with the
worker's manipulation of tools and techniques, led to changes
in equipment and processes. More recently, "human engineering" and "industrial psychology" promise to have direct impact
on apparatus. Traditional social organization of work also
interacts with tasks and tools.

176   Forbes, Robert James. THE CONQUEST OF NATURE: TECHNOLOGY
AND ITS CONSEQUENCES. A Britannica Perspective. New York:
Frederick A. Praeger Publishers, 1968. 142 p.

An attempt to explain "the principles and trends of the technological order," which characterize today's society, by examining the historical development of technology and the subsequent
changes inflicted upon man and his environment. Because
"there is a constant interchange between technological achievements and human values," the author's answer to whether that
technology will be beneficial or problematic lies in mankind's
"inner faith."

177   Heilbroner, Robert L. "Do Machines Make History?" TECHNOLOGY
AND CULTURE 8 (July 1967): 333-45.

Concerned with "the effect of technology in determining the
nature of the socioeconomic order," the author makes a case
for "a determinate pattern of technological evolution" and
concludes that the "technology of a society imposes a determinant pattern of social relations on that society." Not a
simplistic Marxist view or explanation of determinism.

178   "The Historiography of Technology." TECHNOLOGY AND CULTURE
15 (January 1974): 1-48.

A historiographical theme issue in which Robert Multhauf exam-
ines the large-scale histories including Singer's HISTORY OF
TECHNOLOGY (no. 218) and Kranzberg and Pursell's TECH-
NOLOGY IN WESTERN CIVILIZATION (no. 210). Eugene
Ferguson suggests using the social context and attendant value

judgments as the organizational theme for the history of technology, while Edwin Layton stresses the need to perceive technology as a body of knowledge. Summary comments by Derek De Solla Price.

179   McClary, Andrew. BIOLOGY AND SOCIETY: THE EVOLUTION OF MAN AND HIS TECHNOLOGY. New York: Macmillan, 1975. x, 320 p. Illus., maps, bibliog.

An evolutionary survey from the beginnings of man to modern Western technology. The preface states that "this book was written with one aim in mind: to argue that we can make more sense out of the thorny problems facing our technological society if we view them from an evolutionary perspective."

180   Morison, Elting E. MEN, MACHINES, AND MODERN TIMES. Cambridge: M.I.T. Press, 1966. ix, 235 p.

A study of the process of technological development and social change based upon studies of several technological innovations including naval gunfire and ships, the process of bureaucratization, computers, and nineteenth-century steel-making. The final chapter offers suggestions as to how to keep technical developments within "human dimensions."

181   Morison, George S. THE NEW EPOCH AS DEVELOPED BY THE MANUFACTURE OF POWER. Boston: Houghton Mifflin, 1903. Reprint. Technology and Society Series. New York: Arno Press, 1972. xi, 134 p.

A good turn-of-the-century discussion of technology by an engineer. The author's new epoch is that of the control of power as symbolized by the steam engine. In this context, his specifically related concerns are transportation, communication, manufacturing, capital, government, civil engineering, and education.

182   Mumford, Lewis. "From Erewhon to Nowhere." NEW YORKER, 8 October 1960, pp. 180-97.

In an article that is only in part a review of Singer's HISTORY OF TECHNOLOGY (no. 218), Mumford suggests that if we are to regain control of our mechanized society, we must learn more about the history of technology itself. His major complaint with the Singer volumes is that they generally fail to analyze the cultural environment which gives human significance to the technological events, a tendency only too prevalent in society at large. Typical Mumford.

183   _____. THE MYTH OF THE MACHINE. Vol. 1: TECHNICS AND

HUMAN DEVELOPMENT. New York: Harcourt, Brace and World,
1967. ix, 342 p. Illus., bibliog. Vol. 2: THE PENTAGON OF
POWER. New York: Harcourt Brace Jovanovich, 1970. 496 p. Illus.,
bibliog.

That man is primarily a toolmaker is a myth. Rather, it is
man's mind, with its powers expressed in dreams and symbols,
that is the "ultimate criterion of man's biological and cultural
success." A widened interpretation of the entire course of
human development is presented with the purpose of questioning
the present commitment to technical progress as an end in itself.

184 _____. TECHNICS AND CIVILIZATION. New York: Harcourt,
Brace and Co., 1934. Reprint. New York: Harcourt, Brace, and
World, 1963. 495 p. Illus., bibliog.

An early Mumford work which, while critical of technology's
impact on Western civilization, is also important for its statement of his originally favorable attitude toward technology:
"the machine itself makes no demands and holds out no promises: it is the human spirit that makes demands and keeps
promises." Since the tenth century, technics have been divisi-
ble into three eras based on source of power and basic material
used: eotechnic (water and wood), paleotechnic (coal and
iron), and neotechnic (electricity and alloy). Includes a list
of important inventions and bibliography with brief annotations.

185 _____. THE TRANSFORMATIONS OF MAN. World Perspectives Series,
vol. 7. New York: Harper, 1956. Reprint. New York: Collier,
1966. 192 p.

Mumford calls this book "the best summation of my general outlook." He traces the evolution of mankind from its primitive
origins to the present and offers two possible scenarios for the
future: that of a "post-historic man" characterized by depersonalization, totalitarianism, and machine technics, or that of
a new and more promising "world culture."

186 Pyke, Magnus. THE SCIENCE CENTURY. New York: Walker and Co.,
1967. 183 p. Illus.

Despite its somewhat misleading title, this book discusses the
development and impact of technology upon society from approximately 1850 to 1950. Pyke surveys the changes in medicine, warfare, transportation, light, communication, industrialization, urbanization, food, and the associated thought patterns
and theories of belief.

187 _____. THE SCIENCE MYTH. New York: Macmillan, 1962. 179 p.

The title of this popularized study is misleading in that the
book deals primarily with technology. Starting with the Pro-
crustean myth of fitting everyone to an average length bed--
in this allusion, the bed is that of scientific technology and
industrialism--Pyke analyzes the problems individuals encounter
in accommodating themselves to modern society in the areas of
work, war, materialism, psychology, advertising, consumerism,
religion, food, transportation, and communication. Resistance
to averageness is the author's answer.

188   Rosen, S. McKee, and Rosen, Laura. TECHNOLOGY AND SOCIETY:
THE INFLUENCE OF MACHINES IN THE UNITED STATES. New York:
Macmillan, 1941. xiv, 474 p. Illus., maps, bibliog.

A popularized, social science account of technology's economic,
social, and political impact, based in part on the depression-
induced 1937 National Resources Committee report (no. 1145).
Although dated now, the study reveals prewar thinking.

189   Rürup, Reinhard. "Reflections on the Development and Current Problems
of the History of Technology." TECHNOLOGY AND CULTURE 15
(April 1974): 161-93.

Primarily a historiographical article tracing the growth of the
history of technology as a discipline. Rürup believes historians
have something special to contribute as social scientists in
terms of explaining the changing relations between technology
and society and in "creating the conditions under which technological progress can be socially planned." To this end he
suggests promising areas of study.

190   "Symposium: The Historiography of American Technology." TECHNOL-
OGY AND CULTURE 11 (January 1970): 1-35.

In an insightful article, "The Big Questions in the History of
American Technology," George Daniels suggests a number of
fundamental areas in which to focus future studies. His question is whether technology causes social change or vice versa,
to which he suggests in conclusion that peoples' preferences or
values have a great deal to do with the development of their
technology. Generally supportive comments by John Burke
and Edwin Layton follow.

191   White, Lynn, Jr. "The Legacy of the Middle Ages in the American Wild
West." SPECULUM 40 (April 1965): 191-202.

White draws upon examples of technology prevalent in the
American West--the revolver (gunpowder), barbed wire, and
the windmill--which had their origins in medieval Europe, and
our emphasis on pluralism to suggest that we are in many ways
closer to the Middle Ages than to the Reformation.

192   Wiebe, Robert H. THE SEARCH FOR ORDER, 1877-1920. The Making of America Series, vol. 5. New York: Hill and Wang, 1967. xiv, 333 p. Bibliog.

> Somewhat controversial, this is an excellent and provocative survey of a period of rapid economic, industrial, and social change. It is Wiebe's thesis that a middle-class bureaucracy of centralized authority emerged in answer to the problems of industrialization, urbanization, and immigration faced by the many autonomous "island communities" characteristic of the Reconstruction era. Valuable bibliographical essay.

C. HISTORY OF TECHNOLOGY

193   Burlingame, Roger. BACKGROUNDS OF POWER: THE HUMAN STORY OF MASS PRODUCTION. New York: Charles Scribner's Sons, 1949. xi, 372 p. Bibliog.

> The third volume of the author's trilogy in which he is concerned with both the benefits and potential dangers of automated production. "We start with one conviction and one only: as we believe that the proper study of the machine is man, so we believe also that the proper study of machine production is society."

194   _____. ENGINES OF DEMOCRACY. New York: Charles Scribner's Sons, 1940. xviii, 638 p. Illus., bibliog.

> The second volume in the author's social history of American technology, covering the period since 1865, analyzes the simultaneous development of inventions and their relationship to social impulses. He sees U.S. history as "fundamentally a history of invention."

195   _____. MACHINES THAT BUILT AMERICA. New York: Harcourt, Brace, 1953. 214 p. Reprint. New York: New American Library, 1964. 166 p.

> A brief history of inventors and inventions which had a major impact on American economic and social development, covers such nineteenth-century individuals as Oliver Evans, Eli Whitney, Samuel Slater, Cyrus McCormick, Samuel Colt, and Elias Howe, with a final chapter on Henry Ford and the mass-produced automobile.

196   _____. THE MARCH OF THE IRON MEN: A SOCIAL HISTORY OF UNION THROUGH INVENTION. New York: Charles Scribner's Sons, 1938. Reprint. New York: Grosset and Dunlap, 1960. 516 p. Illus., maps.

In this first volume of his trilogy on American invention, the author chronologically traces technological developments as the primary means by which a unified society developed in a new land by 1865.

197   Byrn, Edward W. THE PROGRESS OF INVENTION IN THE NINE-TEENTH CENTURY. New York: Munn, 1900. Reprint. New York: Russell and Russell, 1970. 476 p. Illus.

An older but still valuable general survey of nineteenth-century technology and invention, but one which does not deal extensively with social impact. Included is a chronology of leading inventions, and it is very well illustrated with woodcuts and some photographs.

198   Calder, Ritchie [Lord]. AFTER THE SEVENTH DAY: THE WORLD MAN CREATED. New York: Simon and Schuster, 1961. 448 p.

Man's technological adaptation to his environment through the ages is the author's concern in this series of somewhat disconnected sketches. He concludes: "With the resources of modern science and technology, tempered by wisdom, we can escape from the limitations of past civilizations and succeed where they failed."

199   _____. THE EVOLUTION OF THE MACHINE. The Smithsonian Library Series. New York: American Heritage Publishing Co., 1968. 160 p. Illus., bibliog.

A brief popularized history of the machine from the beginnings of man to the present also considers energy sources and conversion, materials, and the diffusion of ideas. A chronology of important dates, biographical sketches of important inventors, and suggestions for further reading are included.

200   Chase, Stuart. MEN AND MACHINES. New York: Macmillan, 1929. 354 p. Illus., bibliog.

In a popular, sweeping survey of the machine age, Chase reviews its history to the last nut and bolt and considers the machine's role in the process of industrialization. Basically optimistic, he admits worry about the effects of automation, but remains confident that the worst effects of industrialization, even boredom of factory work, are subsiding.

201   Crowther, James Gerald. DISCOVERIES AND INVENTIONS OF THE TWENTIETH CENTURY. 5th ed. New York: E.P. Dutton, 1966. 434 p. Illus., maps.

Twentieth-century technological and scientific developments are surveyed. Photographs and line drawings illustrate this revised and updated version of the earlier compilations of the author and his predecessors, Edward Cressy. Topics include steam-power, internal combustion, electricity, chemistry, transportation, radio, atomic energy, and spaceflight, among many others.

202   Derry, T.K., and Williams, Trevor I. A SHORT HISTORY OF TECH-NOLOGY, FROM THE EARLIEST TIMES TO A.D. 1900. New York: Oxford University Press, 1961. xviii, 782 p. Illus., bibliog.

A shorter, redesigned narrative version of Singer's HISTORY OF TECHNOLOGY (no. 218) attempts to relate the history of technology to man's general history. The first half covers the period to 1750 and will have little to interest the strictly American historian. The second half covers the industrial revolution through 1900 and provides a good factual introduction.

203   Forbes, R[obert].J[ames]. MAN THE MAKER: A HISTORY OF TECH-NOLOGY AND ENGINEERING. Rev. ed. New York: Henry Schuman, 1958. 355 p. Illus., bibliog.

A good but brief survey of the history of engineering and technology and their effects upon mankind, although only the latter half contains information on the American experience.

204   Forbes, R[obert]. J[ames]., and Dijksterhuis, E.J. A HISTORY OF SCIENCE AND TECHNOLOGY. 2 vols. Baltimore: Penguin Books, 1963. 534 p. Illus., bibliog.

Volume 1 covers ANCIENT TIMES TO THE SEVENTEENTH CENTURY while volume 2 highlights THE EIGHTEENTH AND NINETEENTH CENTURIES. A very thin treatment arranged topically for the most part.

205   Fuller, Edmund. TINKERS AND GENIUS: THE STORY OF YANKEE INVENTORS. American Procession Series. New York: Hastings House, 1955. xii, 308 p. Illus., bibliog.

The author sees Yankee inventiveness or creativity as a state of mind which was a part of a larger general élan then prevalent. He discusses water power and early mills, metalworking, the early years of Benjamin Franklin's career, steamboats, spinning and weaving, Eli Whitney's cotton gin, arms making, clock making and bridge building, among other topics.

206   Giedion, Sigfried. MECHANIZATION TAKES COMMAND: A CONTRI-BUTION TO ANONYMOUS HISTORY. New York: Oxford University Press, 1948. Reprint. New York: W.W. Norton, 1969. 743 p.

Giedion observes "the coming of mechanization from the human standpoint" through the technique of "anonymous history," and discusses the impact of major developments such as the assembly line and scientific management. His minute account of mechanization's transformation of the artifacts and organization of daily life leads to many original conclusions.

207   Gies, Joseph, and Gies, Francis. THE INGENIOUS YANKEES: THE MEN, IDEAS, AND MACHINES THAT TRANSFORMED A NATION, 1776-1876. New York: Thomas Y. Crowell Co., 1976. viii, 376 p. Illus., bibliog.

Generally a factually sound survey of the first century of U.S. technological development, the study is perhaps slightly marred by its organization around important inventors and innovators, which tends to emphasize the "great man theory." See Darwin Stapleton's perceptive review in TECHNOLOGY AND CULTURE 19 (January 1978): 121-22 on potentially misleading historiographical assumptions.

208   Keir, Malcolm. THE EPIC OF INDUSTRY. Vol. 5: THE PAGEANT OF AMERICA, A PICTORIAL HISTORY OF THE UNITED STATES. New Haven, Conn.: Yale University Press, 1926. 329 p. Illus., maps.

The value of this survey is not in the text, but in the large number (758) of woodcuts, photographs, and paintings of individuals, machines, and factories gathered together in one source. Arrangement is by industry with brief textual descriptions of inventors, inventions, and techniques.

209   Kranzberg, Melvin, and Davenport, William H., eds. TECHNOLOGY AND CULTURE: AN ANTHOLOGY. New York: Schocken, 1972. 364 p.

The anthology comprises twenty-one important articles from the first decade of TECHNOLOGY AND CULTURE, journal of the Society for the History of Technology. Arranged in four sections, "Technology and Society," "Technology and the Humanities," "Man and Machines," and "Invention and Innovation," the volume provides a useful introduction and survey of the field. Not limited to American history.

210   Kranzberg, Melvin, and Pursell, Carroll W., Jr., eds. TECHNOLOGY IN WESTERN CIVILIZATION. 2 vols. New York: Oxford University Press, 1967. 802, 772 p. Illus., bibliog.

This lengthy, compressed, and heavily illustrated anthology originated as part of a project in curriculum development for the Armed Forces. The first volume covers the emergence of industrial society from earliest times to 1900, while volume 2 concentrates on twentieth-century developments in the United States. Articles treat not only technological advances but

also the socio-cultural impact of those advances. A very
good text with excellent bibliographical suggestions.

211   Layton, Edwin T., Jr. TECHNOLOGY AND SOCIAL CHANGE IN
AMERICA. Interpretations of American History Series. New York:
Harper and Row, 1973. vii, 181 p. Bibliog.

Technology's relation to society is dealt with in a collection
of ten major articles, focusing on the origin and nature of
technological change and an assessment of its impact on
society.

212   Lilley, Samuel. MEN, MACHINES AND HISTORY: THE STORY OF
TOOLS AND MACHINES IN RELATION TO SOCIAL PROGRESS.
Rev. ed. New York: International Publishers, 1966. xiv, 352 p.
Illus.

Lilley covers the history of technology and its social impact
from the beginnings of agriculture in about 8,000 B.C. to
the mid-1960s, but concentrates on the period since the
industrial revolution. He believes "technological development is the single greatest factor in promoting and directing
social change."

213   Morison, Elting E. FROM KNOW-HOW TO NOWHERE: THE DEVEL-
OPMENT OF AMERICAN TECHNOLOGY. New York: Basic Books,
1974. xiii, 199 p. Bibliog.

While not particularly intended for the scholarly historian,
the book covers the development of American technology
through case examples of early canal building, iron manufacturing and the tungsten filament as reflected respectively
in the work of three engineers: John Jervis, John Fritz, and
William Coolidge. Believing technology has outstripped our
"vision" of what the human condition should be, the author
modestly proposes the establishment of small groups of concerned citizens to deal with specific technological developments, ultimately resulting in a new "common law."

214   Oliver, John W. HISTORY OF AMERICAN TECHNOLOGY. New
York: Ronald Press, 1956. viii, 676 p.

A survey of technology and its impact on American culture
includes some material on scientific developments. Arrangement is topical within each of four major time periods--
colonial, Revolution to Civil War, Civil War to 1900, and
twentieth century. Due to the study's breadth, treatment is
often thin. Not well-received in general.

215   Pursell, Carroll W., Jr., ed. READINGS IN TECHNOLOGY AND

AMERICAN LIFE. New York: Oxford University Press, 1969. ix, 470 p. Graphs, bibliog.

A solid collection of primary material ranging from the colonial period to the mid-1960s, with brief introductions accompanying each selection. Some specific authors and sources include William Byrd, Oliver Evans, Frederick W. Taylor, Herbert Hoover, Vannevar Bush, SCIENTIFIC AMERICAN, and ENGINEERING NEWS.

216   _____ . "Two Hundred Years of American Technology." TECHNOLOGY AND CULTURE 20 (January 1979): 1-195.

The collection of nine articles originally offered at the Society for the History of Technology's Bicentennial Meeting in late 1975 reflects the current state of the art. Eugene Ferguson's opening piece, "The American-ness of American Technology," offers an exceptionally clear statement on the humanistic aspects of technological change. Two other broad perspectives are provided by Nathan Rosenberg in "Technological Interdependence in the American Economy," and Ruth Cowan in "From Virginia Dare to Virginia Slims: Women and Technology in American Life." The remainder of the articles portray narrower slices of the picture and include Edwin Layton's "Scientific Technology, 1845-1900: The Hydraulic Turbine and the Origins of American Industrial Research," Reynold Wik's "Benjamin Holt and the Invention of the Track-Type Tractor," Bruce Sinclair's "Canadian Technology: British Traditions and American Influences," Thomas P. Hughes's "The Electrification of America: The System Builders," Carroll Pursell's "Government and Technology in the Great Depression," and John Burke's "Wood Pulp, Water Pollution, and Advertising."

217   Routledge, Robert. DISCOVERIES AND INVENTIONS OF THE NINETEENTH CENTURY. 13th ed. London: George Routledge and Sons, 1900. xv, 820 p. Illus., maps.

A popular account of important nineteenth-century discoveries and inventions which describes their principles and operation but notes little of the social context. Topics covered include steam engines, iron and steel, railroads, firearms, canals, bridges, printing, light, electricity, photography, explosives, and oil and minerals.

218   Singer, Charles, et al., eds. A HISTORY OF TECHNOLOGY. 5 vols. New York: Oxford University Press, 1954-58. lxiv, 827; lix, 802; xxxvii, 766; xxxiii, 728; xxxviii, 888 p. Illus., maps, bibliog.

The extensive overview of the history of technology primarily covers the Near East, Europe, and the United States up to 1900. Hundreds of illustrations contribute to the value of this work, as do bibliographical suggestions at the end of chapters.

Individual volume titles and their time periods are: Vol. 1: FROM EARLY TIMES TO FALL OF ANCIENT EMPIRES; Vol. 2: THE MEDITERRANEAN CIVILIZATIONS AND THE MIDDLE AGES, c. 700 B.C. to c. A.D. 1500; Vol. 3: FROM THE RENAISSANCE TO THE INDUSTRIAL REVOLUTION, c. 1500- c. 1750; Vol. 4: THE INDUSTRIAL REVOLUTION, c. 1750 to c. 1850; Vol. 5: THE LATE NINETEENTH CENTURY, c. 1850 to c. 1900. A "classic" starting point in the field.

219   Struik, Dirk. YANKEE SCIENCE IN THE MAKING. Boston: Little, Brown, 1948. Rev. ed. New York: Collier Books, 1962. 544 p. Bibliog.

Struik's somewhat random study of pre-civil War New England science and technology covers a wide range of individuals, inventions, and discoveries including their social context. . Although Eli Whitney erroneously receives credit as the inventor of interchangeable parts, this volume is still valuable.

220   White, Lynn, Jr. MACHINA EX DEO: ESSAYS IN THE DYNAMISM OF WESTERN CULTURE. Cambridge: M.I.T. Press, 1968. xi, 186 p.

The eleven essays revised for this collection are an important examination of the cultural context, mainly Hellenic and Christian, from which our science and technology has evolved. In a key essay, "The Historical Roots of Our Ecologic Crisis," originally appearing in SCIENCE (see no. 1414), the author explains that the merging of aristocratic science and empirical, work-oriented technology was a democratic revolution which fused brain and hand into a "functional unity," with not always positive results in terms of man's control over nature.

D. HISTORY OF ENGINEERING

221   Bathe, Greville, and Bathe, Dorothy. OLIVER EVANS: A CHRONICLE OF EARLY AMERICAN ENGINEERING. Philadelphia: Historical Society of Philadelphia, 1935. xx, 362 p. Illus., maps.

Including and depending heavily upon the known letters of Evans, 1755-1819, this biography offers insights not only into the improver of early milling techniques and the builder of early steam engines but also into the state of engineering in the late eighteenth and early nineteenth centuries. Well illustrated.

222   Calhoun, Daniel Hovey. THE AMERICAN CIVIL ENGINEER: ORIGINS AND CONFLICT. Cambridge: M.I.T. Press, 1960. xiv, 295 p. Map, bibliog.

In the standard study of early American civil engineering covering the period from roughly 1816 to 1846, Calhoun seeks to

answer the question, "How independent was the nineteenth-
century engineer?" The "conflicts" of professional and organizational loyalty suggest the early strength of corporate
America.

223   Calvert, Monte A. THE MECHANICAL ENGINEER IN AMERICA,
1830-1910: PROFESSIONAL CULTURES IN CONFLICT. Baltimore:
Johns Hopkins Press, 1967. xviii, 296 p. Illus., bibliog.

The author uses sociological methods to analyze the rise of
mechanical engineering as a profession and the impact of industrialization on this group. Two contrasting points of view--
that of the small shop, elitist entrepreneurs who dominated the
profession in the mid-nineteenth century, and their gradual replacement by those with a more formalized engineering educa-
tion--dominate the story.

224   Ferguson, Eugene S., ed. EARLY ENGINEERING REMINISCENCES
(1815-40) OF GEORGE ESCOL SELLARS. Washington, D.C.: Smithsonian Institution, 1965. xix, 203 p. Illus., maps.

Ferguson has carefully edited an extremely interesting and
valuable collection of reminiscences regarding early nineteenth-
century machines and mechanical skills. Well-selected illustrations accompany the text.

225   Finch, James Kip. ENGINEERING AND WESTERN CIVILIZATION.
New York: McGraw-Hill, 1951. x, 397 p. Illus., maps, bibliog.

Although touching upon earlier periods and countries, the author
concentrates on Victorian England and the United States in this
optimistic expression of faith in engineering advances and resultant social and economic progress. The United States has
been the leading light of Western civilization, the future of
which will continue to depend upon science and engineering.
Excellent annotated bibliography, although somewhat dated.

226   _____. THE STORY OF ENGINEERING. Garden City, N.Y.: Doubleday, 1960. xxvii, 528 p. Illus.

This volume provides a general, brief overview of engineering
by concentrating on the personalities involved. Finch's scope
is from the ancient world of Egyptians, Greeks, and Romans to
that of the twentieth-century skyscraper. Emphasis is on civil
engineering although other fields are included.

227   Gregory, Malcolm S[pencer]. HISTORY AND DEVELOPMENT OF ENGI-
NEERING. London: Longmans, 1971. x, 166 p. Illus., bibliog.

A brief survey of the engineer as designer through the ages.
Useful bibliographical references.

228   Kirby, Richard Shelton, and Laurson, Philip Gustave. THE EARLY YEARS OF MODERN CIVIL ENGINEERING. New Haven, Conn.: Yale University Press, 1932. xvi, 324 p. Illus., maps, bibliog.

> A thematic history of civil engineering in both Europe and the United States covering roughly the period from 1750 to 1850. Among topics included in the study are surveying, canals, roads, railroads, bridges, tunnels and subways, waterworks, sewers, river and harbor improvements, and materials. Brief biographical outlines of over one hundred early "civil engineers."

229   Kirby, Richard Shelton, et al. ENGINEERING IN HISTORY. New York: McGraw-Hill, 1956. vii, 530 p. Illus., bibliog.

> More than just America is covered in this introductory survey of engineering developments in Western civilization. While not particularly oriented toward the technical, the survey includes some sense of the relationship of the field "to other human activities because engineering has not evolved in a vacuum."

230   Layton, Edwin T., Jr. THE REVOLT OF THE ENGINEERS: SOCIAL RESPONSIBILITY AND THE AMERICAN ENGINEERING PROFESSION. Cleveland: Case Western Reserve University Press, 1971. xiv, 286 p. Bibliog.

> "The story of the professional development of American engineering from 1900 to 1940 is in large part the story of the clash between. . .two traditions": "conservatives" who believed themselves part of the business community and "progressives" who viewed themselves as an independent profession. This clash was epitomized by the attempt of the latter to solve the country's problems in the 1920s and 1930s by applying engineering principles to society as pitted against the conservative response by business groups, which ultimately resulted in a lapse into social apathy for many years. Good comparative bibliographic essay.

231   _____. "Veblen and the Engineers." AMERICAN QUARTERLY 19 (Spring 1962): 64-72.

> Layton labels Thorstein Veblen's belief that engineers would emerge as the revolutionary class in America "one of the strangest predictions in the history of social thought." Veblen was apparently misled by the increasing ambition, professionalism, and self-consciousness exhibited by engineers at the turn of the century. A move to preserve middle-class professional status was misconstrued by Veblen as an inclination to revolution.

232   Lewis, Gene D. CHARLES ELLET, JR.: THE ENGINEER AS INDIVID-
       UALIST, 1810-1862. Urbana: University of Illinois Press, 1968. ix,
       220 p. Illus., maps.

       Lewis sees his subject as typifying a struggle against the grow-
       ing specialization of engineering. Ellet was a civil engineer
       involved in the design and building of canals, suspension
       bridges, railroads, river improvements and flood control, and
       even military engineering. The biography suggests a great deal
       about the mobility and flexibility of at least some antebellum
       engineers.

233   McMahon, A. Michal. "Corporate Technology: The Social Origins of
       the AIEE." PROCEEDINGS OF THE INSTITUTE OF ELECTRICAL AND
       ELECTRONICS ENGINEERS 64 (September 1976): 1383-90.

       McMahon believes the "founding of the AIEE resulted from so-
       cial forces creating standardization and narrow specialties
       throughout American society." The Institute sought to central-
       ize and nationalize rapidly expanding electrical knowledge in
       late nineteenth-century America; its drive for professionalism
       was "a bureaucratic response to knowledge."

234   Merritt, Raymond H. ENGINEERING IN AMERICAN SOCIETY, 1850-
       1875. Lexington: University Press of Kentucky, 1969. xii, 199 p.
       Bibliog.

       The key to understanding the nineteenth-century origins of
       American leadership in industry and technology lay in the
       areas of transportation and communication and with the engi-
       neers involved therein. These engineers were largely respon-
       sible for societal advances and a concomitant set of new
       values, urban and cosmopolitan in nature. This interdisciplin-
       ary approach combines technical, social, intellectual, and
       economic history.

235   Morgan, Arthur E. DAMS AND OTHER DISASTERS: A CENTURY OF
       THE ARMY CORPS OF ENGINEERS. Boston: Porter Sargent, 1971.
       xxv, 422 p. Illus.

       Morgan, a hydraulic engineer and at times in conflict with the
       Corps, writes a critical history of the Army Corps of Engineers.
       He attributes many of its failures to its West Point tradition of
       education, which he believes unsuitable to civil projects.

236   Rothstein, William G. "The American Association of Engineers."
       INDUSTRIAL AND LABOR RELATIONS REVIEW 22 (October 1968):
       48-72.

       In a survey of the AAE from 1919 to 1923, the author views
       its ultimate failure as a reflection of the engineering profession

with differing, often competitive, fields, views, and occupational roles. The AAE was primarily an economic organization but also served as a lobbying group and was interested in engineer licensing and ethics.

237   Roysdon, Christine, and Khatri, Linda A. AMERICAN ENGINEERS OF THE NINETEENTH CENTURY: A BIOGRAPHICAL INDEX. New York: Garland, 1978. 250 p.

The index provides access to biographies of over 2400 American engineers, manufacturers, and inventors published in thirty-one nineteenth-century trade periodicals of wide national circulation. Each entry includes a brief description of the individual's contribution, birth and death dates, journal references, and biographical cyclopedia citations.

238   Sinclair, Bruce. PHILADELPHIA'S PHILOSOPHER MECHANICS: A HISTORY OF THE FRANKLIN INSTITUTE, 1824-1865. Baltimore: Johns Hopkins Press, 1974. xiv, 354 p. Illus., bibliog.

This history of the institutionalization of technology utilizes Philadelphia's Franklin Institute as its story vehicle. The Franklin Institute was the major technical organization prior to the Civil War involved in teaching, research, and publication. The author discusses the increasing role of government and the concepts of specialization and professionalism in technology. A valuable contribution.

239   Spence, Clark E. MINING ENGINEERS AND THE AMERICAN WEST: THE LACE-BOOT BRIGADE, 1849-1933. Yale Western Americana Series vol. 22. New Haven, Conn.: Yale University Press, 1970. xiii, 407 p. Illus., maps.

This survey of the growth of the mining profession and the rise of the academically trained engineer covers such topics as training, consulting, mine management, mining law, specialization, foreign endeavors, as well as personal, social, and political aspects.

240   Wisely, William A. THE AMERICAN CIVIL ENGINEER, 1852-1974: THE HISTORY, TRADITIONS, AND DEVELOPMENT OF THE AMERICAN SOCIETY OF CIVIL ENGINEERS. New York: American Society of Civil Engineers, 1974. ix, 464 p.

The preface states: "The chief aim of this book is to provide an accurate documentary reference to the broad range of ASCE activity since the founding of the society." Because Wisely treats the society as a detached whole, rather than dealing with individuals, the how's and why's of historical development are not as well developed as they might be. The work is arranged thematically rather than chronologically. Includes extensive appendixes.

E. HEALTH SCIENCES

1. Medicine

241   Dowling, Harry F. FIGHTING INFECTION: CONQUESTS OF THE TWENTIETH CENTURY. Cambridge, Mass.: Harvard University Press, 1977. x, 339 p.

Dowling, a participating physician in many of the events, describes the development of drugs and vaccines and the attendant social forces involved in fighting infectious disease.

242   Duffy, John A. THE HEALERS: THE RISE OF THE MEDICAL ESTABLISH-MENT. New York: McGraw-Hill, 1976. ix, 385 p. Bibliog.

An objective survey of the history of medicine and its social and ethical context. Specific topics include native American medicine, colonial medicine and physicians, surgery, military medicine, "irregular" practices, medical education and licensing, public health, the role of women and minorities in medicine, and the state of the art today. Inherent is the role of technology and technique. A good bibliographical essay provides hints for further reference.

243   Marks, Geoffrey, and Beatty, William K. THE STORY OF MEDICINE IN AMERICA. New York: Charles Scribner's Sons, 1973. xi, 416 p. Illus., bibliog.

A broad survey of medicine in the United States since 1600 includes chapters on medical practices, education, public health, and recent developments such as aerospace and nuclear medicine.

244   Marti-Ibañez, Felix, ed. HISTORY OF AMERICAN MEDICINE: A SYMPOSIUM. MD International Symposia Series. New York: MD Publications, 1959. 181 p. Bibliog.

The thirteen essays in this collection provide a reasonable survey of important developments in American medicine; a brief bibliography is appended to each. In addition to introductory and concluding summaries, specific topics include native American Indian medicine; colonial disease and medical practices; the development of medical education, research, societies, and journals; the physician as research scientist; and trends in public health.

245   Meade, Richard Hardaway. AN INTRODUCTION TO THE HISTORY
       OF GENERAL SURGERY. Philadelphia: W.B. Saunders Co., 1968.
       xi, 403 p. Illus.

    The title accurately describes this volume. After several intro-
    ductory chapters on general topics such as anatomy, infection,
    fractures, anesthesia, and blood transfusion, the author devotes
    a chapter to each specific area of surgical concentration. In-
    cludes non-American developments.

246   Packard, Francis R. HISTORY OF MEDICINE IN THE UNITED STATES.
       2 vols. New York: Paul B. Hoeber, 1931. xxxvi, 1,323 p. Illus.,
       bibliog.

    This standard work emphasizes the institutional development of
    American medicine from the colonial period to the beginnings
    of specialization.

247   Reiser, Stanley Joel. MEDICINE AND THE REIGN OF TECHNOLOGY.
       New York: Cambridge University Press, 1978. xi, 317 p. Illus.,
       bibliog.

    Reiser describes many of the technological advances of the past
    four centuries which have not only altered the practice of
    medicine but also changed the physician-patient relationship.
    "Objective" evidence has replaced the "subjective" evidence
    of the patient's sensations and the physician's observations in
    diagnostic judgments. Emphasis is on American and British
    developments including the microscope, stethoscope, thermom-
    eter, increasing knowledge of bacteriology and biological
    medicine, X-ray devices, electrocardiographs, and computers.
    Useful bibliography of material infrequently found elsewhere.

248   Rosen, George. PREVENTIVE MEDICINE IN THE UNITED STATES,
       1900-1975: TRENDS AND INTERPRETATIONS. New York: Science
       History Publications, 1975. 94 p. Illus.

    Rosen selectively traces the ideology, institutionalization, and
    techniques of preventive medicine in this century and outlines
    "the significance of current developments for future preventive
    action." Excellent bibliographical footnotes.

249   _____. THE SPECIALIZATION OF MEDICINE: WITH SPECIAL REFER-
       ENCE TO OPHTHALMOLOGY. New York: Froben Press, 1944. Re-
       print. New York: Arno Press, 1972. ix, 94 p.

    Medical specialization is a product of scientific and technologi-
    cal developments within medicine itself, but also of social
    change--for example, urbanization, which allows a physician
    to concentrate on a specific problem area because of the large
    numbers of afflicted people. Rosen examines not only the

technological and social emergence of specialization, but also
the attitudes surrounding it and some of the resultant problems.
Includes non-American information.

250   Shafer, Henry Burnell. THE AMERICAN MEDICAL PROFESSION, 1783
TO 1850. Studies in History, Economics and Public Law, vol. 417.
New York: Columbia University Press, 1936. Reprint. New York:
AMS Press, 1968. 271 p.

"The revolution in medicine after 1850 was made possible by
changes occurring between 1783 and 1850." Shafer surveys
these changes, which included technological developments in
the areas of cheaper publication for medical texts and journals,
improved means of communication and transportation, and the
trend toward specialization.

251   Shryock, Richard Harrison. THE DEVELOPMENT OF MODERN MEDI-
CINE: AN INTERPRETATION OF THE SOCIAL AND SCIENTIFIC FAC-
TORS INVOLVED. Philadelphia: University of Pennsylvania Press,
1936. xv, 442 p. Illus.

A path-breaking book in the social history of medicine.
Shryock was a leader in developing the history of medicine
from mere anecdotal and biographical sketches to encompass
"the interplay of social and internal factors." Information on
Europe as well as America is included. Although science plays
a larger role, technology is not ignored.

252   _____. MEDICINE AND SOCIETY IN AMERICA, 1660-1860. New
York: New York University Press, 1960. ix, 182 p.

The four chapters of this book were originally prepared as the
Anson G. Phelps Lectures at N.Y.U. Analysis of the origins
of the medical profession, the development of medical thought,
and public health converge in the final chapter on the transition period, 1820-1860, in which the author believes can be
seen the first signs of real medical progress.

253   _____. MEDICINE IN AMERICA, HISTORICAL ESSAYS. Baltimore:
Johns Hopkins Press, 1966. xviii, 346 p.

Sixteen important works of this noted scholar of the social history of medicine and public health comprise this volume. To
the author's introductory comment that "medical history involves
social and economic as well as biological content and presents
one of the central themes in human experience," one might
add technological content. In addition to a summary history of
American medicine, specific topics include public health,
scientific thought and medical research, women in medicine,
the physician, and medical historiography.

254   Stern, Bernhard J. MEDICINE IN INDUSTRY. Studies of the New
York Academy of Medicine Committee on Medicine and the Changing
Order. New York: Commonwealth Fund, 1946. xv, 209 p.

Industrialization has greatly affected health by creating new
diseases and modifying existing ones, while at the same time
contributing to a higher standard of living of which health
and medical care are important factors. Stern provides the
social, economic, legal, and professional settings of developments in industrial medicine through World War II.

255   Stevens, Rosemary. AMERICAN MEDICINE AND THE PUBLIC INTER-
EST. New Haven, Conn.: Yale University Press, 1971. xiii, 572 p.
Bibliog.

Medical specialization is examined in light of its effect on
the organization and politics of health services. Technological advance lies at the base of this specialization and improved health care but often creates problems of effective and
equitable distribution.

2. Public Health

256   Blake, John B[allard]. "The Origins of Public Health in the United
States." AMERICAN JOURNAL OF PUBLIC HEALTH 38 (November
1948): 1539-50.

The rise of public health in the second half of the nineteenth
century was directly connected to rapid urbanization and industrialization. Blake summarizes the highlights of sanitary
engineering, water supply and purification, and changing medical theory. A brief bibliography is appended.

257   _____. PUBLIC HEALTH IN THE TOWN OF BOSTON, 1630-1822.
Harvard Historical Studies, vol. 72. Cambridge, Mass.: Harvard University Press, 1959. xv, 275 p. Illus., maps, bibliog.

One of the best monographic studies of public health in a
particular city covers the period ending prior to the sanitary
reform movement of the mid-nineteenth century. Blake reveals a great deal about attitudes toward disease and health
as well as other social and political questions, not only for
Boston but for early America in general.

258   Cassedy, James H. CHARLES V. CHAPIN AND THE PUBLIC HEALTH
MOVEMENT. Cambridge, Mass.: Harvard University Press, 1962.
x, 310 p. Illus., bibliog.

Cassedy uses Chapin of Providence, R.I., as a biographical
tool with which to investigate the public health movement in
the quarter centuries on either side of 1900. He believes the

movement was typified more by Providence than by a giant
city like New York. Chapin played a major role in the
move from environmental sanitation as a "cure-all," important
as it was, to modern understanding of communicable disease
based on germ theory.

259   Duffy, John A. A HISTORY OF PUBLIC HEALTH IN NEW YORK CITY.
       Vol. 1: 1625-1866. Vol. 2: 1866-1966. New York: Russell Sage
       Foundation, 1968, 1974. xix, 619; xxi, 690 p. Illus., maps,
       bibliog.

       Social history dealing with the technological as well as the
       political and economic factors affecting public health in New
       York is examined from the city's beginnings as a colonial
       town to its position as the nation's largest urban center. The
       history was written as part of the one-hundredth anniversary of
       the 1866 establishment of the Metropolitan Board of Health, a
       model for many other urban health departments.

260   Galishoff, Stuart. SAFEGUARDING THE PUBLIC HEALTH: NEWARK
       1895-1918. Westport, Conn.: Greenwood Press, 1975. xv, 191 p.
       Bibliog.

       Newark's response to the major health problems created by
       rapid urbanization and extensive industrialization are examined
       in this case study. In particular, the Newark Board of Health
       and the control of contagious diseases reflected growing gov-
       ernment responsibility for public health and the growing inter-
       action of medicine and society.

261   Kramer, Howard D. "The Beginnings of the Public Health Movement
       in the United States." BULLETIN OF THE HISTORY OF MEDICINE 21
       (May-June 1947): 352-76.

       The beginnings of public health which emerged during the
       1840s and 1850s in response to rapid industrialization and
       urbanization are summarized.

262   Rosen, George. A HISTORY OF PUBLIC HEALTH. New York: MD
       Publications, 1958. 551 p. Bibliog.

       The most comprehensive study of public health covers the
       ancient world and Europe as well as the United States. The
       lack of a published survey solely on American developments
       makes this study indispensable. A bibliography and appendix
       material on memorable figures, health societies, and schools
       of public health add to the value of this survey.

263   Rosenkrantz, Barbara Gutman. PUBLIC HEALTH AND THE STATE:
       CHANGING VIEWS IN MASSACHUSETTS, 1842-1936. Cambridge,

Mass.: Harvard University Press, 1972. xiv, 259 p. Bibliog.

Rosenkrantz depicts changing theories of disease and the development of state responsibility for health by examining the interplay of moral reform, humanitarian zeal, and scientific objectivity. Valuable bibliographic essay.

F. INTELLECTUAL ATTITUDES

264 Abell, Aaron I[gnatius]. "American Catholic Reaction to Industrial Conflict: The Arbitral Process, 1885-1900." CATHOLIC HISTORICAL REVIEW 41 (January 1956): 385-407.

Abell contends that after 1885 the Catholic Church paid increased attention to the labor movement, generally in support, based upon the assumption that workers sought only the reform of working conditions, not revolt. The Church believed Christian social ethics must accompany industrialization. Largely narrative.

265 Adams, Henry. THE EDUCATION OF HENRY ADAMS. Edited by Ernest Samuels. Boston and New York: Houghton Mifflin Co., 1918. Rev. ed. 1973. xxx, 705 p. Bibliog.

The transformation of life by technology permeates Adams' consciousness. It was his belief that "the whole social, political, and economic problem is the resultant of the mechanical development of power." The shift in power from Nature and man to the machine is effectively realized in the chapter "The Dynamo and the Virgin," an account of the author's visit to the Gallery of Machines at the Paris Exhibition of 1900. This work offers a sensitive, contemporary view of a world pushed into violent flux by technology.

266 Akin, William E. TECHNOCRACY AND THE AMERICAN DREAM: THE TECHNOCRAT MOVEMENT, 1900-1941. Berkeley and Los Angeles: University of California Press, 1977. xvi, 227 p. Bibliog.

In answer to cultural questions posed by the Great Depression arose a group called the Technocrats. They believed America's inability to cope with modern technology in terms of production and distribution caused the Depression and, as the way out, "urged a doctrine of radical social engineering." Akin traces the rise of this group and the importance of the questions they raised regarding technology in modern society. He suggests their collapse was the result of an inability to develop a political philosophy compatible with democracy.

267 Bates, Ralph S. SCIENTIFIC SOCIETIES IN THE UNITED STATES. 3rd rev. ed. Cambridge: M.I.T. Press, 1965. 326 p. Bibliog.

"Scientific societies are among the outstanding agencies for increasing and diffusing the world's store of knowledge, [and
they] have been a potent force in the intellectual life of the
American people." Not so much a history, the work is a
reference guide to the more than two thousand societies
broadly concerned in some fashion with science and technology.

268   Beaver, Donald de B.   "Altruism, Patriotism, and Science: Scientific
Journals in the Early Republic." AMERICAN STUDIES 12 (Spring 1971):
5-19.

Expected success or financial profit fail to account for the dis-
proportionate rise of scientific and technical journals in the
early years of the republic. Rather, scientific and technical
knowledge "was regarded as the foundation and ally of the
useful arts," and was seen as the basis for future American
growth, both economically and politically. Scientific periodicals were used altruistically not only to disseminate knowledge,
but also to bring together and increase isolated scientific enterprise within the new republic. They also served as a place
to display both regional and national patriotic pride in scientific achievements.

269   Brown, Richard D.   "Modernization: A Victorian Climax." AMERICAN
QUARTERLY 27 (December 1975): 533-48.

Brown highlights the process of nineteenth-century "modernization"--the internalization of "a value structure emphasizing
rationalization, specialization, efficiency, cosmopolitanism,
and interest in a [better] future." Modernization is closely
linked with urbanization and industrialization, which are in
turn dependent upon technological improvements in transportation and communication.

270   Burner, David, and West, Thomas R.   "A Technocrat's Morality: Conservatism and Hoover the Engineer." In THE HOFSTADTER AEGIS,
edited by Stanley Elkins and Eric McKitrick, pp. 235-56. New York:
Alfred A. Knopf, 1974.

Burner and West analyze Hoover's early engineering career for
what it reveals about the philosophy of conservatism. Hoover
sought both an orderly structuring of society and a democratic
voluntarism. His sense of community involved a collective
methodology based upon American technology and suggests a
"classical conservative sensibility."

271   Callahan, Raymond E.   EDUCATION AND THE CULT OF EFFICIENCY.
Chicago: University of Chicago Press, 1962. vi, 273 p.

The adoption of business values and practices in public education from 1900 to 1930 is investigated along with the impact

of scientific management theory. The author concludes with
a call for more professional autonomy among educators based
on improved training and adequate financial support.

272   Chambers, Clarke A. "The Belief in Progress in Twentieth-Century
America." JOURNAL OF THE HISTORY OF IDEAS 19 (April 1958):
197-224.

A belief in progress has been a basic tenet throughout American history. Central to this belief were the material goods
produced through science and technology, of which the machine was a dominant symbol. The article traces the ups and
downs of the idea through twentieth-century progressivism,
depression, reform, war, and prosperity. Excellent footnotes.

273   Diamond, Sigmund, ed. THE NATION TRANSFORMED: THE CREATION
OF AN INDUSTRIAL SOCIETY. New York: George Braziller, 1963.
xiv, 528 p. Bibliog.

The collection of primary sources from "The Gilded Age"
(1876-1904) encompasses the broad social, economic, and
intellectual spectra characterizing the coming of age of the
industrial society. Selections include articles which had a
direct transforming influence, as well as commentary and interpretive pieces. Some authors represented are Frederick W.
Taylor, Henry Demarest Lloyd, Samuel Gompers, Jane Addams,
and William Graham Sumner. Introductory essays help place
the material in context.

274   Diggins, John P. THE BARD OF SAVAGERY: THORSTEIN VEBLEN
AND MODERN SOCIAL THEORY. New York: Seabury Press, 1978.
xiii, 257 p.

The most recent intellectual biography of Veblen, in which
the author seeks to establish his subject's place as one of the
great social theorists. Veblen was harshly critical of industrial capitalism and sought to explain its nature and development with an eye toward ending, through social planning, the
depredations and conspicuous consumption which it engendered.

275   Dorfman, Joseph. THORSTEIN VEBLEN AND HIS AMERICA. New
York: Viking Press, 1934. 556 p. Illus., bibliog.

A standard study of Veblen, his work, and its impact on American society and values. Includes a bibliography of Veblen's
work (see also no. 274 and no. 300).

276   Elsner, Henry, Jr. THE TECHNOCRATS: PROPHETS OF AUTOMATION.
Syracuse, N.Y.: Syracuse University Press, 1967. vii, 252 p. Illus.,
bibliog.

Elsner provides a historical, sociological study of the Technocracy movement (1932/33), which he believes originated primarily with the work of Thorstein Veblen. Technocrats sought to end the depression with a "scientific" ordering of society, business, and the economy, with control in the hands of a "technocracy," but they clearly had little real influence on American history, due to the radical nature of their proposals and the more moderate appeal of the New Deal.

277 Fisher, Marvin M. WORKSHOPS IN THE WILDERNESS: THE EUROPEAN RESPONSE TO AMERICAN INDUSTRIALIZATION, 1830-1860. New York: Oxford University Press, 1967. ix, 238 p. Bibliog.

An attempt is made to explain the changing American mythical image from "garden" to factory "workshop" as seen through European eyes. Most observers believed American progress to be assured by technology and industrialization, although some noted its attendant problems as well. The bibliography contains primary travel accounts.

278 Gilbert, James [B]. DESIGNING THE INDUSTRIAL STATE: THE INTELLECTUAL PURSUIT OF COLLECTIVISM IN AMERICA, 1880-1940. Chicago: Quadrangle Books, 1972. xi, 335 p. Bibliog.

Gilbert reviews the "collectivist" thinking that bound together a half-century of "progressive" reform movements characterized by a desire for social engineering in response to the industrial centralization of the American political economy. Four introductory chapters are followed by brief intellectual biographies of Edmond Kelly, King Gillette, Charles Steinmetz, William English Walling, Reinhold Niebuhr, and James Burnham. Valuable bibliographic essay.

279 _____. WORK WITHOUT SALVATION: AMERICA'S INTELLECTUALS AND INDUSTRIAL ALIENATION, 1880-1910. Baltimore: Johns Hopkins University Press, 1977. xv, 240 p. Illus.

Gilbert investigates the intellectual reactions to the problems of alienated work, individualism, and splintered community at the turn of the century. In particular, the thought of William James reflected the difficulty society had in grappling with the idea of a work ethic which no longer explained or satisfied American society.

280 Glicksburg, C.I. "Henry Adams and the Modern Spirit." DALHOUSIE REVIEW 27, no. 3 (1947-48): 299-309.

Glicksburg sees in Adams a transitional figure, one of the first moderns, and believes this explains his appeal to recent thought. Despite his failure to formulate a comprehensive theory of society, he challenges the twentieth century with his chronic cultural doubt, a preoccupation with science as the answer, and when that failed, the search for religious faith. THE EDUCATION OF HENRY ADAMS (no. 265) appeals to us not for its solutions, for there were none, but for the problems he posed and with which he struggled.

281   Hahn, Herbert F. "THE EDUCATION OF HENRY ADAMS Reconsidered." COLLEGE ENGLISH 24 (March 1963): 444-49.

Hahn suggests that Adams' dominant theme of a cultivated personality maladjusted to increasingly mechanized civilization was a literary device which reflected not his own problems of adjustment but rather those of a changing world. Adams did find some ground for faith in the human value of thought, for it was aspiration and striving that gave meaning to human existence.

282   Handlin, Oscar. "Science and Technology in Popular Culture." DAEDALUS 94 (Winter 1965): 156-70.

Handlin tries to unravel the tangled historical threads of popular attitudes toward science and technology, attitudes which at once confuse the two and both praise and mistrust them. Traditional understanding was undermined by rapid migration, urbanization, and industrialization, while changes in the ways of knowing offered both promises of perfectibility and problems of comprehension. Uneasiness "will be quieted only if science [including technology] is encompassed within institutions which legitimate its purpose and connect its practitioners with the populace."

283   Higham, John. "Hanging Together: Divergent Unities in American History." JOURNAL OF AMERICAN HISTORY 61 (June 1974): 5-28.

In an intellectual foray into the nature and quality of social cohesion, Higham finds three forms of unity in American society: (1) primordial unity--a corporate feeling of oneness, (2) ideological unity or explicit systems of general beliefs, and (3) a technical unity which emerged in the mid-nineteenth century and is largely characteristic of today's society. The latter "endorses a certain kind of interdependence, embodied in the image of the machine"; however, all three are necessary to a smoothly functioning society. Valuable references.

284   Hopkins, Charles Howard. THE RISE OF THE SOCIAL GOSPEL IN AMERICAN PROTESTANTISM, 1865-1915. New Haven, Conn.: Yale University Press, 1940. xii, 352 p.

Post-Civil War industrialization and its attendant problems

spurred the spread of the Social Gospel Movement with its
concern for social and economic injustice rather than just doctrine. Hopkins traces in detail the movement's development,
especially in the Unitarian, Congregational, and Episcopal
faiths.

285 Hughes, Thomas Parke, ed. CHANGING ATTITUDES TOWARD AMERI-
CAN TECHNOLOGY. New York: Harper and Row, 1975. ix, 340 p.

Twenty-four contemporary and historical interpretations of technology from 1832 to 1969 include not only negative and
positive attitudes but also ambivalent views. Selections are
largely from "middle-brow" popular literature in order "to
capture the sentiments. . .of the intelligent and literate layman." Introductory notes and a conclusion analyze writers
such as Henry David Thoreau, Theodore Roszak, Henry Adams,
Bertrand Russell, Archibald MacLeish, and other lesser-known
authors.

286 Hushbeck, Judy. "The Impact of Technology on Consciousness: Some
Viewpoints on the American Case, 1875-1930." SOCIAL SCIENCE 49
(Winter 1974): 19-32.

Late nineteenth- and early twentieth-century attitudes toward
American industrialization are illuminated through this study
of representative period writers and publications. The optimistic views of David A. Wells, Carroll D. Wright, and
Frederick W. Taylor not only enhanced the reputation of the
machine and its gifts, but also made factory discipline and
mechanization attractive. In such publications as SCIENTIFIC
AMERICAN, the machine assumed the status of a cultural
symbol of material and social equality. The approbation of
engineers and scientists, voiced by such social thinkers as
Thorstein Veblen and John Dewey, added to their aura of
virtue.

287 Kaplan, Sidney. "Social Engineers as Saviours: Effects of World War
I on Some American Liberals." JOURNAL OF THE HISTORY OF IDEAS
17 (June 1956): 347-69.

The idea of intelligence applied and directed by social engineers as the key to progress survived the Great War, albeit
in somewhat altered form, in the personages of John Dewey,
Randolph Bourne, Walter Lippmann, and Herbert Croly.
Kaplan briefly traces the development in thinking of these
four intellectual precursors of the Technocracy movement.

288 Kasson, John F. CIVILIZING THE MACHINE: TECHNOLOGY AND
REPUBLICAN VALUES IN AMERICA, 1776-1900. New York: Grossman
Publishers, 1976. xiv, 274 p.

An excellent analysis of the intellectual and social bases surrounding the growth of machine technology and the process of industrialization. Kasson concentrates on five selected themes: the introduction of domestic manufactures in the Revolutionary and Federal periods; the model factory town of Lowell, Massachusetts; Ralph Waldo Emerson's thoughts on technology; the aesthetic response to machinery; and the utopian-dystopian novels of the 1880s and 1890s.

289 Kranzberg, Melvin, and Gies, Joseph. BY THE SWEAT OF THY BROW: WORK IN THE WESTERN WORLD. New York: G.P. Putnam's Sons, 1975. 248 p.

Kranzberg and Gies trace Western ideas regarding work from their preindustrial origins in ancient agriculture and craftsmanship through the industrial factory of mass production to today's automation. A popular, but historically well-grounded survey with notes to guide readers to the more detailed secondary literature.

290 May, Henry F. PROTESTANT CHURCHES AND INDUSTRIAL AMERICA. New York: Harper and Brothers, 1949. Reprint. New York: Octagon, 1963. x, 297 p. Bibliog.

May examines the social thought, especially the social gospel theory, of the Protestant church, which emerged in response to the rapid industrialization of the latter third of the nineteenth century. The Presbyterian, Congregationalist, Baptist, Methodist, and Episcopalian denominations of the eastern and midwestern areas are considered.

291 Meier, Hugo A. "American Technology and the Nineteenth-Century World." AMERICAN QUARTERLY 10 (Summer 1958): 116-30.

Meier notes that nineteenth-century America was not at all isolationist with respect to its technology. This fact explains in part the development of nationalism, the struggle for international prestige, and, by 1900, an increased concern with the social goals of democracy for the world.

292 _____. "Technology and Democracy, 1800-1860." MISSISSIPPI VALLEY HISTORICAL REVIEW 43 (March 1957): 618-40.

Meier explores how technology came to be intellectually seen as providing "the physical means of achieving democratic objectives of political, social, and economic equality." He concludes that community support was the essential ingredient wherein technology became the central factor in an American faith in progress, blending the ideas of republicanism and democracy.

293   Miller, Perry. "The Responsibility of Mind in a Civilization of Machines." AMERICAN SCHOLAR 31 (Winter 1961): 51-69.

An important historian of American thought grapples with our seeming lack of intellectual concern in a machine culture. Drawing upon the nineteenth century for analogy, Miller advocates a responsibility of mind in dealing with a utilitarian society which by no means need be overpowered by machines.

294   Mondale, Clarence. "Daniel Webster and Technology." AMERICAN QUARTERLY 14 (Spring 1962): 37-47.

In an analysis of Webster's statements on technology and its consequences, Mondale suggests that his commentary, shifting as it did from a negative to a positive view with respect to government support for manufactures and the protective tariff, makes most sense when viewed as political oratory.

295   Mumford, Lewis. "Apology to Henry Adams." VIRGINIA QUARTERLY REVIEW 38 (Spring 1962): 196-217.

In order to reveal problems in today's society, Mumford tries to explain "the fatal inertness of Adams' contemporaries when confronted with his most challenging and penetrating insights into the prospects of our civilization." Mumford's plea for the restoration of "human feeling" and balance in a technologically dehumanized society stems in part from his fear of nuclear disaster. He finds parallels to his apprehension in Adams' reaction to the machine.

296   Nelson, John R., Jr. "Alexander Hamilton and American Manufacturing: A Reexamination." JOURNAL OF AMERICAN HISTORY 55 (March 1979): 971-95.

Nelson examines Hamilton's role as a premier advocate of American manufacturing, concluding that, despite certain platitudes to the contrary, he was generally unresponsive to domestic manufacturers. Reveals the politics and financial background surrounding the early development of American industrialization.

297   Oleson, Alexandra, and Brown, Sanborn C., eds. THE PURSUIT OF KNOWLEDGE IN THE EARLY AMERICAN REPUBLIC: AMERICAN SCIENTIFIC AND LEARNED SOCIETIES FROM COLONIAL TIMES TO THE CIVIL WAR. Baltimore: Johns Hopkins University Press, 1976. xxv, 372 p.

The first of three proposed volumes, this collection of nineteen invited papers on learned scientific and technical societies provides an up-to-date summary of research on this facet of intellectual history. Well-written essays with valuable footnotes include information on general developments as well as specific societies such as the Royal Society of London in America, the Franklin Institute, and the American Society for the Advancement of Science.

298   Ostrander, Gilman M. AMERICAN CIVILIZATION IN THE FIRST MACHINE AGE 1890-1940. New York: Harper and Row, 1970. 414 p. Bibliog.

Ostrander's thesis is that American society has been greatly affected by technology, which has produced a unique experience. This change was realized in an intellectual shift after 1890 which emphasized a "filiarchal" faith in youth and a machine culture at the expense of older values of age and experience. Based primarily on secondary sources.

299   Rezneck, Samuel. "The Rise and Early Development of Industrial Consciousness in the United States, 1760-1830." JOURNAL OF ECONOMIC AND BUSINESS HISTORY 4 (August 1932): 784-811.

Rezneck chronicles the early rise of an industrial consciousness, which often predated actual manufacture, from the political and economic stress of the revolutionary era, through the reports of Tench Coxe and Alexander Hamilton, to the industrial fairs, societies for the encouragement of manufacturing, and technical journals which marked "a more mature stage of development."

300   Riesman, David. THORSTEIN VEBLEN: A CRITICAL INTERPRETATION. New York: Charles Scribner's Sons, 1953. Reprint 1960. xvii, 221 p. Bibliog.

Riesman views Veblen as being in the vein of Populist thought and considers, among other things, his subject's attitudes toward technology. Veblen believed society must accommodate itself to the machine and that a viable and humane post-industrial society was possible. A chronology, a list of Veblen's books, and a useful annotated bibliography of secondary literature on Veblen are included.

301   Rodgers, Daniel T. THE WORK ETHIC IN INDUSTRIAL AMERICA, 1850-1920. Chicago: University of Chicago Press, 1974. xv, 300 p.

Traditional values of work were shaken by evolving industrial forms. As a result, many people questioned the factory system and the direction of progress. Rodgers discusses the origin of the work ethic and its changing expression in debates over wages, creativity, leisure, feminism, children's literature, and political rhetoric. Good intellectual history, with valuable footnotes.

302   Rosenberg, Charles E. NO OTHER GODS, ON SCIENCE AND AMERI-
       CAN SOCIAL THOUGHT. Baltimore: Johns Hopkins University Press,
       1976. xiii, 273 p. Bibliog.

       Concentrating on the scientist and his role in society, Rosenberg
       attempts to fathom "the relationship between social thought,
       social policy, and the prestige and data of science." Science
       is broadly defined herein, and should be of some interest to
       historians of technology. Most chapters appeared as articles
       but have been revised for this volume.

303   Samuels, Ernest. HENRY ADAMS: THE MAJOR PHASE. Cambridge,
       Mass.: Harvard University Press, 1964. xv, 687 p. Bibliog.

       The third volume of the author's study of Adams covers the
       years from 1890 to 1918. Several chapters analyze the auto-
       biographical commentary, THE EDUCATION OF HENRY
       ADAMS (no. 265).

304   Sanford, Charles [L.]. "The Intellectual Origins and New Worldliness
       of American Industry." JOURNAL OF ECONOMIC HISTORY 18
       (March 1958): 1-16.

       Early factory developers had to convince society that European
       mistakes of poverty and worker degradation would not be re-
       peated in America. As a consequence, a moralizing influence
       characterized the development of American industry. Interest-
       ing intellectual history reveals contemporary attitudes up to
       the mid-nineteenth century, although it might be debatable
       how far this argument can be carried.

305   Schultz, Stanley K. THE CULTURE FACTORY: BOSTON PUBLIC
       SCHOOLS, 1789-1860. New York: Oxford University Press, 1973.
       xviii, 394 p. Illus., maps.

       Adapting the factory metaphor used by nineteenth-century
       schoolmen, Schultz sees the public school being used to incul-
       cate American values in both native and immigrant children in
       a nation experiencing social turmoil as it underwent rapid ur-
       banization and industrialization. Educators fashioned a bureau-
       cracy and "system" of schools to grapple with moral disloca-
       tion. An excellent treatment.

306   Sibley, Mulford Q. "Utopian Thought and Technology." AMERICAN
       JOURNAL OF POLITICAL SCIENCE 17 (May 1973): 255-81.

       Sibley searches the history of utopian-dystopian writing from
       the classic treatment of Plato's REPUBLIC to Aldous Huxley's
       recent ISLAND (1962) for clues to an understanding of our
       technology. He believes we must stop and answer the questions
       of the utopists: "Why? To what ends? Within what priori-

ties? Under what controls? With what consequences? With what effects on human beings? Why go faster and faster?"

307 Smith, Henry Nash, ed. POPULAR CULTURE AND INDUSTRIALISM, 1865-1890. Documents in American Civilization Series. New York: New York University Press, 1967. xxvii, 522 p.

Ninety primary documents exemplify the commonplace attitudes and thoughts that most Americans took for granted. Focus is on both their faith in technology, hard work, progress, and the subsequent disillusionment with the negative effects or technology's impact on society. Included are sections on industrialism, the city, immigrants, protest, the arts, and religion.

308 Wagar, W. Warner. GOOD TIDINGS: THE BELIEF IN PROGRESS FROM DARWIN TO MARCUSE. Bloomington: Indiana University Press, 1972. ix, 398 p.

Wagar deals with the intellectual concept of progress since about 1880 in both Europe and North America, bringing it up to the present. Both prophets and naysayers are examined. Wagar personally believes man generally has progressed during his stay on earth but has by no means reached perfection. The problem in the twentieth century is the great explosion of mankind--beliefs and institutions have not kept up with knowledge, power, commodities, people, desires, and wastes.

Part 3

THE INNOVATIVE PROCESS

A. BIBLIOGRAPHIES

309   Rothenberg, Albert, and Greenberg, Bette. THE INDEX OF SCIENTIFIC WRITINGS ON CREATIVITY; GENERAL: 1566-1974. Hamden, Conn.: Archon Books, 1976. xviii, 274 p.

> Although this unannoted bibliography covers the process of creativity in world literature from the sixteenth century to the present, several chapters include citations relevant to science and technology in America: "Creativity--General"; "Creativity and Psychopathology"; "Developmental Studies"; "Scientific Creativity"; "Creativity in Industry, Engineering, and Business"; and "Facilitating Creativity through Education." The stated purpose of the bibliography is to assist interdisciplinary research on the topic. Writings cited include medical, psychological, and psychiatric studies; case studies; biographical and theoretical approaches; empirical observations by scientists, engineers, social scientists, and educators; and systematic theories.

310   Schorr, Alan Edward. EXPERTISE AND TECHNOLOGICAL INNOVATION: 1960-1970. Exchange Bibliography no. 567. Monticello, Ill.: Council of Planning Librarians, 1974. 15 p.

B. BOOKS AND ARTICLES

311   Aitken, Hugh G.J., ed. EXPLORATIONS IN ENTERPRISE. Cambridge, Mass.: Harvard University Press, 1965. x, 420 p.

> The eighteen articles comprising this collection are drawn primarily from the journal EXPLORATIONS IN ENTREPRENEURIAL HISTORY with an excellent introduction by the editor. Many of the subjects included are non-American and hence provide a good comparative framework.

312   Benson, Barbara E., ed. BENJAMIN HENRY LATROBE AND MONCURE
       ROBINSON: THE ENGINEER AS AGENT OF TECHNOLOGICAL TRANS-
       FER. Greenville, Del.: Eleutherian Mills Historical Library, 1975.
       71 p.   Illus.

       In the proceedings of a 1974 Eleutherian Mills Regional Con-
       ference in Economic History, Edward Carter and Darwin
       Stapleton, through the biographical approach, reveal the indi-
       vidual as the primary agent of technological transfer in ante-
       bellum America. Their respective analyses of Latrobe, a civil
       engineer, and Robinson, a railroad engineer, are followed by
       a commentary by John B. Rae.

313   Birr, Kendall. PIONEERING IN INDUSTRIAL RESEARCH: THE STORY
       OF THE GENERAL ELECTRIC RESEARCH LABORATORY. Washington,
       D.C.: Public Affairs Press, 1957. ix, 204 p. Bibliog.

       An institutional study of a modern industrial research lab con-
       centrates on organization and administration rather than on the
       process of invention.

314   Bright, James R. "Opportunity and Threat in Technological Change."
       HARVARD BUSINESS REVIEW 41 (November-December 1963): 76-86.

       Business management must develop means to respond to and
       anticipate technological innovation. Bright examines techno-
       logical trends and discusses the means of advance and impact
       in seven areas including computers, alteration of materials,
       preservation, energy, and transportation. Further consequences
       are forecast. Examples are somewhat dated.

315   _____, ed. RESEARCH, DEVELOPMENT, AND TECHNOLOGICAL
       INNOVATION. Homewood, Ill.: Richard D. Irwin, 1964. xvii,
       783 p. Illus., bibliog.

       Graduate educational training for managers dealing with "radi-
       cal" technological change and its interactions with social,
       economic, and political factors was initiated with this first
       text on the subject. Bright emphasizes the necessity for reali-
       zation of the social implications of rapid technological innova-
       tion. Five parts address the process of innovation, case studies
       in the use of advanced technology, evaluation of technological
       opportunities, planning and forecasting.

316   Buhl, Lance C. "Mariners and Machines: Resistance to Technological
       Change in the American Navy, 1865-1869." JOURNAL OF AMERICAN
       HISTORY 61 (December 1974): 703-27.

       The Navy's condemnation of the steamship WAMPANOAG in
       1869 and a parallel decision to depend primarily upon sail pow-
       er form the basis for an examination of resistance to technol-

ogy, which the author believes to be more than a technical dispute or a psychological and intellectual argument for the maintenance of a life-style. It also included a sociopolitical dimension, with many officers fearing a loss of status, authority, or control.

317   Burlingame, Roger. INVENTORS BEHIND THE INVENTOR. New York: Harcourt, Brace, and Co., 1947. 211 p. Illus.

Burlingame dispels some of the myths surrounding older hero-inventors and tries to explain changes in the process of invention which have led to their demise. Chapters on the individuals behind great inventors such as Franklin, Fulton, Morse, Bessemer, Ford, and Edison show that even then, but especially now, the complexities of science and technology "belie an heroic age of invention."

318   Constant, Edward W. II. "A Model for Technological Change Applied to the Turbojet Revolution." TECHNOLOGY AND CULTURE 14 (October 1973): 553-72.

A model of "presumptive anomaly" for describing innovation or change is based on the development of the turbojet as a case example. Constant suggests that scientific insight or advance is frequently more important than economic pressure in inducing certain kinds of technological advance.

319   Danhoff, Clarence H. GOVERNMENT CONTRACTING AND TECHNOLOGICAL CHANGE. Washington, D.C.: Brookings Institution, 1968. xiii, 472 p.

Widespread federal support of science and technology has been a major development of the post-World War II years. This is primarily an internal study of the government contract system, in itself revealing much about recent changes in the process of technological innovation; however, the final chapter touches upon ethical and value questions suggesting several avenues for fruitful investigation.

320   Daniels, George H., ed. NINETEENTH-CENTURY AMERICAN SCIENCE: A REAPPRAISAL. Evanston, Ill.: Northwestern University Press, 1972. xv, 274 p.

Although most of these papers are devoted to critiques of the historiography of American science and analyses of scientific research, four articles by Charles Rosenberg, Edwin Layton, Carroll Pursell, and Bruce Sinclair deal with the interrelationships between science, technology, and entrepreneurship. Specific topics include the late nineteenth-century agricultural experiment stations, relationships between science and technology and science and industry, and technical education.

321   DeCamp, L. Sprague. THE HEROIC AGE OF AMERICAN INVENTION.
       Garden City, N.Y.: Doubleday, 1961. 290 p. Bibliog.

       Most of the volume is devoted to describing particular indi-
       viduals and their technical contributions in the traditional
       mode of heroic inventors and includes chapters on Samuel
       Morse and the telegraph, Cyrus McCormick and the reaper,
       Alexander Bell and the telephone, Thomas Edison and the
       electric light, George Selden and the automobile, and R.A.
       Fessenden and Lee DeForest and the radio. To be fair,
       DeCamp does note that "most invention is a matter of many
       men's making successive improvements."

322   Ferguson, Eugene S. "On the Origin and Development of American
       Mechanical 'Know-How.'" MIDCONTINENT AMERICAN STUDIES
       JOURNAL 3 (Fall 1962): 3-15.

       In searching for an explanation behind the "know-how" neces-
       sary for the development of an American industrial complex,
       the author suggests the existence of a mechanical community
       of knowledge, in which information was freely passed among
       its members. Other important components were European
       mechanical and engineering influences, American travels to
       Europe to gather information, and an inherent ability and self-
       reliance.

323   Fox, Frank W. "The Genesis of American Technology 1790-1860; An
       Essay in Long-Range Perspective." AMERICAN STUDIES 17 (Fall 1976):
       29-48.

       American inventive genius and the intimate association between
       technology and culture can only be understood from a broad
       study of social, environmental, and individual motivation.
       Elements of the American inventive man include individualism,
       incredible mobility in career and geographic location, free
       exchange of information among "tinkers," a conviction that
       mechanical inventiveness led to success, and "an unqualified
       confidence in the future." Valuable references.

324   Gilfillan, S. Colum. "Social Implications of Technological Advance."
       CURRENT SOCIOLOGY 1, no. 4 (1953): 191-265.

       The social context of invention is more complex than historians
       have tended to believe. It is difficult to isolate an invention's
       origin in time, hard to define it exclusively, and generally
       impossible to assign it to a unique inventor. Thus it is difficult
       as well to measure its effects precisely. This paper serves as
       an introduction to a lengthy annotated bibliography by Gilfillan
       and Alfred B. Stafford (pp. 211-65), covering chiefly literature
       published after World War II.

325 _____. THE SOCIOLOGY OF INVENTION. Chicago: Follett Publishing Co., 1935. Reprint. Cambridge: M.I.T. Press, 1970. xiii,
185 p. Bibliog.

This sociological classic opens with a list of thirty-eight
"social principles of invention," comprehending the origins
and sources of innovation, the "life cycle" of inventions, and
the role of personalities versus larger social forces. In the
light of these principles, the author examines the development
of the merchant ship. He concludes that social planning is
needed to guide inventions and control their impact. Massive
bibliography.

326 _____. SUPPLEMENT TO THE SOCIOLOGY OF INVENTION. San
Francisco: San Francisco Press, 1971. x, 229 p. Bibliog.

Chapter-by-chapter notes update the original work, along with
a controversial chapter on national and racial factors in invention and brief history. The bibliography of the original work
is somewhat updated.

327 Habakkuk, H.J. AMERICAN AND BRITISH TECHNOLOGY IN THE
NINETEENTH CENTURY: THE SEARCH FOR LABOUR-SAVING INVEN-
TIONS. New York: Cambridge University Press, 1962. ix, 222 p.

An interesting, but controversial, speculative argument suggests
that American industrialization resulted from and was characterized by a ready acceptance of inventions and technical
innovations due to labor shortages. Habakkuk concentrates his
argument on the first half of the century but believes the process continued, albeit to a lesser degree, after 1850.

328 Hacker, Louis M. THE WORLD OF ANDREW CARNEGIE: 1865-1901.
New York: J.B. Lippincott Co., 1968. xxxvii, 473 p. Bibliog.

An extension of the ideas set forth in Hacker's earlier work,
THE TRIUMPH OF AMERICAN CAPITALISM (1940), the present
study uses Carnegie as a focus for a broader examination of
industrialization. He uses the concepts of entrepreneurship
and William Graham Sumner's folkways or cultural mores to
explain the process which really began only after 1865.

329 Hughes, Thomas Parke. ELMER SPERRY: INVENTOR AND ENGINEER.
Baltimore: Johns Hopkins University Press, 1971. xvii, 348 p. Illus.

This is an excellent biography of an inventor, engineer, and
entrepreneur involved in the field of automatic or feedback
controls from 1880 to 1930. Hughes views Sperry as a transitional figure in the change from an age of heroic invention
to the beginnings of organized "R and D." The study reveals
much about the process of innovation and entrepreneurship.

330   ___, ed. "The Development Phase of Technological Change."
TECHNOLOGY AND CULTURE 17 (July 1976): 423-81.

The special issue is oriented around the comparatively un-
studied theme of technological development as opposed to
invention and innovation. Hughes provides an introduction
to three main articles--Lynwood Bryant's "The Development
of the Diesel Engine," Thomas M. Smith's "Project Whirlwind:
An Unorthodox Development Project," and Richard G. Hewlett's
"Beginnings of Development in Nuclear Technology." There is
also a summary comment by Charles Susskind.

331   "Innovation in Science." SCIENTIFIC AMERICAN 199 (September
1958): 58-178.

An article by Jacob Bronowski on the creative process introduces this special issue. Discussions of innovation in four
basic fields of science--mathematics, physics, biology, and
technology--are followed by analyses of the imagination from
physiological and psychological viewpoints.

332   Jeremy, David J. "British Textile Technology Transmission to the United
States: The Philadelphia Region Experience, 1770-1820." BUSINESS
HISTORY REVIEW 47 (Spring 1973): 24-52.

A useful summary of the complexity of textile technology
transfer and its application. Textile technology, at this time,
had a "non-verbal" character because of the lack of published
operating procedures and representative drawing. For this
reason, the immigrating artisan who could operate smuggled
machinery or build it from memory or with the aid of models
and parts was the most important component in technology
transfer.

333   ___. "Innovation in American Textile Technology during the Early
19th Century." TECHNOLOGY AND CULTURE 14 (January 1973):
40-76. Illus.

The process of innovation in American textile production from
1812 to 1840 was affected by crowded product markets and
large-scale, vertically integrated manufacturing operations combined with a shortage of unskilled labor. Concentration on
inexpensive, low-to-medium grade standardized goods and a
variety of technical improvements resulted in principles which
would later contribute to American mass production in the
twentieth century.

334   Jewkes, John; Sawers, David; and Stillerman, Richard. THE SOURCES
OF INVENTION. New York: St. Martin's Press, 1958. Reprint.
New York: W.W. Norton, 1969. xii, 428 p.

Written from an economic point of view, this study of the conditions which have stimulated invention also impinges on the fields of history, science, technology, and law. The inventive process in the nineteenth century is compared to that of recent times. Elements in the industrial setting which seem to encourage or stifle innovation are analyzed. The individual inventor also receives attention. Part 2 consists of brief case histories of a large number of inventions, such as the cotton picker, ballpoint pen, cyclotron, jet engine, insulin, safety razor, zipper, rockets, television, and synthetic detergents.

335 Josephson, Mathew. EDISON: A BIOGRAPHY. New York: McGraw-Hill, 1959. xii, 511 p. Illus.

Edison, in the mode of "heroic inventor," is seen as a transitional figure bridging the gap between crude mechanical inventors of an earlier day and the systematic experimentation of twentieth-century research laboratories. The volume also details relationships between the process of invention and the economics of the day.

336 _____. THE ROBBER BARONS: THE GREAT AMERICAN CAPITALISTS, 1861-1901. New York: Harcourt, Brace and Co., 1934. Reprint. New York: Harcourt, Brace, and World, 1962. ix, 474 p. Bibliog.

Josephson characterizes the business leaders of the post-Civil War era as "Robber Barons," not ethical agents of material progress despite their many contributions.

337 Kelly, Patrick, and Kranzberg, Melvin, eds. TECHNOLOGICAL INNOVATION: A CRITICAL REVIEW OF CURRENT KNOWLEDGE. San Francisco: San Francisco Press, 1978. xviii, 390 p. Bibliog.

This state-of-the-art study was compiled under a National Science Foundation grant to understanding of "R and D." Part 1 covers "The Ecology of Innovation," while part 2 covers "Aspects of Technological Innovation." Among the contributors are Kranzberg, Frederick Rossini, Nathan Rosenberg, Paul Strassman, James Bright, Thomas Parke Hughes, and Simon Kuznets. There is a lengthy bibliography which, although not annotated, contains a wealth of material.

338 Layton, Edwin [T., Jr.]. "Mirror-Image Twins: The Communities of Science and Technology in Nineteenth-Century America." TECHNOLOGY AND CULTURE 12 (October 1971): 562-80.

Layton notes the incompleteness of the traditional model of the scientific creation of new knowledge which technologists then apply. Rather, he finds an adoption in various technological fields of scientific methodology, creating a "mirror image." The author also deals briefly with the values of the two communities and their impact upon social responsibility.

339   Livesay, Harold C. ANDREW CARNEGIE AND THE RISE OF BIG BUSINESS. Library of American Biography. Boston: Little, Brown, 1975. xi, 202 p. Illus., bibliog.

Livesay's major contribution in this brief biography is to describe Carnegie within a perspective of late nineteenth-century industrial development.

340   Mansfield, Edwin. THE ECONOMICS OF TECHNOLOGICAL CHANGE. New York: W.W. Norton and Co., 1968. x, 257 p. Illus.

The creation and assimilation of new products and processes as well as the role of innovations in economic growth is analyzed in this overview. Research in areas of economics, social sciences, management, and operations research is consulted. Written for an audience wider than specialized professionals, Mansfield ranges from research and development, productivity's reliance on technological change, and the diffusion of new techniques, to sociological considerations of labor displacement by automation and public policy on technology.

341   _____, et al. RESEARCH AND INNOVATION IN THE MODERN CORPORATION. New York: W.W. Norton and Co., 1971. x, 239 p.

Reporting research done by Mansfield and his graduate students over a five-year period, the focus of this study is technological innovation in the individual firm. The process is followed from research, project selection, factors influencing costs, and time to diffusion. Coexisting issues, such as the problems of small business in obtaining government "R and D" contracts, the lag between invention and innovation, and time and cost overruns in commercialization are considered.

342   Michaelis, Michael. "Technology for Society." AMERICAN ECONOMIC REVIEW 58 (May 1968): 492-501.

An interplay between technological and social change is essential to the continued economic viability of technological innovation. The traditional social mechanism, the market, which translates innovations into use will not be adequate in the future. Value-laden traditional culture must interact with the value-free superculture of technology to lessen resistance to change and create a "functional" rather than product-oriented corporate society.

343   Murphy, John Joseph. "Entrepreneurship in the Establishment of the

American Clock Industry." JOURNAL OF ECONOMIC HISTORY 26 (June 1966): 169-86.

> Clockmaking, because of its early reliance upon a division of labor and use of measuring devices, was important to the introduction of the "American System" of interchangeable parts. By drawing upon the work of Eli Terry of Connecticut, Murphy makes some interesting suggestions regarding the process of innovation and transfer of technological knowledge.

344 National Bureau of Economic Research. THE RATE AND DIRECTION OF INVENTIVE ACTIVITY: ECONOMIC AND SOCIAL FACTORS. Princeton, N.J.: Princeton University Press, 1962. x, 635 p.

> These conference papers present economic and social analyses of factors determining inventive effort or the output of inventive activity. While all of the papers are written by leading economists interested in economic growth and efficiency, key factors such as intellect, scientific discovery, welfare, "R and D" management, and market demand receive attention. Case studies of the petroleum and aluminum industries, the transistor, and Dupont's innovations also appear.

345 Orth, Charles D. III; Bailey, Joseph C.; and Wolek, Francis W. ADMINISTERING RESEARCH AND DEVELOPMENT: THE BEHAVIOR OF SCIENTISTS AND ENGINEERS IN ORGANIZATIONS. Homewood, Ill.: Robert D. Irwin and Dorsey Press, 1964. x, 585 p. Illus.

> By joining numerous case studies with research reports, the authors isolate those unique aspects of management of professionals in research and development. The climate which must be dealt with arises largely from rapid innovation and obsolescence, the brilliant individual, and uncertainty of role concept. Research studies and pragmatic examples from industry include considerations of the values of managers, scientists, and engineers; factors affecting creativity; conflict and cooperation; barriers to innovation; and dual hierarchy.

346 Passer, Harold C. "The Electric Light and the Gas Light: Innovation and Continuity in Economic History." EXPLORATIONS IN ENTREPRENEURAL HISTORY 1 (March 1949): 1-9.

> A brief analysis of Edison's invention of the central station lighting system points out that the breakthrough was the conceptual one of imitating with electricity the distribution of the existing gas light industry. Edison combined inventiveness and entrepreneurship to "subdivide the electric light."

347 Porter, Glenn. THE RISE OF BIG BUSINESS, 1860-1910. Crowell American History Series. New York: Thomas Y. Crowell Co., 1973. vii, 119 p. Bibliog.

In a short but useful summary of the coming of big business in an institutional framework, Porter neatly ties this to advances in technology and the changing social-value structures of the era. Excellent bibliographical essay.

348   Prout, Henry G[oslee]. A LIFE OF GEORGE WESTINGHOUSE. New York: American Society of Mechanical Engineers, 1921. Reprint. Technology and Society Series. New York: Arno Press, 1972. xiii, 375 p. Illus.

This topical biography is primarily arranged by type of invention with several chapters on the impact of the developer of the airbrake, who also held numerous patents in such other areas as electricity, traction, turbo-generation, and natural gas. Westinghouse left no personal written record, therefore, much of the volume was compiled with the assistance of his friends and associates who contributed information and impressions. The appendix contains a list and description of Westinghouse patents.

349   Pursell, Carroll W., Jr. EARLY STATIONARY STEAM ENGINES IN AMERICA: A STUDY IN THE MIGRATION OF A TECHNOLOGY. Washington, D.C.: Smithsonian Institution Press, 1969. viii, 152 p. Illus., bibliog.

A brief but excellent account of technology transfer discusses the introduction of the stationary steam engine in America from the colonial period to the mid-nineteenth century. Pursell concentrates on the individuals involved in bringing the steam engine to this country and the subsequent uses to which the engines were put, rather than presenting a technical history per se.

350   Rae, John B. "The 'Know-How' Tradition: Technology in American History." TECHNOLOGY AND CULTURE 1 (Winter 1959): 139-50.

In this early article in the then-emerging field of the history of technology, the author makes three points regarding the structure of technology and its profound effect on American society: the recognition that American technology has largely been pragmatic, the need to understand the "interrelationship between technological development and industrial applications," and the suggestion that historians "must give more attention to the role of technology in the growth and organization of industry."

351   Ray, William, and Ray, Marlys. THE ART OF INVENTION: PATENT MODELS AND THEIR MAKERS. Princeton, N.J.: Pyne Press, 1974. xii, 132 p. Illus., bibliog.

"A tribute to the ingenuity and imaginative spirit of the nineteenth century American inventor" as seen in patent models. The numerous illustrations are largely chosen for aesthetic rather than historical reasons but are revealing of the inventive process.

352   Rosenberg, Nathan. "The Direction of Technological Change: Inducement Mechanisms and Focusing Devices." ECONOMIC DEVELOPMENT AND CULTURE CHANGE 18 (October 1969): 1-24.

Rosenberg suggests several alternatives regarding problem solving in industrialization. While noting the ultimate incentive as economic in nature, he suggests that technology itself, in terms of labor disruption or constraints on supply, such as those brought on by war or legal proceedings, may well explain more about the specific directions of technological innovation.

353   _____. "Economic Development and the Transfer of Technology." TECHNOLOGY AND CULTURE 11 (October 1970): 550-75.

Rosenberg provides a number of historical examples from late nineteenth- and early twentieth-century Britain and the United States to illustrate potential problems in technology transfer, not only internationally but also from one industry to another. Problems include how the processes of learning and specialization can be institutionalized, public acceptance and taste for products, producer initiative in mass production, and the ability to fulfill contracts. He concludes that the highest research priority should be finding the most suitable means to an individual country's ends.

354   _____. "Factors Affecting the Diffusion of Technology." EXPLORATIONS IN ECONOMIC HISTORY 10 (Fall 1972): 3-33.

The diffusion of technology, including its timing, is important to understanding economic growth. By drawing upon historical examples from Great Britain and the United States, Rosenberg outlines a framework for understanding some of the supply limitations to the adoption of "new" inventions: incremental developments in the technology itself, associated human skills relative to its adoption, the necessity for complementary inventions and improvements in competing "old" technologies.

355   _____. "On Technological Expectations." ECONOMIC JOURNAL 86 (September 1976): 523-35.

Technological dynamism, rather than producing rapid innovation in industry and business, leads instead to a period of "lag" in which changes are not readily adopted. Entrepreneurs and managers, sensitive that a decision to implement an improvement may result in their being saddled with a "soon-to-be-obsolete-technology," will wait until the rate of change slows and the product stabilizes.

356 _____. "Science, Invention and Economic Growth." ECONOMIC JOURNAL 84 (March 1974): 90-108.

Since Schmookler's analysis in INVENTION AND ECONOMIC GROWTH (no. 358), economists have considered invention to be dependent on market demand. Rosenberg contends that inventive activity is also related to the state of scientific and technical knowledge at any given time. He demonstrates, with numerous examples, that economic forces do not act within a vacuum in shaping the direction of technical progress but work in concert with knowledge, complementarity of processes, and the corresponding cost of producing a successful invention.

357 Ruttan, Vernon W. "Usher and Schumpeter on Invention, Innovation and Technological Change." QUARTERLY JOURNAL OF ECONOMICS 73 (November 1959): 596-606.

Ruttan attempts to clarify the meaning of invention, innovation, and technological change by using a comparison of Joseph A. Schumpeter (no. 361) and Abbot P. Usher (no. 367) as his focus of analysis. The article is valuable more for the concise presentation of the thought of these two theorists than for his own suggestions regarding definitions of this terminology.

358 Schmookler, Jacob. INVENTION AND ECONOMIC GROWTH. Cambridge, Mass.: Harvard University Press, 1966. xv, 332 p. Illus., bibliog.

Although the influence of technological innovation on economic growth is established, Schmookler analyzes the obverse--the effects of economic growth on technology. His theories are essentially based on an examination of patent statistics. Relationships covered are important inventions as causes of further invention, market demand and innovation, and "inevitability" of certain inventions. Appendixes list references to important inventions in agriculture, paper, petroleum, and railroad industries.

359 _____. PATENTS, INVENTION, AND ECONOMIC CHANGE. Cambridge, Mass.: Harvard University Press, 1972. xvii, 292 p. Illus., bibliog.

Papers not published in Schmookler's INVENTION AND ECONOMIC GROWTH (no. 358) are included in this volume. The five articles consider the relationships between inventive activity, technological change, industrial growth, and the

market structure. Detailed tables which classify patents by
year, type, industry, and probable use are appended.

360   Schon, Donald A. TECHNOLOGY AND CHANGE: THE NEW HERA-
CLITUS. New York: Delacorte Press, 1967. xix, 248 p. Bibliog.

The author sees industrial invention as a metaphor for change
in American society. Schon builds from a consideration of the
process of invention, to technological innovation in the corporation, patterns of technological change within industries, and
finally to the consequences of such change for social values
and norms. Our view of technological innovation as part of
orderly, planned progress, that is, as a manageable, rational
force, is constantly resisted by the irrationality of invention,
interindustry invasion, and the undermining of technological
values. Case studies of change in the textile, machine tool,
and building industries are appended.

361   Schumpeter, Joseph A. BUSINESS CYCLES: A THEORETICAL, HISTORI-
CAL, AND STATISTICAL ANALYSIS OF THE CAPITALIST PROCESS. 2
vols. New York: McGraw-Hill, 1939. xxv, 1,095 p.

This "classic" theoretical study, despite many recent critical
responses, has served as an inspiration or take-off point for
many subsequent entrepreneurial historians. It is Schumpeter's
thesis that business cycles have a direct relationship to great
technological innovations and entrepreneurial breakthroughs.

362   Strassmann, W. Paul. RISK AND TECHNOLOGICAL INNOVATION:
AMERICAN MANUFACTURING METHODS DURING THE NINETEENTH
CENTURY. Ithaca, N.Y.: Cornell University Press, 1959. xii,
249 p. Bibliog.

Strassmann is concerned with the interaction between social
forces of business enterprise and technological change. He
sees the entrepreneur as a creative factor in economic development who in general operated in a low-risk or predictable
social, political, and business atmosphere conducive to innovation. Examples are drawn from industries such as iron and
steel, textiles, machine tools, and electric power. Useful
bibliography.

363   "Technological Progress and Economic Institutions." AMERICAN ECO-
NOMIC REVIEW 44 (May 1954): 161-200.

Two articles plus discussion are contained in this section of
the papers and proceedings of the sixty-sixth annual meeting
of the American Economic Association. Irving H. Siegel, in
"Conditions of American Technological Progress," surveys the
major forces which shaped technological progress in this

country and those which will have influence in the future.
Among these are control of nature, aspects of the American
character (mechanical ability, optimism, mobility, and competitiveness), scarcity of labor, private economic institutions,
and educational system. Future growth will depend on research, further mechanization, government policy, and resources. W. Rupert MacLaurin, in "Technological Progress
in Some American Industries," analyzes whether large industries tend to create rapid technological progress or conservatism. Highest rate of technical innovation is linked to
research effort, patents, monopoly, state of engineering art,
and entrepreneurial leadership.

364   Temin, Peter. "Labor Scarcity and the Problem of Industrial Efficiency
        in the 1850s." JOURNAL OF ECONOMIC HISTORY 26 (September
        1966): 277-98.

        Historians have frequently argued, based on mid-nineteenth
        century British observation, that extensive American adoption
        and development of machine-based manufacturing was due to
        a scarcity of labor. By examining interest rates and the
        availability of land and capital, Temin can find no evidence
        to support this thesis. Instead, he suggests that an asymmetry
        in communications and information flow between two countries
        employing essentially the same technology ultimately resulted
        in a divergence of American technology.

365   _____. "Steam and Waterpower in the Early Nineteenth Century."
        JOURNAL OF ECONOMIC HISTORY 26 (June 1966): 187-205.

        This paper examines the use of stationary steam engines in
        America about 1840 by detailing the nature of the machines
        used and the factors underlying the decision to use steam or
        water power in particular industries such as iron, textiles,
        lumber, and food processing. Temin finds that the local
        rather than national market was a prime consideration in de-
        cisions regarding power and that pressure to favor labor-saving
        innovations such as the steam engine was not evident.

366   Uselding, Paul J. "Henry Burden and the Question of Anglo-American
        Technological Transfer in the Nineteenth Century." JOURNAL OF
        ECONOMIC HISTORY 30 (June 1970): 312-37.

        Uselding uses the career of Henry Burden to illustrate the role
        of the emigré in the process of diffusion of mechanical tech-
        niques cross-culturally and within a particular nation. Burden
        was involved in arms manufacture at the Springfield Armory,
        was an entrepreneur in the forging of nails, railroad spikes,
        and horseshoes, and was also an inventor of machinery utilized
        in the production of bar iron from 1820 through the Civil War.

367   Usher, Abbott P. A HISTORY OF MECHANICAL INVENTIONS. New
       York: McGraw-Hill, 1929. Rev. ed. Cambridge, Mass.: Harvard
       University Press, 1954. Reprint. Boston: Beacon Press, 1959. xiv,
       450 p. Illus., bibliog.

       A classic study of the process of innovation as it is related to
       economic history emphasizes continuity and the origin of new
       inventions as based in earlier developments to which no indi-
       vidual is indispensable. Chapters on specific subjects expli-
       cating this thesis cover water wheels, windmills, clocks,
       printing, textile machinery, and machine tools. Valuable
       despite the fact that most of the examples do not pertain to
       the United States.

368   Vanderbilt, Byron M. INVENTING: HOW THE MASTERS DID IT.
       Durham, N.C.: Moore Publishing Co., 1974. ix, 375 p. Illus.

       This examination of the process of invention through brief
       case studies of Charles Goodyear, Alexander Graham Bell,
       Thomas A. Edison, George Westinghouse, Edward Goodrich
       Acheson, and Alfred Bernhard Nobel, emphasizes personal
       backgrounds and research methods. Three concluding chapters
       summarize this material and relate it to more recent develop-
       ments and views regarding the process of invention.

369   Wall, Joseph F. ANDREW CARNEGIE. New York: Oxford University
       Press, 1970. xii, 1,137 p. Illus.

       The most complete and revealing biography of Carnegie, the
       iron and steel magnate.

370   Welch, Walter L. CHARLES BATCHELOR: EDISON'S CHIEF PARTNER.
       Syracuse, N.Y.: Syracuse University Press, 1972. x, 118 p. Illus.

       Welch's brief biography of Edison's associate and chief labora-
       tory assistant emphasizes the relationship between the two men
       and Batchelor's contributions to the inventive process. The
       author based his work on the Batchelor papers housed at the
       Edison National Historical Site.

371   White, George R., and Graham, Margaret B.W. "How to Spot a '
       Technological Winner." HARVARD BUSINESS REVIEW 56 (March-April
       1978): 146-52.

       High-level managers must accept the responsibility for assessing
       the merit of a potentially radical technological innovation.
       A framework for evaluation, based on retrospective study of
       the transistor and the subsonic jet engine, is presented. The
       assessment method is also applied to currently developing
       technologies--the computerized car and the supersonic jet.

372   Wilkinson, Norman B. "Brandywine Borrowings from European Technology." TECHNOLOGY AND CULTURE 4 (January 1963): 1-13.

The article focuses on industries along the Brandywine River as an example of the unrecognized dependence of American industry upon European methods, machinery, and "know-how" for the period from 1791 to the first protective tariff of 1816. The author also discusses the nature of this technology transfer.

Part 4

INDUSTRIALIZATION

A. SURVEYS

1. Bibliography

373   Lovett, Robert W. AMERICAN ECONOMIC AND BUSINESS HISTORY:
       A GUIDE TO INFORMATION SOURCES. Management Information
       Guide Series, no. 23. Detroit: Gale Research Co., 1971. 323 p.

       Lovett's selective, but wide-ranging, annotated bibliography
       includes the following major divisions: economics, business,
       agriculture, labor, science and technology, and general refer-
       ence works. Some works on Canadian history are included
       but the emphasis is on the United States, in particular books
       published from 1948 to 1970. Although not particularly
       values-oriented, there is a wealth of background material on
       the process of industrialization included herein.

2. Books and Articles

374   Bishop, J[ohn]. Leander. A HISTORY OF AMERICAN MANUFACTURES
       FROM 1608-1860. 3 vols. 3d ed. 1868. Reprint. Reprints of Economic
       Classics. New York: Augustus M. Kelley, 1966. 702, 654, 574 p.
       Illus.

       A large part of this older standard survey of American manu-
       facturing up to the Civil War is biographical. Volume 1
       covers the colonial period and the early Republic and is still
       valuable for its general description of industries, while volume
       2 takes a somewhat similar approach for the remainder of the
       period. Volume 3 is less successful by today's standards and
       contains brief descriptions of specific individuals and manufac-
       turing concerns that, incidentally, were financial contributors
       to the volume. The lack of a table of contents and of clear
       organization is a problem, but there is an index for each vol-
       ume.

375   Bolles, Albert S. THE INDUSTRIAL HISTORY OF THE UNITED STATES.
       3d ed. Norwich, Conn.: Henry Bill Publishing Co., 1878. Reprint.
       Reprints of Economic Classics. New York: Augustus M. Kelley, 1966.
       x, 936 p. Illus.

       An old but still useful survey. The author's topical division
       includes: agriculture and horticulture; manufactures; shipping
       and railroads; mines, mining, and oil; banking, insurance,
       and commerce; trade unions and the eight-hour movement; and
       a final chapter on Canadian industries. Approximately three
       hundred engravings.

376   Clark, Victor Seldon. HISTORY OF MANUFACTURES IN THE UNITED
       STATES. Contributions to the Economic History of the United States,
       Carnegie Institution of Washington. 3 vols. Rev. ed. New York:
       McGraw-Hill, 1929. 607, 566, 467 p. Illus., maps, bibliog.

       A standard history for anyone interested in the economic impact
       of technology provides good coverage of most aspects of manu-
       facturing and industry from 1607 to 1928. An extensive bib-
       liography lists many late nineteenth- and early twentieth-
       century sources.

377   Cole, Arthur Harrison, ed. INDUSTRIAL AND COMMERCIAL CORRES-
       PONDENCE OF ALEXANDER HAMILTON ANTICIPATING HIS REPORT
       ON MANUFACTURES. Library of Early American Business and Industry,
       vol. 24. Chicago: A.W. Shaw, 1928. Reprint. Reprints of Economic
       Classics. New York: Augustus M. Kelley, 1968. xxviii, 334 p. Illus.

       The collection of letters and other sources from which Hamilton
       prepared his famous 1791 REPORT ON MANUFACTURES in-
       cludes the REPORT itself. Together with Cole's introductions,
       these documents provide an important picture of domestic in-
       dustry in the early national period.

378   Hays, Samuel P. THE RESPONSE TO INDUSTRIALIZATION, 1885-1914.
       The Chicago History of American Civilization. Chicago: University of
       Chicago Press, 1957. ix, 211 p. Bibliog.

       Hays analyzes the impact of industrialization upon individual
       farmers, workers, and businessmen and their variety of responses
       in this thematic survey treatment of the Populist-Progressive
       period. The dichotomy of individualism versus organization
       and bureaucracy, the rapid growth of cities, southern and
       western protest, political change, and foreign policy were
       major themes in the adjustment to industrialism and are covered
       herein. A list of important dates is provided.

379   Jaher, Frederic Cople, ed. THE AGE OF INDUSTRIALISM IN AMERICA.
       New York: Free Press of Glencoe, 1968. x, 400 p.

Twelve articles dealing with selected aspects of industrialization and the resulting social change and search for community during the period from approximately 1870 to 1930 are chosen for this anthology. Specific topics include: economic growth and laissez-faire; political leadership in the United States Senate; immigration; black response; Atlanta in the Progressive era; metropolitanism and western urban elites; Boston Brahmins; class and status; American trade unionism; Horatio Alger; the World's Fairs of 1876, 1893, and 1933; and the Protestant response to social change.

380   Mitchell, Broadus, and Mitchell, George Sinclair. THE INDUSTRIAL REVOLUTION IN THE SOUTH. Baltimore: Johns Hopkins University Press, 1930. xiv, 298 p.

Twenty-seven articles on the social effects of southern cotton manufacturing. Industrial development was typified by three stages--a concentration on technical problems, the reaction of workers against exploitation, and industrial maturity defined as "the establishment of a certain balance of power between human and mechanical forces." Most of the articles concentrate on the middle stage, although the authors then believed the industry was about to enter the third stage.

381   Nelson, Daniel. MANAGERS AND WORKERS: ORIGINS OF THE NEW FACTORY SYSTEM IN THE UNITED STATES, 1880-1920. Madison: University of Wisconsin Press, 1975. x, 234 p. Bibliog.

Nelson examines developments in the evolution of the factory system and the emergence of modern industrial administration, the dominant themes of which were "the substitution of formal, centralized controls for ad hoc, decentralized controls and the increasing influence of the management over the factory and its labor force." The focus is on the changing relationship between manager and employee, especially in larger manufacturing industries.

382   Preyer, Norris W. "Why Did Industrialization Lag in the Old South?" GEORGIA HISTORICAL QUARTERLY 55 (Fall 1971): 378-96.

An agrarian ideal, closely tied to a fear of abolition, which emphasized the debilitating physical, moral, and psychological effects of the factory system, explains the South's reluctance to industrialize.

383   Tryon, Rolla Milton. HOUSEHOLD MANUFACTURES IN THE UNITED STATES, 1640-1860: A STUDY IN INDUSTRIAL HISTORY. Chicago: University of Chicago Press, 1917. xii, 413 p. Bibliog.

Tryon describes the family system of household manufactures and . its relationship to social, political, and general industrial history and traces its development through the shop to factory stage. Only goods formerly made in the home or on the plantation from self-produced raw materials are discussed. Thus, the "putting out" system, for example, is excluded.

384   Veblen, Thorstein. THE THEORY OF BUSINESS ENTERPRISE. 1904. 2d ed. New York: Charles Scribner's Sons, 1915. vii, 400 p.

The modern capitalist industrial system is dominated by the machine process and investment for profit. Veblen analyzes the nature of the interlocking, standardized procedures which form the machine process as well as the financial manipulations of entrepreneurs. He then discusses the effect of these developments on culture. The machine process inculcates regularity and mechanical precision in habits of life while it masters and disciplines the worker's actions and thought processes. Mental patterns resort to cause and effect. The workman is adapted to his work; he too must be standardized and interchangeable. Anthropomorphic habits of thought are eliminated.

385   Weisberger, Bernard A. THE NEW INDUSTRIAL SOCIETY. American Republic Series, vol. 5. New York: John Wiley and Sons, 1969. ix, 162 p. Illus., maps.

What was different about America in 1900 from a generation before? Was the America of 1900 "new" in comparison to the America of the 1870s? Weisberger attempts to unravel the effect of industrialization upon the economic, urban, intellectual, and political realms of social change. A valuable concluding historiographical essay sets this theme into the broader scope of history.

386   Wright, Carroll D. THE INDUSTRIAL EVOLUTION OF THE UNITED STATES. 1895. Reprint. New York: Russell and Russell, 1967. 362 p. Illus., maps.

The final third of this older survey of the development of mechanical industries during the colonial period and the nineteenth century covers the impact of machinery upon labor and the growth of the labor movement. Wright concludes: "The centers devoted to industrial pursuits are the centers of thought, of mental friction, of intelligence, and of progress."

387   _____. REPORT ON THE FACTORY SYSTEM OF THE UNITED STATES. Tenth Census, 1880. Washington, D.C.: Government Printing Office, 1883. v, 78 p. Illus., bibliog.

An important early study of the factory system includes information on its development; impact on wages, prices, and pro-

duction; and legislation. The report focuses on cotton textiles
and provides some comparative material on the British system
and its influence. Thirteen plates illustrate worker housing.
Wright optimistically concludes that "the factory system has
not affected society so badly as has been generally believed."

B. PRE-INDUSTRIAL TECHNOLOGY

388   Bedini, Silvio A. THINKERS AND TINKERS: EARLY AMERICAN MEN
OF SCIENCE. New York: Charles Scribner's Sons, 1975. xix, 521 p.
Illus., bibliog.

The history of American science from settlement to approximately
1825 is told from the point of view of little-known men, the
"mathematical practitioners," who contributed in great measure
to the development of the American nation. An expansion of
the author's EARLY AMERICAN SCIENTIFIC INSTRUMENTS
AND THEIR MAKERS (1964), this volume covers the work of
map makers, surveyors, navigators, science teachers, and the
makers of mathematical instruments. Well illustrated with a
glossary of terms.

389   Bridenbaugh, Carl. THE COLONIAL CRAFTSMAN. New York: New
York University Press, 1950. Reprint. Chicago: University of Chicago
Press, 1961. x, 214 p. Illus.

Six lectures on the American craftsman in the preindustrial
era cover his work in the rural areas of the North and South
and the urban city. The artisan as businessman, and his position in society and role as citizen are also covered. Intriguing
social history, although somewhat lacking by recent standards
in analytical modeling.

390   Carroll, Charles F. THE TIMBER ECONOMY OF PURITAN NEW
ENGLAND. Providence, R.I.: Brown University Press, 1973. xiii,
221 p. Maps.

The almost universal use of wood in every phase of seventeenth-
century New England life is emphasized in this wide-ranging
social history. Although lacking in detailed technical material,
this is a valuable overview.

391   Hindle, Brooke, ed. AMERICA'S WOODEN AGE: ASPECTS OF ITS
EARLY TECHNOLOGY. Tarrytown, N.Y.: Sleepy Hollow Restorations,
1975. vii, 218 p. Illus., maps, bibliog.

Six original articles and the editor's introduction on the social
and economic importance of wood in American life note the
prevalent use of this abundant material resource until the mid-

nineteenth century. Subjects covered include the early
seventeenth-century exploitation of the primeval forest, the
link between woodworking machinery and building technology
in the early nineteenth century, a pictorial essay on early
lumbering techniques, wooden instrument making, a description of colonial watermills, and the theme that water power
continued to play an important technological and economic
role long after the development of the steam engine. Well
illustrated with drawings and photographs.

392   . THE PURSUIT OF SCIENCE IN REVOLUTIONARY AMERICA,
1735-1789. Chapel Hill: University of North Carolina, 1956. xi,
410 p. Illus., bibliog.

Technology (in colonial terms, "useful knowledge") is often
intimately related to science, and Hindle explicates this relationship well, especially in chapter 10, "American Improvement." "It was one of the articles of faith of the Enlightenment that science could be applied to the improvement of the
material conditions of life."

393   Olton, Charles S. ARTISANS FOR INDEPENDENCE: PHILADELPHIA
MECHANICS AND THE AMERICAN REVOLUTION. Syracuse, N.Y.:
Syracuse University Press, 1975. 172 p. Bibliog.

While much of the content of this brief study of Philadelphia's
master craftsmen in the period from 1765 to 1790 relates to
revolutionary politics, there is some valuable information on
preindustrial artisanship and the manner in which craftsmen
lived.

394   Sloane, Eric. A MUSEUM OF EARLY AMERICAN TOOLS. New York:
Wilfred Funk, 1964. Reprint. New York: Ballantine Books, 1973.
xvi, 108 p. Illus.

A collection of brief informal descriptions of early American
hand tools and the manner in which each was used is presented.
Excellent pen-and-ink sketches by the author accompany each
subject clarifying the techniques. Also interesting is the
author's A REVERENCE FOR WOOD (1965, 1974).

395   Tunis, Edwin. COLONIAL CRAFTSMEN AND THE BEGINNINGS OF
AMERICAN INDUSTRY. Cleveland: World Publishing Co., 1965.
159 p. Illus.

Forty-eight skilled artisan trades in the colonial period each
receive a one to five page general summary, which is accompanied by several very useful pen-and-ink sketches drawn by
the author.

396   Weiss, Harry B., and Weiss, Grace M. FORGOTTEN MILLS OF EARLY

NEW JERSEY. Trenton: New Jersey Agricultural Society, 1960.
94 p. Illus., bibliog.

Brief sketches of a variety of milling activities in late
eighteenth- and early nineteenth-century New Jersey include
such specific types as oil, plaster, bark, indigo, tanning, tilt,
rolling and slitting, nail and screw making.

397   Zimiles, Martha, and Zimiles, Murray. EARLY AMERICAN MILLS.
New York: Bramhall House, 1973. xii, 290 p. Illus., maps, bibliog.

The primary theme of this visual survey of New England and
New York mills is the aesthetic, although some attention is
given to the technology itself. Especially useful for its more
than 350 illustrations, both historical and contemporary.

C. MACHINE TOOLS AND INTERCHANGEABLE PARTS

398   Green, Constance McL[aughlin]. ELI WHITNEY AND THE BIRTH OF
AMERICAN TECHNOLOGY. The Library of American Biography.
Boston: Little, Brown, 1956. viii, 215 p. Bibliog.

A standard biography of Whitney, the study helps to perpetuate
the myth of his invention of the system of interchangeable
parts.

399   Howard, Robert A. "Interchangeable Parts Reexamined: The Private
Sector of the American Arms Industry on the Eve of the Civil War."
TECHNOLOGY AND CULTURE 19 (October 1978): 633-49.

Howard explores the private arms industry to clarify the extent
of interchangeability within the "American System." Because
private manufacturers were more interested in producing inexpensive, high-quality arms than in achieving interchangeability
as "a proper goal," they turned to the more economical hand-
fitting method. Military needs required interchangeability and
cost was not a major consideration. Thus, the "attainment of
interchangeability was a function of the precision required in
the mechanism being produced and the market's desire for this
feature."

400   Lincoln, Jonathan Thayer. "The Beginnings of the Machine Age in New
England: David Wilkinson of Pawtucket." NEW ENGLAND QUARTERLY
6 (December 1933): 716-32.

Behind the oft-told story of the New England textile industry
was that of the early machine builders. One of the earliest
and most important was Samuel Slater's brother-in-law,
Wilkinson. His blacksmith's shop served as a training-school
for other mechanics, inventors, and builders. Lincoln also

gives at least partial credit to Wilkinson for developing the slide-lathe, an important component of all machine tools.

401 Mirsky, Jeannette, and Nevins, Allan. THE WORLD OF ELI WHITNEY. New York: Macmillan, 1952. xvi, 346 p. Illus., bibliog.

Based on the Whitney papers at Yale, this biography goes beyond the mere personal life of the inventor and includes several chapters on the social and economic import of the cotton gin and his work on interchangeable parts. The reader should be cautious of claims for Whitney's "invention" of the latter concept.

402 Roe, Joseph Wickham. ENGLISH AND AMERICAN TOOL BUILDERS. New York: McGraw-Hill, 1916. Reprint. New York: McGraw-Hill, 1926. xv, 315 p. Illus., maps, bibliog.

This early but valuable history of English and American machine-tool builders covers the major developments in the field. Arrangement is generally by important individuals and places. Approximately two-thirds is devoted to the American scene.

403 _____. "Interchangeable Manufacture." TRANSACTIONS OF THE NEWCOMEN SOCIETY 17 (1936-37): 165-74.

A brief summary of the development of interchangeable parts is valuable only for its sense of overview. Individual aspects of the development have been analyzed more completely elsewhere.

404 Rolt, L.T.C. A SHORT HISTORY OF MACHINE TOOLS. Cambridge: M.I.T. Press, 1965. 256 p. Illus., bibliog.

In a solid survey of the metal-cutting machine-tool industry in Britain and the United States starting with the Industrial Revolution, Rolt emphasizes broad development rather than technical details, but he does not analyze social and economic effects in any depth.

405 Rosenberg, Nathan. "Technological Change in the Machine Tool Industry, 1840-1910." JOURNAL OF ECONOMIC HISTORY 23 (December 1963): 414-46.

The specialized machine-tool industry played an important role in the industrialization process, which depended upon the development and spread of similar technological innovations. The nature and growth of this "technological convergence" is examined with examples drawn from the firearms, sewing machine, bicycle, and automobile industries. Includes a comment by W. Paul Strassmann.

406 ____, ed. THE AMERICAN SYSTEM OF MANUFACTURES. Edinburgh: University Press, 1969. 440 p. Illus.

Rosenberg contributes a lengthy introductory analysis to three important British documents which describe the "American System" of manufacturing by interchangeable parts. The documents were the result of investigations regarding the suitability of the system to British needs and include the REPORT OF THE COMMITTEE ON THE MACHINERY OF THE UNITED STATES, 1855, and the SPECIAL REPORTS of George Wallis and Joseph Whitworth, 1854.

407 Sawyer, John E. "The Social Basis of the American System of Manufacturing." JOURNAL OF ECONOMIC HISTORY 14 (Winter 1954): 361-79.

Mid-nineteenth-century Europeans and post-World War II British "productivity teams" sent to look at American industries recorded similar observations. Analysis leads Sawyer to conclude that sociocultural conditions and pressures such as education, the absence of class and craft restraints, an emphasis on individualism, the mobility and adaptability of Americans, and a belief in progress were extremely important influences on industrial activity.

408 Sinclair, Bruce. "At the Turn of a Screw: William Sellars, the Franklin Institute, and a Standard American Thread." TECHNOLOGY AND CULTURE 10 (January 1969): 20-34.

The development of a standard system of screw threads, a significant contribution to the American system of mass production, is the subject of this brief case study. In the decade of the 1860s, when the United States was expanding into international industrial competition, the support of the federal government as well as private interests such as the Franklin Institute were important to the successful adoption of this innovation.

409 Smith, Merritt Roe. "John H. Hall, Simeon North, and the Milling Machine: The Nature of Innovation among Antebellum Arms Makers." TECHNOLOGY AND CULTURE 14 (October 1973): 573-91.

The development of the milling machine was a crucial phase in the rise of the "American System" of interchangeable parts and "provides an apt illustration of the migration and diffusion of mechanical ideas during the formative period of American industrialization." Smith argues against the heroic theory of invention. Illustrated.

410 Steeds, W[illiam]. A HISTORY OF MACHINE TOOLS, 1700-1910.

London: Oxford University Press, 1969. xx, 181 p. Illus.

The history of the chronological development of metal-working machine tools concentrates on British and American developments. Approximately 200 figures and plates contribute to the clarity of this volume.

411   Uselding, Paul [J.]. "Elisha K. Root, Forging, and the 'American System.'" TECHNOLOGY AND CULTURE 15 (October 1974): 543-68.

Root's active career spanned the period from the late 1830s to the late 1850s and reveals the contribution of die forging to the development of interchangeable parts in the manufacturing of axes and revolvers. Uselding's particular interest is with the theory that diminishing economic returns from increased inventiveness in a given technological approach provide incentive for alternative technologies, in this case from milling machinery to die forging. Revealing of the development of special-purpose machinery and the transfer of technical knowledge from one industry to another.

412   Woodbury, Robert S. "The Legend of Eli Whitney and Interchangeable Parts." TECHNOLOGY AND CULTURE 1 (Summer 1960): 235-54.

The author debunks a common theory in American history that Eli Whitney was the originator of the system of interchangeable parts within the firearms industry. The article provides important background to one of the vital aspects of the "American System" of manufacturing.

413   _____. STUDIES IN THE HISTORY OF MACHINE TOOLS. Cambridge: M.I.T. Press, 1972. v, 135, 191, 107, and 124 p. Illus., bibliog.

The collection of four excellent technical studies of specific machine tools was originally published in the Society for the History of Technology's monograph series. The titles are self-explanatory: HISTORY OF THE GEAR-CUTTING MACHINE: A HISTORICAL STUDY IN GEOMETRY AND MACHINES (1958); HISTORY OF THE GRINDING MACHINE: A HISTORICAL STUDY IN TOOLS AND PRECISION PRODUCTION (1959); HISTORY OF THE MILLING MACHINE: A STUDY IN TECHNICAL DEVELOPMENT (1960); and HISTORY OF THE LATHE TO 1850; A STUDY IN THE GROWTH OF AN INDUSTRIAL ECONOMY (1961).

D. THE MACHINE IN EXHIBITION

414   Burg, David F. CHICAGO'S WHITE CITY OF 1893. Lexington: University Press of Kentucky, 1976. xvi, 382 p. Illus.

The World's Columbian Exposition, also known as the Chicago

World's Fair of 1893, was an event of "genuine cultural import" which this study attempts to evaluate. Although it reflected a spirit of internationalism, it was also a symbol of America's achievement of maturity in both arts and industries. The volume describes more than analyzes the event.

415 Greeley, Horace, ed. ART AND INDUSTRY: AS REPRESENTED IN THE EXHIBITION AT THE CRYSTAL PALACE NEW YORK--1853-4. New York: Redfield, 1853. xxv, 386 p.

Articles by various hands which appeared in the NEW YORK TRIBUNE during the exhibition at the Crystal Palace are collected in this volume. Nineteenth-century Americans' love of their machines is evident in this celebration of useful, work-related objects as art. Criteria for excellence is indicative of the "practical" industrial spirit: "novelty, efficiency, economy, and social utility." Enthusiasm for mechanical ingenuity is everywhere evident.

416 Hirschfeld, Charles. "America on Exhibition: The New York Crystal Palace." AMERICAN QUARTERLY 9 (Summer 1957): 101-16.

America's first world's fair, the 1853 Crystal Palace Exhibition, reflected the country's achievements, its ideals, values at mid-century. Industry displayed its manufactures and revealed a certain democratic faith in technology and progress. Hirschfeld briefly describes the organization, architectural design, construction, displays, meaning, and fiery end of the Crystal Palace.

417 Hirschl, Jessie Heckman. "The Great White City." AMERICAN HERITAGE 11 (October 1960): 8-21, 75.

The 1893 Chicago World's Fair contained many industrial exhibits and architectural feats indicative of the age, its values, and its dreams. The chief advantage of this brief summary is the accompanying illustrations.

418 Maass, John. THE GLORIOUS ENTERPRISE: THE CENTENNIAL EXHIBITION OF 1876 AND H.J. SCHWARZMANN, ARCHITECT-IN-CHIEF. Watkins Glen, N.Y.: American Life Foundation, 1973. 156 p. Illus., bibliog.

A valuable history of the Philadelphia Centennial Exhibition uses chief architect and engineer H.J. Schwarzmann as the focal point. Maass makes excellent use of drawings and photographs to discuss both the architecture and social meaning of this important celebration.

419 THE MASTERPIECES OF THE CENTENNIAL INTERNATIONAL EXHIBI-

TION. Vol. 2: INDUSTRIAL ART, by Walter Smith. Vol. 3:
HISTORY, MECHANICS, SCIENCE, by Joseph M. Wilson. Philadelphia: Gebbie and Barrie, 1877-78. 521, 375 p. Illus.

Mechanical devices and the products of their manufacturing
processes are well illustrated in these catalogs. Late
nineteenth-century sentiments which declare the necessity of
education in skilled industrial arts are evident in the accompanying texts. The development of labor-saving devices is
not considered an adequate or honorable end. The creation
of beautiful objects, by machine, is lauded as a goal, which
will create independence from Europe and an American culture.

420   Post, Robert C., ed. 1876: A CENTENNIAL EXHIBITION. Washington, D.C.: Smithsonian Institution, 1976. 223 p. Illus., bibliog.

Post has brought together an excellent collection of photographs and brief articles by present-day scholars describing
the varied components of the Philadelphia "Centennial" to
accompany and set the tone for the Smithsonian's bicentennial
recreation in the Arts and Industries Building.

E. SELECTED CASE STUDIES OF INDUSTRIES AND COMPANIES

421   Anderson, Oscar Edward. REFRIGERATION IN AMERICA: A HISTORY
OF A NEW TECHNOLOGY AND ITS IMPACT. Princeton, N.J.:
Princeton University Press, 1953. Reprint. Port Washington, N.Y.:
Kennikat Press, 1972. 344 p. Illus., bibliog.

This introductory survey of the history of refrigeration takes a
cultural approach by studying the social effects as well as the
major technological changes. The wide-reaching effects of
refrigeration with respect to urbanization, diet, reduced spoilage, and decreased soil erosion due to a wider variety of
marketable crops are mentioned as are the technical developments in ice making, refrigeration, and storage from 1830 to
1950.

422   Arnold, Horace Lucien, and Faurote, Fay Leone. FORD METHODS
AND THE FORD SHOPS. New York: Engineering Magazine Co.,
1915. Reprint. Technology and Society Series. New York: Arno
Press, 1972. x, 440 p. Illus.

This early study of the Ford Motor Company and the industrial
process of its Highland Park Plant was not intended to deal with
the social effects of the automobile; however, it contains much
information on the assembly process and its impact on the
worker. Liberally illustrated, including fold-out floor plans of
the plant.

423   Bining, Arthur Cecil. PENNSYLVANIA IRON MANUFACTURE IN THE
       EIGHTEENTH CENTURY. 1938. 2d ed. Harrisburg: Pennsylvania
       Historical Commission, 1973. vi, 215 p. Illus., bibliog.

       "The chief purpose of this study is to present in some detail
       an account of the origin and progress of the Pennsylvania
       iron industry during its first century of development, especially
       its social and economic aspects." The author admirably suc-
       ceeds in his stated purpose.

424   Brandon, Ruth. A CAPITALIST ROMANCE: SINGER AND THE SEWING
       MACHINE. Philadelphia: J.B. Lippincott Co., 1977. xiii, 244 p.
       Illus., bibliog.

       The study serves as a popular biography and social history of
       Isaac Singer, a major innovator and popularizer of the sewing
       machine. Singer also made use of early mass-production tech-
       niques and installment purchasing.

425   Bright, Arthur Aaron, Jr. THE ELECTRIC-LAMP INDUSTRY: TECHNO-
       LOGICAL CHANGES AND ECONOMIC DEVELOPMENTS FROM 1800
       TO 1947. M.I.T. Studies of Innovation. New York: Macmillan,
       1949. Reprint. New York: Arno Press, 1972. xxviii, 526 p. Illus.,
       bibliog.

       A broad survey of the industry attempts to understand "the
       direction, extent, and timing of technological advances" there-
       in, as part of a larger theory of economic development.
       Bright finds the patent system and the organization of the lamp
       industry especially important.

426   Cole, Arthur H[arrison]. THE AMERICAN WOOL MANUFACTURE.
       2 vols. Cambridge, Mass.: Harvard University Press, 1926. Reprint.
       The Allan Nevins Reprints in American Economic History. New York:
       Harper and Row, 1969. xix, 392; viii, 328 p. Illus., bibliog.

       Ferguson, in his BIBLIOGRAPHY OF THE HISTORY OF TECH-
       NOLOGY (no. 152) calls this "a major work in economic
       and business history which pays balanced attention to technical
       problems and machines." Volume 1 covers the period from
       1830 to the full growth of the factory in 1870, while volume
       2 describes the succeeding era of industrial maturity to 1920.

427   Cole, Arthur H[arrison]., and Williamson, Harold F. THE AMERICAN
       CARPET MANUFACTURE: A HISTORY AND AN ANALYSIS. Harvard
       Economic Studies. Cambridge, Mass.: Harvard University Press, 1941.
       xvii, 281 p. Illus., bibliog.

       An industry-wide survey covers the social changes witnessed
       by the spread of carpet from the upper classes to all levels

of society, and technical developments such as carpet power
looms, as well as industrial organization, labor, marketing,
and competition.

428   Commons, John R[ogers]. "American Shoemakers, 1648-1895: A
Sketch of Industrial Evolution." QUARTERLY JOURNAL OF ECO-
NOMICS 24 (November 1909): 39-84.

Commons analyzes the various economic stages of industrial
development in shoemaking by means of brief sketches of the
shoemakers' labor organizations. The groups include: Company of Shoomakers [sic], Boston 1648; Society of the Master
Cordwainers, Philadelphia, 1789; Federal Society of Journey-
men Cordwainers, 1794; United Beneficial Society of Journey-
men Cordwainers, Philadelphia, 1835; The Knights of St.
Crispin, 1868; and the Boot and Shoe Workers' Union, 1895.

429   Cooper, Grace Rogers. THE SEWING MACHINE: ITS INVENTION
AND DEVELOPMENT. Washington, D.C.: Smithsonian Institution,
1976. ix, 238 p. Illus., bibliog.

A greatly expanded version of the author's earlier work of a
similar title, THE INVENTION OF THE SEWING MACHINE
(1968). The short text with lengthy appendixes and many
excellent illustrations clearly explains the development of the
sewing machine but does not deeply analyze its impact on
clothing and other related industries. Lists of American sew-
ing-machine manufacturers and short biographical sketches are
included.

430   Copeland, Melvin Thomas. THE COTTON MANUFACTURING INDUS-
TRY OF THE UNITED STATES. Harvard Economic Studies, vol. 8.
Cambridge, Mass.: Harvard University Press, 1912. Reprint. Library
of Early American Business and Industry, no. 17. New York: Augustus
M. Kelley, 1966. xii, 415 p. Bibliog.

A two-part history, on the one hand, depicts the past and
present organizations of the American cotton industry and, on
the other, places it in a European comparative framework.
Although there are two chapters on technical developments,
the emphasis is on markets and trade.

431   Cummings, Richard O. THE AMERICAN ICE HARVESTS: A HISTORICAL
STUDY IN TECHNOLOGY, 1800-1918. Berkeley: University of
California Press, 1949. x, 184 p. Illus., bibliog.

A brief survey (the text is only 113 pages) of natural ice
harvesting covers techniques, marketing and distribution, and
the impact of the industry on associated areas of dairy, fruit,
vegetable, and meat storage and transportation.

432 Deyrup, Felicia Johnson. ARMS MAKING IN THE CONNECTICUT VALLEY: A REGIONAL STUDY OF THE ECONOMIC DEVELOPMENT OF THE SMALL ARMS INDUSTRY, 1798-1870. Smith College Studies in History, vol. 33. Northampton, Mass.: Smith College, 1948. Reprint. York, Pa.: George Shumway, 1970. vi, 290 p.

Deyrup's study reveals several important aspects of the rise of industrialization--specialization, interchangeable parts and precision measurement, machine-tool production, and the transfer of technological knowledge. While not as sophisticated, especially with respect to interchangeability, as Smith's more recent HARPER'S FERRY ARMORY AND THE NEW TECHNOLOGY (no. 449) the study is valuable. The research was based largely on the records of the Federal Springfield Armory and was originally published as ARMS MAKERS OF THE CONNECTICUT VALLEY.

433 Downard, William L. THE CINCINNATI BREWING INDUSTRY: A SOCIAL AND ECONOMIC HISTORY. Athens: Ohio University Press, 1973. 173 p. Illus., bibliog.

The case study explores an urban industry and its relationship to the city's economic and social life, the development of national markets and marketing techniques.

434 Fagen, M[orton].D., ed. A HISTORY OF ENGINEERING AND SCIENCE IN THE BELL SYSTEM: THE EARLY YEARS, 1875-1925. Murray Hills, N.J.: Bell Telephone Laboratories, 1975. xiii, 1,073 p. Illus., bibliog.

An in-house history of the science and technology of the first half century of telephone development is written by present or retired members of the company's technical staff. This first volume of a series covers the conception of Bell's "Grand System," subsequent technical developments in its perfection, and the origins of scientific research in the Bell System.

435 _____. A HISTORY OF ENGINEERING AND SCIENCE IN THE BELL SYSTEM: NATIONAL SERVICE IN WAR AND PEACE (1925-1975). Murray Hill, N.J.: Bell Telephone Laboratories, 1978. xv, 757 p. Illus., bibliog.

The central topic of the second volume of the history of the Bell System and its contributions to science and telecommunications technology is the application of systems engineering in communications to national defense needs both in peace and war.

436 Gibb, George Sweet. THE SACO-LOWELL SHOPS: TEXTILE MACHINERY BUILDING IN NEW ENGLAND, 1813-1949. Harvard Studies in

Business History, vol. 16. Cambridge, Mass.: Harvard University Press, 1950. Reprint. New York: Russell and Russell, 1969. xxxvi, 835 p. Illus.

While this business history emphasizes organization and administrative policy, technology and the work process receive adequate treatment. A detailed text, extensive tables, and ninety pages of appendix material make this an extremely valuable work. It supplements the work of Thomas R. Navin on the Whitin Machine Works (no. 445).

437   Hazard, Blanche Evans. THE ORGANIZATION OF THE BOOT AND SHOE INDUSTRY IN MASSACHUSETTS BEFORE 1875. Harvard Economic Studies, vol. 23. Cambridge, Mass.: Harvard University Press, 1921. x, 293 p. Illus., maps, bibliog.

A study of the development of the factory system in one industry traces four stages: the home stage of the frontier, the handicraft stage typical until the mid-eighteenth century, the domestic stage of industrial organization until the mid-nineteenth century, and the first factory stage to 1875. The human element in shoemaking is briefly considered, including the formation of the Order of the Knights of St. Crispin, an early shoemakers' trade union.

438   HISTORY OF STANDARD OIL COMPANY (New Jersey). Vol. 1: PIONEERING IN BIG BUSINESS, 1882-1911, by Ralph W. Hidy and Muriel E. Hidy. Vol 2: THE RESURGENT YEARS, 1911-27, by George Sweet Gibb, and Evelyn H. Knowlton. Vol 3: NEW HORIZONS, 1927-50, by Henrietta M. Larson, Evelyn H. Knowlton, and Charles S. Popple. New York: Harper, 1955-71. xxx, 839 p.; xxi, 754 p.; xxv, 945 p. Illus., maps.

A detailed business history describes the exploration, transportation, production and processing, and marketing of petroleum products as well as financial, management, and personnel decisions. Volume 1 covers Standard Oil's origins and its development as a trust and holding company down to the U.S. Supreme Court decision for dissolution in 1911. The second volume analyzes the period of renewed growth of the New Jersey group due to the impetus of the automobile, war, and foreign competition. The emergence of industry consciousness and the development of new patterns of employee relations also receive attention. Volume 3 continues the study to 1950.

439   Kaufman, Morris. THE FIRST CENTURY OF PLASTICS: CELLULOID AND ITS SEQUEL. London: Plastics Institute, 1963. 130 p. Illus.

A brief in-house survey of the development of the plastics industry begins with Alexander Parkes's 1862 invention of celluloid. Information on European and American developments is provided and a chronology of important dates is included.

440 Kidwell, Claudia B., and Christman, Margaret C. SUITING EVERY-
ONE: THE DEMOCRATIZATION OF CLOTHING IN AMERICA.
Washington, D.C.: Smithsonian Institution Press, 1974. 208 p. Illus.,
bibliog.

> The "spirit of egalitarianism" evident in members of the aspir-
> ing middle class of nineteenth-century America, who con-
> sidered themselves as good as anyone else and wanted the
> clothing to prove it, was responded to by the emergence of
> skilled craftsmanship in textile technology. The result was
> "ready-made clothing of a quality which made it possible for
> the lowest of men to look not unlike the highest of men."
> The authors consider diverse elements, in addition to advances
> in machinery, which spurred the progress of the industry: im-
> migration brought people with skills and retailing talents as
> well as the workers who "manned" the industry, and the spring-
> ing up of department stores and mail-order houses made mass
> distribution possible.

441 Knowlton, Evelyn H. PEPPERELL'S PROGRESS: HISTORY OF A COTTON
TEXTILE COMPANY, 1844-1945. Harvard Studies in Business History,
vol. 13. Cambridge, Mass.: Harvard University Press, 1948. xxix,
511 p. Illus., map.

> A traditional business history deals with the financing, supply
> procurement, production and marketing for a medium-sized
> textile company, the Pepperell Manufacturing Co., originally
> of Biddeford, Maine, and later expanding into Georgia and
> Alabama. Knowlton credits Pepperell's executive management
> for the company's success.

442 Lathrop, William Gilbert. THE BRASS INDUSTRY IN THE UNITED
STATES: A STUDY OF THE ORIGIN AND THE DEVELOPMENT OF THE
BRASS INDUSTRY IN THE NAUGATUK VALLEY AND ITS SUBSEQUENT
EXTENSION OVER THE NATION. Shelton, Conn.: W.G. Lathrop,
1909. Rev. ed. Mt. Carmel, Conn.: William G. Lathrop, 1926.
Reprint. Technology and Society Series. New York: Arno Press, 1972.
vii, 174 p. Illus.

> An early history provides a survey of the nineteenth-century
> brass industry centered primarily in Connecticut, where approxi-
> mately three quarters of the country's brass was then produced.

443 Lewis, W. David. IRON AND STEEL IN AMERICA. Greenville, Del.:
Hagley Museum, 1976. 64 p. Illus., bibliog.

> Lewis furnishes a brief but accurate introduction to the history
> of iron and steel production in America from the colonial
> period to 1945.

444 Mitchell, Broadus. THE RISE OF COTTON MILLS IN THE SOUTH.
Baltimore: Johns Hopkins Press, 1921. Reprint. The American Scene,

Comments and Commentators. New York: DaCapo Press, 1968. xi, 281 p. Bibliog.

Originally a Johns Hopkins dissertation in political economy, Mitchell's work describes the birth of the southern cotton industry, concentrating on Georgia and the Carolinas during the last two decades of the nineteenth century. Most interesting are two chapters on the reasons for southern industrialization and on the labor factor.

445   Navin, Thomas R. THE WHITIN MACHINE WORKS SINCE 1831, A TEXTILE MACHINERY COMPANY IN AN INDUSTRIAL VILLAGE. Harvard Studies in Business History, vol. 15. Cambridge, Mass.: Harvard University Press, 1950. xxix, 654 p. Illus., graphs, maps.

The detailed business history of a small, family-operated firm provides valuable information on factory development, management, and labor. A good companion piece to G.S. Gibb's study of the Saco-Lowell shops (no. 436).

446   Passer, Harold C. THE ELECTRICAL MANUFACTURERS, 1875-1900: A STUDY IN COMPETITION, ENTREPRENEURSHIP, TECHNICAL CHANGE, AND ECONOMIC GROWTH. Studies in Entrepreneurial History. Cambridge, Mass.: Harvard University Press, 1953. Reprint. New York: Arno Press, 1972. xviii, 412 p. Illus., bibliog.

In a study of "change and the entrepreneur" in the electrical manufacturing industry, as particularly applied to apparatus for lighting and power, the author notes the rapid growth of the industry due to wide-spread applications of its products, the importance of the engineer-entrepreneur, a growing technical complexity, and a trend toward product standardization. Valuable bibliography.

447   Roberts, Kenneth D. ELI TERRY AND THE CONNECTICUT SHELF CLOCK. Bristol, Conn.: Ken Roberts Publishing Co., 1973. xvi, 320 p. Illus., bibliog.

Roberts presents a technically detailed and well-illustrated study of the Connecticut clock industry from the 1790s through the mid-nineteenth century. A checklist of Connecticut shelf-clock firms through 1833 is provided.

448   Scoville, Warren C. REVOLUTION IN GLASSMAKING: ENTREPRENEURSHIP AND TECHNOLOGICAL CHANGE IN THE AMERICAN INDUSTRY, 1880-1920. Cambridge, Mass.: Harvard University Press, 1948. xvii, 398 p. Illus., bibliog.

The development of glassmaking in many ways paralleled the general pattern of industrial expansion. From its largely handicraft nature in 1880, Scoville traces the process of growth in an industry which had become largely mechanized with few skilled workers by 1920. Concentration is on Toledo area companies.

449 Smith, Merritt Roe. HARPER'S FERRY ARMORY AND THE NEW TECHNOLOGY, THE CHALLENGE OF CHANGE. Ithaca, N.Y.: Cornell University Press, 1977. 363 p. Illus., maps, bibliog.

A "must" book for understanding the process of technological innovation and the development of the "American System" of manufacturing, this provocative and well-written study of the arms industry challenges long-held assumptions concerning the ready acceptance of mechanization in antebellum America.

450 Taylor, George Rogers, ed. THE EARLY DEVELOPMENT OF THE AMERICAN COTTON TEXTILE INDUSTRY. New York: Harper and Row, 1969. xxxvi, 146 p. Illus.

Taylor combines a lengthy introduction with two mid-nineteenth century classic histories of the growth of the cotton industry: Nathan Appleton's INTRODUCTION OF THE POWER LOOM AND ORIGIN OF LOWELL (1858) and Samuel Batchelder's INTRODUCTION AND EARLY PROGRESS OF THE COTTON MANUFACTURE OF THE UNITED STATES (1863). Both Appleton and Batchelder discuss the "Waltham System" as employed particularly in Lowell, Massachusetts.

451 Temin, Peter. IRON AND STEEL IN NINETEENTH CENTURY AMERICA: AN ECONOMIC ENQUIRY. M.I.T. Monographs in Economics. Cambridge: M.I.T. Press, 1964. ix, 304 p. Bibliog.

Temin approaches his subject by studying the quantity and composition of the goods sold, the methods of production including machinery, and the nature of the firms comprising the industry. He finds the most important influence on the industry's development to have been the combination of a growing demand for iron and steel, especially rails, which led to the use of the Bessemer process, and an increased sophistication in the use of heat.

452 Ware, Caroline Farrar. THE EARLY NEW ENGLAND COTTON MANU-FACTURE, A STUDY IN INDUSTRIAL BEGINNINGS. Boston, New York: Houghton Mifflin Co., 1931. Reprint. New York: Russell and Russell, 1966. 349 p. Bibliog.

The development of the cotton industry reveals a great deal about the early factory system and the general process of industrialization in America. This standard work contains information on the initial founding, subsequent growth, financing, marketing, labor, and working conditions of New England cotton manufacturing.

453   Williamson, Harold F., et al. THE AMERICAN PETROLEUM INDUSTRY.
       Vol. 1: THE AGE OF ILLUMINATION, 1859-1899. Vol. 2: THE
       AGE OF ENERGY, 1899-1959. Evanston, Ill.: Northwestern University
       Press, 1959, 1963. xvi, 864 p., xx, 928 p. Illus., maps.

       Volume 1 briefly covers the era before Drake's discovery of
       oil in Pennsylvania but concentrates on production techniques,
       distribution, and business organization, in particular with
       respect to Standard Oil. In like fashion, volume 2 relates
       the change of emphasis upon oil as a source of lighting to a
       source of energy. An excellent study of an important industry.

F. MANAGEMENT

454   Aitken, Hugh G.J. TAYLORISM AT WATERTOWN ARSENAL: SCIEN-
       TIFIC MANAGEMENT IN ACTION, 1908-1915. Cambridge, Mass.:
       Harvard University Press, 1960. 269 p.

       Taylorism as instituted at the government-owned Watertown
       Arsenal in Boston is examined in an excellent case study.
       The author is interested in the development of management
       and its impact on traditional modes of business and sees such a
       complex social change as reflective of the stresses inherent in
       an ever-changing industrial process.

455   Bell, Daniel. WORK AND ITS DISCONTENTS: THE CULT OF EFFI-
       CIENCY IN AMERICA. Boston: Beacon, 1956. Reprint. New York:
       League for Industrial Democracy, 1970. 56 p.

       In these brief essays, Bell's primary concern and point of con-
       tention is the American acceptance, indeed, almost worship,
       of the notion of efficiency. He believes the twentieth-century
       trends of scientific management, human relations techniques,
       and automation to be in essential conflict with values empha-
       sizing the welfare, creativity, and dignity of the worker.

456   Bendix, Reinhard. WORK AND AUTHORITY IN INDUSTRY: IDEOLO-
       GIES OF MANAGEMENT IN THE COURSE OF INDUSTRIALIZATION.
       New York: John Wiley and Sons, 1956. 466 p. Illus.

       Industrialization has been accompanied by the development of
       managerial ideologies which seek to justify the subordination
       of workers to factory discipline and excessive authority.
       Bendix compares Communistic and non-Communistic patterns of
       totalitarian subordination by contrasting economic enterprises
       in early industrialized Great Britain with czarist Russia, and
       modern America with contemporary East Germany. In the
       West, the change in industrial structure shifts from idealization
       of the entrepreneur to tense labor-management relations.

457 Brandes, Stuart D. AMERICAN WELFARE CAPITALISM, 1880-1940.
Chicago: University of Chicago Press, 1976. ix, 210 p. Bibliog.

A near neutral treatment of "welfare capitalism," itself a pro-
business term, concentrates primarily on the first third of this
century. If not a result, at least a parallel development with
American industrial growth, the phenomenon had specific realizations in housing, education, religion, recreation, profit
sharing and stock ownership, medical care, pensions, social
work, and employee representation, all of which are herein
analyzed.

458 Chandler, Alfred, D[upont]., Jr. "The Coming of Big Business." In
THE COMPARATIVE APPROACH TO AMERICAN HISTORY, edited by
C. Vann Woodward, pp. 220-37. New York: Basic Books, 1968.

Chandler's thinking on the years of rapid, large-scale industrialization and merger in the late nineteenth and early twentieth
centuries is presented in an excellent summary article. Giant,
vertically integrated, joint-stock corporations, managed by
professional executives became the norm because of the ineffec-
tiveness of cartels and the poor marketing network previously
available.

459 _____. STRATEGY AND STRUCTURE: CHAPTERS IN THE HISTORY
OF INDUSTRIAL ENTERPRISE. Cambridge: M.I.T. Press, 1962. xiv,
463 p.

Chandler examines the organizational structure or technique
of business administration used to take strategic advantage of
the "opportunities and needs created by changing population,
income, and technology." Based primarily on case studies of
Dupont, General Motors, Standard Oil of New Jersey, and
Sears Roebuck, the study focuses on the innovation of the
modern multidivisional or "decentralized" form. A comparison
with approximately seventy other large corporations adds further
perspective.

460 _____. THE VISIBLE HAND: THE MANAGERIAL REVOLUTION IN
AMERICAN BUSINESS. Cambridge, Mass.: Harvard University Press,
1977. xvi, 608 p. Maps.

A monumental study of the changing processes of production
and distribution concentrates on the rise of modern business
enterprise and its management, "the visible hand," from the
1840s to the 1920s. Chandler's major theme is "that modern
business enterprise took the place of market mechanisms [Adam
Smith's invisible hand] in coordinating the activities of the
economy and allocating its resources." Expanding markets and
technological developments such as the railroad and mass production were crucial to the timing and direction of this phenomenon.

461   Cochran, Thomas C[hilds]. 200 YEARS OF AMERICAN BUSINESS.
        New York: Basic Books, 1977. xvi, 288 p. Bibliog.

        Cochran provides a synthesis of American business history from
        the Revolution to 1976, concentrating on the decision-making
        process in management in which he emphasizes the importance
        of social values and market demand rather than supply or
        production to explain new or expanded use of organization and
        technology. Comparisons with France, Germany, Great Britain,
        and Japan further clarify the American experience.

462   Copley, Frank Barkley. FREDERICK W. TAYLOR, FATHER OF SCIEN-
        TIFIC MANAGEMENT. New York: Harper and Brothers, 1923. Re-
        print. Library of Early American Business and Industry. 2 vols. New
        York: Augustus M. Kelley, 1969. 467, 472 p. Illus.

        This standard biography of Taylor concentrates on his contribu-
        tion to scientific management, which was closely intertwined
        with his early work in high-speed tool steel and metal cutting.

463   Drury, Horace Bookwalter. SCIENTIFIC MANAGEMENT: A HISTORY
        AND CRITICISM. Columbia University Studies in History, Economics,
        and Law, vol. 65, no. 2, 1915. 3d ed. New York: Columbia Uni-
        versity, 1922. 222 p.

        An earlier but still valuable history of scientific management
        is generally favorable toward the system but recognizes that it
        is not a panacea for industrial and social ills.

464   Frederick, Christine. HOUSEHOLD ENGINEERING: SCIENTIFIC
        MANAGEMENT IN THE HOME. Chicago: American School of Home
        Economics, 1920. 527 p. Illus., bibliog.

        The principles of scientific management are applied to such
        household tasks as cooking and food preparation, laundry,
        finances and record-keeping, management of servants, health
        care, planning, and purchasing. Designed as a text for cor-
        respondence courses, it reveals something of the widespread
        impact of the movement.

465   Gould, Jay M. THE TECHNICAL ELITE. New York: Augustus M.
        Kelley, 1966. 178 p. Graphs.

        The reasoning which led Veblen to conclude that technologists,
        interested in maximizing output and innovation, are better
        equipped to manage business than conservative entrepreneurs
        is reviewed in this concise study. Gould documents the
        emergence of technicians (scientists, engineers) in top man-
        agement and evaluates their influence on social and industrial
        organization. His research on the education and background

of one thousand top managers indicates that the need for
technicians has overcome barriers which once kept lower social
classes out of management.

466   Haber, Samuel. EFFICIENCY AND UPLIFT: SCIENTIFIC MANAGE-
MENT IN THE PROGRESSIVE ERA, 1890-1920. Chicago: University of
Chicago Press, 1964. xiii, 181 p. Bibliog.

A central characteristic of Progressivism was efficiency, epitomized by F.W. Taylor's scientific management, which frequently supported the era's tendency toward elitism. Efficiency came to have four possible meanings: a personal
characteristic, the energy output-input ratio of a machine,
commercial efficiency measured in dollar profit, and social
harmony or efficiency among men. The latter, the focus of
Haber's study, was particularly important for those who
mouthed the ideals of democracy but desired to maintain societal control.

467   Hoxie, Robert Franklin. SCIENTIFIC MANAGEMENT AND LABOR.
New York, London: D. Appleton, 1915. Reprints of Economic Classics.
New York: Augustus M. Kelley, 1966. x, 302 p.

The report of a study of scientific management shops undertaken by Hoxie for the U.S. Commission on Industrial Relations presents a generally positive view of the movement while
taking cognizance of real labor concerns. Includes a lengthy
questionnaire and appendixes covering the points of contention
between labor and management.

468   Jaffe, William J. L.P. ALFORD AND THE EVOLUTION OF MODERN
INDUSTRIAL MANAGEMENT. New York: New York University Press,
1957. xxi, 366 p. Illus., bibliog.

Leon Pratt Alford was an engineer, editor, author, and educator, and in all capacities an exponent of the principles of
scientific management. The author uses Alford as a vehicle
to explore the development of industrial management from the
turn of the century to about 1940. The bibliography contains
excellent primary sources on scientific management.

469   Jenks, Leland H. "Early Phases of the Management Movement."
ADMINISTRATIVE SCIENCE QUARTERLY 5 (December 1960): 421-47.

Examples of industrial management prior to Frederick W.
Taylor's "scientific management" show that the time was ripe
for his ideas, which were of limited scope in terms of direct
application. Jenks discusses in some detail "the works
management movement," which had its origins among mechanical engineers in the late 1890s.

470   Kakar, Sudhir. FREDERICK TAYLOR: A STUDY IN PERSONALITY
       AND INNOVATION. Cambridge: M.I.T. Press, 1970. xiii, 221 p.

       An interesting but controversial psychobiography views Taylor
       as an "obsessive-compulsive" personality with inner conflicts
       regarding authority and control which were crucial in his
       creativity and development of scientific management. For a
       generally negative review, see Edwin Layton, TECHNOLOGY
       AND CULTURE 12 (October 1971): 666-68, who criticizes
       the author for failing to take into full account the historical
       period in which Taylor worked.

471   Lee, Frederic S. THE HUMAN MACHINE AND INDUSTRIAL EFFI-
       CIENCY. New York: Longmans Green, 1918. Reprint. Easton, Pa.:
       Hire Publishing Co., 1974. vii, 119 p. Illus., bibliog.

       The theories of scientific management are applied in this
       treatise on industrial physiology. Lee contends that the
       "worker is a physiological mechanism and must be treated as
       such." He proceeds to call for an extension of scientific
       experimentation to the factory. The abilities of workers should
       be determined by exact tests, and a combination of inspection
       and measurement should be utilized to determine working con-
       ditions. Lee provides recommendations regarding fatigue,
       length of working day, efficiency of women compared with
       men, and industrial accidents. The volume serves as a prime
       illustration of the attitude which views "the combined body
       and mind of the worker as itself a machine."

472   Litterer, Joseph A. "Systematic Management: The Search for Order
       and Integration." BUSINESS HISTORY REVIEW 35 (Winter 1961):
       461-76.

       Contemporary literature on systematic internal management of
       industrial firms, especially metalworking from 1870 to 1900,
       is analyzed. Businessmen of the period believed themselves
       faced with problems of workers and their productivity, the use
       of machinery, and general business organization. An increase
       in the size of firms, specialization, and the growth of a
       managerial hierarchy required improved coordination and stan-
       dard procedures, especially in the area of control.

473   Nadworny, Milton J. SCIENTIFIC MANAGEMENT AND THE UNIONS,
       1900-1932: A HISTORICAL ANALYSIS. Cambridge, Mass.: Harvard
       University Press, 1955. ix, 187 p.

       Nadworny's interest is the reaction of organized labor to the
       system of scientific management and management's attitude to-
       ward resulting union practices. In general, unions reacted
       with hostility to the movement until 1920 when a period of
       collaboration emerged which lasted throughout the subsequent
       decade until the Depression diluted attention to such matters.

474   Nelson, Daniel. "Taylorism and the Workers at Bethlehem Steel, 1898–1901." PENNSYLVANIA MAGAZINE OF HISTORY AND BIOGRAPHY 101 (October 1977): 487–505.

Rather than providing evidence of the efficacy of scientific management's time-study and differential piece rate, the reorganization of Bethlehem's workers was a "modest affair" that demonstrated "haphazard, unsystematic methods" as well as the dehumanization of the worker. Taylor designated the capacity of a "first class" man by the output of ten carefully chosen men observed for just one day.

475   Noble, David F. AMERICA BY DESIGN: SCIENCE, TECHNOLOGY AND THE RISE OF CORPORATE CAPITALISM. New York: Knopf, 1977. xxvi, 384 p.

It is Noble's contention that the expansion of scientific technology from approximately 1880 to 1930, during which time the engineer played an important role, was central to the development of modern, systematic industrial capitalism and its concomitant social transformations. This work is an extraordinarily good attempt to show technology "as the human enterprise that it is."

476   Taylor, Frederick Winslow. THE PRINCIPLES OF SCIENTIFIC MANAGEMENT. New York, London: Harper and Brothers, 1911. Reprint. New York: W.W. Norton and Co., 1967. 144 p.

A general discussion of Taylor's principles of efficiency and managerial techniques, not as technical or specific as his earlier SHOP MANAGEMENT (no. 478). Taylor carried out experiments to determine the most efficient method of performance for each operation, set quotas on workers, created clear division between management and the worker, and introduced systems in organizations. The concepts of systematic management expressed herein served as the precursor of modern organization and administrative theory. He transformed management into a science.

477   _____. SCIENTIFIC MANAGEMENT. New York: Harper and Brothers, 1947. Reprint. 3 vols. in 1. Westport, Conn.: Greenwood Press, 1972. 207, 144, 287 p.

Contains Taylor's three comments on scientific management: SHOP MANAGEMENT (no. 478), THE PRINCIPLES OF SCIENTIFIC MANAGEMENT (no. 476), and TESTIMONY BEFORE THE SPECIAL HOUSE COMMITTEE (1912). Includes a brief foreword by Harlow S. Person, former head of the Taylor Society.

478   _____. SHOP MANAGEMENT. New York: McGraw-Hill, 1911. 143 p. Illus.

Taylor's experiments and observations in time study, his piece-rate system, division of labor, the "task idea" in management, and systems planning, are delineated in detail in this technical treatise which originally appeared in the TRANSACTIONS of the American Society of Mechanical Engineers. Most of Taylor's work recorded herein took place at Bethlehem Steel Corporation.

479   Thompson, C. Bertrand. THE THEORY AND PRACTICE OF SCIENTIFIC MANAGEMENT. Boston: Houghton Mifflin, 1917. vii, 319 p. Bibliog.

After brief sketches of Frederick W. Taylor and Taylorism, Thompson analyzes at some length the practice, economics, and literature of the movement. Extensive unannotated bibliography of early management material.

480   Veblen, Thorstein. THE ENGINEERS AND THE PRICE SYSTEM. New York: B.W. Huebsch, 1921. 169 p.

Six essays which originally appeared in the DIAL during 1919 consider the structure of large-scale mechanized industry. Veblen discusses the role of the captain of industry or entrepreneur; the rise of the engineer and scientific management specialists; the use of "sabotage," defined as techniques which restrict, obstruct, and delay production; and the inefficiency resulting from restriction of technologists by dictatorial financial controllers. Recognizing that twentieth-century technology has outgrown the existing system of vested interests, Veblen advocates gradual changes resulting in the elevation of production engineers to control of industry.

481   Yost, Edna. FRANK AND LILLIAN GILBRETH, PARTNERS FOR LIFE. New York: American Society of Mechanical Engineers, 1949. xii, 372 p. Illus.

Yost presents a laudatory biography of Frank Gilbreth, a disciple of Frederick W. Taylor, and his wife Lillian Gilbreth, a psychologist, who as a team devoted their careers to motion study and the field of scientific management. Contends that the Gilbreths were ultimately concerned with the human element in work.

G. MECHANIZATION OF AGRICULTURE

482   Berry, Wendell. THE UNSETTLING OF AMERICA: CULTURE AND AGRICULTURE. San Francisco: Sierra Club Books, 1977. xi, 228 p.

Berry argues against modern large-scale exploitative agriculture and all that it represents; good farming involves cultural development and spiritual discipline. His suggestions include an emphasis on diversity and appropriate technology.

483 Bidwell, Percy Wells, and Falconer, John I. THE HISTORY OF AGRICULTURE IN THE NORTHERN UNITED STATES, 1620-1860. Washington: Carnegie Institution of Washington, 1925. Reprint. Library of Early American Business and Industry, vol. 59. Clifton, N.J.: A.M. Kelley, 1973. xii, 512 p. Illus., maps, bibliog.

The fifth volume of the Contributions to American Economic History series is a basic work in the history of agriculture, including much more than just the mechanical apparatus of farming. Other topics include crops, livestock, land tenure, trade patterns, and transportation.

484 Bogue, Allan G. FROM PRAIRIE TO CORN BELT: FARMING ON THE ILLINOIS AND IOWA PRAIRIES IN THE NINETEENTH CENTURY. Chicago: University of Chicago Press, 1963. 310 p. Maps, bibliog.

Bogue's survey of midwestern farming in two states emphasizes the period from 1830 to 1890. Valuable information on agricultural technology is provided in chapter 8, "How to Farm Sitting Down."

485 Casson, Herbert N[ewton]. CYRUS HALL MCCORMICK, HIS LIFE AND WORK. Chicago: A.C. McClurg and Co., 1909. xii, 264 p. Illus.

McCormick is seen as the central figure in the development and manufacture of modern farm machinery, especially the reaper, in this old but still valuable biography which concentrates on McCormick's work rather than his personal and social life.

486 Cavert, William L. "The Technological Revolution in Agriculture, 1910-1955." AGRICULTURAL HISTORY 30 (January 1956): 18-27.

With emphasis on the tractor, automobile, and truck, the author concludes that mechanization by means of the gasoline engine revolutionized American farm life in the first half of the twentieth century. In addition, electricity, crop technology, fertilizers, and irrigation have created trends toward better management, specialization, larger farm units with less labor, and increased land values. Contrast with Earle D. Ross's treatment included below (no. 499).

487 Danhoff, Clarence H. CHANGE IN AGRICULTURE: THE NORTHERN UNITED STATES, 1820-1870. Cambridge, Mass.: Harvard University Press, 1969. xii, 322 p. Bibliog.

Agricultural development in the period from 1820 to 1870 supported and paralleled the process of industrialization as its orientation shifted from the subsistence farm to a largely commercial market. Reaction to new techniques and technical innovations in agricultural implements receive major attention in this important study.

488 _____. "Gathering the Grass." AGRICULTURAL HISTORY 30 (October 1956): 169-73.

A major change in the history of American agriculture in the first half of the nineteenth century was the shift from human to animal power. Particularly important to this shift was the development of the hayrake, which increased the amount of hay that could be harvested and thereby the number of animals that could be wintered. Acceptance of the change prepared the way for other horse-powered devices for reaping, mowing, and threshing.

489 Gates, Paul W[allace]. THE FARMER'S AGE: AGRICULTURE, 1815-1860. The Economic History of the United States, vol. 3. New York: Holt, Rinehart and Winston, 1960. xix, 460 p. Illus., maps, bibliog.

Gates details the last period in which farmers were able to dominate American politics; by 1860 "the great age of the American farmer was drawing to a close." Several chapters deal with technology, especially as applied to farm machinery and the impact of railroads. Good bibliographical essay.

490 Gray, Lewis Cecil. HISTORY OF AGRICULTURE IN THE SOUTHERN UNITED STATES TO 1860. 2 vols. Washington, D.C.: Cambridge Institution of Washington, 1933. Reprint. Library of Early American Business and Industry, vol. 47. New York: Augustus M. Kelley, 1973. xxx, 1,086 p. Maps, bibliog.

What Bidwell and Falconer did for agricultural history in the antebellum North (no. 483), Gray has done for the South in this detailed overview. Arranged both chronologically and topically, the author covers, in addition to general trends, individual crops and livestock, slavery, the plantation system, and land policies. Emphasis is on economics, but much technological material is included.

491 Hayter, Earl W. THE TROUBLED FARMER, 1850-1900: RURAL ADJUSTMENT TO INDUSTRIALISM. DeKalb: Northern Illinois Press, 1968. vii, 349 p. Illus., bibliog.

Lacking communication and the means to make educated decisions, many farmers used to traditional agricultural ways were not prepared for the impersonal world of the city and industrialization. Consequently many were duped or cheated with respect to new procedures and technology such as washing machines, lightning rods, and instruments to dehorn cattle. A limited but interesting view of people trying to adjust to changing technology.

492 Hilliard, Sam B. "The Dynamics of Power: Recent Trends in Mechanization on the American Farm." TECHNOLOGY AND CULTURE 13 (January 1972): 1-24.

Mechanization is particularly representative of American agriculture and is an ongoing process. The author focuses his attention on the power revolution and the trend toward ever-larger tractors and self-propelled machinery. Illustrated.

493 Hutchinson, William T. CYRUS HALL MCCORMICK. Vol. 1: SEED-TIME, 1809-1856. New York, London: Century Co., 1930. Vol. 2: HARVEST, 1856-1884. New York, London: Century Co., 1935. Reprint. The American Scene: Comments and Commentators. New York: DeCapo Press, 1968. xiii, 493; ix, 793 p. Illus., map, bibliog.

A standard biography of McCormick, who is generally given credit for developing the mechanical reaper.

494 McCallum, Henry D., and McCallum, Frances T. THE WIRE THAT FENCED THE WEST. Norman: University of Oklahoma Press, 1965. xv, 285 p. Illus., bibliog.

The story of barbed wire includes information on the various types of wire fencing, the development of the industry, and the impact of its use--for example, with respect to the spread of agriculture and the enclosure of the open range.

495 Perkins, John H. "Reshaping Technology in Wartime: The Effect of Military Goals on Entomological Research and Insect-Control Practices." TECHNOLOGY AND CULTURE 19 (April 1978): 169-86.

A war effort can be a stimulus to the rapid advancement of nonmilitary as well as military technology. Though first utilized by Swiss farmers, DDT's development became the wartime object of the entire entomological profession, eager to help the effort through perfecting the substance for such uses as louse control and mosquito repellency. Only after the war was the substance developed for agricultural use. As a result of wartime research, the insecticide trade grew enormously and the nature of insect-control research greatly changed. Traditional research and programs in biological control and habitat sanitation were abandoned for the pursuit of quick-fix synthetic insecticides.

496   Rasmussen, Wayne D. "Advances in American Agriculture: The
       Mechanical Tomato Picker as a Case Study." TECHNOLOGY AND
       CULTURE 9 (October 1968): 531-43.

       The mechanical tomato picker serves as a case study of modern
       agriculture, which is based on a "system approach" or "pack-
       age" of technical advances to increase productivity in contrast
       to traditional individual developments. Not only was the
       technical machinery developed but also a redesigned, machine-
       harvestable tomato.

497   _____. "The Impact of Technological Change on American Agriculture,
       1862-1962." JOURNAL OF ECONOMIC HISTORY 22 (December
       1962): 578-99.

       Rasmussen generally believes agricultural development to have
       been evolutionary except during the Civil War period and the
       post-World War II era in which he finds revolutionary change.
       In both cases increases in demand, prices, and the use of
       new technology coincided with shortages of manpower to pro-
       duce change, an understanding of which is vital to future
       agricultural planning. Followed by comments from Clarence
       Danhoff and H.C. Knoblauch.

498   Rogin, Leo. THE INTRODUCTION OF FARM MACHINERY IN ITS
       RELATION TO THE AGRICULTURE OF THE UNITED STATES DURING
       THE NINETEENTH CENTURY. University of California Publications in
       Economics, vol. 9. Berkeley and Los Angeles: University of California
       Press, 1931. Reprint. New York: Johnson Reprint Corp., 1966. ix,
       260 p. Illus., bibliog.

       By analyzing two areas of development in agricultural equip-
       ment--the plow and other tillage equipment and the various
       seeders, harvesters, and threshers used in wheat production--
       the author attempts to answer questions as to the amount of
       time from their introduction to utilization, and the related
       change in man-hour requirements for specific crop production.

499   Ross, Earle D. "Retardation in Farm Technology before the Power Age."
       AGRICULTURAL HISTORY 30 (January 1956): 11-18.

       Many examples of trial and error show that transitions in farm
       technology have been gradual, halting, and uneven--seldom,
       if ever, "revolutionary." "If there was any sort of revolution
       in the coming of farm machinery, it was entrepreneurial rather
       than mechanical." Contrast this view to that of William L.
       Cavert above (no. 486).

500   Rossiter, Margaret W. THE EMERGENCE OF AGRICULTURAL SCIENCE:
       JUSTUS LIEBIG AND THE AMERICANS, 1840-1880. New Haven, Conn.:

Yale University Press, 1975. xiv, 275 p. Illus., map, bibliog.

A solid study of agricultural science, in particular chemistry, and its transfer to the United States from Germany, culminating in research laboratories by 1880. Rossiter notes the importance of Justus Liebig for American agriculture, both through his writing and the Americans who travelled to Germany to study under his tutelage.

501   Schlebecker, John T. WHEREBY WE THRIVE: A HISTORY OF AMERICAN FARMING, 1607-1972. Ames: Iowa State University Press, 1975. x, 342 p. Illus., bibliog.

A survey of American agriculture based primarily on secondary sources. Schlebecker uses five major time periods to tell his story--1607-1783, 1783-1861, 1861-1914, 1914-45, and 1945-72--and in each period covers the recurrent themes of land policy, technology and science, marketing, and farm practices.

502   _____, ed. THE USE OF THE LAND: ESSAYS ON THE HISTORY OF AMERICAN AGRICULTURE. Lawrence, Kans.: Coronado Press, 218 p. Bibliog.

Ten of the eleven essays contained herein are reprinted and bring together Schlebecker's ideas on agricultural history. "Agriculture comprises those human activities by which men intentionally regulate biological events in order to secure food, industrial products, and amelioratives. We force nature with harrow and plow." The theme of technological change is recurrent but not dominant. Not intended as a comprehensive history of agriculture.

503   Shannon, Fred A. THE FARMER'S LAST FRONTIER; AGRICULTURE, 1860-1897. The Economic History of the United States series, vol. 5. New York: Holt, Rinehart, and Winston, 1945. Reprint. New York: Harper and Row, 1968. xii, 434 p. Illus., graphs, bibliog.

Although not a technical history of agriculture, Shannon does deal with transportation, markets, railroad land grants, farm mechanization, and the farmer's political response to societal change in this period.

504   Shover, John L. FIRST MAJORITY--LAST MINORITY: THE TRANSFORMING OF RURAL LIFE IN AMERICA. Minorities in American History. DeKalb: Northern Illinois University Press, 1976. xix, 338 p. Illus., bibliog.

In a study of the transformation of a nation of individual farmers to an "agro-industrial empire," a change almost unnoticed in its extent and impact, Shover's approach is through a series of case studies concentrating on the post-World War

II period, but without failing to note earlier changes as well. Information on technological changes and their impact is provided.

505   Steward, John F[letcher]. THE REAPER: A HISTORY OF THE EFFORTS OF THOSE WHO JUSTLY MAY BE SAID TO HAVE MADE BREAD CHEAP. New York: Greenburg, 1931. xviii, 382 p. Illus.

An attempt to balance earlier studies, most notably H.N. Casson's ROMANCE OF THE REAPER, (1908), which over-emphasized the role of Cyrus McCormick. Steward includes information on Obed Hussey, William Deering, the Marsh brothers, John F. Appleby, and others.

506   Street, James H. THE NEW REVOLUTION IN THE COTTON ECONOMY: MECHANIZATION AND ITS CONSEQUENCES. Chapel Hill: University of North Carolina Press, 1957. xvi, 294 p. Illus., maps, bibliog.

The rise of mechanical cotton pickers symbolizes the complete mechanization of cotton production, which has resulted in changes in population movement, land tenure, farm organization, and labor patterns, especially for children and blacks. Street sees World War II as the major factor in explaining the timing and social consequences of this process.

507   Wik, Reynold M. "Henry Ford's Tractors and American Agriculture." AGRICULTURAL HISTORY 38 (April 1964): 79-86.

Wik outlines the history of the Fordson tractor from the original 1917 production model to its demise in 1927 due to numerous design weaknesses and competition from other manufacturers. He concludes that the "Fordson failed to revolutionize American agriculture for it seems clear the mechanization of farming was inevitable regardless of the part played by the Ford organization." Its significance was in Ford's propagandizing of power farming.

508   _____. STEAM POWER ON THE AMERICAN FARM. Philadelphia: University of Pennsylvania Press, 1953. xi, 288 p. Illus., graphs, bibliog.

The author surveys the uses and benefits of steam power on the American farm. He includes information on the manufacture, distribution, and financing of agricultural steam engines and on threshermen's organizations and schools.

Part 5

LABOR AND THE WORK PROCESS

A. HISTORY

1. Surveys

a. BIBLIOGRAPHIES

509   McBrearty, James C. AMERICAN LABOR HISTORY AND COMPARA-
       TIVE LABOR MOVEMENTS. Tucson: University of Arizona Press, 1973.
       ix, 262 p.

> Over 3,000 items comprise this wide-ranging but generally
> unannotated bibliography. McBrearty separates books from
> articles and then arranges the works for each section into
> basic chronological periods supplemented by specialized topics
> wherein some titles are repeated. Following this is a second
> grouping on comparative labor movements for each section.
> Also included is a section on labor novels which contains
> very brief annotations. There is no grouping for technology
> and labor per se, but many titles have portions that are per-
> tinent. Includes author index. Some titles are included
> under more than one heading.

510   Neufeld, Maurice F. A REPRESENTATIVE BIBLIOGRAPHY OF AMERI-
       CAN LABOR HISTORY. Ithaca, N.Y.: Cornell University Press,
       1964. ix, 146 p.

> The classifications of this selective unannotated bibliography
> cover general works; specific periods of development; city,
> regional, and state materials; theories of American labor; and
> individual occupations, trades, and industries. Neufeld has
> strived to provide a cross-section of opinion. In addition to
> scholarly monographs, he has included popular works, novels,
> plays, government reports, and union documents.

511   Stroud, Gene S., and Donahue, Gilbert E. LABOR HISTORY IN THE

UNITED STATES: A GENERAL BIBLIOGRAPHY. Bibliographic Contributions no. 6. Urbana: University of Illinois Institute of Labor and Industrial Relations, 1961. 167 p.

A successor to Ralph E. McCoy's HISTORY OF LABOR AND UNIONISM IN THE UNITED STATES: A SELECTED BIBLIOGRAPHY, published by the Institute in 1953, this wide-ranging volume covers wages and working conditions, labor-management relations, productivity, unemployment, and government regulation of industrial relations. The 2,000 plus titles are unannotated and arranged alphabetically by author. A reasonable subject index aids in locating material. Fred D. Rose's AMERICAN LABOR IN JOURNALS OF HISTORY: A BIBLIOGRAPHY (1962) also published by the Institute supplements this volume.

b. BOOKS AND ARTICLES

512   Braverman, Harry. LABOR AND MONOPOLY CAPITAL: THE DEGRA-DATION OF WORK IN THE TWENTIETH CENTURY. New York: Monthly Review Press, 1974. xiii, 465 p.

Braverman's study of the impact of monopoly capital upon labor processes is written from a Marxist perspective but includes a variety of traditional sources as well, making it a well-balanced study. Within this framework, technology, scientific management, and mechanization are analyzed in light of their degrading impact upon labor under modern monopoly capitalism.

513   Commons, John Rogers, et al. HISTORY OF LABOR IN THE UNITED STATES. 2 vols. New York: Macmillan, 1918. Rev. ed. Reprints of American Classics. 4 vols. New York: Augustus M. Kelley, 1966. xxv, 623; xx, 620; xxx, 778; viii, 683 p. Bibliog.

This is still the basic history of American labor. Volume 1 covers the colonial period to the Civil War, and volume 2 carries the story forward through the depression of 1896. Volume 3 analyzes working conditions and labor legislation, while volume 4 deals with labor movements. Both of the latter volumes, originally written in 1935, cover the period from 1897 to 1932. Excellent bibliographies accompany each volume.

514   Derber, Milton. THE AMERICAN IDEA OF INDUSTRIAL DEMOCRACY, 1865-1965. Urbana: University of Illinois Press, 1970. xv, 553 p.

Concerned with the pragmatic, collective-bargaining model of industrial democracy as a major theme in the development of industrial relations. That this theme is closely tied to industrial and technological developments should be patently obvious and poses important questions for the future.

515   Pelling, Henry. AMERICAN LABOR. Chicago History of American
       Civilization Series. Chicago: University of Chicago Press, 1960. viii,
       247 p. Illus., bibliog.

       This brief survey of "Americans at work" covers the colonial
       period through the 1950s. Pelling is primarily concerned with
       unions from the Knights of Labor to the AFL-CIO, but he
       also considers indentured servitude, slavery, and some non-
       union workers. He includes a list of important dates.

516   Perlman, Selig. A THEORY OF THE LABOR MOVEMENT. New York:
       Macmillan, 1928. 321 p.

       Perlman develops a sociohistorical theory of labor in which he
       sees labor as an observable group developing in particular
       ways because of forces peculiar to a given situation. Major
       factors are the strength of capitalism, the influence of the
       "intellectual mentality," and the trade-union movement. The
       study is based on a historical comparison of the United States,
       Great Britain, Germany, and Russia.

517   Rayback, Joseph G. A HISTORY OF AMERICAN LABOR. Rev. ed.
       New York: Free Press, 1966. x, 491 p. Bibliog.

       Although Rayback tends to concentrate on union history in
       this excellent labor history text, several of his earlier chapters
       deal with worker reaction to the changes wrought by industri-
       alization.

2. Working and Living Conditions

518   Berthoff, Rowland Tappan. BRITISH IMMIGRANTS IN INDUSTRIAL
       AMERICA 1790-1950. Cambridge, Mass.: Harvard University Press,
       1953. Reprint. New York: Russell and Russell, 1968. xiii, 296 p.
       Maps.

       A large part of this history of British immigrants deals with
       their experience in the textile, mining, iron and steel, and
       several smaller industries. British skills were important in the
       early years of industrialization but eventually declined in
       importance. Berthoff finds that the British enjoyed high eco-
       nomic status, rose freely in the society, and were assimilated
       with relative ease. Despite the title dates, the study concen-
       trates on the nineteenth century.

519   Blumer, Herbert. "Early Industrialization and the Laboring Classes."
       SOCIOLOGICAL QUARTERLY 1 (January 1960): 5-14.

       The author challenges the prevailing view that the early stages
       of industrialization inevitably lead to frustration, aggression,

and rebelliousness. The rural background from which the labor force is derived is not always superior to factory environs, Blumer argues. Nor does the recently displaced worker invariably chafe against factory discipline. While industrialization may coincide temporally with social upheaval in the larger environment, it does not necessarily cause it.

520   Cole, Donald B. IMMIGRANT CITY: LAWRENCE, MASSACHUSETTS, 1845-1921. Chapel Hill: University of North Carolina Press, 1963. xiii, 248 p. Maps.

Although primarily about the immigrant experience, Cole's study of industrial Lawrence reveals much about the processes of urbanization and industrialization in terms of their impact upon the working man's search for security in a new environment. Concludes that largely because of the immigrant cycle in which new waves continually came in at the bottom of the social and economic scale, most were able to find considerable security in family, home, group organizations, the mills themselves and, most important, in being Americans.

521   Dawley, Alan. CLASS AND COMMUNITY: THE INDUSTRIAL REVOLUTION IN LYNN. Cambridge, Mass.: Harvard University Press, 1976. xi, 301 p. Illus., bibliog.

The search for equality by the shoemakers of Lynn, Massachusetts, is documented in this social and economic study of the Industrial Revolution's impact on labor and community. Using an analytical framework of class, the author concludes that politics acted as a "safety valve" for class conflict.

522   Dawley, Alan, and Faler, Paul. "Working-Class Culture and Politics in the Industrial Revolution: Sources of Loyalism and Rebellion." JOURNAL OF SOCIAL HISTORY 9 (June 1976): 466-80.

The Industrial Revolution gave birth to individualism and concurrently the twin themes of loyalism and opposition to the new industrial capitalism. This article analyzes the impact of traditional and modern values of industrial morality in the United States based on a study of Lynn, Massachusetts, shoemakers in the period from 1820 to 1890.

523   Dew, Charles B. "David Ross and the Oxford Iron Works: A Study of Industrial Slavery in the Early Nineteenth Century." WILLIAM AND MARY QUARTERLY 31 (April 1974): 189-224.

Based on the recent discovery of a letter book kept by David Ross, owner of the Oxford Iron Works in Campbell County, Virginia, in the years 1812 and 1813, this article describes slave working and living conditions and the operations of this early industry.

524   Ehrlich, Richard L., ed. IMMIGRANTS IN INDUSTRIAL AMERICA,
      1850-1920. Charlottesville: University Press of Virginia, 1977. xiv,
      218 p.

      In contrast to the more traditional melting-pot thesis, ethnicity
      emerges as the key factor in explaining immigrant reaction to
      the urban-industrial environment of the late nineteenth and
      early twentieth centuries in these ten papers from a 1973 joint
      conference sponsored by the Balch Institute and the Eleutherian
      Mills-Hagley Foundation.

525   Erickson, Charlotte. AMERICAN INDUSTRY AND THE EUROPEAN
      IMMIGRANT, 1860-1885. Cambridge, Mass.: Harvard University
      Press, 1957. xi, 369 p.

      Contract labor, particularly that involving large numbers of
      unskilled laborers for industry, was rare in the twenty-year
      period following the Civil War until its abolishment in 1885.
      Labor's attitude toward immigration is analyzed in depth in
      light of the process of industrialization.

526   Faler, Paul. "Cultural Aspects of the Industrial Revolution: Lynn,
      Massachusetts, Shoemakers and Industrial Morality, 1826-1860." LABOR
      HISTORY 15 (Summer 1974): 367-94.

      The process of industrialization brought with it a new moral
      and cultural code which emphasized a sober, self-disciplined,
      and orderly society in which the values of work and industry
      were paramount. This paper examines the new code and the
      Lynn shoemakers' response in terms of poverty and dependency,
      temperance, recreation, and education.

527   Fitch, John A. THE STEELWORKERS. Vol. 3 of THE PITTSBURGH
      SURVEY, edited by Paul Underwood Kellogg. New York: Charities
      Publications, 1911. xiii, 380 p. Illus., map.

      Fitch presents a sociological study of the city conducted in
      the early years of the twentieth century. He covers steel-
      making techniques, unionization, working conditions, and
      social attitudes. Margaret F. Byington's volume in the series,
      HOMESTEAD: THE HOUSEHOLDS OF A MILL TOWN (1910),
      provides a complement focusing on the family and home life
      of a steel-working residential community.

528   Ginger, Ray. "Labor in a Massachusetts Cotton Mill, 1853-1860."
      BUSINESS HISTORY REVIEW 28 (March 1954): 67-91.

      The condition of wage earners in New England textile mills,
      in particular skilled Scottish female immigrants, is analyzed
      based on records of the Lyman Mills, Holyoke, Massachusetts.
      High wages (women could save from ten to twenty-five percent

of their earnings) and a high degree of labor mobility contributed to the lack of a permanent wage-earning class with
a group consciousness, a condition which in turn resulted in
few effective strikes.

529   Gitelman, Howard M. "The Waltham System and the Coming of the
Irish." LABOR HISTORY 8 (Fall 1967): 227-53.

"This article has two interrelated purposes: first, a reconstruction of the founding and developing of the Waltham system
and second, an analysis of the movement of the Irish into the
Boston Manufacturing Company." Gitelman believes economic
reasons may have been more important than employer mag-
nanimity in the creation of the Waltham system and that high
numbers of American-born workers continued to labor in the
textile industry alongside a heterogeneous and highly mobile
Irish component.

530   _____. WORKINGMEN OF WALTHAM: MOBILITY IN AMERICAN
URBAN INDUSTRIAL DEVELOPMENT, 1850-1890. Johns Hopkins University Press, 1974. xvi, 192 p. Illus., maps.

Of the recent mobility studies, Gitelman's is the most directly
related to industrialization and labor. He concludes that, in
general, "the opportunities for occupational mobility in
Waltham appear to have increased steadily over time."

531   Graebner, William. COAL-MINING SAFETY IN THE PROGRESSIVE
PERIOD. Lexington: University Press of Kentucky, 1976. xii, 244 p.
Bibliog.

A "persistence of decentralization and disorganization" characterized coal-mining safety in the Progressive period rather than
the generally accepted thesis of national organization. An
interesting combination of legislative, technological, and reform history in which the author finds that commercial and
social efficiency were central to the safety movement. Recipi-
ent of the Organization of American Historians' Frederick
Jackson Turner Award.

532   Gutman, Herbert G. "The Worker's Search for Power: Labor in the
Gilded Age." In THE GUILDED AGE: A REAPPRAISAL, edited by
H. Wayne Morgan, pp. 38-68. Syracuse: Syracuse University Press,
1963.

Traditional histories of labor in the Gilded Age have stressed
the development of trade unions rather than an understanding
of non-unionized wage earners and their communities. Gutman
sets out to rectify this failing and finds that industrial capitalism was less readily accepted in smaller towns than in the city

because of the differences in the social structure which emphasized the human element more fully.

533   _____, ed. WORK, CULTURE, AND SOCIETY IN INDUSTRIALIZING
AMERICA: ESSAYS IN AMERICAN WORKING-CLASS AND SOCIAL
HISTORY. New York: Alfred A. Knopf, 1976. xiv, 360 p.

A series of seven articles by the author which provide an
overview of the reaction of labor to the process of industrialization. In addition to an excellent synthesis, specific themes
include the Protestant response, class and the social origins
of manufacturers in Paterson, New Jersey, black coal miners
and the U.M.W., railroad strikes and violence, and Pennsylvania mines and coal company towns. Very good labor history
in its social setting.

534   Hareven, Tamara K. "The Laborers of Manchester, New Hampshire,
1912-1922: The Role of Family and Ethnicity in Adjustment to Industrial
Life." LABOR HISTORY 16 (Spring 1975): 249-65.

"Workers, in their efforts to retain their own work habits and
traditions, relied on two important resources: family and kin-
ship ties, and ethnicity." In an attempt to develop a permanent labor force which identified with the corporation, the
Amoskeag textile mills developed an efficiency plan and welfare program typical of other early twentieth-century experiments. Hareven outlines the interaction of these forces in the
acculturation process in which labor responded with strength
and resourcefulness.

535   Hareven, Tamara K., and Langenbach, Randolph. AMOSKEAG: LIFE
AND WORK IN AN AMERICAN FACTORY-CITY. New York: Pantheon Books, 1978. xiii, 395 p. Illus.

This fine combination of oral histories and photographs is
woven around a narrative warp of factory life in the Amoskeag textile mills of Manchester, New Hampshire. The
authors focus on the first third of the twentieth century and
include a glossary of textile terminology.

536   Harvey, Katherine A. THE BEST-DRESSED MINERS: LIFE AND LABOR
IN THE MARYLAND COAL REGION, 1835-1910. Ithaca, N.Y.:
Cornell University Press, 1969. xiv, 488 p. Illus., map, bibliog.

Harvey finds the western Maryland coal fields and towns atypi-
cal of the more common poverty of other contemporary Eastern
mining regions. Well-educated northern European and, later,
native American workers predominated; however, their experience with unionization was similar to that of other miners
throughout the country. A good combination of the social,
economic, and labor sides of mining history.

537   Korman, Gerd. INDUSTRIALIZATION, IMMIGRANTS, AND AMERI-
       CANIZERS: THE VIEW FROM MILWAUKEE, 1866-1921. Madison:
       State Historical Society of Wisconsin, 1967. x, 225 p. Illus., bibliog.

       This case study in industrial relations "examines the process
       by which a polyglot population evolved the techniques for
       coping with the problems of an emerging industrial society."
       Korman's topical organization deals with Milwaukee's indus-
       trial makeup, the labor force, its industrial leadership, and
       the themes of Americanization, industrial safety, and welfare
       programs.

538   Lahne, Herbert J. THE COTTON MILL WORKER, New York: Farrar
       and Rinehart, 1944. xiii, 303 p. Bibliog.

       Survey of the twentieth-century cotton mill operative covers
       labor unions and strikes, the industrial structure, composition
       of the work force, labor conditions, living standards, social
       values, and government policy. It includes data on both
       New England and southern states.

539   Laurie, Bruce. "'Nothing on Compulsion': Life Styles of Philadelphia's
       Artisans, 1820-1850." LABOR HISTORY 15 (Summer 1974): 337-66.

       Pre-industrial working class habits and culture were altered
       from 1820 to 1850 in particular by the effect of transportation
       improvements, especially canals and railroads, which opened
       up new markets and allowed mass production in textiles,
       shoes, and clothing. Nativism and its attendant values of
       sobriety and self-discipline gradually replaced the pre-
       industrial blend of work and leisure.

540   Lipset, Seymour Martin, and Bendix, Reinhard. SOCIAL MOBILITY
       IN INDUSTRIAL SOCIETY. Berkeley and Los Angeles: University of
       California Press, 1959. xxii, 309 p.

       Comparative sociological analysis of social mobility debunks
       the traditional theory that the role of American mobility has
       been greater than in Europe and that mobility declines with
       industrial maturation. Suggests rather that "a high rate of
       social and labor mobility is a concomitant of industrialization
       regardless of political conditions."

541   Montgomery, David. "The 'New Unionism' and the Transformation of
       Workers' Consciousness in America, 1909-22." JOURNAL OF SOCIAL
       HISTORY 7 (Summer 1974): 509-29.

       Montgomery finds that two levels of working-class struggle
       emerged during this period, one by skilled craftsmen over the
       issue of job control touched off by new managerial tactics

and another by laborers and operatives over wages and the rising cost of living. These currents tended to fuse during and after World War I.

542   _____. "Workers' Control of Machine Production in the Nineteenth Century." LABOR HISTORY 17 (Fall 1976): 485-509.

Concerned with the second and third generations of industrial experience and workers' control of production. Analyzes three levels of development: (1) functional autonomy of the craftsman, (2) union work rules, and (3) mutual support of diverse trades in rule enforcement and sympathetic strikes. The new methods of industrial management which emerged early in the twentieth century undermined these courses of worker strength.

543   _____. "The Working Classes of the Pre-Industrial American City, 1780-1830." LABOR HISTORY 9 (Winter 1968): 3-22.

In this exploratory foray into the lower working classes of Boston, Philadelphia, New York, and Baltimore, Montgomery suggests parameters for questions regarding the sources, size, and character of pre-industrial labor and its "ideological baggage," questions whose answers are necessary before we can truly understand labor's response to industrialism. In particular, he calls for careful study of each individual group of urban workers. Despite much valuable literature since the appearance of this article, a great deal of work yet remains.

544   Rodgers, Daniel T. "Tradition, Modernity, and the American Industrial Worker." JOURNAL OF INTERDISCIPLINARY HISTORY 7 (Spring 1977): 655-81.

Rodgers' analysis of recent labor history generally makes use of a modernization hypothesis--seeing the process of industrialization as a transition from "traditional" society to one of "modernity" in which the needs of the new community are internalized. He uses select examples of factory workers in the period from 1865 to 1919 to suggest such acculturation was not as complete nor as uniform as some historians claim. Valuable footnotes.

545   Rosen, George. "The Medical Aspects of the Controversy over Factory Conditions in New England, 1840-50." BULLETIN OF THE HISTORY OF MEDICINE 15 (May 1944): 483-97.

Rosen shows that, at least in terms of health, working conditions under the Waltham system were not as good as Lowell propagandists and apologists would have had their contemporaries believe.

546   Rosenbloom, Richard S. "Men and Machines: Some 19th-Century
       Analyses of Mechanization." TECHNOLOGY AND CULTURE 5 (Fall
       1964): 489-511.

       A series of discussions by nineteenth-century observers of
       factory mechanization and its impact upon the worker. Con-
       centrates on European thinkers (Charles Babbage, Andrew Ure,
       and Karl Marx) but includes sections on the Americans David
       Wells and Carroll Wright, and concludes that all were too
       close to the events to provide "a successful 'grand theory' on
       the effects of mechanization."

547   Silvia, Philip T., Jr. "The Position of Workers in a Textile Com-
       munity: Fall River in the Early 1880s." LABOR HISTORY 16 (Spring
       1975): 230-48.

       Silvia provides a brief overview of industrial textile workers
       in Fall River, Massachusetts, covering working conditions,
       technical developments, wages, and housing.

548   Starobin, Robert S. INDUSTRIAL SLAVERY IN THE OLD SOUTH.
       New York: Oxford University Press, 1970. xiii, 320 p. Illus.,
       bibliog.

       Starobin investigates the political, economic, and social his-
       tory of the approximately five percent of black slaves em-
       ployed in industrial pursuits such as manufacturing, mining,
       lumbering, agricultural processing, and the building and
       operation of transportation facilities. Of particular interest
       are sections on working conditions for industrially employed
       slaves and their attitudes toward work routines.

549   Stearns, Peter N., and Walkowitz, Daniel J., eds. WORKERS IN
       THE INDUSTRIAL REVOLUTION: RECENT STUDIES OF LABOR IN THE
       UNITED STATES AND EUROPE. New Brunswick, N.J.: Transaction
       Books, 1974. x, 442 p. Bibliog.

       These fifteen reprinted essays emphasize the social and cul-
       tural rather than the more traditional aspects of labor adapt-
       ing to the process of industrialization. There are seven selec-
       tions on American events including contributions by David
       Montgomery, Stephen Thernstrom, Herbert Gutman, Walkowitz,
       and Melvin Dubofsky.

550   Sullivan, William A[rnold]. THE INDUSTRIAL WORKER IN PENNSYL-
       VANIA, 1800-1840. Harrisburg: Pennsylvania Historical and Museum
       Commission, 1955. Reprint. New York: Johnson Reprint, 1972. vii,
       253 p. Bibliog.

       Sullivan examines "the impact of the Industrial Revolution on
       the Pennsylvania wage earner and his reaction to it." With-

out slighting other trade areas, the study focuses on the iron and textile industries in Philadelphia, Lancaster, and Pittsburgh as the major centers of industry in the state during this early period. Valuable information on early strikes and attempts at labor organizations is also included.

551 Thernstrom, Stephen. THE OTHER BOSTONIANS: POVERTY AND PROGRESS IN THE AMERICAN METROPOLIS, 1880-1970. Harvard Studies in Urban History. Cambridge, Mass.: Harvard University Press, 1973. xviii, 345 p.

A study of the common citizen contains some interesting findings on occupational mobility. Thernstrom suggests a more "fluid" social order existed than in Europe, where class-based protest movements were impeded which otherwise might have sought basic societal and economic changes.

552 _____. POVERTY AND PROGRESS: SOCIAL MOBILITY IN A NINE-TEENTH CENTURY CITY. Cambridge, Mass.: Harvard University Press, 1964. xii, 286 p.

This path-breaking study of social mobility in Newburyport, Massachusetts, sets the tone methodologically for most subsequent mobility studies. Thernstrom concludes that during the period from 1850 to 1880, a time of rapid-industrial and urban growth, there was little chance for real social mobility, especially for the common laborer.

553 Thompson, E.P. "Time, Work Discipline, and Industrial Capitalism." PAST AND PRESENT 38 (December 1967): 56-97.

Although reflecting the British experience, this article should not be overlooked. Thompson shows how industrialization created a different sense of time and contributed to work discipline. Also useful for comparative purposes is the author's THE MAKING OF THE ENGLISH WORKING CLASS (1963).

554 Walker, Joseph E. HOPEWELL VILLAGE: A SOCIAL AND ECONOMIC HISTORY OF AN IRON-MAKING COMMUNITY. Philadelphia: University of Pennsylvania Press, 1966. 526 p. Illus., bibliog.

This study is a social and economic history of a nineteenth-century, rural charcoal-iron furnace and the attendant community. Walker includes information on operations, labor conditions, and the social life of a community in which many workers lived in company houses and purchased their daily necessities in the company store. (Hopewell Village, which is located in southeastern Pennsylvania, is presently a restored National Historical Site).

555 Wallace, Anthony F.C. ROCKDALE: THE GROWTH OF AN AMERI-

CAN VILLAGE IN THE EARLY INDUSTRIAL REVOLUTION. New York: Alfred A. Knopf, 1978. xx, 553 p. Illus., maps, bibliog.

Wallace examines the impact of early industrial capitalism on Rockdale, Pennsylvania, a small cotton-manufacturing town, from 1825 to 1865. Based on a "paradigmatic process" model of cultural change, he reveals a religious paternalism and sense of moral stewardship which shaped the emerging industrialism and transformed "the workers into Christian soldiers," resulting in a dominant ideology of "Christian capitalism."

3. Labor Response

556 Baker, Elizabeth Faulkner. DISPLACEMENT OF MEN BY MACHINES: EFFECTS OF TECHNOLOGICAL CHANGE IN COMMERCIAL PRINTING. New York: Columbia University Press, 1933. Reprint. Work, Its Rewards and Discontents Series. New York: Arno Press, 1977. xxii, 284 p. Illus., bibliog.

This case study of commercial printing pressrooms made to determine the nature and extent of technological unemployment finds the phenomenon to exist but believes it to be as much cultural as technological and suggests the phrase "technocultural unemployment" would be more accurate. Covers the period from 1913 to 1928.

557 Barnett, George E. CHAPTERS ON MACHINERY AND LABOR. Cambridge, Mass.: Harvard University Press, 1926. vii, 161 p.

Barnett looks at four machines--the linotype, the stoneplaner, the semi-automatic bottle machine, and the automatic bottle machine--to determine the nature and impact of the machinery upon skilled labor. Subsequent chapters analyze the specific facts in light of general theory and appropriate trade-union policy regarding displacement, defined to include lowered wages as well as loss of employment.

558 Brody, David. "The Emergence of Mass-Production Unionism." In CHANGE AND CONTINUITY IN TWENTIETH-CENTURY AMERICA, edited by John Braeman et al., pp. 221-62. Columbus: Ohio State University Press, 1964.

This preliminary investigation of the rise of unionism in the mass-production industries--iron and steel, rubber, chemicals, petroleum, and food-processing--in the decade after the mid-1930s focuses more on the internal developments than on the technological changes in industry which led to this kind of unionization.

559 _____. STEELWORKERS IN AMERICA: THE NONUNION ERA. Cam-

bridge, Mass.: Harvard University Press, 1960. x, 303 p. Bibliog.

Life as a steelworker in the period from 1890 to 1929 is
examined for the changes inflicted by the technology of steel-
making as well as by immigration, managerial goals, and
periodic unemployment. The effect was to create a period
of stability, broken only by the great 1919 steel strike.
Primarily labor history.

560   Cottrell, W[illiam]. Fred. TECHNOLOGICAL CHANGE AND LABOR
IN THE RAILROAD INDUSTRY. Lexington, Mass.: D.C. Heath and
Co., 1970. x, 160 p.

Cottrell compares the impact of technological change upon
railroad workers in the United States, Great Britain, and
New Zealand. In particular, three developments are analyzed: motive power, changes in track signaling, and rolling
stock. Cottrell's ultimate aim is an understanding of the relationship between technology and value systems.

561   Fledderus, Mary L., and Kleeck, Mary van. TECHNOLOGY AND
LIVELIHOOD: AN INQUIRY INTO THE CHANGING TECHNOLOGI-
CAL BASIS FOR PRODUCTION AS AFFECTING EMPLOYMENT AND
LIVING STANDARDS. New York: Russell Sage Foundation, 1944.
237 p.

Depression, technologically induced unemployment, and wartime productivity led the authors to examine basic technological changes and their effects on employment. Factually based
on the 1937 National Resources Committee report, TECHNO-
LOGICAL TRENDS AND NATIONAL POLICY, INCLUDING
THE SOCIAL IMPLICATIONS OF NEW INVENTIONS (no.
1145).

562   Grob, Gerald N. WORKERS AND UTOPIA: A STUDY OF IDEOLOGI-
CAL CONFLICT IN THE AMERICAN LABOR MOVEMENT, 1865-1900.
Evanston, Ill.: Northwestern University Press, 1961. xiii, 220 p.

"Unions are a microcosm of a large whole" and "reflect the
dominant standards and values of American culture." Upon
this assumption Grob analyzes the two ideologies which
dominated the late nineteenth-century labor movement--reform
unionism, which looked backward to a pre-industrial era, and
trade unionism, the ultimate victor, which accepted the inevitability of industrialization. Includes a valuable bibliographical essay on labor history.

563   Nelson, Daniel. "The New Factory System and the Unions: The National Cash Register Company Dispute of 1901." LABOR HISTORY 15
(Spring 1974): 163-78.

Late nineteenth-century changes in technology and organization, including "systematic management," drastically altered management-labor relations in the first third of the twentieth century for mass production industries. This article examines the specifics of this general trend for the NCR Company in which control of the work process moved more completely into the hands of management. An elaborate welfare and benefits program was central to the process at NCR.

564   Ozanne, Robert. A CENTURY OF LABOR-MANAGEMENT RELATIONS AT McCORMICK AND INTERNATIONAL HARVESTER. Madison: University of Wisconsin Press, 1967. xvii, 300 p. Illus., bibliog.

In a revealing case study of labor and its relationship to management in terms of working conditions and wages during the period from 1860 to 1960, Ozanne finds "a far earlier and greater impact of the union on management-labor relations, personnel policies, and wage policies than had hitherto been suspected."

565   Pessen, Edward. "The Workingmen's Movement of the Jacksonian Era." MISSISSIPPI VALLEY HISTORICAL REVIEW 43 (December 1956): 428-43.

Pessen sets forth evidence of legitimate Working Men's parties in Philadelphia, New York, and New England, which developed during the late 1820s and 1830s largely in response to extensive poverty and misery. However, such parties were only in a very general sense part of the Jacksonian reform movement, for they held very distinct, often contradictory views on the means by which to solve what they perceived as "asocial" institutional problems of monopolies, banks, paper money, machines, and the factory system.

566   Terkel, Louis [Studs]. WORKING. PEOPLE TALK ABOUT WHAT THEY DO ALL DAY AND HOW THEY FEEL ABOUT WHAT THEY DO. New York: Pantheon Books, 1974. xlix, 589 p.

Terkel's ability to encourage people to take emotional risks and expose the ambivalence in their psyches is precious. These interviews with workers from garbage man and parking jockey to film critic and conglomerate president create one overpowering impression: man, taking his identity from the work he does, must achieve a sense of dignity. Reading these interviews leads to the disturbing realization that the human need for creativity begets self-deception and the love of slavery. Workers trapped on assembly lines or in jobs eliminating personal expression are broken, frustrated, tense victims of paranoia. Those resigned to their inability to break free focus their hopes on their children.

567   Ware, Norman [J.]. THE INDUSTRIAL WORKER, 1840-1860: THE REACTION OF AMERICAN INDUSTRIAL SOCIETY TO THE ADVANCE OF THE INDUSTRIAL REVOLUTION. Boston, New York: Houghton Mifflin Co., 1924. Reprint. Chicago: Quadrangle Books, 1964. xxi, 259 p. Bibliog.

> There were two interrelated aspects of the American industrial revolution--the development of a modern factory system and a "social revolution in which sovereignty in economic affairs passed from the community as a whole into the keeping of a special class." It was against this latter change that workers and reformers at first reacted defensively (1840s) and then aggressively (1850s) through strikes and other means.

568   _____. THE LABOR MOVEMENT IN THE UNITED STATES, 1860-1895: A STUDY IN DEMOCRACY. New York: Vintage, 1929. Reprint. Gloucester, Mass.: Peter Smith, 1959. xviii, 409 p. Bibliog.

> This traditional labor history in the J.R. Commons mode covers primarily the Order of the Knights of Labor, although Ware also treats the emergence of trade unions and the AFL. The order, whose major principle was that of solidarity, was a popular movement and in that sense "democratic." "It failed, and its failure was perhaps a part of the general failure of democracy--or is it humanity?"

569   Yellowitz, Irwin. INDUSTRIALIZATION AND THE AMERICAN LABOR MOVEMENT, 1850-1900. Port Washington, N.Y.: Kennikat Press, 1977. 183 p. Bibliog.

> A fine labor history which avoids concentrating solely on strikes but instead outlines organized craftworkers' responses to rapid industrialization during the last half of the nineteenth century. Craft unions generally accepted technological and industrial developments but tried to ameliorate the resulting displacement of skill, fluctuating employment, and reduced wages by countering with the eight-hour day, reasonable production levels, and limitations on competitive apprentice, immigrant, child, and female labor.

570   _____. "Skilled Workers and Mechanization: The Lasters in the 1890s." LABOR HISTORY 18 (Spring 1977): 197-213.

> Lasters were one of the final groups of hand craftsmen in the shoe industry to be affected by mechanization. Although there were differences over tactics, the Lasters Protective Union accepted reality and was willing to accept technological innovation in the form of lasting machines if the interests of the existing work force were considered as well as those of the employer and consumer. Good labor history reflecting the impact of the mechanization upon the work process.

4. Women at Work

a. BIBLIOGRAPHIES

571 Bickner, Mei Liang. WOMEN AT WORK: AN ANNOTATED BIBLIOG-
RAPHY. Los Angeles: Institute of Industrial Relations, University of
California, 1974. Unpaged.

Bickner includes scholarly material primarily economic and
sociological in outlook which was published during the period
from 1960 to mid-1973.

572 Soltow, Martha Jane; Forché, Carolyn; and Massare, Murray. WOMEN
IN AMERICAN LABOR HISTORY, 1825-1935: AN ANNOTATED BIB-
LIOGRAPHY. East Lansing: Michigan State University, School of
Labor and Industrial Relations, 1972. iv, 150 p.

Emphasizes women in craft unions but includes such related
topics as worker education, legislative lobbying, and supportive interest groups.

b. BOOKS AND ARTICLES

573 Abbott, Edith. WOMEN IN INDUSTRY: A STUDY IN AMERICAN
ECONOMIC HISTORY. New York and London: D. Appleton and Co.,
1910. Reprint. New York: Source Book Press, 1970. xxii, 409 p.
Bibliog.

This early but useful study of women's work in nineteenth-
century industry also includes a chapter on child labor.
Abbott covers wages, development of the factory system, and
conditions of employment in general and of the cotton, boot
and shoe, cigar, clothing, and printing industries in particular.

574 Baker, Elizabeth Faulkner. TECHNOLOGY AND WOMAN'S WORK.
New York: Columbia University Press, 1964. xvi, 460 p. Bibliog.

The evolution of women's work in America from Hamilton's
report on manufactures in 1791 to the 1960s is examined in
detail. The impact of technological developments such as
interchangeable parts, electricity, typewriter, telephone,
radio tube, and mass marketing is considered by industry and
occupation. Baker concludes with a discussion of economic
adjustments to women in the labor force.

575 Brownlee, W. Elliot, and Brownlee, Mary M. WOMEN IN THE
AMERICAN ECONOMY: A DOCUMENTARY HISTORY, 1675 TO 1929.
New Haven, Conn.: Yale University Press, 1976. viii, 350 p.

The Brownlees' collection of primary sources outlines the diversity of women's attitudes toward work. Approximately a third of the material is on the process of industrialization. A lengthy preface provides a useful overview, and brief introductions precede each set of documents.

576 Butler, Elizabeth Beardsley. WOMEN AND THE TRADES: PITTSBURGH, 1907-1908. Vol. 1 of THE PITTSBURGH SURVEY, edited by Paul Underwood Kellogg. New York: Charities Publications, 1909. Reprint. American Labor, From Conspiracy to Collective Bargaining. New York: Arno Press, 1969. 440 p. Illus., bibliog.

Butler surveys women workers in such trades as canning, cigar making, garments and needle work, laundries, metals, glass, printing, telephone, and telegraph. Summaries of the women's social lives and health, working and economic conditions follow analyses of the specific trades. The study forms part of the PITTSBURGH SURVEY funded by the Russell Sage Foundation in which Pittsburgh is viewed as somewhat typical of other large American industrial cities. (See also no. 527.)

577 Cantor, Milton, and Laurie, Bruce, eds., CLASS, SEX, AND THE WOMAN WORKER. Contributions in Labor History, vol. 1. Westport, Conn.: Greenwood Press, 1977. ix, 253 p.

Woman as worker serves as the theme to tie together ten topically and chronologically diverse but valuable essays. Historians of technology will be particularly interested in articles by Thomas Dublin and Lise Vogel on New England textile operatives. Caroline Ware's introduction provides an integrative framework.

578 Cowan, Ruth S. "The 'Industrial Revolution' in the Home: Household Technology and Social Change in the 20th Century." TECHNOLOGY AND CULTURE 17 (January 1976): 1-23.

At least for middle-class, nonrural American women, technological developments between the wars, such as electric irons, washing machines, stoves, canned food, and running water, have had somewhat unexpected results. The housewife's tasks actually increased in number, and she became a household "manager" with an advertisement-induced and heightened sense of self-worth. Largely based on evidence found in the better-quality women's magazines.

579 Foner, Philip S., ed. THE FACTORY GIRLS. Chicago: University of Illinois Press, 1977. xxvii, 360 p.

Although Foner includes samples from the genteel factory women in this collection of primary writings by New England

factory "girls" of the 1840s, most selections are from the
militant female operatives. Introductions to the book and
individual chapters set the material in historical context.

580   Huber, Joan. "Toward a Sociotechnological Theory of the Women's
       Movement." SOCIAL PROBLEMS 23 (April 1976): 371-88.

       A measure of the degree of sexual stratification is the extent
       to which males dominate the distribution of resources outside of
       the home. Though the Industrial Revolution simplified house-
       hold tasks, it transferred the locus of production from home to
       factory, resulting in a net loss of power for women. Only
       after married women entered the work force in great numbers
       during World War II did the women's movement gain momentum.

581   Josephson, Hannah. THE GOLDEN THREADS: NEW ENGLAND'S
       MILL GIRLS AND MAGNATES. New York: Duell, Sloan, and Pearce,
       1949. ix, 325 p. Bibliog.

       Lowell, Massachusetts, and its textile mills is the primary
       focus of this study. Josephson takes a generally positive view
       of the Boston business associates and the living and working
       conditions of female operatives in the model city's more
       idyllic period. However, the increasing problems of the
       1840s and 1850s--low wages and long hours, speed-ups, social
       status--are not glossed over.

582   Kleinberg, Susan J. "Technology and Women's Work: The Lives of
       Working Class Women in Pittsburgh, 1870-1900." LABOR HISTORY 17
       (Winter 1976): 58-72.

       Pittsburgh's philosophy and legislation requiring that municipal
       services must be paid for directly by the users resulted in their
       unequal distribution by class. This had a direct impact on
       working-class women, who suffered from a relative lack of
       sewers, paved streets, and abundant clean water and who were
       also unable to purchase domestic technological developments
       such as washing machines, toilets, and ice boxes.

583   O'Neill, William L., ed. WOMEN AT WORK. Chicago: Quand-
       rangle Books, 1972. xix, 360 p.

       O'Neill brings together two selections on working women in
       order to show the advances but also the remaining similiarities
       and limitations of such work. Dorothy Richardson's THE LONG
       DAY: THE STORY OF A NEW YORK WORKING GIRL (1905)
       relates the author's experience in the early sweatshops, while
       Elinor Langer's INSIDE THE NEW YORK TELEPHONE COM-
       PANY (1970) analyzes the technical bureaucracy typical of
       many of today's clerical positions.

584   Ryan, Mary P. WOMANHOOD IN AMERICA, FROM COLONIAL
       TIMES TO THE PRESENT. New York: Franklin Watts, 1975. 496 p.

       This speculative history of American women, organized around
       the theme of attitudes, has much to say about the impact of
       industrialization upon women with respect to their work roles.
       Useful as a course text.

585   Smuts, Robert W. WOMEN AND WORK IN AMERICA. New York
       Columbia University Press, 1959. Rev. ed. New York: Schocken
       Books, 1971. xxi, 176 p.

       In this general account of the changing role of women in the
       work force during the twentieth century, information on
       women's work vis-à-vis technological change is not a major
       theme, but it can be gleaned by the reader. Researched
       under the auspices of the Conservation of Human Resources
       Project at Columbia University during the 1950s.

586   Sumner, Helen L. HISTORY OF WOMEN IN INDUSTRY IN THE
       UNITED STATES. Vol. 9: REPORT ON CONDITION OF WOMAN
       AND CHILD WAGE-EARNERS IN THE UNITED STATES. Washington,
       D.C.: Government Printing Office, 1910. Reprint. Women in
       America, From Colonial Times to the 20th Century. New York: Arno
       Press, 1974. 277 p.

       Survey of women's changing role as workers from the home to
       the factory, especially in the textile, sewing, and clothing
       industries, includes information on mechanization, specializa-
       tion, hours, wages, conditions of work, the industrial educa-
       tion and efficiency of women, and the effect of women's
       work upon men.

587   Vanek, Joann. "Household Technology and Social Status: Rising
       Living Standards and Status and Residential Differences in Housework."
       TECHNOLOGY AND CULTURE 19 (July 1978): 361-75.

       With mass production and urbanization came a trend toward
       more equal distribution of goods and an easing of social strati-
       fication based on purchases among housewives. Standardiza-
       tion of household goods and practices accompanied the replace-
       ment of servants by appliances and electricity, also an
       egalitarian trend. As reinforcement for new values, the
       media preached standards for cleanliness and nutrition. Not
       household consumption, Vanek argues, but education and em-
       ployment became status markers for women.

588   Wertheimer, Barbara Mayer. WE WERE THERE: THE STORY OF WORK-
       ING WOMEN IN AMERICA. New York: Pantheon, 1977. xx,
       427 p. Illus., bibliog.

Wage-earning women, rather than those at the professional
level or active in social and reform activities, are the focus
of this survey. Wertheimer includes material on the colonial
period and slave system, although the emphasis is on factory
employment and trade unions. Arranged topically within
standard chronological divisions. Useful bibliography.

589   "Women in the Age of Science and Technology." IMPACT OF SCI-
        ENCE ON SOCIETY 20 (January–March 1970): 3-105.

Most of the papers in this issue are concerned with the employment of women as scientists, though some have a
broader viewpoint. Pertinent papers include a discussion of
the female capacity for technical activity by the first woman
in space, Valentina Terechkova Nikolayeva, and Madeleine
Guilbert's "Women and Work III: The Effects of Technological Change."

B. SOCIOLOGY

1. Industry, Occupations, and Work

a. BIBLIOGRAPHY

590   Taviss, Irene, and Gerber, William.   TECHNOLOGY AND WORK.
        Research Review Number 2. Cambridge, Mass.: Harvard University
        Program on Technology and Society, 1969. 47 p.

The selective, annotated bibliography concentrates on studies
of the effect of technological change on the occupational
distribution of the labor force, work patterns and skills,
social implications and public policy. Most items published
between 1966 and 1969.

b. BOOKS AND ARTICLES

591   Baritz, Loren. THE SERVANTS OF POWER: A HISTORY OF THE USE
        OF SOCIAL SCIENCE IN AMERICAN INDUSTRY. Middleton, Conn.:
        Wesleyan University Press, 1960. xii, 273 p. Bibliog.

Industrial social sciences developed as industrialists recognized
that for optimum productivity and profitability it was necessary
to manage workers as well as machines. Baritz follows the
history of these disciplines from their initial applications in
advertising through successive developments of Taylorism, the
industrial relations movement, and the "human relations movement." He observes that throughout this history, management
maintained firm control over social scientists and their results.
Baritz fears that as social scientists move ever closer to a

science of behavior, the result could be "more fearful than anything previously hinted."

592   Berger, Peter L., ed. THE HUMAN SHAPE OF WORK: STUDIES IN THE SOCIOLOGY OF OCCUPATIONS. New York: Macmillan, 1964. vii, 241 p.

Presents the work-lives of those engaged in a variety of occupations from janitor to assembly-line worker to business executive. The most penetrating essay may be that on the advertiser whose "virtuosity in fraud" is meticulously exposed.

593   Best, Fred, ed. THE FUTURE OF WORK. Englewood Cliffs, N.J.: Prentice-Hall, 1973. x, 179 p.

Best's contention is that "work's evolution will be determined by the priorities of human needs as they are felt and acted upon within the constraints and opportunities of the time." In part 1, C. Wright Mills briefly reviews the evolutionary history of work. Part 2 looks at changing goals of work, away from material goals toward the seeking of fulfillment. Issues of tomorrow--such as automation, changing leisure, and continuing education--provide topics for part 3. In part 4, alternative features of work, from machine slavery to life-work integration, are projected. Authors include Abraham Maslow, Peter Drucker, Robert Theobald, Jacques Ellul, and Ernest Callenbach.

594   Beum, Robert. "From Millenium to Malaise: Reflections on Modern Work." MODERN AGE 22 (Winter 1978): 54-63.

Beum finds the failure "to make distinct" the process by which traditional attitudes toward work changed and became today's "radically different" attitudes typical of even the best sociologies of work. He feels the twelfth-century Biblicist, Joachim of Flora, may be the connection. The millenarist spirit emphasized by Joachim and reinforced by the Reformation and democratic competitiveness exalted work and made a religion of it. Today's malaise results from the totalitarianism of the millenarist dogma of "socially useful work."

595   Blau, Peter M., and Duncan, Otis Dudley. THE AMERICAN OCCUPATIONAL STRUCTURE. New York: John Wiley and Sons, 1967. xvii, 520 p.

"Occupational structure is the foundation of the stratification system of contemporary industrial society." The analysis of American occupational structures and the factors influencing social mobility is based on questionnaires sent to a sample of 20,000 men between the ages of twenty and sixty-four in 1962.

596   Blauner, Robert. ALIENATION AND FREEDOM: THE FACTORY
      WORKER AND HIS INDUSTRY. Chicago: University of Chicago
      Press, 1964. xvi, 222 p. Illus.

      The worker's relationship to the organization of the work pro-
      cess and the social organization of the factory can determine
      whether or not he experiences that blend of futility, isolation,
      and discontent known as alienation. Drawing principally
      upon the findings of the 1947 Roper job-attitudes survey,
      Blauner found that alienation was unevenly distributed in the
      industries covered, dependent on organization of specific
      work processes.

597   Chinoy, Ely. AUTOMOBILE WORKERS AND THE AMERICAN DREAM.
      New York: Doubleday, 1955. xx, 139 p.

      The disparity between the American dream of success and the real-
      ity of limited opportunities for workers provides the theme of this
      book. In interviewing auto workers, Chinoy found that they lacked
      ambition, on the whole, but lacked as well the social or education-
      al skills needed to pursue other occupational goals. In adapting to
      limited capabilities, workers assign success a less prominent place
      in their lives, centering instead on collective well-being through
      unionism and an improved living standard.

598   Cotgrove, Stephen. "Technology and Work." TECHNOLOGY AND
      SOCIETY 8 (July 1973): 70-74.

      In advanced society, the need to work has become institu-
      tionalized in spite of the fact that technology has rendered
      contemporary work intrinsically unrewarding. Recent programs
      aimed at job enlargement or enrichment, while meritorious,
      cannot change the basically instrumental meaning of factory
      work. Though freedom from the coercive economic system
      might be gained through total automation, critics suggest that
      such a development may be accompanied by technological
      dominance over personal life as well.

599   Cottrell, W[illiam].F[red]. "Of Time and the Railroader." AMERICAN
      SOCIOLOGICAL REVIEW 4 (April 1939): 190-98.

      The exigencies of the arrival-departure schedule have dominated
      the life of the railroader. An occupational dependence on the
      clock made it impossible to plan other relationships, particu-
      larly at home, and rendered participation in regular civic or
      social groups difficult.

600   _____. THE RAILROADER. Stanford, Calif.: Stanford University
      Press, 1940. ix, 145 p.

      From a railroading family, and himself a one-time railroad
      worker, Cottrell draws from experience and research in writing
      this sociological study of railroaders. Various railroad occupa-

tions are described, and the nature of occupational status and the effect of mobility are examined. A chapter on railroad language and a glossary add color.

601 Davis, Louis E., and Cherns, Albert B., eds. THE QUALITY OF WORKING LIFE. Vol. 1: PROBLEMS, PROSPECTS AND THE STATE OF THE ART. Vol. 2: CASES AND COMMENTARY. New York: Free Press, 1975. xiii, 450 p.; xi, 387 p.

Thirty-six original papers discuss factors which affect the work environment and suggest means for improvement. Ways of measuring and defining working life quality are described, followed by analyses of the impact of such factors as organizational configuration, technological change, and worker values. The second volume presents case studies from a number of countries and industries documenting the impact of changes in organizational structure and job design on the job satisfaction of workers in diverse occupations.

602 Dubreuil, Henri. ROBOTS OR MEN. New York: Harper and Brothers, 1930. x, 248 p. Illus.

Dubreuil, a Frenchman, spent a year in American factories working and observing. Though a Socialist, he was favorably surprised by the blend of scientific management and worker relations that he found governing the American factory. The life of the worker in factory and home is examined. Dubreuil concludes that the switch to the assembly line had been achieved without loss of pride in work.

603 Fairfield, Roy P., ed. HUMANIZING THE WORKPLACE. Buffalo, N.Y.: Prometheus Books, 1974. 265 p.

The many inadequacies of the work environment--social, philosophical, and legal--are brought to light by the papers in this volume. The first part deals with general issues of worker discontent and alienation, in the context of general doubts about the impact of technology. A second part turns to specific problems encountered by workers in offices, coal mines, and auto and pet-food factories. The concluding part suggests new directions in work organization, stressing flexibility and consideration for the special problems of women.

604 Faunce, William A. PROBLEMS OF AN INDUSTRIAL SOCIETY. New York: McGraw-Hill, 1968. xiv, 180 p.

Inherent in the structure of industrial society are alienation, ambiguity, and social flux. Industrial society is by nature normless, poorly integrated, and unstable. Through automation, a post-industrial society that can achieve stability may be created, Faunce suggests.

605 _____, ed. READINGS IN INDUSTRIAL SOCIOLOGY. New York: Appleton–Century–Crofts, 1967. viii, 599 p. Bibliog.

This collection of classic studies in the field of industrial sociology demonstrates the continuing relevance of the subdiscipline. Papers cover the social impact of industrialization, industrial bureaucracy, major industrial work roles, work groups, and the future of the industrial order. Many noted authors are represented. A substantial bibliography follows each chapter.

606 Faunce, William A., and Form, William H., eds. COMPARATIVE PERSPECTIVES ON INDUSTRIAL SOCIETY. Boston: Little, Brown and Co., 1969. vi, 277 p. Illus.

This collection examines the social structural characteristics peculiar to industrial society and the contribution of industrialization to the development of those characteristics. Considerations of changes for the individual, the process of urbanization, the changing division of labor, mobility, and social strife culminate in the question: will industrialization lead to a homogeneous world culture?

607 Form, William H. BLUE COLLAR STRATIFICATION: AUTOWORKERS IN FOUR COUNTRIES. Princeton, N.J.: Princeton University Press, 1976. xx, 335 p. Bibliog.

Form selected for his study four countries differing in degree of industrialization: India, Argentina, Italy, and the United States. Samples of skilled, semiskilled and unskilled autoworkers in each country were compared in an attempt to discover how the technology to which workers have been exposed affects their behavior in work group, union, political party, and social network. Problems in social relations and anomie were directly related to the degree of technological complexity of the factory. But, regardless of nation, workers reported, on the whole, contentment with and interest in their work.

608 Friedmann, Georges. THE ANATOMY OF WORK: LABOR, LEISURE AND THE IMPLICATIONS OF AUTOMATION. New York: Free Press of Glencoe, 1964. 203 p. Bibliog.

The psychological consequences of excessive specialization and routinization of industrial labor are examined. Friedmann finds that such specialization has resulted in a decline of job knowledge and skill as well as widespread alienation. Reflecting on a number of British, American, and European experiments, he relates efforts in job enlargement and work-group creation that have ameliorated detrimental aspects.

609 Heisler, W[illiam].J., and Houck, John W., eds. A MATTER OF

DIGNITY: INQUIRIES INTO THE HUMANIZATION OF WORK.
Notre Dame, Ind.: University of Notre Dame Press, 1977. 214 p.

The monotony of jobs is largely due to the fact that involvement in the workplace belongs to the machine, not the
worker. These papers from a lecture series at Notre Dame
consider the design of more humanistic work from an interdisciplinary perspective. Contributors are from the fields of
philosophy, theology, human resource accounting, sociology,
and history, even a union bargainer is in the group. The
role of work in human existence, the effects of work on the
laborer, and the role of the organization in work humanization are the major themes.

610   Kaufmann, Carl B. MAN INCORPORATE: THE INDIVIDUAL AND
       HIS WORK IN AN ORGANIZED SOCIETY. New York: Doubleday,
       1967. 281 p.

       An "ethic of work" is necessary if labor is to provide a sense
       of commitment and dignity. Kaufmann explores whether our
       highly automated and organized corporate structure can offer
       such rewards. A history of economic organization and the
       development of significant technologies is followed by an
       examination of attitudes toward work. A report on the indi-
       vidual in a corporation and on what such organizations have
       done to society ends with a call for individualism amidst
       standardization.

611   Lodahl, Thomas M. "Patterns of Job Attitudes in Two Assembly Tech-
       nologies." ADMINISTRATIVE SCIENCE QUARTERLY 8 (March 1964):
       482–519.

       Job attitudes of workers from two assembly technologies,
       women producing high-quality electronic tubes and men work-
       ing along auto conveyer lines, are studied to relate emotional,
       technological, and performance variables. Satisfaction comes
       from the feeling of performing well, while motivation is re-
       lated to the struggle to achieve a better self-concept through
       work despite the absence of advancement possibilities. Tech-
       nological and emotional factors which impede job satisfaction
       are determined. Lodahl believes it is only the manager who
       can see beyond the "trained incapacity of the specialist" to
       create change.

612   Mayo, Elton. THE SOCIAL PROBLEMS OF AN INDUSTRIAL CIVILIZA-
       TION. Boston: Division of Research, Graduate School of Business
       Administration, Harvard University, 1945. xvii, 150 p.

       Through a review of research on social relations in industry,
       Mayo demonstrates that, in the absence of an adequate social
       organization, incentive wages and improved working condi-

tions do not operate to enhance worker productivity. Rather, it seems that efficiency and productivity are the result of worker solidarity.

613   Meissner, Martin. TECHNOLOGY AND THE WORKER: TECHNICAL DEMANDS AND SOCIAL PROCESSES IN INDUSTRY. San Francisco: Chandler Publishing Co., 1969. xiii, 264 p. Illus.

The effect of technical conditions of production on the social behavior of workers is explored. The author describes the functional, temporal, and perceptual restraints imposed by a number of industrial operations from weaving to shoe bottoming.

614   Merton, Robert K. "The Machine, The Worker, and the Engineer." In SOCIAL THEORY AND SOCIAL STRUCTURE, pp. 562-73. Glencoe, Ill.: Free Press, 1957.

With the introduction of new productive processes in the factory that render old skills obsolescent, workers suffer a loss of social relations and job identity. Through introducing novelty, technology becomes a means of keeping workers down and of producing sharper industrial social stratification. Engineers, through their removal to a small bureaucratic elite, have become separated from the effects of their innovations. Merton calls for more broadly focused social research in industry.

615   Miller, Delbert C., and Form, William H. INDUSTRIAL SOCIOLOGY. New York: Harper and Row, 1963. xxii, 873 p.

Industrial sociology encompasses all forms of economic activity, including the study of occupations and of more general relations between work and other forms of social behavior. This standard text covers the origins and history of industrial sociology, the structure of work organization, the individual's place in the organization, and the application of sociological findings to management philosophies.

616   Moore, Wilbert E[llis]. INDUSTRIAL RELATIONS AND THE SOCIAL ORDER. New York: Macmillan, 1951. 660 p. Bibliog.

This text in industrial sociology entails "a systematic dissection and analysis of the industrial system as a social organization and of the industrial way of life." The development of modern industry, particularly of industrial management and its various philosophies, is followed. Workers' relationships with each other and with machines also receive considerable attention.

617   Nosow, Sigmund, and Form, William H., eds. MAN, WORK AND

SOCIETY. New York: Basic Books, 1962. 612 p. Bibliog.

Spanning several decades of publications in the field of occupational sociology, this large anthology gives considerable space to papers concerning man-machine relations. Other principal topics include economic, industrial, and occupational systems and personal adjustment in the factory. The profiles of occupations collected in chapter 14 include one of railroad workers by W.F. Cottrell.

618   Parker, S.R., et al. THE SOCIOLOGY OF INDUSTRY. New York: Praeger Publishers, 1967. 182 p. Bibliog.

This general survey begins with a selection of articles examining relationships between industry and other subsystems of society, specifically the economy, education, the family, and social structure. A second part dissects the internal structure of industries in order to define roles played by individuals and relations between them. The final section contrasts work and nonwork roles of individuals. British slant.

619   Peterson, Richard M. THE INDUSTRIAL ORDER AND SOCIAL POLICY. Englewood Cliffs, N.J.: Prentice-Hall, 1972. x, 159 p. Illus., bibliog.

In a highly organized, simply phrased work, Peterson conducts an examination of the industrializing process. The growth of industry and its relations to changes in social structure is traced from the congested mills of Great Britain to the sparsely populated contemporary automated factory. Forms of industrial organization are described, with attention to the perspective of the individual. Anecdotal illustrations highlight the text.

620   Purcell, Theodore V. BLUE COLLAR MAN: PATTERNS OF DUAL ALLEGIANCE IN INDUSTRY. Werheim Publications in Industrial Relations. Cambridge, Mass.: Harvard University Press, 1960. xviii, 300 p. Illus.

As the result of approximately 800 oral interviews with workers from three Swift and Company meatpacking plants, the author finds a much greater incidence of dual allegiance to both company and union than generally perceived.

621   Roethlisberger, F[ritz].J[ules]., and Dickson, William J. MANAGEMENT AND THE WORKER; AN ACCOUNT OF A RESEARCH PROGRAM CONDUCTED BY THE WESTERN ELECTRIC COMPANY, HAWTHORNE WORKS, CHICAGO. Cambridge, Mass.: Harvard University Press, 1939. Reprint. Cambridge, Mass.: Harvard University Press, 1947. xxiv, 615 p.

The Hawthorne experiments, conducted jointly by Harvard

University and the Western Electric Company, have become
a classic in the field of industrial management. Related
and analyzed in this volume, the experiments were the first
extensive attempts to use scientific methods in the measurement of the effect of working conditons on human morale and
productive efficiency. The following variables are studied:
rest periods, length of work day and week, fatigue, monotony,
wage incentive. The report also formulates a methodology for
understanding employee dissatisfaction, looks at social organization of workers, and presents applications of the research
to practice.

622   Rose, Michael. INDUSTRIAL BEHAVIOUR: THEORETICAL DEVELOP-
MENT SINCE TAYLOR. London: Allen Lane, 1975. 304 p.

In a historical review of the literature of industrial sociology,
Rose follows the evolution and decline of theories beginning
with Taylor's "machine-man," as rebutted by the British human-
factors school. The human relations approach, which for many
years dominated the field, is criticized as insufficiently attentive to the role of technology and of extra-factory social
relations in shaping worker behavior. Recent studies attuned
to these larger considerations, which adopt "action" approaches,
are favorably surveyed.

623   Schneider, Eugene V. INDUSTRIAL SOCIOLOGY: THE SOCIAL RE-
LATIONS OF INDUSTRY AND THE COMMUNITY. New York:
McGraw-Hill, 1957. 559 p. Bibliog.

Schneider opens with an overview of historical changes in the
organization and social structure of modern industry. Labor-
management relations and the labor movement are treated at
length. Closing chapters consider industry's place in larger
social systems. A lengthy bibliography follows.

624   Shostak, Arthur B., and Gomberg, William, eds. BLUE-COLLAR
WORLD: STUDIES OF THE AMERICAN WORKER. Englewood Cliffs,
N.J.: Prentice-Hall, 1964. xviii, 622 p.

Intended to serve four purposes: to look at the worker as a
person rather than an instrument, to encourage an integrated
approach to studies of the worker, to stress the contemporary
situation of the worker, and to encourage a reexamination of
older materials with this freshened viewpoint. Changes in
working class, life-style, family roles, community participation, and health and working patterns are treated by a sizable
group of prominent sociologists.

625   Simon, Yves R.M. WORK, SOCIETY AND CULTURE. New York:
Fordham University Press, 1971. xvi, 234 p. Bibliog.

A philosopher, Simon calls for a culture based not on leisure but on work-like activities. Technology has the potential to dispel the "irksomeness" of work, for, "the more the technique at his disposal, the greater the possibility for creative choices open to any worker."

626   "Technology, the Labor Process, and the Working Class." MONTHLY REVIEW 28 (July-August 1976): 1-118.

Marxist considerations of the effect of technology on the working class focus on the role of women workers, division of labor in the computer field, efficiency as perceived by capitalist and socialist points of view, relations of production and consumption, the consciousness of the worker, Marx's views on technology, and the approaches of Marx and Adam Smith to division of labor.

627   Walker, Charles Rumford. STEEL TOWN. New York: Harper, 1950. xv, 284 p. Illus., maps.

When U.S. Steel decided to move its tube plant from Ellwood City, Pennsylvania, to Gary, Indiana, Walker took the opportunity to use the move as an industrial case history of the conflict between progress and security. Plotting the historical and community setting, he describes work life in the mill as background for the crisis. Yet he reported, with surprise and satisfaction, that cooperation among all elements characterized the shift.

628   Walker, Charles [Rumford], and Guest, Robert H. THE MAN ON THE ASSEMBLY LINE. Cambridge, Mass.: Harvard University Press, 1952. 180 p. Illus.

The job satisfaction of assembly-line workers is the subject of this pilot study. One hundred and eighty workers were interviewed at home on job experiences and attitudes, and social relations. The authors found that while most disliked the mechanized pacing, social isolation, and repetitiveness of their jobs, they liked the pay and security well enough to remain.

629   Whyte, William Foote. MEN AT WORK. Irwin-Dorsey Series in Behavioral Science in Business. Homewood, Ill.: Dorsey Press and Richard D. Irwin, 1961. 593 p. Illus., bibliog.

Human relations in industry are studied by the examination of specific individuals in jobs, groups, organizations, and case studies. Whyte uses his personal experience in field research for this analysis of the worker. The influence of the following factors on the worker are studied in detail: social and economic environment, technology, automation, unions, management, technological innovation, and organization. Case studies come from restaurant, hotel, steel, automobile, glass, and petroleum industries.

630 _____. THE ORGANIZATION MAN. New York: Simon and Schuster, 1956. 429 p.

An important product of industrial society is Whyte's "organization man," who belongs spiritually and physically to self-perpetuating bureaucracies. Whyte describes the dehumanizing training, pressures to conform, loyalty requirements, and lack of imagination that he deems typical of the ideal organization man, in the hope of stirring disaffection for this image. There is an appendix, mockingly titled: "How to Cheat on Personality Tests."

631 Widick, B.J., ed. AUTO WORK AND ITS DISCONTENTS. Baltimore: Johns Hopkins University Press, 1976. ix, 112 p. Bibliog.

Contributors, all of whom have worked in the auto industry, conclude that the concepts of job satisfaction and alienation "do not offer a satisfactory explanation for the degree of conflict, change, or challenge found in the workplace environment." Workers, they find, are pitiable or dehumanized only in the eyes of middle-class observers.

2. Automation

632 Bowen, Howard R., and Mangum, Garth L., eds. AUTOMATION AND ECONOMIC PROGRESS. Englewood Cliffs, N.J.: Prentice-Hall, 1966. 170 p. Illus.

A condensation of the report of the U.S. Commission on Technology, Automation, and Economic Progress, entitled TECHNOLOGY AND THE AMERICAN ECONOMY, is presented along with selections from the six volumes of supplementary studies. The Commission concludes that unemployment is caused less by automation than by "passive fiscal policies," and that problems center primarily on decision-making and policymaking mechanisms. Among the supplementary studies are considerations of computers, development and diffusion of technologies, and leisure. The report also addresses social problems considered amenable to technological solutions: health care, urban transportation, housing, pollution, and work environment.

633 Bright, James R. AUTOMATION AND MANAGEMENT. Boston: Graduate School of Business Administration, Harvard University, 1958. xv, 270 p. Illus.

Field study of many major industrial plants resulted in this analysis of the implications of automation. Bright finds that novelty rather than automation is often the cause of troubles, the degree of advance over the former system is significant, and skill requirements for workers decrease with automation. Specific areas of investigation are evolution of automation in certain industries, descriptions of automation programs at plants, development of systems, impact of downtime, effect on workers, sales, and role of management.

634   Buckingham, Walter. AUTOMATION: ITS IMPACT ON BUSINESS AND PEOPLE. New York: Harper and Brothers, 1961. ix, 196 p.

The economic and social consequences of automation are analyzed in this nontechnical study. An examination of the principles, history, motives, and limits of automation is followed by considerations of its effects on the theory and practice of management, as well as its impact on industrial organization, employment, prices, and economic growth. The social implications for leisure time and cultural progress are then discussed.

635   Diebold, John. BEYOND AUTOMATION; MANAGERIAL PROBLEMS OF AN EXPLODING TECHNOLOGY. New York: McGraw-Hill, 1964. x, 220 p.

A "pioneer" in the application of computers to industrial and governmental operations stresses the social and economic implications of automation. Although the contents of this volume were originally addresses and presented papers, they have been edited into an integrated whole. Diebold devotes the major portion of the book to problems in management, specifically those related to the application of information technology, education of managers for change, and systems research. He then turns to policy issues on the state and national political levels.

636   Dunlop, John T., ed. AUTOMATION AND TECHNOLOGICAL CHANGE. Englewood Cliffs, N.J.: Prentice-Hall, 1962. 184 p. Bibliog.

A historical perspective and factual information on the impact of automation and technological change are provided in this collection of essays. Robert L. Heilbroner presents the historic debate while other contributors look at the educational consequences, organizational and managerial impacts, economic considerations, the "industry" of technological innovation, and the role of creativity.

637   Friedmann, Georges. INDUSTRIAL SOCIETY: THE EMERGENCE OF

THE HUMAN PROBLEMS OF AUTOMATION. Glencoe, Ill.: Free
Press, 1955. 436 p. Bibliog.

A noted French sociologist concentrates on difficulties associated with the mechanization of industry, indicting particularly
the rigid tradition of Taylorism. The problems of monotony
and boredom are given particular attention through a review
of research on those aspects of modern labor.

638   Jacobson, Howard Boone, and Roucek, Joseph S., eds. AUTOMATION
AND SOCIETY. New York: Philosophical Library, 1959. 553 p.

Thirty-two contributed papers consider three dimensions of
automation: industrial applications, management responsibility,
and effects on society. There are case studies of automation
in automotive, electronics, communications, railroad, education, accounting, and other industries. Edward R. Murrow
and Fred W. Friendly muse on its benefits and problems.
Social aspects discussed include its impacts on leisure, education, employment, politics, work, and class stratification.

639   Lipstreu, Otis, and Reed, Kenneth A. TRANSITION TO AUTOMATION:
A STUDY OF PEOPLE, PRODUCTION, AND CHANGE. Boulder: University of Colorado, 1964. 156 p. Graphs.

The effects of automation on workers and management are
analyzed through research which combines a questionnaire survey and observation of a company undergoing major technological change. The authors document implications for organizations, personnel, management, workers, trade unions, and
production. The questionnaire was distributed to top management in the 500 largest U.S. corporations. Hypotheses were
tested on a before and after basis through case study in an
unnamed company.

640   Mann, Floyd C., and Hoffman, L. Richard. AUTOMATION AND THE
WORKER: A THEORY OF SOCIAL CHANGE IN POWER PLANTS.
New York: Holt, 1960. xiv, 272 p. Illus., bibliog.

Attitudes of workers toward automation of a large power plant
are examined through contrasting workers in nonautomated and
automated plants of the same company. Though reactions were
complex, it appeared to the authors that they were on the
whole favorable to automation, given proper preparation.

641   Marcson, Simon, ed. AUTOMATION, ALIENATION AND ANOMIE.
New York: Harper and Row, 1970. 479 p.

Drawing from important publications in sociology, economics,
and social psychology, this reader offers a comprehensive
overview of literature on the effects of technology on the

work environment. The many impacts of automation are dili-
gently pursued--from the more obvious effects on workers and
work organization to more subtle changes. The meaning of
alienation and its relation to changes in modes of production
also receive considerable deliberation.

642   Philipson, Morris, ed. AUTOMATION: IMPLICATIONS FOR THE
       FUTURE. New York: Vintage Books, 1962. 456 p.

       This useful anthology reprints many noted papers concerned
       with the broader implications of computers and communication
       techniques as well as with the immediate effects of factory
       automation. The book is divided into seven parts, each de-
       voted to an economic or social institution affected by new
       technologies. Among the many prominent authors represented
       are John Diebold, Norbert Wiener, Peter F. Drucker, Diana
       Crane, Simon Ramo, and Paul Goodman.

643   Seligman, Ben B. MOST NOTORIOUS VICTORY: MAN IN AN AGE
       OF AUTOMATION. New York: Free Press, 1966. xviii, 430 p.
       Bibliog.

       Seligman does not attribute the direction of technological
       growth to chance; rather, he feels that technology, an inter-
       nal drive, has come to condition man and his works. The
       present collection of essays, some previously published, studies
       the economic, social, psychological, and philosophical impli-
       cations of automation, from the Industrial Revolution to com-
       puter technology.

644   Shils, Edward B. AUTOMATION AND INDUSTRIAL RELATIONS. New
       York: Holt, Rinehart and Winston, 1963. 360 p. Graphs.

       The impact of automation and the computer on management
       and economics is analyzed by looking at the challenges posed
       for government and by examining the attitudes and experiences
       in six leading industries. The influence of automation on
       skill requirements is singled out for special attention. Case
       studies of the adoption of automatic technologies are provided.

645   Somers, Gerald G.; Cushman, Edward L.; and Weinberg, Nat, eds.
       ADJUSTING TO TECHNOLOGICAL CHANGE. New York: Harper and
       Row, 1963. viii, 230 p.

       The combined editorship of a professor of economics, a vice
       president of a major auto company, and a labor union officer
       results in a collection of essays which presents an integrated,
       nonemotional survey of the impact of industrial automation on
       labor, management, and the community. To understand the
       process of adjustment to technological change, costs are

weighed against gains, unions and displaced employees are considered, and the experience at Armour and Company is scrutinized as a case study.

646   Theobald, Robert. "Should Men Compete with Machines?" NATION 202 (9 May 1966): 544–50.

The problem of automation replacing laborers and computers replacing knowledge-workers will not subside. Therefore, Theobald reasons, we should question not whether man can but whether he should compete with machines. The author argues for a fundamental change in the distribution of goods to allow for machine displacement; he calls it BES, or Basic Economic Security. This program will "lead to cultural, social and political advances on an unprecedented scale."

647   U.S. National Commission on Technology, Automation, and Economic Progress. TECHNOLOGY AND THE AMERICAN ECONOMY: APPEN-DIX VOLUMES 1–6. Washington, D.C.: 1966. Y3.T22:2T22/app/I–VI.

The series of commissioned studies deals with the implications of technological change on American society. Titles of volumes and brief indication of topics covered follows. Vol. 1: THE OUTLOOK FOR TECHNOLOGICAL CHANGE AND EMPLOYMENT. 373 p. Policy requirements for full employment, computers, automation, information processing networks. Vol. 2: THE EMPLOYMENT IMPACT OF TECHNOLOGICAL CHANGE. 399 p. Technological changes in banking, steel, agriculture; skill requirements; diffusion of technology; hours of work and leisure. Vol. 3: ADJUSTING TO CHANGE. 275 p. Forecasting; technology's role in assisting minorities, unskilled. Vol. 4: EDUCATIONAL IMPLICATIONS OF TECHNOLOGICAL CHANGE. 151 p. Application of computers (no. 1036). Vol. 5: APPLYING TECHNOLOGY TO UNMET NEEDS. 291 p. Urban planning, housing, aerospace industry, pollution, transportation, solid waste, health care. Vol. 6: STATEMENTS RELATING TO THE IMPACT OF TECHNOLOGICAL CHANGE. 309 p. Statements by representatives of industry, labor unions, professional organizations.

648   Weeks, Robert P., ed. MACHINES AND THE MAN: A SOURCEBOOK ON AUTOMATION. New York: Applecton–Century–Crofts, 1961. xiii, 338 p.

Thirty-five articles, speeches, book excerpts, and works of literature discussing the many aspects of automation. Designed for student use in writing undergraduate research papers, the volume presents a balanced view. Discussion questions and suggested research topics are included.

649   Zeitlin, Irving. "Aspects of the Scientific-Industrial Revolution in
        America." CAHIERS D'HISTOIRE MONDIALE 9, no. 4 (1969):
        1009-19.

        Is automation just another quantitative advance in a long line
        of technological advances dating from the Industrial Revolution,
        or is it qualitatively different? Based on man's decreased con-
        trol of the production process, Zeitlin concludes the latter is
        the more convincing theoretical position and offers several
        examples of potential societal changes.

3. Leisure

a. BIBLIOGRAPHY

650   Starbuck, James C. THEME PARKS: A PARTIALLY ANNOTATED
        BIBLIOGRAPHY OF ARTICLES ABOUT MODERN AMUSEMENT PARKS.
        Exchange Bibliography no. 953. Monticello, Ill.: Council of Planning
        Librarians, 1976. 20 p.

b. BOOKS AND ARTICLES

651   De Grazia, Sebastian. OF TIME, WORK AND LEISURE. New York:
        Twentieth Century Fund, 1962. 559 p. Bibliog.

        Science and technology have failed to produce an overall
        improvement in the quality of human life, as the leisure time
        promised by the machine has been eaten up in commuting and
        job changing. The desire for contemplative leisure has been
        supplanted by that for material goods, a want that can be
        satisfied only by money--and therefore, more work and time.
        It is ironic, De Grazia observes, that faith in the machine,
        which is to take away work, is founded on a doctrine that
        awards status only for work.

652   Douglass, Paul F., ed. "Recreation in the Age of Automation."
        ANNALS OF THE AMERICAN ACADEMY OF POLITICAL AND SOCIAL
        SCIENCES 313 (September 1957): 1-147.

        Modern life is characterized by what Douglass calls "unsold
        time," time not consumed in production and thus available
        for other purposes, notably leisure. This volume opens with
        background papers on the history, philosophy, and economics
        of leisure. Four papers ponder the relationship between edu-
        cation and leisure. Forms of leisure from local camping to
        international travel, as promoted by public and commercial
        agencies, are surveyed in the remaining parts.

653   Ducassé, Pierre. "Science, Technology and Leisure." IMPACT OF SCI-
        ENCE ON SOCIETY 3 (Spring 1952): 26-42. Bibliog.

In its initial stages, the Industrial Revolution reduced the amount and quality of leisure available to both workers and upper classes. As industrial society matured, it offered increasing time for leisure. Such leisure would be best spent, the author suggests, on scientific research. An annotated bibliography of important studies on technology and leisure concludes the article.

654 Friedmann, Georges. "Leisure and Technological Civilization." INTERNATIONAL SOCIAL SCIENCE JOURNAL 12, no. 4 (1960): 509-21.

One of the basic features of technological civilization is the vacation, a scheduled period of time off from work. Modern society has not developed appropriate institutions to constructively deal with leisure. Leisure is now usurped by commuting, fatigue, higher standards of home maintenance, and second jobs. A major task of industrial society has become education for leisure.

655 Gabor, Dennis. "Technology, Life and Leisure." NATURE 200 (9 November 1963): 513-18.

Among current problems created by technology, chief is the problem of increasing leisure time, more threatening than overpopulation and automation. Technology itself can supply a partial solution to the problem through offering opportunities for education and self-expression.

656 Kaplan, Max, and Bosserman, Phillip, eds. TECHNOLOGY, VALUES AND LEISURE. Nashville, Tenn.: Abingdon Press, 1971. 256 p.

The book opens with "Perspectives on Leisure," a set of general essays on technology and social values authored by Robert Theobald, Emmanuel Mesthene, and Harrison Brown. Authors in the second part reflect on the positive implications of leisure for government, education, and the public. It is pointed out that leisure also holds negative connotations for the slum dweller, for youth, and for the aged. A concluding survey of research on leisure covers recent and ongoing projects.

657 Kasson, John F. AMUSING THE MILLION: CONEY ISLAND AT THE TURN OF THE CENTURY. New York: Hill and Wang, 1978. 120 p. Illus.

Coney Island's history dramatizes the effects of the rise of urban-industrial civilization on the American masses. Kasson presents an insightful exploration of the illumination Coney's heyday casts on the cultural upheaval during the early decades of this century, revealing how the entertainment which developed there reflected the lives of the urban millions.

658   Larrabee, Eric, and Meyersohn, Rolf, eds. MASS LEISURE. Glencoe,
       Ill.: Free Press, 1958. x, 429 p. Bibliog.

       Through the spread of industrialization, leisure has become
       available on an ever-increasing scale. This anthology reveals
       the forms that leisure has assumed in American life, from
       sports to solitude. It offers as well papers reflecting on the
       past, future, and values of leisure. Articles directly con-
       cerned with the role of technology include Robert Dubin,
       "Industrial Workers' Worlds"; David Riesman, "Work and
       Leisure in Post-Industrial Society"; and Clement Greenberg,
       "Work and Leisure Under Industrialism." A comprehensive
       bibliography on leisure by Meyersohn, covering the years
       1900-58, completes the volume.

659   Mangels, William F. THE OUTDOOR AMUSEMENT INDUSTRY: FROM
       EARLIEST TIMES TO THE PRESENT. New York: Vantage Press, 1952.
       206 p. Illus.

       The development of amusement parks as well as mechanized
       thrill and fun devices is chronicled with attention to social
       forces which influenced design. The carousel, roller coaster,
       Ferris wheel, oscillating swings, and illusion rides receive
       detailed attention along with a discussion of the growth of
       the most pervasive resort area, Coney Island. Rare illustra-
       tions of seventeenth- through nineteenth-century entertainment
       machines add to the work's value as still the most substantial
       sourcebook on the subject.

660   Martin, Thomas W., and Berry, Kenneth J. "Competitive Sport in Post-
       Industrial Society: The Case of the Motocross Racer." JOURNAL OF
       POPULAR CULTURE 8 (Summer 1974): 107-20.

       Motocrossing is described as an innovative working-class re-
       sponse to the stresses of postindustrial society. In motocrossing,
       a euphoric man-machine unity is achieved without sacrifice of
       rugged individualism and pride in physical manhood, values
       still important in working-class socialization.

661   Segal, Julius. "The Lure of Pinball." HARPER'S MAGAZINE, October
       1957, pp. 44-47.

       Pinball's psychological "pay off" is a result of the "delicate
       balance between success and failure" deliberately built into
       the machine, the cheating achieved through "gunching"
       (rocking the machine), and the satisfaction of manipulating
       and mastering an industrial mechanism. Players become big
       winners by amassing enormous numbers of points, beat their
       industrial masters, vent frustrations, and make "the world be-
       have"--for a nickel.

662   Sharpe, Roger C., et al. PINBALL! New York: E.P. Dutton, 1977. 190 p. Ill.

> This informal historical survey of pinball provides a comprehensive account of the development of the mechanical amusement from its origins in bagatelle in the late nineteenth century to today's arcades. Detailed diagrams and explanations of such implements as "tilt," "bumpers," and "free play" are provided. Lavishly illustrated with color photographs by James Hamilton, interactions of game, machine, and player are accentuated. The author recognizes his own involvement in a romantic fantasy: "I can feel myself merging with the machine, hands and eyes in perfect coordination. I take a deep breath. . . . Playing pinball is like making love: it demands the complete concentration and total emotional involvement of the player, nothing else will do." Includes an exhaustive, chronological list of games and manufacturers.

663   Smigel, Erwin O., ed. WORK AND LEISURE: A CONTEMPORARY SOCIAL PROBLEM. New Haven, Conn.: College and University Press, 1963. 208 p.

> Primarily written by sociologists, this collection of papers on leisure includes many previously published writings. Bennet M. Berger reviews theoretical issues related to the sociology of leisure. Robert Dubin identifies the "critical life interests" of workers; Louis H. Orzach does the same for professionals. The impact of automation is covered by William A. Faunce. Other papers study the impact of changing work hours and occupations on leisure choices. The book concludes with a projection of future issues in leisure by Robert S. Weiss and David Riesman, and a statistical appendix documenting postwar leisure growth for American workers by Peter Henle.

664   Snow, Robert E., and Wright, David E. "Coney Island: A Case Study in Popular Culture and Technical Change." JOURNAL OF POPULAR CULTURE 9 (Spring 1976): 960-75.

> The growth and demise of Coney Island reveals the effect of both mechanization on popular culture and of pop styles on the implementation of new technologies. "Mechanized leisure" allowed people to "participate vicariously in the myth of progress, and to use technology for escape."

665   Somers, Dale A. "The Leisure Revolution: Recreation in the American City 1820-1920." JOURNAL OF POPULAR CULTURE 5 (Summer 1971): 125-47.

> "Enthusiasm for recreation on a great scale developed rapidly as the United States shifted from a rural-agrarian to an urban-industrial society." Somers traces the growth and impact of commercial and organized amusement during a century of adjustment.

666   Wright, David E., and Snow, Robert E. "Las Vegas: Metaphysics in the Technological Society." CENTENNIAL REVIEW 23 (Winter 1979): 40-61.

As in the case of the Egyptian Pyramids or Chartres, the money, energy, and technological know-how of American society has been marshalled for the building of Las Vegas--a shrine to our dominant metaphysic of technological-secular progress. Las Vegas has been successful because it provides a release from the pressures of technological society while it, paradoxically, affirms technological values. The authors review the history of the city with its development related to railroads and Hoover Dam and explore its present inability to fulfill imaginative needs as it once did. Its allure has been "mechanized extrication from our lock-step world to a land of luxury, release and celebration." But, increasingly, it is becoming an ambivalent symbol of isolation, thoughtless demands on resources, and blind adherence to faith in the technological fix.

Part 6

ECONOMICS OF TECHNOLOGY

A. HISTORICAL SURVEYS

667   Anderson, E.H. "The Scientific Revolution and its Impact on Modern
       Economics." SOUTHERN ECONOMIC JOURNAL 23 (January 1957):
       227-44.

       The process by which the methodology of science was applied
       to agriculture, industry, engineering, medicine, marketing,
       and management in America from 1880 to World War I is
       termed a "scientific" rather than a technological or industrial
       revolution. Factors examined include technological develop-
       ment; systems of operation, i.e., mass production and mass
       marketing; institutional changes in education and bureaucracy;
       and new economic theories.

668   Bruchey, Stuart Weems. THE ROOTS OF AMERICAN ECONOMIC
       GROWTH, 1607-1861: AN ESSAY IN SOCIAL CAUSATION. New
       York: Harper and Row, 1965. 2d ed. 1968. xxviii, 234 p. Bibliog.

       An original synthesis of the then recent literature on American
       economic history finds that the central factor in American
       economic growth was industrialization, "together with a con-
       stellation of conditions that made it possible." Analysis of
       the interrelationships among social values, technological
       change, government, private capital, education, and an
       emerging national market results in a causal explanation of
       American industrialism.

669   Cochran, Thomas Childs, and Miller, William. THE AGE OF ENTER-
       PRISE: A SOCIAL HISTORY OF INDUSTRIAL AMERICA. New York:
       Macmillan, 1942. Rev. ed. New York: Harper and Row, 1961. x,
       394 p. Bibliog.

       Cochran's economic and social history of American industry is
       based on then existing monographic material. He presents
       a synthesis primarily for the nonprofessional reader, and in

addition to industrialization itself includes related information on transportation, labor, urbanization, and the rise of commercial agriculture.

670   David, Paul A. TECHNICAL CHOICE, INNOVATION, AND ECONOMIC GROWTH: ESSAYS ON AMERICAN AND BRITISH EXPERIENCE IN THE NINETEENTH CENTURY. London: Cambridge University Press, 1975. x, 334 p. Graphs, bibliog.

An interesting collection of micro-economic essays presents broad implications on the role of nineteenth-century technological innovation in economic growth. Conceptual background and theories of generation, diffusion, and ramifications are covered; specific topics include labor scarcity, cotton textiles in New England, the mechanization of reaping in the mid-West, mechanical grain farming in Britain, and the impact of the railroad in antebellum America.

671   Fogel, Robert W[illiam]., and Engerman, Stanley L., eds. THE RE-INTERPRETATION OF AMERICAN ECONOMIC HISTORY. New York: Harper and Row, 1971. xxiv, 494 p.

A collection of thirty-six articles takes an econometric approach to history. Several of the pieces deal with important technologies and innovations such as the iron industry, cotton textiles, railroads, the mechanization of reaping, steampower, and urbanization. Useful for both historians and economists to broaden the scope of their course readings. Includes guides for classroom use.

672   Hacker, Louis M. THE COURSE OF AMERICAN ECONOMIC GROWTH AND DEVELOPMENT. American Economic History Series. New York: John Wiley and Sons, 1970. xxvi, 382 p. Bibliog.

The survey deals with the social and institutional factors underlying American economic growth and development. Hacker is suspicious of modern economic theory and statistical analysis, preferring instead to rely on concepts of entrepreneurship and cultural mores.

673   Heilbroner, Robert L. THE ECONOMIC TRANSFORMATION OF AMERICA. New York: Harcourt Brace Jovanovich, 1977. xi, 276 p. Illus., maps, bibliog.

A textbook survey of American economic history places heavy emphasis on the role of technology and industrialization. Heilbroner's central theme is that expansion was the major motivating force in our economic history.

674   Higgs, Robert. THE TRANSFORMATION OF THE AMERICAN ECON-

OMY, 1865-1914: AN ESSAY IN INTERPRETATION. New York: John Wiley and Sons, 1971. xvi, 143 p. Maps, bibliog.

Higgs's theoretical interpretation notes the important contribution of technological progress as intellectual capital to the growth of the American economy. He deals with the economic themes of growth, transformation, rural and urban institutional changes, and inequality in the distribution of income and wealth.

675   Kirkland, Edward C[hase]. A HISTORY OF AMERICAN ECONOMIC LIFE. Crofts American History Series. 1932. 4th ed. New York: Appleton-Century-Crofts, 1969. xv, 767 p. Maps, bibliog.

The human aspects of economic history receive full play in this survey as does the technology of agriculture, industry, and transportation. The revised edition takes into account recent trends in the writing of economic history.

676   _____. INDUSTRY COMES OF AGE: BUSINESS, LABOR, AND PUBLIC POLICY, 1860-1897. Economic History of the United States, vol. 6. New York: Holt, Rinehart and Winston, 1961. x, 445 p. Bibliog.

A broad-ranging economic survey in which the author takes a rather positive approach to the accomplishments of the so-called Robber Barons. Kirkland approaches the period "through the eyes of contemporaries." Good bibliographical essay.

677   Nettels, Curtis P. THE EMERGENCE OF A NATIONAL ECONOMY, 1775-1815. Economic History of the United States, vol. 2. New York: Holt, Rinehart and Winston, 1962. Reprint. New York: Harper and Row, 1969. xiv, 424 p. Illus., map, bibliog.

This volume in the generally fine economic history series contains useful general information on transportation, industry, agriculture, and labor.

678   North, Douglass C. THE ECONOMIC GROWTH OF THE UNITED STATES, 1790-1860. Englewood Cliffs, N.J.: Prentice-Hall, 1961. New York: W.W. Norton and Co., 1966. xvi, 304 p. Maps.

An examination of economic growth prior to the Civil War is based on the thesis that "U.S. growth was the evolution of a market economy where the behavior of prices of goods, services and productive factors was the major element in any explanation of economic change." Particular emphasis is placed on the importance of cotton exports and industrialization.

679   _____. GROWTH AND WELFARE IN THE AMERICAN PAST: A NEW

ECONOMIC HISTORY. Englewood Cliffs, N.J.: Prentice-Hall, 1966. 2d ed. 1974. xiv, 210 p. Maps.

The "major trends and issues in American economic history are summarized." Several chapters relate to industrialization and economic growth. While technology is a major ingredient for economic growth, human capital and efficiency of economic organization are also of importance.

680   Rosenberg, Nathan. TECHNOLOGY AND AMERICAN ECONOMIC GROWTH. New York: Harper and Row, 1972. xi, 211 p.

This exploration of the interrelationship between technological change and the long-term growth of the American economy and society attempts to provide an interpretive framework. Basically optimistic about the role of science and technology in society, the author believes the ills which do result from technology remain because "we have chosen not to reduce the unpleasant side-effects of our technology," either by devoting too little in the way of resources or by choosing technological alternatives "less costly in terms of money outlays but which generate higher levels of pollution."

681   Weeden, William B. ECONOMIC AND SOCIAL HISTORY OF NEW ENGLAND, 1620-1789. 2 vols. 1890. Reprint. New York: Hillary House, 1963. xxx, 964 p.

This wide-ranging survey of economic and social developments in colonial New England is still valuable for its accounts of early manufacturing, transportation, and commerce.

682   Williamson, Harold F., ed. THE GROWTH OF THE AMERICAN ECONOMY: AN INTRODUCTION TO THE ECONOMIC HISTORY OF THE UNITED STATES. New York: Prentice-Hall, 1944. xiii, 804 p. Maps, bibliog.

Taking a largely thematic approach, Williamson includes chapters on agricultural technology, heavy and light industries, business organization, and transportation. Each chapter is written by a different expert in the field and is followed by selected bibliographical references.

B. THEORY

683   Ayres, Clarence E. "The Role of Technology in Economic Theory." AMERICAN ECONOMIC REVIEW, PAPERS AND PROCEEDINGS OF THE SIXTY-FIFTH ANNUAL MEETING OF THE AMERICAN ECONOMIC ASSOCIATION 43 (May 1953): 279-87.

Social scientists must assimilate technology into theories of

social systems function. When the significance for human behavior of machines and technological modes of doing is adequately realized, changes in the economic process will be
necessary.

684   Galbraith, John K[enneth]. AMERICAN CAPITALISM: THE CONCEPT
OF COUNTERVAILING POWER. Boston: Houghton Mifflin, 1952.
217 p.

The rise of concentration of market power in large industrial
organizations has provided a favorable climate for technological innovation. Galbraith contends that the development of
industrial conglomerates and monopolies operates for the public
interest within the market economy. Independent, disadvan-
taged groups such as farmers turn to government intervention.
Therefore, "positive" use of government power is an essential
element in economic balance. In Galbraith's opinion, American capitalism has produced reasonably acceptable results.

685   _____. THE NEW INDUSTRIAL STATE. Boston: Houghton Mifflin,
1967. Rev. ed. 1971. xiv, 423 p.

The industrial state is the expression of technology, and in it
the controlling economic power shifts from consumers and markets to the needs of corporations and business organizations.
Run by a "technostructure," that is, by committees of scientists,
engineers, and managers, the profit motive is replaced by
concern for the growth of the organization. With efficient
coordination of machines and men, markets and governmental
policy are manipulated. Galbraith wants to use the university
elite to change the industrial elite through education for new
values.

686   Heilbroner, Robert L. "Economic Problems of a 'Postindustrial' Society."
DISSENT 20 (Spring 1973): 163-76.

Scrutinizing the concept of postindustrial society, Heilbroner
finds inadequacies in views on the size of the service sector,
quality of information growth, the end of capitalism. Trends
to be expected include the concentration of technological innovation in the service sector, business-state coordination, and
problems with ecological adjustment. The ultimate mark of
the coming era will be a stage of socioeconomic development
in which the future is determined not by "lawlike mechanisms,"
but by the political selection of goals.

687   _____. THE LIMITS OF AMERICAN CAPITALISM. New York:
Harper and Row, 1966. 150 p.

Speculating on the end of capitalism, Heilbroner foretells the
demise of the present society because it cannot control or

resolve the forces of technology. A system which abdicates its decision making to the rule of profit is unable to apply rationality to technological and social changes. He advocates rule by a scientific elite who are attracted to science rather than to acquisition. In two generations, scientists will control population, genetic quality, care of children, choice of life-work, and duration of life.

688   Lederer, Emil. "Has Capitalism Failed?" AMERICAN SCHOLAR 3 (Summer 1934): 294-301.

In this early statement on the failure of capitalism, Lederer explains that the ideals of social harmony, humanitarianism, and free trade have not been realized by this economic system. Mankind is now threatened by the machinery that has been built. People must accept whatever form of work is offered, and even the efforts of white-collar workers and scientists must be directed toward what can be produced and sold. The "structural contradictions" within capitalism base production on technique, which in turn requires huge investments that demand immense output. Growth is constantly essential. Only a planned economic system can save the modern economic structure. Democracy is not compatible with capitalism.

689   Rostow, W[alter].W. THE STAGES OF ECONOMIC GROWTH: A NON-COMMUNIST MANIFESTO. Cambridge: Cambridge University Press, 1961. xii, 179 p.

In his famous, if somewhat controversial, framework of economic growth, Rostow sets forth five stages: the traditional society, preconditions for take-off, take-off, the drive to maturity, and the age of high mass-consumption. The author compares the historic economies of the U.S. and the USSR in laying out his theory and relating economic to social and political forces.

C. GROWTH AND QUALITY OF LIFE

1. Bibliographies

690   Agelasto, Michael A. II, and Perry, Patricia R. THE NO-GROWTH CONTROVERSY. Exchange Bibliography no. 519. Monticello, Ill.: Council of Planning Librarians, 1974. 28 p.

691   Geiger, H. Kent. NATIONAL DEVELOPMENT 1776-1966: A SELECTIVE AND ANNOTATED GUIDE TO THE MOST IMPORTANT ARTICLES IN ENGLISH. Metuchen, N.J.: Scarecrow Press, 1969. vi, 247 p.

Cultural, economic, political, and social aspects of development are represented in this selective, highly annotated bibliography of 350 books and articles. An emphasis is placed on evaluation of the publications included. Geiger provides ratings for each entry and also compiles lists of the most important publications, as determined through citation analysis, republication, and other methods. Most of the publications included appeared after 1950.

2. Books and Articles

692   Chase, Richard X. "Economic Analysis and Environmental Quality." AMERICAN JOURNAL OF ECONOMICS AND SOCIOLOGY 31 (July 1972): 271-82.

The development of an economic framework for analyzing the effects of pollution must recognize the costs of the stabilization of environmental quality. Despite alternatives of subsidies, fines, or government regulation, society will bear a large portion of the clean-up bill. The cost for our priority of values is likely to be unevenly distributed among the population.

693   Dorfman, Robert, and Dorfman, Nancy S. ECONOMICS OF THE ENVIRONMENT: SELECTED READINGS. New York: W.W. Norton and Co., 1972. xl, 427 p. Illus., bibliog.

Economic principles related to the environment are explained as a preface to an assessment of environmental degradation and its causes in technological development. The authors consider the effect of public policy and economic disregard of nonmarket externalities. Methods of measuring the social and economic consequences of environmental damage are analyzed, and the viability of means of alleviation, such as effluent charges, is assessed.

694   Edison Electric Institute. ECONOMIC GROWTH IN THE FUTURE: THE GROWTH DEBATE IN NATIONAL AND GLOBAL PERSPECTIVE. New York: McGraw-Hill, 1976. xiv, 434 p. Illus.

The point of view of the power industry regarding the growth issue emerges from this study by consultants in technical and business fields. An analysis of the present economic situation, population, consumption, energy supply and demand is followed by views on the future of growth and discussion of alternative growth patterns. The issues of concern to the electric utility industry are presented. The report concludes that growth can be sustained with improvement in quality of life, attempts to halt growth would require authoritarian measures, energy demand will grow more slowly than GNP, and nuclear reactors and deep seabed mining are the solution to the energy problem.

695   Faramelli, Norman J. "Perilous Links between Economic Growth, Justice and Ecology: A Challenge for Economic Planners." ENVIRON-MENTAL AFFAIRS 1 (April 1971): 218-27.

Improvement in environmental quality will result in expansive applications of pollution control technology or a reduction in production of material goods. Either case will result in severe problems for the poor. Faramelli explores the relationship between ecological responsibility and economic justice. He questions who should pay for pollution control and problems associated with unemployment. Challenges to be faced are a redistribution of income with shorter work hours and a guaranteed annual income, and a transformation of the "American value schema" toward new life-styles and an antimaterialist growth model.

696   Galbraith, John K[enneth]. "Economics and the Quality of Life." SCIENCE 145 (10 July 1964): 117-23.

Although economic concerns are paramount for poor societies, they remain the major force guiding political and social thought and action for affluent societies. Economic goals are erroneously considered immutable and are supported by vested interests. Growth consists of luxury consumption, and the enjoyment of such luxury becomes an "index of national virtue" since economic growth is the primary national goal. Economics is reluctant to admit underlying social change. Preoccupation with problems no longer primary, first production then unemployment, destroys the possibility of prescribing for the most urgent present problem--the quality of life.

697   Goldman, Marshall I., ed. CONTROLLING POLLUTION: THE ECONOMICS OF A CLEANER AMERICA. Englewood Cliffs, N.J.: Prentice-Hall, 1967. xii, 175 p.

The readings in this collection are written in a popular tone and deal with economic aspects of water, air, and scenic pollution. Most originally appeared in nonscholarly journals such as SATURDAY REVIEW and PETROLEUM TODAY. The role of government in matters relating to environmental quality is also considered. Useful only to nonspecialized students, the articles consider the nature of the pollution problem, the social costs of industry, specific case studies of pollution of the Ohio River and Lake Erie, and Pittsburgh's attempts to clean its environs.

698   Henderson, Hazel. CREATING ALTERNATIVE FUTURES: THE END OF ECONOMICS. New York: Berkeley Publishing Corp., 1978. x, 404 p. Illus.

A personal view of the transition of our society from mass-consumption-based industrialism to less energy-oriented alternative life-styles is presented by Henderson's collected writings. In part 1, "The End of Economics," the problems of transcending traditional economic practice are confronted. Assumptions about resource exploitation, growth, competition, inflation, and corporate political power are dissected. The essays in part 2, "Creating Alternative Futures," describe Henderson's activist efforts to organize public interest groups and describe ways to revision our future. Aspects of our culture discussed are organizational redesign, media's democratization of taste, global equity, and technology assessment.

699   Hjalte, Krister; Lidgren, Karl; and Stahl, Ingemar. ENVIRONMENTAL POLICY AND WELFARE ECONOMICS. Translated by Curt Wells. New York: Cambridge University Press, 1977. vii, 111 p. Illus., bibliog.

The application of theories and tools of welfare economics to the problem of allocation of environmental resources for human needs is explored in this concise study. An analytical framework is developed and applied to a range of environmental problems, such as recreation, water resources, recycling, sewage, and industrial waste. Protection agencies, institutional systems, and international implications are discussed in regard to the decision and policymaking process.

700   Kapp, K[arl]. William. THE SOCIAL COSTS OF PRIVATE ENTERPRISE. Cambridge, Mass.: Harvard University Press, 1950. xii, 287 p. Illus.

An early detailed economic examination of the social costs of private enterprise is provided herein. The concern is with those costs not entered in the calculations of firms and not reflected in entrepreneurial outlays. They are "social" because they are paid by unassociated individuals or public agencies. Among the social costs examined are economic losses from industrial accidents, air and water pollution, energy and environmental depletion, technological change, depressions, monopoly, and transportation.

701   Leonard, Norman. "Economic Technology and the Liberal-Humanist Dream." SOCIAL SCIENCE 48 (Summer 1973): 142-51.

Economic growth through technology is creating social conditions and institutions not compatible with a liberal-humanistic society. The goal of economic technology is efficient use of natural resources, while the essential humanist value is the individual. Leonard looks to the philosophy of science to attempt to find concepts which will bring the two goal systems closer together. Philosophical ideas considered are the perspective of the observer, environment as cause, and field theory. Humanism and economics present differing perspectives on these concepts, yet a merger may be possible through inclusive cost-benefit analysis. A Social Welfare Index would assist the planning of mutually supporting technology and humanism.

702   Madden, Carl H. "The Greening of Economics." VIRGINIA QUARTERLY REVIEW 50 (Spring 1974): 161-74.

The scientific revolution is changing people's values so that the "industrial world view" is being replaced by a new culture. Former beliefs in the scientific method, the merger of scientific and technological advance, and dominance of economic considerations in policymaking are giving way to a world view stressing holism, naturalism, and immanentism. We have become aware of the dangers economic and scientific success has created, i.e., pollution, devastating war, overpopulation, urbanization, and dehumanization of work; thus, a new social contract is demanded which calls for a balance of environment and growth, and for the social responsibility of corporations.

703   Meier, Richard L. SCIENCE AND ECONOMIC DEVELOPMENT: NEW PATTERNS OF LIVING. Cambridge and New York: Technology Press of Massachusetts Institute of Technology and John Wiley and Sons, 1956. 266 p. Illus.

The program for economic development traced in this study is less dated than would be expected. Scientific and technical innovations such as protein synthesis and solar energy are utilized to analyze the world situation and to prepare programs for world development. The concepts and quantitative methodologies chosen are understandable to both natural and social scientists. Social as well as economic impacts of new technologies are carefully assessed. The problems of food and fuel receive primary focus.

704   Mishan, E.J. THE ECONOMIC GROWTH DEBATE: AN ASSESSMENT. London: George Allen and Unwin, 1977. 277 p. Bibliog.

A close consideration of the social consequences of continued economic growth leads Mishan to conclude that technology and change have undermined the institutions and myths which gave civilization stability and cohesion. Book 1 reviews the economic growth debate, focusing on the limitations of theories in favor of growth. Book 2 explores the basic material and psychological needs of man, then concentrates on the impacts of specific technological developments on social well-being. Any political endeavor to move society toward a steady state would encounter extreme resistance.

705 _____. "Whatever Happened to Progress." JOURNAL OF ECONOM-
IC ISSUES 12 (June 1978): 405-25.

The idea of progress, which encompasses the forces of knowledge and wealth, has been institutionalized by the "Established Englightenment." While the credits of progress are
undeniable, they run counter to human needs of physical
activity, security, love, trust, self-respect, and group be-
longing. Mishan briefly discusses the social costs of the
automobile and other transport technologies. Our civilization will not be saved by the young because they too are
"maximizers," plunderers with "unchecked gluttony" in regard to self-indulgence. A move away from the growth path
is not politically feasible because of conventional rationalization, entrenched interests, and international distrust.

706 National Academy of Sciences and National Academy of Engineering.
THE IMPACT OF SCIENCE AND TECHNOLOGY ON REGIONAL
ECONOMIC DEVELOPMENT. Washington, D.C.: 1969. xiii, 112 p.
Bibliog.

The effect of national policies regarding research and development on regional economic growth is assessed. Objectives
of federal policy for "R and D" are outlined, then the study
turns to factors affecting the introduction and assimilation of
high technology. The effect of technological innovation and
transfer on institutions and society is considered. Contributions to the regional economy are outlined: improved processes, products, skill development, and utilization of natural
resources. Methods of implementation of regional goals in
"R and D" are discussed.

707 Nelson, Richard R.; Peck, Merton J.; and Kalachek, Edward D. TECH-
NOLOGY, ECONOMIC GROWTH, AND PUBLIC POLICY. Washington,
D.C.: Brookings Institution, 1967. xiii, 238 p. Illus., bibliog.

The adaptation of the economy to technical change and the
problems encountered in the process are considered. An
analysis of factors determining technological innovation, "R
and D" concentration, and the adoption of new technologies
is followed by a consideration of the social and economic
consequences of changes. Adjustment in the social framework
receives considerable attention. The authors then turn to an
examination of policymaking and present a framework for the
development of criteria to assess the value of research programs.

708 "The No-Growth Society." DAEDALUS 102 (Fall 1973): entire issue.

The problem of zero population and economic growth as well
as their implications for our political and economic systems
are explored. E.J. Mishan and Richard Zeckhauser consider

the ills and risks of continued growth. The means to achieve
zero growth and its effects are analyzed by Kingsley Davis,
Norman B. Ryder, and William Alonzo. Harvey Brooks reveals why no-growth requires more sophisticated technologies.
Lester Brown and Willard R. Johnson provide the perspective
of poor countries. Growth versus no-growth is weighed by
economists Kenneth Boulding, Marc J. Roberts, and Roland N.
McKean.

709   Pirages, Dennis Clark, ed. THE SUSTAINABLE SOCIETY: IMPLICA-
TIONS FOR LIMITED GROWTH. New York: Praeger Publishers, 1977.
xv, 342 p. Illus.

The transition from rapid industrial growth to a post-industrial
"sustainable society" is explored by examining the social
and economic issues attendant to the change. Studies by contributors are grouped around four problem areas: energy
choices, economic and political planning, and social innovations. Among specific components of the steady state society
receiving attention are alternative energy sources, evaluation
of alternative futures, property, business, economic inequality,
life styles, and developing countries.

710   Resources for the Future. ENVIRONMENTAL QUALITY IN A GROW-
ING ECONOMY: ESSAYS FROM THE SIXTH RESOURCES FOR THE
FUTURE FORUM. Edited by Henry Jarrett. Baltimore: Johns Hopkins
Press for Resources for the Future, 1966. xv, 173 p.

Pairs of essays in six topic areas present a paper by one expert and a response by another. Topics include resource development, health in urban environments, the market economy,
current economic research in environmental problems, public
attitudes, and public policy. Among the contributors are
Kenneth Boulding, René Dubos, and Allen Kneese.

711   Rosenberg, Nathan. PERSPECTIVES ON TECHNOLOGY. New York:
Cambridge University Press, 1976. 353 p.

The economic process of the diffusion of technological change
in America is scrutinized through interdisciplinary analysis in
this collection of fifteen of Rosenberg's best articles written
in the 1960s and 1970s. Part 1 provides a historical discussion of forces accounting for the growth of machine tools and
woodworking machines in the nineteenth century. The author
then moves to an exploration of the "conceptual apparatus"
with which economists analyze new technologies. Part 3
turns to an identification of the determinants of the speed of
diffusion of technologies. The final section places technological change in environmental contexts.

712   _____. "Technology and the Environment: An Economic Exploration."

TECHNOLOGY AND CULTURE 12 (October 1971): 543-61.

Looking at the technology-environment problem from an economic perspective, Rosenberg explores the issues in both urban and natural environment contexts. The urban experience,
coupled with modern technology, has created inefficient patterns of resource use, and cost/benefit interdependencies between members of the community. Technology has deprived
us of any technological excuse for failing to fulfill ideals such
as the eradication of poverty. In the natural setting ecological disruptions have largely been caused by the adoption of
cheapest techniques for production.

713 "Special Section on Economics and the Environment." ENVIRONMEN-
TAL AFFAIRS 2 (Winter 1972): 580-637.

Four articles consider the integration of economic, social, and
environmental factors in policymaking. Warren J. Samuels
considers power and ecosystem policy; James J. Sullivan and
H. Fernando Arias discuss the principles of environmental
economics; Haynes C. Goddard attempts to merge economic
and environmental policy. The interdependence of factors in
a actual issue is illustrated by Walter Hecox's analysis of the
viability of voluntary recycling.

714 Theobald, Robert. "The Implications of American Physical Abundance."
ANNALS OF THE AMERICAN ACADEMY OF POLITICAL AND SOCIAL
SCIENCE 378 (July 1968): 11-21.

According to Theobald, the principal issue confronting responsible Americans is whether there must be fundamental change
in the American socioeconomic system in order for all to
benefit from technology. Automation, the computer, and
other advances offer the promise of all the necessities, but
they do not ensure equal distribution.

715 Vatter, Harold G., and Will, Robert E. "Technology and the New
Philosophy of Poverty." SOUTHERN ECONOMIC JOURNAL 33 (April
1967): 559-71.

Technological progress has transformed the philosophy of poverty. The traditional perspective, developed in an atmosphere
where technology was capital absorbing and profits were expended on production capacity, sees poverty as a functional
phenomenon amenable only to slight amelioration. Concomitant with this view is a psychology of workers emphasizing
laziness and the propensity to procreate. Advanced electrical,
petrochemical, and automation technologies have created a
new situation in which technology is capital saving. More
capital is available and is being expended on education of
laborers. Social theory now places the blame for poverty on
external conditions and the status of the group rather than on

the individual. Poverty is seen as dysfunctional, and its
elimination is possible.

716   Weintraub, Andrew; Schwartz, Eli; and Aronson, J. Richard, eds. THE
       ECONOMIC GROWTH CONTROVERSY. White Plains, N.Y.: Interna-
       tional Arts and Sciences Press, 1973. xv, 229 p.

       A symposium held at Lehigh University explores the problems
       of economic growth. Participants find the issues surrounding
       the possibility, necessity, and desirability of growth to be
       inextricably related to the social values and economic institu-
       tions of our society. E.J. Mishan, Robert M. Solow, Melvin
       Kranzberg, Lester Thurow, Abraham Gerber, and others discuss
       growth and antigrowth, the doomsday Club of Rome report,
       the ability of technological progress to provide for the future,
       energy as a factor in growth, environmental problems, zero
       economic growth, and population.

717   Wilson, Kenneth D., ed. PROSPECTS FOR GROWTH: CHANGING
       EXPECTATIONS FOR THE FUTURE. New York: Praeger Publishers,
       1977. xiv, 349 p. Illus.

       The pattern of changing expectations regarding economic
       growth is presented in this anthology commissioned by the Edi-
       son Electric Institute. Essays examining the growth debate are
       organized in a four-part structure. The nature and origins of
       the controversy are described in part 1. Part 2 presents quali-
       tative analyses of alternative methods of managing the present.
       Forecasts and economic analyses appear in part 3. The need
       for a steady state and the futility of growth are argued in the
       concluding section. Specific factors of growth receiving at-
       tention are energy policy, space stations, and quality of life.
       Among the contributors are E.J. Mishan, Gerald K. O'Neill,
       Daniel Bell, and Kenneth Boulding.

718   Wingo, Lowdon, and Evans, Alan, eds. PUBLIC ECONOMICS AND
       THE QUALITY OF LIFE. Johns Hopkins Press for Resources for the
       Future, 1977. xv, 327 p. Bibliog.

       The papers from the International Research Conference on
       Public Policy and the Quality of Life in Cities, 1975, support
       and establish the credibility of the quality of life concept as
       a "viable public policy construct." Divergent definitions of
       quality of life emerge from the contributors with economists
       looking at markets and production while political scientists
       and planners turn to social factors such as health, education,
       income, and working life. The potential role of government
       intervention is considered to be of prime importance to future
       economic directions. Many of the fifteen papers address the
       assessment of needs and attempt to provide models for measure-
       ment.

Part 7

URBANIZATION

A. GENERAL

1. Bibliographies

719   Appleyard, Donald. THE URBAN ENVIRONMENT: SELECTED BIB-
LIOGRAPHY. Exchange Bibliography no. 291. Monticello, Ill.:
Council of Planning Librarians, 1972. 60 p.

720   Bryfogle, R. Charles. CITY IN PRINT: A BIBLIOGRAPHY. Agincourt,
Ontario: General Learning Press, 1974. iv, 324 p.

Books, reports, journals, and audio-visual materials are cited
in this extensive, annotated, selective bibliography. "Urban
studies" is viewed with a wide-ranging perspective, thus the
categorization comprises urban history, planning, architecture,
transportation, the city as human process, urban geography,
urban environment, demographics, cybernetics, fiction, and
art. Annotations are critical, discuss content, and evaluate
usefulness for research, personal or professional use.

721   Feaver, Douglas D., and Gallagher, Edward J., eds. HUMANISTIC
PERSPECTIVES ON THE CITY: A SELECT BIBLIOGRAPHY. Exchange
Bibliography no. 934. Monticello, Ill.: Council of Planning Librarians,
1975. 62 p.

Several faculty members involved in a "Life and Work Habitat"
seminar at Lehigh University contributed to this annotated bibliography which provides basic readings for an interdisciplinary
approach to the "complex problems posed by the city." The
subject is seen from the viewpoints of various humanities disciplines: American history, American literature, science fiction, fine arts, economics, classics, philosophy, religion, social
relations, urban studies, visual media, work, and leisure.

722   Taviss, Irene; Burbank, Judith; and Rothschild, Joan. TECHNOLOGY

AND THE CITY. Research Review no. 5. Cambridge, Mass.: Harvard University Program on Technology and Society, 1970. 53 p.

The impact of technological change on the American city is surveyed in this extensively annotated, selective literature review. Sections cover the general technology-city relationship, housing, transportation, planning and new towns, and urban information systems. Taviss concludes that the literature is confused because values and goals are in conflict and political mechanisms are deficient.

723 U.S. Department of Housing and Urban Development. Library. ENVIRONMENT AND THE COMMUNITY: AN ANNOTATED BIBLIOGRAPHY. Washington, D.C.: 1971. 66 p.

The partially annotated bibliography selects materials which discuss or attempt to alleviate the deterioration of the environment of cities. Designed as a resource tool for city planners, architects, and concerned citizens, listed materials are books, articles, reports, and films. Suggested journals and organizations are also provided. Subject breakdown includes architecture and urban design, environmental quality, planning, housing, pollution, land use, recreation, transportation, and working conditions, as well as the present and future roles of technology.

724 Wolf, C.P. ALTERNATIVE URBAN FUTURES. Exchange Bibliography no. 1142. Monticello, Ill.: Council of Planning Librarians, 1976. 31 p.

2. Books and Articles

725 Abrams, Charles. THE CITY IS THE FRONTIER. New York: Harper and Row, 1965. 394 p.

Abrams reviews the major problems of cities: suburban flight, racial friction, and transportation, and then charts the history and inadequacies of renewal efforts. He is particularly critical of housing efforts and failures of relocation programs. Stressing the cultural and convenience advantages of the city as evidence that it merits revival, he advocates a new philosophy for cities that encourages preservation, a unity of city and suburb, and a greater federal role in support.

726 Berry, Brian J.L. THE HUMAN CONSEQUENCES OF URBANIZATION: DIVERGENT PATHS IN THE URBAN EXPERIENCE OF THE TWENTIETH CENTURY. The Making of the 20th Century. New York: St. Martin's Press, 1973. xv, 205 p. Map, bibliog.

Although Berry's general theoretical overview of twentieth-century urbanization devotes primary attention to the United States, it also has comparative chapters on Europe and the Third World. North American urbanization is seen as "being driven by both a technological and social dynamic under conditions of competitive bargaining and interest group politics."

727   Cousins, Albert N., and Nagpaul, Hans, eds. URBAN MAN AND SOCIETY: A READER IN URBAN SOCIOLOGY. New York: Alfred A. Knopf, 1970. xi, 486 p. Bibliog.

This balanced collection of classic writings on the city includes empirical studies, reports, and essays. Forty-five papers cover urban history, sociology, social psychology, urban problems and planning, and future directions. Particularly relevant to the student of technology are chapters on industrialization and the urban physical environment.

728   Donaldson, William V. "How to Use Technology to Solve City Problems." NATIONAL CIVIC REVIEW 62 (November 1973): 543-47.

Self-proclaimed experts in urban technology often have no idea how a city works or what its problems are. Fundamental problems such as fire-fighting and waste disposal, for example, are still suffering from antiquated technology and hopeless inefficiency. Technology transfer to cities must address these sorts of genuine needs, rather than those "problems that fit technologists' already developed solutions and programs." Mutual understanding between city officials and technologists must precede any program. To work, a program will need to be long-term, responsive to failures, and small-scale enough to be governable.

729   Doxiadis, C[onstantinos].A. ANTHROPOPOLIS: CITY FOR HUMAN DEVELOPMENT. New York: W.W. Norton and Co., 1975. xx, 398 p. Illus., bibliog.

Doxiadis' study of the development of the humane city is accompanied by papers from the symposium on the City for Human Development held in Athens in 1972. In order to give shape to the city for man, the author details hypotheses related to man's basic needs, considers the city as a system, delineates man's requirements throughout his life cycle, and projects planning proposals. Part 2, the symposium, includes Doxiadis' eighteen hypotheses for optimum urban life, and papers by Dennis Gabor, René Dubos, Margaret Mead, Erik Erikson, and others.

730   _____. BETWEEN DYSTOPIA AND UTOPIA. Hartford, Conn.: Trinity College Press, 1966. Reprint. N.p.: Athens Publishing Center,

1974. xii, 92 p. Illus., maps, bibliog.

In three lectures delivered at Trinity College, Doxiadis attempts
to provide connections between the "dystopias" that are our
existing cities and the dreams of utopia which have been
presented in literature. He hopes that an exploration of
dreams and realities will help toward the visualization of a
city that satisfies the scientist, architect, resident, and
dreamer. Instead of "no-place," this "in-place" will be
"entopia." Utopian literature discussed ranges from classical
to contemporary, including the visions of Le Corbusier, Frank
Lloyd Wright, B.F. Skinner, Ray Bradbury, Tommaso
Cambanella, Thomas More, Aldous Huxley, and H.G. Wells.

731   Eberhard, John P. "Technology for the City." INTERNATIONAL
SCIENCE AND TECHNOLOGY 57 (September 1966): 18-29.

The history of the city and of technological growth reveal the
two to be "inexorably related." Technology made possible a
high density setting through the provision of skyscrapers, ele-
vators, electric lights, refrigerators, and numerous other innovations. The auto, however, has so altered the city that the
basic solutions of the 1930s no longer suffice. A new "systems" approach must be taken that envisons the city as an
aggregate of people, hardware, and software accomplishing
certain functions. The author distinguishes major hardware and
software systems, noting necessary characteristics needed by
each system.

732   Eckbo, Garrett. "The Quality of Urbanization." CENTENNIAL RE-
VIEW OF ARTS AND SCIENCE 10, no. 3 (1966): 305-26.

A theoretical article discusses the interrelationships among open
space, buildings, vehicles, and pedestrians in an urban setting.
Eckbo suggests that urbanism is a product of social pressures
interacting with structural technology. Its quality is a direct
reflection of the society of which it is a part.

733   Eldredge, H[anford]. Wentworth. "Alternative Possible Urban Futures."
FUTURES 6 (February 1974): 26-41.

The twenty-first century will exhibit a variety of urban forms.
Eldredge specifies two types. Type A, described as "present
forms almost certain to continue," includes the center city,
megalopolis, the small city, and inner and outer suburbs.
Type B, labelled "far-out potential environments," encompasses
Paolo Soleri-type megastructures, underground habitats, and
social experiments such as communes. These enticing visions
notwithstanding, Eldredge forsees basically "more of the same"
for the near future.

734   _____, ed. TAMING MEGALOPOLIS. 2 vols. Garden City, N.Y.:
Anchor Books, 1967. xv, 1,166 p.

An anthology considers what megalopolis is and what it could
be. In the first part, the configuration, environment, and
roles of American cities are surveyed. Articles in the second
part encompass the whole planning arena, touching on urban
renewal, new towns, social planning, and citizen participation. Final chapters consider urbanization in developing nations and in Europe. Many distinguished urban specialists are
represented.

735   Gale, Stephen, and Moore, Eric G., eds. THE MANIPULATED CITY:
PERSPECTIVES ON SPATIAL STRUCTURE AND SOCIAL ISSUES IN
URBAN AMERICA. Chicago: Maaroufa Press, 1975. xiii, 366 p.
Illus., bibliog.

A cross-disciplinary perspective is provided on the spatial
organization of the metropolis. Essays in part 1 are concerned
with the influence of social, economic, and political institutions on urban structures. In part 2, the focus is shifted to
the urban infrastructure of housing, buildings, and transportation.

736   Gottmann, Jean. MEGALOPOLIS, THE URBANIZED NORTHEASTERN
SEABOARD OF THE UNITED STATES. New York: Twentieth Century
Fund, 1961. xi, 810 p. Illus., maps.

Gottmann attempts to understand the changing dynamics of urban
growth in the densely populated northeastern seaboard from
Boston to Washington, D.C., in order to provide some help
and understanding for future decisions about urban life. He
covers the historical process of the area's urbanization, the
changing nature of land use, the impact of manufacturing and
transportation, as well as social responsibility and interchange.

737   Greer, Scott A. THE EMERGING CITY: MYTH AND REALITY. New
York: Free Press of Glencoe, 1962. vii, 232 p.

Images of the city, folk and pragmatic alike, are found to be
weak in explanatory power. A new, balanced image of the
city must be fashioned, within a larger metropolitan framework.
Greer dissects the components of city life, including lifestyles,
social bonds, and organizational ties of citizens. Three types
of urban citizens are identified: isolates, neighbors, and community actors who control public affairs. In a concluding discussion of metropolitan problems, Greer criticizes proponents of
two extreme solutions: the "ideologists of return" who seek a
true city united through mass transit, and the opponents of
megalopolis, who, unrealistically, according to Greer, seek a
return to small communities.

738   Hauser, Philip M., and Schnore, Leo F., eds. THE STUDY OF URBAN-
       IZATION. New York: John Wiley and Sons, 1965. viii, 554 p.

       In this interdisciplinary collection of social-science articles
       on the process of urbanization, the following selections are
       especially valuable: Charles N. Glaab, "The Historian and
       the American City: A Bibliographic Survey"; Gideon Sjoberg,
       "Cities in Developing and in Industrial Societies: A Cross-
       Cultural Analysis"; and Eric E. Lampard, "Historical Aspects
       of Urbanization."

739   Higbee, Edward Counselman. A QUESTION OF PRIORITIES: NEW
       STRATEGIES FOR OUR URBANIZED WORLD. New York: William
       Morrow and Co., 1970. xxxiv, 214 p. Bibliog.

       Only through increasing urbanization, writes Higbee, can the
       Earth's growing population be accommodated. The author
       foresees a limitless expansion of production and population
       that must be met with continuous urban expansion.

740   Jacobs, Jane. THE DEATH AND LIFE OF GREAT AMERICAN CITIES.
       New York: Random House, 1961. 458 p.

       In this now classic attempt to introduce new principles of city
       planning and redevelopment, Jacobs looks closely at how
       cities work, how ordinary things like sidewalks, streets, parks,
       and neighborhoods contribute to the atmosphere and dynamics
       of city life. The author finds that the need for diversity of
       uses which provides constant intertwining economic and social
       support is the basis for successful city areas. After consider-
       ing the social behavior of people in cities, and urban eco-
       nomic activity, Jacobs examines aspects of decay and regenera-
       tion, then suggests changes in housing, traffic, design, plan-
       ning, and administrative practices.

741   Lynch, Kevin. THE IMAGE OF THE CITY. Cambridge: M.I.T. Press,
       1960. 194 p. Illus., bibliog.

       The visual quality of the urban landscape is the subject of this
       study. The mental image of a city is determined by the ease
       or difficulty with which its parts can be organized into a co-
       herent pattern. Lynch examines the physical forms of Boston,
       Jersey City, and Los Angeles and interviews inhabitants to
       determine the role of urban environments in their lives. He
       then presents design criteria for the creation of harmonious city-
       scapes.

742   National Academy of Sciences. SCIENCE, ENGINEERING AND THE
       CITY. Washington, D.C.: 1967. vii, 142 p. Maps, bibliog.

       The current and potential interaction of technology with the city is the concern of these conference papers. Authors focus on social requirements for urban design, urban transportation, urban construction, urban experimentation and research.

743   Perloff, Harvey S., ed. THE QUALITY OF THE URBAN ENVIRON-MENT: ESSAYS ON NEW RESOURCES IN AN URBAN AGE. Washington, D.C.: Resources for the Future, 1969. vii, 332 p.

A state-of-the-art on the urban environment is presented. Opening papers consider elements in policymaking. Robert U. Ayres and Allen V. Kneese demonstrate that waste, for example, must be treated as an important ecological feature of a highly interrelated urban system. Subsequent papers are concerned with the nature of urban space and its two- and three-dimensional uses. The broader influences on the urban environment are analyzed in Brian J.L. Berry and Elaine Neil's study of industrial imperatives, and F. Stuart Chapin, Jr. and Thomas H. Logan's study of household activity patterns and their implications.

744   Soleri, Paolo. ARCOLOGY: THE CITY IN THE IMAGE OF MAN. Cambridge: M.I.T. Press, 1969. v, 122 p. Illus.

Seeking "an environment suitable for the species of man, a coherence that may be historically valid," Soleri defines his architecture, urban planning, and design theories based on organic principles. His "arcologies" are one-structure systems-- habitats for life, work, education, culture, and leisure for hundreds of thousands of people per square mile. Like a biological system, the urban structures seek wholeness and respect the earth's ecology. Thirty arcology schemes are illustrated including plans for Arcosanti. The student is cautioned that the graphics are symbolic.

745   Strauss, Anselm L., ed. THE AMERICAN CITY: A SOURCEBOOK OF URBAN IMAGERY. Chicago: Aldine Publishing Co., 1968. xiv, 530 p. Illus.

The city's image in recent history is portrayed through a generous sampling of older and more recent stances toward the metropolis. Contrasting conceptions of the same city, Chicago, and predictions of city destiny reflect changing American aspirations. Among other themes studied are city perils, real and imagined; city subcultures and social worlds from barroom to bohemia; the rural versus urban dialogue; and urban governance and reform.

746   Wilson, James, Q., ed. THE METROPOLITAN ENIGMA: INQUIRIES INTO THE NATURE AND DIMENSIONS OF AMERICA'S "URBAN CRISIS." Cambridge, Mass.: Harvard University Press, 1968. xii, 338 p. Illus.

This anthology surveys numerous urban problems from housing, urban design, and social conflict to education and poverty. For the student of technology, three papers are especially pertinent: John F. Kain on the movement of jobs and industry, John R. Meyer on urban transportation, and Roger Revelle on pollution and cities.

747   Wood, Robert C. SUBURBIA: ITS PEOPLE AND THEIR POLITICS. Boston: Houghton Mifflin, 1958. xi, 340 p.

Wood examines suburban political ideology, which he finds not the epitome of twentieth-century culture, but rather unfortunately resistant to change and clinging to outmoded traditions of physically limited communities and conditions of intimacy.

B. HISTORICAL OVERVIEW

1. Bibliography

748   Stewart, Ian R. THE AMERICAN CITY: 1800-1920; A PRIMER BIBLIOGRAPHY IN AMERICAN URBAN HISTORY. Exchange Bibliography no. 796. Monticello, Ill.: Council of Planning Librarians, 1975. 16 p.

2. Books and Articles

749   Abell, Aaron Ignatius. THE URBAN IMPACT ON AMERICAN PROTESTANTISM, 1865-1900. Harvard Historical Studies, vol. 54. Cambridge, Mass.: Harvard University Press, 1943. x, 275 p. Bibliog.

Rapid urbanization and industrialization created a situation in which increased demands for industrial and economic guidance were placed upon the Protestant Church. Abell describes the philanthrophic response of Christian Socialism, the Salvation Army, mission and tracts societies, and groups such as the YMCA and YWCA.

750   Armstrong, Ellis L., ed. HISTORY OF PUBLIC WORKS IN THE UNITED STATES, 1776-1976. Chicago: American Public Works Association, 1976. xv, 736 p. Illus., bibliog.

Armstrong's overview of the history of public works will probably be the standard work for a long time. The study is organized by type of public work with chapters devoted to: waterways; roads, streets, and highways; highway structures and traffic controls; railroads; urban mass transportation; airways and airports; community water supply; flood control and drainage; irrigation; light and power; sewers and wastewater treatment; solid wastes; public buildings; educational facilities; public housing; parks and recreation; military installations; and aerospace. A brief bibliography follows each chapter.

751   Blake, Nelson Manfred. WATER FOR THE CITIES: A HISTORY OF THE URBAN WATER-SUPPLY PROBLEM IN THE UNITED STATES. Syracuse, N.Y.: Syracuse University Press, 1956. x, 341 p. Illus., maps.

The social history of the development of centralized water supplies is analyzed primarily for the cities of Philadelphia, New York, Boston, and Baltimore during the period 1790-1860. Blake stresses a city's dependence upon water for a smoothly functioning urban existence and the recognition of this precondition as factors which permitted the great growth of American cities during the nineteenth century.

752   Callow, Alexander B., Jr., ed. AMERICAN URBAN HISTORY: AN INTERPRETIVE READER WITH COMMENTARIES. New York: Oxford University Press, 1969. Rev. ed. 1973. xiv, 684 p.

Callow has provided a useful compendium of urban articles, in which Joel Tarr's "From City to Suburb: The 'Moral' Influence of Transporation" is particularly intriguing. Tarr finds that the rationale for improved transportation included not only economic benefits but also an expected solution to slum congestion and the social evils of city life through the removal of workers and the poor to a more rural and hence virtuous and healthful suburbia.

753   Chudacoff, Howard P. THE EVOLUTION OF AMERICAN URBAN SOCIETY. Englewood Cliffs, N.J.: Prentice-Hall, 1975. viii, 280 p. Illus., maps, bibliog.

Chudacoff's social survey does not deal as completely with technology and industrialization as some other texts; however, his chapter entitled "The Birth of the Modern City: Mass Transit and Industrial Growth" is quite good. Brief bibliographical essays follow each chapter and cover the standard works.

754   Cross, Robert D., ed. THE CHURCH AND THE CITY, 1865-1910. American Heritage Series. Indianapolis: Bobbs-Merrill, 1967. xlv, 359 p. Bibliog.

Cross has compiled a series of contemporary pieces on the city's impact upon the church preceded by an excellent introductory essay. He fails to find evidence of "de-Christianization" but rather four modes of "churchly response" to urbanism and secularism: transformations, transplantations, adaptations, and reintegrations.

755   Fries, Sylvia Doughty. THE URBAN IDEA IN COLONIAL AMERICA.
       Philadelphia: Temple University Press, 1977. xviii, 218 p. Illus.,
       maps, bibliog.

       A look at the "conceptual framework of our understanding of
       the origin of American ideas of the city" examines the late
       seventeenth- and eighteenth-century pre-industrial cities of
       Boston, New Haven, Philadelphia, Williamsburg, and Savan-
       nah. For many settlers "civilization was nourished and mani-
       fest in cities," and the city became a tool for societal re-
       construction.

756   Furer, Howard B. "The American City: A Catalyst for the Women's
       Rights Movement." WISCONSIN MAGAZINE OF HISTORY 52 (Summer
       1969): 285-305.

       Despite an overemphasis on the Nineteenth Amendment as the
       ultimate victory of women's rights, the author clearly corre-
       lates the rise of the movement with that of industrialization
       and urbanization. With respect to work, leisure and politics,
       industry and the city provided the opportunity and experience
       for women to move outside the home and to escape the influ-
       ence of the "agrarian myth" which personified her as "the
       paragon of American innocence, who must be defended, pro-
       tected, and sheltered from the hard realities and evils of life
       at all costs."

757   Glaab, Charles N. "Metropolis and Suburb: The Changing American
       City." In CHANGE AND CONTINUITY IN TWENTIETH-CENTURY
       AMERICA: THE 1920'S, edited by John Braeman et al., pp. 399-437.
       Columbus: Ohio State University Press, 1968.

       Glaab surveys the spread of and response to decentralized
       suburbia and the rise of the "super-city" during the 1920s,
       which was based in large part on the technology of cheap
       electricity, communication improvements like the telephone,
       the automobile, and rapid transit systems.

758   Glaab, Charles N., and Brown, A. Theodore. A HISTORY OF URBAN
       AMERICA. Rev. ed. New York: Macmillan, 1976. xi, 350 p.
       Bibliog.

       A thematic rather than a political periodization is the approach
       of this survey of American urban history. Although the colo-
       nial and early national periods are considered, emphasis is on
       the period from 1860 to the mid-1960s, but with little in-
       cluded for the last decade. Technology's role in shaping the
       urban environment is adequately set forth. Good suggestions
       for further reading.

759   Goheen, Peter G. "Industrialization and the Growth of Cities in

Nineteenth-Century America." AMERICAN STUDIES 14 (Spring 1973): 49-66.

Goheen's theoretical argument makes use of changing factors of production and geographic location to explain the principal themes characterizing urbanization: population growth, industrial productivity, and transportation technology. He concludes that "industrialization is a concept which summarizes a basic change which overtook the city's economic character and revolutionized the urban social and spatial structure" particularly in terms of developing class distinctions, territorial segregation of population, and loss of local control over production.

760   Goist, Park Dixon. FROM MAIN STREET TO STATE STREET: TOWN, CITY, AND COMMUNITY IN AMERICA. Port Washington, N.Y.: Kennikat Press, 1977. 180 p. Bibliog.

Goist focuses on the changing sense of community as expressed by novelists, advertisers, sociologists, journalists, social reformers, and city planners during the period of rapid urbanization from 1890 to 1940.

761   Gorman, Mel. "Charles F. Brush and the First Public Electric Street Lighting System in America." OHIO HISTORICAL QUARTERLY 7 (April 1961): 128-44.

Street lighting is indicative of the nature of urban social life, and it received its first systematic electrical implementation in Cleveland in 1879. Development by Brush of a dynamo, arc light, and shunt coil and their subsequent integration for lighting are detailed, providing some insight into the process of invention and innovation.

762   Handlin, Oscar, and Burchard, John [Ely], eds. THE HISTORIAN AND THE CITY. Cambridge: M.I.T. Press and Harvard University Press, 1963. xii, 299 p. Bibliog.

This collection of twenty-one articles is based on a 1961 conference held by the Harvard-M.I.T. Joint Center for Urban Studies to explore the nature and needs of the then new field of urban history. Technology's relation to the city is one of the basic themes. In addition to an excellent introduction by Handlin, there are contributions by Sam Bass Warner, Morton White, Frank Friedel, Kenneth Boulding, Eric Lampard, and John Burchard. Covers some non-American cities.

763   Hays, Samuel [P.]. "The Politics of Reform in Municipal Government in the Progressive Era." PACIFIC NORTHWEST QUARTERLY 55 (October 1964): 157-69.

Hays finds the principal sources of Progressivism in upper-class

businessmen and professionals. Municipal reform was a bureaucratic attempt to apply the techniques of efficiency and rational control to the urban environment.

764   Hoy, Suellen M., ed. ESSAYS IN PUBLIC WORKS HISTORY. Chi-
       cago: Public Works Historical Society, 1976-- . Irregular.

       This ongoing series of pamphlet-length essays--brief but not
       superficial--on varied public works topics includes the follow-
       ing titles: James C. O'Connell, CHICAGO'S QUEST FOR
       PURE WATER (1976) 19 p.; Abel Wolman, GEORGE WARREN
       FULLER: A REMINISCENCE (1976) 30 p.; Edward C. Carter
       II, BENJAMIN HENRY LATROBE AND PUBLIC WORKS:
       PROFESSIONALISM, PRIVATE INTEREST, AND PUBLIC POL-
       ICY IN THE AGE OF JEFFERSON (1976) 29 p.; Martin V.
       Melos, PRAGMATIC ENVIRONMENTALIST: SANITARY ENGI-
       NEER GEORGE E. WARING, JR. (1977) 30 p.; Larry D.
       Lankton, THE "PRACTICABLE" ENGINEER: JOHN B. JERVIS
       AND THE OLD CROTON AQUEDUCT (1977) 30 p.; and
       Joel A. Tarr, TRANSPORTATION INNOVATION AND
       CHANGING SPATIAL PATTERNS IN PITTSBURGH, 1850-1934
       (1978) 64 p.

765   Jackson, Kenneth T. "The Crabgrass Frontier: 150 Years of Suburban
       Growth in America." In THE URBAN EXPERIENCE: THEMES IN
       AMERICAN HISTORY, edited by Raymond A. Mohl and James F.
       Richardson, pp. 196-221. Belmont, Calif.: Wadsworth Publishing
       Co., 1973.

       Jackson briefly examines the suburbanizing trend of wanting
       to own one's home as it is shaped and facilitated by industrial
       impact, mass transportation systems, the automobile and the
       highway, and such "social technologies" as municipal zoning
       and long-term, low-interest mortgages. Includes a brief anno-
       tated bibliography.

766   Jackson, Kenneth T., and Schultz, Stanley K., eds. CITIES IN
       AMERICAN HISTORY. New York: Alfred A. Knopf, 1972. xi,
       508 p. Bibliog.

       An excellent collection of articles on the American city,
       several of which were written especially for this volume. Of
       special interest to the student of technology are Robert Higgs,
       "Cities and Yankee Ingenuity, 1870-1920"; Allan Pred,
       "Manufacturing in the American Mercantile City, 1800-1840";
       Roger Lutchin, "San Francisco: The Patterns and Chaos of
       Growth"; and Glen E. Holt, "The Changing Perception of
       Urban Pathology: An Essay on the Development of Mass Tran-
       sit in the United States." The volume concludes with a good
       bibliographical essay.

767   Lampard, Eric E. "The History of Cities in the Economically Advanced
        Areas." ECONOMIC DEVELOPMENT AND CULTURAL CHANGE 3
        (January 1955): 81-136.

        Lampard was one of the first historians to seek a framework
        for understanding the process of urbanization. He believes
        "specialization provides an essential link between the techni-
        cal and spatial conditions of economic progress," and is
        important to understanding urban-industrial growth. In his
        analysis, there are three stages of urban growth--pre-industrial,
        industrial, and metropolitan.

768   McKelvey, Blake. THE EMERGENCE OF METROPOLITAN AMERICA,
        1915-1966. New Brunswick, N.J.: Rutgers University Press, 1968.
        xiii, 311 p. Illus., maps, bibliog.

        A sequel to his earlier volume, THE URBANIZATION OF
        AMERICA, 1860-1915, (no. 769) this study examines the con-
        tinued growth of American cities. McKelvey concentrates on
        the responsibilities and relationships of city, state, and federal
        governments in attempts to solve recurrent urban problems.

769   _____. THE URBANIZATION OF AMERICA, 1860-1915. New
        Brunswick, N.J.: Rutgers University Press, 1963. xiv, 370 p. Illus.,
        maps, bibliog.

        This early survey goes beyond mere city biography in an at-
        tempt to provide a frame of reference for uban development
        as a whole. McKelvey is not unaware of industrial and tech-
        nological forces in the shaping of American cities. Good,
        although somewhat dated bibliography.

770   Miller, Zane L. THE URBANIZATION OF MODERN AMERICA: A
        BRIEF HISTORY. Harbrace History of the United States. New York:
        Harcourt Brace Jovanovich, 1973. xiv, 241 p. Illus., maps, bibliog.

        Another survey attempts to synthesize the "internal" growth
        of specific cities with their "external" relationships to other
        urban, political, and economic developments. Miller sees
        four periods in American urban growth: the preindustrial era
        of the eighteenth and early nineteenth centuries, the industri-
        alizing city of mid-century, the industrial city of the late
        nineteenth and early twentieth centuries, and today's post-
        industrial city. Standard bibliographical references, with con-
        cise annotations, follow each chapter.

771   Mumford, Lewis. THE CITY IN HISTORY: ITS ORIGINS, ITS TRANS-
        FORMATIONS, AND ITS PROSPECTS. New York: Harcourt, Brace,
        and World, 1961. xi, 657 p. Illus., bibliog.

        Mumford's excellent general history of the city in Western

civilization includes material on Egypt, Rome, Greece, the Middle Ages, and the modern world. In an expansion of the historical portion of his earlier work, THE CULTURE OF CITIES (1938), the author takes a cautiously optimistic view of the future role of the city in "expressing and actualizing the new human personality--that of 'One World Man.'" Lengthy bibliography with brief annotations.

772 _____. THE URBAN PROSPECT. New York: Harcourt, Brace, and World, 1968. xx, 255 p.

In a more future-oriented study than his other works on the city, Mumford suggests the need for regionally organized towns and metropolises which would take advantage of technical developments in transportation and communication in contrast to the haphazardly organized Megalopolis. However, Mumford sees as even more important the necessity to realize truly human needs and goals in a complete overhaul of society.

773 Pred, Allan R. THE SPATIAL DYNAMICS OF U.S. URBAN-INDUSTRIAL GROWTH, 1800-1914: INTERPRETIVE AND THEORETICAL ESSAYS. Regional Science Studies Series vol. 6. Cambridge: M.I.T. Press, 1966. x, 225 p. Maps.

Economic and geographic location theories are taken into account in this conceptual view of the urbanization process. Pred is particularly interested in the spatial interaction between industrialization--in particular, invention and the diffusion of innovation--and urbanization. Valuable footnotes.

774 _____. URBAN GROWTH AND THE CIRCULATION OF INFORMATION: THE UNITED STATES SYSTEM OF CITIES, 1790-1840. Harvard Studies in Urban History. Cambridge, Mass.: Harvard University Press, 1973. xiv, 348 p. Maps.

Pred discusses the means by which large cities influence one another's growth by examining information circulation (and indirectly the technology of pre-telegraphic communications) which is so much a part of the economic actions and location decisions of urban growth. Today's regionally prominent cities had already emerged as such in the settled areas by 1840, lending support to a characterization of long-term urban stability.

775 Rosenberg, Carroll Smith. RELIGION AND THE RISE OF THE AMERICAN CITY: THE NEW YORK CITY MISSION MOVEMENT, 1812-1870. Ithaca, N.Y.: Cornell University Press, 1971. x, 300 p. Bibliog.

Christian missions were one of society's answers to the problems of poverty resulting from urbanization, industrialization, and immigration. Rosenberg describes the organized mission effort, which changed from that of an evangelical disseminator of religious truth prior to the Panic of 1837 to an instrument for dealing with the social problems of the poor.

776   Schlesinger, Arthur Meier. THE RISE OF THE CITY, 1878-1898. A History of American Life, vol. 10. New York: Macmillan, 1933. Reprint. Chicago: Quadrangle Books, 1971. xvii, 494 p. Illus., bibliog.

Although there has been much criticism of and reaction to this book, it remains an important early work in urban history. Schlesinger views the central development of the period as "the momentous shift of the center of national equilibrium from the countryside to the city."

777   Schnore, Leo F., ed. THE NEW URBAN HISTORY. Quantitative Studies in History. Princeton, N.J.: Princeton University Press, 1975. xi, 284 p.

Although the volume contains several articles that are highly quantitative, there is good material on the relationship of the city to inventiveness, the diffusion of innovations, religion, and economic growth. It is revealing of the varied methodology employed in the "new urban history." Contributors include Martyn J. Bowden, Kathleen Neils Conzen, Claudia Dale Goldin, Robert Higgs, Kenneth T. Jackson, Zane L. Miller, Allan R. Pred, Gregory H. Singleton, Joseph A. Swanson, and Jeffrey G. Williamson.

778   Schultz, Stanley K., and McShane, Clay. "To Engineer the Metropolis: Sewers, Sanitation and City Planning in Late-Nineteenth-Century America." JOURNAL OF AMERICAN HISTORY 65 (September 1978): 389-411.

The role of the engineer in the physical and political changes in the administration of American cities during the latter decades of the nineteenth century and early twentieth century is traced. Proving their worth through technical expertise, efficiency, and comprehensive planning, municipal engineers, aloof from politics, emerged as a "strategic elite." Through an effective professional communications network, competence and experience was transmitted. Engineers became so valued and necessary that they soon were developing comprehensive city and regional plans which involved the "interaction of technology with the social, economic, and political structure of cities."

779   Wakstein, Allen M., ed. THE URBANIZATION OF AMERICA: AN

HISTORICAL ANTHOLOGY. Boston: Houghton Mifflin, 1970. 502 p. Bibliog.

This is a standard anthology in the field with articles covering historiography, industrialization, urban services, and metropolitanization among other topics.

780   Ward, David. CITIES AND IMMIGRANTS: A GEOGRAPHY OF CHANGE IN NINETEENTH-CENTURY AMERICA. New York: Oxford University Press, 1971. xv, 164 p. Illus., maps, bibliog.

An excellent synthesis of urban geography covers the century of mass immigration, 1820-1920. Ward traces economic growth and population movements with respect to the spatial characteristics of urbanization both nationally and locally. Technology in terms of transportation and industry has a great effect upon the location of jobs and residence. Valuable bibliography.

781   Warner, Sam Bass, Jr. THE URBAN WILDERNESS: A HISTORY OF THE AMERICAN CITY. New York: Harper and Row, 1972. xvii, 303 p. Illus., maps, bibliog.

Warner devotes reasonable attention to technology's role, especially that of transportation, in the process of urbanization in this fine one-volume interpretive survey. Major examples provided are New York, 1820-70; Chicago, 1870-1920; and Los Angeles, 1920-70. Contains a useful bibliographical essay.

C. SELECTED CASE STUDIES OF SPECIFIC CITIES AND TOWNS

782   Albion, Robert Greenhalgh. THE RISE OF NEW YORK PORT, 1815-1860. New York: Charles Scribner's Sons, 1939. Reprint. New York: Charles Scribner's Sons, 1961. xiv, 485 p. Illus., maps, bibliog.

In the introduction to this classic study of New York and its relationship as a port city with the interior of the nation and world commerce, the author notes: "Plenty of books tell how the old ships sailed; too few tell why they sailed." This book answers those questions and suggests much more, with some reference to the technologies of harbors, ships, and steam. Thirty-one appendixes contain extensive data on tonnage, dollar value, immigration, and other pertinent commercial information.

783   Armstrong, John Borden. FACTORY UNDER THE ELMS: A HISTORY OF HARRISVILLE, NEW HAMPSHIRE, 1774-1969. Cambridge: M.I.T. Press, 1970. xx, 320 p. Illus., maps.

Armstrong's case study of a small industrial community dependent upon textile manufacturing includes, in addition to technological change and the economics of business history, sections on politics, religion, education, and social activities. Although offering little in the way of comparative history, it should, when combined with others such as Stephen Thernstrom's POVERTY AND PROGRESS (no. 552), provide new insight into the broad impact of industrial development.

784 Barth, Gunther Luther. INSTANT CITIES: URBANIZATION AND THE RISE OF SAN FRANCISCO AND DENVER. New York: Oxford University Press, 1975. xxvi, 310 p. Maps, bibliog.

Barth has taken an original approach to urban history based, not on the social science of census data, but on the newspapers and published contemporary sources which reveal the quality of human life. Finding ancient and medieval antecedents, the author places the rise of San Francisco and Denver, "instant cities," into the broader context of western civilization and the history of the American urban West in particular. Technology plays an important role in this story.

785 Baskin, John. NEW BURLINGTON: THE LIFE AND DEATH OF AN AMERICAN VILLAGE. New York: New American Library, 1976. 260 p. Illus.

Excellent social history of a small southwestern Ohio town is achieved through oral interviews. Although technology is not the primary theme, insights thereon frequently appear with respect to skills, jobs, attitudes, and values. New Burlington no longer exists; all that remains is a history and an Army Corps of Engineers reservoir.

786 Brook, Anthony. "Gary, Indiana: Steel Town Extraordinary." JOURNAL OF AMERICAN STUDIES 9 (April 1975): 35-53.

"Gary represented the failure of large-scale industrial city planning." This brief social and urban survey reflects the impact of the new, turn-of-the-century, midwestern steel industry, in particular U.S. Steel, on the people, resources, and growth of a previously unsettled region. A brief bibliography is included. In a similar vein, see also Raymond A. Mohl's and Neil Betten's "The Failure of Industrial City Planning: Gary, Indiana, 1906-1910," JOURNAL OF THE AMERICAN INSTITUTE OF PLANNERS 38 (July 1972): 202-15.

787 Buder, Stanley. PULLMAN, AN EXPERIMENT IN INDUSTRIAL ORDER AND COMMUNITY PLANNING, 1880-1930. New York: Oxford University Press, 1967. xvi, 263 p. Illus.

George Pullman, known for his development of the sleeping

car, was also an innovator in industrial and community planning. The "model town" bearing his name was a social reform aimed at solving nineteenth-century industrial strife. The Pullman strike of 1894 and the town's ultimate failure reveal a great deal concerning the social aspects of urbanization and industrialization.

788   Cain, Louis P. SANITATION STRATEGY FOR A LAKEFRONT METROPOLIS: THE CASE OF CHICAGO. DeKalb: Northern Illinois University Press, 1978. xv, 173 p. Illus., maps, bibliog.

Sanitation systems are "crucial" to the city-building process, determining in part the direction of urban growth. Cain examines the problem of sanitation in Chicago from the perspective of an economic historian, concluding that decisions regarding water supply, sewage disposal, and drainage evolved "rationally," given the city's location and history.

789   Condit, Carl W. CHICAGO, 1910-1929: BUILDING, PLANNING, AND URBAN TECHNOLOGY. Chicago: University of Chicago Press, 1973. xiv, 354 p. Illus., maps, bibliog.

In a unique approach, Condit combines the history of building, planning, and technology to tell the story of Chicago's growth from the adoption of the Burnham Plan of development in 1910 to the start of the Depression. His "technical biography" concludes that much more could have been done for the poor, if planners and architects had had the desire.

790   _____. CHICAGO, 1930-1970: BUILDING, PLANNING, AND URBAN TECHNOLOGY. Chicago: University of Chicago Press, 1974. xvi, 351 p. Illus., bibliog.

In this continuation of his earlier volume on Chicago, the author picks up the story of the city during the Depression, when there were more problems than solutions. The reasons for decay included building, urban renewal, and transportation failures. Nonetheless, Chicago continued to play a leading role in architectural design. Very well illustrated.

791   _____. THE RAILROAD AND THE CITY: A TECHNOLOGICAL AND URBANISTIC HISTORY OF CINCINNATI. Columbus: Ohio State University Press, 1977. xii, 335 p. Illus., maps, bibliog.

Condit considers how the network of rails and position of tracks, bridges, and interlocking systems dictated the urban fabric and the pattern of land use in Cincinnati. The architecture of the railway station and its evolution into an "urbanistic institution" are carefully analyzed.

792   Coolidge, John. MILL AND MANSION: A STUDY OF ARCHITEC-
       TURE AND SOCIETY IN LOWELL, MASSACHUSETTS, 1820-1865.
       Columbia Studies in American Culture, no. 10. New York: Columbia
       University Press, 1942. Reprint. New York: Russell and Russell,
       1967. xiii, 261 p. Illus., maps, bibliog.

       More than just a history of Victorian architecture in Lowell,
       Coolidge has provided a different focus on the rise of mid-
       nineteenth-century urbanization and industrialization. The
       architecture, as reflected through the mills, city planning,
       management, and worker housing, serves as a "mirror of
       communal ideas."

793   Fogelson, Robert M. THE FRAGMENTED METROPOLIS: LOS ANGELES,
       1850-1930. Cambridge: Joint Center for Urban Studies of M.I.T. and
       Harvard University, Harvard University Press, 1967. xviii, 362 p.
       Illus., maps, bibliog.

       The history of Los Angeles reflects a tension between the rise
       of a "populous, urbanized, and industrialized settlement" and the
       subsequent "rejection of the metropolis in favor of its suburbs."
       The author includes a great deal of material on the role of
       the electric railway and the automobile in the urbanization
       process.

794   Green, Constance McLaughlin. HOLYOKE, MASSACHUSETTS, A
       CASE HISTORY OF THE INDUSTRIAL REVOLUTION IN AMERICA.
       Yale Historical Publications, vol. 34. New Haven, Conn.: Yale Uni-
       versity Press, 1939. xiii, 425 p. Illus., maps, bibliog.

       Connecticut River water-power accounted in large part for
       Holyoke's rise as an industrial city featuring cotton and paper
       mills. In addition to the interconnections of urban and indus-
       trial growth, the author covers labor-management relations,
       education, religion, and the city's social life. The study
       ends with 1922.

795   Greer, Edward. "Monopoly and Competitive Capital in the Making of
       Gary, Indiana." SCIENCE AND SOCIETY 40 (Winter 1976-77):
       465-78.

       While U.S. Steel built Gary, political control was vested in
       a group of Protestant entrepreneurs who could be counted on
       to support the free-enterprise system. The corporation built
       the homes for skilled laborers but never housed the unskilled
       "new immigrants." As a result, within eight years, decentral-
       ized Gary included four times as much land as that owned by
       the company. The social structure of the city continues to the
       present to be dominated by a "petty bourgeois stratum."

796   Hoffecker, Carol E. WILMINGTON, DELAWARE: PORTRAIT OF AN

INDUSTRIAL CITY, 1830-1910. Charlottesville: University Press of Virginia for the Eleutherian Mills-Hagley Foundation, 1974. xvi, 187 p. Illus., maps, bibliog.

In this concise, well-illustrated history of urbanization and industrialization, the author fails to discover the "privatism" or fragmentation evident in Sam Bass Warner's study, PRIVATE CITY (no. 800). Rather, she describes a sense of community, based in large part upon a skilled middle-class and concerned businessmen, that grew with industrialization.

797   Lynd, Robert S., and Lynd, Helen M. MIDDLETOWN: A STUDY IN MODERN AMERICAN CULTURE. New York: Harcourt, Brace and Co., 1929. Reprint. New York: Harcourt, Brace, and World, 1956. xi, 550 p.

In this well-known social anthropology study, the Lynds investigate Muncie, Indiana, as a "typical" small American city in the mid-1920s. Although technology is not the authors' primary concern, it receives frequent mention in the areas of human activity considered: making a living and a home, training the young, using leisure, and engaging in religious practices and community activities. A follow-up study, MIDDLETOWN IN TRANSITION, appeared in 1937.

798   Shlakman, Vera. ECONOMIC HISTORY OF A FACTORY TOWN: A STUDY OF CHICOPEE, MASSACHUSETTS. Smith College Studies in History, vol. 20, no. 1-4. Northampton, Mass.: Smith College, 1934-35. Reprint. New York: Octagon Books, 1969. 264 p. Map, bibliog.

Shlakman traces the rapid development of a rural village into a textile factory town due to outside capital investment. Special attention is given to labor and the rise of a middle class within the context of the process of industrialization and subsequent growth for the period from 1825 to the early years of the Depression.

799   Simon, Roger D. THE CITY-BUILDING PROCESS: HOUSING AND SERVICES IN NEW MILWAUKEE NEIGHBORHOODS, 1880-1910. Transactions of the American Philosophical Society, vol. 68, pt. 5. Philadelphia: American Philosophical Society, 1978. 64 p. Illus., maps, bibliog.

Taking a somewhat similar but expanded approach to that contained in Warner's STREETCAR SUBURBS (no. 801), Simon analyzes the city-building process in Milwaukee for selected wards by examining housing stock; city services such as water, sewers and streets; and residential segregation.

800   Warner, Sam Bass, Jr. THE PRIVATE CITY: PHILADELPHIA IN THREE

PERIODS OF ITS GROWTH. Philadelphia: University of Pennsylvania Press, 1968. xiii, 236 p. Illus., maps.

Warner analyzes Philadelphia as typical of many large American cities for three periods of its growth: 1770-80, 1830-60, and 1920-30. He believes that the concept of privatism or the search for personal wealth has been the major historical shaping force in urban growth. The failure of American cities, and of Philadelphia in particular during the years 1830-60, has been the failure of this private market to accommodate to big city needs.

801 ____. STREETCAR SUBURBS: THE PROCESS OF GROWTH IN BOSTON, 1870-1900. Cambridge: M.I.T. Press and Harvard University Press, 1962. Reprint. New York: Atheneum, 1969. xxi, 208 p. Illus., bibliog.

An excellent pioneering study in the new urban history analyzes the impact of streetcar lines and the subsequent extension of city services on suburban growth patterns for the towns of Roxbury, West Roxbury, and Dorchester. Warner also considers the impact of the rural ideal, the ethnicity of neighborhoods, and architectural styles of house-building.

D. AGRARIAN-URBAN TENSIONS

802 Bender, Thomas. TOWARD AN URBAN VISION: IDEAS AND INSTITUTIONS IN NINETEENTH-CENTURY AMERICA. Lexington: University Press of Kentucky, 1975. xv, 275 p. Bibliog.

The intellectual and institutional responses to unprecedented nineteenth-century urban and industrial growth are examined. Bender draws upon case studies of Lowell, Massachusetts, and the work of Frederick Law Olmsted and Charles Loring Brace in making his general observation that many more people than previously recognized were touched by and had to deal with a crisis in which traditional cultural ideals could not keep pace with social and physical change. The urban vision of mid-nineteenth-century America sought the possibility of bringing "city and country, and the values they respectively stand for, into a contrapuntal relationship." Includes an excellent bibliographical essay.

803 Brownell, Blaine A. "The Agrarian and Urban Ideals: Environmental Images in Modern America." JOURNAL OF POPULAR CULTURE 5 (Winter 1971): 576-87.

An urban ideal, as well as an agrarian ideal, is prevalent in American popular culture. Both image patterns are "myths" in the sense that they do not correspond to reality. Rather than polar opposites, the ideals contain similar values, i.e., self-reliance, individualism, frugality, hard work, progress, and law and order, and they provide a frame of orientation which promotes the realization of identity. These ideals should be treated as "complex, shifting environmental preferences that existed to meet certain deeply-rooted cultural and psychological needs."

804   James, Henry. THE AMERICAN SCENE. London: Chapman and Hall, 1907. Reprint. Bloomington: Indiana University Press, 1968. xxiv, 486 p.

Disorientation greeted James upon return to his native land after a twenty years' absence. A "vast crude democracy of trade" and a New York poxed with early skyscrapers demanded a reassessment of his relationship with his homeland. James's means is a "quest for metaphor to reflect the teeming, exploding, materialistic, unhistorical here-and-now continent." He depicts the vulgarity of commerce and industry, affluence, and materialism through an elaborate symbolic structure where gold is the central image. The skyscrapers overtopping Trinity Church are stuck "anywhere and anyhow," but they are the "triumphant payers of dividends." The buildings, mansions, ghettos, and booming frontier, as well as the social structure all built on business values foretell a "blight" where human and city decay go hand in hand.

805   Jefferson, Thomas. NOTES ON THE STATE OF VIRGINIA. 1785. Edited by William Peden. Chapel Hill: University of North Carolina Press, 1955. xxv, 315 p. Maps.

In his famous and often reprinted contribution to American scientific writing, Jefferson described the physical attributes of his native Virginia. Much of the anti-urban feeling of the nineteenth-century stems from statements made herein as to the value of an agrarian and rural existence for Republican ideals and institutions.

806   Nash, Roderick. WILDERNESS AND THE AMERICAN MIND. New Haven, Conn.: Yale University Press, 1967. 256 p.

The term "wilderness" designates a quality, a changing personal meaning that makes it a state of mind. Through literary and historical works, as well as case studies, Nash interprets the fluctuating American conceptions of the idea and the symbolism which has developed around it. A feeling of "appreciation" has largely replaced an earlier view in which wilderness was regarded as "a moral and physical wasteland fit only for conquest and fructification in the name of progress, civilization, and Christianity." At the same time, the alien, threatening aspects are recognized in the midst of a longing for a sanctuary from mechanized lifestyles. Nash traces attitudes from their Old World roots, through romantic conceptions, to wilderness preservation activities and the driving need for uncontrolled refuges from civilization.

807   Pollack, Norman. THE POPULIST RESPONSE TO INDUSTRIAL AMERICA: MIDWESTERN POPULIST THOUGHT. Cambridge, Mass.: Harvard University Press, 1962. 166 p.

Agrarianism is generally considered a retrogressive social force in the face of industrialization. Pollack believes the Populists were an exception and accepted industrialism, opposing only the economic and social inequities of the capitalistic system. An interesting intellectual study of the agrarian side of America's industrial transformation.

808   Schmitt, Peter J. BACK TO NATURE: THE ARCADIAN MYTH IN URBAN AMERICA. Urban Life in America Series. New York: Oxford University Press, 1969. xxiii, 230 p.

The back-to-nature, "Arcadian" myth which emerged at the turn of the century was not an agrarian rejection of the city, but rather an attempt to integrate the spiritual urge for a rugged, outdoor life with modern urbanization. It took form in the development of city and national parks, landscape architecture, suburbia, country clubs, vacation homes, and summer camps for youths. Schmitt examines fiction, nonfiction, and especially popular-culture magazine writing in a comprehensive overview of these developments.

809   Shideler, James H. "FLAPPERS AND PHILOSOPHERS, and Farmers: Rural-Urban Tensions of the Twenties." AGRICULTURAL HISTORY 47 (October 1973): 283-99.

Philosophers such as Lewis Mumford and Walter Lippman and writers like F. Scott Fitzgerald and Sinclair Lewis noted and reflected a growing modernism in direct contrast to the older rural agrarianism of previous generations. Shideler outlines the particularly sharp tensions of change during the 1920s in which he sees the rural as bound to lose to the urban due to economic and social disadvantages.

810   Smith, Henry Nash. VIRGIN LAND: THE AMERICAN WEST AS SYMBOL AND MYTH. Cambridge, Mass.: Harvard University Press, 1950. viii, 311 p.

Smith traces "the impact of the West. . .on the consciousness of Americans and follows the principal consequences of this impact in literature and social thought" down to Turner's frontier thesis. Although technology is not a major consideration in this study, the themes of the West, the frontier, and agrarianism have important interconnections with the development of industrialization and urbanization.

811   Thomas, John L. "Utopia for an Early Age: Henry George, Henry Demarest Lloyd and Edward Bellamy." In PERSPECTIVES IN AMERICAN HISTORY, vol. 6, edited by Donald Fleming and Bernard Bailyn, pp. 135–63. Cambridge, Mass.: Charles Warren Center for Studies in American History, Harvard University, 1972.

Thomas finds that George, Lloyd, and Bellamy had nearly identical concerns with the transformation of an older, liberal agrarian society to a modern, industrialized urban state. They struck a responsive chord in Americans used for the most part to living in a decentralized rural republic, yet each recognized in the coming societal complexity and concentration, a perceived need for increased governmental action. Their utopias were attempts to harmonize these antithetical perceptions which carried over into many of the Progressive and New Deal reforms of this century.

812   Weimer, David R., ed. CITY AND COUNTRY IN AMERICA. New York: Appleton–Century–Crofts, 1962. xvi, 399 p. Illus., bibliog.

Weimer has collected statements on the city from three major traditions: the agrarian, urban defenders, and those attempting a rational synthesis. He includes selections from St. John De Crevecoeur, Thomas Jefferson, Henry David Thoreau, Edward Bellamy, John Ruskin, Frederick Law Olmsted, Lewis Mumford, Le Corbusier, Frank Lloyd Wright, and Robert Moses. Includes study questions.

813   White, Morton, and White, Lucia. THE INTELLECTUAL VERSUS THE CITY: FROM THOMAS JEFFERSON TO FRANK LLOYD WRIGHT. Cambridge: Harvard University Press and M.I.T. Press, 1962. x, 270 p.

The Whites study the reactions to the American city of our most celebrated thinkers from the eighteenth century to the first half of the twentieth century. The intellectual roots of "anti-urbanism and ambivalence" toward city life found in the writings of figures who represent major tendencies in American thought are analyzed. Writers chosen are Jefferson, Franklin, Crevecoeur, Emerson, Thoreau, Hawthorne, Poe, Melville, Henry Adams, Henry and William James, Howells, Frank Norris, Dreiser, Jane Addams, Robert Park, John Dewey, Josiah Royce, George Santayana, and Frank Lloyd Wright.

E. PLANNING AND RENEWAL

1. Bibliographies

814   Agarwal, Bhoo; Piasetzki, [J.]. Peter; and Aasen, Clarence. A HU-
MANISTIC APPROACH TO QUALITY OF LIFE: A SELECTED BIBLIOG-
RAPHY. Exchange Bibliography no. 1052, 1053, 1054. Monticello,
III.: Council of Planning Librarians, 1976. 147 p.

Books and journal articles are cited in this selective but unannotated bibliography which concern the improvement of
quality of life in the urban environment and which will assist
in the development of a conceptual understanding of "humanistic ideals for urban form." Entries are arranged under six
major sections: rediscovering human potential, urbanites'
experiences, man-environment relationships, desirable urban
qualities, urban futures, and alternative planning approaches.

815   Alexander, Ernest F.; Sawicki, David S.; and Catanese, Anthony J.,
eds. URBAN PLANNING: A GUIDE TO INFORMATION SOURCES.
Urban Studies series, vol. 2. Detroit: Gale Research Co., 1979.
xiv, 165 p.

The annotated bibliography emphasizes the comprehensive planning process and draws from the literature of various fields.
The volume can serve as an update to Melville Branch's bibliography (no. 817).

816   Bell, Gwen; Randall, Edwina; and Roeder, Judith, E.R. URBAN EN-
VIRONMENTS AND HUMAN BEHAVIOR: AN ANNOTATED BIBLIOG-
RAPHY. Stroudsburg, Pa.: Dowden, Hutchinson and Ross, 1973. xvi,
271 p.

Addressed to architects, urban designers, and planners, as well
as to educators, this highly selective bibliography brings together publications from several disciplines which consider the
interrelationships between urban design and behavior. Part 1
examines the literature related to perceptions of citizens and
designers in the planning process. Social interaction, human
ecology, time and activity analysis are included in part 2.
Part 3 looks at subsets of the urban environment: neighborhoods, shopping centers, new towns, dwelling groups, high-
rise living, and rooms. Key periodicals and bibliographies in
the field are listed.

817   Branch, Melville C. COMPREHENSIVE URBAN PLANNING: A
SELECTIVE ANNOTATED BIBLIOGRAPHY WITH RELATED MATERIALS.
Beverly Hills, Calif.: Sage Publications, 1970. 477 p.

Planning publications which consider all primary components of
the urban situation are cited in this work. Fifteen-hundred

entries focusing on cities in the United States are included. References, including books, articles, reports, and pamphlets, are grouped under the following headings: background, process, theory, information–communication, research–analysis, methodology, institutionalization, management, effectuation, systems elements, subsystems, and forms of urban planning. The annotations are limited to material in the table of contents of the publication. Author and extensive subject indexes are provided.

818   Clapp, James A. NEW TOWNS: AN EMPHASIS ON THE AMERICAN EXPERIENCE. Exchange Bibliography no. 982. Monticello, Ill.: Council of Planning Librarians, 1976. 101 p.

819   Glance, Richard, and Freund, Eric C. THE URBAN ENVIRONMENT AND RESIDENTIAL SATISFACTION WITH AN EMPHASIS ON NEW TOWNS--AN ANNOTATED BIBLIOGRAPHY. Exchange Bibliography no. 429. Monticello, Ill.: Council of Planning Librarians, 1973. 72 p.

820   Golany, Gideon. NEW TOWNS PLANNING AND DEVELOPMENT: A WORLD-WIDE BIBLIOGRAPHY. ULI Research Report 20. Washington, D.C.: Urban Land Institute, 1973. 256 p. Illus.

      A substantial portion of this unannotated bibliography is composed of references to publications dealing with new towns in the United States. Aspects of the subject covered are planning, economics, finance, social organization, housing, communication, industry, land use, legislation, urbanization process, and power structure. Publications are also arranged by specific locality.

821   Hulchanski, John David. CITIZEN PARTICIPATION IN URBAN AND REGIONAL PLANNING: A COMPREHENSIVE BIBLIOGRAPHY. Exchange Bibliography no. 1297. Monticello, Ill.: Council of Planning Librarians, 1977. 60 p.

822   _____. HISTORY OF MODERN TOWN PLANNING, 1800-1940: A BIBLIOGRAPHY. Exchange Bibliography no. 1239. Monticello, Ill.: Council of Planning Librarians, 1977. 24 p.

823   Kemper, Robert V.; Osgood, Donna; and Schouten, RoseMary. ANNOTATED EXPLORATORY BIBLIOGRAPHY ON NEW TOWNS. Exchange Bibliography no. 956. Monticello, Ill.: Council of Planning Librarians, 1976. 57 p.

      Sociocultural dimensions, resident characteristics, and ideologies of planners of new towns are emphasized in this selective bibliography. The sixty-seven entries are books and journal articles. Topical and geographic indexes are provided.

824 Zeitlin, Morris. GUIDE TO THE LITERATURE OF CITIES: ABSTRACTS AND BIBLIOGRAPHY, PART 10: CITY PLANNING—THEORY AND PRACTICE. Exchange Bibliography no. 314-315. Monticello, Ill.: Council of Planning Librarians, 1972. 83 p.

A century of city planning reveals two schools of thought: the anti-city and the pro-city. Zeitlin surveys the literature of the field with attention to the attitudes and ideologies of planners. The shifts in areas of concern from the field's domination by architects and engineers to the more contemporary leadership of social scientists is also documented.

2. Books and Articles

825 Anderson, Stanford, ed. PLANNING FOR DIVERSITY AND CHOICE: POSSIBLE FUTURES AND THEIR RELATIONS TO THE MAN-CONTROLLED ENVIRONMENT. Cambridge: M.I.T. Press, 1968. xii, 340 p. Bibliog.

Studies included here were originally presented at a 1966 M.I.T. conference as preparation for a research project on architectural education in the United States. I.C. Jarvie discusses the pertinence of utopian thinking for the architect. Other papers treat social phenomena relevant to planners, including population, resources, and leisure. A more theoretical social and philosophical content is offered in papers by Hasan Ozbekhan, Raymond Bauer, and Paul A. Feyeraband.

826 Arnold, Joseph L. THE NEW DEAL IN THE SUBURBS: A HISTORY OF THE GREENBELT TOWN PROGRAM, 1935-1954. Columbus: Ohio State University Press, 1971. xiii, 272 p. Bibliog.

Greenbelt towns with their projected safety, convenience, beauty, and sense of community were a response to the unplanned crowded condition of urban-industrial growth. Arnold's analysis of the New Deal program attributes its failure to the "radical challenge to fundamental patterns of urban growth and real estate practice."

827 Aronovici, Carol. COMMUNITY BUILDING: SCIENCE, TECHNIQUE, ART. New York: Doubleday, 1956. 354 p. Bibliog.

The purpose of planning is to create an effective balance between the new forces of technology and the human personality. Aronovici begins her broad study with a general introduction and historical survey of community planning, and then considers specifics such as land, regionalism, conservation, zoning,

transportation, the neighborhood, and atomic energy. The
planner's roles as technician and humanist are stressed. There
is an extensive, annotated bibliography.

828   Barnett, Jonathan. URBAN DESIGN AS PUBLIC POLICY: PRACTICAL
        METHODS FOR IMPROVING CITIES. New York: Architectural Record,
        McGraw-Hill, 1974. 200 p. Illus.

        A member of the Urban Design Group working for Mayor John
        Lindsay and New York City, Barnett describes the urban de-
        sign techniques and projects developed within the context of
        city politics. The book serves as a model of a methodology
        for anticipating the consequences of urban growth and turning
        plans into positive results through the political system. Con-
        centrating on gradual change and conservation, Barnett dis-
        cusses safeguarding the public interest, the use of zoning to
        design new areas without displacement of buildings, preserva-
        tion of landmarks, neighborhood planning and community parti-
        cipation, city centers as competition for suburbs, transportation,
        environmental quality, and the conduct of design review
        studies.

829   Branch, Melville C., ed. COMPREHENSIVE URBAN PLANNING
        THEORY. Stroudsburg, Pa.: Dowden, Hutchinson and Ross, 1975.
        xii, 596 p. Illus.

        Essays serve as introductions to the elements comprising the
        wide-ranging scope of urban planning and are organized under
        topic headings such as design, information systems, process,
        analysis, simulation, management, and environment. The
        breadth of the field is demonstrated by the inclusion of works
        from architecture, engineering, urban planning, economics,
        sociology, political science, psychology, business and political
        management, and law. Serves as a companion to Branch's
        major bibliography (no. 817). Among the contributors are
        Kevin Lynch, Eliel Saarinen, Rexford G. Tugwell, Ian L.
        McHarg, Stanley Milgram, and Dennis L. Meadows.

830   CITIZEN'S POLICY GUIDE TO ENVIRONMENTAL PRIORITIES FOR
        NEW YORK CITY 1974-1984. PART 2: TOWNSCAPE. New York:
        Council on the Environment of New York City, 1974. 78 p. Illus.

        Distinguished New Yorkers consider the role of environmental
        aesthetics in the social life of their city. Urban aspects
        which should influence city planners are discussed: the social
        uses of buildings and other structures, the benefits of pedes-
        trian streets, the importance of neighborhoods, parks and
        recreation, and design for environmental quality. Among the
        authors of the eight essays are René Dubos, William H. Whyte,
        and Ada Louise Huxtable.

831   Doxiadis, Constantinos A. EMERGENCE AND GROWTH OF AN
URBAN REGION: THE DEVELOPING URBAN DETROIT AREA. 3
vols. Detroit: Detroit Edison Co., 1966-70. Illus., bibliog.

Commissioned by the Detroit Edison Company, the project
analyzes the nature and magnitude of urban growth in the
Detroit area, then attempts to understand the problems created
by "dynamic developments." The purpose is to provide a comprehensive planning framework for future expansion and energy
needs. Titles of the three volumes are ANALYSIS, FUTURE
ALTERNATIVES, and A CONCEPT FOR FUTURE DEVELOP-
MENT.

832   Fein, Albert, ed. LANDSCAPE INTO CITYSCAPE; FREDERICK LAW
OLMSTED'S PLANS FOR GREATER NEW YORK CITY. Ithaca, N.Y.:
Cornell University Press, 1967. 490 p. Illus.

Convinced that the city would shape the lives, thoughts, and
values of future Americans, Olmsted pioneered the professions
of landscape architecture and city planning in this country.
Beginning in the latter half of the nineteenth century,
Olmsted attempted to create urban environments conducive to
social harmony and cultural and intellectual activity. Docu-
ments produced by Olmsted and his partners Calvert Vaux and
J. James R. Croes, which contain theories, surveys, and
plans for greater New York City, are anthologized herein.
Included are plans for Central Park, Prospect Park, Riverside
Park, a transit system, and suburbs Staten Island and Rockaway
Point.

833   Goodman, Percival, and Goodman, Paul. COMMUNITAS; MEANS
OF LIVELIHOOD AND WAYS OF LIFE. New York: Vintage Books,
1960. 248 p. Illus., maps.

An attempt is made to clarify the issues important to community building and to determine the criteria necessary to
successful planning. In part 1, several modern plans are
analyzed: green belt, industrial plans, and integrated plans.
The authors discuss how these plans approach the following
factors: technology, work and leisure, domestic life, education, aesthetics, politics, and economics. Part 2 presents
three analytical models of regional schemes which demonstrate
value choices regarding the relationships of the above factors.
The schemes strive for either "efficient consumption," elimination of the difference between production and consumption,
or planned security with minimum regulation.

834   Horvath, R.J. "Machine Space." GEOGRAPHICAL REVIEW 64
(April 1974): 167-88.

"Machine space" represents territory designated for use by

machines rather than by people. In modern American cities, such as Detroit, Horvath contends automobile territory has impinged on human space to a crisis point. Expanding machine space must be recognized as a threat to the individual and to the solidarity of the community.

835   McHarg, Ian L. DESIGN WITH NATURE. Garden City, N.Y.: Doubleday, Natural History Press, 1969. viii, 198 p. Illus., maps.

From the viewpoint of a city planner-landscape architect, McHarg examines the ecology of urbanized areas and provides a prescription for improvement of the environment. He examines such areas as Staten Island, Richmond Parkway, the Potomac Basin, and Washington, D.C., incorporating geology, ecological processes, urban development, and potential social values. He emphasizes the dynamic aspect of ecosystems and the potential for life-enriching use of land through understanding of natural processes.

836   MacKaye, Benton. FROM GEOGRAPHY TO GEOTECHNICS. Edited by Paul T. Bryant. Urbana: University of Illinois Press, 1968. 194 p. Maps.

MacKaye utilizes social planning, conservation, technical knowledge, and human values in his regional development work. He applies an Emersonian belief in "self-realization through harmony with society and nature" to urban as well as wilderness environments. This collection of his essays spans the period from his work for Roosevelt, through the Tennessee Valley Authority (TVA) to the 1950s. As a government planner he advocated programs in which technology would do the heavy work, community planning would ensure social interaction, and regions would be considered as integrated entities. The rise of nonfunctional suburbs is, for MacKaye, the primary curse on our culture.

837   _____. THE NEW EXPLORATION: A PHILOSOPHY OF REGIONAL PLANNING. New York: Harcourt, Brace and Co., 1928. Reprint. Urbana: University of Illinois Press, 1962. 243 p. Illus.

Influenced by Thoreau and Mumford, MacKaye presents planning theories which attempt judicious use of natural, technical, and urban resources without disruption of ecology. While the originator of the plan for the Appalachian Trail, MacKaye is aware of the cultural value of cities. Distinguishing between the indigenous urban center and metropolitan sprawl, the process of "metropolitan flow," in which suburbanization depletes the city and destroys the surrounding environment, is analyzed. The planning concepts outlined here, in regard to transportation and use of natural resources, are designed to promote growth rather than expansion.

838   Mitchell, Robert B., ed. "Building the Future City." ANNALS OF THE AMERICAN ACADEMY OF POLITICAL AND SOCIAL SCIENCE 242 (November 1945): 1-162.

In a postwar look at the American city, a number of prominent authorities make forecasts and suggest directions for urban planning. Glenn E. McLaughlin considers the role of industrial expansion, while Otis W. Freeman assesses the importance of natural resources. Bernhard Stern measures the "challenge of advancing technology," and Harold G. Mayer reviews developments in intercity transportation.

839   _____. "Urban Revival Goals and Standards." ANNALS OF THE AMERICAN ACADEMY OF POLITICAL AND SOCIAL SCIENCE 352 (March 1964): 1-151.

The many social factors that must be taken into account in planning urban change are considered. Ian McHarg opens with an assessment of the place of nature in the city. Authors who follow consider factors such as urban mental and physical health, social differentiation, social change, urban governance, transportation, and education.

840   Mumford, Lewis. FROM THE GROUND UP: OBSERVATIONS ON CONTEMPORARY ARCHITECTURE, HOUSING, HIGHWAY BUILDING, AND CIVIC DESIGN. New York: Harcourt Brace Jovanovich, 1956. viii, 243 p.

In this collection of twenty-six essays previously published in the NEW YORKER from 1947 to 1955, Mumford deals with building and town planning in the New York City area. Specific problems are examined with searching analyses of causes and probable implications. The United Nations complex should proclaim a new world order. He calls for buildings designed for privacy as well as social interaction. Discussions of traffic problems, new housing developments, and super-skyscrapers create a bleak view of a hopeless urban mess, but Mumford keeps working.

841   Myhra, David. "Rexford Guy Tugwell: Initiator of America's Greenbelt New Towns, 1935 to 1936." JOURNAL OF THE AMERICAN INSTITUTE OF PLANNERS 40 (May 1974): 176-88.

The development of Tugwell's greenbelt towns is documented with emphasis on his economic and planning ideologies. Roosevelt's director of the Resettlement Administration adopted a pragmatic outlook and hoped to accomplish his goals through an experimental approach. The four towns he planned and built as satellite suburbs were keyed to the availability and impact of the automobile. The towns, Tugwell believed, would demonstrate that urban ills could be eliminated through

planning for orderly growth, management, and control of
populations.

842   Newton, Norman T. DESIGN ON THE LAND: THE DEVELOPMENT
       OF LANDSCAPE ARCHITECTURE. Cambridge, Mass.: Belknap Press of
       Harvard University Press, 1971. 714 p. Illus., bibliog.

       Defining landscape architecture as the "art or science of
       arranging land, together with the spaces and objects upon it,
       for safe, efficient, healthful, pleasant human use," Newton
       traces work in this field and its effects from ancient times
       to the middle of the twentieth century. Most of this volume
       is devoted to an examination of parks and city planning in
       America. Attention is given to the values implicit in the
       work of Olmsted, Vaux, and other designers of city open
       spaces; the national park system and town planning are dis-
       cussed in detail.

843   Owen, Wilfred. THE ACCESSIBLE CITY. Washington, D.C.: Brook-
       ings Institution, 1972. viii, 150 p. Illus., bibliog.

       For the contemporary city, the advantages of the automobile
       versus public transportation remains a central dilemma. Owen
       documents the impact of the auto on urban areas, showing
       meanwhile how efforts to revive public transit have failed to
       coordinate it with the auto. Such an effort is essential for
       the revival of the congested metropolis.

844   _____. CITIES IN THE MOTOR AGE. New York: Viking Press,
       1959. xv, 176 p. Illus.

       In a synthesis of the proceedings of a 1957 conference, Owen
       addresses the need for an attack on urban problems to eradi-
       cate blight, crowding, ugliness, and noise. Central to the
       discussion is the automobile and highway, although the atti-
       tude expressed here is ambivalent.

845   "Psychology and Urban Planning: Perception, Behavior, and Environ-
       ment." JOURNAL OF THE AMERICAN INSTITUTE OF PLANNERS 38
       (March 1972): 65-122.

       The contribution of psychology to the planner's ability to
       understand the social, economic, and physical interactions be-
       tween man and his environment is the subject of this special
       issue. Erich Fromm, in "Humanistic Planning," suggests that
       planning has been guided by "technical feasibility" and has
       overlooked the "development and fulfillment of man." Other
       articles consider crowding, environmental quality of city
       streets, housing preferences, attitudes of blacks toward their
       environment, and conceptualization of the city.

846   Reiner, Thomas A. THE PLACE OF THE IDEAL COMMUNITY IN
URBAN PLANNING. Philadelphia: University of Pennsylvania Press,
1963. 194 p. Illus., bibliog.

The use of nineteenth- and twentieth-century utopias or ideal
communities, which "incorporate description and analysis of
the physical environment," as tools in contemporary city planning is explored. The creations of Le Corbusier, Richard
Neutra, Frank Lloyd Wright, Walter Gropius, Hugh Ferriss,
and several others serve such purposes as assessing the
validity of propositions, providing a synoptic view of the interrelated urban environment, and crystallizing policy alternatives.
Reiner assesses this literature in regard to form of urban environment, flow and physical layout, population density,
neighborhood formation, and contribution to value concepts.

847   Reps, John W. THE MAKING OF URBAN AMERICA: A HISTORY OF
CITY PLANNING IN THE UNITED STATES. Princeton, N.J.: Princeton University Press, 1965. xv, 574 p. Illus., maps, bibliog.

Reps traces urban plans and the planning process from the
European colonial settlements to World War I. Half of the
study is devoted to a chronological look at the colonial and
early national periods, while the remainder covers major
design forms and special influences on city planning such as
industrialization and the railroad, especially during the nineteenth century.

848   Scott, Mel. AMERICAN CITY PLANNING SINCE 1890. California
Studies in Urbanization and Environmental Design. Berkeley and Los
Angeles: University of California Press, 1971. xxii, 745 p. Illus.,
maps, bibliog.

Scott's comprehensive history of city planning also covers the
changing intellectual and social milieus.

849   Spreiregen, Paul D. URBAN DESIGN: THE ARCHITECTURE OF TOWNS
AND CITIES. New York: McGraw-Hill, 1965. xi, 243 p. Illus.,
bibliog.

Composed of revised articles which originally appeared in the
AIA JOURNAL, this guide for urban design strives to combine
an appreciation for nature with the use of computerized technology and an aesthetic rooted in the history of cities and
design. Spreiregen blends the visions of George Perkins
Marsh, Lewis Mumford, and Benton MacKaye. A discussion
of basic principles and techniques of urban design is followed
by considerations of parts or aspects of the city, such as
residential areas and transportation. The comprehensive role
of urban design is then approached. Extensive bibliography.

850   Stein, Clarence S. TOWARD NEW TOWNS FOR AMERICA. Liver-
       pool, Engl.: University Press of Liverpool, 1951. Rev. ed., 1957.
       Reprint. M.I.T. Press, 1966. 263 p. Illus., maps, bibliog.

       This survey of garden city and new town theory and practice
       beginning with the Sunnyside Gardens experiment of the
       1920s in New York City was written by one of the major
       architect/planners in the field.

851   Tunnard, Christopher, and Pushkarev, Boris. MAN-MADE AMERICA:
       CHAOS OR CONTROL? AN INQUIRY INTO SELECTED PROBLEMS
       OF DESIGN IN THE URBANIZED LANDSCAPE. New Haven, Conn.:
       Yale University Press, 1963. xii, 479 p. Illus., maps, bibliog.

       Aesthetic failures in the appearance of rapidly developing
       urban regions are analyzed in an attempt to raise the visual
       sensitivity of planners and nondesigners who are decision-
       makers. Utilitarian problems, such as land use, financing,
       and legal problems, are also brought to the attention of de-
       signers. The components of the urban scene studied are low-
       density suburban housing, freeway form, industrial development,
       recreation, and historic preservation.

852   Tunnard, Christopher, and Reed, Henry Hope. AMERICAN SKYLINE:
       THE GROWTH AND FORM OF OUR CITIES AND TOWNS. Boston:
       Houghton Mifflin, 1955. xviii, 302 p. Illus., maps, bibliog.

       The authors defer from the theory that American townscapes
       emerged haphazardly. Rather, cities depict the premedita-
       tion and planning behind the industries, homes, skyscrapers,
       hotels, highways, and parking lots of the American urban
       scene from 1607 to the early 1950s in which technology has
       played a major role. Includes a chronological listing of
       important factors and developments in the growth of the
       American city.

853   Twombly, Robert C. "Undoing the City: Frank Lloyd Wright's Planned
       Communities." AMERICAN QUARTERLY 24 (October 1972): 538-49.

       Wright recognized that the factors which once made the city
       necessary were forcing its demise in the mid-twentieth century.
       Protection from nuclear weapons demands dispersion, and
       transportation systems eliminate the necessity of proximity for
       business and social life. His plans for new towns were im-
       practicable, however. The emphasis was placed on aesthetic
       values at the expense of political and economic practicalities.
       The structure of his plans emphasized his conservative social
       thinking: homes for the affluent were separated from those for
       workers, and social contact between classes was discouraged.
       All social ills, he felt, could be solved by an aesthetically
       beneficial environment.

854   Von Eckardt, Wolf. A PLACE TO LIVE: THE CRISIS OF THE CITIES. New York: Dell Publishing Co., 1967. xviii, 430 p. Illus., bibliog.

> The crisis of contemporary cities is their failure to provide a sense of place for inhabitants, for which architecture holds much of the blame. However, skilled architects who are builders, artists, and planners may solve the problems. This survey explains how architects have destroyed the sense of place, reviews attempts to merge art and technology for a livable environment, and discusses urban design and renewal programs, as well as recent humanistic approaches to community design in new towns.

855   Wilson, James Q., ed. URBAN RENEWAL: THE RECORD AND THE CONTROVERSY. Cambridge: M.I.T. Press, 1966. xx, 683 p.

> Twenty-six reprinted papers provide a representative selection of writings on urban renewal. Seven sections cover urban economics; renewal history; local programs; relocation programs; government and citizen participation in renewal; planning and design considerations; critiques and praises, and the future.

856   Zucker, Paul, ed. NEW ARCHITECTURE AND CITY PLANNING: A SYMPOSIUM. New York: Philosophical Library, 1944. xv, 694 p. Illus.

> The expression of sociological conditions through form is the theme addressed. The integration of buildings with social culture is considered the prime objective of planners concerned with architecture and urban systems. Value questions such as the primacy of functionalism or individual creativity and the appeal of standardization through industrialization must be debated by decision makers. Contributors look at new materials, building types, housing, city and regional planning, and education for citizens as well as engineers and architects. Among the participants are Carol Aronovici, Louis Kahn, Laszlo Moholy-Nagy, and Richard Neutra.

F. URBAN SOCIOLOGY

1. Bibliographies

857   Allen, Irving Lewis. THE SOCIOLOGY OF NEW TOWNS AND NEW CITIES: A CLASSIFIED BIBLIOGRAPHY. Exchange Bibliography no. 518. Monticello, Ill.: Council of Planning Librarians, 1974. 19 p.

858   Gutman, Robert. URBAN SOCIOLOGY: A BIBLIOGRAPHY. New Brunswick, N.J.: Urban Studies Center, Rutgers University, 1963. xii, 44 p.

This is a selective bibliography designed to reflect "the major traditional and emerging concerns of urban sociology." Well-selected, unannotated entries are divided into nine sections: the nature and function of urban sociology; space and land use in urban society; the social organization of urban society; the culture of urban settlements; social organizations and the functions of the local community; the organization of the metropolitan system; urban growth and development; sociology and urban planning; and the future of urban society.

859   Seaton, Richard W. SOCIAL FACTORS IN ARCHITECTURAL AND URBAN DESIGN. Exchange Bibliography no. 201. Monticello, Ill.: Council of Planning Librarians, 1971. 13 p.

860   Wood, James L.; Ng Wing Cheung; and Wood, Patricia A. URBAN SOCIOLOGY BIBLIOGRAPHY. Exchange Bibliography no. 1336. Monticello, Ill.: Council of Planning Librarians, 1977. 52 p.

2. Books and Articles

861   Appleyard, Donald, and Lintell, Mark. "The Environmental Quality of City Streets: The Resident's Viewpoint." JOURNAL OF THE AMERICAN INSTITUTE OF PLANNERS 38 (March 1972): 84-101.

The effect of traffic on the livability of city streets in San Francisco is observed. Investigators find that traffic intensity creates noise, stress, and pollution, as well as impinging on social interaction, territorial extent, environmental awareness, and safety. Increases in traffic were followed by departures of families. Information was gathered through interviews and observations.

862   Booth, Alan. URBAN CROWDING AND ITS CONSEQUENCES. New York: Praeger Publishers, 1976. xiv, 139 p. Bibliog.

This comprehensive study covers the effects of crowded household and neighborhood conditions on the health, family life, and sense of well-being of those who inhabit such areas. Data collected from interviews, medical records, and observations made in Toronto, Canada suggest that crowded conditions have little adverse effect.

863   Cobb, James C. "Urbanization in the Changing South." In SOUTH ATLANTIC URBAN STUDIES, vol. 1, edited by Jack R. Censer, N. Steven Steinert, and Amy M. McCandless, pp. 253-66. Columbia: University of South Carolina Press, 1977.

Though several differing explanations of the South's uniqueness have been offered by historians, most scholars have agreed that the region's distinctive patterns of thought and behavior would be weakened by urbanization and industrialization. However, recent studies, Cobb remarks, have suggested that urbanization has failed to become a "way of life" in the Wirthian sense, capable of breaking down southern class barriers or conservative politics.

864   Dobriner, William M., ed. THE SUBURBAN COMMUNITY. New York: G.P. Putnam's Sons, 1958. xii, 416 p.

Noted sociologists cover the growth, sociology, and social organization of the suburb. Suburban life-styles, with the emphasis on familism, leisure, and the automobile are studied, using Levittown as a case history. Suburban problems of education, transportation, and race conflict also receive attention. A closing paper by David Riesman ponders "the suburban sadness."

865   Fischer, Claude S. THE URBAN EXPERIENCE. New York: Harcourt Brace Jovanovich, 1976. x, 309 p. Illus., bibliog.

Three theories of urban life are presented and explored. The determinist (Wirthian) notion holds that urban living weakens social cohesion and causes alienation. An opposing view, as explained by Fischer, contends that urbanization is less important than other social factors in causing social disruption. A third synthetic theory, the author's own, suggests that urbanism does not weaken social groups, rather, it creates them.

866   Gans, Herbert J. THE URBAN VILLAGERS. New York: Free Press of Glencoe, 1962. xvi, 367 p. Illus., bibliog.

The West End of Boston, an inner-city neighborhood of primarily Italian heritage, was declared a slum in 1953 and razed between 1958 and 1960. Gans conducted a participant-observation study of the area between the time of its condemnation and its demise. He concluded that the West End was no slum, but an area of life and character. Its denizens, Gans decided, held positive values that should be understood by single-minded planners.

867   Gutman, Robert, and Popenoe, David, eds. NEIGHBORHOOD, CITY AND METROPOLIS. New York: Random House, 1970. xii, 942 p.

These papers, by many major urban scholars, address a number of areas in urban sociology. The opening section, concerned with theories and approaches, offers several classic papers. Other sections cover urbanism and urbanization, process and impact, urban differentiation, urban ecology, urban local groups, urban environment, social behavior, and urban policy and planning.

868   Hatt, Paul K., and Reiss, Albert J., Jr., eds. READER IN URBAN SOCIOLOGY. 1951. CITIES AND SOCIETY: THE REVISED READER IN URBAN SOCIOLOGY. 2d ed. Glencoe, Ill.: Free Press, 1957. 852 p. Bibliog.

Divided into five parts, this compilation covers the nature of the city, the nature and extent of urbanization and population redistribution, the history of urban settlement, spatial and temporal patterns of cities, and demographic structures and vital processes. A large selection of papers and many classic works, are included.

869   McKee, James B. "Urbanism and the Problem of Social Order." CENTENNIAL REVIEW OF ARTS AND SCIENCE 10, no. 3 (1966): 382-99.

The American intellectual's decidely one-sided negative interpretation of the city has bestowed legitimacy on the popular anti-urbanism that long ruled American culture. Because sociologists have been so preoccupied with the city it surprises the author that they, too, remained for many years mired in an intellectual perspective that viewed the city as a symbol of social disorder. The development of anti-urbanism is traced from its nineteenth-century romantic and conservative origins to Louis Wirth's 1938 essay "Urbanism as a Way of Life" (no. 875). The impact of Wirth's view of the city as transitory, superficial, and depersonalized has waned only recently.

870   Mead, Margaret. "Values for Urban Living." ANNALS OF THE AMERICAN ACADEMY OF POLITICAL AND SOCIAL SCIENCE 314 (November 1957): 10-14.

Through developments in communication and transportation, the city's role as a nexus for business connections and industrial convenience has disappeared. Rather than sacrificing commuters and transferees to the changing urban configuration, Mead suggests that businesses be made the societal gamepieces, with the "work parts of life set up as movable factories and offices being composed of interchangeable, dismountable and easily constructed units." With population stable and happily dispersed, decongested cities would assume a role as cultural centers or vacation spots.

871   Ottensmann, John R. "Social Behavior in Urban Space: A Preliminary Investigation using Ethnographic Data." URBAN LIFE 7 (April 1978): 3-22.

Using ethnographic studies of sections of cities, this article looks at relationships between the physical environment of urban neighborhoods, social classes of urban residents, and patterns of social interaction. Eleven studies of twelve residential sections in American and British cities were selected for review. Two types of physical environment,--high-density urban and low-density suburban; two social classes,--lower-working and middle; and two types of social interaction,-- street-life and neighboring, were considered. Findings yielded a high relationship between neighboring and density, with results complicated by class factors.

872   Park, Robert E.; Burgess, Ernest W.; and McKenzie, Roderick D. THE CITY. 1925. The Heritage of Sociology. Reprint. Chicago: University of Chicago Press, 1967. x, 239 p.

From about 1915 to about 1940, the Chicago school of urban sociology enjoyed great influence. This volume presents a cross-section of its more noted writings. The city was viewed not as a mere artifact but as an embodiment of human nature, almost alive. Among concerns which surface here are the human ecology of the city, city growth, and unique residents such as hobos. A useful sixty-page bibliography of the urban community by Louis Wirth closes the volume.

873   Popenoe, David, ed. THE URBAN-INDUSTRIAL FRONTIER: ESSAYS ON SOCIAL TRENDS AND INSTITUTIONAL GOALS IN MODERN COMMUNITIES. New Brunswick, N.J.: Rutgers University Press, 1969. xi, 176 p.

Essays focus on the major institutions in society that impact the individual and family residing in an urban-industrial community. Arthur J. Naftalen emphasizes the role of changing technology in creating and aggravating urban problems. An essay by Kenneth Boulding concerns technology and the changing social orders. Urban planner Ian McHarg reminds the reader of the ecological considerations in urban development.

874   Schneider, Kenneth R. "Do American Cities Destroy Freedom?" EKISTICS 44 (September 1977): 151-55.

In the midst of confusing change, Americans have failed to build defenses of personal freedom into the urban fabric. According to the author, "freedom resides in self-reliant individuals behaving confidently in self-determining organizations." Three aspects of contemporary cities mitigate against freedom: the misuse of urban space, mass escape to the suburbs that imprisons the poor, and the chaos of urban personal relations that results in isolation and defensive privacy. To counteract these trends, urban space should be dense with buildings, but infused with nature, diverse but less traversed.

875   Wirth, Louis. "Urbanism as a Way of Life." AMERICAN JOURNAL
       OF SOCIOLOGY 44 (July 1938): 1-24.

       The rapidity of urbanization in the United States accounts for
       the severity of its urban problems. Sociology, Wirth argues,
       lacks a sociological definition of the city. He proposes a
       scheme by which the characteristics of urban life and the
       differences between cities of various types can be explained
       on the basis of three variables: size, density, and degree of
       heterogeneity. A widely reprinted, highly influential article.

Part 8

SOCIOLOGY AND PSYCHOLOGY

A. THEORY

876   Adelman, Maurice. "Toward a Sociology of Technology?" TECHNOL-
OGY AND SOCIETY 8 (August 1974): 123-27.

Evidence is presented that suggests a need to separate a new
sociology of technology from the sociology of science. Differing in origins, development, activities, and outlooks, science and technology represent two different realms—one of
knowledge and one of doing. The lead taken by philosophers
of technology in developing a distinct discipline should be
followed by sociologists.

877   Gella, Aleksander; Jensen, Sue Curry; and Sabo, Donald F., Jr.
HUMANISM IN SOCIOLOGY: ITS HISTORICAL ROOTS AND CON-
TEMPORARY PROBLEMS. Washington, D.C.: University Press of
America, 1978. xiii, 250 p.

Depicting humanistic sociology in an embattled position among
positivism and behaviorism, or "scientism," the authors attempt
to promote their subdiscipline. Opening with a historical
review, they turn to humanistic sociology's potential for alleviating problems of man in technological society through stimulating concern for morals and values. There is an appendix,
"Humanistic Trends in Recent Sociology: A Guide to Literature."

878   Gendron, Bernard. TECHNOLOGY AND THE HUMAN CONDITION.
New York: St. Martin's Press, 1977. viii, 263 p.

In a critical review of the writings of representative writers
on the social role of technology, Gendron asks whether technology should be viewed as a progressive or regressive social
force, or as neutral. Three views of technology are summarized: the utopian, dystopian, and socialist. The last
view, as favorably described by the author, sees technological

growth as essential for alleviating social ills, but dependent
for effectiveness on optimum political conditions.

879   Horowitz, Irving L. "Sociological and Ideological Conceptions of
Industrial Development." AMERICAN JOURNAL OF ECONOMICS AND
SOCIOLOGY 23 (October 1964): 351-74.

The history of the concept of change from the Greeks to the
present is briefly reviewed. In their own attitudes to change,
sociologists have displayed ambivalence. But there is general
agreement that technology is disruptive of older norms, encouraging a shift from an ideology based on tradition to one
built on expertise and novelty, with accompanying social
disintegration.

880   Leiss, William. THE LIMITS TO SATISFACTION: AN ESSAY ON
THE PROBLEMS OF NEEDS AND COMMODITIES. Toronto: University
of Toronto Press, 1976. x, 159 p. Bibliog.

The problem of isolating genuine human needs in the high intensity contemporary industrial society is a difficult one.
Marketing has transcended its original function to become a
social bond. Rising consumption has emerged as the highest
societal aim. The development of this consumer ethic is
traced, with observations on its impact on the natural environment.

881   Lloyd, Henry Demarest. WEALTH AGAINST COMMONWEALTH. New
York: Harper and Brothers, 1894. iv, 563 p.

In this late nineteenth-century utopian criticism of monopoly
and the wealthy in society based on unequal distribution of
technology, Lloyd called for just social laws in a classless
society.

882   Marcuse, Herbert. "Some Social Implications of Modern Technology."
STUDIES IN PHILOSOPHY AND SOCIAL SCIENCE 9 (March 1941):
414-39.

Technology is defined as a social process or a mode of organization and production in which machines play a subsidiary
role. Marcuse views the machine age as an organizing
principle for contemporary thought, social relationships, and
behavior. The individual is motivated and guided by the
external standards and measures of technological rationality.
Thus, man has become obedient to the machine instead of the
reverse.

883   Merton, Robert K. "Civilization and Culture." SOCIOLOGY AND
SOCIAL RESEARCH 21 (November 1936): 103-31.

Merton criticizes William F. Ogburn's idea, as expressed in SOCIAL CHANGE (no. 884), that the material side of culture invariably serves as the source of change on the nonmaterial side. He finds a division of culture into material and nonmaterial an illogical and useless distinction, and challenges the notion that a meaningful measure of social change has yet been devised. A more useful distinction is suggested to be that between "civilization" (knowledge) and "culture" (values).

884   Ogburn, William F[ielding]. SOCIAL CHANGE, WITH RESPECT TO CULTURE AND ORIGINAL NATURE. New York: W.B. Huebsch, 1922. Rev. ed. New York: Viking Press, 1950. viii, 393 p.

This sociological classic provides a general overview of change phenomena, including biological change, innovation, diffusion, adjustment and maladjustment, cultural lag. The book is important for its strong and influential emphasis on technological determinism, phrased in Ogburn's conviction of the "preeminence of material culture as a factor in changing society today."

885   Rollins, Peter C. "The Whorf Hypothesis as a Critique of Western Science and Technology." AMERICAN QUARTERLY 24 (December 1972): 563-83.

Whorf is responsible for a theory of linguistic relativity that claims that the categories and structures of a given language largely determine the way in which the native speaker perceives the world and his experiences in it. Rollins, substantially agreeing with the Whorf hypothesis, believes that the Western mind is locked by language into a traditional logic that makes technological abuse inevitable. He suggests the study of non-Western language as an antidote.

886   Sklair, Leslie. ORGANIZED KNOWLEDGE: A SOCIOLOGIST'S VIEW OF SCIENCE AND TECHNOLOGY. St. Albans, Engl.: Hart-Davis MacGibbon, 1973. 284 p.

Technology has assumed great importance, as it is now capable of yielding mass destruction or mass salvation. Government involvement in science and technology has grown correspondingly. Sklair's purpose is to expose the workings of science and technology, to "strip it of mystique." Main currents in the sociology of science, from Marxist thought to the structural-functionalist approach of Merton are critiqued. A somewhat gloomy overview of the political consequences of science and technology is brightened by a final chapter showing alternative futures that might be achieved through participatory democracy.

887   Stern, Bernhard J. HISTORICAL SOCIOLOGY. New York: Citadel Press, 1959. 433 p. Illus.

In part 2, "The Social Aspects of Technology," Stern shows that scientific and technical developments are often impeded or aborted by social and cultural obstacles. The author reveals the nature of these obstacles, from psychological resistance to more overt measures such as patent suppression. He reviews as well the role of war and other political events in channeling technological growth.

888   Veblen, Thorstein. THE THEORY OF THE LEISURE CLASS. 1899. New ed. New York: Macmillan, 1915. viii, 404 p.

Veblen's highly influential thesis is that those blessed with an income above the subsistence level do not use this surplus for constructive purposes, but, rather, for their own pleasure. Veblen coined the term "conspicuous consumption" as an umbrella term for behaviors from the purchase of luxury goods or connoisseurship in food and drink to the pursuit of elitist higher education. Such consumption is a central characteristic of the "pecuniary standard of living" that has accompanied industrialization, and that denigrates such traditional values as quality of workmanship.

889   Wilson, H.T. THE AMERICAN IDEOLOGY: SCIENCE, TECHNOLOGY AND ORGANIZATION AS MODES OF RATIONALITY IN ADVANCED WESTERN SOCIETIES. London: Routledge, Kegan Paul, 1977. vii, 355 p.

Wilson contends that the social sciences have furthered the domination of rationality in the ideology of contemporary America. Central postulates of this American ideology are described from the works of Max Weber, Karl Mannheim, John Kenneth Galbraith, Peter Drucker, and Daniel Bell. The intellectual orientation of modern science, as revealed in the conflicting work of Karl Popper and Thomas S. Kuhn, has gradually been assimilated by sociology.

B. STUDIES OF TECHNOLOGY AND SOCIAL CHANGE

890   Abels, Sonia Leib; Abels, Paul; and Richmond, Samuel A. "Ethics Shock: Technology, Life Styles and Future Practice." JOURNAL OF SOCIOLOGY AND SOCIAL WELFARE 2 (Winter 1974): 140-54.

Certain contemporary trends must be taken into account by the social work profession in the planning of future practice. These include: the influence of lower fertility on the quality of life; an increasing gap between rich and poor; and genetic engineering and behavior control techniques. Ethical dilemmas

between individual and social good have been exacerbated.
The authors urge the study of ethics as an essential component
of continuing education in social work.

891   Allen, Francis R. "Technology and Social Change: Current Status and
Outlook." TECHNOLOGY AND CULTURE 1 (Winter 1959): 48-59.

Through reviewing accomplishments thus far in the study of
technology and social change, Allen uncovers promising directions for research. Most urgent, he feels, are studies of the
social effects of aviation, nuclear energy and military technology, and of the cumulative effects of television viewing.

892   _____, ed. TECHNOLOGY AND SOCIAL CHANGE. New York:
Appleton-Century-Crofts, 1957. 529 p. Illus.

Technology and applied science, Allen believes, are the
dominant forces in causing social change in Western society.
Sociological papers collected here corroborate this view.
Theoretical papers by the work's other contributors, William F.
Ogburn, Hernell Hart, Meyer F. Nimkoff, and Delbert C.
Miller, are followed by case studies of the social effects of some
major inventions such as the automobile and the motion picture. Subsequent papers discuss social theory and research on
the influence of technology on institutions and social problems.

893   Bauer, Raymond A., ed. SOCIAL INDICATORS. Cambridge: M.I.T.
Press, 1966. xxi, 357 p.

Five prominent social scientists examine the potential for and
problems of developing statistical tools appropriate for assessing the nation's social well-being. The larger questions are
explored in the course of examining the difficulties of anticipating secondary effects of the U.S. space program.

894   Berger, Peter L.; Berger, Brigitte; and Kellner, Hansfried. THE
HOMELESS MIND: MODERNIZATION AND CONSCIOUSNESS. New
York: Random House, 1973. ix, 258 p.

A case is made that technology leads inevitably to a destruction of man's sense of place in society and public life. The
abstract, instrumental cognitive style required for technological
production further compartmentalizes social relations. In the
light of these observations, the authors look at the process of
modernization in the Third World and at the elements of disaffection in industrial society.

895   Bernard, Jessie. "Technology, Science and Sex Attitudes." IMPACT
OF SCIENCE ON SOCIETY 18 (October-December 1968): 213-27.

To the study of the impact of such technological innovations

as contraceptives on sex values should be added studies on the
effect of sex attitudes on science and technology. But because of the persistence of repressive attitudes, sex as a subject of scientific study has lagged.

896   Cottrell, W[illiam].F[red]. "Death by Dieselization: A Case Study in
the Reaction to Technological Change." AMERICAN SOCIOLOGICAL
REVIEW 16 (June 1951): 358-65.

The town that is the subject of this case study was built to
meet the service needs of railroad engines traversing an
isolated portion of the American Southwest. Just after World
War II, technological improvements involving a switch to
dieselization increased engine efficiency to the extent that
this stop, and the town around it, were rendered obsolete.
Cottrell traces the town's futile attempts at self-preservation
and its evolving philosophy toward the railroad company.

897   _____. TECHNOLOGY, MAN AND PROGRESS. Columbus, Ohio:
Merrill, 1972. vi, 194 p.

This collection of papers from the noted railroader-turned-
sociologist are mostly reprinted. Chapter 1 compares technological with evolutionary progress. An update on the town of
Caliente profiled in "Death by Dieselization" (no. 896) discusses such later adaptations as tourism and agriculture. Final
papers consider technology's relation to the aging process and
to the possibilities for world peace.

898   Ellis, John. THE SOCIAL HISTORY OF THE MACHINE GUN. New
York: Pantheon, 1973. 186 p. Illus., bibliog.

Ellis investigates man's relationship to military technology
using the machine gun as his vehicle of analysis. It is his
contention that mass mechanized killing helped to create an
irrelevance and irreverence for human individuality. With
wide-ranging implications, the study concentrates on the
period from the Civil War to World War I and includes European events.

899   Keniston, Kenneth. THE UNCOMMITTED: ALIENATED YOUTH IN
AMERICAN SOCIETY. New York: Harcourt, Brace, and World,
1965. viii, 500 p. Illus., bibliog.

A landmark book on the concept of alienation is based on
the comparative study of three groups of Harvard students
identified through testing as "alienated," "middle," and
"unalienated." Keniston studies personal and social sources
of their rejection of society and finds technology and its
demands to be greatly at fault: "The values, requirements,

and virtues of technology are not in themselves bad, but their unquestioned supremacy is human social misfortune."

900   McHale, John. "Science, Technology and Change." ANNALS OF THE AMERICAN ACADEMY OF POLITICAL AND SOCIAL SCIENCE 373 (September 1967): 120-40.

The narrowing interval between scientific discovery and social use has had the effect of accelerating the rate of social change. Monitors that have been developed to measure change in the various sectors of society--science indicators, social indicators, economic indicators--are no longer ade-quate. Indicators must be redesigned, McHale urges, to provide more suitable early warnings.

901   Miller, Sanford A. "The Kinetics of Diet and Culture." TECHNOLOGY REVIEW 80 (August-September 1978): 38-45.

With the aid of technology, man has overcome technical barriers to producing enough food for the world's population. But cultural patterns of food consumption and production have proven problematic. For example, in industrialized and de-veloping societies alike, an increased intake of animal protein and total calories has become a status symbol that is linked to development, even at the expense of good nutrition.

902   Moore, Wilbert Ellis. ORDER AND CHANGE: ESSAYS IN COMPARA-TIVE SOCIOLOGY. New York: John Wiley and Sons, 1967. viii, 313 p.

This selection of previously published articles by a noted so-ciologist encompasses his ideas on forecasting the social future. Included also are the articles "Social Aspects of In-dustrial Civilization" and "The Individual in an Organizational Society."

903   Odum, Howard W. "Notes on the Technicways in Contemporary Society." AMERICAN SOCIOLOGICAL REVIEW 2 (June 1937): 336-46.

In contemporary civilization, folkways and mores are supplanted as the rate of social evolution accelerates. Byproducts of science and technology, "technicways" impose artificial be-havior patterns and structure on traditional societies, hastening social disintegration and centralization of power.

904   Ogburn, William Fielding. "How Technology Changes Society." SOCIOLOGY AND SOCIAL RESEARCH 36 (November-December 1951): 75-83.

Conditions in society modify science and vice versa, Ogburn states. As war created the atomic bomb, it has in return made war a reality for civilian populations. Ogburn briefly mentions effects of other innovations on society, dwelling especially on the automobile. Relations between society and technology are compared with a game of billards or a linked chain, occasionally so entangled that they appear "like the chain armor of the middle ages."

905 _____. ON CULTURE AND SOCIAL CHANGE: SELECTED PAPERS. Edited by Otis Dudley Duncan. Chicago: University of Chicago Press, 1964. xxii, 360 p. Bibliog.

A selection of major papers by a prominent sociologist reveals an overriding interest in the relationship between technological and social change. Of particular interest are papers studying the role of technology on government change and on the standard of living. An innovative selection views technology as an environment; another paper, based on Ogburn's extensive work in that area, provides suggestions for predicting the future. A bibliography of the author's principal works is included.

906 Ogburn W[illiam].F[ielding]., and Nimkoff, M.F. TECHNOLOGY AND THE CHANGING FAMILY. Boston: Houghton Mifflin, 1955. v, 329 p.

Ogburn and Nimkoff cite technology as the principal impetus for recent changes in family structure, function, and composition. New methods of birth control have reduced family size. With industrial growth, the family has lost its productive functions. But discomfort is temporary. For the future family, the authors project a technological bounty of creature comforts and recreation devices.

907 Parker, Frederick B. "Social Control of the Technicways: Relative Strengths of the Folkways and Technicways." SOCIAL FORCES 22 (December 1943): 163-68.

In another study following the lead of Howard Odum, the manifestation of folkways versus "technicways" in the life of the individual is studied. Folkways, the author concludes, are internalized into the supergo, their power reinforced by ritual and shared values. In contrast, "technicways" exercise the internal, rationalized control of the time clock.

908 President's Research Committee on Social Trends. RECENT SOCIAL TRENDS IN THE UNITED STATES. 2 vols. New York: McGraw-Hill, 1933. xcv, 1568 p. Illus., maps.

In 1929 President Hoover called upon a number of eminent social scientists to explore and report on social change to serve as a basis for national policy development. Among the twenty-nine chapters, those concerned with technology include William F. Ogburn, "The Influence of Invention and Discovery"; Ralph G. Hurlin, "Shifting Occupational Patterns"; and Malcolm M. Willey, "The Agencies of Communication."

909 Schroeter, James. "Technology and the Sexual Revolution." YALE REVIEW 62 (Spring 1973): 392-405.

According to Freud, civilization curbs and represses sexuality. Schroeter argues that, on the contrary, the growth of industrial civilization has brought about sexual liberation. Previous pressures for control, such as preservation of family wealth through marriage ties or the economic need to bear many children, have been eliminated. From an examination of recent literature, the author concludes that while industrial society has set sex free, it has at the same time trivialized it, cutting its power over population, evolution, and the psyche.

910 Shinbach, Kent D. "Technology and Social Change: Choosing a Near Future." MENTAL HYGIENE 52 (April 1968): 276-83.

Modern as well as primitive cultures are suffering the stress of acculturation in adapting to such revolutionary devices as the computer. Three types of effects of new inventions are identified: expected, unexpected, and effects of the "aura of introduction," the sense of involvement in change that accompanies the diffusion of a major innovation.

911 "The Social Consequences of Technological Progress." INTERNATIONAL SOCIAL SCIENCE BULLETIN 4 (Summer 1952): 243-346. Bibliog.

A select group of international scholars presents general and theoretical viewpoints from a number of disciplines. William F. Ogburn and Wilbert E. Moore present the stance of the sociologist, while Einar Thorsrud provides a psychological and Rene Savatier a legal approach. Anthropologist A.P. Elkin summarizes the early effects of Western technology imported to the Australian aborigines. An introduction by Georges Friedmann and conclusion by Harold Lasswell lend coherence to the presentation.

912 "Utopias." DAEDALUS 94 (Spring 1965): 271-517.

In what has become a well-known number of this prestigious journal, authors including Lewis Mumford, Northrop Frye, Judith Shklar, Bertrand de Jouvenel, and John R. Pierce present their individual perspectives on utopia. Literary, historical, socialist, pragmatic, and electronic utopias are described. Uses that have been made of utopia, particularly for reform, are reviewed.

913   Wilkening, Eugene A. "Change in Farm Technology as Related to Familism, Family Decision-Making and Family Integration." AMERICAN SOCIOLOGICAL REVIEW 9 (February 1954): 29-37.

> This study suggests that family relationships, as exemplified by integration, familism, and father-centered decision-making, have little direct influence on the acceptance of innovations or improvements in farming.

914   Winthrop, Henry. "The Alienation of Post-Industrial Man." MID-WESTERN QUARTERLY 9 (January 1968): 121-37.

> The Beat and Teenage generations believed that their conflict with their elders was a new social phenomenon. Winthrop analyzes this and other beliefs and values of the subculture: pleasure, a scorn of convention and patriotism, and an alienation from bureaucracy. He views the conflict not as generational in the traditional sense but as a conflict between the values of industrial and post-industrial man.

915   _____. "Some Instabilities and Moral Deficiencies of the 'Post-Industrial' Society." AMERICAN JOURNAL OF ECONOMICS AND SOCIOLOGY 35 (October 1976): 373-89.

> In the author's opinion, the current discussion of the post-industrial society devotes excess attention to planning and policy for the material aspects of life, and insufficient attention to social, psychological, and spiritual issues. An inner-oriented society (IOS) should supplant the post-industrial society. Major features of such a society are outlined.

C. SELECTED ANTHROPOLOGICAL AND ETHNIC STUDIES

916   Anderson, S.E. "Science, Technology and Black Liberation." BLACK SCHOLAR 5 (March 1974): 2-8.

> The growth of technology has broadened black dependence on white America. Though there are a few promising developments, black participation in the sciences has been small. In order to attract blacks to science, curricula must be humanized, with attention paid to third world problems and the dangers of "neoeugenics."

917   Bernard, H. Russell, and Pelto, Pertti J., eds. TECHNOLOGY AND SOCIAL CHANGE. New York: Macmillan, 1972. vii, 354 p. Bibliog.

> Case studies compare the impact of two kinds of technological development on cultural change in developing countries and small-scale societies, some located in the United States. The

potential social consequences of "macrotechnological" developments, like the Karibu Dam on the Zambezi, are generally reviewed, sometimes planned for. On the other hand "micotechnological" changes, meaning commercially introduced goods such as tools, vehicles or housing forms, are rarely prepared for. The studies demonstrate that social upheaval caused by microtechnological change is often greater and should receive equal preparatory attention.

918   Bigart, Robert James. "Indian Culture and Industrialization." AMERICAN ANTHROPOLOGIST 74 (October 1972): 1180-88.

The western factory is structured by impersonal relationships of dominance and submission. In contrast, American Indian society is based on group loyalty with individual autonomy. Thus Indian values appear incompatible with traditional factory organization. If a reservation factory is to succeed, the author suggests, it should offer individual, precision craft work, flexible hours, and worker participation in decision making.

919   Boskoff, Alvin. "Negro Class Structure and the Technicways." SOCIAL FORCES 29 (December 1950): 124-31.

As folkways dissolve in response to technological change, new social patterns compatible with the technological order are instituted. In the case of black class structure, Boskoff asserts, social distinctions based on criteria such as racial or immediate slave ancestry were replaced by those based on occupational success and family stability.

920   Clarke, Robin, and Hindley, Geoffrey. THE CHALLENGE OF THE PRIMITIVE. New York: McGraw-Hill, 1975. 240 p. Bibliog.

A prominent proponent of alternative technology, Clarke believes that in primitive life can be found some answers to problems presented by life in a technological society. Western man, given over to an ethic of progress, has lost his ability to find happiness. The authors' ethnographic survey suggests that one need not to destroy the environment nor prey upon fellow citizens in order to enjoy good health, a comfortable home, and sound social relations.

921   Furman, Necah. "Technological Change and Industrialization among the Southern Pueblos." ETHNOHISTORY 22 (Winter 1975): 1-14.

Prompted by population pressures and diffusion of ideas through the media and education, the pueblos are gradually undergoing a transition from agrarianism to industrialization and urban-style living. The nature and speed of the transition varies widely among pueblos. Debates are being waged over the merits of native-operated versus other-operated industry. Beneficial changes such as electrification have been balanced by new problems such as language loss and auto deaths.

922   Graburn, Nelson H.   ESKIMOS WITHOUT IGLOOS: SOCIAL AND ECONOMIC DEVELOPMENTS IN SUGLUK.   Boston: Little, Brown 1969.   x, 244 p.   Illus., maps, bibliog.

In a record of changes among a group of Hudson Strait Eskimos, emphasis is placed on the effect of changes in subsistence on the rest of the traditional culture.   Large-boat fishing, overhunting, and exhaustion of game led to wage employment and, in turn, to enlarged, permanent settlements.   Education and social life were modified accordingly.

923   Hall, Edwin S.   "The 'Iron Dog' in Northern Alaska."   ANTHROPOLOGICA 13, no. 1-2 (1971): 237-54.

The introduction of the snowmobile to the Alaskan Eskimos has stimulated profound cultural change, as illustrated by this paper on Noatak Village.   Among outstanding changes have been a greater efficiency in caribou hunting and more frequent intra-village social interaction.   Hall projects changes to come, mostly in the direction of acculturation to the larger society.

924   Henderson, L.J.   "Public Technology and the Metropolitan Ghetto."   BLACK SCHOLAR 5 (March 1974): 9-18.

Two related problems face the American city, the metropolitanization of black communities and a growing need for the application of technology to urban problem-solving.   To date, blacks have not been employed in technological occupations or involved in technology assessment or decision-making.   The author calls for a new assessment of the potential applications of technology to the city, with maximum black involvement.

925   Ritzenthaler, Robert G.   "The Impact of Small Industry on an Indian Community."   AMERICAN ANTHROPOLOGIST 55 (January-March 1953): 143-48.

Until 1946, the Lac Du Flambeau Chippewa gained most of their small income from the tourist trade.   The introduction of an electric meter manufacturing company offered permanent lucrative employment, but for the first few years there were major conflicts between traditional Indian values and the demands of the time clock and the wage-hour system.   While encouraging reservation industry, the authors suggest careful preparation for its introduction.

926   Spicer, Edward H., ed.   HUMAN PROBLEMS IN TECHNOLOGICAL

CHANGE. New York: Russell Sage Foundation, 1952. 301 p. Illus.

This casebook includes some classic papers--examining the impact of the introduction of Western technologies to under-developed groups in America and elsewhere. American cases focus on the impact of the wagon on Papago culture, of hybrid corn in New Mexico, and advances in reindeer herding in Alaska.

D. SOCIAL TECHNOLOGY

927 Attinger, Ernst O., ed. GLOBAL SYSTEM DYNAMICS: INTERNA-TIONAL SYMPOSIUM, CHARLOTTESVILLE, VA., 1969. New York: S. Karger, 1970. xiv, 353 p. Illus., bibliog.

At a meeting concerned with systematic approaches to the analysis of social systems, papers focused on the complex interactions between health, education, economic progress, and population growth. Part 1 treats methodology, part 2, the human factor in systems planning. Integration and analy-sis of large complex systems is covered in the third part, and a collection of analyses of specific social systems closes the volume.

928 Boguslaw, Robert. THE NEW UTOPIANS: A STUDY OF SYSTEMS DE-SIGN AND SOCIAL CHANGE. Englewood Cliffs, N.J.: Prentice-Hall, 1965. 213 p.

The "new utopians" of our time are the systems engineers, computer programmers, and operations researchers. Boguslaw explores the characteristics of the field of systems design that he believes can promote social change and the parameters that social change may, in turn, impose on systems develop-ment.

929 Chen, Kan, ed. TECHNOLOGY AND SOCIAL INSTITUTIONS. New York: IEEE Press, 1974. xii, 212 p. Bibliog.

Assembled in this volume are invited papers, workshop sum-maries, and project reports originally presented at the Engi-neering Foundation Conference on Technology and Social Institutions held in May, 1973. Participants included indus-trial and labor leaders, government officials, academics, and other researchers. The focus of the conference was on the utilization of technology to aid urban and regional planning and problem-solving.

930 Chen, Kan; Ghausi, Mohammed S.; and Sage, Andrew P., eds. "So-cial Systems Engineering." PROCEEDINGS OF THE INSTITUTE OF

ELECTRICAL AND ELECTRONICS ENGINEERS 63 (March 1975): 340-534.

"Social systems engineering" is defined by the editors as the application of systems engineering to social problems. Papers discuss such community topics as scenarios for urban revitalization, social service delivery, and community dialogue technology. More general methodological and philosophical issues and problems of environmental and energy planning are also addressed.

931   Etzioni, Amitai, and Remp, Richard. TECHNOLOGICAL SHORTCUTS TO SOCIAL CHANGE. New York: Russell Sage Foundation, 1973. 235 p.

Many studies have demonstrated the primary effect of technology on the rate and direction of social change in industrial society. The question raised here is whether it may be possible to initiate and accelerate desired social change through technological means. Histories of several "technological shortcuts" are outlined, including the rise of methadone in treating heroin addicts, and "antabuse" for alcoholics.

932   Jones, Daniel P. "From Military to Civilian Technology: The Introduction of Tear Gas for Civil Riot Control." TECHNOLOGY AND CULTURE 19 (April 1978): 151-68.

The circumstances surrounding the transfer of tear gas from its origin as a military weapon to local police as a means of civil control is analyzed. Jones concludes that the use of tear gas for civil riot control was more humane in the sense that it resulted in fewer deaths and injuries than with conventional weapons, but it also "meant a loss of power to any group opposing established order."

933   Michael, Donald N. "Technology and the Human Environment." PUBLIC ADMINISTRATION REVIEW 28 (January 1968): 57-60.

Dealing with the social implications of new technologies will require the use of more technology. Social technology, the application of the behavioral sciences, will develop with the aid of government programs and the computer. In its developed state, enriched with data and methodology, it should be able to analyze the implications of new technologies.

934   Weinberg, Alvin M. "Can Technology Replace Social Engineering?" BULLETIN OF THE ATOMIC SCIENTISTS 22 (December 1966): 4-8.

Traditional methods employed to resolve social problems--based on persuasion or force--have proved frustrating. Social engineers aim to use social knowledge to invent legal, moral, and educational devices to change behavior in predictable ways;

however, their success is not easy to assess. Weinberg feels that technologists can broaden the options for social engineers through the provision of such products as birth control devices or water desalination equipment.

E. PSYCHOLOGICAL CHANGE

935   Bertalanffy, Ludwig von. ROBOTS, MEN AND MINDS: PSYCHOLOGY IN THE MODERN WORLD. New York: George Braziller, 1968. x, 150 p. Bibliog.

A biologist and systems theorist, Bertalanffy describes a "scientific organismic approach" by means of which man may be studied in relation to his total environment. The book strays into a long, digressive critique of behaviorism, whose tenets the author believes have contributed heavily to the current manipulative use of the mass media.

936   Bettleheim, Bruno. "Joey: A Mechanical Boy." SCIENTIFIC AMERICAN 200 (March 1959): 116-27.

The case history of a schizophrenic child who believed himself to be a machine exemplifies a fascinating if bizarre response to infant neglect and emotional deprivation. Refusing all human contact not mediated by machine, Joey "plugged himself in," shifted through gears, and went mechanically "haywire." During his slow recovery, as revealed in his drawings, he was transformed from an electric papoose to the machine's master. Bettleheim observes, "It is unlikely that Joey's calamity could befall a child in any time and culture but our own."

937   Daly, Robert. "The Spectres of Technicism." PSYCHIATRY 33 (November 1970): 417-32.

Three contemporary orientations to technological phenomena are examined: the traditional view that technology is dominated by some nontechnical reality; the technicist view that technological innovation is the supreme human activity; and a "spectral" view of technology as linked to mysterious, dominant forces. The manifestations of the spectral view are exemplified through a number of psychiatric case histories.

938   Houston, Jean. "Prometheus Rebound: An Inquiry into Technological Growth and Psychological Change." TECHNOLOGICAL FORECASTING AND SOCIAL CHANGE   9, no. 3 (1976): 241-58.

The technological environment has had a profound influence on the human psyche and body. Houston argues that this influence has been a negative one. A new kind of nurturing is needed for body and mind to recapture latent capabilities of imagistic thinking and movement.

939   Katz, Solomon H. "Toward a New Science of Humanity." ZYGON
       10 (March 1975): 12-31.

   The adoption of the cognitive styles that underlie the evolution
   of modern technology may have been costly in terms of other
   basic brain activities and cognitive needs that are no longer
   satisfied. The domination of left hemisphere functions, which
   are logical, analytical, and linear, over the spatial, artistic,
   and holistic functions controlled by the right hemisphere has
   rendered man incomplete. Katz suggests that an understanding of both rational and irrational modes of thought must be
   incorporated into a new science of humanity that will better
   reflect the complexities of human nature.

940   Koestler, Arthur. THE GHOST IN THE MACHINE. New York: Mac-
       millan, 1967. xiv, 384 p. Bibliog.

   In a heavy critique of behaviorist psychology, Koestler postulates his own formula for the nature of man as a being
   possessing both self-assertive and integrative potential. As a
   cure-all for the "schizophysiology" inherent in man's nature,
   Koestler suggests a pill designed to enhance mental well-
   being and stability.

941   Mankin, Donald. TOWARD A POST-INDUSTRIAL PSYCHOLOGY:
       EMERGING PERSPECTIVES ON TECHNOLOGY, WORK, EDUCATION
       AND LEISURE. New York: John Wiley and Sons, 1978. xc, 212 p.
       Bibliog.

   The transformation of industrial psychology from a tool of management into an "agent for post-industrial change" will require
   rethinking of the purpose and practice of the discipline.
   Mankin takes a broad look at such areas as unemployment,
   quality of work life, leisure, and retirement in attempting to
   identify potential contributions of a revised industrial psychology toward furthering a humanistically planned future.

942   Parr, Albert E. "Mind and Milieu." SOCIOLOGICAL INQUIRY 33
       (Winter 1963): 19-24.

   Modern technology is so changing our physical surroundings as
   to shake the individual's sense of self reliance and security
   in the knowledge of his environmental and personal niche.
   With external aids for environmental adaptation removed,
   psychological, inner-directed adjustment assumes greater import. The author advises the use of advanced media techniques, particularly film, in the study of psychological reactions to the man-made environment.

943   Ruesch, Jurgen. "Technological Civilization and Human Affairs."
       JOURNAL OF NERVOUS AND MENTAL DISEASE 145 (September 1967):
       194-205.

In order to adapt to technological change, man has undergone psychological and social transformations. A world organized around individuals is being changed to a world structured around systems and collectives, a tendency manifested in such diverse phenomena as job teamwork, a decline in privately owned homes, and group therapy.

F. BEHAVIOR CONTROL

944   Bedau, Hugo Adam. "Physical Interventions to Alter Behavior in a Punitive Environment: Some Moral Reflections on New Technology." AMERICAN BEHAVIORAL SCIENTIST 18 (May-June 1975): 657-78.

Four techniques of "physical intervention"--psychosurgery, chemotherapy, aversion techniques, and sensory deprivation are considered in the context of criminology and penology. At present, such techniques are used surreptitiously, sometimes with deleterious and irreversible effects. Given the nature of incarceration, no prisoner can truly give voluntary consent; in its absence, Bedau argues, no such techniques should be used.

945   Delgado, Jose [M.R.] PHYSICAL CONTROL OF THE MIND: TOWARD A NEW PSYCHOCIVILIZED SOCIETY. New York: Harper and Row, 1969. xxi, 280 p. Illus.

In relation to other areas, psychic life and emotional reactions remain little understood. However, technology for the exploration of mental activities is developing rapidly. Through such techniques as electronic stimulation of the brain (ESB), described at length in this volume, total mind and personality control may eventually be achieved. Though Delgado expresses some ethical reservations about potential misuses of such techniques, he suggests that humans have never been in control: "generally we are not masters but slaves of milleniums of biological history."

946   Erickson, Richard. "Walden III: Toward an Ethic of Changing Behavior." JOURNAL OF RELIGION AND HEALTH 16 (January 1977): 7-14.

The author contends that behavior modification procedures have been "misrepresented by enthusiasts and misunderstood by opponents." Three significant points are made. Erickson contends that free will is not, as some behaviorists have contended, illusory; that behaviorists must respond more readily to changing views of man's nature; and that the term behavior "control" should be softened to "influence." However, he remains committed to the belief that behavior modification can be employed to the betterment of both individual and community.

947   Gaylin, William.   "Skinner Redux."   HARPER'S, October 1973,
       pp. 48-56.

       A psychiatrist suggests that interest in behavior control is on
       the rise, made palatable by B.F. Skinner's assurances that such
       control offers security at the expense of a freedom that is only
       an illusion.   Gaylin is skeptical about the validity of deter-
       minist views shared by behaviorists and psychoanalysts.   He
       is also doubtful that the values required for future living can
       be well enough predicted to permit appropriate conditioning
       of children.

948   Halleck, Seymour L.   "Legal and Ethical Aspects of Behavioral Con-
       trol."   AMERICAN JOURNAL OF PSYCHIATRY 131 (April 1974):
       381-85.

       New drugs and techniques to change behavior have inspired
       the fear that such advances will be universally adopted to
       decrease aggressiveness in favor of conformity.   Halleck dis-
       cusses three classes of situations and the appropriateness of
       therapy for ill or criminal patients in each case: (1) the
       patient does not consent to therapy, (2) he consents under
       duress, and (3) he requests therapy.   The author concludes
       that there is never justification for deceiving patients, or for
       punishing those who refuse treatment, but that mild coercion
       may be warranted with dangerous or self-destructive persons.

949   Holland, James.   "Ethical Considerations in Behavior Modification."
       JOURNAL OF HUMANISTIC PSYCHOLOGY 16 (Summer 1976):   71-78.

       Drugs, electrical stimulation of the nervous system and operant
       conditioning have emerged as powerful means of controlling
       human behavior.   Though committed to behavior modification,
       Holland is concerned about the "cooptation of science in the
       service of elites."   Though selfish manipulation is not inherent
       in the science of behavior, it is intrinsic to the present social
       and political systems in which scientists must work.

950   Ingraham, Barton L., and Smith, Gerald W.   "The Use of Electronics
       in the Observation and Control of Human Behavior and Its Possible
       Use in Rehabilitation and Parole."   ISSUES IN CRIMINOLOGY 7
       (Fall 1972):   35-53.

       Surveillance devices represent a breakthrough in penology, as
       they will permit the release of many more parolees than has
       been traditionally possible.   Specific monitoring devices are
       described, including electrocardiogram monitors, "endroradio-
       sondes" that measure various physiological variables, and
       implants for ESB (electronic stimulation of the brain).   Argu-
       ing against those critics who suggest that such devices will
       make robots of men, the authors conclude that behavior con-

trol technology represents perhaps the first possibility for
stimulating positive evolutionary change since Homo sapiens
emerged as a species.

951   Karlins, Marvin, and Andrews, Lewis M., eds. MAN CONTROLLED:
       READINGS IN THE PSYCHOLOGY OF BEHAVIOR CONTROL. New
       York: Free Press of Glencoe, 1972. x, 277 p. Bibliog.

       Readings describe "some promising and not-so-promising"
       methods for controlling behavior, including behavior modifi-
       cation, brain stimulation, genetic engineering, drugs, adver-
       tising, environmental design, hypnosis, and brainwashing.
       The effect of group pressures, and cultural and dispositional
       factors in behavior control also receive attention. Among
       authors represented are Jose M.R. Delgado, Herman Muller,
       David Krech, Stanley Milgram, Carl Rogers, B.F. Skinner,
       and Leonard Krassner.

952   Kelman, Herbert C. "Manipulation of Human Behavior: An Ethical
       Dilemma for the Social Scientist." JOURNAL OF SOCIAL ISSUES 21
       (April 1965): 31-46.

       As knowledge of human behavior grows, the behavioral sci-
       entist must confront the ethical questions surrounding the use
       of that knowledge. The author describes manipulative tech-
       niques used by psychotherapists, industrial sociologists, and
       pollsters. Three measures are proposed to mitigate the de-
       humanizing effects of new knowledge: heightened awareness
       of the nature of manipulation, development of mechanisms for
       protection against manipulation, and emphasis on personal
       freedom as a societal value.

953   Kinkade, Kathleen. A WALDEN TWO EXPERIMENT: THE FIRST
       FIVE YEARS OF TWIN OAKS COMMUNITY. New York: William
       Morrow and Co., 1972. xii, 271 p.

       Founded by the author and seven others on a rural Virginia
       farm, the community was set up according to the principles
       of Skinnerian behavioral psychology, with common property
       and communal, nonfamily living. The book consists of an
       account of daily life, detailing behavioral conditioning
       techniques and "scientific" problem-solving techniques used to
       maintain order.

954   Klerman, Gerald L. "Behavior Control and the Limits of Reform."
       HASTINGS CENTER REPORT 5 (August 1975): 40-45.

       New technologies originating from the behavior and biological
       sciences are now being considered as means for controlling
       deviant behavior in "total institutional" settings. The con-
       sideration of such techniques brings up the question of the

rights of patients and prisoners. Until legal and ethical quandaries are resolved, behavior control technologies can not be utilized advantageously.

955   London, Perry. BEHAVIOR CONTROL. New York: Harper and Row, 1969. x, 241 p. Bibliog.

For contemporary society, behavior control is "scientifically inevitable, socially necessary and psychologically prepared for." What remains to be considered, according to London, are appropriate purposes, rules of use, and authorization procedures for behavior control. The status of techniques for "control by information" and "control by coercion" is surveyed.

956   Mabe, Alan R., ed. "New Technologies and Strategies for Social Control: Ethical and Practical Limits." AMERICAN BEHAVIORAL SCIENTIST 18 (May-June 1975): 595-722.

Ethical and practical limits of new techniques of social control, particularly as applied in institutions, are discussed. Frank Ervin reviews biological intervention techniques, while John Atthowe summarizes research in behavior modification and environmental design. That the use of physical intervention techniques on prisoners is a legal and ethical dilemma is stressed in essays by Hugo Bedau, David Wexler, and C.R. Jeffrey and Ina A. Jeffrey.

957   Neville, Robert [C.] "The Limits of Freedom and the Technology of Behavior Control." HUMAN CONTEXT 4 (Autumn 1972): 433-46.

As new techniques in behavior control are developed, their impact on values must be considered. Neville summarizes but does not critique the Skinnerian position on the relationship between behavior control and freedom. According to Neville, B.F. Skinner grants that, through controlling the environment of a person, one limits his range of potential behavior. However, he asserts, within those restrictions, people retain freedom to act, while gaining freedom from hesitancy and frustration.

958   _____, ed. "Controlling Behavior Through Drugs." HASTINGS CENTER STUDIES 2 (1974): 65-112.

Papers originally presented at a symposium held in 1972 present various angles on behavior modification through drugs. Gerald L. Klerman summarizes the state of the art of drugs for treating mental illness, while Paul H. Wender considers the long-range emotional and psychological consequences of behavior-altering drugs. Other papers consider the effects of hallucinogenic drugs on the nontherapeutic user.

959 Nolan, J. Dennis. "Freedom and Dignity: A Functional Analysis." AMERICAN PSYCHOLOGIST 29 (March 1974): 157-60.

B.F. Skinner has suggested that behavior control techniques be used in the design of entire cultures. Nolan challenges this suggestion, criticizing basic premises of the behaviorist position. In dismissing freedom and disregarding other values, he states, one allows technology itself to dictate society's goals and directions. Behavior control technology would become an end in itself.

960 Rogers, Carl R., and Skinner, B.F. "Some Issues Concerning the Control of Human Behavior." SCIENCE 124 (30 November 1956): 1057-66.

Rogers and Skinner debate the philosophical and practical implications of behavior control. Arguing that Western man has been too long dominated by ". . .what Andrew Hacker has called 'the spectre of predictable man'," Skinner produces arguments for the social necessity for behavior controls. Rogers' primary objection is that he believes Skinner underestimates the threat of power abuse inherent in such controls.

961 Russell, E.W. "The Power of Behavior Control: A Critique of Behavior Modification Methods." JOURNAL OF CLINICAL PSYCHOLOGY MONOGRAPH SUPPLEMENT 43 (April 1974): 1-30.

The potential claimed for recently developed techniques of behavior control has been greatly inflated, Russell believes. Behavior therapies have derived their power from nonspecific placebo effects. "Brainwashing" techniques, for example, have little effect in a noncoercive situation, he asserts. Thus, Russell sees little ground for fear of the appearance of a Skinnerian utopia.

962 Saleebey, Dennis. "Pigeons, People and Paradise: Skinnerian Technology and the Coming of the Welfare Society." SOCIAL SCIENCE REVIEW 50 (September 1976): 388-401.

The utopian vision of the sixties, the Welfare State, will require for realization large social as well as technological and economic resources. The author suggests that the behavioral technology of B.F. Skinner, which offers the replacement of coercive socialization by operant socialization, has much to offer this effort.

963 Schrag, Peter. MIND CONTROL. New York: Pantheon Books, 1978. xviii, 327 p.

In a popular, but well-documented account, Schrag identifies a fundamental shift in the nature of institutional control of behavior from such crude measures as physical punishment and threats to the softer methods of drugs, psychosurgery, behavior modification, and electronic surveillance. The book broadly surveys the nature and use of such methods in many institutional contexts. While motives may be humane, Schrag contends, the growth of behavior control technology must ultimately be viewed as "a subtle seductive process, a process of mystification, which teaches every individual that his mind and behavior are subject to chemical or other organic processes not fully within his control."

964   Shapiro, Michael H. "The Uses of Behavior Control Techniques: A Response." ISSUES IN CRIMINOLOGY 7 (Fall 1972): 55-93.

In response to an article by Ingraham and Smith (no. 950), Shapiro questions a number of statements and assumptions made by advocates of behavior control. He argues that the potential power of control technologies is unknown and thus to be feared. Skeptical about the appropriateness of behavior modification as a means of rehabilitation, he is also dubious about society's competence to delegate authority over control techniques. Questions concerning consent, privacy, and abuse of power have not, to his mind, been satisfactorily answered.

965   Skinner, B.F. BEYOND FREEDOM AND DIGNITY. New York: Alfred A. Knopf, 1971. 225 p.

In a highly controversial book, Skinner contends that while modern society has succeeded in solving many technical problems, it has not succeeded with problems related to human behavior. Society has failed because it has not chosen to apply the knowledge of behavioral science to those problems. Defending an environmental explanation of behavior that can become the basis for such a technology, Skinner dismisses present ideas about "freedom" and "dignity" as deceptive, illusory, and self-destructive.

966   _____. "Freedom and the Control of Men." AMERICAN SCHOLAR 25 (Winter 1955-56): 47-65.

In defense of behavior technology, Skinner argues that the growth of a science of man is a consistent and unavoidable development for Western democracy. We object to planned improvements of human behavior and culture, yet, he contends, our current beliefs about freedom have been carefully engineered.

966   Smith, W. Lynn, and Kling, Arthur. ISSUES IN BRAIN/BEHAVIOR CONTROL. New York: Spectrum Publications, 1976. 157 p.

Who is responsible for the treatment of overly aggressive,

violent, antisocial persons, and for the side effects of treatment? These are questions addressed by this volume. The origins of violent behavior are sought in cerebral dysfunction and genetic abnormalities. Legal implications of psychosurgery and the meaning of brain control for a democratic society also receive discussion.

968   Spece, Roy G., Jr. "Conditioning and Other Technologies Used to 'Treat?' 'Rehabilitate?' 'Demolish?' Prisoners and Mental Patients." SOUTHERN CALIFORNIA LAW REVIEW 45 (Spring 1972): 618-84.

Concise paragraph-length descriptions of a number of behavior control techniques, including drug therapy, electronic stimulation of the brain, electroconvulsive therapy, lobotomy, and milieu therapy provide an excellent overview of recent developments. Spece examines applications of such techniques in selected California penal institutions as background for a lengthy discussion of legal questions and decisions concerning prisoners' and mental patients' right to receive or refuse such treatments.

969   Tarter, Donald. "Heeding Skinner's Call: Toward the Development of a Social Technology." AMERICAN SOCIOLOGIST 8 (November 1973): 153-58.

Because sociology has avoided technology, choosing to focus on data gathering, observing, and abstracting rather than on practical application, the discipline has grown stagnant, Tarter believes. To remedy this situation, sociologists must turn to experimental psychology and embrace behaviorism, adopting ideas also from engineering and systems science. In these disciplines can be found the essentials for social intervention techniques that will make the profession useful.

970   Ulrich, Roger; Strachnik, Thomas; and Mabry, John, eds. CONTROL OF HUMAN BEHAVIOR. Vol. 1: EXPANDING THE BEHAVIORAL LABORATORY. Glenview, Ill.: Scott, Foresman and Co., 1966. 349 p. Bibliog.

A broad range of contributions to the control of human behavior is surveyed, along with assumptions underlying behavior analyses and fallacies in interpretation. Implications of behavior control receive attention, particularly those addressing the question of values. A judicious selection of papers reprinted from a number of scholarly journals.

971   _____. CONTROL OF HUMAN BEHAVIOR. Vol. 2: FROM CURE TO PREVENTION. Glenview, Ill.: Scott, Foresman and Co., 1970. 378 p.

The implications of the experimental analysis of behavior for clinical and institutional practice are addressed. The editors suggest that the alternate goal of behavioral science should be the amelioration of behaviors disruptive to individuals and to the larger society. Current methods for remediation of behavior problems in prisons, mental institutions, clinics, and classrooms are surveyed. Authors in part 3 address the subject of prevention of future behavior problems, recognizing the dangers inherent in such methods.

972   Wheeler, Harvey, ed. BEYOND THE PUNITIVE SOCIETY; OPERANT CONDITIONING: SOCIAL AND POLITICAL ASPECTS. San Francisco: W.H. Freeman and Co., 1973. viii, 274 p. Bibliog.

The storm of controversy that followed the publication of Skinner's BEYOND FREEDOM AND DIGNITY (no. 965) prompted the appearance of this collection of papers offering an overview of operant conditioning and a critical evaluation of Skinner's work. Among the eighteen contributors are John R. Platt, Dennis O. Pirages, Nathan Rotenstreich, and John Wilkinson. In the closing paper, B.F. Skinner responds with "Answers for My Critics."

G. ENVIRONMENTAL PSYCHOLOGY

1. Bibliographies

973   Bell, Gwen, and MacGreevey, Paula. BEHAVIOR AND ENVIRON-MENT: A BIBLIOGRAPHY OF SOCIAL ACTIVITIES IN URBAN SPACE. Exchange Bibliography no. 123. Monticello, Ill.: Council of Planning Librarians, 1970. 64 p.

974   Brown, Linda. AN ANNOTATED BIBLIOGRAPHY OF THE LITERATURE ON LIVABILITY, WITH AN INTRODUCTION AND AN ANALYSIS OF THE LITERATURE. Exchange Bibliography no. 853. Monticello, Ill.: Council of Planning Librarians, 1975. 60 p.

An extensive introduction to the issues and questions surrounding the livability concept precedes the bibliography. Subject categories are: attitudes toward and perceptions of the city and neighborhood, environmental influences on behavior, measurement, density and overcrowding, urban design, urban form, relocation and the journey to work, territory and personal space, noise, and landscape preferences.

975   Chang, Diana. SOCIAL AND PSYCHOLOGICAL ASPECTS OF HOUSING, A REVIEW OF THE LITERATURE. Exhange Bibliography no. 557. Monticello, Ill.: Council of Planning Librarians, 1974. 20 p.

976   Hollander, Arnold Peter. HIGH DENSITY ENVIRONMENTS: SOME
       CULTURAL, PHYSIOLOGICAL AND PSYCHOLOGICAL CONSIDERA-
       TIONS--AN ANNOTATED BIBLIOGRAPHY. Exchange Bibliography
       no. 221. Monticello, Ill.: Council of Planning Librarians, 1971.
       34 p.

977   Jenkins, Thomas H., and Fouty, Lon. SOCIAL FACTORS AND EN-
       VIRONMENTAL DESIGN: RECIPROCAL RELATIONS OF SOCIETY
       AND MAN-MADE ENVIRONMENT. Exchange Bibliography no. 1511.
       Monticello, Ill.: Council of Planning Librarians, 1978. 41 p.

978   Sanoff, Henry, and Burgwyn, Henry. SOCIAL IMPLICATIONS OF THE
       PHYSICAL ENVIRONMENT WITH PARTICULAR EMPHASIS ON HOUS-
       ING AND NEIGHBORHOOD CHARACTERISTICS: A BIBLIOGRAPHY.
       Exchange Bibliography no. 145. Monticello, Ill.: Council of Planning
       Librarians, 1970. 16 p.

2. Books and Articles

979   Archea, John, and Eastman, Charles, eds. EDRA 2: PROCEEDINGS
       OF THE SECOND ANNUAL ENVIRONMENTAL DESIGN RESEARCH
       ASSOCIATION CONFERENCE. Stroudsburg, Pa.: Dowden, Hutchin-
       son and Ross, 1970. xi, 399 p. Illus.

       Research which is considered to be outstanding in the field of
       environmental design is presented. Topics of the forty papers
       range from measurement of response to buildings, environ-
       mental preferences, and evaluation of architectural determi-
       nants of satisfaction or dissatisfaction, to design for behavior,
       urban systems planning theory, and computer-aided design.

980   ARCHITECTURE FOR HUMAN BEHAVIOR: COLLECTED PAPERS FROM
       A MINI-CONFERENCE. Philadelphia: American Institute of Archi-
       tects, 1971. 81 p. Illus., bibliog.

       Exposure to the complex relationships between the built en-
       vironment and human behavior is provided by participants, who
       attempt to merge the information produced in the field of
       environmental psychology with the changing social values of
       architecture and planning professionals. Topics considered
       are research in environmental psychology, fitting architecture
       to behavior, values related to planning for the nonpaying
       client, institutional buildings, and behavioral observation in
       a high-technology undersea habitat.

981   Baum, Andrew, and Valins, Stuart. ARCHITECTURE AND SOCIAL
       BEHAVIOR: PSYCHOLOGICAL STUDIES OF SOCIAL DENSITY. Hills-
       dale, N.J.: Lawrence Erlbaum Associates, 1977. ix, 112 p. Illus.,
       graphs, bibliog.

The relationship between architectural design and social density, that is, crowding behavior, is studied through research in dormitory settings. Interior design variables which arrange space and social resources are seen to affect quality of life. Through analysis of the impacts of settings on group phenomena and social experience, the authors attempt to develop generalizations which will aid in the development of building environments congruent with human needs.

982   Carson, Daniel H., ed. MAN-ENVIRONMENT INTERACTIONS: EVALUATIONS AND APPLICATIONS. PROCEEDINGS OF EDRA 5. 3 vols. Stroudsburg, Pa.: Dowden, Hutchinson and Ross, 1974. 198 p., 288 p., 211 p. Illus., bibliog.

The large collection of contributed essays is arranged under such chapter headings as social impact assessment, human factors in architectural design, privacy, computers and architecture, cognition and perception, and "childhood city." Essays narrow the focus to specific topics including the social effects of nuclear power plants and stripmining, architectural design for crime prevention, alienation from urban environments, and design of playgrounds and day-care facilities. A valuable collection.

983   Conway, Donald, ed. HUMAN RESPONSE TO TALL BUILDINGS. Stroudsburg, Pa.: Dowden, Hutchinson and Ross, 1977. xii, 362 p. Illus.

Empirical research on the impact of tall buildings on surrounding environments and on inhabitants or users is herein gathered. Three major areas are addressed: the effect of tall buildings on immediate surroundings and the community; the viability of tall buildings for children, working adults, and the elderly; and responses to emergencies in high-rise structures by people and the buildings themselves.

984   Deasy, C.M. DESIGN FOR HUMAN AFFAIRS. New York: John Wiley and Sons, 1974. 183 p. Illus., bibliog.

A practicing architect explores results of the merger between behavioral scientists and architects--"behavior-based design." Deasy demonstrates conventional concepts of the design and planning professions that create behavior problems and reports research and procedures that consider or demonstrate how actions and attitudes are influenced by surroundings. Projects produced by his own firm are utilized as examples.

985   Dubos, René. SO HUMAN AN ANIMAL. New York: Charles Scribner's Sons, 1968. xiv, 267 p. Bibliog.

How man's physical and mental characteristics are shaped by his surroundings and experiences is explored in this eloquent study. Dubos believes it is possible to "deal scientifically with the living experience of man" and he appeals for holism in the approach of science to man's problems. He considers not only interaction with natural surroundings but also with the technological world. The effects of buildings, cities, and urban social attitudes are emphasized.

986   "Environment and Culture." ARTS IN SOCIETY 9, no. 1 (1972): 1-144.

An attempt to define an environmental aesthetic for the urban industrial environment is the aim of this issue. Urban design with environmental psychology in view is the concern of Gyorgy Kepes, Edmund N. Bacon, and Louis I. Kahn. The effect of urban environmental factors on man's attitudes is discussed by Robert Ginsberg and Olgerts Puravs. Aesthetics is discussed by Willis H. Truitt, Ihab Hassan, John Burchard, and Rudolf Arnheim.

987   Ewald, William R., ed. ENVIRONMENT FOR MAN: THE NEXT FIFTY YEARS. Bloomington: Indiana University Press, 1967. ix, 308 p. Illus.

The first volume of papers from the American Institute of Planners two-year consultation, "The Next Fifty Years 1967-2017," centers on "Optimum Environment With Man as Measure." Papers concern "the physiological, psychological, and sociological impact of the physical environment." Primarily considering cities, contributors such as René Dubos, John Dyckman, Christopher Alexander, William Wheaton, Stephen Carr, and Moshe Safdie discuss topics from planning, architecture, and Habitat '67 to urban social networks, politics, and the role of big business in shaping environments.

988   Griffin, William V.; Mauritzen, Joseph H.; and Kasmar, Joyce V. "The Psychological Aspects of the Architectural Environment: A Review." AMERICAN JOURNAL OF PSYCHIATRY 125 (February 1969): 1057-62.

The literature on the effect of the man-made environment on psychological and social behavior is reviewed. Studies related to experimentation with animals, effects of design and space on human behavior, and the influence of architecture in psychiatric hospitals are discussed.

989   Gutman, Robert, ed. PEOPLE AND BUILDINGS. New York: Basic Books, 1972. xix, 471 p. Illus., graphs, bibliog.

Studies by behavioral scientists and designers concerned with
the "behavioral science mold" focus on the effects of the design of the built environment on human psychology and social
activity. Articles deal with situations in which special and
other physical considerations have direct implications in regard to health, attitudes, and social interaction, i.e., the
design of a toilet, forced removal from an old neighborhood,
furniture arrangement as indicative of roles, effects of
aesthetic surroundings, dormitory rooms, privacy, and social
mechanisms of the city. Contributors include James Fitch,
Abraham Maslow, Thorstein Veblen, and Alexander Kira.
Extensive annotated bibliography.

990   Heilweil, Martin, ed. "Student Housing, Architecture, and Social
       Behavior." ENVIRONMENT AND BEHAVIOR 5 (December 1973):
       375-513.

       The interaction of architecture with behavior in student
       dormitories is investigated in this special issue. A review
       article is followed by three studies of suite structure, a con-
       sideration of crowding, a report on student-built polyurethane
       foam dome-shaped housing, and a reminder of the need for
       low-cost minimal housing. The focus on suites reveals a
       trend toward "smallness, intimacy, and support," and a move
       away from competition, independence, and intellectuality.

991   Heimsath, Clovis. BEHAVIORAL ARCHITECTURE: TOWARD AN
       ACCOUNTABLE DESIGN PROCESS. New York: McGraw-Hill, 1977.
       x, 203 p. Illus., bibliog.

       Environmental psychology, social behavior patterns, and sys-
       tems are coordinated in order to present a new design method-
       ology for architects and planners. The three sections of this
       study deal with the problems in the current state of the art
       of design; issues related to behavior, systems and buildings;
       and techniques available for implementing behavioral design.

992   Holahan, Charles J. ENVIRONMENT AND BEHAVIOR: A DYNAMIC
       PERSPECTIVE. New York: Plenum Press, 1978. xvi, 188 p. Graphs,
       bibliog.

       A text for students of environment and behavior focuses on
       the "dynamic perspective," that is, the positive and adaptive
       ways in which people cope with environments. Three sections
       examine distinct reaction processes. "Environmental coping"
       is illustrated by studying how people deal with environmental
       challenges in a public housing project, a high-rise dorm, a
       psychiatric ward. "Social accommodation" is exemplified by
       reactions to negative impacts in a hospital and urban setting.
       The imposition of personal meaning, "environmental schematiza-
       tion," is discussed through examples of sex differences in en-
       vironmental perception, and errors in cognitive mapping.

993 Ittelson, William H., ed. ENVIRONMENT AND COGNITION. New York: Seminar Press, 1973. xii, 187 p. Illus.

Psychologists, geographers, and architects approach the problems of environmental perception and cognition with interdisciplinary perspectives. Modes of psychological inquiry integrate the studies. Theoretical considerations of human spatial behavior and projective techniques in geographic research accompany analyses of the effect of the architecture of Las Vegas; the design of hospital facilities; and perceptions of cities, highways, and natural environments.

994 Kates, R.W., and Wohlwill, J.F., eds. "Man's Response to the Physical Environment." JOURNAL OF SOCIAL ISSUES 22 (October 1966): 1-140.

Three major themes are addressed: the impact of man's behavior on the stimulus properties of the environment, adaptation, and man's use of and conception of space. Contrasting opinions are held by the contributors. A.E. Parr suggests that cities lack stimulating visual interest, while Julian Wolpert implies that they possess too much. Concluding papers consider planning implications of studies of human behavior from architectural programming to wilderness policy.

995 Lang, Jon, et al., eds. DESIGNING FOR HUMAN BEHAVIOR: ARCHITECTURE AND THE BEHAVIORAL SCIENCES. Stroudsburg, Pa.: Dowden, Hutchinson and Ross, 1974. xiii, 354 p. Illus., bibliog.

Changes in architectural philosophy which embrace the field of environmental psychology are documented and considered. Realizations that traditional architectural theory and a reliance on "sensitivity" are inadequate to produce enjoyable environments are followed by papers relating the processes of environmental psychology to architecture. The methodological contribution of the behavioral sciences to architectural programming and evaluation is the subject of the third section. Specific topics include personal space, light, the house, group dynamics, surveys, and building evaluation.

996 Leonard, Michael. "Humanizing Space." PROGRESSIVE ARCHITECTURE 50 (April 1969): 128-33.

Architecture has psychological effects on man and influences his physical actions. For example, man reacts to openness or enclosure by degrees of muscular tension, gestures of excitement or depression; and buildings without obvious centers impart a negative lack of orientation on inhabitants. An observer interacts most completely with surrounding space when enclosure elements are implied rather than physically stated. The shaping of space can also foster or discourage activities which influence relationships. The architect can learn much about the dynamics of movement from the dancer.

997   Mehrabian, Albert, and Russell, James A. AN APPROACH TO ENVI-
RONMENTAL PSYCHOLOGY. Cambridge: M.I.T. Press, 1974. xii,
266 p. Bibliog.

Through a developed theoretical approach, the field of environmental psychology is defined. Human emotional responses are
linked to the environment and to the behaviors elicited. The
effects of stimulus components in the environment on basic
emotional responses are the basis of the study. Chapters focus
on the emotional impact of environments, sources of emotion,
interrelations between internal and external stimulus components, and approach-avoidance behavior. The reader needs
familiarity with psychological research methods.

998   Moore, Gary T., and Golledge, Reginald G., eds. ENVIRONMEN-
TAL KNOWING: THEORIES RESEARCH, AND METHODS. Strouds-
burg, Pa.: Dowden, Hutchinson and Ross, 1976. xxii, 442 p.
Illus., bibliog.

Centered on theory and research, the studies in this volume
concern the reactions of people to the natural and built
environments. Theories and methodologies from scientific,
humanistic, and behavioral disciplines are used to assist in
the understanding of the interchange between person, social
group, and spatial environment. Environmental "cognition"
or "knowing" is what individuals believe about the sociopolitical environment. Studies work with theories of information
processing, personal construct, and development. Extensive
bibliography.

999   Moos, Rudolf H. THE HUMAN CONTEXT: ENVIRONMENTAL DETER-
MINANTS OF BEHAVIOR. New York: John Wiley and Sons, 1976.
xiv, 444 p.

Existing knowledge about environmental influences on behavior
is integrated in this study. Moos considers how people shape
environments as well as how environments mold behavior. The
four parts present an historical overview of scholarship: the
impact of natural and man-made physical environments, including such factors as weather, architecture, population, crowding, noise and air pollution; the social setting; organizational
structure, types of people, and human ecology; and a discussion of the value of utopias as models for coping with or
changing the environment.

1000   Perin, Constance. WITH MAN IN MIND: AN INTERDISCIPLINARY
PROSPECTUS FOR ENVIRONMENTAL DESIGN. Cambridge: M.I.T.
Press, 1970. 185 p. Illus., bibliog.

Interdisciplinary connections between the human sciences and
environmental design are developed. Perin hopes to move
social and behavioral scientists toward awareness and involve-

ment in the human properties of the physical environment.
Architects, planners, and developers have proceeded too long
without adequate understanding of the people inhabiting their
buildings and neighborhoods. Assessment of limitations of the
current state of the art of environmental design is followed
by an analysis of possible collaboration and opportunities in
research. Extensive bibliography.

1001 Proshansky, Harold M.; Ittelson, William H.; and Rivlin, Leanne G.
ENVIRONMENTAL PSYCHOLOGY: MAN AND HIS PHYSICAL SET-
TING. New York: Holt, Rinehart and Winston, 1970. xi, 690 p.
Illus., bibliog.

Designed to "define and establish" the field of environmental
psychology, this extensive volume of readings draws from the
writings of psychologists, sociologists, anthropologists, architects, urban planners, geographers, and designers. Introductions to each of the six parts integrate diverse materials.
Major topic areas are theory, research methods, psychological
processes, individual needs, social institutions, and environmental planning.

1002 Sanoff, Henry, and Cohn, Sidney, eds. EDRA 1: PROCEEDINGS OF
THE FIRST ANNUAL ENVIRONMENTAL DESIGN RESEARCH ASSOCIA-
TION CONFERENCE. Stroudsburg, Pa.: Dowden, Hutchinson and
Ross, 1970. xvii, 360 p. Illus.

Designed to facilitate collaboration between scientists and
environmental designers, the conference focuses on the development of parameters, models, and methodologies for the
discipline of environmental design. Papers are grouped under
topics such as attributes of the environment, environmental
quality, methods for determining human response to the environment, models for planning, decision-making, and design
education.

1003 Stokols, Daniel. PERSPECTIVES ON ENVIRONMENT AND BEHAVIOR:
THEORY, RESEARCH, AND APPLICATIONS. New York: Plenum
Press, 1977. xiv, 360 p. Illus.

Attempting to define the field of environmental psychology,
the volume provides a historical overview of environmentally
oriented research in psychology; discusses the "theoretical
underpinnings and methodological strategies" of such research;
and presents reviews of the literature, empirical developments,
and future trends in the field. Existing research on response
to crowding and noise, environmental simulation, and applications of behavioral research to architecture and urban planning
are discussed.

1004 Van der Ryn, Sim, and Silverstein, Murray. DORMS AT BERKELEY:
AN ENVIRONMENTAL ANALYSIS. New York: Educational Facilities

Laboratories, 1967. 89 p. Illus.

Studying the effect of the built environment on the user and inhabitant, the authors evaluate activities and processes within the dormitory setting and determine the influence of design decisions. Rather than quantitative building standards, the report represents a functional critique of student high-rise housing at Berkeley. Research methods employed were observation, interview, questionnaire, student log, and literature search.

Part 9

EDUCATION

A. EDUCATIONAL TECHNOLOGY

1005 Ashby, Eric. ADAPTING UNIVERSITIES TO A TECHNOLOGICAL
SOCIETY. San Francisco: Jossey-Bass Publishers, 1974. xvi, 158 p.

According to Ashby, the West is at the eve of unprecedented
crisis for three reasons: lack of new resources, a damaging
philosophy of progress, and a realization of the limits to
growth. Education, he concludes, must lead the adjustment
to a steady-state world through training scientists and technologists to emphasize humanist concerns.

1006 Brickman, William W., and Lehrer, Stanley, eds. AUTOMATION,
EDUCATION AND HUMAN VALUES. New York: School and Society
Books, 1966. 419 p. Illus., bibliog.

The general question posed to contributors to this volume is
the humanistic implications for education of the pervasive
impact of technological change, particularly of the computer.
Educators, government officials, and noted scholars consider
larger relationships between man, his work and automation;
the meaning of automation for humanistic education; applications of technology to education; and the relation between
creativity and technology.

1007 Carnegie Commission on Higher Education: THE FOURTH REVOLUTION:
INSTRUCTIONAL TECHNOLOGY IN HIGHER EDUCATION; A REPORT
AND RECOMMENDATIONS. New York: McGraw-Hill, 1972. ix,
106 p.

The "fourth revolution," as defined by Eric Ashby, consists of
developments in electronics, particularly radio, video, and
computing. Convinced that a significant portion of higher
education will be conducted by means of information technology by the year 2000, Commission delegates review and critique pertinent developments in instructional technology.

Specific recommendations are made urging the development of materials, encouragement of faculty who produce them, and the establishment of media centers. Goals for 1980, 1990, and 2000 are suggested.

1008   Davies, Ivor Kevin, ed. CONTRIBUTIONS TO AN EDUCATIONAL TECHNOLOGY. New York: Crane, Russak, 1972. 294 p. Illus.

The term "educational technology" has two distinct meanings, both addressed by articles in this volume: the application of technology to instructional processes, i.e., hardware, and the application of scientific or psychological principles to instruction. Authors in the first section, who include B.F. Skinner and R.M. Gagné, seek a theoretical basis for educational technology. Other sections study current techniques, applications, and evaluation methods.

1009   DeCecco, John, ed. EDUCATIONAL TECHNOLOGY. New York: Holt, Rinehart and Winston, 1964. 479 p.

Two developments in programmed instruction are addressed: Skinner's model of operant conditioning, and programmed instruction as part of educational technology. Theoretical discussions by psychologists and educators emphasize relations between the psychology of learning and practical applications. Major techniques and devices are also introduced. Supplementing the volume is a glossary of teaching machine terms.

1010   Evans, Luther, and Arnstein, George, eds. AUTOMATION AND THE CHALLENGE TO EDUCATION. Washington, D.C.: National Education Association, 1962. x, 190 p.

As part of a larger study of the educational implications of automation, contributors to this symposium take different sides on the meeting's theme. The hypothesis debated is, "automation will continue to be introduced, with gains in productivity and a shorter work week," time that could be captured by educators for expanding the trained labor force and enlarging leisure horizons. Contributors number business people, social scientists, labor officials, and educators.

1011   Feinberg, William, and Rosemont, Henry, Jr., eds. WORK, TECHNOLOGY AND EDUCATION. Urbana: University of Illinois Press, 1975. 222 p.

The editors' thesis is that education has succeeded all too well in transforming the young into dutiful and compliant members of a conformist, corporate, technological society, in which imagination is not prized. Articles included in this volume share this viewpoint. The role of technology is considered in three papers: Kenneth D. Benne, "Technology and Community: Conflicting Bases of Educational Authority"; Max Wartofsky, "Art and Technology: Conflicting Models of Education?"; and Don Ihde, "A Phenomenology of Man-Machine Relations."

1012   Frankel, Charles. "Education and Telecommunications." JOURNAL OF HIGHER EDUCATION 41 (January 1970): 1-15.

The introduction of technology in the educational setting has evoked two stereotypic responses: fear and resentment, or a love of novelty for its own sake. Technology will never solve some needs of education, such as the need for personal attention. But technology does have a role in education, Frankel asserts, if only to acquaint students with its potential and to facilitate educational resource sharing.

1013   Goldberg, Maxwell H. "The Impact of Technological Change on the Humanities." EDUCATIONAL RECORD 46 (Fall 1965): 389-99.

Technology has triggered the imagination of those involved in humanities disciplines. The humanities offer to the technologist a structured imagination, a sense of wholeness, and a forum for discussion of ethics. The author calls upon scholars to reassess the boundaries of their disciplines and to encourage what could be a healthy cross-fertilization.

1014   Goshen, Charles E. "Humanizing Education through Technology." ENGINEERING EDUCATION 61 (November 1970): 133-38.

In a summary report on the Conference on Humanizing Education Through Technology, Goshen emphasizes the holistic view of the teaching-learning system developed by participants. Educational technology is deemed valuable only to the extent that it can serve to humanize education. Specific guidelines for appropriate uses are developed.

1015   Grayson, Lawrence P. "Education, Technology and Individual Privacy." EDUCATIONAL COMMUNICATION AND TECHNOLOGY 26 (Fall 1978): 195-206.

Modern technology offers increased opportunities for educational delivery, through individual instruction or widely beamed satellite transmission. But there are drawbacks, reminds Grayson. Educational privacy, an essential element, can be disrupted technologically through improper use of student records, surveillance of student or teacher behavior, or abuse of developing behavior modification techniques. The need to preserve privacy is stressed.

1016 _____. "Educational Satellites: A Goal or a Gaol?" IEEE TRANS-
ACTION ON EDUCATION E 19 (May 1976): 38-45.

Communication satellites may serve as a vehicle for providing
high-quality education to currently isolated populations.
However, Grayson warns, it is important to consider the
potentially detrimental political or cultural effects of such
broadcasts. Dealing with cultural, ethnic, and ethical
differences will require diversity in program content. The
challenge will be to accommodate such differences while
keeping costs low enough to ensure wide availability of educational opportunity.

1017 _____. "Instructional Technology: On Diversity in Education."
AV COMMUNICATIONS REVIEW 24 (Summer 1976): 117-34.

In the educational field, instructional technology was at first
conceptualized as a mere supplement to the teacher's lecture.
Now it is viewed as an essential part of a total systems
approach to education that will encourage uniformity in instructional content and method. Such uniformity, in Grayson's
opinion, is a serious threat to the diversity and freedom vital
to the educational process.

1018 Heinich, Robert. TECHNOLOGY AND THE MANAGEMENT OF
INSTRUCTION. Washington, D.C.: Association for Educational Communications and Technology, 1970. 198 p. Illus., bibliog.

Thomas Kuhn's model of scientific revolutions, Heinich contends, is applicable to nonscientific fields as well. Because
of technological advances, an anomaly exists in education
that can only be resolved through arriving at new paradigms.
Emerging technologies of education must not be conceived
and managed as extensions of traditional teaching methods.

1019 Hencley, Stephen P. FUTURISM IN EDUCATION: METHODOLOGIES.
Berkeley, Calif.: McCutchan Publishing Corp., 1974. xii, 510 p.
Illus., bibliog.

The study of the future and the development of appropriate
methodologies has been characterized by a dominant interest
in industrial fields. This volume assesses futurist methods
and their appropriate application to problems in education.
Methods reviewed range from force analysis and impact
matrices to Delphi forecasting and technology assessment.
Appendixes clarify the technical material. A glossary is also
included.

1020 Hoban, Charles F. "Educational Technology and Human Values." AV
COMMUNICATIONS REVIEW 25 (Fall 1977): 221-42.

Of the two classes of technology, physical and social, the latter is viewed by the author as more dominant in the classroom and, to some extent, as a determinant of machine instructional technology. A review of the place of values in the classroom and in educational technology leads to the following conclusion: "A symbiotic relationship exists between educational technology and values and in this symbiosis human values should be invariably transcendent."

1021 Hostrop, Richard W., ed. FOUNDATIONS OF FUTUROLOGY IN EDUCATION. Homewood, Ill.: ETC Publications, 1973. vi, 249 p.

Brief undocumented papers, reprinted from a number of sources, introduce basic forecasting techniques and major conceptual views of the future to educational practitioners. The volume includes contributions by Alvin Toffler, Robert Theobald, and Willis W. Harman, along with discussions of such techniques as Delphi forecasting. Speculations about the future of education focus on perceived trends toward increasingly individual, innovative and broad-based instruction.

1022 Klinge, Peter L., ed. AMERICAN EDUCATION IN THE ELECTRIC AGE: NEW PERSPECTIVES IN MEDIA AND LEARNING. Englewood Cliffs, N.J.: Educational Technology Publications, 1974. xv, 203 p.

Composed of original articles and restructured interviews, this text seeks to examine the role of mass media in the educational process. Authors including Alvin Toffler, Charles E. Silberman, and Herbert J. Gans reflect on the media as educational tool and institution, and as extracurricular mindmanipulator. Several articles evaluate the relatively recent impact of public broadcasting.

1023 Kvale, Steinar. "The Psychology of Learning as Ideology and Technology." BEHAVIORISM 4 (Spring 1976): 97-116.

From those areas in which theoretical advances in the psychology of learning have been greatest, Kvale contends, few practical applications have been derived. It is the less theoretical work of such researchers as B.F. Skinner that has had the largest impact on the practice of teaching. Learning theories have served, nevertheless, the ideological function of making a technological approach to learning acceptable and inevitable.

1024 Lumsdaine, A.A., and Glaser, Robert, eds. TEACHING MACHINES AND PROGRAMMED LEARNING: A SOURCE BOOK. Washington, D.C.: National Education Association, 1960. xii, 724 p. Bibliog.

Though old, this volume remains a useful source on teaching machines and associated instructional techniques. Two review

papers provide an overview of the field. These are followed
by original papers that serve as a guide to historical developments. Stress is placed on the seminal work of such figures
as Sidney L. Pressey and B.F. Skinner. Lengthy bibliographical appendixes supplement the collection.

1025   Oettinger, Anthony G. RUN, COMPUTER, RUN: THE MYTHOLOGY
       OF EDUCATIONAL INNOVATION. Harvard Studies in Technology
       and Society. Cambridge, Mass.: Harvard University Press, 1969.
       xx, 302 p. Bibliog.

       From a critical evaluation of the effectiveness of technological
       tools as teaching devices, Oettinger concludes that computers
       and audiovisual equipment will not solve contemporary educa-
       tional problems. Major institutional change is needed, he
       states, that will encourage experimentation and flexibility in
       the stolid schools. This must be accomplished before new
       technological devices can be used advantageously.

1026   Piele, Philip K., and Eidell, Terry L., eds. SOCIAL AND TECHNOL-
       OGICAL CHANGE: IMPLICATIONS FOR EDUCATION. Eugene,
       Oreg.: Center for the Advanced Study of Educational Administration,
       1970. xv, 333 p.

       State-of-the-art papers cover the educational implications of
       social and technological change in America. Willis W.
       Harman, making general predictions about the future, con-
       cludes that educators will have to adapt to one of two social
       configurations: the "person-oriented society" or the "second-
       phase industrial society." Also reviewed are systems approaches
       to educational planning and the educational relevance of de-
       velopments in information processing.

1027   Pula, Fred John, and Goff, Robert J., eds. TECHNOLOGY IN EDU-
       CATION: CHALLENGE AND CHANGE. Worthington, Ohio:
       Charles A. Jones Publishing Co., 1972. x, 262 p.

       These essays provide a basis for understanding the potential
       role of technology in education. A discussion of pertinent
       learning and communications theories leads into papers con-
       cerned with selection, integration, and uses of media mate-
       rials and equipment. Educational, social, and psychological
       ramifications are considered. Contributors include Ralph W.
       Tyler, Robert Gagné, and Robert Heinich.

1028   Pulliam, John D., and Bowman, Jim R. EDUCATIONAL FUTURISM:
       IN PURSUANCE OF SURVIVAL. Norman: University of Oklahoma
       Press, 1974. viii, 164 p. Bibliog.

       Main tenets of futurism and the global problems that must be
       faced are succinctly set forth. Appropriate directions for edu-

cation are suggested that will lead to "lifelong synergistic education." The authors feel that change is urgent and overdue: "If political and economic institutions are not ready for the future, the schools are not ready for the present, much less the future."

1029   Rossi, Peter H., and Biddle, Bruce J., eds. THE NEW MEDIA AND EDUCATION: THEIR IMPACT ON SOCIETY. Chicago: Aldine Publishing Co., 1966. x, 417 p. Bibliog.

Essays speculate on the roles that may be played by new educational media of the next few decades. Following a recount of recent and projected developments in instructional media, including simulation devices, games, teaching machines, and programmed instruction, the impact of such devices on school and society is assessed.

1030   Schon, Donald A. BEYOND THE STABLE STATE: PUBLIC AND PRIVATE LEARNING IN A CHANGING SOCIETY. New York: Random House, 1971. 254 p. Illus.

While continuing transformation has become the central fact of modern life, learning has become the principal skill. Social institutions must become effective "learning systems," Schon believes, and capable of leading creative adaptation.

1031   Skinner, B.F. "Teaching Machines." SCIENCE 128 (24 October 1958): 969-77.

A brief sketch of the development of teaching machines stresses the advantages of the machine tutor: constant interchange between program and student, step-by-step learning, and immediate reinforcement. Examples of programs are provided, with a discussion of the difficulties encountered in composing them. Skinner concludes that teaching machines will supplement but never replace human teachers.

1032   _____. THE TECHNOLOGY OF TEACHING. New York: Appleton-Century-Crofts, 1968. ix, 271 p. Illus., bibliog.

Schools are failing to provide proper reinforcement in the learning process, reinforcement that can be provided through the use of teaching machines. Such machines will not displace, but will supplement teachers' efforts, maximizing the human relation between teacher and student while minimizing the need for such aversive stimuli as corporal punishment and lack of individual attention. Types of teaching machines and appropriate uses are described.

1033   "Symposium on the Application of Technology to Education." ENGI-

NEERING EDUCATION 59 (February 1969): 471-514.

Eleven brief papers have been selected from those presented at a symposium sponsored by the American Society for Engineering Education. Three topics are discussed: the role of computers in education, systems analysis in education, and managing change. Both hardware and software aspects receive attention.

1034   Toffler, Alvin, ed. LEARNING FOR TOMORROW: THE ROLE OF THE FUTURE IN EDUCATION. New York: Vintage Books, 1974. xxvi, 421 p.

Eighteen noted psychologists, educators, futurists, humanists, and other social scientists discuss the integration of a future consciousness into the learning process. Specific topics addressed include the psychology of the future, the future-view of the black child, the place of futures in the curriculum, and teaching methods, including games, simulations, and science fiction. Sample syllabi and a directory of futures studies serve as supplements.

1035   Tyler, I. Keith, and Williams, Catherine M., eds. EDUCATIONAL COMMUNICATION IN A REVOLUTIONARY AGE. Worthington, Ohio: Charles A. Jones Publishing Co., 1973. 150 p.

In a volume dedicated to Edgar Dale, a major figure in the field, numerous implications of technology for education are discussed. Robert J. Havighurst suggests that a revolution in education will be concomitant with three other revolutions: in politics, economics, and communications. William Pearson writes on educational film, Mitjoi Nishimoto on the potential for broadcast college education, and Ralph Tyler on improvements in evaluation.

1036   U.S. National Commission on Technology, Automation and Economic Progress. TECHNOLOGY AND THE AMERICAN ECONOMY. Appendix Vol. 4: EDUCATIONAL IMPLICATIONS OF TECHNOLOGICAL CHANGE. Washington, D.C.: 1966. v, 151 p. Y3.T22:2T22/app/ IV.

Three studies treating the educational implications of technological change are presented. Don D. Bushnell and others review computer applications in education. Karl L. Zinn more narrowly specifies appropriate systems for computer-aided instruction. A broad state-of-the art review of the emerging technology of education by James D. Finn concludes the first part. Part 2 of the appendix volume offers specific proposals for government action.

1037   Witt, Paul W.F., ed. TECHNOLOGY AND THE CURRICULUM. New

York: Teacher's College Press, 1968. 147 p.

Originally presented at a curriculum conference held at Columbia University, these nine papers are concerned with the demands placed on education by the technological establishment. Alice Mary Hilton discusses the general impact of cybernetics on society. Eli Ginzberg and Robert E. Slaughter assess changing requirements placed by industry on educational systems. Remaining articles treat the development of educational technology and training of specialists in the field.

B. ENGINEERING AND TECHNICAL EDUCATION

1038   Chen, Kan. "Exploring New Directions for Engineering Education." ENGINEERING EDUCATION 63 (November 1972): 128-31.

New directions for engineering education are discussed in relation to projected societal trends and changing university structures. The advent of a "person-oriented" society will require the increasing use of technology for fulfilling diverse human needs. Engineering education, and indeed the entire future university, should be devoted to sociotechnological engineering. Chen provides suggestions for appropriate changes in curriculum.

1039   Davenport, William H. "Engineering and the Applied Humanities: The Recent Past." TECHNOLOGY AND SOCIETY 5 (July 1969): 24-32.

As technology grew more complex following World War II, it became apparent that engineering as a discipline had to undergo modification. Early attempts to make curriculum changes added no more than "thin veneers of culture," in the form of humanities and social science distribution requirements. Davenport presents criteria for setting up a humanities and social science "stem" for engineers that will prove viable, revolving around engineering history, a sizable humanities component, with an applied bent, and encouragement of creativity and continuing education.

1040   DeSimone, Daniel V. "Education for Innovation." IEEE SPECTRUM 5 (January 1968): 83-89.

Innovation and invention are the "business of engineering." Creativity should be stimulated by engineering education. The computer, in removing the tedium of calculation, has released time for students to develop creative powers. Engineering education, according to DeSimone, should "encourage students to strive for the mastery of fundamentals, the discovery of the relatedness of things and the cultivation of excellence."

1041 _____, ed. EDUCATION FOR INNOVATION. Oxford: Pergamon Press, 1968. ix, 180 p.

Papers from a conference sponsored by several government agencies examine the processes of invention and innovation, exploring means for encouraging creativity in engineering education. Contributors include a number of noted engineering educators.

1042 Douglas, Paul H. AMERICAN APPRENTICESHIP AND INDUSTRIAL EDUCATION. New York: Columbia University Press, 1961. Reprint. New York: AMS Press, 1968. 348 p. Bibliog.

The decline of the apprenticeship system lent especial importance to the industrial education movement of the 1910s and early 1920s. Douglas suggests a complex scheme of educational reform to fit the needs of both industry and the individual. He is particularly adamant about the need for lengthened compulsory schooling, on-the-job training, and improved pay for instructors in the industrial arts.

1043 "Engineering Education. . .Impact on Life." ENGINEERING EDUCATION 63 (May 1973): 567-91.

Six articles discuss the larger social context of engineering and of engineering education. John W. Davis reviews technology assessment, while Dorothy Nelkin recounts the controversial history of the civilian industrial technology program (CITP). The humanist's view as provided by William A. Marra is supplemented by George Bugliarello's concept of engineering as "sociotechnology." Applications of engineering to problems encountered in suburban and inner-city areas serve as case studies.

1044 Fisher, Berenice M. INDUSTRIAL EDUCATION: AMERICAN IDEALS AND INSTITUTIONS. Madison: University of Wisconsin Press, 1967. xiv, 267 p.

This historical and sociological study of industrial education begins with the pre-Civil War era, when such instruction was viewed as a remedy for crime and vagrancy and as a means of support for the flagging independent artisan. After the Civil War, industrial education was institutionalized in two forms: as professional training for engineers and as manual training in trade and public schools. Fisher follows the twentieth-century changes in manual training, noting its constant reorientation to suit the needs of industry and the status requirements of society.

1045 Florman, Samuel C. ENGINEERING AND THE LIBERAL ARTS: A TECHNOLOGIST'S GUIDE TO HISTORY, LITERATURE, PHILOSOPHY,

ART, AND MUSIC. New York: McGraw-Hill, 1968. x, 278 p.
Bibliog.

Designed to promote and assist education in the liberal arts
for engineers, Florman's guide consists of broad outlines of the
content of humanistic disciplines. The humanities are approached as interdisciplinary bridges between the two cultures;
thus Florman explores the history of technology, the engineer
in fiction, philosophy of science, utility as related to beauty,
and sound, as well as literature, philosophy, art, and music
in general. Each chapter includes recommended reading
(and viewing, listening).

1046 Grayson, Lawrence P., and Biedenbach, Joseph M. FRONTIERS IN
EDUCATION CONFERENCE, 5TH, GEORGIA INSTITUTE OF TECHNOL-
OGY, 1975. PROCEEDINGS. New York: IEEE, 1975. xx, 428 p.

The future of engineering education and recent innovations in
instruction, from teaching modules to industrial internships,
are surveyed in numerous brief papers. Section 4.2 studies
the "humanities-engineering bridge," reviewing diverse interactions from policy to music. The engineer's role in technology assessment is analyzed in the following section.

1047 Hertz, David. "The Technological Imperative--Social Implications of
Professional Technology." ANNALS OF THE AMERICAN ACADEMY
OF POLITICAL AND SOCIAL SCIENCE 389 (May 1970): 95-106.

Engineers and technologists have always been captains in the
struggle against nature. Their very success has engineered a
misplaced faith in the ability of technology to solve all problems, even those created by technology, Hertz states. A
new approach to technological development must be adopted
by engineers, one that involves technology assessments of a
new breadth. Training for this visionary role should begin
with a reconstructed engineering curriculum.

1048 Holloman, J. Herbert. "Modern Engineering and Society: The Marriage between Technical Ability and Social Needs." CHEMICAL AND
ENGINEERING NEWS 42 (29 June 1964): 66-71.

In contrast to those posed by the military-space world, problems involved in applying science and technology to the
"real" world are not technical at all but social, political,
and economic. Current four-year engineering curricula are
inadequate for dealing with the complexities of social problems.

1049 Lynn, Walter R. "Engineering and Society Programs in Engineering
Education." SCIENCE 195 (14 January 1977): 150-54.

Through striving to provide a strong analytical base, engineering educators have given insufficient attention to the professional development of the student. Particularly in design courses, Lynn stresses, it is important to emphasize the real-life context of engineering work. At present, humanities courses are too overspecialized and science-technology-society courses not well-enough integrated into the technical curriculum. Reform is needed.

1050 Massachusetts Institute of Technology. School of Engineering. Center for Policy Alternatives. FUTURE DIRECTIONS FOR ENGINEERING EDUCATION: SYSTEMS RESPONSES TO A CHANGING WORLD. Washington, D.C.: American Society for Engineering Education, 1975. 108 p. Illus., bibliog.

Changing social conditions, marked by economic stabilization, environmental concerns, and resource scarcity, have created a new environment for engineering education. Engineering students retain their generally authoritative, activity-oriented, upwardly mobile character, a character incompatible with the requirements of an ambiguous, complex society. Ways of altering this outlook include more design coursework, clinical and academic exposures, and the enrollment of students from other fields in engineering programs.

1051 Pletta, Dan H. "Social Science Emphasis in Engineering Education." PROCEEDINGS OF THE AMERICAN SOCIETY OF CIVIL ENGINEERS 101, no. EI14 (October 1975): 509-19.

In current engineering curricula, greater emphasis is being placed on the social sciences in order to prepare graduates to communicate with experts from other fields. Examples of programs are cited and critically summarized. Pletta suggests that appropriately educated technical experts would become the logical candidates for leadership roles in industrial society.

1052 "Rounding Out the New Engineer." ENGINEERING EDUCATION 68 (April 1978): 721-34.

Brief articles discuss the desirable nonengineering components in engineering education. Stephen K. Huber, a lawyer, writes about the teaching of professional ethics, while James A. Kent suggests that the liberal arts component must be made more meaningful in the context of the professional aspirations of engineering students. Barry Hyman, in discussing the need to educate engineers in public policy issues, states that engineers have had, to date, too little, not too much, political power.

1053 Salvadori, M.G. "Social Concern and Engineering Education." CIVIL ENGINEERING 44 (June 1974): 70-73.

After two decades of militarily oriented work, Salvadori states, the engineer's new battle is against those technological forces that have been unleashed in the course of improving the American standard of living. The reorientation of the profession must begin in engineering schools, through the teaching of multidisciplinary "technology and society" courses and through interdisciplinary case-study ventures. Exemplary programs and courses are cited.

1054 Schrader, Charles R. "Engineering Education and a Professional Ethic." ASCE PROCEEDINGS 97, no. PP1 (October 1971): 147-52.

Though science and technology have much to offer society, the engineer must change in order to aid in their appropriate application. An awareness of the humanities and the social sciences is necessary to understanding social needs. The narrow disciplinary boundaries that now prevail in engineering schools must be eliminated in favor of a professional ethic aimed at the elimination of suffering.

1055 "Symposium: Technology for Man." TECHNOLOGY AND CULTURE 10 (January 1969): 1-19.

W.E. Howland presents the argument that engineering education, transformed through an infusion of the liberal arts, should prepare engineers for social leadership. Samuel Florman suggests, in response, that a well-constructed liberal arts curriculum might prove a more powerful stimulant to engineers than is generally realized. While James C. Wallace agrees with Howland in principle, he warns that such an education, badly administered, could lead to the creation of a dogmatic, pseudointellectual "ignoramus, of colossal size and major consequence."

1056 Tribus, Myron. THE THREE FACES OF TECHNOLOGY AND THE CHALLENGE TO ENGINEERING EDUCATION. Morgantown: College of Engineering, West Virginia University, 1975. 18 p. Illus.

The practice of engineering is portrayed as a cube with three faces. One face shows "-ics" (academics, scientific); one, "-ing" (managing, designing, doing); the third, "-tion," indicating needs of society to be served--nutrition, education, transportation, and so forth. Tribus suggests that engineers must be better educated to make decisions at the "-tion" face which they now would prefer to avoid.

1057 Woodbury, Robert S. "Science, Engineering and the Humanities." TECHNOLOGY REVIEW 61 (January 1959): 147-49, 154, 156.

Faced with the expansion of scientific and engineering training which occurred after Sputnik, Woodbury pleads for the development of educated scientists and engineers rather than technicians. Technicians, he feels, exist in all fields, even history and literature. Rather than merely acquiring highly developed skills, an educated person recognizes the interrelations between his field and the whole. Studies in the history of science and engineering are recommended as effective bridges to an integrated education.

Part 10

TECHNOLOGY POLICY

A. OVERVIEWS

1. Bibliography

1058　Caldwell, Lynton K[eith]., ed.　SCIENCE, TECHNOLOGY AND PUBLIC POLICY: A SELECTED AND ANNOTATED BIBLIOGRAPHY. 3 vols.　Bloomington: Indiana University Press, 1968-70.　xi, 492; xii, 544; xii, 868 p.

> Excellent coverage is provided for books, monographs, government documents, and periodical articles on public affairs and public policies related to science and technology.　Volumes 1 and 2 cover the period 1945-67; volume 3, 1968-70.　Some coverage is also given to philosophy and history of science and technology, and to science, the humanities, and religion.

2. Books and Articles

1059　Baker, Robert F.; Michaels, Richard M.; and Preston, Everett S. PUBLIC POLICY DEVELOPMENT: LINKING THE TECHNICAL AND POLITICAL PROCESSES.　New York: John Wiley and Sons, 1975. xi, 315 p.

> In the past, technician and policymaker have frequently failed to communicate and to act jointly in the public interest.　Through a study of the relative roles of technologist and policymaker in the context of an overall review of the policymaking process, the authors hope to facilitate needed communications.　Case studies of highway safety, underground construction, and energy conservation illustrate more specific problems.

1060　Basiuk, Victor.　"The Impact of Technology in the Next Decades." ORBIS 14 (Spring 1970): 17-42.

> The unveiling of new technologies in the next twenty-five

years will have enormous political ramifications, most significant a decline in the deterministic effect of the location of natural resources as the technological resource base diversifies and moves away from fossil fuels. With this shift will dawn a truly global, geotechnical independent world marked by the growth of nonmilitary technology for social needs.

1061   Boyle, Godfrey; Elliott, David; and Roy, Robin, eds. THE POLITICS OF TECHNOLOGY. New York: Longman, 1977. xiv, 351 p. Bibliog.

A fine reader offers selections touching on many aspects of the question of control over technology. Specifically, sections address: social control; government control; public participation in technological decision-making; and decentralization and community technology. Contributors include Roger Williams, Barry Commoner, Hazel Henderson, Lawrence Tribe, Joseph Coates, and other noted writers. Concludes with a brief guide to the literature.

1062   Branscomb, Lewis M. "Taming Technology: A Plea for National Regulation in a Social Context." SCIENCE 171 (12 March 1971): 972-77.

The worry about technology stems from its complex, pervasive, elusive nature, and the fact that the individual seems removed from the technological decision making process. Power over technology is diffused through a number of institutions; the locus of decision making is difficult to discern. Yet somehow scientists must be included in the decision making process.

1063   Brooks, Harvey. THE GOVERNMENT OF SCIENCE. Cambridge: M.I.T. Press, 1968. vii, 343 p.

Papers written between 1960 and 1967 deal with various aspects of the relationship between science and government, with special attention to policymaking in the area of research support. The sweep is broad, from federal support of research in universities to the interplay of technology with the economy and with education.

1064   Carroll, James D. "Participatory Technology." SCIENCE 171 (19 February 1971): 647-53.

Because the public interest is substantially affected by technological choices, people should be included in the process of developing, implementing, and regulating technology. Carroll sees three possible means of involvement at present: lawsuits, technology assessments, and citizen's organizations.

1065   Carroll, James D., and Henry, Nicholas, eds. "Symposium on Knowl-
        edge Management." PUBLIC ADMINISTRATION REVIEW 35 (November-
        December 1975): 567-602.

>   Seven articles question whether man can "increase his under-
>   standing of how to develop, regulate and use knowledge more
>   effectively for the achievement of public values and objec-
>   tives." Three specific topics are considered: relationship be-
>   tween knowledge, society, and bureaucracy; implications of
>   knowledge management for public administration; and implica-
>   tions of knowledge management in relation to specific policy
>   and administrative developments. Contributors include Lynton K.
>   Caldwell, Nicholas Henry, James D. Carroll, George
>   Frederick Goerl, Bruce C. Gates, William Thomas Keating,
>   and Jerry McCaffrey.

1066   Chase, Edward T. "Politics and Technology." YALE REVIEW 52
        (March 1963): 321-39.

>   It is rapid technological change rather than ideology or
>   economics that now foments political crisis. The market
>   mechanism, though still an effective interpreter of public de-
>   sires, is no longer capable, in Chase's opinion, of conjuring
>   up the long-range values that should dictate the sensible use
>   of new technology. Recent thinking about the kind of politi-
>   cal controls that are necessary and possible is summarized.

1067   Dickson, David. "Technology and the Construction of Social Reality."
        RADICAL SCIENCE JOURNAL 1 (January 1974): 29-50. Revised
        version, DIALECTICAL ANTHROPOLOGY 1 (November 1975): 25-41.

>   Technology is a social institution encompassing both machines
>   and their users. Technological development is, at font, a
>   political process. In a capitalist society, Dickson believes,
>   it serves to reinforce the position of the dominant social
>   classes, though its political nature is disguised by the preva-
>   lent ideology of efficiency and competition.

1068   Elliott, David, and Elliott, Ruth. THE CONTROL OF TECHNOLOGY.
        New York: Springer-Verlag, 1976. xv, 241 p. Bibliog.

>   Developed from a course in the design and technology of
>   man-made futures, the authors discuss the forces which con-
>   trol the interaction of modern society and technology. It is
>   emphasized that man is not limited to a dichotomous choice
>   between an authoritarian, interdependent high technology and
>   a self-determining low technology. Some radical "blueprints"
>   for societies in which the application of technology is under
>   direct control are considered as well as the type of social and
>   economic structure which would foster advantageous control of
>   future technological advances.

1069   Etzioni, Amitai. "Agency for Technological Development for Domestic Programs." SCIENCE 164 (4 April 1969): 1-4.

In recent years, technology has aided in ameliorating some social problems, such as crime and drug rehabilitation. Etzioni proposes the establishment of an Agency for Technological Development (ATD) to coordinate and promote such efforts. The creation of such an agency would also reduce the waste and duplication of current, widely dispersed research and development efforts.

1070   Eulau, Heinz. TECHNOLOGY AND CIVILITY: THE SKILL REVOLUTION IN POLITICS. Stanford, Calif: Hoover Institution Press, 1977. xiv, 114 p.

Through collecting his previously published papers, Eulau conveys a coherent composite of his advocacy of representative government based on continuity of the past and the use of the civil politics of compromise. He is distrustful of com-com (computer-communications) engineers, the advocates of a technological fix, who obviate the democratic process.· But he is equally skeptical of the idea of participatory democracy and the irrational left. The ideal would be an incorporation of skill (expertise) as a credential for representative office.

1071   _____. "Technology and the Fear of the Politics of Civility." JOURNAL OF POLITICS 35 (May 1973): 367-85.

Writings on the effects of technology on society have displayed a leaning to hyperbole, as well as a tendency to deride "the politics of civility." Civil politics is defined as "the broad range of behavior patterns expressed by persuading, soliciting, consulting, advising, compromising, etc." The technologist views this process with impatience and distrust; the utopian despises its compromising and pragmatic quality. Nevertheless, the author believes, civil politics represents our best hope for proper use of technology.

1072   Ewald, William R., Jr., ed. ENVIRONMENT AND CHANGE: THE NEXT FIFTY YEARS. Bloomington: Indiana University Press, 1968. xvi, 397 p.

Resulting from the American Institute of Planners consultation, "The Next Fifty Years," this extensive anthology focuses on "The Future Environment of a Democracy." Contributors explore the values by which goals are set and the means available to achieve them and attempt to delineate priorities for a democratic society. Papers are grouped within four topics: creating the future environment; change; role of planning; and youth, technology, and the world. Prestigious authors include Herman Kahn, Anthony Wiener, Emmanuel Mesthene, Robert

Theobald, John Burchard, Gunnar Myrdal, David Bazelon, and R. Buckminster Fuller.

1073 _____. ENVIRONMENT AND POLICY: THE NEXT FIFTY YEARS. Bloomington: Indiana University Press, 1968. xiv, 459 p.

Designed to accompany ENVIRONMENT AND CHANGE (no. 1072), the contributors of studies included in this volume were asked to provide "explicit statements of policy and program" over a fifty-year time span in areas of importance to American life. Each paper is followed by two critiques. It is hoped that deliberately planned policies will promote more rationally structured environments. Problems considered include minorities, education, health services, leisure, cities, transportation, housing, natural resources, research, and national development policy.

1074 Ferkiss, Victor C. THE FUTURE OF TECHNOLOGICAL CIVILIZATION. New York: George Braziller, 1974. 369 p. Bibliog.

Ferkiss opens with a violent attack on liberalism, which he blames for making economic and technical growth the ultimate end of society. Liberalism has in the end proved an inadequate philosophy, in its failure to provide approaches to such problems as nonrenewable resources and persistent social inequity. Rejecting conservatism, anarchism, and "antipolitics," Ferkiss offers "ecological humanism," a political philosophy based on a balanced relationship with nature and an egalitarian social order.

1075 Ferry, Wilbur H. "Must We Rewrite the Constitution to Control Technology?" SATURDAY REVIEW 51 (2 March 1968): 50-54.

The regulation of technology has become the most important intellectual and political task on the American agenda. Particularly worrisome is the encroachment on privacy, pollution, and schools. The author calls for a revamping of government in order to direct technology, utilizing a constitutional amendment if necessary.

1076 Greenberg, Daniel S. THE POLITICS OF PURE SCIENCE. New York: New American Library, 1967. xiv, 303 p.

In this account of the scientific community's continuing quest for recognition and funding, Greenberg stresses the surge in federal interest brought about by World War II. To document the increasingly political nature of "pure" science, he details the history of three projects: the "Mohole" (a deep drilling into the earth), MURA (Midwestern University Research Association), and the SLAC (Stanford Linear Electron Accelerator).

1077   Haberer, Joseph, ed. SCIENCE AND TECHNOLOGY POLICY: PER-
        SPECTIVES AND DEVELOPMENTS. Lexington, Mass.: Lexington Books,
        1977. ix, 216 p.

        Haberer laments the fact that technology policy as a field of
        study has been the intellectual stepchild of the study of
        science policy. This volume represents a significant step to-
        ward independence. Part 1, "Perspectives in Science and
        Technology," is followed by "Developments in Technology
        Policy," part 2, which brings together papers on federal con-
        trols, foreign and regional policymaking, and appropriate
        technology. A third part reviews the "R and D" process in
        relation to policy concerns. Authors represented include
        Derek de Solla Price, Dorothy Nelkin, Edward Wenk, and
        Albert H. Teich. Most papers were previously published in
        POLICY STUDIES JOURNAL 5 (December 1976): 154-227.

1078   Hollomon, J.H[erbert]. "Technology Policy: The U.S. Picks its Way."
        IEEE SPECTRUM 7 (August 1972): 72-81.

        The need for new technology, the need to eliminate unde-
        sired effects of old technologies, and the need to cure the
        ills of technologically based businesses are three reasons
        Hollomon cites for a renewed interest in the development of
        an American science and technology policy. The relationship
        between government and technology offers, in his opinion,
        eight options for action ranging from laissez-faire to direct
        government measures to support high-risk ventures, improve
        technology transfer, and ameliorate undesirable consequences.

1079   Khozin, G.S. "Science and Technology: Ideology and Politics in
        the U.S.A." SOVIET STUDIES IN PHILOSOPHY 12 (Winter 1973-74):
        50-67.

        Khozin's critical examination of U.S. technology policy be-
        gins with the 1940s and 1950s. During those decades, sci-
        entific and technological advances were placed quickly at the
        service of the military. The space program of the sixties
        differed in its broadened military-civilian scope and emphasis
        on international cooperation. But the program failed to have
        the desired effect of stirring the public imagination, Khozin
        contends. Instead, it provoked an outcry for a more appro-
        priate use of such massive resources.

1080   Lambright, W. Henry. GOVERNING SCIENCE AND TECHNOLOGY.
        New York: Oxford University Press, 1976. xiii, 218 p.

        This study of the broad interaction of government with science
        and technology focuses on the key "technoscience agencies"
        of the executive branch, including NASA, ERDA, DOD, and
        NIH. The process through which science and technology pro-

grams are established, implemented, and terminated is followed, with an assessment of the role of technoscience agencies in each phase. Lambright concludes that while the inertia of such agencies may prove a positive virtue in accomplishing such long-range objectives as the moon-shot, only through a unified national policy can new programs be swiftly initiated and obsolete ones eliminated.

1081 Lapp, Ralph E. THE NEW PRIESTHOOD: THE SCIENTIFIC ELITE AND THE USES OF POWER. New York: Harper and Row, 1965. 244 p.

Democracy faces its most severe challenge in the increasing political power wielded by the scientific and technical elite. World War II is identified as "the cauldron in which two initially quite different potions of power were mixed," those brews being science and the military. From nonelective, advisory positions, Lapp warns, decisions of great import with regard to future government-sponsored research and development in all areas are being made.

1082 MacPherson, C.B. "Technical Change and Political Decision: Introduction." INTERNATIONAL SOCIAL SCIENCE JOURNAL 12, no. 3 (1960): 357-68.

The interrelations of technical change and politics are exceedingly complex. Political decisions determine the rate of advance; yet, conversely, the growth of technology has increased the complexity of political decision making and affected adversely the democratic quality of that process.

1083 Mazur, Allan. "Opposition to Technological Innovation." MINERVA 13 (Spring 1975): 58-81.

In comparing the controversy about fluoridation with the more recent debate over nuclear power, Mazur finds some similarities. Neither issue initially appeared controversial or of national interest. Both were scientifically as well as politically debatable. Local opposition groups, loosely linked by newsletters and networks, were formed by politically active, genuinely concerned individuals. Despite waning of national interest in the fluoridation issue, opposition groups have remained persistent.

1084 Melman, Seymour. OUR DEPLETED SOCIETY. New York: Holt, Rinehart, and Winston, 1965. x, 366 p. Bibliog.

Melman analyzes the social and economic cost of the Cold War and its military technology. He finds the military quest for security "self-defeating" and argues for a conversion to peace-time production. A little dated now.

1085 Nelson, Richard R. THE MOON AND THE GHETTO: AN ESSAY ON PUBLIC POLICY. New York: W.W. Norton and Co., 1977. 159 p.

Nelson identifies three major intellectual traditions that have contributed to the American curse of technological wizardry linked to social ineptitude: "rational analysis," the "systems perspective," and the "research and development orientation." The faltering policy process of the present is observed through case studies of day-care and the supersonic transport. The author presents an alternative framework for social problem analysis.

1086 Nelson, William R., ed. THE POLITICS OF SCIENCE: READINGS IN SCIENCE, TECHNOLOGY AND GOVERNMENT. New York: Oxford University Press, 1968. x, 495 p.

The heavy financial commitment of government to science and technology is a relatively recent phenomenon. Through these readings, the history and organizational manifestation of that commitment is scrutinized. Studies reveal the poor integration of the opinions of scientists and the public into the policy-making process. Contributors include scientists, reporters, government officials, and experts on science policy.

1087 Rotenstreich, Nathan. "Technology and Politics." INTERNATIONAL PHILOSOPHICAL QUARTERLY 7 (June 1967): 197-212.

Technology has direct and indirect influences on politics. In altering the ruling classes through changes in the money economy, championing industrial innovation, and promoting equality in the standard of living, technology indirectly influences politics. Direct influences described are the rise of industrial management in government and the impact of television's coverage of political events and personages. Most important, technology has furthered war and domination. Rotenstreich makes a plea for the use of technology in the service of life.

1088 Strasser, Gabor, and Simons, Eugene M., eds. SCIENCE AND TECH-NOLOGY POLICIES: YESTERDAY, TODAY AND TOMORROW. Cambridge, Mass.: Ballinger Publishing Co., 1973. xxvi, 286 p.

Speeches from a Battelle Institute-sponsored science policy colloquium and articles from Battelle's journal SCIENCE POLICY REVIEW have been assembled to provide a spectrum of opinion of noted thinkers in science and technology policy. Organized into four parts, the collection covers science-technology-society interactions, national science and technology policies, applied science and technology policies, and an assessment of "Where Are We Now?" Among authors represented are Frederick Seitz, J. Herbert Hollomon, Emilio Q. Daddario, Derek de Solla Price, and Chauncey Starr.

1089   Theobald, Robert. BEYOND DESPAIR: DIRECTIONS FOR AMERICA'S THIRD CENTURY. Washington, D.C.: New Republic, 1976. xviii, 169 p. Bibliog.

Theobald expresses general concern about the challenges facing Americans in the transition from an industrial to a communications era. He is particularly adamant that there be the widest possible public participation in decision making, and that society maintain its diversity despite diminishing resources. As elsewhere, Theobald includes a plea for a guaranteed basic income program.

1090   U.S. Federal Council for Science and Technology. PUBLIC TECHNOLOGY: A TOOL FOR SOLVING NATIONAL PROBLEMS. Washington, D.C.: Government Printing Office, 1972. ix, 60 p.

Science and technology are now being applied to problems that are the responsibility of state and local government. This report contends that states are not equipped to manage science and technology and recommends several remedies to this situation, particularly state involvement in every step of science and technology policymaking, greater information dissemination, and strengthening of the ability of local governments to perform and apply research.

1091   Wenk, Edward, Jr. "Political Limits in Steering Technology: Pathologies of the Short Run." TECHNOLOGY IN SOCIETY 1 (Spring 1979): 27-36.

A commitment to the "quick fix" has marred political efforts to steer technology. This "pathology of the short run" is traced to a number of causes, including the exigencies of political expediency, the uncertainty and complexity of technological decisions, bureaucratic resistance to change and a tendency to risk avoidance. New institutions created to infuse a more long-range perspective, such as the Office of Technology Assessment, have met with only limited success. Wenk warns that "the benign neglect of the future may undermine even the future capacity to decide."

1092   Williams, Roger. POLITICS AND TECHNOLOGY. London: Macmillan, 1971. 79 p.

Williams recognizes three "imperatives of technology": a stable economy, state-involvement in risk-laden research, and a reorganization of the educational system to meet technological needs. Such imperatives imply a special technocratic class working within a highly specialized "technocomplex." Following a review of the ideas of principal negative and positive viewpoints on technology, Williams concludes that while technology may expand worldwide material expectations precipitiously, it retains a strong, pleased following.

B. SELECTED THEMES

1. Legal Process

a. BIBLIOGRAPHY

1093   Cohen, Morris L.; Stepan, Jan; and Ronen, Naomi. LAW AND SCI-
ENCE: A SELECTED BIBLIOGRAPHY. Cambridge, Mass.: Science,
Technology, and Human Values, Harvard University, 1978. 143 p.

> Bibliography of the literature on the interface of science,
> technology, and the legal process includes books, journal
> articles, and government publications in 1655 entries. Mate-
> rial is drawn from fields of the sciences, law, political sci-
> ence, sociology, and philosophy. Journals and looseleaf
> current-awareness services of use to researchers in the field
> are listed in separate sections. Topic headings include com-
> puters, scientific evidence, medicine and the law, legal
> control of health hazards, privacy, controls on natural re-
> sources, space law, law of the sea, arms control, taxation
> of research operations, and legal protection for the distribu-
> tion of scientific and technical information.

b. BOOKS AND ARTICLES

1094   Aultman, Mark. "Technology and the End of Law." AMERICAN JOUR-
NAL OF JURISPRUDENCE 17 (1972): 46-79.

> For a legal system to be truly effective, legal thought must
> be sensitive to social change, and to impelling forces such as
> technology. Recalling the message of Jacques Ellul on law
> and the nature of technology, the author concurs that there
> is not evidence that technology will ultimately benefit man.
> Law, for most of this century a mere tool of state, must be
> used to control change for man's benefit.

1095   Baram, Michael S. "Social Control of Science and Technology."
SCIENCE 172 (7 May 1971): 535-39.

> Baram questions whether our present legal system is capable
> of imposing control over new technologies before they can
> inflict considerable harm; law, it appears, functions only
> retroactively. Because large-scale commitments to new tech-
> nologies are generally made before citizen groups can orga-
> nize and take legal action, such groups are generally ren-
> dered ineffectual. Legislation must be passed that will slow
> the process of technological development to encourage debate
> and minute assessment.

1096   Baxter, William F. "The SST: From Watts to Harlem in Two Hours."

STANFORD LAW REVIEW 21 (November 1968): 1-57.

The criteria for allocating the social cost of the sonic boom produced by the supersonic transport are delineated. Baxter notes the inadequacies of present legal and administrative systems and proposes adjustments. Following an explanation of the causes, characteristics, and physical and psychological effects of the sonic-boom phenomena, the author considers the concept of "economic externalities" and legal recourse.

1097 Bazelon, David L. "Coping with Technology through the Legal Process." CORNELL LAW REVIEW 62 (June 1977): 817-32.

Neither the courts nor scientists and technologists have the qualifications to make "painful value choices" related to technological innovations. Concerned over the decision-making process, this judge asks who should be involved and what procedures should be followed. He advocates broadened public participation and widely informed regulatory agencies. Excellent documentation of recent court cases and government publications.

1098 "Implications of Science-Technology for the Legal Process." DENVER LAW JOURNAL 47, no. 4 (1970): 549-680.

The role of law and law education in meeting the exigencies presented by technological and scientific activity is the focus of a symposium held at the University of Denver. Papers consider the social control of science and technology, the law school as center for policy analysis, the adversary positions of law versus technology, and political adaptation to a technological culture.

1099 Loth, David, and Ernst, Morris L. THE TAMING OF TECHNOLOGY. New York: Simon and Schuster, 1972. 256 p.

The regulation of technology through law is demonstrated. The authors deal mainly with legal methods of lessening the effects of technology on the environment. Cases related to air or water pollution, medicine, computers, energy, waste disposal, and radiation are discussed. A table of cases is appended.

1100 "Science, Technology and the Law." IMPACT OF SCIENCE ON SOCIETY 21 (July-September 1971): 193-278.

A number of legal aspects of present and potential technological developments are touched upon. Liability for technological misfortunes is discussed by Laurence H. Tribe, while the complications that will be created by advances in human reproduction and communications also receive attention. Two legally uncharted new frontiers, the oceans and space, will soon demand jurisprudence.

1101   Tribe, Laurence H. CHANNELING TECHNOLOGY THROUGH LAW. Chicago: Bracton Press, 1973. xviii, 644 p.

The ways in which the legal process can be utilized to influence the evolution of technologies is explored. The possibilities for intervention aimed at early stages of technological development is Tribe's interest. He begins with a delineation of technology assessment and legal strategies. Succeeding parts apply the strategies to specific technologies: supersonic transport; genetic engineering, primarily cloning; electronic monitoring and neurological manipulation; and computerized information systems. Recommendations for a system of technological decision making proposed by the National Academy of Sciences concludes the volume.

2. Role of Scientists and Technologists

1102   Bugliarello, George. "A Technological Magistrature." BULLETIN OF THE ATOMIC SCIENTISTS 34 (January 1978): 34-37.

Problems having to do with values are pervasive in technology, but the question of how to make technology responsive is complicated by society's inability to agree upon and articulate values. In the past, engineers have planned technological change only at the tactical level, leaving values discussions to other sectors. In order to unite the "two great forces" of government and technology, Bugliarello proposes the establishment of a "technological magistrature," essentially a technocracy with humanist leanings.

1103   Casper, Barry M. "Technology Policy and Democracy." SCIENCE 194 (1 October 1976): 29-35.

Kantrowitz's idea of a science court (no. 1104) does not solve the problem of controlling technology democratically. In Casper's opinion, the scheme has several serious problems. The choice of issues and timing of hearings might be subject to political abuse. Separating scientific from political or values questions would often be a difficult task. What is needed is not a science court but an improved forum for public debate that will provide open access to scientific information and viewpoints.

1104   Kantrowitz, Arthur. "Controlling Science Democratically." AMERICAN SCIENTIST 63 (September-October 1975): 505-9.

Two methods that can be used to control technology are contrasted: "paternalistic" control by the technical elite and democratic control. Kantrowitz suggests a compromise involving a separation of scientific and ethical components of crucial issues. As a forum for debating issues, he suggests the creation of an institution that can utilize adversary procedures developed by the legal profession. Through such a science court, Kantrowitz believes, "experts can make objective judgments regarding the scientific parts of the question, leaving the determination of what is good and what is evil to the democratic "process."

1105 Mazur, Allan. "Science Courts." MINERVA 15 (Spring 1977): 1-14.

On some recent controversial issues, such as fluoridation, supersonic transport, and nuclear power plants, technical experts have adopted contrasting positions. "Science courts" have been suggested as a public arena for debating these differences, though no decision reached could be final, as it might be confounded at any time by new evidence. Nevertheless, a hearing could serve to summarize and clarify current knowledge of an issue, with results published in a form useful to policymakers and the public at large.

1106 Nelkin, Dorothy. "The Political Impact of Technical Expertise." SOCIAL STUDIES OF SCIENCE 5 (February 1975): 35-54.

With the growth of the environmental and consumer movements, scientists have become increasingly involved in controversial areas. Two disputes are described in which the testimony of scientists was used by advocates on either side of the question: the Cayuga Lake nuclear power plant, and a proposed runway for Boston's Logan Airport. Nelkin found that the impact of "experts" was reduced if there was conflict between their testimonies.

1107 Perrucci, Robert. "Engineering: Professional Servant of Power." AMERICAN BEHAVIORAL SCIENTIST 14 (March-April 1971): 492-506.

Projections of an emerging technocratic elite rest, Perrucci argues, on two false assumptions: that engineers are homogenous, sharing the same values, and that engineers constitute an independent power base capable of deciding the work to which engineering talents are assigned. On the contrary, the author contends, the profession is neither independent nor autonomous, and it lacks a unified professional stance or ethic. However, "the growing centrality of engineering activities calls for a profession with strong technical skills and a commitment to human welfare."

1108 Primack, Joel, and Von Hippel, Frank. "Scientists, Politics, and the

SST: A Critical Review." BULLETIN OF THE ATOMIC SCIENTISTS 28 (April 1972): 24-30.

The role played by scientists in exerting pressure on government in the interests of the general public is studied through the case of the supersonic transport. Through the years of its development, the SST was represented as an inevitable advance, despite abundant negative evidence about noise levels and profitability. Scientists became active and influential in the process of citizen group formation and action that led to the eventual demise of the project. The case of the SST points to the need for early scrutiny by citizen-professionals of such major projects.

1109   Tribus, M[yron]. "Along the Corridors of Power: Where are the Engineers?" MECHANICAL ENGINEERING 98 (April 1976): 24-28.

At present, those trained in science and technology are generally lacking in real political power. Yet, Tribus argues, engineers can offer a process for dealing with technical matters which is superior to the currently dominant adversary mode. Recent examples of difficulties in environmental and energy policymaking are cited, with suggestions of the way engineering involvement in decision making might have simplified matters.

1110   Weinberg, Alvin M. "Science and Trans-Science." MINERVA 10 (April 1972): 209-22.

Debates concerning the responsibility of the scientist generally assume that for any given issue a neat division can be made between the scientific and political aspects of an issue. Weinberg feels that such a view is oversimplified and proposes a new term, "trans-scientific," to describe questions "which can be asked of science and yet cannot be answered by science." Examples of such questions are biological effects of low-level radiation and the probability of such extremely improbable events as earthquakes or catastrophic reactor accidents. The engineer, especially, must frequently deal with the "trans-scientific" in that "he cannot afford the luxury of examining every question to the degree which scientific rigor would demand." Implications of the "trans-science" concept for policymaking are discussed.

3. International Relations

1111   Basiuk, Victor. TECHNOLOGY, WORLD POLITICS AND AMERICAN POLICY. New York: Columbia University Press, 1977. xv, 409 p. Bibliog.

The future impact of technology on international relations,

especially in developed regions, is studied. The first part of
the book identifies five trends in the technological transformation of the globe over the next twenty-five years: a lessened
importance of resource location, technological integration, a
greater political importance attached to technology, heightened
scale and cost, and accelerating change. Specific trends,
prospects, and problems in the United States, the Soviet Union,
Western Europe, and Japan are treated. In the long-range
view, Basiuk believes that America's goal must be the "task
of producing progressive human evolution."

1112 Dahlberg, Kenneth A. "The Technological Ethic and the Spirit of International Relations." INTERNATIONAL STUDIES QUARTERLY 17
(March 1973): 55-88.

Most analyses of the relationship between technology and international relations have studied the impact of diffused technologies, e.g., weapons or fertilizers. Such an approach,
the author states, is too narrow. He argues that the introduction of large-scale applications of technology is invariably
linked to the simultaneous transmission of a technological
ethic, characterized by rationality, specialization, efficiency,
social dissolution, and exploitative control. The international
implications of this ethic merit study.

1113 Haskins, Caryl P. "Technology, Science and American Foreign Policy."
FOREIGN AFFAIRS 40 (January 1962): 224-43.

The Sputnik space-shot demonstrated that outstanding technological achievement can be extraordinarily powerful in cementing
a people's sense of solidarity and national pride. In America,
Sputnik stimulated a reorganization of and explosion of growth
in science; in Europe, a proliferation of international organizations.

1114 Skolnikoff, Eugene B. THE INTERNATIONAL IMPERATIVES OF TECH-
NOLOGY: TECHNOLOGICAL DEVELOPMENT AND THE INTERNA-
TIONAL POLITICAL SYSTEM. Berkeley: Institute of International Stud-
ies, University of California, 1972. ix, 194 p.

In recent years, science and technology have taken on a new
meaning internationally as a source of wealth, rapid social
change, and superpower status. Skolnikoff conjectures about
changes that can be expected from continued rapid development, particularly in areas that will require international regulation such as telecommunications, climate modification, and
use of pesticides. Specific recommendations are made for
strengthening international agencies to meet additional regulatory responsibilities.

1115 U.S. Congress. House. Committee on International Relations. SCIENCE, TECHNOLOGY AND AMERICAN DIPLOMACY: AN EX- TENDED STUDY OF THE INTERACTIONS OF SCIENCE AND TECH- NOLOGY WITH AMERICAN FOREIGN POLICY. 3 vols. 95th Cong., 1st sess. Washington, D.C.: 1977. Bibliog. Y4.In 8/16: Sci 2/3/ v.1-3. xvii, v, v, 2107 p.

Recognizing the increasing importance of science and technol- ogy in policymaking, the study describes and analyzes the formulation of American diplomatic policies that have signifi- cant scientific or technological components. Volume 1 offers six case studies from the control of atomic energy (Baruch Plan) to recent U.S.-Soviet commercial relations. In the second volume, case studies illustrate relations between the United States and multinational bodies with regard to such issues as food, medicine, and the "brain drain." Cases are analyzed and principal policy implications are derived in the third volume. A selected, annotated bibliography by Genevieve Knezo touches on all concerns of the report.

C. RISK AND TECHNOLOGY ASSESSMENT

1116 Bauer, Raymond A., ed. SECOND-ORDER CONSEQUENCES: A METHODOLOGICAL ESSAY ON THE IMPACT OF TECHNOLOGY. Technology, Space and Society. Cambridge: M.I.T. Press, 1969. xii, 240 p.

In an early technology assessment study, the social impact of the American space program receives close scrutiny. Among "second-order effects" analyzed are those on the imagination, on employment, and on the growth of science and technology as a whole. Documents the way space technology has dif- fused through society. Appended are documents of societies sponsoring this methodological study.

1117 Cetron, Marvin J., and Bartocha, Bodo, eds. THE METHODOLOGY OF TECHNOLOGY ASSESSMENT. New York: Gordon and Breach, 1972. viii, 235 p. Illus.

Intended as a state-of-the-art synthesis, this collection of papers briefly considers both qualitative and quantitative as- pects of technology assessment. Various matrix techniques are presented and analyzed for effectiveness. On the "soft" side, the roles of law, social indicators, and social goals in tech- nology assessment receive attention.

1118 _____ . TECHNOLOGY ASSESSMENT IN A DYNAMIC ENVIRON- MENT. London: Gordon and Breach Science Publishers, 1973. xiv, 1,036 p.

A review of technology assessment in the United States and elsewhere is presented through the contributions of forty authors. Part 1 considers the scope, rationale, and use of technology assessment. Part 2 reviews methodology, and part 3 presents case studies of applications in particular fields such as food production and waste utilization. A concluding section speculates on the future of technology assessment.

1119 Coates, Joseph F. "Some Methods and Techniques for Comprehensive Impact Assessment." TECHNOLOGICAL FORECASTING AND SOCIAL CHANGE 6 (October 1974): 341-57.

A step-by-step guide to the process of technology assessment enumerates components, methods, and goals. Concise, paragraph-length descriptions are provided for such methods as Delphi, cross-impact analysis, trend extrapolation, and cost benefit analysis. Transcending the analytical niceties, Coates stresses that "the goal of technology assessment is less the conventional scientific one of nailing down the facts or testing a theory than it is developing a degree of public wisdom."

1120 _____. "Technology Assessment and Public Wisdom." JOURNAL OF THE WASHINGTON ACADEMY OF SCIENCE 65 (March 1975): 3-11.

Technological planning in the United States has until recently addressed only concerns for immediate feasibility, profitability, and safety, neglecting to consider long-ranging consequences. Technology assessment may help to enlarge foresight, Coates believes. He expands upon government organizations and methodological steps crucial to adequate assessment, listing a number of benefits--from risk clarification to regulation--that can be the result of a proper assessment.

1121 Ebel, Roland, H.; Wagoner, William; and Hrubecky, Henry F. "Get Ready for the L-Bomb: A Preliminary Social Assessment of Longevity Technology." TECHNOLOGICAL FORECASTING AND SOCIAL CHANGE 13 (February 1979): 131-48.

The societal impacts in the United States of the "retardation of the cellular aging process in men and women" are considered. Recent biomedical and genetic technologies indicate the life span may be considerably expanded. The impacts on employment, income, resource consumption, education, social institutions, and legal problems are analyzed for life spans in ten year segments up to an age limit of 110. Demographic and econometric computer models are utilized.

1122 Fischhoff, Baruch. "Cost-Benefit Analysis and the Art of Motorcycle Maintenance." POLICY SCIENCES 8 (June 1977): 177-202.

Due to the watchful eyes of environmental and consumer groups, the process of technological regulation has been made public. Meanwhile, the methodology for technology assessment has undergone some development. The author critically evaluates such techniques as cost-benefit analysis, decision analysis, and risk assessment, calling for a formalization of public criticism in such analyses.

1123   Fischhoff, Baruch; Slovic, Paul; Lichtenstein, Sarah; Read, Stephen; and Combs, Barbara. "How Safe is Safe Enough? A Psychometric Study of Attitudes toward Technological Risks and Benefits." POLICY SCIENCES 9 (April 1978): 127-52.

The public acceptance of risk-taking as a necessary sacrifice for an adequate power supply has been a rising topic in social science literature. Chauncey Starr's "revealed preference method" has yielded laws relating acceptable risk to perceived benefit. Psychometric procedures used by the authors elicited judgments about perceived risks and benefits for a number of innovations and activities. Unlike Starr, Fishhoff and co-authors found no evidence for "laws."

1124   Freeman, Christopher. "Technology Assessment and Its Social Context." STUDIUM GENERALE 24 (September 1971): 1038-50.

Though skepticism about the benefits of science and technology is by no means new, recent threats, particularly population growth, nuclear energy, and pollution, have added urgency to the debate. The resolution of crises depends on improving institutional mechanisms through which social choices are made; "laissez-innover," the indiscriminate development and application of new technologies, must cease. A framework for technology assessment is presented.

1125   Freeman, David [M.]. TECHNOLOGY AND SOCIETY: ISSUES IN ASSESSMENT. Chicago: Rand McNally College Publishing Co., 1974. xx, 181 p.

This general text on technology-society interrelations is particularly concerned with planning issues. A discussion of valuation issues compares what measures are preferable socially, economically, and politically. In the light of these valuation criteria, issues in planning and technology assessment are reviewed. The present system of technology assessment is criticized as being too slow in response to technological advancement. Freeman suggests that improvements need to be made in prediction, data gathering, and standards.

1126   Green, Harold P., ed. "Cost-Risk Benefit Analysis and the Law." GEORGE WASHINGTON LAW REVIEW 45 (August 1977): 901-1150.

Though technology assessment has received intense discussion, an Office, and some related legislation, the movement has languished. In its place has emerged cost–benefit or risk–benefit analysis. This form of assessment, the editor states in his introduction, can be useful only if values are considered more than monetary costs. Among the authors that follow, Amory Lovins expresses skepticism about the value of such assessments in solving energy problems; Raphael Kasper holds similar reservations about environmental issues. Joel Yellin criticizes regulatory agencies, principally the Nuclear Regulatory Commission, while William D. Rowe and Jeffrey M. Albert supply, respectively, a historical and an epistemological background. Notes on specific issues and problems follow.

1127 Hetman, François. SOCIETY AND THE ASSESSMENT OF TECHNOLOGY. Paris: Organization for Economic Cooperation and Development, 1973. 420 p. Illus., bibliog.

Modern disenchantment with technology and technologists has led to rising public demands for control and participation in decision making. In this general survey of technology assessment, its potential for aiding the achievement of public goals is studied. Hetman cites specific potential areas for "TA" applications and places the method in an institutional framework. Tables and charts clarify the text.

1128 Inoue, Arlene, and Susskind, Charles. "Technological Trends and National Policy, 1937: The First Modern Technology Assessment." TECHNOLOGY AND CULTURE 18 (October 1977): 593–621.

As the authors observe, "one sign that technology assessment is making the transition from invisible college to institution is the growing corpus of investigations into its history." This paper critically examines a report issued by the Roosevelt administration as an early piece of technology assessment. Written by major social scientists, academicians, and technologists, the volume opened with discussions of innovation, basic research, and other theoretical issues; the body of the report analyzed specific industries. The authors of the present review conclude, as did William Ogburn, the coordinator of the project, that the report was strong on description but weak on prediction.

1129 Kasper, Raphael G., ed. TECHNOLOGY ASSESSMENT: UNDERSTANDING THE SOCIAL CONSEQUENCES OF TECHNOLOGICAL APPLICATIONS. New York: Praeger Publishers, 1972. x, 291 p.

A product of the Program of Policy Studies at George Washington University, this seminar volume focuses on the role of Congress, the President, and other pertinent government agencies in the process of technology assessment. Whether technology assessment serves as an important vehicle for citizen participation or simply constitutes "technology harassment" is also debated through case studies evidence.

1130　Keating, W.T. "Politics, Energy and the Environment: The Role of Technology Assessment." AMERICAN BEHAVIORAL SCIENTIST 19 (September–October 1975): 37–74.

Attempts made since 1946 to assess the desirability of nuclear power are reviewed in the light of current opinion on costs, benefits, and social and environmental effects of nuclear energy. With an eye to growing public concern for adequate assessment, the author compares three possible courses for future regulation: stronger government authorities, continuation of the present loose system, and institutional change to permit expanded public participation in decision making.

1131　Kloman, Erasmus H., ed. "A Mini Symposium: Public Participation In Technology Assessment." PUBLIC ADMINISTRATION REVIEW 35 (January–February 1975): 67–80.

Public participation, technology assessment, and the relations between the two serve as topics for papers in this issue. Joseph F. Coates reveals why public participation is essential to the assessment process. John Dixon and Sherry R. Arnstein discuss means for encouraging participation. Philosophical and legal underpinnings are considered by Walter A. Hahn and Hazel Henderson.

1132　Koopmans, Tjalling C. "Economics among the Sciences." AMERICAN ECONOMIC REVIEW 69 (March 1979): 1–13.

The problems which evolve in the collaboration of professionals involved in interdisciplinary study of society's important problems are discussed. Koopmans considers three issues approached by groups of engineers, scientists, social scientists, and economists, namely, helium storage, future energy supply and use, and automobile emission control. Differences in outlook among the professionals and use of evaluation and verification methodologies cause the most serious problems. Distinctions in values become evident. Illuminating quotations from participants are included.

1133　Lowrance, William W. OF ACCEPTABLE RISK: SCIENCE AND THE DETERMINATION OF SAFETY. Los Altos, Calif.: William Kaufman, 1976. 180 p.

Based on the premise that "risks to health and safety are becoming more acute in nature and degree," this volume studies the processes through which policy decisions on safety are reached. Defining safety as a measure of acceptability of risk, the author discusses the problems of measuring and of appraising the acceptability of risk, as well as the difficulties of applying knowledge in devising safeguards. DDT is offered as a case study through which issues introduced in previous pages can be reviewed. The author concludes with a warning that as the time for decision making is growing short, responsibilities must be assigned with haste.

1134   Michael, Donald N. "An Aesthetic for Technology Assessment." ALTERNATIVE FUTURES 1 (Spring 1978): 19-28.

Because social change defies unswervingly rational analysis, the process of technology assessment cannot be envisioned as a purely formal technical activity. It is also to be viewed and esteemed, Michael suggests, as a form of art. A holistic, systems perspective must be adopted as the basis for the assessment of technology's social effects.

1135   Pursell, Carroll [W., Jr.]. "Belling the Cat: A Critique of Technology Assessment"; "A Savage Struck by Lightning: The Idea of a Research Moratorium"; and "'Who to Ask Besides the Barber'--Suggestions for Alternative Assessments." LEX ET SCIENTIA 10 (October-December 1974): 121-78.

In three papers given at Lehigh University in 1974 as the first Andrew W. Mellon Lectures in the History of Science and Technology, Pursell analyzes the field of technology assessment. Before engineers can provide society with reliable guidelines, there must develop wider perspectives within engineering education itself and some increased level of job security for those involved in assessments. Contains questions and answers.

1136   Rowe, William D. THE ANATOMY OF RISK. New York: John Wiley and Sons, 1977. xii, 488 p. Bibliog.

The means by which society's agents in government set levels of acceptable risks for technological systems and programs are examined. The book opens with a general discussion of what risk is, and how acceptable risk levels are arrived at by individuals and society. Formal methods for risk estimation and valuation are described, followed by a discussion of methodological problems and approaches in the quantification of risks.

1137   Skolimowski, Henryk. "Technology Assessment in a Sharp Social Focus." TECHNOLOGICAL FORECASTING AND SOCIAL CHANGE 8, no. 4 (1976): 421-25.

In its first few years, technology assessment suffered from a pro-technology bias, due to the vested interests of practitioners. Skolimowski suggests a set of three laws for technology assessment, which state: no system can adequately assess itself; a quantitatively satisfactory assessment is not necessarily socially satisfactory; and assessment must terminate in values statements. His conclusion is that "real expertise in technology assessment is social and moral and not technical."

1138 Starr, Chauncey. "Social Benefit Versus Technological Risk." SCIENCE 165 (19 September 1969): 1232-38.

The evaluation of technical approaches to societal problem-solving involves cost-benefit analysis. Starr describes several quantitative approaches to risk analysis, defined as a determination of socially acceptable levels of accidental deaths sacrificed for a technical advance. Levels are arrived at through study of historical situations in which such a tradeoff between utility and risk has been satisfactorily achieved.

1139 Starr, Chauncey; Rudman, Richard; and Whipple, Chris. "Philosophical Bases for Risk Analysis." ANNUAL REVIEW OF ENERGY 1 (1976): 629-62.

Inherent in all technical systems is the implicit acceptance of a level of public risk. The incorporation of estimates of risk is at an early stage of methodological development. The authors suggest that risk-benefit analysis should be better utilized in decisions about expansions of current technologies, in choices between technologies, and in developing performance criteria. Methods for measuring risk are presented and critiqued.

1140 Stober, Gerhard J., and Schumacher, D., eds. TECHNOLOGY ASSESSMENT AND QUALITY OF LIFE. New York: Elsevier Scientific Publishing Co., 1973. 302 p. Illus.

Papers in this volume were originally presented at the 1972 international conference of SAINT (Salzburg Assembly: Impact of the New Technology). Gerhard Stober opens with a consideration of the scope and elements that define the "quality of life." Clark C. Abt reviews the social role of technology, while François Hetman describes the way social objectives may be matched to desirable new technologies. James S. Wilson describes the relations between quality of life and the industrial process as a whole.

1141 Tarr, Joel A., ed. RETROSPECTIVE TECHNOLOGY ASSESSMENT-- 1976. San Francisco: San Francisco Press, 1977. x, 326 p. Graphs.

Retrospective technology assessment is a historical technique which may help contemporary technology assessors "ask the right kinds of questions" and provide "a sense of depth in time" by drawing instructive parallels. Tarr has edited the proceedings of a 1976 interdisciplinary conference on retrospective "TA" which included sixteen exploratory papers on methodology, case studies, and values. Useful references.

1142   "Technology Assessment and the Law: Introduction and Perspectives." GEORGE WASHINGTON LAW REVIEW 36 (July 1968): 1105-37.

The purpose of this symposium was to stimulate the interest of the legal profession in technology assessment. Emilio Q. Daddario introduces the subject, while Marvin J. Cetron and Alan Weiser present the perspective of the corporate "R and D" manager. Through reviewing the history of the SST, weather modification, and fluoridation, Michael Wollen demonstrates how vested interests in government prevent the construction of truly thorough technology assessments. A concluding paper by Edmund S. Muskie defines the Congressional role in controlling technological advance.

1143   Tribe, Laurence H. "Legal Frameworks for the Assessment and Control of Technology." MINERVA 9 (April 1971): 243-55.

Scientists and technologists have been largely unaware of the central role that law must play in any effort to steer the development of technology in human directions. Lawyers, in a similar vein, have failed to perceive their roles as including such areas. Tribe, attempting to encourage dialogue, presents and compares three models of legal controls appropriate to influencing technological development.

1144   U.S. Congress. House. Committee on Science and Astronautics. TECHNOLOGY: PROCESSES OF ASSESSMENT AND CHOICE. 91st Congr., 1st sess. Report of the National Academy of Sciences. Washington, D.C.: July 1969. 163 p.

A distinguished panel that includes Harvey Brooks, Melvin Kranzberg, Gerard Piel, and Herbert A. Simon reviews the objectives, problems, and pitfalls of technology assessment.

1145   U.S. National Resources Committee. Subcommittee on Technology. TECHNOLOGICAL TRENDS AND NATIONAL POLICY, INCLUDING THE SOCIAL IMPLICATIONS OF NEW INVENTIONS. Washington, D.C.: 1937. viii, 388 p. Illus., maps.

Assembled by a stellar group of scientists, technologists, and social scientists, this famous document profiles technology in the Roosevelt era. Part 1 studies the social aspects of invention, linking innovation in industry to such social phenomena as unemployment. The third part offers expansive surveys of and forecasts for agriculture, mining, transportation, communication, construction, power, metallurgy, the chemical industry, and electrical manufacture. Based on its study, the committee recommended studies of the projected impact of certain recent innovations, attention to technological unemployment, and the founding of the National Resources Board to coordinate planning.

1146 White, Lynn, Jr. "Technology Assessment from the Stance of a Medieval Historian." AMERICAN HISTORICAL REVIEW 79 (February 1974): 1-13.

White's 1973 American Historical Association presidential address offers a brief survey of medieval technical innovations as examples of problems in technology assessment in order to demonstrate what they might reveal about our own concerns with "TA." His thesis is that "technology assessment, if it is not to be dangerously misleading, must be based as much, if not more, on careful discussion of the imponderables in a total situation as upon the measurable elements. Systems analysis must become cultural analysis, and in this historians may be helpful."

Part 11

TRANSPORTATION

A. GENERAL

1147   Meyer, Bathasar Henry, ed. HISTORY OF TRANSPORTATION IN THE
        UNITED STATES BEFORE 1860. Washington, D.C.: Carnegie Institu-
        tion, 1917. xi, 678 p. Illus., maps, bibliog.

   A lengthy survey on roads, canals, and railroads is in most
   ways superseded by Taylor's TRANSPORTATION REVOLUTION
   (no. 1148). The footnotes and bibliography are useful.

1148   Taylor, George Rogers. THE TRANSPORTATION REVOLUTION: 1815-
        1860. New York: Holt, Rinehart, and Winston, 1951. Reprint.
        Economic History of the United States, vol. 4. New York: Harper
        and Row, 1968. xvi, 490 p. Illus., maps, bibliog.

   An extremely important survey of American economic history
   emphasizes the importance of transportation developments in
   the areas of roads, canals, steamboats, and railroads, but
   also covers industrialization, domestic and foreign trade, and
   labor. The excellent bibliographical essay is a must.

1149   Winther, Oscar O. THE TRANSPORTATION FRONTIER: TRANS-
        MISSISSIPPI WEST, 1865-1890. Histories of the American Frontier.
        New York: Holt, Rinehart, and Winston, 1964. xiv, 224 p. Illus.,
        maps, bibliog.

   In a traditional descriptive study covering all forms of land
   transportation, but especially the stage coach, steamboat, and
   railroad, Winther includes information on routes, the technology of each mode, and the social effects.

B. CANALS

1150   Condon, George E. STARS IN THE WATER: THE STORY OF THE
        ERIE CANAL. Garden City, N.Y.: Doubleday, 1974. xix, 338 p.
        Illus., bibliog.

Condon has provided a well-written, semipopular account of the building of the Erie Canal.

1151 Goodrich, Carter. GOVERNMENT PROMOTION OF AMERICAN CANALS AND RAILROADS, 1800-1890. New York: Columbia University Press, 1959. x, 382 p. Map, bibliog.

Goodrich surveys federal, state, and local promotional activity from the earliest national projects of internal improvements to the completion of the railway network. His "main theme is the relation between public and private activity in the creation of canals and railroads," focusing on the issue of "competition and cooperation between government and business."

1152 _____, ed. CANALS AND AMERICAN ECONOMIC DEVELOPMENT. New York: Columbia University Press, 1961. viii, 303 p. Map.

In part 1 of his study of canal building and its impact upon the antebellum economy, Goodrich focuses on New York's Erie, Pennsylvania's Mainline, and New Jersey's Delaware, Raritan and Morris Canals and the political decisions to build. In part 2 he analyzes the cycles of construction of the canal system as a whole and its positive impact upon American economic growth.

1153 Rubin, Julius. CANAL OR RAILROAD? IMITATION AND INNOVATION IN THE RESPONSE TO THE ERIE CANAL IN PHILADELPHIA, BALTIMORE, AND BOSTON. Transactions of the American Philosophical Society, vol. 51, pt. 7. Philadelphia: American Philosophical Society, 1961. 106 p. Map, bibliog.

Rubin traces the different competitive reactions of Philadelphia, Boston, and Baltimore in their debates over building canals or railroads across the Appalachians in order to gain advantages of western trade similar to those which accrued to New York City because of the Erie Canal. He finds that differences in attitude toward uncertainty and delay with respect to the railroad and canal as symbols accounted for the different approaches within each region.

1154 Sanderlin, Walter S. THE GREAT NATIONAL PROJECT: A HISTORY OF THE CHESAPEAKE AND OHIO CANAL. Baltimore: Johns Hopkins Press, 1946. Reprint. Companies and Men, Business Enterprise in America. New York: Arno Press, 1976. 331 p. Map, bibliog.

Although never ultimately completed to the Ohio River, the Chesapeake and Ohio Canal was "something of a symbol in the campaign for improved communications with the West." Sanderlin chronicles the background, building, operation, and economic relationships of the canal, primarily for the period from 1822 to 1889.

1155   Shaw, Ronald E. ERIE WATER WEST: A HISTORY OF THE ERIE
        CANAL, 1792–1854. Lexington: University Press of Kentucky, 1966.
        xiv, 449 p. Illus., maps, bibliog.

> Shaw relates not only the history of the Erie Canal's origin
> and construction, but also its operation and social and cultural
> significance. He sees the canal as more than just a state-
> level endeavor; "it was by its very nature a national enter-
> prise."

C. STEAMBOATS

1156   Boyd, Thomas Alexander. POOR JOHN FITCH, INVENTOR OF THE
        STEAMBOAT. New York: G.P. Putnam's Sons, 1935. Reprint.
        Freeport, N.Y.: Books for Libraries, 1971. 315 p. Illus., bibliog.

> Slightly more than half of this undocumented biography deals
> with Fitch's involvement with the development of the steam-
> boat. Based upon, among others, the Fitch papers and the
> inventor's own account, the study concludes that although the
> steamboat was the result of work by many men, "John Fitch
> worked earliest on the proper principles with the greatest
> mechanical success and the least financial reward."

1157   Burke, John G. "Bursting Boilers and the Federal Power." TECHNOL-
        OGY AND CULTURE 7 (Winter 1966): 1–23.

> This case study raises the question of the sanctity of private
> property as opposed to the federal government's duty to act
> positively in the public's behalf. The development and use
> of high pressure steam engines for marine transportation re-
> sulted in frequent boiler explosions and death. The author
> discusses the parallel rise in federal regulatory power during
> the period from 1816 to 1852.

1158   Dickinson, H[enry W.]. ROBERT FULTON, ENGINEER AND ARTIST.
        London: John Lane, 1913. Reprint. Freeport, N.Y.: Books for
        Libraries, 1971. xiv, 333 p. Illus.

> This early biography attempts to present a balanced view of
> Fulton's contributions in canals, submarines, and especially
> steamboats. The author includes a brief chapter on Fulton's
> early years as a miniature portrait painter in Philadelphia.

1159   Flexner, James Thomas. STEAMBOATS COME TRUE: AMERICAN IN-
        VENTORS IN ACTION. New York: Viking Press, 1944. x, 406 p.
        Illus.

> A popular history of the steamboat's invention concentrates on
> John Fitch, James Rumsey, and Robert Fulton. Flexner notes

that invention is a process involving many individuals, but he
ultimately credits Fulton because of his commercial success.

1160 Haites, Erik F.; Mak, James; and Walton, Gary M. WESTERN RIVER
TRANSPORTATION: THE ERA OF EARLY INTERNAL DEVELOPMENT,
1810-1860. Johns Hopkins University Studies in Historical and Political
Science 93d ser., 2. Baltimore: Johns Hopkins University Press, 1975.
xi, 209 p. Map, bibliog.

Quantitative economic analysis of early western river transportation and its nature as a particular market offers several
new or modified conclusions. Chief among these are that
competition was generally characteristic of the market, costs
were greatly reduced by the introduction of steam and subsequent technical improvements, absolute steamboat tonnage
increased right up to 1860, and private rather than public
investment characterized river system developments.

1161 Hunter, Louis C. "The Invention of the Western Steamboat." JOUR-
NAL OF ECONOMIC HISTORY 3 (November 1943): 201-20.

Hunter debunks the commonly held notion that the development
of the steamboat, America's first major contribution to modern
technology, was the result of a single heroic inventor. Detailed research shows that Henry Shreve, often called "the
father of western steamboating," was singly responsible for
only one of the five basic features of the western steamboat
engine, although he was clearly important in other capacities
such as river improvements.

1162 _____. STEAMBOATS ON THE WESTERN RIVERS: AN ECONOMIC
AND TECHNOLOGICAL HISTORY. Cambridge, Mass.: Harvard
University Press, 1949. xv, 684 p. Illus., maps.

The "classic" study of Western steam navigation includes information on the technology, operation, and social, political,
and economic impact of the steamboat. Hunter concentrates
on the years from 1815 to 1890. For the latter period he
also describes the comparative development and competition
of the railroad.

1163 Morgan, John S. ROBERT FULTON. New York: Mason, Charter,
1977. xi, 235 p. Illus., bibliog.

This biography of Fulton includes information on his submarine,
torpedo, and roles as a jeweler's apprentice and painter.
However, the volume concentrates on his work with canals
and steamboats. As such, it offers little that is new and is a
summary contribution to the history of transportation.

D. BRIDGES

1164 McCullagh, David. THE GREAT BRIDGE. New York: Simon and Schuster, 1972. 636 p. Illus., map, bibliog.

The Brooklyn Bridge was a cultural symbol as well as a technological feat which represented the promise of a changing America. McCullagh covers the engineering, politics, personalities, and symbolic impact of the bridge in this wide-ranging popular, but valuable, study.

1165 Schuyler, Hamilton. THE ROEBLINGS: A CENTURY OF ENGINEERS, BRIDGE-BUILDERS, AND INDUSTRIALISTS. THE STORY OF THREE GENERATIONS OF AN ILLUSTRIOUS FAMILY, 1831-1931. Princeton, N.J.: Princeton University Press, 1931. xx, 425 p. Illus.

Schuyler's study is not so much a history of the Brooklyn and other Roebling designed and built bridges as it is a three-generation biography of these important men, who were not only excellent engineers and bridge builders, but also owned and operated a major wire manufacturing industry. Written primarily for the layman.

1166 Steinman, David B. THE BUILDERS OF THE BRIDGE: THE STORY OF JOHN ROEBLING AND HIS SON. New York: Harcourt, Brace, and Co., 1945. xi, 457 p. Illus., bibliog.

The building of the Brooklyn Bridge is herein told by means of a biographical approach to John and Washington Roebling, the father-son design and building team.

1167 Steinman, David B., and Watson, Sara Ruth. BRIDGES AND THEIR BUILDERS. New York: G.P. Putnam's Sons 1941. Rev. ed. New York: Dover Publications, 1957. Reprint. Technology and Society Series. New York: Arno Press, 1972. xvi, 401 p. Illus., bibliog.

Bridges are creative representations of man's attempt to conquer physical or natural forces and ignorance. As such, they are representative of the times in which they were built. The authors chronicle the development of bridge building from ancient to modern times, drawing upon a variety of bridges such as the London, Eads, Brooklyn, and George Washington bridges as particular examples of vision, design, technique, and material.

1168 Trachtenberg, Alan. BROOKLYN BRIDGE: FACT AND SYMBOL. New York: Oxford University Press, 1965. ix, 182 p. Illus.

The Brooklyn Bridge has long served as a cultural symbol in America, especially of the change from a largely rural to a predominantly urban-industrial society. Trachtenberg's purpose is to examine the bridge both as symbol and as artifact.

E. BICYCLES

1169   Aronson, Sidney H. "The Sociology of the Bicycle." SOCIAL FORCES 30 (March 1952): 305-12.

The bicycle's social and technological legacy is subtle but pervasive. To the auto it bequeathed standardized factories, repair shops, and road lobbies; to all Americans, a new mobility. Especially gracious were its gifts to American women, who found in the bicycle a vehicle for defying traditions in dress and permissible feminine movement.

1170   Smith, Robert A. A SOCIAL HISTORY OF THE BICYCLE: ITS EARLY LIFE AND TIMES IN AMERICA. New York: American Heritage Press, 1972. xii, 269 p. Illus., bibliog.

A popularized look at the bicycle craze of the 1890s covers the technology and manufacture of the bicycle, its economic effects, the attendant clothing revolution, safety, cycle racing, the drive for better roads, and the bicycle as an instrument of social change.

1171   Tobin, Gary Alan. "The Bicycle Boom of the 1890's: The Development of Private Transportation and the Birth of the Modern Tourist." JOURNAL OF POPULAR CULTURE 7 (Spring 1974): 838-49.

The bicycle provided a mechanical transition with respect to individual transportation for at least some segments of society during the transition from horses to automobiles. The technical development of bicycles with two equally sized wheels and balloon tires created a boom with a social and economic impact upon roads, clothing styles, leisure activities including touring, and even a decline in church attendance and piano playing.

F. RAILROADS

1172   Bruce, Alfred W. THE STEAM LOCOMOTIVE IN AMERICA: ITS DEVELOPMENT IN THE TWENTIETH CENTURY. New York: W.W. Norton and Co., 1952. xii, 443 p. Illus.

Written toward the end of steam engine power, this is primarily a reference volume and technical history of the last half-century of development of the steam locomotive. The growth of railroads and the history of the locomotive-building industry receive only limited attention.

1173 Chandler, Alfred D[upont]., Jr., ed. THE RAILROADS: THE NA-
TION'S FIRST BIG BUSINESS: SOURCES AND READINGS. Forces in
American Economic Growth Series. New York: Harcourt, Brace, and
World, 1965. ix, 213 p. Maps, bibliog.

Chandler has brought together a useful collection of readings
which, combined with his introductions, provides a clear
picture of the leading role the railroads played in the development of modern organizational, financial, and operational business techniques during the latter half of the nineteenth century.

1174 Cootner, Paul H. "The Role of the Railroads in United States Economic
Growth." JOURNAL OF ECONOMIC HISTORY 23 (December 1963):
477-528.

Although admitting that railroads played an important part in
nineteenth-century U.S. economic history, the author takes a
"skeptical" attitude toward their role as an initiator of
economic growth. Instead, he suggests the root cause was
the shifting worldwide demand for goods and services, which
frequently capitalized on products more efficiently produced
here than elsewhere. Brief comments by Matthew Simon and
Harry N. Scheiber follow.

1175 Fishlow, Albert. AMERICAN RAILROADS AND THE TRANSFORMATION
OF THE ANTEBELLUM ECONOMY. Harvard Economic Studies, vol.
127. Cambridge, Mass.: Harvard University Press, 1965. xvi, 452 p.
Maps, graphs, bibliog.

An attempt to quantify the impact of the railroads through
forward and backward linkages emphasizes their importance to
the antebellum economy, and further shows they were not
built "ahead of demand" but rather developed simultaneously
with economic growth. An interesting contrast with the item
which follows.

1176 Fogel, Robert William. RAILROADS AND AMERICAN ECONOMIC
GROWTH: ESSAYS IN ECONOMETRIC HISTORY. Baltimore: Johns
Hopkins Press, 1964. xv, 296 p. Maps, bibliog.

Fogel's counterfactual econometric argument was developed to
show that "the railroad did not make an overwhelming contribution to the production potential of the economy" in the sense
that "no single innovation was vital for economic growth during the nineteenth century." A controversial work, resulting
in a great deal of comment, criticism, and subsequent study.

1177 Gates, Paul Wallace. THE ILLINOIS CENTRAL RAILROAD AND ITS
COLONIZATION WORK. Harvard Economic Studies, vol. 42. Cambridge, Mass.: Harvard University Press, 1934. xvi, 374 p. Illus.,
maps, bibliog.

The impact of the Illinois Central, a land-grant railroad, on settlement and colonization policies, land sales, agricultural developments, town promotion, and immigration are examined in this social and economic history.

1178   Glaab, Charles N. KANSAS CITY AND THE RAILROADS: COM-MUNITY POLICY IN THE GROWTH OF A REGIONAL METROPOLIS. Madison: State Historical Society of Wisconsin, 1962. xii, 260 p. Illus., maps, bibliog.

Kansas City from the 1850s to the 1880s was "the story of railroad planning and promotion," a theme central for many Western communities. The author investigates the motivating forces, community ideology regarding the West and transporta-tion, organization and operation of local railroad programs, and relationships between entrepreneurship, geography, and community planning.

1179   Overton, Richard C. BURLINGTON WEST: A COLONIZATION HIS-TORY OF THE BURLINGTON RAILROAD. Cambridge, Mass.: Harvard University Press, 1941. xxi, 583 p. Illus., maps, graphs, bibliog.

A detailed story of the Burlington Railroad's role in promoting settlement of Western lands during the half-century from 1856 to 1906 provides an interesting comparison with Gates's study, above.

1180   Scott, Roy V. "American Railroads and Agricultural Extension, 1900-1914: A Study in Railway Developmental Techniques." BUSINESS HISTORY REVIEW 39 (Spring 1965): 74-98.

Railroads served not only to expand settlement through land sales to farmers, but also promoted agricultural education as part of their business activities. Techniques included free or reduced rates for travelers on educational business, pamphlets on crop growing, educational demonstration trains and farms, county agents, and support for the Smith-Lever extension pro-gram.

1181   Stover, John F. AMERICAN RAILROADS. Chicago History of Ameri-can Civilization. Chicago: University of Chicago Press, 1961. x, 302 p. Illus., maps, bibliog.

A good brief survey of American railroads concentrates on the "Golden Age" from 1850 to 1916. Stover includes a list of important dates and briefly annotated suggestions for further reading.

1182   _____. IRON ROAD TO THE WEST: AMERICAN RAILROADS IN THE

1850s. New York: Columbia University Press, 1978. xii, 266 p. Illus., maps, bibliog.

It is Stover's belief "that no decade was more important in the history of American railroads than the ante-bellum 1850s." He describes the technological, political, and economic aspects of the railroad network as it developed east of the Mississippi. Unannotated but useful bibliography.

1183 _____. THE LIFE AND DECLINE OF THE AMERICAN RAILROAD. New York: Oxford University Press, 1970. xi, 324 p. Illus., maps, bibliog.

In a scholarly but nontechnical treatment, Stover surveys American railroading from the formation of the pioneer Baltimore and Ohio in 1827 to the late 1960s. Some of the topics covered include the use of railroads during wartime, competition with other forms of transportation, problems of freight and passenger service, and the use of computer systems in moving and classifying cars.

1184 Taylor, George Rogers, and Neu, Irene D. THE AMERICAN RAILROAD NETWORK, 1861-1890. Studies in Economic History. Cambridge, Mass.: Harvard University Press, 1956. ix, 113 p. Maps.

Taylor and Neu attempt to clarify misconceptions regarding the degree of physical integration of the pre-Civil War railroad system. The authors are particularly interested in tracing the crucial development of a standard-gauge during the next thirty years before integration was complete. Three excellent maps detail the railroads and gauges as they existed in 1861.

1185 Walker, James Blaine. FIFTY YEARS OF RAPID TRANSIT, 1864-1917. New York: Law Print Co., 1918. Reprint. Rise of Urban America. New York: Arno Press, 1970. iii, 291 p. Illus.

Walker covers rapid-transit technology, construction, and politics in New York City for elevated trains and the subways, but not single streetcars or trolleys.

1186 White, John H., Jr. AMERICAN LOCOMOTIVES: AN ENGINEERING HISTORY, 1830-1880. Baltimore: Johns Hopkins University Press, 1968. xxiii, 504 p. Illus., bibliog.

A definitive technical study of the first half-century of American locomotives is written primarily for the expert. Three sections cover fundamental design, components, and case histories of representative locomotives. Many drawings contribute to the value of this study.

1187 _____. THE AMERICAN RAILROAD PASSENGER CAR. Johns Hopkins
Studies in the History of Technology. New Series, no. 1. Baltimore:
Johns Hopkins University Press, 1978. xiii, 699 p. Illus., bibliog.

A detailed, well-written, and lavishly illustrated history covers
what passenger cars looked like, who made them and of what
materials, how they were arranged and used, and what they
cost. Emphasis is on the nineteenth century. Included are
brief biographical sketches of car designers and builders, and
a chronology of important events.

G. AUTOMOBILES

1188 Anderson, Rudolph E. THE STORY OF THE AMERICAN AUTOMOBILE:
HIGHLIGHTS AND SIDELIGHTS. Washington, D.C.: Public Affairs
Press, 1950. vii, 301 p. Illus.

An interesting social history of the automobile by an editor of
the journal of the National Automobile Dealers Association
emphasizes lesser-known aspects such as early nineteenth-
century road vehicles, advertising, racing, sex appeal, and
the automobile in song and theater.

1189 "Automobiles." JOURNAL OF POPULAR CULTURE 8 (Summer 1974):
121-84.

These articles on the automobile's place in American culture
combine the whimsical and the insightfully critical. Glen
Jeansonne's "The Automobile and Social Morality" probes
relationships between changing social standards and the use of
the auto. Other papers explain the rise and decline of styles
(e.g., "woodies" and tailfins), trace the evolution of ideas
of motion and comfort, and analyze the appeal of drag racing.

1190 Barrett, Paul. "Public Policy and Private Choice: Mass Transit and
the Automobile in Chicago between the Wars." BUSINESS HISTORY
REVIEW 49 (Winter 1975): 473-97.

The interplay between intellectual inertia regarding the value
of mass transit, including poor management, and the pressures
of engineers, business interests, automobile dealers, and own-
ers' associations to solve immediate crises played a crucial role
in the rise of the automobile at the expense of public transportation in Chicago.

1191 Berger, Michael L. "The Influence of the Automobile on Rural Health
Care, 1900-1929." JOURNAL OF THE HISTORY OF MEDICINE AND
ALLIED SCIENCES 28 (October 1973): 319-35.

Although bringing mixed blessings, on balance, the rise of the automobile in the early twentieth century contributed to improved, even if more complex, health care for the still largely rural population. The rise of rural hospitals, expanded public health services, and the increased mobility of physicians more than offset the move of many doctors to small towns and the consequent depersonalization of medicine and rise of "irregular" doctors.

1192 Black, Stephen. MAN AND MOTOR CARS: AN ERGONOMIC STUDY. New York: W.W. Norton and Co., 1966. 373 p. Illus., bibliog.

Black's study considers the genesis of design--a synthesis of biology and engineering--with respect to the nature of the motor car. He investigates the economic and psychological implications of the motor car, which clearly is not designed to answer man's biological needs.

1193 Borth, Christy. MANKIND ON THE MOVE: THE STORY OF HIGH-WAYS. Washington, D.C.: Automotive Safety Foundation, 1969. vi, 314 p. Illus.

Borth's history of "roads" and their relationship to vehicular traffic starts with the ancient world and includes a great deal of information on Europe. The latter third of the volume covers America and its twentieth-century automobile culture.

1194 Brownell, Blaine A. "A Symbol of Modernity: Attitudes toward the Automobile in Southern Cities in the 1920's." AMERICAN QUARTERLY 24 (March 1972): 20-44.

The rapid adoption of the automobile in Southern cities during the 1920s, as in other regions, included a complex array of attitudes which cut across class and racial lines, ranging from complete acceptance to deep suspicion. The automobile, as with other technologies, was seen as a fundamental force in society and thus a symbol of modernity.

1195 Buel, Ronald A. DEAD END: THE AUTOMOBILE IN MASS TRANSPORTATION. Englewood Cliffs, N.J.: Prentice-Hall, 1972. 231 p.

Buel looks critically at the urban transportation network where the automobile plays the primary determining role. The auto has had a negative effect upon society in terms of economic waste, violence, land use, pollution, and energy consumption. Suggested alternatives include rapid-transit systems, bicycles and walking, buses, taxis, car pools, and restrictions upon autos such as purposely induced congestion.

1196 Chandler, Alfred D[upont]., Jr., ed. GIANT ENTERPRISE: FORD,

GENERAL MOTORS AND THE AUTOMOBILE INDUSTRY. Forces in American Economic Growth Series. New York: Harcourt, Brace, and World, 1964. xiii, 242 p. Bibliog.

A collection of introductory readings reveals the development and workings of the automobile industry--its technology, markets, business, and labor organization. Chandler provides valuable introductions and a brief conclusion to set the selections in context for the reader.

1197   Cohn, David L[ewis]. COMBUSTION ON WHEELS: AN INFORMAL HISTORY OF THE AUTOMOBILE AGE. Boston: Houghton Mifflin, 1944. 272 p. Illus.

The subtitle is an accurate description of this discussion of the daily life and habits surrounding the use of the automobile prior to World War II.

1198   Flink, James J. AMERICA ADOPTS THE AUTOMOBILE, 1895-1910. Cambridge: M.I.T. Press, 1970. xii, 343 p. Illus., bibliog.

Flink's excellent social history of the impact of the automobile on American life is based upon contemporary periodical literature. Sections on automobile clubs, increasing regulation, ancillary services such as roads and garages, industrial organization, and the development of a mass market emphasize the existence of an American car culture prior to the opening of Ford's Highland Park plant.

1199   _____. THE CAR CULTURE. Cambridge: M.I.T. Press, 1975. x, 260 p.

In an expansion of an earlier article (no. 1200), the author presents a provocative and "controversial" case for automobility as an alternative approach to a "Presidential Synthesis" of American history since 1890. The three stages of the automobile in America are: from its nineteenth-century introduction to the opening of the Ford Highland Park plant in 1910, a second period in which the motor car received mass idolization and dramatically altered American society, and, third, the period since 1950, in which the auto has been seen not as a progressive force for change but, rather, as a social problem.

1200   _____. "Three Stages of American Automobile Consciousness," AMERICAN QUARTERLY 24 (October 1972): 451-73.

Although expanded upon in his book, THE CAR CULTURE, (no. 1199), this article is worth noting for its concise statement of Flink's viewpoint.

1201   Ford, Henry. MY LIFE AND WORK. New York: Doubleday, 1922. 289 p.

   Not a complete autobiography, this work offers Ford's personal ideas on human needs, business and work, progress, and the machine. Central to his analysis are the "primary functions" of agriculture, manufacture, and transportation. The autobiography was written in collaboration with Samuel Crowther. Subsequent volumes of similar nature by Ford are TODAY AND TOMORROW (1926) and MOVING FORWARD (1930).

1202   Foster, Mark S. "The Model-T, the Hard Sell, and Los Angeles's Urban Growth: The Decentralization of Los Angeles during the 1920's." PACIFIC HISTORICAL REVIEW 44 (November 1975): 459-84.

   Forces shaping the twentieth-century American city were vastly different from those affecting nineteenth-century urbanization. The flexibility of an inexpensive, mass-produced automobile readily available to a rapidly growing population, in contrast to the more limited trolley car, made possible the decentralization of Los Angeles. The nature of the decentralization process is examined.

1203   Gustin, Lawrence R. BILLY DURANT: CREATOR OF GENERAL MOTORS. Grand Rapids, Mich.: William B. Eerdmans, 1973. 285 p. Illus., bibliog.

   Gustin's popularized but solid account of Durant's personal role in the founding of G.M. and his relationship with the auto industry generally is based on previously unpublished Durant manuscripts and oral interviews.

1204   Jerome, John. THE DEATH OF THE AUTOMOBILE: THE FATAL EFFECT OF THE GOLDEN ERA, 1955-1970. New York: W.W. Norton and Co., 1972. 288 p. Illus.

   Although a popular polemic against the present-day automobile, which the author believes must go if we are to rebalance our society, this is a thoughtful piece written by a one-time automotive journalist.

1205   Keats, John. THE INSOLENT CHARIOTS. New York: J.B. Lippincott Co., 1958. 233 p. Illus.

   Keats' satiric but thoughtful diatribe on the disillusionment with the automobile industry in the late 1950s is written for a popular audience.

1206   Kennedy, Edward D. THE AUTOMOBILE INDUSTRY: THE COMING OF AGE OF CAPITALISM'S FAVORITE CHILD. New York: Reynal and Hitchcock, 1941. 333 p.

Although superseded by the works of Rae and Flink, this is still a useful summary of the first half-century of the American automobile from 1890 to 1940.

1207 Leland, Mrs. Wilfred C., and Millbrook, Minnie Dubbs. MASTER OF PRECISION: HENRY M. LELAND. Detroit: Wayne State University Press, 1966. 296 p. Illus.

This biography of the developer of the Cadillac, Lincoln, and the self-starter is based on the Leland papers and is written by his son Wilfred's wife. It is revealing of developments in the early automobile industry.

1208 May, George S. A MOST UNIQUE MACHINE: THE MICHIGAN ORIGINS OF THE AUTOMOBILE INDUSTRY. Grand Rapids, Mich.: William B. Eerdmans, 1975. 408 p. Illus., bibliog.

May's study of the automobile industry from its beginnings in the mid-1890s to 1909 suggests why Michigan and Detroit, in particular, took the lead in automobile manufacturing: available finances, an appropriate labor force, and pre-existing carriage and gasoline industries. The author concentrates on the manufacture and business developments rather than on the impact of the auto on society. The bibliographical essay covers primary sources only.

1209 _____. R.E. OLDS: AUTO INDUSTRY PIONEER. Grand Rapids, Mich.: William B. Eerdmans, 1977. viii, 458 p. Illus., bibliog.

May resurrects the career of Ransom Olds from the shadow of Henry Ford and places it within the context of the developing automobile industry. Olds was an early pioneer in the development of steam, electric, and gasoline automobiles, and his "mass-produced" curved-dash Oldsmobile predated Ford's Model T by several years.

1210 Nevins, Allan, and Hill, Frank Ernest. FORD. 3 vols. New York: Charles Scribner's Sons, 1954-63. Reprint. Companies and Men, Business Enterprise in America. New York: Arno Press, 1976. xx, 688; xx, 714; ix, 508 p. Illus., maps, bibliog.

A lengthy history of the Ford Motor Company includes a great deal of biographical information on Ford himself. Volume 1, THE TIMES, THE MAN, THE COMPANY, covers the early years up to 1915 and such developments as the five-dollar day, assembly line, and Model T. Volume 2, EXPANSION AND CHALLENGE, 1915-1933, includes material on the war years, the expansion of the 1920s, including River Rouge and the Model A, and the threat of depression. The third volume, DECLINE AND REBIRTH, 1933-1962, recounts the revival of Ford from near financial disaster and its transformation into the modern industrial corporation it is today.

1211   Niemeyer, Glenn A. THE AUTOMOTIVE CAREER OF RANSOM E. OLDS. MSU Business Studies. East Lansing: Michigan State University Press, 1963. xiii, 233 p. Illus., bibliog.

This biography places Olds's achievements within the automobile industry into comparative perspective much as Nevins and Hill did with FORD (no. 1210). Includes a chronology of Olds's career.

1212   Rae, John B. THE AMERICAN AUTOMOBILE: A BRIEF HISTORY. Chicago History of American Civilization. Chicago: University of Chicago Press, 1965. xv, 265 p. Illus., maps, bibliog.

Rae tells the story of America's adoption and subsequent love affair with the automobile in this excellent survey of the industry and related developments during the years from 1893 to 1963. "The American automobile has become a way of life, and whatever happens to it must profoundly affect the economy and the whole culture of the United States." Includes a list of important dates.

1213   _____. AMERICAN AUTOMOBILE MANUFACTURES: THE FIRST FORTY YEARS. Philadelphia: Chilton, 1959. xii, 233 p. Illus., bibliog.

Rae traces the development of the automobile through the industry's leading manufacturers from its beginnings to 1935. Throughout he stresses the human element in terms of business leadership, considering it the most important factor in the industry's growth.

1214   _____. THE ROAD AND THE CAR IN AMERICAN LIFE. Cambridge: M.I.T. Press, 1971. 404 p. Illus., bibliog.

A generally positive view of the social and economic effects of highway transportation relates the automobile to the road. Rae concludes that "transportation is social progress because it has been throughout history the way in which not only goods and services but ideas as well were exchanged among peoples."

1215   _____, ed. HENRY FORD. Great Lives Observed. Englewood Cliffs, N.J.: Prentice-Hall, 1969. ix, 180 p. Bibliog.

A collection of short essays and excerpts by Ford himself, his contemporaries, and more recent, leading historians provides a balanced perspective of Ford's thinking and personality rather than the impact of his work.

1216   Rothschild, Emma. PARADISE LOST: THE DECLINE OF THE AUTO-INDUSTRIAL AGE. New York: Random House, 1973. ix, 264 p.

Rothschild tries to explain the declining state of the automobile industry by examining such interrelated problems as environmental concerns, urban congestion, rising costs, styling changes, "obsolete" automotive technology, foreign competition, and the collapse of social and institutional support. The "mortality" of the auto industry does not imply economic catastrophe but will necessitate extensive readjustment. The author draws heavily upon G.M. and the Vega as exemplifying the problems of Detroit.

1217 Sanford, Charles L., ed. AUTOMOBILES IN AMERICAN LIFE. Case Studies in the Human Dimensions of Science and Technology. Troy, N.Y.: Rensselaer Polytechnic Institute, 1978. iii, 187 p. Bibliog.

Sanford's collection is the first in a proposed series of inexpensive documentary case studies for use in courses concerned with science/technology-related issues of public policy. Value considerations are assumed to count as much as factual data. Selections include James Flink's excellent "Three Stages of American Automobile Consciousness" (no. 1200), and material from Henry Ford, Studs Terkel, Alfred Sloan, Emma Rothschild, John B. Rae, and Lewis Mumford, among others. A brief bibliographical essay highlights valuable additional sources.

1218 Sloan, Alfred P., Jr. MY YEARS WITH GENERAL MOTORS. Garden City, N.Y.: Doubleday, 1964. xxv, 472 p. Illus.

Sloan's autobiography contains a great deal of valuable information with respect to his participation in major changes at G.M., where he was chief executive officer from 1923 to 1946, including the company restructuring and automotive styling.

1219 Thompson, George V. "Intercompany Technical Standardization in the Early American Automobile Industry." JOURNAL OF ECONOMIC HISTORY 14 (Winter 1954): 1-20.

Thompson traces the growth of intercompany technical standards and the interconnections with changing business conditions from the automotive industry's early years, characterized by many small firms, to about 1930, a period typified by the larger corporation. This study of changing standards and their adoption shows how "technology frequently reflects institutional conditions as well as advances in knowledge."

1220 "Transportation and People." SOCIETY 10 (July-August 1973): 14-49.

Sociological aspects of automobile ownership, use, and misuse are revealed through the varied papers of this issue. Automobiles have been used as a means of permitting youthful hitchhikers to escape from home, while enslaving the daily commuter. They provide a livelihood for taxi drivers, while inhibiting opportunities for car-less ghetto dwellers. Several authors provide suggestions for private automobile transport; of these, John P. Huttman's suggestion of public car rentals is perhaps the most unusual.

1221 White, Lawrence J. THE AUTOMOBILE INDUSTRY SINCE 1945. Cambridge, Mass.: Harvard University Press, 1971. xii, 348 p. Bibliog.

Although there is some attention paid to the technical side of automobile manufacturing, this is primarily an economic, "industrial organization" study with chapters on economies of scale, integration and diversification, pricing, dealership systems, foreign competition, pollution, and safety, among others. White concludes with several recommendations, including the creation of ten new firms to replace the present Big Three.

1222 Wik, Reynold M. HENRY FORD AND GRASS-ROOTS AMERICA. Ann Arbor: University of Michigan Press, 1972. x, 266 p. Illus.

Honesty, thrift, and hard work in addition to an inexpensive automobile earned Henry Ford a hero's reputation among rural Americans. Wik concludes that his fame was based on an "ability to mass produce a practical automobile which had a universal appeal." An honest picture of Ford, his image and impact upon rural America, includes chapters on his attitudes toward ecology, education, politics, and the Great Depression.

H. AVIATION AND SPACE

1223 Bryan, Leslie A. "Social Effects of Aviation." IMPACT OF SCIENCE ON SOCIETY 2 (April-June 1951): 41-46.

After only twenty-five years, air transport in America occupied an important place in public and commercial transport. Bryan considers the economic, political, and social results of that success. Among the changes catalogued are suburbanization, a great importance for inland cities, business and pleasure travel, aviation medicine, and an increasing need for international cooperation.

1224 _____. "Some Impacts of Aviation." IMPACT OF SCIENCE ON SOCIETY 16, no. 2 (1966): 113-30.

In a followup to his 1951 study (no. 1223), Bryan surveys the changes of the subsequent fifteen years. He notes the

surprising emergence of passenger service as the dominant
source of airline revenue, and the marked increases in air
shipment of goods. Politically, air travel has ushered in a
new age of personal diplomacy. Trends projected are essentially the same as in Bryan's earlier article.

1225 Clarke, Arthur C. "The Challenge of the Spaceship." IMPACT OF
SCIENCE ON SOCIETY 4 (Spring 1953): 15-28.

In this pre-Sputnik paper, Clarke makes conservative projections for dates for manned lunar landings and other space
triumphs. He ponders the potential effects of space exploration on the sciences and on human consciousness, concluding,
"the future development of mankind, in the spiritual and no
less the material plane, is bound up with the conquest of
space."

1226 Emme, Eugene M. A HISTORY OF SPACE FLIGHT. New York:
Holt, Rinehart, and Winston, 1965. 224 p. Illus., bibliog.

The first half of this survey provides an introduction to man's
view of the universe and mythical perceptions of flight, as
well as a background on ballooning, early fixed-wing flights,
and the evolution of rocket technology. The remainder covers
the space age from Sputnik through 1964. Includes a chronology of milestones in space flight from 1957 to 1965.

1227 Etzioni, Amitai. THE MOON-DOGGLE: DOMESTIC AND INTERNA-
TIONAL IMPLICATIONS OF THE SPACE RACE. Garden City, N.Y.:
Doubleday, 1964. xv, 198 p.

In a polemical critique of the space program, the author contends that it, and the moon landing especially, has diverted
an inexcusable amount of scientific and economic resources
away from worthier projects, while accomplishing little toward
the goals of increasing national prestige and security. A
thorough reorganization of national science institutions to coordinate a responsible science policy is urged.

1228 Ginsberg, Robert. "Social Aesthetics: The Moonlanding and the
Imagination." JOURNAL OF SOCIAL PHILOSOPHY 7 (April 1976):
1-5.

The author expresses resentment and melancholy at having
been deprived of the moon as a subject worthy of imaginative
wonder. He dreams of possible moon landings, concluding
that the actual landing was so mundane and pedestrian that it
exhibited only our own puniness and inability to soar above
human dilemmas. The discovery of the New World by the
Europeans was an infinitely richer experience.

1229 Howard, Frank, and Gunston, Bill. THE CONQUEST OF THE AIR. New York: Random House, 1972. 264 p. Illus., bibliog.

Although balloons and rockets are briefly considered in this popular survey from man's earliest myths and legends regarding flight to today's space travel, the bulk of the volume is concerned with winged aircraft. Lavishly illustrated.

1230 Kelly, Fred C. THE WRIGHT BROTHERS. New York: Harcourt, Brace and Co., 1943. xi, 340 p. Illus.

Kelly's authorized biography of the Wright Brothers is aimed at the nontechnical reader and concentrates on the decade from 1900 to 1910. Orville Wright contributed suggested changes in the manuscript.

1231 Levy, Lillian, ed. SPACE: ITS IMPACT ON MAN AND SOCIETY. New York: W.W. Norton and Co., 1965. 228 p.

This collection represents an attempt to examine some of the political, economic, religious, and philsophical questions posed by space exploration. A piece by Lyndon B. Johnson, then President, appropriately opens the volume with a discussion of the politics of space. Space exploration effects on such diverse social phenomena as language and women's rights are followed by articles concerned with moral and religious dilemmas.

1232 Logsdon, John M. THE DECISION TO GO TO THE MOON: PROJECT APOLLO AND THE NATIONAL INTEREST. Cambridge: M.I.T. Press, 1970. xiii, 187 p.

Following an historical reconstruction of events leading up to the lunar-landing decision, Logsdon probes deeper into the values, motivations, and decision-making processes that resulted in the moonshot program. He concludes that the "Apollo approach" might well be used in addressing other, nontechnical problems.

1233 Mailer, Norman. OF A FIRE ON THE MOON. Boston: Little, Brown and Co., 1970. 472 p.

Despite an education in aeronautical engineering, Mailer bemoans his inability to relate to the Apollo 11 moon mission until he succeeds in restoring "magic and psyche" to the technological venture. He believes a "psychology of machines" is essential because there are spirits in the technological appliances which give them a "mind of their own, harboring waywardness, self-will, and even magic." Mailer presents the hypothesis that the colossal moon venture could prove to be an exploration, via technology, to discover the passions and instincts which have made man worship the machine throughout history.

1234   Mazlish, Bruce, ed. THE RAILROAD AND THE SPACE PROGRAM:
        AN EXPLORATION IN HISTORICAL ANALOGY. Technology, Space,
        and Society. Cambridge: M.I.T. Press, 1965. ix, 223 p.

   The collection of eight essays was sponsored by the American
   Academy of Arts and Sciences under NASA funding to help
   determine the potential impact of the space program upon
   society by means of an historical analogy with nineteenth-
   century railroads. Contributions by Mazlish, Thomas Parke
   Hughes, Robert Fogel, Paul Cootner, Alfred Chandler, Stephen
   Salsbury, Thomas C. Cochran, Robert Brandfon, and Leo Marx
   cover railway technology; economic, political, and social
   impacts of the railroad; resulting changes in business administration; and the image of the railroad as a cultural symbol.
   Reveals more about the impact of the railroad than of the
   space program.

1235   Michael, Donald N. "The Beginning of the Space Age and American
        Public Opinion." PUBLIC OPINION QUARTERLY 24 (Winter 1960):
        573-82.

   Contemporary reactions to Sputnik I (1957) are analyzed
   through a review of public reports and informally collected
   data. Michael discovered that opinion about the space-shot
   was inconsistent and often illogical. But it did not resemble
   the psychological shock predicted by some researchers as the
   likely reaction to technological breakthroughs of such magnitude.

1236   Ogburn, William Fielding. THE SOCIAL EFFECTS OF AVIATION.
        Boston: Houghton Mifflin, 1946. vi, 755 p. Illus., bibliog.

   In an ambitiously wide-ranging study, Ogburn forecasts the
   impact of the developing aviation industry on American society.
   Technical developments toward greater speed, comfort, and
   safety would lead, he prophesized, to an expansion of airmail
   and of passenger travel. Perhaps overly influenced by the
   history of the automobile, he foresaw a helicopter in every
   far-flung suburban home, air ambulances, and airborne law-
   enforcement vehicles.

1237   Rae, John B. CLIMB TO GREATNESS: THE AMERICAN AIRCRAFT
        INDUSTRY 1920-1960. Cambridge: M.I.T. Press, 1968. xiii, 280 p.
        Illus., bibliog.

   The history of the modern American aircraft industry is political
   as well as technological because of the close involvement of
   the federal government as its chief customer. After 1960 the
   industry changed and became dominated by aerospace interests.

1238   Ritner, Peter. THE SOCIETY OF SPACE. New York: Macmillan,
        1961. 144 p.

Loosely written essays present discourse on three types of "spaces": that inside the human mind, the opportunities created by the technological revolution, and the extraterrestrial environment. Ritner celebrates the rejuvenation of idealism about space ushered in with the Kennedy era, and the simultaneous resuscitation of art and enthusiasm.

1239 Swenson, Lloyd S. "The 'Megamachine' behind the Mercury Spacecraft." AMERICAN QUARTERLY 21 (Summer 1969): 210-27.

In a study of government-industry relations during the development of the Mercury spacecraft, Swenson focuses on the nature and function of the Mercury "team." The space organization is viewed as a "megamachine" of people, its coordination an achievement comparable to the space-flight itself.

1240 Taubenfeld, Howard Jack, ed. SPACE AND SOCIETY: STUDIES FOR THE SEMINAR ON PROBLEMS OF OUTER SPACE, SPONSORED BY THE CARNEGIE ENDOWMENT FOR INTERNATIONAL PEACE. Dobbs Ferry, N.Y.: Oceana Publishers, 1964. xviii, 172 p.

The mutual impact of space on man and man on space serves as the topic for this collection. From a consideration of the politics and science of space exploration, authors consider competing claims to and uses for outer space, with special emphasis on the military and on communications. Contributors include Robert Jastrow and Richard Falk.

1241 Van Dyke, Vernon. PRIDE AND POWER: THE RATIONALE OF THE SPACE PROGRAM. Urbana: University of Illinois Press, 1964. xii, 285 p.

In this analysis of the American space program, Van Dyke focuses principally on motives. The most powerful, he discerned, were national prestige and pride. The author builds his case through detailed study of the program's history, and its technological and economic ramifications.

1242 Von Braun, Wernher, and Ordway, Frederick I. III. HISTORY OF ROCKETRY AND SPACE TRAVEL. 1966. 3d rev. ed. New York: Thomas Y. Crowell Co., 1975. xii, 308 p. Illus., bibliog.

This popular but detailed history of astronautics from the early years of Chinese rocketry to recent manned space flights is international in scope, although the emphasis for the modern period is understandably on the U.S. and USSR. Very well illustrated with color as well as black-and-white photographs and drawings.

Transportation

1243   Ward, John W. "The Meaning of Lindbergh's Flight." AMERICAN
        QUARTERLY 10 (Spring 1958): 3-16.

        An especially insightful analysis of Lindbergh's 1927 trans-
        Atlantic flight asks the questions, "Was the flight the achieve-
        ment of a heroic, solitary, unaided individual? Or did the
        flight represent the triumph of the machine, the success of
        an industrially organized society?" In Lindbergh, the people
        could celebrate both, and the conflict remains unresolved to-
        day.

Part 12

COMMUNICATIONS

A. GENERAL

1. Bibliographies

1244   Blum, Eleanor. BASIC BOOKS IN THE MASS MEDIA. Urbana: University of Illinois Press, 1972. ix, 252 p.

An annotated, selective bibliography covers general communications, publishing, broadcasting, and film. There are 665 entries in all, supplemented by a list of scholarly and professional periodicals.

1245   Gordon, Thomas F., and Verna, Mary Ellen. MASS COMMUNICATION EFFECTS AND PROCESSES: A COMPREHENSIVE BIBLIOGRAPHY, 1950-1975. Beverly Hills, Calif.: Sage Publications, 1978. 227 p.

A partially annotated research bibliography covers over 2700 books, journal articles, and reports on media processes, use, content, and effects. Arrangement is by author, with access provided through a literature overview, subject index, and index of nonprimary authors.

1246   Hansen, Donald A., and Parsons, J. Herschel. MASS COMMUNICATIONS: A RESEARCH BIBLIOGRAPHY. Santa Barbara, Calif.: Glendessary Press, 1968. 144 p.

Three hundred citations, unannotated, are included. Entries are organized in the following categories: bibliographies and reference materials, research and methods, media, contents, media organizations, the audiences, and diffusion effects and functions.

2. Books and Articles

1247   Albanese, Catherine L. "Technological Regligion: Life-Orientation and THE MECHANICAL BRIDE." JOURNAL OF POPULAR CULTURE 10 (Summer 1976): 14-27.

Albanese finds in McLuhan's study of advertising and media, THE MECHANICAL BRIDE (no. 1273), examples of an American "technological religion, a life-orientation system centered around the machine, its products, its values, the modes of consciousness and unconsciousness it encourages, and the forms of action it applauds." She traces the tensions of this "religion" through McLuhan's ads, concluding that, whatever the outcome, we are intimately involved.

1248 Bagdakian, Ben H. THE INFORMATION MACHINES: THEIR IMPACT ON MEN AND THE MEDIA. New York: Harper and Row, 1971. xxxvi, 359 p.

From a study of present trends, Bagdakian projects the future of news selection and presentation, assessing the potential role of new technologies in creating change. The future of print versus broadcast media is discussed at length, along with projections of content of future news.

1249 Bauer, Raymond A., and Bauer, Alice H. "America, Mass Society and Mass Media." JOURNAL OF SOCIAL ISSUES 16, no. 3 (1960): 1-88.

In considering the relationship of the mass media to American society, the authors challenge the concept of a passive "mass society" victimized by successive waves of technological innovation. They point to research that indicates a growing recognition of the role of personal interaction in determining response to mass media. While acknowledging television's seductive draw as a substitute for real experience, the authors conclude that there is no clear evidence of television's deleterious effects.

1250 Boorstin, Daniel J[oseph.] THE IMAGE: OR, WHAT HAPPENED TO THE AMERICAN DREAM. New York: Atheneum Press, 1962. vi, 315 p. Bibliog.

Americans are feeding upon illusions, from abridged books to television, in a world of self-created "pseudo-events." Stemming from the graphic revolution of the nineteenth century, "the image," assembled through American wealth, literacy, and technology, has clouded our vision of reality and our power to shape it.

1251 Bowers, Raymond; Lee, Alfred M.; and Hershey, Cary, eds. COMMUNICATIONS FOR A MOBILE SOCIETY: AN ASSESSMENT OF NEW TECHNOLOGY. Beverly Hills, Calif.: Sage Publications, 1978. 432 p.

A state-of-the-art study of land mobile communications systems encompasses the history, current uses, capabilities, and future commercial and public potential of citizen's-band radios and similar devices. Special attention is given to legal and safety issues. An admirably well-rounded technology assessment.

1252   Bowes, John E.   "Media Technology: Detour or Panacea for Resolving Urban Information Needs?"   JOURNAL OF BROADCASTING 20 (Summer 1976):   333-43.

Before the complexities of urban living can be ameliorated by media technology in the form of information utility and low-cost computing, a number of problems must be solved.   Interface difficulties and the threat of "information overload" have thus far stayed a media "revolution."   It will be necessary to design file structures and control language to meet public rather than specialized needs.

1253   Carey, James W., and Quirk, John J.   "The Mythos of the Electronic Revolution."   AMERICAN SCHOLAR 39 (Spring-Summer 1970):   219-41, 391-424.

An increasingly prevalent and popular brand of futurism identifies electronics and cybernetics with the prospect for a new birth of community, decentralization, ecological balance, and social harmony.   Prophets of this electronic utopia--such as Buckminster Fuller, John Cage, Marshall McLuhan, and Zbigniew Brzezinski--have such diverse cultural and political views that their unity of vision in this matter seems surprising. And yet, the authors submit, visible effects to date of electronic advances suggest that they are all wrong--that the "electronic revolution" will bring centralized power, erosion of regional culture, and new forms of pollution.

1254   "Communications Explosion."   ARTS IN SOCIETY 9 (Summer-Fall 1972): 177-338.

The effect of the pervasiveness of electronic communications on society and art is the topic of this issue.   Several contributors consider the role of various art forms as communications mediums.   Articles include: "Art Beyond the Communications Explosion," by Vytautas Kavolis; "Sensibility under Technocracy: Reflections On The Culture of Processed Communications," by Kingsley Widmer; and "Dr. Jekyll and the Bride of Frankenstein: Socio-Historical Aspects of Man-Machine Interaction," by John McHale.   Social roles of cable television, documentary film, and electronic music are also discussed.

1255   "Communications vs. Powers."   SOCIETY 12 (September-October 1975): 26-71.

The meaning of developments in telecommunications for personal privacy, cultural integrity, and political power is assessed.   Several authors, including Paul Laskin, Emile G. McAnany, and Ithiel de Sola Pool are concerned with the impact of American broadcasting worldwide on the values and

traditions of other nations, particularly those in the developing world. Marguerite and Jacques Bouvard fear for the protection of individual rights; Jerrold Oppenheim optimistically
suggests that UHF television may prove to be the best means
of "breaking the monolith" of the communications industry.

1256 Dexter, Lewis Anthony, and White, David Anthony, eds. PEOPLE,
SOCIETY AND MASS COMMUNICATIONS. New York: Free Press of
Glencoe, 1964. xii, 595 p. Bibliog.

A well-selected anthology assesses the strengths, weaknesses,
and social roles of the mass media. The seven parts, each
offering five or six prefaced articles, cover social perspectives, audience makeup and behavior, social institutions as
communications networks, and communications research.
Among the well-known writers featured are Franklin Fearing,
Elihu Katz, Ithiel de Sola Pool, Raymond Bauer, and Ben
Bagdakian. There is an appendix entitled "A Critique of
Bibliographic Matter in Mass Communications."

1257 "The Electronic Revolution." AMERICAN SCHOLAR 35 (Spring 1966):
189-374.

A giant special issue brings together papers delivered at the
conference Vision 65. Among the twenty-five or so essays
are contributions by Marshall McLuhan, Buckminster Fuller,
Jacob Bronowski, Loren Eiseley and other luminaries. Visionary interests roam music, poetry, television and film, computers, and cybernetics.

1258 Ewen, Stuart. CAPTAINS OF CONSCIOUSNESS: ADVERTISING AND
THE SOCIAL ROOTS OF THE CONSUMER CULTURE. New York:
McGraw-Hill, 1976. x, 261 p. Bibliog.

A study of mass consumption and modern advertising in our
twentieth-century industrial society from a Marxist perspective.
Today's "mass culture" is viewed as a result of the desire for
industrial stability through complete social control. Useful
bibliography.

1259 Fuller, Wayne E. THE AMERICAN MAIL: ENLARGER OF THE
COMMON LIFE. Chicago History of American Civilization. Chicago:
University of Chicago Press, 1972. xi, 378 p. Bibliog.

It is the author's hope to rescue the role of the mail within
our communications system from historical oblivion. He shows
the intimate relationship between the mail and transportation
developments and reveals that new communications techniques
seldom displaced the old, but rather redefined them. Annotated bibliography.

1260 _____. RFD, THE CHANGING FACE OF RURAL AMERICA. Bloomington: Indiana University Press, 1964. xii, 361 p. Illus., map.

Rural Free Delivery for mail radically changed the nature of rural life in the early decades of this century. From its early horse and buggy days to those of the automobile and improved roads, the RFD system decreased the isolation of the American farmer.

1261 Gerbner, George H.; Gross, Larry P.; and Melody, William H., eds. COMMUNICATIONS TECHNOLOGY AND SOCIAL POLICY: UNDERSTANDING THE NEW CULTURAL REVOLUTION. New York: John Wiley and Sons, 1973. xiii, 573 p.

The purpose of this anthology is to discuss ways of harnessing the "tidal wave of communications technology" for the realization of public goals. Contributors reflect on the social, economic, and cultural implications of new technologies. The first part discusses the capabilities of such new technologies as cable television and communications satellites. Subsequent parts cover national and international regulation, educational technology, urban communications systems, applications in developing countries, and the need for continuing impact assessment.

1262 Goldhamer, Herbert, ed. THE SOCIAL EFFECTS OF COMMUNICATIONS TECHNOLOGY. Santa Monica, Calif.: Rand Corp., 1970. vii, 31 p.

Concise two-paragraph descriptions, written in nontechnical language, introduce the reader to the technological foundations of the communications revolution--e.g., transistors, integrated circuits, and computers, and resultant devices--cable technology, videophones, communications satellites, and others. Present and projected effects on education, political behavior, privacy, and lifestyles are crisply presented. The author urges further research on the social effects of communications technology.

1263 Greenberg, Bradley S., and Dervin, Brenda. USES OF THE MASS MEDIA BY THE URBAN POOR: FINDINGS OF THREE RESEARCH PROJECTS. New York: Praeger Publishers, 1970. xvi, 251 p. Bibliog.

The first part reports the results of three research projects on the mass communications behavior of poor adults, adolescents, and children. Some eighty previous studies on the communication behavior of the poor are reviewed in the following part. The mass media, especially television, are found to be heavily utilized by the improverished, constituting their prin-

cipal link to the larger society. There is a lengthy annotated
bibliography, pp. 130-249.

1264   Horton, Donald, and Wohl, R. Richard. "Mass Communication and
        Parasocial Interaction." PSYCHIATRY 19 (August 1956): 215-29.

        One of the most striking characteristics of mass media--partic-
        ularly radio, television and the movies--is that they promote
        the illusion of face-to-face relationships between performer
        and audiences. For the lonely and disaffected, the distinction
        between such parasocial and genuinely social relationships be-
        comes blurred.

1265   Katzman, Natan. "Impact of Communication Technology: Some Theo-
        retical Premises and Their Implications." EKISTICS 38 (August 1974):
        125-30.

        Six theoretical premises about the social implications of new
        communications technologies are presented and discussed. The
        introduction of new techniques increases the amount of informa-
        tion transmitted and received by individuals, but especially by
        those already information-rich. Thus new information, Katzman
        concludes, actually advances social inequality through widening
        information gaps.

1266   Klapper, Joseph T. THE EFFECTS OF MASS COMMUNICATION.
        Glencoe, Ill.: Free Press, 1960. 302 p. Bibliog.

        In a broad, authoritative survey of the literature, covering over
        one thousand studies, Klapper synthesizes social research treating
        mass media and its consequences. Opinion-formation research
        consumes a good part of the book, as do such topics as media-
        related crime and violence, and media-induced escapism and
        passivity. Based on his review, Klapper assigns to media
        only a secondary role in influencing opinion and exacerbating
        social ills.

1267   Lamberton, Donald M., ed. "The Information Revolution." ANNALS
        OF THE AMERICAN ACADEMY OF POLITICAL AND SOCIAL SCIENCE
        412 (March 1974): 1-162.

        Viewing the exponential growth of information as a revolution-
        ary development, the editor offers an interdisciplinary collec-
        tion as an attempt to analyze the beginnings of this nascent
        upheaval. The first part encompasses general considerations,
        with a paper on the need for citizen participation in communi-
        cations planning. The second part, "Social and Economic
        Developments," reflects on information impacts on business,
        economic analysis, and property rights. A third part looks at
        ways in which information technologies might aid in the provi-

sion of social services, while closing papers treat information policy issues.

1268   Larsen, Otto N., ed. VIOLENCE AND THE MASS MEDIA. New York: Harper and Row, 1968. 310 p.

Contributors assess the social effects of the portrayal of violence in a wide spectrum of communications forms. Selections have been drawn from speeches, news reports, and articles in popular and scholarly journals dating from 1954 to 1966. The efficacy of regulation and control is stressed through solid documentation of events that precipitated the voluntary coding of movies and comic books.

1269   Leone, Mark. "Modern American Culture: The Decline of the Future." JOURNAL OF POPULAR CULTURE 4 (Spring 1971): 863-80.

Our cultural institutions do not appear to be capable of generating the social and ideological unity needed for successful adaptation to technology. McLuhan has suggested that we are being retribalized and homogenized by the media. Television and spectator sports, Leone suggests, have become the institutions that reinforce American values, while ideology has been reduced to a set of beliefs generated by each individual for his own use, and synthesized from "bits and pieces of conceptual baggage."

1270   McHale, John. THE CHANGING INFORMATION ENVIRONMENT. Boulder, Colo.: Westview Press, 1976. x, 117 p. Bibliog.

Recent advances in information technology have been viewed in two ways: as a universal panacea, or as the onset of an Orwellian nightmare. As he analyzes such developments, McHale considers the appropriateness of these opposing visions. What he views as the crucial nexus is the convergence of computer systems with concurrently developing information technologies. Together, they will form a radically new information environment of yet unknown meaning.

1271   _____. "The Future of Art and Mass Culture." FUTURES 10 (June 1978): 178-90.

The advent of mass culture has been linked to technologies of communication, i.e., radio, television, and cinema. Although there are few historical precedents from which to extrapolate future directions of mass culture, some changes in art and social culture can be argued. Mechanical reproduction has dematerialized the artifact so that art is no longer "in the frame." It moves toward combines, happenings, and lifestyles. Communication and information technologies alter the concept of mass culture from vertical levels to horizontal interaction and broaden the concept of art until it includes even the work experience.

1272　McLuhan, [Herbert] Marshall. "At the Flip Point of Time--The Point of More Return?" JOURNAL OF COMMUNICATION 25 (Autumn 1975): 102-6.

Until the beginning of this century, the continual intensifica-tion of visual experience through print and art pushed auditory and oral experience into the background. Electronic media have not only returned these senses to a state of importance, but, through eliminating time and space in the media experi-ence, have created a "fourth world." The "mass man" is in-volved with everyone and with all problems. Mass participa-tion in societal problem-solving should yield quick solutions that would elude the elite.

1273　_____. THE MECHANICAL BRIDE: THE FOLKLORE OF INDUSTRIAL MAN. New York: Vanguard Press, 1951. 157 p. Illus.

In an epigrammatic, sarcastic treatment of artificiality in American life, McLuhan ridicules the mass media, advertising, and more respectable institutions such as life insurance com-panies and funeral homes. Large reproductions of advertise-ments illustrate the text.

1274　_____. UNDERSTANDING MEDIA: THE EXTENSIONS OF MAN. New York: McGraw-Hill, 1964. vii, 395 p.

The well-known premise of this study is that it is the form of any medium, rather than the content, that determines what is communicated. McLuhan studies speech, writing, movies, phonographs, and television to determine how these "extensions of the human nervous system" affect the patterning of human associations.

1275　McLuhan, [Herbert] Marshall, and Fiore, Quentin. THE MEDIUM IS THE MASSAGE. New York: Random House, 1967. 157 p. Illus.

With a text photo-illustrated and graphically scrambled for emphasis, McLuhan reiterates that electronic communication technology is restructuring patterns of individual and social thought and behavior. Impacts on family and home, educa-tion, employment, and more general considerations of the media as extensions of human capabilities are presented.

1276　Parker, Edwin B., and Dunn, Donald A. "Information Technology: Its Social Potential." SCIENCE 176 (30 June 1972): 1392-99.

The technology of cable television, video, and computer information systems is now ripe, the authors believe, for the creation of an "information utility." The utility would provide equal access to public information on topics from entertainment to job opportunities, and would function as library, newspaper, theater, and classroom. Though Parker and Dunn believe that development funds should come from the private sector, they urge federal funding of pilot projects to demonstrate the feasibility of an information utility.

1277 Pool, Ithiel de Sola. TALKING BACK: CITIZEN FEEDBACK AND CABLE TECHNOLOGIES. Cambridge: M.I.T. Press, 1973. xiii, 325 p.

This collection opens with a broad consideration of the social context into which new technologies for individualized communication will be introduced. Descriptions of the technical attributes and potentials of cable systems lead into conjectures of social applications of two-way interactive systems. Suggested uses include group dialogues of various sorts, citizen feedback at "public" meetings, and increasingly personalized information selection.

1278 Rosenberg, Bernard, and White, David Manning, eds. MASS CULTURE: THE POPULAR ARTS IN AMERICA. Glencoe, Ill.: Free Press, 1957. Reprint. Glencoe, Ill.: Free Press, 1962. 561 p.

The fifty-one contributors to this anthology concerned with the social effects of mass media on American life are from various disciplines: literary criticism, social sciences, communications, journalism, and art criticism. The essays are grouped around the following topics: perspectives on mass culture, mass literature (books, detective fiction, comic books and cartoons, magazines), motion pictures, television and radio, "divertissement" (popular songs, jazz, card playing, Broadway), advertising, and overviews. Designed as a reader for college courses in popular culture and/or mass media.

1279 Rovere, R.H. "Invasion of Privacy: Technology and the Claims of Community." AMERICAN SCHOLAR 27 (Fall 1958): 413-21.

Through devices from the telephone to the tape recorder, technology has permitted the increase of two sorts of invasion of privacy: tapping and bugging of telephones, and abuse of presumably legitimate rights by the press. The only recent invention to safeguard privacy has been soundproofing. Though Americans tend to be gregarious and open, the need for privacy must be better recognized and preserved.

1280 Sackman, Harold, and Nie, Norman, eds. THE INFORMATION UTILITY AND SOCIAL CHOICE. Montvale, N.J.: AFIPS Press, 1970. 284 p.

Concerned with the social and political implications of a
mass information society, the volume includes a brief history
of public utilities and traces the emergence of a computer-
service society. Case histories, some autobiographical, illustrate problems in man-computer interactions that must be
solved for an effective utility. Various options for "social
reconstruction" in accordance with the needs of individuals
are offered.

1281 Schiller, Herbert I. "Mind-Management: Mass Media in the Advanced
Industrial State." QUARTERLY REVIEW OF ECONOMICS AND BUSI-
NESS 11 (Spring 1971): 39-52.

The mass media, and especially television and radio, have become a powerful source of manipulation and control over the
American working class, functioning to reinforce the values of
the "goods economy." Examples of manipulative techniques
are furnished.

B. TELEGRAPH AND TELEPHONE

1282 Boettinger, Henry. THE TELEPHONE BOOK: BELL, WATSON, VAIL
AND AMERICAN LIFE, 1876-1976. Croton-on-Hudson, N.Y.: River-
wood, 1977. 192 p. Illus.

A lavishly illustrated popular history of the telephone and the
Bell System is worth looking at for the drawings and photographs alone. Written by a member of the Bell "family," the
account contains some valuable social insights.

1283 Bruce, Robert V. BELL: ALEXANDER GRAHAM BELL AND THE CON-
QUEST OF SOLITUDE. Boston: Little, Brown and Co., 1973. xi,
564 p. Illus.

Bruce's extensive biography is based largely on the Alexander
Graham Bell Collection held by the National Geographic
Society, as well as on other smaller collections. Large por-
tions deal with the invention of the telephone and Bell's work
with speech and the deaf.

1284 Harlow, Alvin F. OLD WIRES AND NEW WAVES: THE HISTORY OF
THE TELEGRAPH, TELEPHONE, AND WIRELESS. New York: Appleton-
Century, 1936. xiv, 548 p. Illus., bibliog.

The subtitle of this communications history is misleading in
that the author devotes the bulk of his presentation to the
early years of the telegraph.

1285 Hounshell, David A. "Elisha Gray and the Telephone: On the Disadvantages of Being an Expert." TECHNOLOGY AND CULTURE 16 (April 1975): 133-61.

> Hounshell investigates a case example of the problem of parallel invention and why one inventor becomes a folk hero and another remains obscure. Gray, an inventor in the field of telegraphic apparatus, failed to recognize the importance and commercial value of the telephone because of his professional ties, while Alexander Graham Bell, an amateur, succeeded precisely because he did not hold the experts' biases. Illustrated.

1286 Mabee, Carleton. THE AMERICAN LEONARDO: A LIFE OF SAMUEL F.B. MORSE. New York: A.A. Knopf, 1943. Reprint. New York: Octagon Books, 1969. xxi, 435 p. Illus., bibliog.

> Samuel F.B. Morse was more than just the inventor of the telegraph; he was also a painter, businessman, and politician. Mabee analyzes all facets of Morse's varied career.

1287 Pool, Ithiel de Sola, ed. THE SOCIAL IMPACT OF THE TELEPHONE. Cambridge: M.I.T. Press, 1977. vii, 502 p. Illus., bibliog.

> These papers were originally presented at a series of seminars held at M.I.T. celebrating the centennial of the telephone. Contributors recognized that there have been few previous studies assessing the role of this everyday device in social change. An opening historical section provides a backdrop for papers examining the effect of the telephone on daily life. The papers concur that, through the telephone, oral discourse has reemerged as the major form of communication. New patterns of social interaction which developed, from telephone etiquette to crisis intervention centers, are also discussed. Contributors include Sidney H. Aronson, Colin Cherry, John R. Pierce, Jean Gottman, and other prominent scholars.

1288 Thompson, Robert Luther. WIRING A CONTINENT: THE HISTORY OF THE TELEGRAPH INDUSTRY IN THE UNITED STATES, 1832-1866. Princeton, N.J.: Princeton University Press, 1947. Reprint. Technology and Society Series. New York: Arno Press, 1972. xviii, 544 p. Illus., maps, bibliog.

> A case study of this important communications industry encompasses its early years of reckless growth, to consolidation in six major companies, and the ultimate triumph of Western Union as "the nation's first great industrial monopoly."

C. RADIO

1289 Aitken, Hugh G.J. SYNTONY AND SPARK: THE ORIGINS OF RADIO. New York: John Wiley and Sons, 1976. xviii, 347 p. Illus.

Winner of the Dexter Prize in 1976, this case study of the
development of the radio prior to 1914 deals with the interrelationships between science, technology, and the economy.
More than just a study of the contributions of three major
figures, Heinrich Hertz, Oliver Lodge, and Guglielmo
Marconi, the volume considers the development of a new technology and the means by which it is incorporated into the
economy. The Dexter Prize citation reads in part, "a first
step toward a general theory of human creativity."

1290   Barnouw, Erik. A HISTORY OF BROADCASTING IN THE UNITED
        STATES. 3 vols. New York: Oxford University Press, 1966-70.
        344, 390, 396 p. Illus., bibliog.

        A history of radio and television focusing on "what has been
        broadcast by whom, and why." Volume 1, A TOWER OF
        BABEL, TO 1933, details the period of independent radio sta-
        tions, each in competition with all others; while volume 2,
        THE GOLDEN WEB, 1933-53, considers the development of
        network organizations first of voice and sound, and by the
        end of the period, of pictures as well. Volume 3, THE
        IMAGE EMPIRE, FROM 1953, concentrates on television and
        its social impact, including the international ramifications.

1291   Bliven, Bruce. "How Radio is Remaking Our World." CENTURY 108
        (June 1924): 147-54.

        In a relatively conservative, early essay predicting the future
        of radio, the author foresees an important role for the medium
        in creating national solidarity and influencing national poli-
        tics. Bliven downplays radio's potential for education, for
        competing with the newspaper in reportage, and for advancing
        world understanding.

1292   Cantril, Hadley, and Allport, Gordon W. THE PSYCHOLOGY OF
        RADIO. New York: Harper and Brothers, 1935. x, 276 p.

        The first attempt by psychologists to depict, from their view-
        point, the altered mental world created by radio. An analy-
        sis of the general psychological and cultural factors shaping
        programming and listener response is followed by a review of
        five experiments studying the mental processes of the listeners.
        Suggesting practical applications for these findings, the authors
        conclude that "the psychological and social significance of
        radio is all out of proportion to the meager intelligence used
        in planning for its expansion."

1293   Culbert, David Holbrook. NEWS FOR EVERYMAN: RADIO AND
        FOREIGN AFFAIRS IN THIRTIES AMERICA. Westport, Conn.: Green-
        wood Press, 1976. xvi, 238 p. Bibliog.

Culbert discusses the broadcasting careers of six depression newscasters: Boake Carter, H.V. Kaltenborn, Raymond Gram Swing, Elmer Davis, Fulton Lewis, Jr., and Edward R. Murrow. The study reveals the impact of radio technology in shaping public opinion; "radio news came to serve as an integrating force in America by helping to create a national foreign policy consensus."

1294   Field, Harry, and Lazarsfeld, Paul F. THE PEOPLE LOOK AT RADIO. Chapel Hill: University of North Carolina Press, 1946. ix, 158 p.

The results of the first nationwide investigation of public attitudes toward radio are reported here. The survey yielded generally favorable attitudes toward the medium, though it indicated directions for improvement. Appendixes include data on the sample and a copy of the questionnaire.

1295   Havid, Alan, ed. "Radio, In-Depth." JOURNAL OF POPULAR CULTURE 12 (Fall 1978): 217-367.

Thirteen articles focus on the heyday of radio as popular entertainment. Following a survey of radio as a field of study, contributors look at specific programs and performers including "Vic and Sade," Amos and Andy, Fred Allen, Henry Morgan, and Boake Carter; use of the medium for propaganda; censorship; daytime programming for the homemaker; women radio pioneers; and radio drama. A concluding article lists sources for obtaining old programs. It is necessary to note that the date "Fall 1979" has been misprinted on this issue.

1296   Hettinger, Herman S. "Radio: The Fifth Estate." AMERICAN ACADEMY OF POLITICAL AND SOCIAL SCIENCE ANNALS 177(January 1935): 1-219.

Social services and problems of radio broadcasting are analyzed. An overview of broadcasting in various parts of the world serves as a background for a consideration of the medium's impact on music, the humanities, public opinion, children, religion, advertising, and other areas.

1297   Koppes, Clayton. "The Social Destiny of the Radio: Hope and Disillusionment in the 1920's." SOUTH ATLANTIC QUARTERLY 68 (Summer 1969): 363-76.

In its infancy, radio was hailed as a means of achieving many previously unattainable goals--world peace, political truth, mass education, and heightened culture. But as the twenties advanced, the radio became a conservative, censored, manipulated industry. It became "not the exposer but the purveyor of bunk."

1298   Maclaurin, W[illiam]. Rupert. INVENTION AND INNOVATION IN
        THE RADIO INDUSTRY. New York: Macmillan, 1949. Reprint.
        New York: Arno Press, N.Y. Times, 1971. xxi, 304 p. Illus.,
        bibliog.

        This history of radio communications includes not only research
        and invention but also the practical commercial applications
        as well. Eugene Ferguson refers to it as the "standard work."
        Reveals more about the process of invention and innovation
        than about social impact.

1299   Siepmann, Charles A. RADIO, TELEVISION AND SOCIETY. New
        York: Oxford University Press, 1950. viii, 410 p. Maps, bibliog.

        The first part of the book chronicles the history of radio,
        and to a lesser extent, television broadcasting, concentrating
        on the development of federal regulation of the industry. The
        second part considers the social implications of broadcasting,
        from its role in shaping values and cultural traits to its impact
        on free speech.

D. TELEVISION

1. Bibliographies

1300   Comstock, George A. TELEVISION AND HUMAN BEHAVIOR: THE
        KEY STUDIES. Santa Monica, Calif.: Rand Corp., 1975. ix, 251 p.

        Four hundred and fifty items representing key studies on tele-
        vision's social impact have been selected from the larger
        GUIDE (no. 1302) for lengthy annotations.

1301   _____ . TELEVISION AND HUMAN BEHAVIOR: THE RESEARCH HORI-
        ZON, FUTURE AND PRESENT. Santa Monica, Calif.: Rand Corp.,
        1975. x, 120 p.

        In the third part of this research review appears a "current
        bibliography" of publications from 1973 to 1975, and a number
        "in press."

1302   Comstock, George A., and Fisher, Marilyn. TELEVISION AND HUMAN
        BEHAVIOR: A GUIDE TO THE PERTINENT SCIENTIFIC LITERATURE.
        Santa Monica, Calif.: Rand Corp., 1975. ix, 344 p.

        Over two thousand items from scholarly literature, congressional
        hearings, reports of special committees, and noteworthy jour-
        nalism have been authoritatively selected. Items appear in a
        master alphabetical list, then again as entries of eleven spe-
        cialized bibliographies on: TV messages; audience behavior;
        behavioral concomitants of TV; TV and children and youth;

TV and the public: women, minorities, the poor, and the elderly; TV and decision making about politics and purchases; TV and psychological processes; communicator behavior; methodologies for study; and theory, review, and agenda for research. Not annotated.

2. Books and Articles

1303 Bailyn, Lotte. "Mass Media and Children: A Study of Exposure Habits and Cognitive Effects." PSYCHOLOGICAL MONOGRAPHS 73 (1959): 1-48.

The effect of mass media on four cognitive aspects of the child are reviewed: stereotyping, perception of threat, projected self-image, and passivity. Data was collected through questionnaires administered to six hundred children in a Boston suburb. Media effect was found to be closely related to parental permissiveness, IQ, certain psychological characteristics, and sex of the child.

1304 Barnouw, Erik. TUBE OF PLENTY: THE EVOLUTION OF AMERICAN TELEVISION. New York: Oxford University Press, 1975. viii, 518 p. Illus., bibliog.

A condensation of the author's three-volume HISTORY OF BROADCASTING (no. 1290), but updated to cover events since 1970 such as Watergate, this history of television details its technical origins, its coverage of news events, and its role as entertainment. Well-illustrated, but without the larger work's footnotes, this is a popularized account depicting television's impact on society and its reflection of our culture.

1305 Bogart, Leo. THE AGE OF TELEVISION: A STUDY OF VIEWING HABITS AND THE IMPACT OF TELEVISION ON AMERICAN LIFE. 1956. 3d ed. New York: F. Ungar Publishing Co., 1972. xliv, 575 p. Bibliog.

A survey of the literature on the social implications of television comprehensively covers studies conducted by government, industry, and academic researchers to 1956. Television's rapid penetration into the American home and displacement of other media are dramatically documented. Bogart takes a critical look at television's impact on children and on such areas of American life as sports and politics. The 1972 edition includes a large appendix of notes, statistics, and references that update each chapter of the original work (1956).

1306 _____. "Warning: The Surgeon General Has Determined That TV Violence Is Moderately Dangerous to Your Child's Mental Health."

PUBLIC OPINION QUARTERLY 36 (Winter 1972): 491-521.

The report of the Surgeon General concerned with television's effect on children has incited controversy. Bogart relates the history of the project, suggesting ways in which the makeup of the committee and the selection of research projects colored the group's conclusions. Bogart is particularly critical of the specificity of questions raised, and of the proclivity for searching for links between specific programs and specific acts of violence. The real issue, in his opinion, is the deliberate use of cliché violence as a marketable commodity.

1307 Cater, Douglass, and Strickland, Stephen. TV VIOLENCE AND THE CHILD: THE EVOLUTION AND FATE OF THE SURGEON GENERAL'S REPORT. New York: Russell Sage Foundation, 1975. 167 p.

In a journalistic account of the construction and impact of the Report, Cater emphasizes the biases of researchers who contributed, noting their political and business affiliations. He is particularly concerned about what he feels to be contradictory data supplied by the industry, which played down media stimulation of violence but inflated media impact when addressing potential advertisers.

1308 Cawelti, John G. "Some Reflections on the Video Culture of the Future." JOURNAL OF POPULAR CULTURE 7 (Spring 1974): 990-1000.

Television has created a popular culture in which people participate on an unprecedented scale. The further development of videotape recording and cable television may intensify television's role in American life. Cawelti projects three possible models of a future "video culture": McLuhan's "global village," an electronically unified world; a maximally efficient, but private video culture; and a society of video diversity that encourages cultural pluralism.

1309 Elliott, W.Y., ed. TELEVISION'S IMPACT ON AMERICAN CULTURE. East Lansing: Michigan State University Press, 1956. 382 p.

In an early study of television's social impact, Elliott and his collaborators focus on the educational prospects of television, both within the milieu of the commercial industry and in a separate, publicly controlled network. More general influences of television on the American character also receive consideration.

1310 Liebert, Robert M.; Neale, John M.; and Davidson, Emily S. THE EARLY WINDOW: EFFECTS OF TELEVISION ON CHILDREN AND YOUTH. New York: Pergamon Press, 1973. xvi, 193 p. Illus., bibliog.

For the young child, television is the "early window" onto the world. Drawing widely from social psychology research from the 1950s classics to recent findings, the book surveys television availability and use, the nature of programming for children and adults, and effects of programming on children's attitudes, development, and behavior. Adequate support for the hypothesis that television violence increases aggressiveness is found. The authors conclude that commercial interests have failed to make a positive contribution to television, but that educational television may have some prosocial effects.

1311   Maccoby, Eleanor E. "Television: Its Impact on School Children." PUBLIC OPINION QUARTERLY 15 (Fall 1951): 421-44.

This early study examines the effect of television exposure on the personality, family relations, and social interaction of children. Maccoby found that children who were heavy watchers spent less time with playmates and more with family, though not in a socially interactive context. Television served as a pacifier, increasing the child's tolerance for frustration, and interfering with the practice of real-life skills.

1312   Schramm, Wilbur; Lyle, Jack; and Parker, Edwin B. TELEVISION IN THE LIVES OF OUR CHILDREN. Stanford, Calif.: Stanford University Press, 1961. vii, 324 p. Bibliog.

Results of eleven research studies done in various Canadian and American cities are surveyed. Statistics on the amounts and kind of television children watch at various ages open the discussion. Analysis reveals that, influenced by television, children perceive the adult world as heavy with violence and crime and light in intellectual interchange. The authors conclude that though television does not overly frighten, pacify, or otherwise disturb the normal child, its inaccurate portrayal of adult life may adversely effect an already disturbed child. An annotated bibliography supplements.

1313   Schramm, Wilbur; Lyle, Jack; and Pool, Ithiel de Sola. THE PEOPLE LOOK AT EDUCATIONAL TELEVISION. Stanford, Calif.: Stanford University Press, 1963. 209 p.

The origins and early development of noncommercial television are followed. Profiles of nine stations serve as a basis for a study of ETV audience's composition, program preferences, and rationale for watching. The place of educational television within the larger realm of mass media is assessed.

1314   Steiner, Gary A., ed. THE PEOPLE LOOK AT TELEVISION. New York: Alfred A. Knopf, 1963. 422 p.

Results of a study undertaken by Columbia University's Bureau of Applied Research are reported. Over two thousand adults were questioned on the importance of television to their lives, on their viewing behavior, and on opinions of programs and commercials. General satisfaction with the medium was reported, tempered with an element of guilt about watching too much, and annoyance with commercials. There is an appendix containing tables and questionnaires.

1315 TELEVISION AND SOCIAL BEHAVIOR. A Technical Report to the Surgeon General's Scientific Advisory Committee on Television and Social Behavior. 5 vols. Washington, D.C.: 1972.

In 1969, the Department of Health, Education and Welfare initiated a special program, conducted under the auspices of the Surgeon General's Committee, to examine the relations between television violence and the attitudes and behaviors of children. The five volumes report the work of the independent researchers who sent results to the Committee for study.

Vol. 1: MEDIA CONTENT AND CONTROL. Edited by George A. Comstock and Eli A. Rubinstein. v, 546 p.

Violent content in media is quantified and assessed, in the light of a comparative overview of broadcasting in four countries.

Vol. 2: TELEVISION IN SOCIAL LEARNING. Edited by John P. Murray, Eli A. Rubinstein, and George A. Comstock. iv, 371 p.

Relationships between television content and behavior of children are studied.

Vol. 3: TECHNOLOGY AND ADOLESCENT AGGRESSIVENESS. Edited by George A. Comstock and Eli A. Rubinstein. vi, 435 p.

Adolescent viewing habits are related to aggressiveness and deviant behavior.

Vol. 4: TELEVISION IN DAY-TO-DAY LIFE: PATTERNS OF USE. Edited by Eli A. Rubinstein, George A. Comstock, and John P. Murray. vi, 603 p.

Nationwide viewing behavior of children and adults is surveyed, with particular attention to commercials and their impact.

Vol. 5: TELEVISION'S EFFECTS: FURTHER EXPLORATIONS. Edited by George A. Comstock, Eli A. Rubinstein, and John P. Murray. vi, 375 p.

Effects of such variables as race, comparisons with film, and miscellaneous methodological problems are considered.

1316   U.S. Surgeon General's Scientific Advisory Committee on Television and Social Behavior. TELEVISION AND GROWING UP: THE IMPACT OF TELEVISED VIOLENCE. Washington, D.C.: 1972. ix, 279 p.

> The result of a two-year study by a distinguished group of behavioral scientists, this well-known report confirmed that violence is a prominent and pervasive component of television programming. The real question to be answered, in their opinion, was how much of a contribution to the violence in American society could be attributed to extensive viewing of violent programming by youth. Though the committee allowed that watching violent programming can induce mimicry or increased aggressiveness, they concluded that the overall effect is small compared with other sources. Bibliographical and methodological appendixes supplement.

1317   Williams, Raymond. TELEVISION: TECHNOLOGY AND CULTURAL FORM. New York: Schocken Books, 1975. 160 p. Bibliog.

> This social history of television probes the reasons for the channeling of television technology into the development of a medium for home use. The latter part of the book summarizes the effects of television on the behavior of viewers, concluding with an assessment of future uses.

E. COMPUTERS

1. Bibliographies

1318   Anderson, Ronald E., and Fagerlund, E. "Privacy and the Computer: An Annotated Bibliography." COMPUTING REVIEWS 13 (November 1972): 551-59.

> An annotated bibliography covering literature through 1971 is organized into the following divisions: bibliographies, privacy and the computer, privacy and the computer-government information systems, and U.S. government hearings and reports.

1319   Davis, Lenwood G. SOCIAL IMPACT OF CYBERNETICS: A WORKING BIBLIOGRAPHY. Exchange Bibliography no. 1534. Monticello, Ill.: Council of Planning Librarians, 1978. 9 p.

1320   Taviss, Irene, and Burbank, Judith. IMPLICATIONS OF COMPUTER TECHNOLOGY. Research Review no. 7. Cambridge, Mass.: Harvard University Program on Technology and Society, 1971. 55 p.

> Covers the economic, political, and cultural implications of computer technology through a state-of-the-art essay and

lengthy abstracts of selected books and articles. Specific topics covered include automation in industry, office automation, applications in government, citizen feedback, information systems, and computers in humanities, education, science, and social science research.

2. Books and Articles

1321 Adams, J. Mack, and Haden, Douglas H. SOCIAL EFFECTS OF COMPUTER USE AND MISUSE. New York: John Wiley and Sons, 1976. x, 326 p. Illus., bibliog.

A text for nontechnically-oriented readers offers a general introduction to the history of computation, present computer applications, artificial intelligence, and robots. More sophisticated and expansive treatment is accorded social and philosophical questions surrounding computers. An appendix offers a selection of important papers on these issues, by authors including A.M. Turing, Joseph Weizenbaum, Paul Baram, and Bruce Mazlish.

1322 Baer, Robert M. THE DIGITAL VILLAIN: NOTES ON THE NUMEROLOGY, PARAPSYCHOLOGY AND METAPHYSICS OF THE COMPUTER. Reading, Mass.: Addison-Wesley, 1972. 187 p.

A balanced, stylish, and lively account of man's creation of and subsequent interaction with the computer is provided. Part 1 presents a brief historical sketch of the development of the computer and the computer industry, complete with brief biographies of potentates from Mark I (1939-43) to ILLIAC IV (1967-71). The second portion of the book is devoted to the literary reaction to automata and computers, from Capek's R.U.R. to Len Deighton's "Billion Dollar Brain."

1323 Dechert, Charles R., ed. THE SOCIAL IMPACT OF CYBERNETICS. Notre Dame, Ind.: University of Notre Dame Press, 1966. viii, 206 p.

Eight essays selected from a 1964 symposium discuss the implications of cybernetic technologies. Robert Theobald stresses the potential of cybernetics in the task of social reorganization. More general relationships between cybernetics and culture are illuminated by Marshall McLuhan. Other contributors consider computers as tools and metaphors, as a basic component for a "humanistic technology," and in relation to Marxism and international development. Observes the editor: "determining the human values to be served by cybernetics may well be the most critical challenge of this generation."

1324 Fink, Donald G. COMPUTERS AND THE HUMAN MIND. Garden City, N.Y.: Doubleday, 1966. xii, 301 p.

Fink begins with the basics of the computer and data processing: binary arithmetic, hardware, and software. He then
moves on to a comparison of the capabilities of the human
mind versus the computer, concluding with a review of inci-
pient efforts at machine composition of music and poetry. To
the question "can machines create?" he responds with a
qualified "yes."

1325   George, Frank Honywill. MACHINE TAKEOVER: THE GROWING
THREAT TO HUMAN FREEDOM IN A COMPUTER-CONTROLLED SO-
CIETY. Elmsford, N.Y.: Pergamon Press, 1977. xiv, 193 p. Bibliog.

In George's opinion, the greatest societal threat is "information
pollution," defined as the "propagation of false information
through distortion." A related phenomenon is "control pollution," the misuse of information. Examples of control pollution are dossier buildup or data-bank spying, activities conducive, in George's opinion, to totalitarianism. Unless
cautionary measures are taken, the next step, the author fears,
is takeover by a new machine species of symbol-producing,
logical automata.

1326   Hilton, Alice Mary, ed. THE EVOLVING SOCIETY: PROCEEDINGS
OF THE FIRST CONFERENCE ON THE CYBERCULTURAL REVOLUTION--
CYBERNETICS AND AUTOMATION. New York: Institute for Cyber-
cultural Research, 1966. xiv, 410 p.

Philosophical, technical, and socioeconomic aspects of an
imminent cyberculture are tackled by some fifty-four contributors. The role computers and systems will play in fueling the
cybernetic explosion provides the initial discussion. Major
concerns for other authors are labor displacement and corresponding abundant, and equally threatening, leisure time.

1327   Kemeny, John G. MAN AND THE COMPUTER. New York: Charles
Scribner's Sons, 1972. 151 p.

Kemeny surveys the history of computers over the last twenty-
five years and projects future developments. Computer impact
on areas such as education, libraries, and home services are
reviewed. The author views the appearance of time-sharing
networks as the development most crucial to the widespread
and diversified application of computer power.

1328   Lee, Robert S. "Social Attitudes and the Computer Revolution." PUB-
LIC OPINION QUARTERLY 34 (Spring 1970): 53-59.

Popular beliefs about and attitudes toward the computer are
discovered through one hundred intensive interviews, supplemented with psychological analyses of humor depicted in over
two hundred computer cartoons in popular magazines. Surveys

and cartoons alike indicate that the American public views the computer in terms of two independent belief-attitude dimensions: as an instrument of man's purpose and as an autonomous, thinking entity.

1329　McCauley, Carole Spearin. COMPUTERS AND CREATIVITY. New York: Praeger Publishers, 1974. 160 p. Illus., bibliog.

How creative people have utilized the computer is documented. Discussion of the inventive people who developed the computer is followed by considerations of its use in artificial intelligence, graphics, art, film, advertising, music, dance, and literature. Lengthy, annotated bibliography.

1330　Martin, James Thomas, and Norman, Adrian R.D. THE COMPUTERIZED SOCIETY: AN APPRAISAL OF THE IMPACT OF COMPUTERS ON SOCIETY OVER THE NEXT FIFTEEN YEARS. Englewood Cliffs, N.J.: Prentice-Hall, 1970. xii, 560 p. Illus., maps, bibliog.

In an optimistic, technically oriented overview of the close-range future of the computer, the authors predict a sudden massive spread of usage that will affect everyone. The first portion explains basic principles and current applications of computers, from education to transport. The second portion recognizes drawbacks: loss of privacy, computer crime, and unemployment. Closes with suggestions for needed protective legislation.

1331　Michael, Donald N. "Speculations on the Relation of the Computer to Individual Freedom and the Right to Privacy." GEORGE WASHINGTON LAW REVIEW 33 (October 1964): 270-86.

Two principal threats to privacy are posed by the computer. It permits more complete, integrated and cross-correlated records on individuals, records which may be leaked or spied upon. Second, through providing social scientists with more social data, it enhances their ability to predict and perhaps control individual and group behavior. Purely hardware devices, such as pacemakers, also have the potential for being misused for tracking or monitoring individuals. The worst fear that Michael harbors is a societal complacency about these blows to freedom.

1332　Miller, Arthur R. "Personal Privacy in the Computer Age: The Challenge of a New Technology in an Information-Oriented Society." MICHIGAN LAW REVIEW 67 (April 1969): 1091-1246.

The cybernetic revolution has enormous implications for personal privacy. Personal information has been lost to national data banks, credit bureaus, and agencies of surveillance. Miller

stresses the inadequate state of law regarding this problem.
An outline for safeguards and a legal framework are presented.

1333   Mowshowitz, Abbe. THE CONQUEST OF WILL: INFORMATION PRO-
CESSING IN HUMAN AFFAIRS. Reading, Mass.: Addison-Wesley,
1976. xvi, 365 p. Bibliog.

As man has extended his power over the natural world, exer-
cising a "will to power" through the elaboration of technique,
his own will has become enfeebled, Mowshowitz contends.
It is now subject to control by autonomous forces of his own
creation, as exercised most dramatically by computer systems
and data banks. The author argues that the computer has
provided a means for centralizing awesome power "which
could not have been imagined by absolute rulers in the past."
Good bibliography.

1334   Nikolaieff, George A., ed. COMPUTERS AND SOCIETY. New York:
H.W. Wilson Co., 1970. 226 p. Bibliog.

Through brief articles drawn from newspapers, popular magazines, and student technical manuals, Nikolaieff has constructed a useful, if very basic guide to computer history and
developments, operations, and social impacts.

1335   Orcutt, James D., and Anderson, Ronald E. "Social Interaction, Dehumanization and the Computerized Other." SOCIOLOGY AND SO-
CIAL RESEARCH 61 (April 1977): 380-97.

An experiment is described which pits a human (student) in a
game of Prisoner's Dilemma against two opponents, one of
which is allegedly human, the other a computer. In fact,
both responses are computer-generated. Subjects frequently
perceived the "computer opponent" to be "incapable of meaningful play," but often responded themselves in what might be
described as a dehumanized way toward their "human" opponent.

1336   Pylyshyn, Zenon W., ed. PERSPECTIVES ON THE COMPUTER REVOLU-
TION. Englewood Cliffs, N.J.: Prentice-Hall, 1970. 540 p. Bibliog.

This solid, lengthy anthology is aimed at "illuminating the
broader context in which the computer has developed and with
which it is interacting." Part 1, "Development of Computer
Science," studies the heritage of the field and theoretical
ideas concerning algorithms, automata, and cybernetics, including papers by John von Neumann and Claude E. Shannon.
The second portion of the book contains papers on the relationship between man and machine. Among papers in part 3, on
machine intelligence, is Herbert Ginsberg's "The Psychology of
Robots." Part 4, on man-machine partnerships, includes Joseph
Weizenbaum's "Contextual Understanding by Computers."

1337   Sanders, Donald H. COMPUTERS IN SOCIETY. 1973. 2d ed. New York: McGraw-Hill, 1977. xiv, 458 p. Illus.

A textbook for students of the liberal arts and social science provides a readable introduction to the history and evolution of information processing, as well as to the present positive and negative aspects of computers. Uses of computers in government, law, health, education, the humanities, science and engineering, and business are examined. References appear at the end of each chapter. There is an appendix of FORTRAN and BASIC coding.

1338   Seaborg, Glenn T. "The Cybernetic: An Optimist's View." SATUR-DAY REVIEW 50 (28 July 1967): 21-23.

The applications of computers that alter daily life are summarized. While offering great benefits, the computer age threatens an end to privacy and skill. To meet this challenge, education must be reoriented to instruction for "total living."

1339   Taviss, Irene, ed. THE COMPUTER IMPACT. Englewood Cliffs, N.J.: Prentice-Hall, 1970. ix, 297 p.

Intended to provide a "broad sampling of major social issues raised by computer technology," this collection covers developments in computer technology, the expanding role of computers in business and government, and impacts on diverse areas from arts and science fiction to schools and social services.

1340   U.S. Congress. House. Committee on Government Operations. Special Subcommittee on Invasion of Privacy. THE COMPUTER AND THE INVASION OF PRIVACY. Hearings. 89th Cong. 2d sess. Washington, D.C.: Government Printing Office, 1966. 311 p.

The hearings provide a good resource on general questions surrounding computers and privacy. Included are statements by Vance Packard, Charles A. Reich, and other academics and government officials, as well as Donald N. Michael's longer paper, "Speculations on the Relation of the Computer to Individual Freedom and the Right to Privacy." Appendixes deal with the use of economic data and a proposal for a National Data Center.

1341   Weizenbaum, Joseph. COMPUTER POWER AND HUMAN REASON: FROM JUDGMENT TO CALCULATION. San Francisco: W.H. Freeman And Co., 1976. xii, 300 p.

Weizenbaum's warning that computers are becoming overrated and misused merits special attention. Computer researchers have deluded themselves into believing that their programming goal is a recreation of the human mind. Weizenbaum's arguments against this quest center on evidence for computer limitations and the contrasting limitless variety of human thought. Two kinds of research are labelled particularly abhorrent: the experimental linking of animal sensory systems and brains to computers, and computer substitution for humans in positions requiring interpersonal respect and understanding.

1342 _____. "Impact of the Computer on Society." SCIENCE 176 (12 May 1972): 609-14.

The subtle, yet ultimately most important social effects of the computer have not yet been felt, Weizenbaum believes. Because the power of the computer has been so overstated, we are in danger of molding man to the awesome computer's image. In understanding man's mind in terms of the rational computer, "we diminish the moral creature." Technology, he concludes, should not be permitted to answer questions about what is possible and righteous.

1343 Westin, Alan F. PRIVACY AND FREEDOM. New York: Atheneum, 1967. xvi, 487 p. Bibliog.

Technology has furnished a number of new tools for invading privacy, including listening and watching devices and techniques for psychological surveillance. Westin presents five case studies of attempts to control these intrusions on personal freedom. He urges that policy and legal changes be made to restore rights and curtail further encroachments.

1344 _____, ed. INFORMATION TECHNOLOGY IN A DEMOCRACY. Cambridge, Mass.: Harvard University Press, 1970. 499 p. Bibliog.

Fifty essays deal with government's and society's growing reliance on computerized information systems. Part 1 provides descriptions of developing information systems in Detroit, New York State, at various levels of federal and local governments, and in corporations. Part 2 introduces the broad sociopolitical debate about the meaning of such systems through papers by Emmanuel Mesthene, Zbigniew Brzezinski, Harold Lasswell, Eric Fromm, and others. Concluding sections evaluate the merits of specific applications, in areas from urban problems to management science.

1345 Whisler, Thomas L. THE IMPACT OF COMPUTERS ON ORGANIZATIONS. New York: Praeger Publishers, 1970. xiv, 188 p.

Changes in a group of companies in the life insurance industry were studied and analyzed to determine the impact of computers on organizations. Computer technology causes specific changes in organizational structure, decision making, authority and control, and job content. The most imminent and critical problems occur in top-level management. Other clearly recognizable alterations are a narrowing of job content, introduction of rigidity, inflexibility, reliance on quantitative data in decision making, tightening control on individual behavior, and upward shift of power.

1346   Withington, Frederic. THE REAL COMPUTER: ITS INFLUENCE, USES AND EFFECTS. Reading, Mass.: Addison-Wesley, 1969. ix, 350 p.

Written for managers, this book studies computer-caused changes in the structure and behavior of organizations. Computer capabilities, computer-caused changes in management and planning, and computer impacts on individuals are surveyed.

Part 13

ENVIRONMENT

A. GENERAL

1. Bibliographies

1347   Dee, Sandra R. A BASIC ENVIRONMENTAL COLLECTION. Exchange
Bibliography no. 410. Monticello, Ill.: Council of Planning Librarians,
1973. 15 p.

1348   Dunlap, Riley E. SOCIOLOGICAL AND SOCIAL-PSYCHOLOGICAL
PERSPECTIVES ON ENVIRONMENTAL ISSUES: A BIBLIOGRAPHY.
Exchange Bibliography no. 916. Monticello, Ill.: Council of Planning
Librarians, 1975. 37 p.

1349   Paulson, Glenn L., et al., eds. ENVIRONMENT U.S.A.: A GUIDE
TO AGENCIES, PEOPLE, AND RESOURCES. New York: R.R. Bowker
Co., 1974. xii, 451 p.

> The guide to the field of environmental information provides
> data on government agencies, private conservation organiza-
> tions, professional and trade associations, libraries, films,
> bibliographies, and educational programs. Especially helpful
> sections provide names of contact people in companies, radio
> and television stations, as well as science editors for news-
> papers and journals. There are also explanatory chapters on
> fund raising and environmental law.

1350   Sangster, Robert Powell. ENVIRONMENTAL DEGRADATION: A
SELECTED BIBLIOGRAPHY. Exchange Bibliography no. 171. Monticello,
Ill.: Council of Planning Librarians, 1971. 47 p.

1351   Thibeau, Charles E., and Taliaferro, Peter W., eds. NFEC DIRECTORY
OF ENVIRONMENTAL INFORMATION SOURCES. 1971. 2d ed.
Boston: National Foundation for Environmental Control, 1972. 457 p.

Sources of environmental information are listed and annotated in the directory which has been compiled from data in the NFEC's computerized data bank. Organization is by type of source: government agencies, legislative committees, citizens' organizations, professional and trade associations, indexes and bibliographies, documents and reports, journals, books, and films and filmstrips.

2. Books and Articles

1352 "America's Changing Environment." DAEDALUS 96 (Fall 1967): vii, 1013-1225.

Faced with the opportunity to present long-term plans for dealing with environmental problems, the contributors to this issue delineate the changes needed if we are to cope with the problems of an advanced industrial society. The volume begins with discussions of what can be done by ecological researchers, conservation groups, and individuals. Essays then consider the effects of economic development on specific natural resources, agribusiness, and on the question of who should pay for clean air. There are differing opinions on the need for a "new economics based on non-market commodities." Attention then shifts to the design of cities, a call for multidisciplinary planning, and attitudes toward leisure and recreational facilities.

1353 Brown, Lester R. THE TWENTY-NINTH DAY: ACCOMMODATING HUMAN NEEDS AND NUMBERS TO THE EARTH'S RESOURCES. New York: W.W. Norton and Co., 1978. xiii, 363 p.

The deterioration of the Earth's biological system will necessitate far-reaching social changes within the next two decades. In this Worldwatch Institute study, Brown investigates stresses on the environment from factors related to population, energy, food, economics, and national and global distribution of wealth. He then turns to a consideration of the elements and means of accommodation.

1354 Campbell, Rex R., and Wade, Jerry L., eds. SOCIETY AND ENVIRONMENT: THE COMING COLLISION. Boston: Allyn and Bacon, 1972. vii, 375 p. Illus., bibliog.

Attempting to provide a wide perspective on the social causes of environmental problems, the articles in this anthology consider how attitudes, value systems, institutions, and social patterns affect the environment. The volume is organized into major problem areas: the nature of the collision, water, air, problem profusion, and population. A final section considers the needed social and behavior changes. Articles include classics by Lynn White, Robert Heilbroner, Paul Ehrlich, René Dubos, and Garrett Hardin, as well as case studies and philosophical considerations. Each section ends with a bibliography.

1355 Commoner, Barry. THE CLOSING CIRCLE: NATURE, MAN, AND TECHNOLOGY. New York: Alfred A. Knopf, 1972. 326 p.

Understanding of why the collapse of the ecosphere is now a threat and which human acts have "broken the circle of life" is the purpose of this study. Following an explanation of the nature of the ecosphere, specific instances of air, water, earth, and nuclear contamination of our genetic inheritance are analyzed as case studies. Commoner then discusses how the technological development of nondegradable substances and industrial profit motives are more to blame than population and affluence. He argues for rapid change in environmental policy.

1356 _____. SCIENCE AND SURVIVAL. New York: Viking Press, 1966. 150 p.

The impact of science and technology on our daily lives is so intense that the existence of life may be endangered. Commoner discusses instances in which harmful effects of new technologies have not been anticipated before general use. His major focus is on nuclear and chemical pollutants, detergents, and defense. The blame for mistakes falls on the secrecy of scientists and the military, the adverse effects of political and social pressures on scientific integrity, and on ignorance of the relationships in the biosphere.

1357 Darling, F. Fraser, and Milton, John P., eds. FUTURE ENVIRONMENTS OF NORTH AMERICA. Garden City, N.Y.: Natural History Press, 1966. xv, 767 p. Bibliog.

The proceedings of a conference held in 1965 examine the present and potential implications of man's manipulation of the environment. Papers and discussions consider six topic areas: the organic world, regional development, economic forces, social and cultural values, planning, and implementation of policy. Among the thirty-four papers are studies of habitat, impact of increased leisure, stress and creativity, and urbanization.

1358 FITNESS OF MAN'S ENVIRONMENT. SMITHSONIAN ANNUAL 2. Washington, D.C.: Smithsonian Institution Press, 1968. 250 p.

The twelve essays comprising this symposium consider man's relationship and reactions to his environment. The contributors pursue various interests: planning, ecology, architecture, literary criticism, philosophy, biology, and anthropology. A focus on cities includes studies by Leo Marx, Edward Hall, Philip Johnson, and Robert Wood.

1359 Herber, Lewis [Bookchin, Murray]. OUR SYNTHETIC ENVIRONMENT. London: Cape, 1963. 285 p. Bibliog.

The ways in which human health is affected by environmental problems are examined. Herber attempts to develop a point of view which will help to eliminate various ills without the expulsion of the benefits of science and technology. He considers the effects of urbanization, chemicals in food, environmental carcinogens, and radiation.

1360 Klausner, Samuel Z. ON MAN IN HIS ENVIRONMENT: SOCIAL SCIENTIFIC FOUNDATIONS FOR RESEARCH AND POLICY. San Francisco: Jossey-Bass, 1971. xiv, 224 p. Illus., bibliog.

The man-environment interaction is examined from a sociological point of view. Klausner first presents a survey of the responses of sociologists in this area, then provides a theoretical model for sociological research, policymaking, and application of findings toward the alleviation of environmental problems. He then analyzes the effects on man of aspects of technological growth, specifically pollution, noise, and recreation.

1361 _____, ed. "Society and Its Physical Environment." ANNALS OF THE AMERICAN ACADEMY OF POLITICAL AND SOCIAL SCIENCE 389 (May 1970): 1-115.

The relationships between society and its manipulation of the physical environment are explored from sociological, economic, legal, political, and technological points of view. Among the topics discussed are adaptation resulting from environmental threats, the psychological and economic aspects of outdoor recreation, legislative and judicial response to environmental problems, governmental policymaking, and technological intervention to improve environmental quality.

1362 Longgood, William. THE DARKENING LAND. New York: Simon and Schuster, 1972. 572 p. Bibliog.

The interrelationships of pollutants and the life-support systems of the environment are explained in this popular treatment of the damage caused by specific harmful substances, and of major value problems such as population and politics. Longgood discusses air pollutants, e.g., carcinogens, sulfur, automobile emissions; poisons, including DDT, mercury, asbestos, PCBs, nerve gases; and despoiled natural resources.

1363 Sewell, W.R. Derrick, ed. "Environmental Quality." ENVIRONMENT AND BEHAVIOR 3 (June 1971): 119-214.

Behavioral responses to aspects of environmental quality is the concern of this special issue. Contributors appraise the potential for environmental revival, design with people in mind, and public opinion on environmental quality. There are also two case studies of decision making in water management and weather modification.

1364 Shepard, Paul, and McKinley, Daniel, eds. ENVIRON/MENTAL ESSAYS ON THE PLANET AS A HOME. Boston: Houghton Mifflin, 1971. x, 308 p. Illus., bibliog.

Social and psychological consequences of our "past faith in a mechanistic culture" and the equation of development with progress are emphasized in this collection of essays. General discussions of the ecosystem lead to explorations of the psychological effects of overpopulation and urban crowding, philosophical values related to environmental perception, and the role of technology in harming and reclaiming environmental balance. Contributors include Eugene Odum, Walter J. Ong, Paul Shepard, Sibyl Moholy-Nagy, Stanley Milgram, Charles Lindbergh, and Paul Ehrlich. Extensive lists of additional readings.

1365 Ward, Barbara, and Dubos, René. ONLY ONE EARTH: THE CARE AND MAINTENANCE OF A SMALL PLANET. New York: Ballantine Books, 1972. xxix, 288 p.

The "unofficial report commissioned by the Secretary-General of the United Nations Conference on the Human Environment" considers what should be done to maintain the Earth as a suitable habitat for man. The authors advocate a "global state of mind" which will generate a philosophy of "stewardship" for future generations. Central to the report is a consideration of the social and environmental effects of industry and high technology. Among specific areas examined are market versus social costs of pollution, problem of wastes, prosperity and the consumer revolution, third-world development, the green revolution, and policies for growth.

B. CONSERVATION MOVEMENT

1. Bibliography

1366 Buttel, Frederick H., and Morrison, Denton E. THE ENVIRONMENTAL MOVEMENT: A RESEARCH BIBLIOGRAPHY WITH SOME STATE-OF-THE-ART COMMENTS. Exchange Bibliography no. 1308. Monticello, Ill.: Council of Planning Librarians, 1977. 27 p.

2. Books and Articles

1367 Adams, Ansel, and Newhall, Nancy. THIS IS THE AMERICAN EARTH.
San Francisco: Sierra Club, 1960. 111 p. Illus.

Photos by Ansel Adams and others are joined by free verse
poetry by Nancy Newhall in this first publication in the
Sierra Club's series of aesthetic pleas for wilderness conservation. Sections illustrate the endurance of the earth, the
western new world, the effect of the machine on the land,
ecological balance, and the dynamics of nature. The work
assisted in the raising of environmental consciousness in the
early years of the present movement.

1368 Bates, J. Leonard. "Fulfilling American Democracy: The Conservation
Movement, 1907-1921." MISSISSIPPI VALLEY HISTORICAL REVIEW 44
(June 1957): 29-57.

Bates provides a brief, generally complimentary survey of the
conservation movement, which was closely tied to Republican
politics in this period. The acceptance of conservation was
"a tribute to a group of men whose concept of official responsibility for conservation was not a loose, vague theory, nor a
matter of efficiency as such, but a fighting democratic faith."
Conservationists were concerned with economic justice and the
democratic division of resources, not just with prevention of
waste, and, to these ends, believed the federal government
would have to take a leading role.

1369 Hays, Samuel P. CONSERVATION AND THE GOSPEL OF EFFICIENCY:
THE PROGRESSIVE CONSERVATION MOVEMENT, 1890-1920. Harvard
Historical Monographs, vol. 40. Cambridge, Mass.: Harvard University
Press, 1959. Reprint. New York: Atheneum, 1969. 297 p. Bibliog.

This excellent intellectual study emphasizes the scientific and
technical stress on "rational planning to promote efficient development and use of all natural resources" as the major thrust
of the Progressive conservation movement. Hays concentrates
on the ideas and values of conservationists, not on specific
political struggles, and their wider societal implications.

1370 Nash, Roderick, ed. THE AMERICAN ENVIRONMENT: READINGS IN
THE HISTORY OF CONSERVATION. Reading, Mass.: Addison-Wesley,
1968. xix, 236 p. Illus., bibliog.

Essays trace the development of American conservation values
from 1832 through the mid-1960's. Considerations of the value
of nature by George Catlin, H.D. Thoreau, George P. Marsh,
Frederick Law Olmsted, and others are followed by discussions
of the Progressive conservation crusade by such writers as
Gifford Pinchot, Theodore Roosevelt, John Muir, and Nash.

The section on wilderness planning and government conservation programs between the wars includes articles by Benton
MacKaye and Aldo Leopold. The direction then turns to
present concerns of "uglification," Echo Park, pesticides, and
pollution, with contributions by Peter Blake, Wallace Stegner,
and Rachel Carson.

1371 Petulla, Joseph M. AMERICAN ENVIRONMENTAL HISTORY: THE
EXPLOITATION AND CONSERVATION OF NATURAL RESOURCES.
San Francisco: Boyd and Fraser, 1977. 399 p. Illus., maps, bibliog.

A textbook on environmental history based primarily on standard
secondary source material which surveys the American scene
from the first colonists through the early conservation movement
to today's ecological concerns. Each major section--"The
Colonial Period," "The New Nation," "After the Civil War,"
and "The Twentieth Century,"--is preceded by a chronology
of important events, while individual chapters are followed by
references for further reading. A basic introduction to the
field.

1372 Pursell, Carroll [W., Jr.], ed. FROM CONSERVATION TO ECOLOGY:
THE DEVELOPMENT OF ENVIRONMENTAL CONCERN. Problem Studies
in American History. New York: Thomas Y. Crowell Co., 1973. 148 p.
Bibliog.

Presenting a convergence of insights on environmental concern
in America, the essays chosen for this anthology discuss conservation movements from the beginning of the century through
the sixties. While contributors and their topics span the disciplines, a focus on the development of public policy creates
a united whole. Viewpoints are presented by historians,
scientists, economists, sociologists, a literary critic, and a
consumer advocate. Contributors include Roderick Nash,
Stephen Raushenbush, Rachel Carson, Barry Commoner, Leo
Marx, Robert Heilbroner, and Ralph Nader.

1373 Resources for the Future. PERSPECTIVES ON CONSERVATION: ESSAYS
ON AMERICA'S NATURAL RESOURCES. Edited by Henry Jarrett.
Baltimore: Johns Hopkins University Press, 1958. 260 p.

Addressed to the informed general public, the essays examine
the influence of the idea of conservation on national life in
the United States, look for guidance from the record of the
past for future environmental problems, and discuss the important issues of the present. Papers and responses are devoted
to the following aspects of the conservation field: the role of
science and technology, the place of the consumer in resource
conservation, implications of continued urban growth, economic
and political problems, and organization for policymaking.

Extensive essays are by Ernest Griffith, Thomas B. Nolan, John Kenneth Galbraith, Luther Gulick, Edward S. Mason, and Gilbert F. White.

1374   Udall, Stewart L.   THE QUIET CRISIS.   New York: Holt, Rinehart and Winston, 1963.   xiii, 209 p.   Illus.

The quiet conservation crisis of the 1960s is the loss of reverence for the land caused by our technological success.   Udall believes reparation of mistakes can be aided by an understanding of the "history of our husbandry"--of the men and forces which shaped our attitudes toward the land.   To this end, he surveys the conservation movement in America from Thomas Jefferson, Daniel Boone, and Henry David Thoreau to George Perkins Marsh, Carl Schurz, Gifford Pinchot, the Roosevelts, and Frederick Law Olmsted.   He also provides comments on the role of conservation in the future and the development of a land ethic for tomorrow's civilization.

C. INTELLECTUAL ATTITUDES

1. Bibliography

1375   Owings, Loren C.   ENVIRONMENTAL VALUES, 1860-1972: A GUIDE TO INFORMATION SOURCES.   Detroit: Gale Research Co., 1976.   xii, 324 p.

The historical development of attitudes toward nature, or an environmental ethic, in America is documented in this annotated bibliographic guide.   The focus is on values rather than economic or political issues related to depletion of resources.   Owings's coverage is selective; he cites research works, bibliographies, books, articles, government documents, pamphlets, and conference reports.   Arranged by topics indicative of forms of response, chapters include general works on man and nature, travel reports, landscape painting, national parks, conservation, nature writing, nature study, camping, "back to nature" reports, and general reference works.

2. Books and Articles

1376   Bailey, L[iberty].H[yde].   THE HOLY EARTH.   New York: Charles Scribner's Sons, 1915.   Reprint.   New York: Macmillan, 1923.   171 p.

In this classic statement Bailey presents an environmental ethic that views the Earth and the things that grow from it as holy.   He calls for a "moral partition" of resources.   Problems related to a society constructed on trade, industry, and war are discussed. He considers the existence of a group of people who are "separate," that is, unattached to organizations, to be necessary for public policymaking in environmental matters.

1377 Barbour, Ian G., ed. WESTERN MAN AND ENVIRONMENTAL ETHICS: ATTITUDES TOWARD NATURE AND TECHNOLOGY. Reading, Mass.: Addison-Wesley, 1973. 276 p.

The purpose of this anthology is to examine how attitudes toward nature and technology have led to environmental crisis, and how new attitudes may contribute to survival and quality of life on Earth. Part 1 presents classic papers by Lynn White and René Dubos on historical roots of the crisis. In part 2, the relationships between man and nature are explored by Leo Marx and Ian McHarg. Part 3 looks at alternatives for technological development which are compatible with environmental imperatives.

1378 Berry, David. "Preservation of Open Space and the Concept of Value." AMERICAN JOURNAL OF ECONOMICS AND SOCIOLOGY 35 (April 1976): 113-23.

Six major values which people ascribe to open space are identified: utilitarian, functional, contemplative, aesthetic, recreational, and ecological. These values are the result of attitudes shaped by American culture, and are not mutually exclusive, but overlap considerably, and complement each other. Policy related to land use must no longer be based on the single value of utility. The author advocates a multidimensional basis of decision where relative disadvantage to opposing parties is measured.

1379 Braaten, Carl E. "Caring for the Future: Where Ethics and Ecology Meet." ZYGON 9 (December 1974): 311-23.

If mankind is to solve the ecological crises his population and technology have created, then he must develop a "future-oriented ethic." While we have become aware of the finiteness of the environment, our reactions of technological optimism or fear of technology are not useful. If civilization is to survive, new value systems and life styles must be postulated based on a future consciousness complete with new symbols, models, rituals, and myths. A vision of the "essential humanity of man and his natural brotherhood with the world of nature" will need an "army of imagineers" for its realization. Many images of ecological humanism can be found in the religious cultures of the world.

1380 Burch, William R., Jr. DAYDREAMS AND NIGHTMARES: A SOCIO-LOGICAL ESSAY ON THE AMERICAN ENVIRONMENT. New York: Harper and Row, 1971. xiii, 175 p.

The interrelationships between myth, social structure, and
environment are analyzed in an attempt to understand contemporary attitudes toward the environment. Burch examines
the development of the awareness of environmental crises; the
expansion of leisure; the influence of environment on social
structure; rhetorical uses of nature such as primitivism,
transcendentalism, and the arcadian myth; democratic and
conservation values; and the effect of abundance on rationality.

1381   Buttel, Frederick H., and Flinn, William L.   "Social Class and Mass
       Environmental Beliefs, a Reconsideration."   ENVIRONMENT AND BE-
       HAVIOR 10 (September 1978): 433-50.

       Based on a statewide survey of Wisconsin residents conducted
       in 1974, the authors find that previous research which has
       equated environmental concern with upper-middle class status
       may be in error. Their results indicate that the effects of
       education, income, and occupation on environmental attitudes
       are meager. Instead, age and place of residence are better
       predictors. Among the working class, pro-environmental atti-
       tudes are strong in young people and city dwellers.

1382   Ekirch, Arthur A., Jr. MAN AND NATURE IN AMERICA. New
       York: Columbia University Press, 1963. Reprint. Lincoln: University
       of Nebraska Press, 1973. xii, 231 p. Bibliog.

       Ekirch presents a historical study of the relationships between
       man and nature in America. He assembles the viewpoints of
       thinkers of successive eras. The romantic view of an agrarian
       ideal began to be questioned with the equation of technology
       and progress. Emerson's and Thoreau's hopes for harmony were
       found by conservationists to be unrealistic. Proponents of a
       mechanistic philosophy still believe technology will create its
       own balance.   Problems of war, overpopulation, depletion of
       resources, and the effects of machines on the individual are
       explored.

1383   Frederick, Duke; Howenstine, William L.; and Sochen, June, eds.
       DESTROY TO CREATE: INTERACTION WITH THE NATURAL ENVIRON-
       MENT IN THE BUILDING OF AMERICA. Hinsdale, Ill.; Dryden Press,
       1972. 323 p.

       A historical collection of primary readings on attitudes toward
       the American environment includes selections by Lewis and
       Clark, Alexander Hamilton, Walt Whitman, Henry David
       Thoreau, George Catlin, John Wesley Powell, Theodore
       Roosevelt, Gifford Pinchot, John Muir, Stuart Chase, Aldo
       Leopold, Henry A. Wallace, Harrison Brown, Rachel Carson,
       and Paul Ehrlich. Lynn White's often reprinted "The Histori-

cal Roots of our Ecologic Crisis" (no. 1414) serves as an introduction to the collection.

1384   Harblin, Thomas Devaney. "Mine or Garden? Values and the Environment--Probable Sources of Change in the Next Hundred Years." ZYGON 12 (June 1977): 134-50.

To transform American culture from a "mining company" intent on short-term gain from the environment to a culture which functions as a "nurturing" gardener, value changes are necessary. Harblin examines values compromising to environmental quality and those conducive to viable human futures. Impacts of these values are assessed, and the cultural adaptation processes forced by environmental consciousness are surveyed. Uniting political strategy with motivation based on the interaction of science and religion could strengthen "gardener" values.

1385   Klink, William H. "Environmental Concerns and the Need for a New Image of Man." ZYGON 9 (December 1974): 300-310.

A mature relationship with the environment, as conceptualized by Buber's "I-Thou" thesis, demands man's utilization of sophisticated technologies. In the pre-technological world, the environment was seen as a given; but now man can realize how he affects the delicate balance of the Earth. Advanced technology broadens the I-Thou relationship because the environment can be seen as a dynamic system. Effects can be measured and a constant feedback process can be achieved. Man knows the global results of his actions.

1386   Kozlovsky, Daniel G. AN ECOLOGICAL AND EVOLUTIONARY ETHIC. Englewood Cliffs, N.J.: Prentice-Hall, 1974. xi, 116 p. Bibliog.

Maintaining that a human society without environmental problems is possible, Kozlovsky believes changes in behavior, work, life-styles, and values are elemental prerequisites to the achievement of a less-destructive ecology. He attempts to provide a basis for a new philosophical system rooted in biological knowledge of man's relationship with the living world. An overview of biological evolution leads to thoughts on the possibilities for alternative life styles.

1387   Leiss, William. THE DOMINATION OF NATURE. New York: George Braziller, 1972. xii, 242 p. Bibliog.

Beginning with a historical survey of man's attitudes toward nature, Leiss documents the emergence and consequences of the idea of the domination of nature. He then examines the relevant writings of three philosophers, Max Scheler, Edmund Husserl, and Max Horkheimer. Leiss concludes that nature must be liberated through man's adoption of a new purpose for science that is not wedded to the notion of nature's defeat.

1388   Leopold, Aldo. A SAND COUNTY ALMANAC AND SKETCHES HERE AND THERE. 1949. Reprint. New York: Oxford University Press, 1968. 226 p. Illus.

Recognizing that nature and wilderness had little value for Americans until "mechanization assured us of a good breakfast," Leopold finds some diminishing returns in progress. These essays articulate a land ethic. Toward this aim, he relates his family's activities in their "refuge from too-much modernity," recounts episodes in his life which convinced him the constant quest for a higher standard of living is out of step, then presents philosophical discussions of the "conservation aesthetic" and wilderness.

1389   McGinn, Thomas. "Ecology and Ethics." INTERNATIONAL PHILO-SOPHICAL QUARTERLY 14 (June 1974): 149-60.

Levi-Strauss and others have recognized that the environmental predicament demands a values system or ethics that is essentially nonhumanistic. A new "naturalism in Western ethics" would view the natural world as a systematic whole and the primary good in itself. In contrast, humanist ethics assigns value only in regard to human subjectivity; thus nature is seen as for man's use. In a discussion of questions which ecology poses in regard to philosophy of values, McGinn finds that a value system totally based on nature could demand the elimination of man. Without man, however, there can be no values. The potential of a "self-interest ethics" to deal with ecological problems is considered.

1390   Marine, Gene. AMERICA THE RAPED: THE ENGINEERING MENTAL-ITY AND THE DEVASTATION OF A CONTINENT. New York: Simon and Schuster, 1969. 312 p.

Probing the historical and social significance of ecological devastation, Marine condemns the "engineering mentality" in America which looks at problems pragmatically, ignores questions of side effects and works out "solutions" that satisfy only the immediate context of situations. The author has personally seen and discusses many specific ecological catastrophes. Activities of the Army Corps of Engineers are carefully examined. While this account suffers somewhat from reliance on newspaper items and secondary sources, the analysis of attitudes in engineering is vital.

1391 Passmore, John. MAN'S RESPONSIBILITY FOR NATURE: ECOLOGI-
CAL PROBLEMS AND WESTERN TRADITIONS. New York: Charles
Scribner's Sons, 1974. x, 213 p.

Opposing Western traditions which generally consider man as
a despot or steward over nature are described in order to
delineate those which tend to encourage and those which
might curb man's destruction of his environment. Passmore
then examines four major problems: pollution, depletion of
resources, extinction of species, and overpopulation. The
study is brought full-circle with a consideration of which
traditions and resultant trappings must be discarded and which
retained if man is to attempt to solve ecological problems.

1392 Sewell, W.R. Derrick. "Environmental Perceptions and Attitudes of
Engineers and Public Health Officials." ENVIRONMENT AND BEHA-
VIOR 3 (March 1971): 23-59.

In regard to environmental management, reliance is placed on
"experts" to define problems and implement solutions. Studies
have determined that the actions of engineers and public
health officials are affected by differing perceptions of the
environment. For example, engineers see water pollution as
an economic problem to be alleviated by technology, while
health officials look at the effects of human health and find
solutions in regulation. A holistic attitude has not resulted,
despite the recognition of its imporance. Experts are skeptical not only about public involvement in decision making but
also about the participation of other professionals.

1393 Slusser, Dorothy M., and Slusser, Gerald H. TECHNOLOGY--THE
GOD THAT FAILED. Philadelphia: Westminster Press, 1971. 169 p.

Modern man's "technological positivism" has resulted in a
tendency to forget or to leave unnoticed the unproved hypotheses upon which that technology is based. The Slussers find
this attitude most prevalent in man's relationship with the environment. The authors survey the development of technological culture, then examine the damages to the environment.
They conclude with a discussion of man's attitude toward nature and the need for a more adequate environmental ethic.

1394 Swann, James A., ed. "Environmental Education." ENVIRONMENT
AND BEHAVIOR 3 (September 1971): 223-344.

Programs for environmental education are discussed. Articles
present descriptions and evaluations of a "teach-in," a comprehensive program for grades K-12, and a citizen-participation
experiment in the Susquehanna River basin. In a broader
study, critical questions in population education are scrutinized.

1395 Tybout, Richard A., ed. ENVIRONMENTAL QUALITY AND SOCIETY. Columbus: Ohio State University Press, 1975. xii, 316 p. Illus.

The essays in this anthology, drawn from the Conference on Quality of the Environment held in 1970, place environmental issues in a social context. The interdisciplinary considerations are grouped under three topics: "ecolibrium"--the development of an ecological ethic that is acted upon through social processes; the need for a sense of community to replace concern for individual welfare; and economics and policy-making. Man's psychological need for nature and the effects of environmental problems on man's mental health are considered by many of the contributors.

1396 Whisenhunt, Donald W. THE ENVIRONMENT AND THE AMERICAN EXPERIENCE: A HISTORIAN LOOKS AT THE ECOLOGICAL CRISIS. Port Washington, N.Y.: Kennikat Press, 1974. vi, 136 p.

The present environmental crisis is the result of values which have developed from American intellectual, religious, economic, and political heritage. Whisenhunt traces the roots of customs and habits in an attempt to understand American attitudes toward the environment and to create a base upon which to build programs to correct environmental problems. Beliefs in progress, change, growth, faith in the future, division of man from nature, capitalism, disdain for government regulation, and ignorance of the workings of political power are some of the major attitudes which have determined the direction of American culture.

D. TECHNOLOGY OF ECOLOGY

1397 Barbour, Ian G., ed. EARTH MIGHT BE FAIR: REFLECTIONS ON ETHICS, RELIGION AND ECOLOGY. Englewood Cliffs, N.J.: Prentice-Hall, 1972. 168 p.

Eight essays that have as their central goal "the articulation of an ecological theology and an ecological ethic" involve three interwoven strands: "man's unity with nature, God's immanence in nature, and political responsibility for technology." The contributors--Barbour, Frederick Ferré, John J. Compton, Daniel Day Williams, Huston Smith, William Pollard, Harold K. Schilling, and Roger J. Shinn--generally reject technological solutions which do not include fundamental value changes, while holding out hope for significant change with the existing social and economic order. They are particularly concerned with the problems of pollution control, consumption, the redirection of technology, and population growth.

1398 Barnette, Henlee H. THE CHURCH AND THE ECOLOGICAL CRISIS.

Grand Rapids, Mich.: William B. Eerdmans, 1972. 114 p. Bibliog.

Barnette's intent is "to summarize the salient factors in the eco-crisis in the light of the biblical understanding of man and nature." A responsible theology for ecology must include the concept of stewardship. Includes a useful bibliography and lists of environmental films and societies.

1399   Birch, Charles. "Creation, Technology, and Human Survival: Called to Replenish the Earth." ECUMENICAL REVIEW 28 (January 1976): 66-79.

Birch, a biologist, believes our present society is headed for ultimate extinction unless we alter our lifestyles and values. The churches must be involved at more than the spiritual level if we are to extricate society from the scientific-technological vise which grips it. The technocratic view of nature must be abandoned for one which sees "the unity of the whole creation in the light of the Christian understanding of man," an ecology of God.

1400   Black, John. THE DOMINION OF MAN: THE SEARCH FOR ECO-LOGICAL RESPONSIBILITY. Chicago: Aldine Publishing Co., 1970. vii, 169 p.

Black traces the history and consequences of the Biblical notion of man's dominion over nature. Although recognizing serious problems, he fails to find a "crisis" of revolutionary proportions in the present ecological situation. Instead, he sees an evolutionary process which will continue to change as man's expectations regarding his environment change. Very readable.

1401   Cobb, John B. IS IT TOO LATE? A THEOLOGY OF ECOLOGY. Faith and Life Series. Beverly Hills, Calif.: Bruce, 1972. vi, 147 p. Bibliog.

Cobb believes "The major forms of past Christianity are inadequate to our [ecological] needs and must be superseded." They must be replaced by a new form of Christianity in which man, if he is to survive, must recognize his relationship with nature, not dominion over it.

1402   Derrick, Christopher. THE DELICATE CREATION: TOWARDS A THEOLOGY OF THE ENVIRONMENT. Old Greenwich, Conn.: Devin-Adair, 1972. x, 129 p.

Derrick believes Western man must abandon the Manichaean heresy--the view that nature and the world are hostile--which underlies much of our attitude toward the environment, resulting in a tendency toward exploitation and "technomania." He

calls for a "cosmic piety" which would recognize nature and
the environment as both good and vital, to be respected and
preserved even at the cost of certain technological and material advantages.

1403 Dubos, René. A GOD WITHIN. New York: Charles Scribner's Sons,
1972. 326 p.

Dubos documents man's responses to environmental crises
throughout history. Hopeful of a compromise between human
requirements and the stability of nature, he provides the
message that quality of life and culture are distinct from
economic and technological growth. Out of a sense of
"entheos," the belief in the deity or spirit within a place,
a "scientific theology" can be created which will lead to a
balance between civilization, industry, technology, and the
human species.

1404 Elder, Frederick. CRISIS IN EDEN: A RELIGIOUS CRITIQUE OF
MAN AND ENVIRONMENT. Nashville, Tenn.: Abingdon Press,
1970. 172 p. Bibliog.

Elder contrasts two theories of man's relationship to nature--
the "exclusionist," typified by the work of Teilhard de
Chardin, Herbert Richardson, and Harvey Cox, in which
nature is subjugated to and by man; and the "inclusionist,"
best represented by Loren Eiseley, in which man lives in
harmony with nature. Sympathetic to the inclusionists, Elder
proposes the churches, through an environmental theology,
institute a modern asceticism characterized by restraint, an
emphasis upon quality existence, and a reverence for life.
Useful footnotes and bibliography.

1405 Hamilton, Michael, ed. THIS LITTLE PLANET. New York: Charles
Scribner's Sons, 1970. x, 241 p.

Theologians refute Lynn White's contention that the Judeo-
Christian tradition's attitude toward nature is the basis of our
environmental problems. The contributors also search our
religious heritage for positive wisdom and motivation for the
development of an ecological conscience. Pollution, scarcity,
and conservation are discussed by three scientists, after which
three Christian thinkers respond.

1406 Hoffman, Michael W. "Ecology, Religion, and the Counterculture."
ENCOUNTER 38 (Spring 1977): 98-116.

Hoffman believes ecology, religion, and the counterculture
have "essential interconnections." Solutions for the environmental crisis must involve a fundamental change in our philo-

sophical and religious attitudes which will recognize mankind's essential ties to nature. The counterculture in large part embodies just such an organic view. Useful bibliographical footnotes.

1407   Jeffko, Walter G. "Ecology and Dualism." RELIGION IN LIFE 42 (Spring 1973): 117-27.

Jeffko shows how "our current ecological problems stem from modern philosophical dualism going back to Descartes." To solve today's scientifically and technologically induced problems man must reestablish "a positive unity with the world," in which he is transcendent but respectful of his environment.

1408   "Man and His Environment." DIALOG 9 (Summer 1970): 171-235.

A theme issue devoted to material on the environmental crisis includes contributions by Douglas Daetz, H. Paul Santmire, Daniel T. Martensen, Bruce Wrightsman, Ronald S. Laura, and Thomas E. Nutt. Also included is Kenneth A. Alpers' "Starting Points for an Ecological Theology: A Bibliographical Survey," which includes material both on the crisis itself and theological/ethical responses.

1409   "Man's Responsibility for Nature." ZYGON 12 (September 1977): 182-258.

The second of two theme issues is devoted to human responsibility for the system of nature (no. 1410). Paul Abrecht reviews the impact of science and technology upon society and offers brief suggestions for ethical guidelines in answering problems. Hugh Montefore believes the necessary values must come from a theology in which God transcends both man and nature. D. Bryce-Smith distinguishes between human ethics, which are inadequate to the job, and a "moral sense," which can provide an understanding of the reality of God's superhuman creation. Edward Goldsmith concludes the issue with a plea to see religion as "the control mechanism of a stable society" in a given ecosystem.

1410   "Papers from the Institute on Religion in an Age of Science Conference on the Ecosystem, Energy, and Human Values." ZYGON 12 (June 1977): 106-74.

With the conviction that a concept of systems, which would merge practical solutions with abstract ideas, is necessary to resolve environmental problems, the conference explores the "interdependence of physical, biological and socio-cultural value systems in a world of finite resources." Howard Odum, an environmental scientist, considers all phenomena, including human values, to be generated by flows of energy. Thus, his examination of systems of energy interaction relates values to the ecosystem's energy transfer. (His "flow charts" are intriguing.) Sociologist Thomas Harblin discusses the role of values in the development of an energy policy that could transform American culture from a "mining company" extracting short-term gain to "gardeners" tending and nurturing the environment. Whether theological beliefs mold particular attitudes toward the environment is deliberated by Don Marietta.

1411 Santmire, H. Paul. BROTHER EARTH: NATURE, GOD, AND ECOLOGY IN TIME OF CRISIS. New York: Thomas Nelson, 1970. 236 p.

Santmire calls for a Christian ecological theology, an "ethic of responsibility. . .predicated on a vision of the Kingdom of God and His righteousness as the ultimate framework for judging and inspiring moral action." Man must play the role of nature's caretaker.

1412 Schwarz, Hans. "The Eschatological Dimension of Ecology." ZYGON 9 (December 1974): 323-38.

Schwarz sees no evidence that the world has come of age, but rather because of our technology we have reached an environmental crisis of apocalyptic proportions. He believes that for humankind to survive, we must replace our anthropocentric view of nature with the eschatological promises envisioned in the theocentric Judeo-Christian tradition.

1413 Toynbee, Arnold J. "The Genesis of Pollution." HORIZON 15 (Summer 1973): 4-9.

Based upon the belief that technology is neutral, Toynbee sees environmental problems stemming from the monotheistic Christian belief that man has dominion over nature. Man must reintegrate himself with nature religiously or philosophically if he is to survive.

1414 White, Lynn, Jr. "The Historical Roots of Our Ecologic Crisis." SCIENCE 155 (10 March 1967): 1203-7.

In this classic statement, White traces our attitude toward nature to Judeo-Christian teleology. Western traditions of science and technology, basically the "Baconian creed that scientific knowledge means technological power over nature," developed from medieval views of man and nature based on Christian teachings. Unlike Occidental theology, where there is spirit in nature, Christianity is anthropomorphic, sees man as superior to nature, and has implicit faith in perpetual progress. White concludes that "we shall continue to have a worsening ecologic crisis until we reject the Christian axiom that nature has no reason for existence save to serve man."

E. STRATEGY FOR RESTORATION

1. Bibliographies

1415   Meshenberg, Michael J. ENVIRONMENTAL PLANNING: A GUIDE
        TO INFORMATION SOURCES. Man and the Environment, vol. 3.
        Detroit: Gale Research Co., 1976. xx, 492 p.

> With entries selected and annotated for planners on city,
> regional, or state levels, the bibliography focuses on concepts,
> principles, and techniques that promote protection of the en-
> vironment. The more than 1,700 entries include literature
> from engineering and the natural and social sciences. Books,
> journal articles, government studies, and documents are
> arranged under the following topics: ecology, the environ-
> mental planning process, environmental impact analysis, soil,
> geology, water, climate, air pollution, vegetation, wildlife,
> urban growth, environmental design, historic preservation,
> health, noise, environmental law, energy, and land-use plan-
> ning. Journals, newsletters, and indexing-abstracting services
> in the field are listed.

1416   Viohl, Richard C., and Mason, Kenneth G.M. ENVIRONMENTAL
        IMPACT ASSESSMENT METHODOLOGIES: AN ANNOTATED BIBLIOG-
        RAPHY. Exchange Bibliography no. 691. Monticello, Ill.: Council
        of Planning Librarians, 1974. 32 p.

2. Books and Articles

1417   Beckmann, Petr. ECO-HYSTERICS AND THE TECHNOPHOBES.
        Boulder, Colo.: Golem Press, 1973. 216 p. Illus.

> An electrical engineer writes a "doomsday debunker," claim-
> ing that more science and technology are needed to eliminate
> pollution and restore environmental balance. Proponents of
> "apocalyptic holocaustology" do not support their doomsday
> prophecies and often abandon scientific research. Beckmann
> chooses to refute the most impressive targets of the "ecocult":
> population explosion, depletion of resources, pollution, lack
> of energy, and the Club of Rome's report THE LIMITS TO
> GROWTH (no. 2281). This study is not dispassionate and sci-
> entific; instead, the author exhibits the emotional ardor evi-
> dent in his opponents.

1418   Brubaker, Sterling. IN COMMAND OF TOMORROW: RESOURCE
        AND ENVIRONMENTAL STRATEGIES FOR AMERICANS. Baltimore:
        Johns Hopkins University Press for Resources for the Future, 1975. xii,
        177 p.

Beginning with the conviction that resource exhaustion can best be dealt with through technical advances which exploit inexhaustible energy sources and consequently allow continuation of industrial society, Brubaker analyzes the links between resources, environment, and policy. Factors considered are constraints implied by environmental conditions, social attitudes and values which direct goals, instruments available to assist with policymaking, and potential policy directions. Scientific, technical, and value issues related to land use, urbanization, minerals, and pollution are scrutinized.

1419 Burchell, Robert W., and Listokin, David. THE ENVIRONMENTAL IMPACT HANDBOOK. New Brunswick, N.J.: Center for Urban Policy Research, Rutgers University, 1975. iii, 239 p. Bibliog.

The handbook presents a standardized approach to environmental impact statement procedures and requirements. It covers state and local government policies, content, format, the review process, responsibility, guidelines and recommended procedure, and trends in litigation. There is an extensive annotated guide to books, journals, newsletters, and professional organizations concerned with the environment.

1420 Corwin, Ruthann, et al. ENVIRONMENTAL IMPACT ASSESSMENT. San Francisco: Freeman, Cooper and Co., 1975. 277 p. Illus., bibliog.

A team composed of an engineer-biologist, a planner-systems analyst, a geographer, an attorney, an economist, and a journalist-political scientist join to develop a guide for performing the process of environmental impact analysis. An overview of impact assessment is followed by consideration and sources for social and economic analysis, legal requirements, the preparation process, and implementation of the findings. There is a case study of the Warm Springs Dam project and documentation of information sources (journals, research and citizen's groups, government models), as well as federal and state legislation.

1421 DeBell, Garrett, ed. THE ENVIRONMENTAL HANDBOOK: PREPARED FOR THE FIRST NATIONAL ENVIRONMENTAL TEACH-IN. New York: Ballantine Books, 1970. xv, 367 p. Bibliog.

Selections chosen for this anthology present varied approaches to and tactics for combating environmental crises. There are suggestions for an environmental platform and reprinted essays by authorities on economics, ecology, cultural change, and policymaking, as well as bibliographies of books and films. Specific problems addressed are pesticides, the economics of ecosystems, education for environmental values, the SST, auto-

mobiles, recycling, cities, and the media. Two sections
present tactics for environmental change. Classic statements
by Lynn White, Garrett Hardin, Kenneth Boulding, and Lewis
Mumford are included.

1422   Eisenbud, Merril. ENVIRONMENT, TECHNOLOGY, AND HEALTH:
HUMAN ECOLOGY IN HISTORICAL PERSPECTIVE. New York: New
York University Press, 1978. x, 384 p. Illus.

Advocating an environmentalism based on man's needs instead
of religiosity, Eisenbud calls for a perspective in which technology and economic cost-benefit analysis are prominent.
While aware of trade-offs involved, new technologies are
considered the answer to many environmental problems. Pollution is given low priority since the author feels economic
resources have been wasted in efforts toward excessive cleanliness. Considering targets chosen by environmentalists to be
inappropriate, improvements in urban housing are seen as more
urgent than clean air. Some critics accuse Eisenbud of the
same naiveté that characterizes religious environmentalists.

1423   Fuller, R[ichard]. Buckminster. OPERATING MANUAL FOR SPACE-
SHIP EARTH. New York: Simon and Schuster, 1969. 144 p.

Weighing man's future on this planet, Fuller finds the answer
to potential environmental disaster in increased technology,
industrialization, research and development, and the continued
generation of wealth. Man's present tendency toward "oblivion" can be redirected through a move away from specialization to an understanding of systems theory and global perspectives.

1424   Hardin, Garrett. EXPLORING NEW ETHICS FOR SURVIVAL: THE
VOYAGE OF THE SPACESHIP BEAGLE. New York: Viking Press
1972. xii, 273 p.

Employing both nonfiction and science fiction, Hardin explores
the problem of population-environmental quality. Technical
solutions alone can not rescue us from overpopulation. Changes
in values and the acceptance of "mutual coercion" are necessary. In this expansion of the author's famous article, "The
Tragedy of the Commons" (no. 1426), Hardin recognizes that
in matters of the public good, a legitimate legal structure
rather than individual virtue must legislate.

1425   _____. THE LIMITS OF ALTRUISM: AN ECOLOGIST'S VIEW OF
SURVIVAL. Bloomington: Indiana University Press, 1977. 154 p.

If the world is considered in rational terms of reciprocal costs
and benefits, no one "should ever plant a redwood tree."
However, Hardin contends that man insists on acting irrationally.

One of the chief difficulties with obligations to future generations is the considerable gap in time between costs and benefits. Garrett considers large-scale altruistic behavior to be
impossible. Ethical values of decency which serve well in
small groups can not be extended to global problems of population, nuclear war, and developing countries.

1426 _____. "The Tragedy of the Commons." SCIENCE 162 (13 December
1968): 1243-48.

Among those problems that cannot be solved through recourse
to technology, the population problem is most obvious. It is
a values dilemma; while we believe in the individual's right
to make use of the Earth's resources, we realize that, because the Earth is finite, that this right cannot be granted to
all, indefinitely. The "commons" of the Earth must now be
carefully parcelled. Hardin suggests that overpopulation can
only be solved by mutual coercion, not by appeals to reason.

1427 Johnson, Huey D., ed. NO DEPOSIT--NO RETURN; MAN AND HIS
ENVIRONMENT: A VIEW TOWARD SURVIVAL. Reading, Mass.:
Addison-Wesley, 1970. xvi, 351 p.

The papers from the Thirteenth National Conference of the
U.S. National Commission for UNESCO are concerned with
the environment as it relates to many fields. With a scope
limited to environmental problems in the United States, the
volume is a primer for environmental awareness with the purposes to inform and to arouse. Sixty-five interdisciplinary
essays are organized in four parts: natural resources; the role
of institutions in resource management (including government,
industry, media, education, science, law, religion, and art);
youth; and activism. A concluding chapter sets forth action
suggestions.

1428 Kapp, K[arl]. William. "Environment and Technology: New Frontiers
for the Social and Natural Sciences." JOURNAL OF ECONOMIC
ISSUES 11 (September 1977): 527-40.

This paper, read at the International Congress of Scientists on
the Human Environment in 1975 is a plea for "trans-
disciplinary" exploration of environmental disruption and the
complex interaction between the natural environment, the
economy, and social costs. Kapp feels that years of talking
about interdisciplinarity has not resulted in the development
of appropriate "techniques, methods, and attitudes." Attitudes
toward growth and the development of effective social and
environmental indicators to measure disruptions and their effects
are the primary areas of needed change.

1429 Maddox, John. THE DOOMSDAY SYNDROME. New York: McGraw-

Hill, 1972. vii, 293 p. Bibliog.

Scientists and ecologists have juggled facts and expressed conclusions in language designed to scare, instead of encountering
immediate problems and attempting to solve them with beneficial technology. After examining pollution, depletion of
natural resources, ethical problems of biological research, and
economic growth, Maddox concludes that the environment can
be safe for man if energies are spent to correct problems
rather than predict doom. Unfortunately, Maddox counters
pessimism with groundless optimism and often undocumented claims.

1430   Moos, Rudolf [H.] and Brownstein, Robert. ENVIRONMENT AND
UTOPIA: A SYNTHESIS. New York: Plenum Press, 1977. ix, 284 p.

Environmental theory and utopian speculation are merged in
order to present a perspective with which man can restructure
political, economic, and social activities, as well as values
in order to create a balanced interaction with the environment.
A framework which details utopian dealings with issues related to the environment is applied to experimental utopian
communities--Oneida, Israeli kibbutzim, and Columbia, Maryland. One literary utopia, WALDEN TWO (no. 1942) is also
considered. The final section synthesizes environmental and
utopian perspectives, finds them congruent, and indicates directions for future thought and experimentation with human
environments.

1431   Nash, Hugh, ed. PROGRESS AS IF SURVIVAL MATTERED: A HAND-
BOOK FOR A CONSERVER SOCIETY. San Francisco: Friends of the
Earth, 1977. 319 p. Illus.

Political action, litigation in the courts, and lobbying are the
means by which contributors of these essays hope to move toward a conservation society. Each focuses on the beliefs of
environmentalists and attempts to outline goals. Among the
environmental problems considered are energy, population,
nuclear power, jobs, health, transportation, science and
technology, economics, recreation, education, decentralization, the media, war, and environmental law. Contributors
are all associates of Friends of the Earth. There is a "Citizen's Appendix" outlining the process of the introduction
and passage of laws.

1432   National Research Council. Division of Behavioral Sciences. ENVI-
RONMENTAL QUALITY AND SOCIAL BEHAVIOR: STRATEGIES FOR
RESEARCH. Washington, D C.: National Academy of Sciences, 1973.
xiii, 86 p.

The report of an interdisciplinary study conference on research
strategies in the social and behavioral sciences on environ-

mental problems and policies seeks to delineate the kinds of
research that will lead to environmental management and
corrective action. The connections between the results of
research and organizational decision making and governmental
policy formation are stressed. The panel consists of prominent
economists, industrialists, sociologists, political and natural
scientists, legal specialists, and planners.

1433 Ophuls, William. ECOLOGY AND THE POLITICS OF SCARCITY:
PROLOGUE TO A POLITICAL THEORY OF THE STEADY STATE.
San Francisco: W.H. Freeman and Co., 1977. xi, 303 p. Illus.,
bibliog.

To present an "ecological critique of American political institutions and their underlying philosophy," Ophuls draws on
ecology, natural sciences, engineering, technology, the social
sciences, and the humanities. Believing that the environmental crises will doom our present political and economic systems
and their underlying values, the author explains the inadequacies of liberal democracy and individualism, then provides
a base for reform. Ecological scarcity demands a steady-state
balance dependent on technological capacities and social
choices.

1434 Pirages, Dennis C[lark]., and Ehrlich, Paul R. ARK II: SOCIAL
RESPONSE TO ENVIRONMENTAL IMPERATIVES. New York: Viking
Press, 1974. x, 344 p. Bibliog.

The environmental crises that face America necessitate
changes in values, institutions, and behavior. The authors
explain the complex interrelationships between social culture
and environmental problems. They advocate the risking of
mistakes in order to move toward social solutions to meet
impending crises. Affluence, politics, policymaking, education, and information availability receive attention.

1435 Robertson, James, and Lewallen, John, eds. THE GRASS ROOTS
PRIMER. San Francisco: Sierra Club Books, 1975. 287 p. Illus.,
bibliog.

The practical and legal steps taken by "grass roots" environmental groups to preserve their wilderness areas or urban open
spaces are detailed in this handbook. Discussions of local
environmental activists are followed by plans for carrying out
local environmental efforts. Federal and state environmental
laws are listed in digest form; directories of information
sources and projects in the United States and Canada are
cited.

1436 Strausz-Hupé, Robert, ed. "Society and Ecology." AMERICAN BE-

HAVIORAL SCIENTIST 11 (July–August 1968): 1–48.

Ecological problems and the means for their alleviation are the concerns of these essays. The views of the contributors diverge with some finding the solution in more and better science and technology, others rejecting the concept of man's linear progress, and others wondering if sci-tech man can reorder his world with any methods other than that with which he built it. Topics include the politics of ecology, technology of social progress, cities, social planning, technique and institutions, and technology and the human condition. Among the contributors are Jacques Ellul, John McHale, and Stefan Possony.

1437 Vogt, William. ROAD TO SURVIVAL. New York: William Sloane Associates, 1948. xvi, 335 p. Illus., bibliog.

Recognition of the destructive power of technology leads Vogt to an attempt to understand man's relationship to his environment. All societies must recognize their intimate dependence upon the earth and control population while reducing resource consumption. Abuse of applied science has placed man in danger of a catastrophic crash of civilization. Drastic and expensive measures to regain ecological balance are essential. The affluent countries should provide the leadership and resources for the development of an earth company.

F. POLICYMAKING PROCESS

1. Bibliographies

1438 Bowman, James S. POLITICS OF ECOLOGY: THE ENVIRONMENT AND PUBLIC POLICY, A BIBLIOGRAPHY. Exchange Bibliography no. 696. Monticello, Ill.: Council of Planning Librarians, 1974. 39 p.

1439 Chisholm, Joseph. PUBLIC PARTICIPATION IN ENVIRONMENTAL POLICY: AN ANNOTATED BIBLIOGRAPHY. Exchange Bibliography no. 1163. Monticello, Ill.: Council of Planning Librarians, 1976. 17 p.

1440 Dunlap, Riley E. STUDIES IN ENVIRONMENTAL POLITICS AND POLICY: A BIBLIOGRAPHY. Exchange Bibliography no. 917. Monticello, Ill.: Council of Planning Librarians, 1975. 26 p.

1441 Schwartz, Mortimer D. ENVIRONMENTAL LAW: A GUIDE TO INFORMATION SOURCES. Man and the Environment, vol. 6. Detroit: Gale Research Co., 1977. xiii, 191 p.

The field of environmental law is concerned with the protection, preservation, and rehabilitation of the physical environment. The materials listed and annotated herein are limited to books, government publications, proceedings of conferences, and symposia. Journal titles and services substantially devoted to environmental law are included. Arrangement is by topic, e.g., the legal process; air, water, noise, and energy pollution; pesticides; solid waste; conservation of wildlife; land use; and public lands. Lists of environmental action organizations and law libraries are appended.

2. Books and Articles

1442 Baxter, William F. PEOPLE OR PENGUINS: THE CASE FOR OPTIMAL POLLUTION. New York: Columbia University Press, 1974. 110 p.

Developing criteria oriented toward people rather than penguins, Baxter, a law professor at Stanford, advocates an optimal endurance level of pollution. Legislation of the industrial sector through the class-action suit and the effluent tax is seen as more effective than the development of pollution-control technologies. The probable success of various government controls is analyzed; however, Baxter seems unconvinced of the delicacy of the man-ecology interface.

1443 Beard, Daniel P. "United States Environmental Legislation and Energy Resources: A Review." GEOGRAPHICAL REVIEW 65 (April 1975): 229-44.

An overview of the relationships between environmental statutes and energy supply and demand is provided. Relevant government publications, court cases, research studies, and interdisciplinary considerations are cited. The effects of legislation on fuel consumption, fuel switching, delays in construction, changes in technology, land-use conflict, and prices are analyzed.

1444 Brenner, Michael J. THE POLITICAL ECONOMY OF AMERICA'S ENVIRONMENTAL DILEMMA. Lexington, Mass.: Lexington Books, 1973. xx, 179 p.

Basically a work of policy analysis, Brenner's study examines the failure of our public institutions to protect man's habitat. Part 1 examines the connections between the structural characteristics of the industrial system that result in its neglectful attitude toward the environment, and the political and economic theories evolving from social values. This is followed by a detailed assessment of recent public initiatives and possible approaches to the problems. The final two parts look at the practicalities of environmental politics and advocate specific reforms aimed at institutional changes which will lead to altered values.

1445 Caldwell, Lynton Keith. ENVIRONMENT: A CHALLENGE FOR MODERN SOCIETY. Garden City, N.Y.: Natural History Press, 1970. xvi, 292 p.

Convinced that administration of man's environmental relationship must be accepted by government, Caldwell examines the process of implementation from perspectives of policy, tasks, and management. He is primarily concerned with value development in environmental matters so that criteria for choice in policy decisions will be available. The government must administer the purposive shaping of the human environment by man and control human action in relation to the environment. Caldwell explores social attitudes and institutions that would be conducive to the realization of such aims.

1446 _____. "Environmental Policy as a Catalyst of Institutional Change." AMERICAN BEHAVIORAL SCIENTIST 17 (May-June 1974): 711-30.

The "novelty, generality, expansibility, and incompatibility" of environmental issues force alternatives to the traditional politics of compromise and cause changes in institutional structure and behavior. Confrontation and problem-solving are more viable political styles. The multidisciplinary character of environmental problems demands "interconnectedness" of departments rather than line-of-command. Authority of knowledge replaces status, and top directors must be catalysts for cooperation rather than dominant egos.

1447 Graham, Frank, Jr. SINCE SILENT SPRING. Boston: Houghton Mifflin, 1970. xvi, 333 p.

The response to Rachel Carson's SILENT SPRING (no. 1455) is documented in a chronicle which follows the development of pesticide policy and the publications, such as propaganda, government reports, and research, spurred by Carson's work. The controversy demonstrates that reactions and policies evolve from differences in values. Results of use and reactions to such pesticides as chlorinated hydrocarbons, DDT, Dieldrin, Endrin, and Malathion are discussed.

1448 Kirgis, Frederic L., Jr. "Technological Challenge to the Shared Environment: United States Practice." AMERICAN JOURNAL OF INTERNATIONAL LAW 66 (April 1972): 290-320.

Examination of U.S. legal practice in regard to the regulation of the effects of novel technologies on the shared environment can be a first step in fashioning viable international regulatory institutions. The author discusses the Trail Smelter case, and

cases concerning nuclear tests, waste disposal, ocean resources, outer space, and weather modification. U.S.
practice indicates recognition of consideration of environmental
consequences, a duty to consult internationally, reliance on
rough cost-benefit analysis, and little emphasis on national
security considerations.

1449   Laitos, Jan G. "Legal Institutions and Pollution: Some Intersections
Between Law and History." NATURAL RESOURCES JOURNAL 15
(July 1975): 423-51.

A careful review of the reaction of the legal system to air-
pollution problems reveals a hierarchy of values within which
economic market values hold more weight than interests for
clean air. Laitos surveys legal response from 1800 to the
present, with emphasis on the period 1880-1930 when the
legal system began to address long-run social costs. This
period saw the development of tensions affecting the use of
law as a tool for pollution control. Features developed then
continue to limit the law's impact on pollution today.

1450   Longwood, Merle. "The Common Good: An Ethical Framework for
Evaluating Environmental Issues." THEOLOGICAL STUDIES 34 (September 1973): 468-80.

Policymaking in regard to environmental problems requires a
delineation of an ethical framework or set of moral principles
for guidance. Today there is a "poverty of liberalism" which
focuses on distributive concerns (division of goods among individual members of the community) rather than on the aggregate concerns of society. Longwood's proposal for a "modified
version of the traditional concept of the common good"
emphasizes "ideal-regarding" principles rather than the generally emphasized "want-regarding" principles.

1451   National Academy of Sciences and National Research Council. Committee on Resources and Man. RESOURCES AND MAN: A STUDY
AND RECOMMENDATIONS. San Francisco: W.H. Freeman and Co.,
1969. xi, 259 p. Illus., graphs, bibliog.

Focusing on food, minerals, and energy sources from land and
sea, the committee presents an analysis of man's relation to
natural resources and the ecological consequences of actions or
inaction. The detailed, rational assessments and balanced predictions for short-range periods and beyond the year 2000 are
designed to provide a basis for national policy. Recommendations to promote wider use of resources are provided in four
categories: early action, policy, research, and organization.

1452   Roos, Leslie L., Jr. THE POLITICS OF ECOSUICIDE. New York: Holt, Rinehart and Winston, 1971. viii, 404 p. Graphs.

This reader addresses the process of political decision making regarding environmental problems. The essays are divided into major topic concerns: the reactions of business, costs external to the market system, channeling change through institutions, the role of analysis in policymaking, and relationships between the environment and social welfare issues.

1453   Sax, Joseph L. DEFENDING THE ENVIRONMENT: A STRATEGY FOR CITIZEN ACTION. New York: Alfred A. Knopf, 1971. xix, 258 p.

Sax proposes greater citizen participation in environmental matters through the judicial system. He finds government agencies to be often the "most serious obstacles to environmental preservation" because of the intricacies of the administrative process. Citizen initiative in management of the environment can be reasserted through the courts because the individual can receive an equal hearing with organized interests. The Hunting Creek (Alexandria, Virginia) case is examined in detail.

1454   "Symposium on Public Participation in Resource Decisionmaking." NATURAL RESOURCES JOURNAL 16 (January 1976): 1-236.

Contributors consider the culture of participation, sociological interpretation of those involved, legal foundations for public participation, alternative mechanisms for citizen action, and analysis of public input. Case studies of participation in Toronto's Spadina Expressway, the Goldstream controversy, and the Okanagan Basin study are also presented.

G. SELECTED CASE STUDIES

1455   Carson, Rachel. SILENT SPRING. Boston: Houghton Mifflin, 1962. 368 p. Illus., bibliog.

With substantial scientific documentation, Carson demonstrates how the use of chemical insecticides is destroying our environment and wildlife, and is also creating a hazard to man. She documents her findings with case histories such as the gypsy moth campaigns and fire-ant program. Primary attention is given to insecticides, herbicides, and fungicides. Carson discusses and evaluates alternatives of natural manipulation. The controversy which ensued following the publication of this book is in itself of considerable interest. An extensive list of sources is appended.

1456   Constantini, Edmond, and Hanf, Kenneth. "Environmental Concern and Lake Tahoe: A Study of Elite Perceptions, Backgrounds, and Attitudes."

ENVIRONMENT AND BEHAVIOR 4 (June 1972): 209-42.

Since environmental policy is determined through "political combat," the authors survey the reactions of significant actors in the decision-making process in the Lake Tahoe area. Those displaying a high level of environmental concern were professionals and government officials. Businessmen showed less interest.

1457 Dasmann, Raymond F. THE DESTRUCTION OF CALIFORNIA. New York: Macmillan, 1965. 247 p. Illus.

A biologist-conservationist concisely surveys the despoiling of California land which began with the establishment of the chain of Spanish missions in the eighteenth century. He discusses overgrazing on public lands, extermination of wild animals, clear cutting of forests, furnishing increased supplies of potable water to Los Angeles, railroads, automobiles, public utilities, and free enterprise. Dasmann appreciates cities but criticizes those who see the future only in terms of growth.

1458 Davis, Ray Jay, and Grant, Lewis O., eds. WEATHER MODIFICATION: TECHNOLOGY AND LAW. AAAS Selected Symposium, 20. Boulder, Colo.: Westview Press for the American Association for the Advancement of Science, 1978. xviii, 124 p.

The dialog between scientists and lawyers is based on the Conference on the Legal and Scientific Uncertainties of Weather Modification, 1976. Prospects for a viable weather modification technology and the legal problems that will be raised are surveyed in the first two parts. Part 3 then turns to an examination of social impacts. Parts 4 and 5 provide discussions of the interaction between scientists and lawyers.

1459 Feiveson, Harold A.; Sinden, Frank W.; and Socolow, Robert H., eds. BOUNDARIES OF ANALYSIS: AN INQUIRY INTO THE TOCKS ISLAND DAM CONTROVERSY. Cambridge, Mass.: Ballinger Publishing Co., 1976. xiii, 417 p. Illus., bibliog.

How the environmental policy process works is detailed in these essays dealing with the environmental issues of the Tocks Island Dam controversy. The influence of technical analysis on the political process is examined in detail while the human value conflicts are also integrated into the study. The ten essays encompass limitations of discourse in the policy process, the political history of the project, scientific and economic examinations of demands for water, flood control, and electric power in the Delaware River basin, and the viability of technical analytic methods in solving environmental policy problems.

1460 Hummel, Carl F.; Levitt, Lynn; and Loomis, Ross J. "Perceptions of the Energy Crisis: Who is Blamed and How do Citizens React to Environment-Lifestyle Tradeoffs?" ENVIRONMENT AND BEHAVIOR 10 (March 1978): 37-88.

> The goal of this research was to develop a profile of the person who shows behavior-related concern about environmental problems even when confronted by conflicting problems, such as energy. Data were collected as part of a larger 1973 survey of behavior and attitude toward energy and the environment of the noncollege-student population. Findings suggested that clean-air advocates blamed individual consumers for the energy crisis, while energy enthusiasts blamed environmentalists.

1461 McGrath, Dorn C. "Multidisciplinary Environmental Analysis: Jamaica Bay and Kennedy Airport." JOURNAL OF THE AMERICAN INSTITUTE OF PLANNERS 37 (July 1971): 243-52.

> Faced with the dilemma of environmental conservation versus the need for expanded airport facilities in New York City, the Port of New York Authority requested a multidisciplinary study by the National Academies of Sciences and Engineering. The resultant research established techniques for analysis and determined factors necessary for environmental impact studies. The Jamaica Bay Environmental Study Group was composed of professionals from physical and biological sciences, engineering, social and behavioral sciences, urban planning, and law. Each member's participation in at least two subgroups insured interdisciplinary exchange.

1462 Rodda, M. NOISE AND SOCIETY. Edinburgh: Oliver and Boyd, 1967. 113 p. Bibliog.

> Noise is defined as an annoying or unwanted sound. Sources of excess noise in industry and community are identified. Adverse physiological and psychological effects of too much noise are described, with convincing documentation. The author notes that techniques of noise control are well advanced but that economic factors and lack of appropriately trained personnel prevent the widespread application of these techniques.

1463 Rowe, Peter G., et al. PRINCIPLES FOR LOCAL ENVIRONMENTAL MANAGEMENT. Cambridge, Mass.: Ballinger Publishing Co., 1978. xx, 272 p. Illus., bibliog.

> Designed as a handbook to assist local and regional governments in dealing with growth, the study evolved from a National Science Foundation supported environmental analysis for development planning in Chambers County, Texas. It

serves as documentation that university research groups, local government, citizen groups, and corporations can work together to maintain environmental integrity while guiding growth. The resulting handbook covers fundamental environmental management, recent legislation, and local responses to options. Extensive bibliography.

1464 Sewell, W.R. Derrick, ed. HUMAN DIMENSIONS OF WEATHER MODIFICATION. Chicago: Department of Geography, University of Chicago, 1966. xii, 423 p. Illus., maps.

An interdisciplinary look at the identification and measurement of economic and social impacts of weather modification is provided. Papers are organized into nine groups, including a state-of-the-art summary and a review of public attitudes toward weather. Areas of potential impact studied encompass recreation, urban growth, tribal life, and folk beliefs.

1465 Stone, Christopher D. SHOULD TREES HAVE STANDING? TOWARD LEGAL RIGHTS FOR NATURAL OBJECTS. Los Altos, Calif.: William Kaufman, 1974. 103 p.

The development of the Mineral King wilderness area by Walt Disney Enterprises and the resulting suit filed by the Sierra Club were the impetus for Stone's article, which originally appeared in the SOUTHERN CALIFORNIA LAW REVIEW (vol. 45, Spring 1972). Stone's defense of an ethical change in the philosophy of law which would grant rights to natural objects is reprinted herein along with the texts of the Supreme Court decision in the Mineral King case, and the dissenting opinions of Justices Douglas, Brennan, and Blackmun.

1466 Talbot, Allan R. POWER ALONG THE HUDSON: THE STORM KING CASE AND THE BIRTH OF ENVIRONMENTALISM. New York: E.P. Dutton, 1972. 244 p. Maps, bibliog.

Talbot outlines a historical case study of an important conservation struggle to save the scenic beauty of Storm King Mountain from the ravages of a proposed pumped-storage hydroelectric plant. Although environmentalists lost the battle in 1972 after almost a decade of controversy, the case sparked an increased environmental awareness.

1467 Tribe, Laurence [H.]; Schelling, Corinne S.; and Voss, John, eds. WHEN VALUES CONFLICT; ESSAYS ON ENVIRONMENTAL ANALYSIS, DISCOURSE, AND DECISION. Cambridge, Mass.: Ballinger Publishing Co., 1976. xv, 179 p.

At a time when society is no longer sure of priorities among its values, the task of analyzing issues and making policy decisions is exceptionally difficult. The contributors recognize the inadequacy of legal, political, and technological modes of analysis when dealing with competing values. In an attempt to develop a methodology for assessment, the role of values in the controversy over the Tocks Island Dam is studied. The analysis embraces a discussion of the breakdown of discourse, the acceptance of artificial environments and a new rationale for environmental policy, the process of decision making, a history of the Tocks Island controversy, and the rights of abstract "Nature."

1468   Whorton, James [C.]. BEFORE SILENT SPRING: PESTICIDES AND PUBLIC HEALTH IN PRE-DDT AMERICA. Princeton, N.J.: Princeton University Press, 1974. xv, 288 p.

Careless applications of pesticides prior to the 1962 publication of SILENT SPRING (no. 1455) are chronicled. The "self-serving" analyses of the danger of the poisons by agriculturalists and the conflicting reports of medical experts led to government policies based on political and economic considerations. Whorton attempts to provide historical understanding of the regulatory practices and the awareness to danger which existed before Carson.

Part 14

ENERGY

A. SURVEYS

1. Bibliographies

1469   Burg, Nan C. ENERGY CRISIS IN THE UNITED STATES: A SELECTED BIBLIOGRAPHY OF NON-TECHNICAL MATERIALS. Exchange Bibliography no. 500. Monticello, Ill.: Council of Planning Librarians, 1974. 67 p.

1470   _____. ENERGY FOR THE FUTURE: AN UPDATE TO EXCHANGE BIBLIOGRAPHY NO. 776. Exchange Bibliography no. 946. Monticello, Ill.: Council of Planning Librarians, 1975. 19 p.

1471   _____. ENERGY FOR THE FUTURE: A SELECTED BIBLIOGRAPHY ON CONSERVATION. Exchange Bibliography no. 776. Monticello, Ill.: Council of Planning Librarians, 1975. 39 p.

1472   Morrison, Denton E. ENERGY II: A BIBLIOGRAPHY OF 1975-76 SOCIAL SCIENCE AND RELATED LITERATURE. New York: Garland, 1977. 256 p.

   Supplement to title below.

1473   _____, et al. ENERGY: A BIBLIOGRAPHY OF SOCIAL SCIENCE AND RELATED LITERATURE. New York: Garland, 1975. 184 p.

   Several thousand items, alphabetically organized by author, encompass monographs and other professional literature on energy. There is a subject index. In 1977, a supplement appeared (no. 1472).

1474   Piasetzki, J. Peter. ENERGY AND ENVIRONMENTALLY APPROPRIATE TECHNOLOGY: A SELECTIVELY ANNOTATED BIBLIOGRAPHY. Exchange Bibliography no. 1126. Monticello, Ill.: Council of Planning Librarians, 1976. 22 p.

1475 Schnell, John F., and Krannick, Richard S. SOCIAL AND ECONOM-
IC IMPACTS OF ENERGY DEVELOPMENT PROJECTS: A WORKING
BIBLIOGRAPHY. Exchange Bibliography no. 1366. Monticello, Ill.:
Council of Planning Librarians, 1977. 21 p.

1476 Warren, Betty. THE ENERGY AND ENVIRONMENT BIBLIOGRAPHY:
ACCESS TO INFORMATION. Rev. ed. San Francisco: Friends of
the Earth Foundation, 1978. 100 p.

Covering primarily nontechnical literature, this compilation is
concerned with the social and environmental impacts of energy,
alternative energy sources, and conservation measures. Entries
are well chosen and intelligently annotated. Also includes
lists of catalogs, organizations, and agencies.

2. Books and Articles

1477 Anderson, Richard W., and Lipsey, Mark W. "Energy Conservation and
Attitudes toward Technology." PUBLIC OPINION QUARTERLY 42
(Spring 1978): 17-30.

The research reported here has a threefold purpose, the primary
one being to explore attitudes and values underlying the
acceptance of technologies. General attitudes toward technology are compared with beliefs about the energy crisis and
energy conservation behavior exhibited. Some disparities between beliefs and behaviors are noted. The attitudes of
college students are found to be surprisingly similar to those
of the public at large.

1478 Budnitz, Robert J., and Holdren, John P. "Social and Environmental
Costs of Energy Systems." ANNUAL REVIEW OF ENERGY 1 (1976):
553-80.

Available means of evaluating social impacts of energy technologies are considered. The types of impacts and social
costs to be assessed are summarized and charted: coal, for
example, presents different problems in mining (accidents)
from utilization (air pollution). Several impact analysis
methods are critically reviewed, including critical pathways,
economic methodologies, measurement criteria and indexes,
and systems analysis approaches.

1479 Caldwell, Lynton K[eith]. "Energy and the Structure of Social Institutions." HUMAN ECOLOGY 4, no. 1 (1976): 31-45.

Rationing and other short-term efforts to alleviate the energy
crisis are based on misconceptions of the true nature of the
energy problem. All sources of energy are finite or of finite
utility, and the capacity of the environment to absorb residual

effects is also limited. Since no panacea will thus be found, the management of energy problems requires a change in the structure of social institutions to ensure an environmentally appropriate, equitable use of resources. However, Caldwell concludes, no satisfactory solution can be found unless society changes its commitment to endless growth.

1480   Clark, Wilson. ENERGY FOR SURVIVAL: THE ALTERNATIVES TO EXTINCTION. New York: Doubleday, 1975. xvi, 652 p. Illus.

Following a general survey of energy's role in the American economy and home, Clark takes a look at the environmental and economic consequences of the use of various energy sources. He finds that coal and nuclear power pose serious risks and urges research and development on decentralized sources such as solar and wind energy.

1481   Commoner, Barry. THE POVERTY OF POWER: ENERGY AND THE ECONOMIC CRISIS. New York: Alfred A. Knopf, 1976. 314 p. Bibliog.

The United States, Commoner believes, is facing a crisis involving complex interactions among three basic systems: the ecosystem, the productive system, and the economic system. Because energy plays a decisive role in these interactions, it represents the true basis of the crisis. Emphasizing the genuine gravity of the oil situation, Commoner goes on to express serious reservations about coal and nuclear power. A "blind, mindless chain of events" has likewise transformed the technologies of agricultural and industrial production into voracious consumers of capital, energy, and other resources that increase output at an enormous environmental and human cost. In order to survive, there is no choice but a reduced standard of living, for "the powerful have confessed to a poverty of power."

1482   Commoner, Barry; Boksenbaum, Howard; and Corr, Michael, eds. ENERGY AND HUMAN WELFARE. Vol. 1: THE SOCIAL COSTS OF POWER PRODUCTION. Vol. 2: ALTERNATIVE TECHNOLOGIES FOR POWER PRODUCTION. Vol. 3: HUMAN WELFARE: THE END USE FOR POWER. New York: Macmillan Info., 1975. xx, 217 p.; xviii, 213 p.; xvi, 185 p. Illus., bibliog.

These three volumes are the product of the Task Force of the Independent Committee on Environmental Alternatives, which studied at length the environmental effects of power production and explored solutions. Some papers have been reprinted from the periodical ENVIRONMENT. The first volume looks principally at hazards posed by coal extraction, oil spills, and nuclear power. Volume 3 surveys forecasts for future energy consumption in transportation, building, and agriculture.

Two articles are especially concerned with values: Commoner and Corr's "Power Consumption and Human Welfare in Industry, Commerce and the Home;" and Corr's and D. McLeod's "Home Energy Consumption as a Function of Lifestyle."

1483   Connery, Robert H., and Galmour, Robert S., eds. "The National Energy Problem." PROCEEDINGS OF THE ACADEMY OF POLITICAL SCIENCE 31 (December 1973): xii, 1-194.

In discussing diverse aspects of the American energy situation, contributors are unanimous in espousing the need for a national energy policy. Papers cover topics from the energy "crisis" and immediate conservation needs to long-range prospects for nuclear power and international cooperation. Marvin J. Cetron and Vary T. Coates provide a values perspective with their article "Energy and Society."

1484   Cottrell, [William]. Fred. ENERGY AND SOCIETY. New York: McGraw-Hill, 1955. xiii, 330 p.

Cottrell's thesis is that the amounts and types of energy utilized by a society condition not only the material aspects of life, but also set limits on individual achievement and social organization. The author traces man's use of energy and its corresponding cultural implications from the primitive use of plants and animals to steam and electricity.

1485   Davis, David Howard. ENERGY POLITICS. New York: St. Martin's Press, 1974. 211 p.

Energy politics is divided into five arenas. Arranged in order of amount of government regulation, they run from coal, the least regulated to oil, natural gas, electricity and nuclear power, the most regulated. Three sets of independent variables--physical characteristics of the fuel, market forces, and general political environment--interact to form a unique political style and history within each of the five policy arenas.

1486   "Energy." SCIENCE 184 (19 April 1974): 245-389.

The introduction to this special issue poses the crucial question of whether the era of low-cost abundant energy is a "paradise lost." Kenneth Boulding, J.R. Murray, and others review the public, industrial, and government response to the energy crisis. In the second part, brief articles provide technical descriptions of present and potential energy sources. A basic bibliography on energy concludes the offerings.

1487   "Energy." SCIENCE 199 (10 February 1978): 605-64.

This issue brings together a number of brief review articles on promising developments in energy technology and policy.

Papers assess the potential of such oil alternatives as liquid fuels from coal, photovoltaic power systems, and fuel from biomass, while reminding the reader that changes in energy source and use will have a wide-ranging impact on the character of industry.

1488   "Energy and the Environment." AMERICAN BEHAVIORAL SCIENTIST 22 (November–December 1978): 173–320.

Six papers approach the energy-environment relationship from a public policy perspective. James L. Regins follows the rise of energy and the environment as public issues. Erik J. Strenehjem and Edward H. Allen study socioeconomic and institutional constraints on the development of new energy resources. Lettie and Manfred Wenner assess the roles of public participation in energy policy formulation. Helen Ingram suggests that states should be given a larger role in energy policy development.

1489   Energy Policy Project of the Ford Foundation. A TIME TO CHOOSE: AMERICA'S ENERGY FUTURE. Cambridge, Mass.: Ballinger Publishing Co., 1974. xii, 511 p. Bibliog.

The objective of the Energy Policy Project was "to explore the range of energy choices open to the U.S. and to identify policies that match the choices." Three scenarios are presented, with an analysis of policy, industrial, and household implications of each: historical growth (continuation of present trends), "technical fix" (conservation), and "ZEG" (zero energy growth). Rather than advocating rapid development of a new energy source, the authors concentrate on slowing growth and a conservative use of current resources as the most important elements in a sound energy policy.

1490   Freeman, S. David. ENERGY: THE NEW ERA. New York: Walker and Co., 1974. 386 p.

A general treatment of energy issues emphasizes policy questions of energy distribution, pricing and research sponsorship. Changes in use of materials, building efficiency, and alternative transportation are among means suggested for short-term energy conservation. Though the volume's emphasis is conservation, Freeman does review prospects for long-range sources.

1491   Garvey, Gerald. ENERGY, ECOLOGY, ECONOMY. New York: W.W. Norton and Co., 1972. 235 p. Illus.

America's frontier culture fostered patterns of unrestrained use of resources that are still haunting us. Buttressing his ideas with impressive statistics and specific schemes, Garvey suggests that we can, utilizing certain economic and technical skills, develop the nation's oil, coal, and nuclear resources without environmental harm. An optimal "pollution model" is presented.

1492   Georgescu-Roegen, Nicholas. "Energy Analysis and Economic Valuation." SOUTHERN ECONOMIC JOURNAL 45 (April 1979): 1023-58.

The "energetic" dogma which argues that energy is the "only necessary support of the economic system" is refuted in a rather technical article that is largely readable for the non-initiate in econometrics. The author explains the inconsistencies of a theory which fails to consider matter in terms other than energy, and and explains where energy analysis as the basis for economic valuation "goes wrong." He then applies his findings to an investigation of the use of solar radiation. He concludes that such technology is not viable because it is a "parasite" of current technologies that are based on other sources of energy. A thorough "reorientation of our present approach to technology assessment" is demanded.

1493   Hannon, Bruce. "An Energy Standard of Value." ANNALS OF THE AMERICAN ACADEMY OF POLITICAL AND SOCIAL SCIENCE 410 (November 1973): 139-53.

During the past decade there has been a growing disenchantment with the traditional American measure of value in monetary terms. Energy, a finite resource, has been recognized as a critical factor in the functioning of the American system. Hence, public and private development decisions must now be made not only with an eye to dollar cost, but also to energy consumption.

1494   Herber, Lewis [Bookchin, Murray]. "Energy, Ecotechnocracy and Ecology." COMMUNITIES 16 (September-October 1975): 28-33.

In some sectors the phrase "alternate energy" has come to indicate a rite of abstention made necessary by American overconsumption. In other quarters, it represents no more than a redirecting of efforts from traditional large-scale projects like dams or reactors to equally giant windmills and reflectors. Bookchin, in criticizing these views, suggests that the promise of alternate energy lies in the creation of a diversity of small-scale energy sources that can form the basis of a truly balanced ecotechnocracy and of a new aesthetic.

1495   Holdren, John [P.], and Herrera, Phillip. ENERGY. San Francisco: Sierra Club, 1973. 252 p. Illus., bibliog.

Authored by Holdren, a physicist, the first half of the book covers energy sources, supplies and environmental effects. The search for cheap fuels, he believes, should not be allowed to overshadow more important goals such as public health and environmental preservation. Journalist Herrera, in part 2, recapitulates major controversies over nuclear power plant sitings from Bodega Bay, California, to Cayuga Lake, New York.

1496   Illich, Ivan. ENERGY AND EQUITY. New York: Harper and Row, 1974. xxx, 83 p. Bibliog.

Contrary to widespread belief abundant energy is not a panacea for social ills. Beyond a certain threshold, the utilization of high technology and energy invites enslavement in two forms--to machines and to technocracies. A minimum energy economy, based on such people-powered devices as bicycles, is deemed preferable.

1497   Kristofferson, Lars. "Energy in Society." AMBIO 2, no. 6 (1973): 178-85.

The earth's potential energy resources are enormous. Current limitations in access to energy may be ascribed to the uneven distribution of resources. Large-scale political as well as technological change will be necessary to achieve egalitarian global development without environmental degradation. A review of the politics of world energy, focusing on the American import dilemma, convinces the author that a shift to continuous, evenly distributed sources like solar energy will be a necessary step toward achieving a global energy policy based on solidarity.

1498   McGinn, Robert. "Energy and Ethics." STANFORD JOURNAL OF INTERNATIONAL STUDIES 9 (Spring 1974): 246-64.

In the light of energy shortages, the United States set for itself a goal of energy independence by 1980. Little of the public discourse has treated the ethical aspect of the energy situation. The author suggests several neglected moral issues: obligations to the present and future environment, egalitarian energy distribution, and consideration of the needs of future energy users. He concludes: "The reform of the Cowboy culture in the present era of energy-rich and energy-poor is both a moral and a practical necessity."

1499   Mazur, Allan, and Rosa, Eugene. "Energy and Life Style." SCIENCE 186 (15 November 1974): 607-10.

The current American consumption of energy--highest in the world--has long been deemed vital to the maintenance of a high quality of life. In a survey of fifty-five countries relating consumption of energy to twenty-seven variables indicative of the quality of life, Mazur found that only economic indicators showed a consistently high association with energy consumption. Indicators of health, education, culture, and general satisfaction with life did not.

1500 Meador, Roy. FUTURE ENERGY ALTERNATIVES: LONG-RANGE ENERGY PROSPECTS FOR AMERICA AND THE WORLD. Ann Arbor, Mich.: Ann Arbor Science, 1978. ix, 197 p. Illus.

In a cheerful, engaging book, liberally sprinkled with literary quotes, science writer Meador surveys present and future energy sources. An ample section on solar energy features illustrated descriptions of solar heating units and all-solar buildings, concluding with a "solar vocabulary." Fusion energy is seen as the principal hope for "civilized survival."

1501 Morgan, M. Granger, ed. ENERGY AND MAN: TECHNICAL AND SOCIAL ASPECTS OF ENERGY. New York: IEEE Press, 1975. xii, 521 p. Bibliog.

Presented largely from the perspective of the technologist, this collection of papers, reprinted from more popular science journals and from government hearings, addresses various aspects of the energy problem. Opening with overviews of the current global energy-environment situation, the book then turns to the historical and projected use of energy in the United States. The present and future status of principal energy technologies is assessed, with comparative cost/benefit analyses. Bibliographic appendixes supplement.

1502 O'Toole, James. ENERGY AND SOCIAL CHANGE. Cambridge: M.I.T. Press, 1976. xxi, 185 p. Bibliog.

A major forecasting project at the University of Southern California's Center for Futures Research is summarized. With projections based heavily on a Delphi survey, energy futures are predicted--for the near term (to 1990) and long term (beyond 1990). Probable social effects of shortages and rising prices are sketched.

1503 Ross, Charles R. "Electricity as a Social Force." ANNALS OF THE AMERICAN ACADEMY OF POLITICAL AND SOCIAL SCIENCE 405 (January 1973): 47-54.

Until very recently, the level of electricity consumption was cited as an important measure of a country's economic and social prosperity. Efforts were aimed at reducing cost, not waste, a philosophy now in question. A change in values is necessary if society is to survive the restrictions on energy use which may soon be necessary.

1504 Sayre, Kenneth, ed. VALUES IN THE ELECTRIC POWER INDUSTRY.

Notre Dame, Ind.: University of Notre Dame Press, 1977. xvi, 294 p.

Beginning in 1973, a group of engineers, biologists, sociologists, lawyers, and moral philosophers met at Notre Dame to conduct an examination of the role of environmental, social, and economic factors in the decision-making process of two nearby electric power companies. Principal findings are reported here. In addition to making a general ethical analysis, the team studied values in nuclear plant licensing, adherence to the "mandate to serve," and uses of cost-benefit analysis. A list of recommendations follows the papers.

1505 Scheffer, Walter F., ed. ENERGY IMPACTS ON PUBLIC POLICY AND ADMINISTRATION. Norman: University of Oklahoma Press, 1974. xi, 238 p.

Crucial energy problems and suggested avenues for policymaking are discussed by these conference papers. Irvin L. White compares energy impacts on domestic and international policies and priorities. The role of Congress and of the State are addressed, respectively, by James W. Curlen and Robert Tally. Lynton K. Caldwell projects future policy directions.

1506 Solberg, Carl. OIL POWER. New York: Mason, Charter, 1976. xi, 308 p. Bibliog.

A survey history of the development of oil places it in its political, economic, and social contexts. Solberg's message asserts the power of oil and its domination of our lives; however, he believes that its use to excess has exacted a price and that the industry is ready for a downfall.

1507 Steinhart, Carol E., and Steinhart, John S. ENERGY: SOURCES, USE AND ROLE IN HUMAN AFFAIRS. North Scituate, Mass.: Duxbury Press, 1974. xii, 352 p. Illus., bibliog.

This simple but broad treatment of energy problems would be suitable as a text. The first part describes forms of energy and the history of its human use. The second part, concerned with energy and resources, is followed by a discussion of prospects for the future, particularly the options for a national energy policy that can reconcile conflicting public and industrial interests.

1508 _____. THE FIRES OF CULTURE: ENERGY YESTERDAY AND TOMORROW. North Scituate, Mass.: Duxbury Press, 1974. xi, 273 p. Illus.

Through this clearly written overview, broad, nontechnical coverage of the energy problem is provided. The role of energy in human history is traced. In considering energy aspects of food production, the authors stress the finite nature of sources relied heavily upon for this critical activity. Alternative sources are surveyed, and the adoption of a wide variety of such alternatives, with an emphasis on regional, rather than national, planning is advocated.

1509   Thirring, Hans. ENERGY FOR MAN: WINDMILLS TO NUCLEAR POWER. Bloomington: Indiana University Press, 1958. 409 p.

A physicist provides a comprehensive, still valuable survey of possible means of present and future power production. For each source discussed, relevant numerical data and a weighing of merits and drawbacks are furnished. The catalogue of sources encompasses fossil fuels, with a warning about impending shortages, fuels from vegetation, water, solar energy, and tidal power. Atomic research, he notes, has had a paralyzing effect on attempts to use inexhaustible resources. Though Thirring believes that nuclear power will assume increasing importance, he expresses concern about its unknown dangers.

1510   Udall, Stewart L. THE ENERGY BALLOON. New York: McGraw-Hill, 1974. 288 p.

Inspired by the energy crisis of the early seventies, the book traces the history of energy use, and the American tradition of wastefulness from the air conditioner to the suburban auto. Energy alternatives and "leaner lifestyles" are described and encouraged.

1511   Warne, William E., ed. "Symposium: The Energy Crunch of the Late Twentieth Century." PUBLIC ADMINISTRATION REVIEW 35 (July-August 1975): 315-54.

Seven papers focus on the energy problem from the angle of the public administrator organizing to meet energy needs at the national, state, and local levels. The impact of energy needs on environmental goals is discussed by Gerald Garvey, while Glenn T. Seaborg predicts changes in life-styles signaled by the energy crunch. Francis Anderson Gulick critiques energy-related legislation of the Ninety-third Congress, and forthcoming energy proposals.

B. NUCLEAR POWER

1512   American Assembly, Columbia University. THE NUCLEAR POWER CONTROVERSY. Edited by Arthur W. Murphy. Englewood Cliffs, N.J.: Prentice-Hall, 1976. iv, 184 p.

Background papers on the nuclear controversy are presented,

with viewpoints based on three underlying assumptions: that high energy demands must be satisfied, that there can be no easy "technological fix," and that coal is a uniquely attractive American resource. Focus is on the next twenty-five years. Five experts who are pronuclear power, discuss the economics, safety aspects, and regulatory process for that energy source. A concluding paper by George Kistiakowsky, included for balance, provides an essentially antinuclear viewpoint.

1513 Cohen, Bernard L. NUCLEAR SCIENCE AND SOCIETY. Garden City, N.Y.: Anchor, Doubleday, 1974. xii, 268 p. Bibliog.

Intended for students enrolled in a nontechnical course on nuclear power, this volume covers the basics of nuclear energy, nature and effects of radiation, and the generation of nuclear power. Nuclear power is cited as the only practical future source of energy. Cohen rebuts arguments against the source based on predictions of high numbers of accidents or other health hazards. He is optimistic as well about prospects for nuclear weapons control.

1514 Dahl, Robert A., ed. "The Impact of Atomic Energy." ANNALS OF THE AMERICAN ACADEMY OF POLITICAL AND SOCIAL SCIENCE 290 (November 1953): 1-133.

The impact of atomic energy on three areas--weapons, politics, and the individual in society--is discussed. Dahl opens the volume with a consideration of atomic energy's meaning for the democratic process. Among the papers in the second part is Vincent Heath Whitney's analysis of sociological consequences of atomic power. In the final section, Elizabeth Douvan and Stephen B. Whitney study attitudinal consequences of atomic energy, while Wayne A.R. Leys surveys the broader theme of human values in the atomic age.

1515 Duncan, Otis Dudley. "Sociologists Should Reconsider Nuclear Energy." SOCIAL FORCES 57 (September 1978): 1-22.

During the late forties and early fifties, sociologists who considered such matters forecasted, with little dissent, an age of atomic abundance, in which electricity would be as free-flowing as water. Their vision passively mirrored that of contemporary physical scientists. For two decades interest in the energy field was dormant, only to be awakened by the almost unforeseen growth of a public antinuclear movement. It is time, Duncan urges, for sociologists to recapture their research corner from technical experts. The nuclear controversy has demonstrated that many problems initially defined as technical and scientific are eventually recognized to be social and political.

1516   Ebbin, Steven, and Kasper, Raphael [G.]. CITIZEN GROUPS AND
THE NUCLEAR POWER CONTROVERSY: USES OF SCIENTIFIC AND
TECHNOLOGICAL INFORMATION. Cambridge: M.I.T. Press, 1974.
307 p.

Through a long look at the public hearing process, the contribution of current citizen input into the siting of nuclear
power plants is analyzed. The authors find that information
exchanged in such hearings is generally not technically accurate nor sufficiently cognizant of local opinion. To improve the process, they suggest the formation of independent
assessment centers, early announcements of siting plans, and
more frequent, open public hearings.

1517   Garvey, Gerald. NUCLEAR POWER AND SOCIAL PLANNING. Lexington, Mass.: Lexington Books, 1977. xv, 159 p. Bibliog.

Convinced that America's commitment to nuclear power is
irreversible, Garvey questions how best to control nuclear
development. An overview of recent history suggests a
"Promethean progression" toward attainment of ever larger
energy supplies. The task, as Garvey sees it, is to further
this progression while minimizing safety hazards during the
transition from fission to safer fusion power. Power parks,
established within a larger framework of urban development,
are seen as a solution.

1518   Gross, Feliks. "Some Social Consequences of Atomic Discovery."
AMERICAN SOCIOLOGICAL REVIEW 15 (February 1950): 43-50.

In considering these consequences, the author anticipates that
the use of atomic energy will require institutional changes in
the direction of energy ownership and greater interorganiza-
tional cooperation. For society at large, he predicts the
growth of a powerful intelligentsia and the concurrent elimination of manual labor, with a resultant growth in leisure
time.

1519   Hardin, Garrett. "Living with the Faustian Bargain." BULLETIN OF
THE ATOMIC SCIENTISTS 32 (November 1976): 25-29.

The "Faustian bargain" is the utilization of atomic energy,
the risks of which are outlined in this article. Instrumental
risks will remain despite any safeguards, Hardin argues, and
personal risks likewise can never be wholly eliminated. He
worries also about "tribal risks," intergroup rivalries between
"haves" and "have-nots." Atomic addiction, concludes
Hardin, can lead only to totalitarianism.

1520   Hohenemser, Christoph; Kasperson, Roger; and Kates, Robert. "The

Distrust of Nuclear Power." SCIENCE 196 (1 April 1977): 25-34.

At a time when many factors would favor its adoption, there is a growing opposition to nuclear energy. The authors believe fear of atomic power is rooted in the social history of nuclear energy and its association with military high technology. A review of principal safety problems convinces the authors that time is needed to resolve the issues of transport, disposal, and potential sabotage. Meanwhile, a search for alternative energy sources is advised.

1521 LaPorte, Todd R. "Nuclear Waste: Increasing Scale and Sociopolitical Impact." SCIENCE 201 (7 July 1978): 22-28.

Current planning for radioactive waste management is criticized as insufficiently attentive to the environment and ignorant of sociopolitical impact. Public misgivings about waste management systems and community problems have increased as such systems grow in scale.

1522 Lovins, Amory B., and Price, John H. NON-NUCLEAR FUTURES: THE CASE FOR AN ETHICAL ENERGY STRATEGY. Cambridge, Mass.: Ballinger Publishing Co., 1975. xxxii, 223 p. Graphs.

Lovins identifies the technical, social, economic, and political issues surrounding the adoption of nuclear power. The first part of the book looks at the technical basis for concern: risk factors of accident and sabotage. The second part, by Price, presents nuclear power in an economically unfavorable light. Heavily laden with tables and technical appendixes.

1523 Nelkin, Dorothy. NUCLEAR POWER AND ITS CRITICS: THE CAYUGA LAKE CONTROVERSY. Ithaca, N.Y.: Cornell University Press, 1971. x, 128 p. Illus., maps.

In June of 1967, the New York State Electric and Gas Company announced its intention to build a nuclear-fueled generating plan on Cayuga Lake. The ensuing controversy among scientists, public and government agencies, and citizen groups focused on power needs versus environmental and health concerns. This case study carefully documents the development and functioning of opposing groups.

1524 Ogburn, William F[ielding]. "Sociology and the Atom." AMERICAN JOURNAL OF SOCIOLOGY 51 (January 1946): 267-75.

In an article written shortly after World War II, Ogburn is understandably preoccupied with possibilities for social changes that would contribute to a defense against nuclear attack. Among such adaptive changes are deurbanization and international cooperation. But he does note that "the social changes

due to the peacetime uses of atomic energy might become
vastly greater than the social changes that may follow the
bomb alone."

1525   Patterson, Walter. NUCLEAR POWER. Baltimore: Penguin Books,
        1976. 304 p. Illus., bibliog.

        Opening with a lengthy nontechnical description of how nu-
        clear reactors work, the author distinguishes major reactor
        types, citing appropriate British and Canadian examples. Fo-
        cusing on problems of nuclear power, especially health effects,
        the second part documents in detail tragic accidents of the
        early years of nuclear weapons development, and more recent
        near-catastrophes in nuclear power plants. Eying the rapidly
        expanding list of nuclear facilities and their capabilities, the
        author notes the corresponding growth of public questioning of
        the viability of the nuclear option. Appendixes supplement
        the technical material and supply a list of nuclear organiza-
        tions "pro and con." There is a bibliography, "A Nuclear
        Bookshelf."

1526   Weinberg, Alvin M. "Reflections on the Energy Wars." AMERICAN
        SCIENTIST 66 (March–April 1978): 153–58.

        On the subject of man's future energy sources, there is grow-
        ing polarization. Two distinctly opposing groups have
        coalesced: energy "radicals," notably Commoner and Lovins,
        for whom a small, decentralized, solar-based system is essen-
        tial, and energy "conservatives," who favor a course dependent
        on nuclear energy and other "hard" technologies. Weinberg
        analyzes some of the philosophies and scientific issues underly-
        ing the controversy, suggesting a moderate position. The solar
        group's advantage is a safe, clean power source; the nuclear
        option is more in keeping with present settlement patterns.
        Weinberg hopes for the best of both worlds.

1527   _____. "Social Institutions and Nuclear Energy." SCIENCE 177
        (7 July 1972): 27–34.

        Following a brief review of reactor types, hazards and safety
        measures, and transport and waste disposal, Weinberg concludes:
        "We nuclear people have made a Faustian bargain with
        society," offering an inexhaustible source of energy, but re-
        quiring for this gift, eternal vigilance and longevity in social
        institutions.

C. ALTERNATIVE SOURCES

1528   Eccli, Sandy, ed. ALTERNATIVE SOURCES OF ENERGY: PRACTICAL

TECHNOLOGY AND PHILOSOPHY FOR A DECENTRALIZED SOCIETY.
New York: Seabury Press, 1975. 278 p. Illus., bibliog.

This large, heavily illustrated volume offers materials for the
most part extracted from the first two years of ALTERNATIVE
SOURCES OF ENERGY MAGAZINE. Offerings range from
how-to's to quotes, editorials, and documentation of current
educational facilities and projects.

1529   Hayes, Denis. RAYS OF HOPE: THE TRANSITION TO A POST-
PETROLEUM WORLD. New York: W.W. Norton and Co., 1977.
240 p. Bibliog.

From an outline of the petroleum crisis stressing the immanence
of the end of a petroleum-based society, Hayes turns to the
clouded history of the "peaceful" atom. He suggests that the
atom can never offer peace, but will instead heighten man's
vulnerability to terrorism, encourage weapons proliferation, and
foster the appearance of technocratic and authoritarian governments. Reviewing current patterns of consumption and future
needs for energy for homes, transport, industry, and food production, Hayes concludes that such soft technologies as wind,
solar, and biomass are not only attractively flexible and
ecologically sound but practical.

1530   Lovins, Amory. "Energy Strategy: The Road Not Taken?" FOREIGN
AFFAIRS 55 (October 1976): 65-96.

Two energy paths that the United States may follow over the
next fifty years are outlined and contrasted. The first, which
essentially continues the past, features a rapid expansion of
the high technology of nuclear power. The second, favored
by Lovins, poses a commitment to conservation in the short
term, with development of and eventual conversion to renew-
able energy sources. Advantages of the "soft" path, particularly its flexibility, diversity, and inexhaustible supply are
weighed against the dangers to personal freedom and global
survival which Lovins feels are inherent in the "hard" nuclear
path.

1531   _____. SOFT ENERGY PATHS: TOWARD A DURABLE PEACE. Cambridge, Mass.: Ballinger Publishing Co., 1977. xx, 231 p.

Two energy paths "distinguished ultimately by their antithetical
social implications" are compared. Hard energy paths, i.e.,
reliance on nuclear power, are criticized as unnecessarily large-
scale, oligopolistic, inefficient, costly, and risky. Evidence
is presented that soft energy paths, based on solar and wind
energy, can supply sufficient power while encouraging cultural
pluralism and political participation. Foremost in Lovins' concerns, however, is the conviction that nuclear power developed

for any purpose encourages nuclear weapons proliferation and nullifies the hope for enduring world peace. A concise version of Lovins' principal arguments can be found in an article published in FOREIGN AFFAIRS (no. 1530).

1532   Lyons, Stephen, ed. SUN: A HANDBOOK FOR THE SOLAR DECADE. San Francisco: Friends of the Earth, 1978. xiii, 364 p.

A handy compendium of articles and excerpts from books provides an introduction to social, philosophical, political, and economic implications of the use of solar energy. Among the well-known authors represented are Amory Lovins, Murray Bookchin, Ivan Illich, Denis Hayes, and Howard Odum. Authors are united, the editor states, by two beliefs: "that a sustainable future for mankind must be based on technologies that use the regular flow of energy from the sun; that the energy crisis is also an opportunity."

1533   Wallace, Daniel, ed. ENERGY WE CAN LIVE WITH. Emmaus, Pa.: Rodale Press, 1976. xiv, 150 p.

A collection of articles from the Rodale Press publications ORGANIC GARDENING AND FARMING, COMPOST SCIENCE, and ENVIRONMENT ACTION BULLETIN surveys alternative energy sources. The first part features brief articles on sources including the sun, wind, methane, waste, and cellulose. Oriented to homesteaders, the rest offers how-to advice on fireplaces, low-energy agriculture, animal power, and various recycling projects.

1534   Weingart, Jerome Martin. "The 'Helios Strategy': An Heretical View of the Potential Role of Solar Energy in the Future of a Small Planet." TECHNOLOGICAL FORECASTING AND SOCIAL CHANGE 12 (December 1978): 273-315.

Over the next century it will be necessary to make a transition from reliance on fossil fuels to the use of long-term and primary energy forms. Of possible options, Weingart concludes, only the fast breeder reactor and the sun are capable of supplying even the lowest of projected needs. The paper presents an outline of a global solar-energy system that the author believes could support ten billion people enjoying modest energy consumption. This figure is well beyond that typically projected by both opponents and proponents of solar energy.

Part 15

APPROPRIATE TECHNOLOGY

A. BIBLIOGRAPHIES

1535 Carr, Marilyn. ECONOMICALLY APPROPRIATE TECHNOLOGIES FOR
DEVELOPING COUNTRIES: AN ANNOTATED BIBLIOGRAPHY. London: Intermediate Technology Development Group, 1976. 101 p.

Although most of the 291 titles included are of a how-to
nature and directed toward developing nations, American
readers should find some valuable material. Topical divisions
include food production, processing, and nutrition; housing
and building materials; manufacturing; and infrastructure--
power sources, water supply, health, and transport. Includes
a list of twenty-three additional AT (appropriate technology)
bibliographies.

1536 DeMoll, Lane. COMING AROUND: AN INTRODUCTORY SOURCE-
LIST ON APPROPRIATE TECHNOLOGY. Portland, Oreg.: RAIN Magazine, 1976. 12 p.

A good annotated bibliography of books and articles on AT
theory and values also includes guides to more technical
material.

B. BOOKS AND ARTICLES

1537 "Appropriate Technology." IMPACT OF SCIENCE ON SOCIETY 23
(October-December 1973): 251-352.

The theme issue consists of several theoretical articles by
Robin Clarke, Mansur Hoda, and Peter Harper; an interview
with Philippe Arreteau, head of an AT research center in
southern France; and examinations of AT applications for
China and a model Chilean urban community. Useful references for further reading are provided.

1538   Baldwin, J., and Brand, Stewart. SOFT-TECH. New York: Penguin, 1978. 176 p. Illus., bibliog.

The creators of THE WHOLE EARTH CATALOG (no. 1560) and COEVOLUTION QUARTERLY have compiled a useful collection of articles (many from COEVOLUTION QUARTERLY, no. 2311), resources, bibliography, and illustrations. Arranged thematically, the book covers tools, invention, solar, wind, transport, steam, biofuels, building, and integrated systems.

1539   Bender, Tom. SHARING SMALLER PIES. Portland, Oreg.: RAIN Magazine, 1975. 38 p. Illus., bibliog.

Bender provides an excellent primer on the philosophy and economics of appropriate technology, including suggestions for action.

1540   Boyle, Godfrey, and Harper, Peter, eds. RADICAL TECHNOLOGY. New York: Pantheon Books, 1976. 304 p. Illus., bibliog.

A broad-ranging collection of pieces on appropriate technology, some theoretical, some practical, some technical, by the editors of UNDERCURRENTS, also includes an extensive annotated directory-bibliography of organizations, periodicals, and books.

1541   Brace Research Institute and Canadian Hunger Foundation. A HANDBOOK ON APPROPRIATE TECHNOLOGY. Ottawa: Canadian Hunger Foundation, 1976, 1977. 240 p. Illus., bibliog.

A valuable compendium on AT includes essays on general theory, case studies of AT at work in specific developing countries, and an extensive information exchange on tools and equipment, bibliographical material, and interested groups and individuals.

1542   Congdon, R.J., ed. INTRODUCTION TO APPROPRIATE TECHNOLOGY: TOWARD A SIMPLER LIFE-STYLE. Emmaus, Pa.: Rodale Press, 1977. xviii, 205 p. Illus., bibliog.

Previously published by the TOOL Foundation as LECTURES ON SOCIALLY APPROPRIATE TECHNOLOGY (1975), this collection of twelve essays provides an excellent introduction to the field. In addition to several general topics, some of the specifics covered include water technologies, agriculture, building, energy, pedal power, chemical technology, education, and industrial liaison. Valuable for both developed and developing countries.

1543   Darrow, Ken, and Pam, Rick, eds. APPROPRIATE TECHNOLOGY

SOURCEBOOK. Stanford, Calif.: Volunteers in Asia, 1976. 304 p. Illus., bibliog.

> While much of the material contained in this "guide to practical books and plans for village and small community technology" is technical, the introduction and extensive annotations of titles on the philosophy of AT are worthwhile. Specific topics include tools, agriculture, food and crop preservation and storage, energy, water supply, housing, health care, and village industries.

1544 DeMoll, Lane, and Coe, Gigi, eds. STEPPING STONES: APPROPRI-ATE TECHNOLOGY AND BEYOND. New York: Schocken, 1978. 204 p. Illus., bibliog.

> Designed as a philosophical companion piece to the following title (no. 1545) most of the articles in this compendium have appeared elsewhere, but in widely scattered journals. Some of the better-known contributors include Tom Bender, Stewart Brand, E.F. Schumacher, Ivan Illich, Wendell Berry, John Todd, Amory Lovins, and Margaret Mead.

1545 DeMoll, Lane, et al., eds. RAINBOOK: RESOURCES FOR APPROPRI-ATE TECHNOLOGY. New York: Schocken Books, 1977. 251 p. Illus., bibliog.

> An excellent collection of books, films, organizations, and other resources on AT compiled by the editors of RAIN Magazine. General topics include economics, community building, communications, transportation, shelter, agriculture, health, recycling, and energy. Interspersed throughout are short, pithy essays.

1546 Dickson, David. THE POLITICS OF ALTERNATIVE TECHNOLOGY. New York: Universe Books, 1975. 224 p. Bibliog.

> The problems created by technology, Dickson believes, are as much a function of social and political factors as technical ones. An alternative society might be developed to obviate these problems; Dickson indicates the political obstacles to be overcome in realizing such far-reaching change. A number of alternative technologies are theoretically and practically described.

1547 Dorf, Richard C., and Hunter, Yvonne L., eds. APPROPRIATE VI-SIONS: TECHNOLOGY, THE ENVIRONMENT, AND THE INDIVIDUAL. San Francisco: Boyd and Fraser, 1978. xv, 351 p. Illus.

> Most of the appropriate technology-oriented essays in this volume were presented at the "Small Is Beautiful" conference held in February 1977 at the end of E.F. Schumacher's U.S.

tour just prior to his death. Besides Schumacher, who was a
major force at the conference, other contributors include
Richard C. Dorf, Yvonne Hunter, Garrett Hardin, Tom Bender,
Sim Van der Ryn, and Herman Koenig. In addition, there is
a lengthy article by Barry Commoner entitled, "Freedom and
the Ecological Imperative: Beyond the Poverty of Power."

1548   Florman, Samuel C. "Small Is Dubious." HARPER'S MAGAZINE 255
August 1977, pp. 10-12.

In this brief critique of E.F. Schumacher and his followers,
Florman argues for an eclectic, rather than "alternative"
approach to technological problem-solving and planning. He
argues that windmills and solar collectors might better augment
than supplant larger and more reliable extant means of generating power. The choice of technology should be based on
efficiency, not on elegance, aesthetic appeal, or the moral
predilections of a few scholars.

1549   Horvitz, Cathy, and Kahn, Robert, eds. TOOLS FOR A CHANGE:
PROCEEDINGS OF THE NORTHEAST REGIONAL APPROPRIATE TECH-
NOLOGY FORUM. Amherst: School of Business Administration,
University of Massachusetts, 1979. 226 p. Illus.

The PROCEEDINGS are a complete record of a regional AT
forum hosted by the School of Business Administration of the
University of Massachusetts in October 1978 under an NSF
grant. It includes a report of the actual events of the day-
long forum as well as background papers defining AT; its relationship to business, low-income applications, and ownership;
and student attitudes toward AT. A film survey is appended.

1550   Illich, Ivan. TOOLS FOR CONVIVIALITY. World Perspectives,
vol. 47. New York: Harper and Row, 1973. xxv, 110 p.

Illich calls for a society based on appropriate techniques
freely accessible to all. In such a "convivial" society,
technologies would be "responsibly limited," serving individuals
rather than managers, in contrast to mass production, which
fails to fulfill individual freedom.

1551   Jéquier, Nicolas. APPROPRIATE TECHNOLOGY: PROMISES AND
PROBLEMS. Paris: Development Centre of the Organisation for
Economic Co-Operation and Development, 1976. 344 p.

Jequier provides an excellent overview of AT policy issues
followed by nineteen state-of-the-art essays on specific
experiences in developing countries. The author believes "the
appropriate technology movement can probably be viewed as
a cultural revolution." Ken Darrow and Rick Pam in APPRO-

PRIATE TECHNOLOGY SOURCEBOOK, (no. 1543) call this
study "the most significant publication on the subject of
appropriate technology since Schumacher's SMALL IS BEAUTI-
FUL" (no. 1556).

1552   Love, Sam, ed. "Intermediate Technology: An Answer to Many World
Problems?" FUTURIST 8 (December 1974): 264-98.

This special theme issue contains articles on two British
experimental communities and on the Third World's need for
labor-intensive technology, one by E.F. Schumacher entitled,
"Economics Should Begin with People, Not Goods," as well
as a review of his seminal work, SMALL IS BEAUTIFUL,
(no. 1556) and an interview with him. Concludes with a
short piece by guest-editor Love on the interconnectedness of
today's society.

1553   North, Michael, ed. TIME RUNNING OUT? BEST OF RESURGENCE.
Dorset, Engl.: Prism Press, 1976; New York: Universe Books, 1977.
125 p. Illus.

Brief articles from the first decade of the British magazine
RESURGENCE, which is devoted to decentralization and
cooperative self-sufficiency, are herein compiled. Many of
the articles are authored by E.F. Schumacher.

1554   Rivers, Patrick. THE SURVIVALISTS. New York: Universe Books,
1976. 224 p. Bibliog.

Rivers' "survivalists" are the practitioners of appropriate technology, people he met and interviewed on cross-country jour-
neys in Great Britain, Canada, and the United States. In
addition to describing their activities and the opportunities
available for an alternative society, the author includes a
useful bibliography and source list of organizations.

1555   Schumacher, E.F. "A Saner Technology." LIBERATION 12 (August
1967): 15-19.

In developing countries, Schumacher asserts, big technology
creates problems of mass unemployment and mass migration to
ill-prepared cities. In contrast, intermediate technologists
propose to avoid these evils, yet encourage modernization
through introducing indigenous work places, utilizing simple
production methods, and using local materials to make products
for local use.

1556   _____. SMALL IS BEAUTIFUL: ECONOMICS AS IF PEOPLE MAT-
TERED. New York: Harper and Row, 1973. 290 p.

In this now classic study by the "father" of appropriate technology, Schumacher defines AT, or in his words, "intermediate technology," as follows: it makes "use of the best of modern knowledge and experience, is conducive to decentralization, compatible with the laws of ecology, gentle in its use of scarce resources, and designed to serve the human person instead of making him the servant of machines." In the chapter "Buddhist Economics," the author sees work not as an "inhuman chore" to be abolished by automation, but rather something that is needed for the good of man's body and soul. Without it, there is no self-reliance or self-esteem.

1557 "Special Focus: Appropriate Technology." FUTURIST 11 (April 1977): 72-105.

The theme issue devoted primarily to AT includes an article by E.F. Schumacher and a mini-directory of groups and books.

1558 Todd, Nancy, and Todd, Jack, eds. THE BOOK OF THE NEW ALCHEMISTS. New York: E.P. Dutton, 1977. xviii, 174 p. Illus.

Drawing upon the metaphor of metallurgic transformation, the New Alchemy Institute, an experiment in appropriate living located on Cape Cod, seeks "To Restore the Lands, Protect the Seas, and Inform the Earth's Stewards." This is their story--philosophy and practice. Solid material.

1559 Turner, John F.C., and Fichter, Robert, eds. FREEDOM TO BUILD: DWELLER CONTROL OF THE HOUSING PROCESS. New York: Macmillan, 1972. xvi, 301 p. Illus.

The authors examine the level of participation of dwellers in their housing. They conclude that genuine housing values are directly related to the ability of residents to create environments tailored to their personal needs through the "sweat-equity" of dweller autonomy. In addition to the editors, contributors include William C. Grindley, Richard B. Spohn, Rolf Goetze, Hans H. Harms, Peter Grenell, and Ian B. Terner.

1560 Whole Earth Catalog. THE UPDATED LAST WHOLE EARTH CATALOG AND WHOLE EARTH EPILOG. Bladensburg, Md.: Craftsman Press, 1974. 768 p. Illus., bibliog.

From A to Z, if it is worth knowing about, it is somewhere in this compendium of ideas, books, tools, etc. General categories of "Whole Systems," "Shelter," "Industry," "Craft," "Community," "Nomadics," "Communications," and "Learning" and an index will help in locating information, but the serious reader will want to investigate every page of these gems.

1561   Winner, Langdon. "The Political Philosophy of Alternative Technology: Historical Roots and Present Prospects." In ESSAYS IN HUMANITY AND TECHNOLOGY, edited by David Lovekin and Donald Verene, pp. 114-37. Dixon, Ill.: Sauk Valley College, 1978. Reprinted in TECHNOLOGY IN SOCIETY 1 (Spring 1979): 75-86.

> Within the broader context of an emerging philosophy of technology, Winner finds appropriate technology to be in essence a political movement with roots in nineteenth-century utopianism. Despite an ambiguity of meaning and "an annoying tendency toward hardware fetishism," he finds in AT an opportunity for a humane restructuring of society.

1562   Yudelson, John, and Nelson, Lynn. RIGHT LIVELIHOOD, WORK AND APPROPRIATE TECHNOLOGY: A REPORT ON SOCIAL AND ECOLOGICAL PRIORITIES FOR CALIFORNIA. Berkeley, Calif.: Habitat Center, 1976. 128 p. Bibliog.

> In their photo-duplicated report to the California Office of Appropriate Technology on the relationship of employment and economic development to appropriate technology, the editors conclude that jobs should be socially useful and provide "right livelihood." The bibliography contains many otherwise hard-to-find items.

Part 16

PHILOSOPHY AND ETHICS

A. PHILOSOPHY OF TECHNOLOGY

1. Bibliography

1563   Mitcham, Carl, and Mackey, Robert, eds. "Bibliography of the Philosophy of Technology." TECHNOLOGY AND CULTURE 14, no. 2, part 2 (April 1973): xv, S1-S205. Reprint. Chicago: University of Chicago Press, 1973. xvii, 205 p.

In a scholarly volume which effectively posits boundaries for a discipline of the philosophy of technology, the editors present a review of previous bibliographic efforts, followed by a bibliography divided into five major categories: "Comprehensive Philosophical Works," "Ethical and Political Critiques," "Religious Critiques," "Metaphysical and Epistemological Studies," and an appendix of classical documents and background materials. Works by historians, social scientists, scientists, and technologists, as well as philosophers are included. Materials range from highly scholarly to quite popular in content and style. Despite the lack of an author index, the bibliography is an essential resource for those new to or familiar with the field.

2. Books and Articles

1564   Albert, Ethel M. "Conflict and Change in American Values: A Cultural-Historical Approach." ETHICS 74 (October 1963): 19-33.

Drawing on a historical model of cultural diversity, the author suggests that much of America's contemporary value uncertainty is due to significant historical changes occurring at mid-century. The multicultural make-up of America indicates that competing value systems will be in conflict with an earlier assumption of homogeneity. "A generalized theory of values can better follow from than precede an examination of specific problems and solutions."

1565   Anderson, Alan Ross, ed. MINDS AND MACHINES. Englewood Cliffs, N.J.: Prentice-Hall, 1964. viii, 114 p. Bibliog.

A small anthology offers classic and other significant papers on robots and artificial intelligence. Contents include: A.M. Turing's "Computing Machinery and Intelligence," in which he poses his famous "imitation game" as a means for considering the question "can machines think?"; Michael Scriven's "The Mechanical Concept of Mind"; J.R. Lucas's "Mind Machines and Godel"; Paul Ziff's "The Feelings of Robots"; and others. Selected bibliography.

1566   Arbib, Michael A. "Man-Machine Symbiosis and the Evolution of Human Freedom." AMERICAN SCHOLAR 43 (Winter 1973-74): 38-54.

Man has now joined his artifacts in a close symbiotic relationship. He is dependent on them both physiologically and, to some extent, for structuring of social relations. Citing several examples, the author concludes that social problems are now so complex that they cannot be solved without cybernetic aid. But safeguards must be established to ensure that such man-machine networks operate "according to principles embodying a highly refined sense of justice."

1567   Arendt, Hannah. "The Conquest of Space and the Stature of Man." In BETWEEN PAST AND FUTURE, pp. 265-80. New York: Viking Press, 1971.

At one time, the findings of science served to augment and order human sense experience. Now the role of enlarging our world view has been assumed by the space scientist. Even as we reach into space, however, we realize that the potential for exploration is finite, if the universe is not. That realization may bring us an invigorated, prudent "geocentrism," or eventual global despair.

1568   _____. THE HUMAN CONDITION. 1958. Reprint. Chicago: University of Chicago Press, 1969. 332 p.

The "vita activa," according to Arendt, consists of three fundamental human activities: labor, work, and action. Labor is the vital functioning of the body, in contrast to work, which provides an "artificial world of things." Work imposes a rhythm on the laborer; with mechanization, that rhythm also becomes mechanical. Man, ultimately adaptable, has adjusted himself to an environment of machines. But the machine is powerless to effect "the most important task of artifice--offering mortals a more permanent and stable dwelling place than themselves."

1569   Baier, Kurt, and Rescher, Nicholas, eds. VALUES AND THE FUTURE: THE IMPACT OF TECHNOLOGICAL CHANGE ON AMERICAN VALUES. New York: Free Press, 1969. xvi, 527 p. Illus., bibliog.

The unique contribution of this lengthy volume is its combina-tion of philosophical considerations of changes in values with discussions of those operational values used by forecasters, technologists, and planners. Alvin Toffler opens the volume with a description of a profession of the future, that of the "value impact forecaster." Other papers address four forecast-ing concerns: technological developments, trends in social change, economic trends, and values of important groups. Among the distinguished contributors are the editors, Olaf Helmer, Bertrand de Jouvenel, Kenneth Boulding, Bela Gold, James A. Wilson, and John Kenneth Galbraith. A "Bibliog-raphy on Technological Progress and Future Oriented Studies" and "Bibliography on the Theory of Values" close the volume.

1570   Ballard, Edward Goodwin. MAN AND TECHNOLOGY: TOWARD THE MEASUREMENT OF A CULTURE. Pittsburgh: Duquesne University Press, 1978. x, 251 p. Bibliog.

The positive and naturalistic view of science and technology held by such luminaries as Einstein and B.F. Skinner is put aside in favor of an opposing doctrine of humanism. Scientific-technological culture is deemed destructive and self-defeating because it removes men from the self to overly abstract realms. It is only through self-interpretation and contemplation and not through the mimicry of mechanism, that truth and whole-ness can be achieved.

1571   Barrett, William. THE ILLUSION OF TECHNIQUE: A SEARCH FOR MEANING IN A TECHNOLOGICAL CIVILIZATION. Garden City, N.Y.: Anchor Press, Doubleday, 1978. 252 p.

Through a somewhat popular exposition, Barrett sketches the history of twentieth-century philosophy, concentrating on the work of Ludwig Wittgenstein, Martin Heidegger, and William James. To Barrett, Wittgenstein's career demonstrates the ultimate failure of mathematical philosophy to account for the decision and creativity to maintain even the most science-based technological society. Heidegger is found to be a use-ful guide to questions concerning technology, while James's writings on the individual are studied in the concluding portion.

1572   Beck, Robert N. "Technology and Idealism." IDEALISTIC STUDIES 4 (May 1974): 181-87.

The primary problem with technology is not its social effects but the conceptual inadequacy of the values it implies. Technology is guided by causal and means-end principles; its presuppositions about human action have been internalized by advocate and critic alike. There is a need to recognize that technology is only "one of the indefinitely many possibilities of the human spirit."

1573   Brooks, Harvey. "Technology and Values: New Ethical Issues Raised by Technological Progress." ZYGON 8 (March 1973): 17-35.

A values system is an adaptive mechanism which enhances the survival potential of a society. As technology increases societal interdependence, values supporting the welfare of the group against rivals have become less important than those supporting the welfare of the larger system. The choice of technologies therefore implies a values-based decision. Values implicit in some recent decisions are discussed.

1574   Bunge, Mario. "The Five Buds of Technophilosophy." TECHNOLOGY IN SOCIETY 1 (Spring 1979): 67-74.

Technophilosophy is called an "immature and underdeveloped branch of scholarship," at the present time composed mostly of "romantic wailings." Bunge outlines what he sees as the five main research areas for technophilosophy: technoepistemology or technognosiology (the philosophical study of technology); technometaphysics (ontology of technology); technoaxiology (philosophical study of valuations performed by technologists); technoethics (study of the moral issues encountered by technologists); and technopraxiology (philosophical study of human action guided by technology).

1575   _____. "Toward a Technoethics." MONIST 60 (January 1977): 96-107. Also published in PHILOSOPHICAL EXCHANGE 2, no. 1 (1975): 69-79.

Bunge presents a defense of the thesis that technologists are fully and personally responsible for their work and its consequences. While the engineer is torn between the conflicting interests of employers and a larger society, he must be morally responsible for the resolution of that conflict, and should enjoy power commensurate with that burden. Technology, ethically practical, could serve as a model for rational action, the basis of a technoethics of right and efficient conduct.

1576   Burhoe, Ralph Wendell. "Evolving Cybernetic Machinery and Human Values." ZYGON 7 (September 1972): 188-209.

Values are described "mechanistically" as dependent on and

stimulated by the physiology and morphology of the human organism. Three mechanisms of learning are evolving together in homo sapiens: the genotype, the culturetype, and the individual brain, which processes new information. Purposes or goals, derived through this system, can thus be described in the physical language of machinery. Though the computer age poses serious threats to human values, more to be feared, Burhoe believes, is the failure of the human mechanism to envision larger purposes.

1577   Butler, Clark. "Technological Society and its Counter-culture: An Hegelian Analysis." INQUIRY 18 (Summer 1975): 195-212.

The development and collapse of the American counterculture of the sixties and early seventies is viewed as a re-enactment of Hegel's dialectic of "active reason" outlined in the PHENOMENOLOGY OF SPIRIT (1807). Butler concludes that the counterculture represented America's discovery of Hegel's idea of state, but that the discovery came too late to be realizable in an interdependent world.

1578   Caussin, Robert. "The Transfer of Functions from Man to Machine." DIOGENES 28 (Winter 1959): 107-25.

For workers displaced by automation, there are only a few alternatives: evolving along with technology, training for frequent promotion, and accepting frequent lateral moves. More general philosophical dilemmas are suggested by the continuous transferral of functions from man to machine. Caussin is particularly worried about a pervading sense of powerlessness and a society-wide loss of survival skills.

1579   Christiansen, Bente Lis, and Norgard, Jorgen Stig. SOCIAL VALUES AND THE LIMITS TO GROWTH. Hanover, N.H.: Dartmouth College, 1974. 23 p.

Assuming that arguments against continued exponential growth are sound, the authors suggest that changes in values and life-styles are a necessary step toward the attainment of equilibrium. A way must be found to effect a shift in emphasis from values clustering around competition, achievement, efficiency, and material comfort to satisfaction, cooperation, simplicity, and leisure.

1580   Cohen, J.W. "Technology and Philosophy." COLORADO QUARTERLY 3 (Spring 1955): 409-20.

Two views of technology have predominated among Western intellectuals: that technology is dehumanizing and destructive; or that technology is neutral. A third view, that "binds technology to values and which is in fact the distinctive con-

tribution of American thought to the philosophy of technology"
is found in the work of Thorstein Veblen, John Dewey, and
the economist C.E. Ayers.

1581   Cote, Alfred J. THE SEARCH FOR THE ROBOTS. New York: Basic
Books, 1967. viii, 243 p. Illus., bibliog.

Having surveyed developments that might lead to truly lifelike
intelligent automata, Cote concludes that automata may indeed
someday surpass man in abilities. Society will continue to
advance only by competing with the machine, encouraging its
use when beneficial, but restraining it when it threatens.

1582   Cotgrove, Stephen. "Technology, Rationality and Domination." SOCIAL
STUDIES OF SCIENCE 5 (February 1975): 55–78.

Through analyzing the work of a number of scholarly critics of
technology, the author identifies the major issues raised and
constructs an "ideal-type model" of the technological society
debate. Authors considered are of the determinist bent;
Jacques Ellul, Herbert Marcuse, and Theodore Roszak are
typical. Cotgrove becomes particularly involved with the
idea that the nature of the technological threat lies in its
pervasive, subtle, rational dominance.

1583   Delgado, Jose M.R. "Science and Human Values." ZYGON 5
(June 1970): 148–58.

Delgado is concerned with human values and the quality of
life, and he recognizes that not all is well in today's technological society. He believes that biological and ideological
sources of such conflict lie in "the imbalance between the
material and the mental evolution of man." An understanding
of cerebral activity and appropriate education will be vital
in closing the gap.

1584   Dewey, John. INDIVIDUALISM OLD AND NEW. New York: Minton,
Balch and Co., 1930. 171 p.

American idealism professes the theory that man has developed
machines for humane purposes, to further the heritage of
equality and individualism. Dewey contends that the standards of a "pecuniary culture," the insidious influence of
private profit, have perverted these ideals. Instead of encouraging individuality, the machine age has yielded insecur-
ity, conformity, and emptiness. Dewey sees in science and
technology a potentially revolutionary, transforming instrument
for forging a new, realistic individuality, if only the machine
can be seized from the profiteer.

1585   _____. "Science and Free Culture." In FREEDOM AND CULTURE, pp. 131-54. New York: G.P. Putnam's Sons, 1939.

The simple faith of the Enlightenment that the advance of science would, through dispelling ignorance, free man and his institutions is no longer tenable, Dewey suggests. Technological applications have succumbed to the control of corporate powers that have, as a result, come to determine the directions of science itself. Science has destroyed traditional values but has been incapable of generating new ones necessary for social cohesion and moral purpose.

1586   Durbin, Paul T. "Technology and Values: A Philosopher's Perspective." TECHNOLOGY AND CULTURE 13 (October 1972): 556-76.

The simple faith of the Enlightenment that the advance of Technology's role in undermining traditional values has been much debated. Durbin follows the spectrum of that debate from Herbert Marcuse, on the left, who blames all social malfunctions on technology, to Ferdinand Lundberg, on the right, with his idea of the public as self-made victim. Durbin's own view is that value changes of the past thirty years can be linked to changes in social class and structure, and to gains in education, and are only indirectly attributable to technology.

1587   _____, ed. RESEARCH IN PHILOSOPHY AND TECHNOLOGY: AN ANNUAL COMPILATION OF RESEARCH. Vol. 1, 1978. Greenwich, Conn.: JAI Press, 1978. vi, 390 p.

The first of a projected annual review series, the volume opens with an introductory historical survey of the field, with papers describing "methods, frameworks and a practical program" for the philosophy of technology. Part 2 offers papers presented at a 1975 conference at the University of Delaware. Among these, Paul Durbin presents a "social philosophy of technology," while Kai Nelson looks at political and Willis H. Truitt at ethical aspects of science and technology. Definitional papers by Stanley R. Carpenter and Carl Mitcham close the section. A selection of reviews and a lengthy bibliographical update for 1973-74 to Mitcham and Mackey's BIBLIOGRAPHY OF THE PHILOSOPHY OF TECHNOLOGY (no. 1563), compiled by Mitcham and Jim Grote, conclude this valuable volume.

1588   Edge, David [O.] "Technological Metaphor and Social Control." NEW LITERARY HISTORY 6 (Autumn 1974): 135-47.

Because technological devices are significant components of our everyday world, they provide ready-made material for metaphors which lend structure to our thoughts and meanings. Edge identifies three functional types of metaphors and provides technological examples of each. Metaphor, he feels, can be

tyrannical if it constricts our vision or liberating if it expands
it. Edge queries, "what is freedom if not the ability to
choose by which metaphors we will be seized?"

1589   Feibleman, James K. "The Philosophy of Tools." SOCIAL FORCES 45
(March 1967): 329-37.

In comparison to language, tools have been underestimated as
a foundation of culture. Tools are material objects which
alter other objects, including man. Though they tie man to
his environment, they also make it possible for him to achieve
purely human goals. It is through tools manufactured on his
own planet that man will be enabled to engineer an escape
from it.

1590   Ferkiss, Victor. "Political Philosophy and the Facts of Life." ZYGON
9 (December 1974): 272-87.

The new technological man must develop a new philosophical
outlook based on the principles of naturalism, holism, and
immanentism. Only ecological humanism as a political philosophy is appropriate as an approach to current problems.

1591   Goodman, Paul. "Can Technology Be Humane?" NEW YORK REVIEW
OF BOOKS 13 (20 November 1969): 27-34.

In the twentieth century, science and technology emerged as
a new universal system of mass faith. But as people grow
restive with the "anti-life" bent of technology, we advance
closer, Goodman believes, to a "new reformation." Technology is to be viewed as a branch of moral philosophy, lifted
from its low intellectual position as half science, half know-
how. Trained in social science and the humanities, the new
professional technologist must learn to be especially sensitive
to questions of scale in the appropriate application of technology.

1592   _____. "Morality of Scientific Technology." In LIKE A CONQUERED
PROVINCE: THE MORAL AMBIGUITY OF AMERICA, pp. 51-74. New
York: Random House, 1968.

Though critics and proponents alike have assumed that an independent technology will shape the future, Goodman disagrees,
arguing that technology has come increasingly under political,
military, and economic control. Technology must be judged
in terms of criteria appropriate to it as a branch of political
philosophy--by utility, efficiency, flex, relevance, and
modesty. Scientists and engineers must regain control over
their working environment.

1593   Gotesky, Rubin, ed. "Human Dignity." PHILOSOPHY FORUM 9
(June 1971): 165-377.

Three theses relating technology to human dignity are advanced. Ervin Laszlo, interpreting dignity in terms of human needs, calls for a new science of man to define those needs and to bend technology to them. Taking an opposing view, Richard A. Peterson finds that in causing alienation and isolation, technology injures dignity. Richard A. Watson sees technology as a means for achieving an elusive dignity that embraces both being and well-being. A discussion and a symposium of pertinent reviews close the issue.

1594   Haberer, Joseph. "Technology and the Emerging Future: A Framework for Normative Theory." HUMAN CONTEXT 7 (Spring 1975): 130-35.

The destructive potential of technology compels us to think normatively and philosophically about the kind of future we want. To date, futurist and technology assessment studies have restricted their sights to pragmatics and narrow projections. Haberer urges the establishment of a body of normative theory to serve as a guide to the utilization of technology. Such theory should be based on the maximization of individual and community potential and dignity.

1595   Habermas, Jürgen. TOWARD A RATIONAL SOCIETY: STUDENT PROTEST, SCIENCE AND POLITICS. Boston: Beacon Press, 1970. ix, 132 p.

The final three of the six essays of this collection present the central tenets of Habermas's philosophy of technology. In "Technological Progress and the Social Life-World," he suggests that the "irrationality of domination," which has become a threat to life, can be mastered only through public assertiveness. The final essay, dedicated to Marcuse, describes "rationalization" as a process in which work (purposive-rational action) comes to supplant social interaction.

1596   Heidegger, Martin. THE QUESTION CONCERNING TECHNOLOGY, AND OTHER ESSAYS. Translated by William Lovitt. New York: Harper and Row, 1977. xi, 182 p.

In the title essay, Heidegger announces, "We shall be questioning concerning technology, and in doing so we should like to prepare a free relationship to it." The relationship involves intricate and often difficult explorations of the concepts of causality, technology, freedom, and essence. The essence of technology is found to lie in "Enframing," defined in several ways by Heidegger, but perhaps most simply as an "ordaining of destining." The collection also includes the essays "The Word of Nietzsche: 'God is Dead'"; "The Age of the World Picture"; and "Science and Reflection."

1597   Henderson, Hazel. "Science and Technology: The Revolution from

Hardware to Software." TECHNOLOGICAL FORECASTING AND SOCIAL CHANGE 12 (December 1978): 317-24.

Though it will be some time before the earth's physical resources are exhausted, society has already reached its conceptual limits to growth. Industrial society has entered an entropy state in which "the technological process has generated such scale, complexity and interlinkage that it has become unmodelable and hence unmanageable." A reconceptualization of the metaphysical premises of industrialization is needed. Major belief systems based on rationalism, reductionism, and continual expansion must give way to a holistic, balanced world view.

1598   Hook, Sidney, ed. DIMENSIONS OF MIND: A SYMPOSIUM. London: Collier-Macmillan, 1960. 250 p.

Three dimensions of the mind-body relationship are considered: experience and sensation; language habits; and brain physiology, psychology, and cybernetics. The second, most relevant part, entitled "The Brain and the Machine," opens with a summary paper by Norbert Wiener. Michael Scriven debates personhood for robots, and Paul Weiss concludes that it is not cognition but "love that makes the man."

1599   Huchingson, James E. "Toward a Naturalized Technology." ZYGON 8 (September-December 1973): 185-99.

Our culture is currently undergoing an agonizing reassessment, central to which is our attitude toward technology. Huchingson discerns three levels of technology and human awareness: technique, integration of technique with science, and integration of technique with philosophical generalities. Technology must be encompassed in a new scheme comprehending the totality of life.

1600   Ihde, Don. "The Experience of Technology: Human-Machine Relations." CULTURAL HERMENEUTICS 2 (November 1974): 267-79.

A phenomenology of human-machine relations is posed as the basis for possibilities that exist within a technological culture. Ihde specifies several types of relations, with examples: Transperency (chalk), embodiment (auto), and sensory-extension-reduction (telephone). More crucial, however, is the emergence of automata, which indicates a movement from experiencing through machines to witnessing experiences of machines.

1601   _____. TECHNICS AND PRAXIS. Boston: D. Reidel Publishing Co., 1979. xxviii, 150 p.

The phenomenology of instrumentation is explored, leading to a tentative acceptance of "instrumental realism," in which "the instrumentally mediated world becomes the 'real' world." Further insights into the technological transformation of experience are achieved through studies of the impact of the computer, dentist's probe, cinema, and technologically produced music. Concluding essays examine the ideas of Martin Heidegger, Hans Jonas, Emmanuel Mounier, and Paul Ricoeur.

1602 INTERNATIONAL CONGRESS OF PHILOSOPHY, 14TH, VIENNA, AUSTRIA, 1968. AKTEN. 6 vols. Vienna: Herder, 1968.

Colloquium 6, entitled "Cybernetics and the Philosophy of Technical Science," offers several relevant papers written in English: Joseph Agassi's "The Logic of Technological Development"; Herbert L. Dreyfuss's "Cybernetics as the Last State of Metaphysics"; and Henryk Skolimowski's "On the Concept of Truth in Science and Technology."

1603 INTERNATIONAL CONGRESS OF PHILOSOPHY, 15TH, VARNA, BULGARIA, SEPTEMBER 17-22, 1973. PROCEEDINGS. Sofia, Bulgaria: Sofia Press Production Centre, 1973. 395 p.

A considerable part of this event was devoted to the topic "Science, Technology and Man." Plenary session 1 is entitled "Philosophy and Science," while plenary session 3, "Technology and Man," includes W.D. Nietmann's "Technology as a Fact of Life" and R.T. de George's "Technology and Reason in the U.S. Today." Colloquium 3 offers papers on "Knowledge and Values in the Scientific and Technical Era" and Problematika 2 focuses on "Humanism and the Technological Revolution."

1604 Johnston, Edgar G., ed. PRESERVING HUMAN VALUES IN AN AGE OF TECHNOLOGY. Detroit: Wayne State University Press, 1961. 132 p.

The realization that our technological development has outrun our ability to relate to it with traditional Judeo-Christian values is the framework for these lectures. Edward Condon, a physicist, considers the values made possible by science and technology. As a historian, Henry Steele Commager looks at America's unique ideals. The rule of a power elite and the barrenness of democratic thought concern Francis Biddle, a former attorney general. Rabbi Louis Mann explains how modern philosophies have cheapened human life, while Johnston, an educator, asserts that respect for the individual is the basic human value.

1605 Jonas, Hans. PHILOSOPHICAL ESSAYS: FROM ANCIENT CREED TO TECHNOLOGICAL MAN. Englewood Cliffs, N.J.: Prentice-Hall, 1974. xviii, 349 p.

In his later years, Jonas has turned to the philosophical questions surrounding technology. Two previously published essays which provide an overview of his thought are included: Technology and Responsibility; Reflections on the New Tasks of Ethics (no. 1606); and "Seventeenth Century and After: The Meaning of the Scientific Revolution." In "Philosophical Reflections on Experimenting with Human Subjects," he maintains that a quickened pace in the conquest of disease should not be achieved through moral debasement. In "Biological Engineering--a Preview" he deplores the notion that no one will be truly accountable for genetic misdeeds.

1606 _____. "Technology and Responsibility: Reflections on the New Tasks of Ethics." SOCIAL RESEARCH 40 (Spring 1973): 31-54.

Throughout history, ethical thought has assumed human nature as a constant. Jonas ventures that through technology the potential range of human action has been so altered that traditional ethics no longer suffice. All traditional ethics have been anthropocentric and have assumed immediacy of effects of action. The recent discoveries that the environment is fragile and genes mutable suggest that these bases for ethics are inadequate.

1607 _____. "Toward a Philosophy of Technology." HASTINGS CENTER REPORT 9 (February 1979): 34-43.

Two major areas of study in the philosophy of technology are distinguished: the formal dynamics of technology, and the substantive content, or products and objectives, of technology. A third theme is identified as the moral side, the human responsibility for the results of technological activities. Jonas finds technology to be inherently restless, driven by complementary strivings for wealth and knowledge. The transforming power of technology has grown so great that the inevitable last stage appears to be the remaking of man. The best hope for freedom, he concludes, rests in "the spontaneity of human action which confounds all prediction."

1608 Katz, Solomon H. "Dehumanization and Rehumanization of Science and Society." ZYGON 9 (June 1974): 126-38.

Due to the rapidity of technological and social change, the traditional "Purpose" of society has been undermined. Purpose, as defined by Katz, encompasses the "explanation and coherent organization of events of the human life cycle, from conception to death." Individuals bereft of a traditional purpose must devise their own value systems. Recent trends suggest that revitalization movements, similar to those experienced by North American Indians and other people in the nineteenth century, may be underway in the American mainstream.

The author calls for a responsive, humanized science and technology to create a new cultural setting and an alternative to such movements.

1609 Kohanski, Alexander S. PHILOSOPHY AND TECHNOLOGY: TOWARD A NEW ORIENTATION IN MODERN THINKING. New York: Philosophical Library, 1977. x, 203 p.

A review of man's philosophical efforts to establish his physical, intellectual, and spiritual boundaries in the wake of the proliferation of science and technology is attempted. The work of Newton, Kant, and Einstein created a new universe for man which seemed to promise boundless gifts. With some alarm, however, Kohanski views the antireligious dogma of Nietzsche and Sartre. In the past, he concludes, man has been idealized as philosopher-king, philosopher-artist, and philosopher-scientist. He must now be philosopher-technologist.

1610 Kranzberg, Melvin. "Technology and Human Values." VIRGINIA QUARTERLY REVIEW 40 (Autumn 1964): 578-92.

Just at a time when technology seems near to alleviating human needs, it is being castigated as dangerous to values and damaging to the individual. Kranzberg argues that technology has in fact widened individual choice through improvement of the material aspects of life, and through the elimination of slavery and drudgery. It has permitted as well a greater participation in the arts. In the author's opinion, the question remains whether man can master not technology, but himself.

1611 Leiss, William. "Technological Rationality: Marcuse and His Critics." PHILOSOPHY OF THE SOCIAL SCIENCES 2 (March 1972): 31-42.

Marcuse's ideas on technology and its social consequences are evaluated, as they appear in writings dating from 1941 to the present. Leiss is critical of the concept of the "one-dimensional man." He considers the valuable essence of Marcuse's work to be the attempt to explore the contradictory role of technical rationality as both precondition and obstacle to human freedom.

1612 Lenk, Hans. "Technology and Scientism: Remarks Concerning an Ideological Discussion." MAN AND WORLD 5 (August 1972): 253-71.

Lenk believes that the increasing influence of science and technology in society and government is leading to the appearance of a political system in which democracy is replaced by the rule of "experts." He proposes ways in which philosophers might clarify the problems a technocracy would pose, by reintroducing values and goals considerations into discussions of technology.

1613   Levin, Samuel M. "John Dewey's Evaluation of Technology." AMERI-
CAN JOURNAL OF ECONOMICS AND SOCIOLOGY 15 (January
1956): 123-36.

John Dewey's ideas on technology's role in social life and
culture are scattered through his writings. Dewey envisions
technology as an embodiment of man's scientific ability, a
means to utilize nature for man's betterment. His buoyant
faith in the virtue of science diminished fears that technological growth might lead to a mechanization of life, Levin believes.

1614   Lipsey, Mark [W.]. "Adaptation and the Technological Society: A
Value Context for Technology Assessment." ZYGON 13 (March 1978):
2-18.

If one accepts the optimistic view that man can still regulate
technological development, it becomes necessary to address
two tasks: the determination of the range and nature of technology's effects on life, and the elaboration of a values framework yielding standards by which technological consequences
may be evaluated. Adopting an adaptational view of human
behavior, Lipsey notes four domains of human activity vulner-
able to technological disruption: adaptation, competence,
adaptability, and impressionability.

1615   Lovekin, David, and Verene, Donald P., eds. ESSAYS IN HUMANITY
AND TECHNOLOGY. Dixon, Ill.: Sauk Valley College, 1978. xv,
192 p.

The proceedings of a conference held in the spring of 1977
provide a nontechnical, brief, and wide-ranging introduction
to the philosophical questions surrounding technology. Themes
include the experience of travel, the nature of objectivity,
appropriate technology, and the conflict between technical
rationality and other dimensions of human thought and action.
Contributors are Edward Ballard, Langdon Winner, Lionel
Rubinoff, Henry W. Johnstone, Lovekin, and Verene.

1616   Marcuse, Herbert. AN ESSAY ON LIBERATION. Boston: Beacon
Press, 1969. 91 p.

A reasonable use of the tremendous possibilities inherent in
technology could lead to a global utopia free of poverty and
scarcity. However, Marcuse counters, the consumer economy
and the politics of corporate capitalism have so modified the
nature of man that he is tied to commodities. Consumption of

material goods has become almost a biological need. To become liberating, science and technology must themselves be
freed from bondage to materialism.

1617 Mazlish, Bruce. "The Fourth Discontinuity." TECHNOLOGY AND
CULTURE 8 (January 1967): 1-15.

There have been three great shocks to man's image of his
place: the ideas of Copernicus on the universe, of Darwin
on evolution, and of Freud on the human mind. Mazlish
contends that a fourth major discontinuity now exists between
man and machines. "We are now coming to the realization
that man and the machines he creates are continuous and that
the same conceptual schemes that explain the brain also explain the workings of a 'thinking machine.'" Belief in the
sharp discontinuity between man and machine is no longer
tenable.

1618 Melsen, Andrew G. van. SCIENCE AND TECHNOLOGY. Pittsburgh:
Duquesne University Press, 1961. 373 p.

An examination of the philosophy of science and technology
leads to an exploration of its fundamental meaning for human
existence. The first part studies the nature of knowledge
yielded by scientific investigation, characterizing it as non-
reflective, abstract, and exact in comparison with human life
and spirit as a whole. The second part of the work considers
the effect of physical science and technology on culture,
focusing on changes in world view and relations with nature.

1619 Michalos, Alex C., ed. PHILOSOPHICAL PROBLEMS OF SCIENCE
AND TECHNOLOGY. Boston: Allyn and Bacon, 1974. xii, 623 p.

This introductory selection of previously published philosophical
studies of science and technology surveys both abstract philosophical and ethical aspects of the field. The collection
opens with general essays by John Ziman and Mario Bunge.
From essays on the nature of scientific discovery, explanation,
and theory-building, it advances to considerations of the role
of values in science. Joseph Haberer explores scientific leadership and social responsibility, while Michael Baram calls for
greater social control over science and technology. A closing
section considers ethical impacts from birth control to machine
prevention of death.

1620 Mitcham, Carl, and Mackey, Robert, eds. PHILOSOPHY AND TECH-
NOLOGY: READINGS IN THE PHILOSOPHICAL PROBLEMS OF TECH-
NOLOGY. New York: Free Press, 1972. ix, 399 p. Bibliog.

This collection of papers by renowned scholars opens with

"Conceptual Issues," and considers philosophy as an epistemological issue and a driving force in modern thought. Ethical and political critiques form the second part, while a section of religious critiques reveals the contradictory meanings of Christianity for technological man. Existentialist critiques and metaphysical studies close the volume. Fine selective bibliography.

1621   Morris, Bertram. "The Context of Technology." TECHNOLOGY AND CULTURE 18 (July 1977): 395-418.

In primitive societies, Morris writes, technology exists to support life-giving activities. Supported by myth and ritual, which appeal to supernatural aid for skill and success in such activities, technology is central to cultural form. In contrast, technology and science in industrial society are set in the context of a political system that controls the distribution of power and wealth. In such a context, technology no longer lends direct support to life. Morris laments this change, exhorting that technology must be transformed into an "organ mediating science and industry which negates the spurious culture that embraces the ideology of special interests and which affirms a genuine culture that espouses the philosophy of the common interest."

1622   Mueller, Gustav E. SINISTER SAVIOR: TWO ESSAYS ON MAN AND THE MACHINE. Norman, Okla.: Cooperative Books, 1941. 28 p.

Stressing that "we cannot have the benefits without taking the evils," Mueller's first essay stresses the faults of the "sinister savior," technology. His catalog of detrimental effects includes accidents, degradation of work, alienation, regimentation, and conformism. A second essay looks at the history of Western philosophy for the origins of the American cult of efficiency. Three eras of American culture are viewed as crucial to this development: the Puritan encouragement of worldly success, nationalist rationalism and enlightenment, and frontier expansionism. The current era marks a recognition of limitations and of the need to solve the problems of industrialization, which, Mueller suggests, will require "philosophical insight and religious love."

1623   Mumford, Lewis. "Authoritarian and Democratic Technics." TECHNOLOGY AND CULTURE 5 (Winter 1964): 1-8.

From Neolithic times, Mumford claims, two technologies have coexisted. One has been "authoritarian," a system-centered, powerful technology, the other "democratic"--man-centered, weak but clever. The ultimate end of authoritarian technics is the transferral of life attributes to the machine. Combating this trend are such "democratic" developments as "do-it-yourselfing," natural childbirth, and the renewed interest in walking.

1624   Pirsig, Robert M. ZEN AND THE ART OF MOTORCYCLE MAINTEN-ANCE: AN INQUIRY INTO VALUES. New York: William Morrow and Co., 1974. 412 p.

Intended neither as a guide to motorcycles nor Zen, the book ostensibly chronicles a Western motorcycle trip in which the author reviews relationships with his friends, his son, ideas, and technology. Deriving peace from the patient and methodical tuning of the cycle, he discovers the intellectual delight of solving its finite mechanical problems. His harmonious relationship with things technological is contrasted strongly to the suspicious noncomprehension of his friends. Pirsig's long discourses on the theme of quality as it relates to technology are valuable.

1625   Rapp, Friedrich, ed. CONTRIBUTIONS TO A PHILOSOPHY OF TECH-NOLOGY: STUDIES IN THE STRUCTURE OF THINKING IN THE TECHNOLOGICAL SCIENCES. Dordrecht, Holland: D. Reidel Publishing, 1974. xiii, 228 p. Bibliog.

Articles by both Western and Eastern authors, mostly reprinted from journals, serve as a balanced introduction to the field. Emphasis is on methodological and logical musings on technology's social impact. Occasionally, however, values creep into the discussion. Represented authors include Rapp, Mario Bunge, Joseph Agassi, and Henryk Skolimowski.

1626   Rodman, John. "On the Human Question, Being the Report of the Erewhonian High Commission to Evaluate Technological Society." INQUIRY 18 (Summer 1975): 126-66.

A mock commission from "dedeveloped" Erewhon visits the United States in the course of determining its own path of development. The commission's "Report" summarizes the view of "Erewhonian" mechanist and antimechanist philosophers, actually the ideas of Samuel Butler, Arthur C. Clarke, Norbert Wiener, Jacques Ellul, Lewis Mumford, and Marshall McLuhan. The "Commission" concludes that technology is a rigid cultural armor that must be shed to achieve "true emancipation."

1627   Rose, J[ohn]., ed. PROGRESS OF CYBERNETICS: PROCEEDINGS OF THE FIRST INTERNATIONAL CONGRESS OF CYBERNETICS, LONDON 1969. 3 vols. London: Gordon and Breach Science Publishers, 1970. xiv, xiv, xiv, 1,378 p.

The aims of this Congress were to establish cybernetics as a

solidly founded interdisciplinary science and to encourage
international cooperation and an exchange of information
among cybernetic scholars. The main section features eight
papers by eminent cyberneticians surveying the field. Subsequent papers cover the philosophy of cybernetics, neuro-
and bio-cybernetics, relations to industry, economic considerations, cybernetics and artifacts (including art), and impact
on natural and social sciences. Latter sections encompass
some values considerations.

1628   Rubinoff, Lionel. "The Contest between Faust and Prometheus."
PHILOSOPHY IN CONTEXT 3 (1974): 7-22.

Plato favored government by the "best," coincident with
virtuous lovers of wisdom. While such modern utopians as
B.F. Skinner concur with the Platonic notions of government
by experts, they have difficulty comprehending or operational-
izing the notion of the "good." In contemporary thought, the
beautiful and the functional have been divorced. Actions and
items derive value from their role in furthering a given goal,
regardless of whether that goal can be construed as "good."
In striving for well-being through technology, we have ceased
to question the inherent worth of our goals.

1629   Seidenberg, Roderick. POSTHISTORIC MAN. Chapel Hill: University
of North Carolina Press, 1950. x, 246 p.

Seidenberg depicts history as an interplay between instinct and
intelligence in which intelligence has now assumed a dominant
role, with resultant depersonalization and automatism. He
cites, with disapprobation, a trend toward collectivization and
specialization. Individualism, an expression of "a transitional
and unstable cultural amalgam" appears doomed to dissolve.

1630   Shmueli, Efraim. "Freedom and the Predicaments of Self-Realization in
a Technoscientific Age." IDEALISTIC STUDIES 7 (May 1977): 132-50.

From recent advances in science and technology have emerged
new dangers to personal freedom. Aided by computers and
communications devices, social and political agencies possess
the capacity to both manipulate and monitor behavior. Behaviorist psychology is criticized for its reductionist approach
to knowledge which, through dismissing other types of self-
knowledge, also impinges on personal freedom. It is only
through the dialectical interplay of freedom and control,
spontaneity and predictability, that progress is possible.

1631   Shriver, Donald W., Jr. "Invisible Doorway: Hope as a Technological
Virtue." ZYGON 8 (March 1973): 2-16.

Technology represents the "intersection of limit and possibility in the conditions of human life" and "the product of man's dexterity and his hopes." From the time they are conceived by designers, technologies are imbued with hopes. The results of innovation, however, are not predictable. Society is obliged to hope for the best, guided by the wisdom gained through experience.

1632 _____. "Man and His Machines: Four Angles of Vision." TECHNOL-OGY AND CULTURE 13 (October 1972): 531-55.

Four "intellectual predispositions" to the relationship between technology and values are described. "Rational value deter-mination" is the belief that man freely manipulates nature in his own best interests. In contrast, thinkers such as Marshall McLuhan and Jacques Ellul hold that technology runs accord-ing to its own values, while John McDermott and others sug-gest that technology merely reflects the values of controlling corporate interests. An alternative view, proposed by Victor Ferkiss, is that technology may be an aid to human evolution. Which vision is correct, Shriver concludes, depends on the public resolution of conflicting values.

1633 _____. "Technological Change and Multi-valued Choice--a Personal Inquiry." SOUNDINGS 53 (Spring 1970): 4-19.

The question of whether it is best to encourage social change or to modify one's personal lifestyle in response to problems of technology is pondered. To illustrate the dilemma, the author presents a personal values quandary--the decision to own two automobiles. He concludes from this self-examination that individuals must adopt a "multivalued" stance toward change, avoiding entrapment in one mode of action or thought, while developing a sense of universal responsibility.

1634 Sinclair, George. "A Call for a Philosophy of Engineering." TECH-NOLOGY AND CULTURE 18 (October 1977): 685-89.

One reason for studying the history and philosophy of technol-ogy is to achieve an understanding of the nature of technology that will help solve the problems of its impact on society. Sinclair argues that historians, in studying nuts and bolts, and philosophers, in studying abstractions, have ignored the human factor in engineering work. The result is that "the engineer takes little interest in the philosophy of technology because he does not find in it that which would aid him in determin-ing his true role in society."

1635 Skolimowski, Henryk. "The Structure of Thinking in Technology." TECHNOLOGY AND CULTURE 7 (Summer 1966): 371-83.

The philosophy of technology attempts to situate technology in the realm of human knowledge. It is distinct from technological philosophy, which is concerned with the future of society. The author's concern is with the former study. He believes that scientific and technical progress differ in that the latter creates reality, the what-is-to-be, through the pursuit of greater effectiveness. Technology is seen as an independent, complex form of knowledge.

1636 _____. "Towards a Humanistic Technology." RESEARCH MANAGE-MENT 14 (September 1971): 10-23.

Two modern philosophical approaches to technology can be distinguished: the pragmatic (technology as tools), and the intellectual (technology as the shadow of science). Skolimowski presents a third, dialectic approach, which encompasses the ongoing dialogue between society's needs and the potential for technology to satisfy those needs. Valid technological knowledge must serve a social purpose and must be generated by humanistically oriented technologists.

1637 _____. "A Twenty-first Century Philosophy." ALTERNATIVE FUTURES 1 (Fall 1978): 3-31.

In an era of upheaval, survival demands the supplanting of prevailing analytical and empiricist views of the world by a new conceptual framework that more adequately accommodates new social, ecological, ethical, and epistemological problems. Skolimowski's candidate is "ecophilosophy," for which he outlines twelve distinguishing characteristics. Essential features are a commitment to life and nature, and human and social values, reflected in concern with spiritual and physical, rather than material, well-being.

1638 _____. "A Way Out of the Abyss." MAIN CURRENTS 31 (January-February 1975): 71-76.

Western civilization has yielded both great successes and great failure in its uncompromising celebration of quantitative achievement. In order for technology to be complete and sufficient, a change in modes of understanding and in institutions, away from a quantitative instrumental basis of life, is essential.

1639 Stanley, Manfred. THE TECHNOLOGICAL CONSCIENCE. New York: Free Press, 1978. xix, 281 p. Bibliog.

Though Stanley states that he writes "out of a conviction that a literature is now in order eschewing apocalyptic frenzies of doom or salvation in favor of calmer analysis," he admits that

the pessimistic case holds more appeal for him. Stanley's
concept of "technicism" broadly embraces the misuse of scientific and technological modes of reasoning. But his particular concern is with linguistic technicism, defined as the
"misuse of scientific and technological vocabularies with regard to human activities," including metaphor and imagery.
Part 1 follows the historical evolution of technicism, noting
particularly successive challenges to human dignity. Part 2
studies the linguistic and metaphorical excesses of technicism.
The final part turns to the implications for education of the
countertechnicist position.

1640   "Symposium on Technology and Social Criticism." PHILOSOPHY OF
THE SOCIAL SCIENCES 1 (September 1971): 195-257.

Following introductory remarks by Jacob Bronowski appear two
articles, each followed by comments and criticisms. John M.
Roberts considers "expressive aspects" of technological developments, meaning those activities which contribute to such
areas as the conservation of technological knowledge, adjustment to change, and innovation. Examples of expressive
activities include self-testing in driving, museum work, and
games of chance. In the second major paper, Arthur Porter
reflects on the nature and design of systems, with particular
emphasis on educational systems.

1641   "Toward a Philosophy of Technology." PHILOSOPHY TODAY 15
(Summer 1971): 75-156.

A number of philosophical issues surrounding the influence of
technology on contemporary man are addressed. Hans Jonas
considers technology's role in Western intellectual tradition,
while Carl Mitcham and Robert Mackey review the thought of
Jacques Ellul. Four theories about the nature of technology
are critically discussed by Donald Brinkmann. In the concluding essay, Simon Moser looks at contemporary German thought
concerning technology.

1642   "Toward a Philosophy of Technology." TECHNOLOGY AND CULTURE
7 (Summer 1966): 301-90.

Contained in this special issue are a number of important
papers. They include Lewis Mumford's "Technics and the
Nature of Man"; James K. Feibleman's "Technology as Skills";
Mario Bunge's "Technology as Applied Science"; Henryk
Skolimowski's "The Structure of Thinking in Technology"; and
I.C. Jarvie's "The Social Character of Technology: Comments
on Skolimowski's Paper."

1643   Vick, George. "A Decline of Empiricism." PERSONALIST 53 (Summer
1972): 348-56.

Technology's major threat is the "progressive substitution, in our society, of electronically represented experience for. . . 'direct' or 'first hand' experience." Such bad habits as watching television will lead to a decline of empiricism, defined here as the testing of one's ideas or beliefs through individual experience. Truth is increasingly perceived to be the coherent yet incomplete world view projected by the electronic media.

1644 Wiener, Norbert. THE HUMAN USE OF HUMAN BEINGS: CYBER-NETICS AND SOCIETY. Boston: Houghton Mifflin, 1950. 241 p.

Communication, whether transmitted through man or machine, will become increasingly important in society's development, Wiener believes. Understanding advances in communications thus becomes an essential task, central to which is the study of cybernetics, defined here as "the comprehensive study of messages, encompassing computers and automata and the human mental and nervous apparatus." From a comparative study of input, output, and feedback in man and machine, Wiener comes to the conclusion that machines may soon be said to "think."

1645 Wilkinson, John, ed. TECHNOLOGY AND HUMAN VALUES. Santa Barbara, Calif.: Center for the Study of Democratic Institutions, 1966. 42 p.

Short, simply written essays encapsule the technological philosophy of a number of noted thinkers. Dennis Gabor provides hints for fighting existential nausea, while Martin Grotjahn reminds us that technological wizardry notwithstanding, the unconscious remains ageless. Theodore Roszak suggests that the rules of the technological game are so devised that society will always be the loser. Papers were originally presented at a conference on technology and society at Santa Barbara.

1646 Winter, Gibson. "Human Rights in a Technological Society." PHILOS-OPHY IN CONTEXT 1 (1972): 5-8.

Because it misunderstood the nature of technology, the rights movement of the 1960s was doomed to disillusionment. The struggle for human rights is determined to be a confused conflict between those advocating the instrumental use of techno-culture to achieve rights versus those struggling against techno-logical values in order to preserve a humanized world. Education and public participation in decision making are viewed as essential to the maintenance of rights. The author observes ironically that "the paradox of our age is that the more fully men and women participate in this culture, the less free they are to become whole persons and realize their full potentialities."

B. RELIGION

1. Bibliography

1647 McLean, George F. A BIBLIOGRAPHY OF CHRISTIAN PHILOSOPHY AND CONTEMPORARY ISSUES. Philosophy in the 20th Century: Catholic and Christian. Vol. 2. New York: Frederick Ungar Publishing Co., 1967. viii, 312 p.

McLean's bibliography contains a brief chapter, "Philosophy and Technology," with a limited selection of both American and foreign books and articles. Many titles are more directly related to science than to technology. Unannotated.

2. Books and Articles

1648 Abrecht, Paul. "Technology: New Directions in Ecumenical Social Ethics." CHRISTIANITY AND CRISIS 35 (28 April 1975): 92-98.

Abrecht examines religion's fairly recent involvement with technology and social ethics. He suggests likely directions for further investigation by scientists, technologists, and theologians, including the impact of scientific culture upon the relationship among God, nature, and humankind; ideological foundations; the dilemma of developing nations; and socially and environmentally appropriate technologies.

1649 Barbour, Ian G. ISSUES IN SCIENCE AND RELIGION. Englewood Cliffs, N.J.: Prentice-Hall, 1966. Reprint. New York: Harper and Row, 1971. x, 490 p.

A series of essays examines three basic types of issues: the methods of inquiry in science and religion, man's relation to nature, and God's relation to nature. Emphasis is more on science than on technology, but the work is nevertheless useful for understanding technological methodologies and relationships. Largely historical in approach. Useful as a course text.

1650 _____. "Science, Religion, and the Counterculture." ZYGON 10 (December 1975): 380-97.

Barbour responds critically but sympathetically to the ideals of counterculture views on reason, science, technology, and religion. Although there may be an overemphasis on Theodore Roszak as an archetype for the counterculture, Barbour's perceptiveness and readability make this an excellent piece.

1651 _____. SCIENCE AND SECULARITY: THE ETHICS OF TECHNOLOGY. New York: Harper and Row, 1970. 151 p.

Barbour confronts the challenge of science for contemporary religion which he sees posed by six major themes: the scientific method, the autonomy of nature, the technological mentality, and, more specifically, molecular biology, cybernetics, and science policy. He stresses the need for an adequate theology of nature and a humanization of technology.

1652 Bennett, John C[oleman]., ed. CHRISTIAN SOCIAL ETHICS IN A CHANGING WORLD: AN ECUMENICAL THEOLOGICAL INQUIRY. New York: Association Press, 1966. 381 p.

One of four volumes designed for use at the 1966 World Council of Churches' Conference on "Christians in the Technological and Social Revolutions of Our Time." More than just the American experience is considered; thus a useful perspective is provided.

1653 Berdyaev, Nicholas. "Man and Machine." In THE BOURGEOIS MIND AND OTHER ESSAYS, pp. 31-64. London: Sheed and Ward, 1934.

Berdyaev fears that technique will destroy the humanist ideal of man and culture and also that unregenerative rationalist technique will replace natural organic life. But, he also recognizes that no culture is possible without technique. The answer lies in greater religiosity, a stronger spirit united with God which will preserve man in His image.

1654 Bloy, Myron B., Jr. "The Christian Norm." In TECHNOLOGY AND HUMAN VALUES, edited by John Wilkinson, pp. 18-21. Santa Barbara, Calif.: Center for the Study of Democratic Institutions, 1966.

In one of a series of occasional papers published under Center auspices, Bloy suggests that the seeming breakdown of traditional culture by technological innovation, represented by changing sexual mores, cybernation, and the changing role of the family may, in the long run, actually be culturally liberating. Christianity, with Jesus as the model of human adulthood, has the potential of providing the necessary cultural norm, but it must be dynamic, flexible, and rooted in actual life. Also published as "Christian Function in a Technological Culture," CHRISTIAN CENTURY 83 (23 February 1966): 231-4.

1655 _____. THE CRISIS IN CULTURAL CHANGE: A CHRISTIAN VIEWPOINT. New York: Seabury Press, 1963. 139 p.

Bloy attempts to grapple with the rapid technologically induced change in today's society through a religious framework. He sees the need for a cultural self-identity that will view such change as much in a positive as in a negative vein to discover and celebrate "the manifestations of God's grace in life," especially through identification with Christ.

1656 Bonifazi, Conrad. A THEOLOGY OF THINGS: A STUDY OF MAN IN HIS PHYSICAL ENVIRONMENT. Philadelphia: J.B. Lippincott, 1967. 237 p.

Bonifazi is concerned with the relationship of Christian man to the natural world. He believes "the dualism which separates man's destiny from that of the world must be accounted dangerous," and that the concept of the natural as worthy before God must be reinstated.

1657 Brunner, Emil. "Technics." In CHRISTIANITY AND CIVILIZATION vol. 2, SPECIFIC PROBLEMS, pp. 1-15. New York: Charles Scribner's Sons, 1948-49.

Brunner notes and laments the abandonment of spiritual faith which has accompanied technological growth since the Industrial Revolution. Man has rejected salvation through God in return for earthly powers, only to reap boredom, alienation, totalitarianism, loss of individuality and, potentially, ultimate destruction. Christian faith and eternal values are the author's answer.

1658 Buchanan, R.A. "The Churches in a Changing World." In RELIGION IN A TECHNOLOGICAL SOCIETY, edited by Gerald Walters, pp. 1-20. Bath, Engl.: Bath University Press, 1968.

Buchanan calls for today's churches to accept the realities of social change as exemplified by three areas of twentieth-century life: material achievements, increased intellectual understanding of the universe, and a revised notion of authority in which there is no final or revealed truth. This change will require an alteration in religious doctrine and institutions in order to accept the methods and assumptions of science and technology while still providing motivation "to live according to the principle of self-giving love."

1659 Burhoe, Ralph Wendell. "Values via Science." ZYGON 4 (March 1969): 65-99.

Burhoe, the editor of ZYGON (no. 2349), believes the sciences and by implication, technology, can be "the most trustworthy revealers of human values" and suggests that "a reformulation of values in the light of contemporary sciences may be man's best salvation." This is the last of seven articles in this issue devoted to science and human values showing that fact and value involve one another. Extensive commentary is included in the September 1969 issue.

1660   _____, ed. SCIENCE AND HUMAN VALUES IN THE 21ST CENTURY. Philadelphia: Westminster Press, 1971. 203 p.

> Burhoe and four other scientists and theologians prophesy on the future nature of human values in a scientific/technologi- cal world. They are in general agreement on the necessity of science and religion to interact in the transmitting of values. In addition to Burhoe, who wrote half of the chap- ters, the contributors include Langdon Gilkey, O.H. Mowner, Harold K. Schilling, and Robert L. Sinsheimer.

1661   Callahan, Daniel [J.], ed. THE SECULAR CITY DEBATE. New York: Macmillan, 1966. vi, 218 p.

> A collection of reviews, journal debates, and articles both pro and con written in response to Harvey Cox's THE SECU- LAR CITY (no. 1668). There is also a lengthy rejoinder by Cox in which he basically reaffirms his position.

1662   Carothers, J. Edward; Mead, Margaret; McCracken, Daniel D.; and Shinn, Roger L. TO LOVE OR TO PERISH: THE TECHNOLOGICAL CRISIS AND THE CHURCHES. New York: Friendship Press, 1972. 152 p. Illus.

> The report of the United States Task Force on the Future of Mankind and the Role of the Christian Churches in a World of Science-Based Technology concludes that the role of Christianity must be to confront people with the "life and death" issues of the technological crisis.

1663   Cauthen, Kenneth. CHRISTIAN BIOPOLITICS: A CREDO AND STRAT- EGY FOR THE FUTURE. Nashville, Tenn.: Abingdon Press, 1971. 159 p.

> Cauthen's answer for society's future is Christian biopolitics, by which he means a utopian fulfillment of creative life, which will come through a merging of secular futurism and a Christian theology of hope.

1664   _____. SCIENCE, SECULARIZATION AND GOD: TOWARD A THEOLOGY OF THE FUTURE. Nashville, Tenn.: Abingdon Press, 1969. 237 p.

> It is Cauthen's intent "to investigate the relationship of a biblically grounded religion to the science-dominated, secu- larized culture of our time, in pursuit of the thesis that it is possible to be both 'a serious Christian and an intelligent modern.'" His theology of the future is a theology of hope, a naturalistic theism.

1665   Cooper, Brian G. "Religion and Technology--Toward Dialogue."

MAIN CURRENTS IN MODERN THOUGHT 26 (September-October 1969): 10-13.

Technological creativity has changed man's relationship to nature and secularized many religious questions of ultimate meaning. If there is to be a dialogue between religion and technology, as Cooper believes is necessary, the dialogue "must start with mutual criticism, even creative doubt."

1666 Coulson, C.A. SCIENCE, TECHNOLOGY AND THE CHRISTIAN. Nashville, Tenn.: Abingdon Press, 1960. 111 p.

In the first industrial revolution, people were largely uninformed about its consequences for society, much to their and our detriment. If we are to avoid a similar fate in today's second industrial revolution, that of cybernetics, automation, and nuclear energy, we must bring Christian principles to bear on the important decisions which will affect society.

1667 Cox, Harvey. THE FEAST OF FOOLS: A THEOLOGICAL ESSAY ON FESTIVITY AND FANTASY. Cambridge, Mass.: Harvard University Press, 1969. xii, 204 p.

Stemming in part from response to THE SECULAR CITY (no. 1668), this book, while not rejecting the former's emphasis on the secular, pays more attention to the importance of meditation, mysticism, prayer, and ritual. Today's society needs a rebirth of fantasy and festivity, linking the world together in a way in which technology may become a means to fulfillment, not an end in itself.

1668 _____. THE SECULAR CITY: SECULARIZATION AND URBANIZATION IN THEOLOGICAL PERSPECTIVE. 1965. Rev. ed. New York: Macmillan, 1966. xii, 244 p. Bibliog.

A religious "bombshell" when first published, Cox's book views positively certain secular-technological themes--in particular the meaning of urbanization, the role of the church in the city, and Christian response to the issues of work, sex, and learning.

1669 _____. THE SEDUCTION OF THE SPIRIT: THE USE AND MISUSE OF PEOPLE'S RELIGION. New York: Simon and Schuster, 1973. 350 p. Bibliog.

Cox broadly construes mass-media culture as a "religion," a set of values, frequently in conflict with traditional Christian goals. Believing that the human "stories" by which people have traditionally lived are dangerously overbalanced by the systematized "signals" of a specialized secular society, he calls for a new theology of culture.

1670 _____. "The Virgin and the Dynamo Revisited: An Essay on the Symbolism of Technology." SOUNDINGS 54 (Summer 1971): 125-46.

Certain technologies have acquired sacred significance and are among those symbols that have replaced traditional religious ones. For this reason, Cox suggests the need for an understanding of what technology means for us "above and beyond [the] merely technical function. . . .To understand ourselves and our technologies today we need an Adamsian fusion of Yankee shrewdness and gothic fantasy."

1671 Cunliffe-Jones, H[ubert]. TECHNOLOGY, COMMUNITY AND CHURCH. London: Independent Press, 1961. 159 p. Bibliog.

It is the author's contention that "in a world greatly influenced by Science and Technology, plainly the most important fact is the life of persons in community." To this end, both society (government as well as individuals) and the Church must seek to take advantage of the possibilities posed by technology for the enhancement of life.

1672 Douglass, Truman B. "Christ and Technology." CHRISTIAN CENTURY 78 (25 January 1961): 104-7.

"The problem of our so-called 'materialistic' age is not our inventions but man himself and the uses to which he puts his technological achievements." The Church must play a role in determining the goals toward which we direct our technology, but it must also listen to responsible members of the laity for specific answers in solving problems along the way.

1673 Edwards, Scott. "Jesus in the Now: The New Revivalism." HUMANIST 36 (September 1976): 16-19.

Edwards believes the "New Revivalism" has taken on the liberal ethos of our society with its materialism and irrelevance, a concept most specifically illustrated by its exploitation of mass communications technology and its morality.

1674 Faramelli, Norman J. TECHNETHICS: CHRISTIAN MISSION IN AN AGE OF TECHNOLOGY. New York: Friendship Press, 1971. 160 p. Bibliog.

Faramelli believes ethical insight which guides, but yet is shaped by, technology is necessary to survival in today's cybernetic world. Although influential, machines are only an extension of mankind; they do not dominate and may indeed be helpful in achieving societal goals.

1675 Ferré, Frederick. SHAPING THE FUTURE: RESOURCES FOR THE POST-MODERN WORLD. New York: Harper and Row, 1976. xiv, 194 p.

The modern world, which began in the seventeenth century, has reached its climax in the twentieth, and we are on the verge of a post-modern world for which a new philosophical and religious outlook is necessary. If we are to avoid the problems of nuclear war, population growth, pollution, and the depletion of resources, we must abandon the older values of a scientific world view for a new perspective in which religion will guide our choice of values. A hopeful outlook.

1676   Foley, Grover. "Reaping the Whirlwind: The Question of Faith in an Obsolete World." CROSS CURRENTS 23 (Fall 1973): 279-96.

Foley, using examples of war, the energy crisis, and the irrelevance of most knowledge, resoundingly criticizes the optimism of secular theology. He believes a new life-style to be necessary, one which is "consciously un-modern and 'unproductive.'"

1677   Guerin, Wilfred L. "Dynamo, Virgin, and Cyclotron: Henry Adams and Teilhard de Chardin on Pilgrimage." RENASCENCE 28 (Spring 1976): 139-46.

Guerin suggests symbolic parallels between the pessimistic Adams' "The Dynamo and the Virgin" and the optimistic Teilhard's "On Looking at a Cyclotron" as a way of more clearly understanding each.

1678   Gustafson, James M. "Christian Attitudes toward a Technological Society." THEOLOGY TODAY 16 (July 1959): 173-87.

Today's society is disenchanted because of its rationality. Gustafson traces the somewhat ambivalent Christian response to this rationalism.

1679   Haigerty, Leo J., ed. PIUS XII AND TECHNOLOGY. Milwaukee: Bruce Publishing Co., 1962. xxvi, 244 p.

A compilation of speeches by Pope Pius XII on technology and its relationship with humanity represents the Catholic Church's attempt to view technology positively and to search for an acceptable visionary theology which will accommodate, liberate, and guide it. "Technological progress comes from God, and so it can and ought to lead to God."

1680   Hall, Cameron P., ed. HUMAN VALUES AND ADVANCING TECHNOLOGY: A NEW AGENDA FOR THE CHURCH IN MISSION. New York: Friendship Press, 1967. 175 p.

Eleven articles and working group reports which emerged from a 1967 National Council of Churches' project includes contributions by Huston Smith, Robert Theobold, Theodosius

Dobzhansky, Jose M.R. Delgado, and Donald N. Michael. The authors take a generally positive stance toward the solvability through Christian means of values problems raised by advancing technology.

1681 Hamill, Robert H. PLENTY AND TROUBLE: THE IMPACT OF TECHNOLOGY ON PEOPLE. Nashville, Tenn.: Abingdon Press, 1971. 192 p. Bibliog.

Hamill, in examining the impact of technology upon daily life, concludes that sensible Christians must discard those views which see it as either a total answer or as an unmitigated curse, as well as the perception of it as just one more stage in the evolution of humanity. Instead he offers five Christian principles to guide the reader amidst the mixed blessings of technology.

1682 Hanson, Bradley C. "The Counterculture and Theology." LUTHERAN QUARTERLY 23 (February 1971): 32-39.

Hanson sees in the counterculture a search for fulfillment and happiness in life, which includes an openness toward God not readily evident in the lives of many adults. In this search for an imaginative life of nonmaterialistic values, theology and the counterculture must work hand-in-hand to achieve far-sighted and humane goals which make use of but do not succumb to technology.

1683 Hatt, Harold E. CYBERNETICS AND THE IMAGE OF MAN: A STUDY OF FREEDOM AND RESPONSIBILITY IN MAN AND MACHINE. Nashville, Tenn.: Abingdon Press, 1968. 304 p.

With respect to cybernetics, Hatt is particularly concerned with the problem of human freedom and responsibility, which he investigates by relating man as viewed in the image of God to man as viewed in the image of the machine.

1684 Holloway, James Y., ed. INTRODUCING JACQUES ELLUL. Grand Rapids, Mich.: William B. Eerdmans, 1970. 183 p.

Eight interpretive articles analyze Ellul's work and the problems of Christianity and technology. Contributors include Gabriel Vahanian, Christopher Lasch, Julius Lester, Stephen Rose, William Stringfellow, James W. Douglass, and James Branscome. An interview with Ellul conducted by John Wilkinson concludes the volume.

1685 Humbert, Royal. "The Computer and the Mystic." ENCOUNTER 38 (Summer 1977): 227-44.

The challenge of the computerized society and the insight of mystical vision are not mutually exclusive. Indeed, political choices must be made at the center of a triangle of concerns which include the "communal," the "technical," and the "transcendent."

1686   Kuhns, William. THE ELECTRONIC GOSPEL: RELIGION AND MEDIA. New York: Herder and Herder, 1969. 173 p. Bibliog.

Kuhns explores the relationship between electronic media and religion and finds that television in particular has replaced the ritual, mystical, and magical functions of the church. "Men need to understand the nature and ploys of fantasy far more than the structures and demands of religion."

1687   _____. ENVIRONMENTAL MAN. New York: Harper and Row, 1969. 156 p. Bibliog.

Kuhns "explores the significance of man's contemporary environment for theology" by going after the "interfaces" between man and his technology, among them cars, toys, television, and machines. He concludes with suggestions for a new Christian community, one which takes account of this interaction by rejecting the master/matter approach to the environment.

1688   Lee, Robert. RELIGION AND LEISURE IN AMERICA: A STUDY IN FOUR DIMENSIONS. Nashville, Tenn.: Abingdon Press, 1964. 271 p. Bibliog.

Technologically induced leisure is changing the goals of life for those not obsessed by work. The four dimensions in which Lee discusses the subject are: the contemporary, social-psychological, historical, and theological. Christian insights with respect to time may provide a framework to guide us in the use of leisure.

1689   Lynch, William F. CHRIST AND PROMETHEUS: A NEW IMAGE OF THE SECULAR. Notre Dame, Ind.: University of Notre Dame Press, 1970. 153 p.

Lynch calls for a religious image of the secular which will recognize its principles of autonomy, unconditionality, and self-identity without denying the religious goal of unity under God, a secularity in which "the religious imagination can live and breathe."

1690   Metz, Johannes [B.], ed. THE EVOLVING WORLD AND THEOLOGY. Concilium Theology in the Age of Renewal, vol. 26. New York: Paulist Press, 1967. viii, 184 p.

Three articles in this volume on evolution deal with technology. Jacques Ellul believes in accelerated technological evolution rather than revolution. It is a process of causality, not finality, in which Christians may contribute to establishing a desirable future by critical analysis of short-term technological consequences. The essay presents a more positive Ellul than is revealed in THE TECHNOLOGICAL SOCIETY (no. 29). Emmanuel Mesthene maintains man's scientific and technological understanding has freed him from the "tyranny" of nature, enabling him to join God in "doing the work of the world." Religion's role should be to know and reveal God in his eternal possibility to man. Eric Mascall argues that scientific technology is not incompatible with Christian doctrine and may, in fact, contribute to its development. "What is urgently needed today is the development of a theology of the secular."

1691 Mohan, Robert Paul, ed. TECHNOLOGY AND CHRISTIAN CULTURE. Washington, D.C.: Catholic University Press, 1960. vi, 144 p.

Five lectures delivered at Catholic University in 1958 reflect Catholic approaches to dealing with technology in contemporary society. The editor and contributors Rudolf Allers, Thomas P. Neill, Dietrich Von Hildebrand, John C.H. Wu, and Francis J. Connell generally perceive the problem as lying not within technology itself but rather among the people who make use of it.

1692 Nisbet, Robert A. "The Impact of Technology on Ethical Decision-Making." In RELIGION AND SOCIAL CONFLICT, edited by Robert Lee and Martin E. Marty, pp. 9-23. New York: Oxford University Press, 1964.

Nisbet deals with the problem of ethical choice generated by modern "institutionalized" technology which conflicts with other established norms. Technology, through the techniques of abstraction, generalization, and rationalization, reduces normal conflict and threatens individuality, the key to ethical decision making.

1693 Ong, Walter J. AMERICAN CATHOLIC CROSSROADS: RELIGIOUS-SECULAR ENCOUNTERS IN THE MODERN WORLD. New York: Macmillan, 1959. xi, 160 p.

In this selection of six general essays, Ong discusses the relationship of the Catholic tradition to the secular world.

1694 _____. IN THE HUMAN GRAIN: FURTHER EXPLORATION OF CONTEMPORARY CULTURE. New York: Macmillan, 1967. xiii, 207 p.

In this collection of previously published essays, Ong examines literature, technological culture, and religion in a framework oriented around the concept of time. The lack of a truly unifying theme resulted in mixed reviews of this sequel to his earlier work, THE BARBARIAN WITHIN (1962).

1695 _____. "Technology and New Humanist Frontiers." In FRONTIERS IN AMERICAN CATHOLICISM: ESSAYS IN IDEOLOGY AND CULTURE, pp. 86-103. New York: Macmillan, 1957. ix, 125 p.

Ong optimistically views technology as inherently humanistic. The age of technology "can be considered as an [evolutionary] epoch in what we may call the 'hominization' of the world, that is, the taking over of our planet by mankind."

1696 Placher, William C. "The Trinity and the Motorcycle." THEOLOGY TODAY 34 (October 1977): 248-56.

Placher suggests that theologians might find answers to some of the questions regarding technology and society raised in Robert Pirsig's ZEN AND THE ART OF MOTORCYCLE MAINTENANCE: AN INQUIRY INTO VALUES (no. 1624) by returning to the doctrine of the Trinity so long ignored. Although in some ways this essay is one more in a long string stressing the importance of Christian faith in solving contemporary problems, the author does provide a unique slant and concise summary of Pirsig.

1697 Roszak, Theodore. UNFINISHED ANIMAL: THE AQUARIAN FRONTIER AND THE EVOLUTION OF CONSCIOUSNESS. New York: Harper and Row, 1975. xi, 271 p.

Roszak examines the spirituality he believes has emerged as represented by the occult and mystical--the quasi-religious fascinations of today's society. He is critical of, but ultimately encouraged by, this search for meaning, finding it a "healthy sign of spiritual resurgence" for our secularized industrial world.

1698 Schilling, Harold K. THE NEW CONSCIOUSNESS IN SCIENCE AND RELIGION. Philadelphia: United Church Press, 1973. 288 p. Bibliog.

It is Schilling's belief that the "post-modern" world of science and technology is undergoing a revolution of consciousness with respect to reality, wherein many observers have come to recognize a sense of mystery in nature. However, Christianity must also revise its outlook and teaching to incorporate scientific changes, so that it may complement science rationally. A synthesis of contemporary thinking.

1699 Stackhouse, Max L. "Technology and the Supranatural." ZYGON 10 (March 1975): 59-85.

There is a distinction between natural explainable phenomena
and the "supranatural," that which is allowed by the natural,
but which involves ritual, myth, and symbol in its choice
and is therefore unexplainable solely by the former.
Stackhouse believes "both the drive to understand that
eventuates in science and the drive to control that eventuates
in technology are dependent upon fundamental supranatural
decisions." However, all is not lost, for understanding which
decisions "ought" to be made can be aided through the conceptual tools of social axiology, ethics, and theology.

1700   "Symposium on the Human Prospect." ZYGON 10 (September 1975):
215-375.

A theme issue contains six articles presented at a 1974 symposium on Robert Heilbroner's AN INQUIRY INTO THE HUMAN.
PROSPECT (no. 38). Contributors include Langdon Gilkey,
Donald T. Campbell, Victor Ferkiss, Joseph Caggiano,
Edgar S. Dunn, and Ralph Wendell Burhoe, all of whom
comment on the role religion will play in redeeming society's
present predicament. Burhoe's lengthy summary is perhaps
the most complete essay, drawing as it does upon the other
papers, but it is also the most hopeful for the results of a
"scientific theology."

1701   Taylor, Alva W. CHRISTIANITY AND INDUSTRY IN AMERICA.
New York: Friendship Press, 1933. xi, 212 p. Bibliog.

In this depression-era study, the author notes the "social lag,"
in terms of labor conditions, which has accompanied industrialization. Christian principles of justice and charity are
offered as the solution.

1702   Teilhard de Chardin, Pierre. THE PHENOMENON OF MAN. Paris:
Editions du Seuil, 1955. Translated by Bernard Wall. Rev. ed. New
York: Harper and Row, 1965. 320 p.

This is the central work of the famous but frequently disputed
Jesuit paleontologist and philosopher. Teilhard's major concern is with evolution and the explanation of an integrated
world view. Man, nature, science, and technology are parts
of a continually evolving process which will ultimately converge in Christ--the Omega point. There are many evaluations of Teilhard's thought; two of the better brief ones are
Georges Crespy's FROM SCIENCE TO THEOLOGY: AN
ESSAY ON TEILHARD DE CHARDIN (1968) and N.M.
Wildiers' AN INTRODUCTION TO TEILHARD DE CHARDIN
(1960).

1703   Tillich, Paul. "The Person in a Technical Society." In CHRISTIAN

FAITH AND SOCIAL ACTION, edited by John A. Hutchinson, pp. 137-53. New York: Charles Scribner's Sons, 1953. Also in SOCIAL ETHICS AND SOCIETY, edited by Gibson Winter, pp. 120-38. New York: Harper and Row, 1968.

Tillich sees the loss of personhood and human community in modern, competitive, technical society. In an attempt to discover a source of personality and life, he takes his cue from the social criticism of the existential movements. He believes one must transcend industrial society, and even the Church, which has become a part of it, into the New Reality to which the Christian message points.

1704 Vahanian, Gabriel. GOD AND UTOPIA: THE CHURCH IN A TECH-NOLOGICAL CIVILIZATION. New York: Seabury Press, 1977. xxviii, 154 p.

Vahanian compares the eschatological or principal dimension of Christian faith to the utopian dimensions of humanism and technology. He believes technology can "release man's religious drive" in the form of a forward looking theology of utopia in which God is transcendent. An optimistic view of the roles of church and technology in society.

1705 Vaux, Kenneth. SUBDUING THE COSMOS: CYBERNETICS AND MAN'S FUTURE. Richmond, Va.: John Knox, 1970. 197 p. Bibliog.

Vaux reflects on "the ethical significance of electric technol-ogy [cybernetics] and man's use of that power to control envir-onment." Responsible use will involve the Christian ethic of creation. Man as co-creator with God must serve both as master and steward of the world.

1706 _____, ed. TO CREATE A DIFFERENT FUTURE: RELIGIOUS HOPE AND TECHNOLOGICAL PLANNING. New York: Friendship Press, 1972. 144 p. Bibliog.

Of these five papers originally read at the 1972 Houston Con-ference on Technology and a Human Future, Jorgen Rander's paper places the subject in global context, while that of Ivan Illich criticizes the dehumanized or "non-convivial" nature of society. Robert Murray and Robert Francoeur pre-sent discussions of genetic knowledge and sexuality. Vaux contributes a summary paper placing the others in a religious context of hope. Includes commentary.

1707 Wiener, Norbert. GOD AND GOLEM, INC.; A COMMENT ON CERTAIN POINTS WHERE CYBERNETICS IMPINGES ON RELIGION. Cambridge: M.I.T. Press, 1964. ix, 99 p.

Wiener deals with the notion of creativity in the cybernetics

of communication and control, in which machines may learn
and reproduce themselves. Drawing analogies with religious
ethics, he believes men and machines must relate to each
other in creative rather than destructive ways.

C. ENGINEERING ETHICS

1708 APPROACHING THE BENIGN ENVIRONMENT: THE FRANKLIN LEC-
TURES IN THE SCIENCES AND HUMANITIES. University: University
of Alabama Press, 1970. xi, 121 p.

Three essays express concern over the narrow education of
contemporary engineers and scientists. Buckminster Fuller provides "an historical analysis of the extinction implicit in
overspecialization." That the engineering profession has not
accepted its social responsibilities is the concern of Eric
Walker. James Killian advocates an integration of scientists
and humanists spreading from the universities to policymaking
bodies. All three seek a "benign environment" where science
and technology are "directed toward moral and aesthetic
objectives."

1709 Baum, Robert J., and Flores, Albert, eds. ETHICAL PROBLEMS IN
ENGINEERING. Troy, N.Y.: Center for the Human Dimensions of
Science and Technology, 1978. xiii, 335 p.

Designed for engineering courses dealing with ethical issues,
the book begins with a comparative survey of professional
codes of ethics and problems in enforcing them. Case studies
in ethics comprise the second and third parts, covering problems of payoffs, politics, public versus client interests, and
the marketing of professional services. General social concerns and responsibilities of engineers are discussed in the
concluding section. Papers are reprinted from engineering
journals, science and popular magazines, and casebooks.
Good for classroom use.

1710 Davenport, William H., and Rosenthal, Daniel, eds. ENGINEERING:
ITS ROLE AND FUNCTION IN HUMAN SOCIETY. New York:
Pergamon Press, 1967. xii, 284 p.

Conceived by a summer study group of UCLA humanists and
engineers, this anthology can serve as a text for nonengineering students. The editors have allotted equal space to
humanists and scientists presenting their views on technology
and society interrelations. Part 1 introduces humanist views
from John Henry Newman (1852) to D.A. Platt (1964). The
editors suggest that overcoming the science-humanities dichotomy is in the best interest of the humanist, who is able to
translate the public experience of science to private art.

Part 2 presents a portrait of engineering composed of views ranging from the idealist vision of Herbert Hoover to a more restrained characterization by Simon Ramo. Closing sections review the evolution of the man-machine relationship and project its future.

1711 Davies, Duncan S.; Banfield, Tom; and Sheahan, Roy. THE HUMANE TECHNOLOGIST. London: Oxford University Press, 1976. viii, 180 p. Bibliog.

Written for technologists whose educations have been lacking in such areas, this book touches on a number of social concerns. Chapters consider technological planning and growth, emphasizing the use of models; natural resources; energy; management; and the "complete" technological education. Compact and readable, the book is rather conservative in its approach.

1712 Dorf, Richard C. "Engineering Design and Social Indicators." ENGINEERING EDUCATION 61 (November 1970): 110-12.

The engineering designer is obliged to examine the social as well as the material costs of alternative designs. New methods of measuring social costs must be developed, based on social indicators. Teaching the integrated design of a product through consideration of technological, economic, and social constraints is seen as a paramount challenge for engineering education.

1713 Florman, Samuel [C.]. THE EXISTENTIAL PLEASURES OF ENGINEERING. New York: St. Martin's Press, 1975. xi, 160 p.

Florman has prepared an eloquent apology and a paean to his profession and its work. Because they have not been granted the politician's power nor the historian's hindsight, engineers cannot be held responsible for damage done by technology. Yet, Florman seems to feel that technology merits little criticism, as he vigorously confronts the critics of technology, principally Jacques Ellul, René Dubos, Lewis Mumford, and Theodore Roszak. He is particularly sensitive to slurs on the intellectual and spiritual rewards of engineering.

1714 Foecke, Harold A. "Engineering in the Humanistic Tradition." IMPACT OF SCIENCE ON SOCIETY 20 (April-June 1970): 125-35.

It is the engineer, not the scientist or technologist, who should receive criticism for the socially harmful consequences of technology. For it is the engineer's responsibility, Foecke contends, to utilize technology to satisfy human needs in the areas of transportation, communication, nutrition, energy, and recreation. Scientists study what is; technologists, what can be; engineers, Foecke avers, must determine what should be.

1715   Freund, C.J. "Public Concern about Ethics." ENGINEERING EDU-
CATION 60 (June 1970): 951-53.

Two kinds of engineering ethics are distinguished: professional behavior concerning graft, moonlighting, and similar abuses, and the engineer's obligation to help improve the moral standards of Americans. As a result of their technological contributions to society, engineers enjoy a prestige that will make them natural leaders in the struggle to shore up collaps-ing American morality, Freund suggests.

1716   Fruchtbaum, Harold, ed. "The Social Responsibilities of Engineers."
ANNALS OF THE NEW YORK ACADEMY OF SCIENCES 196, no. 10
(28 February 1973): 409-73.

In his opening remarks, Seymour Melman declares that the question of ethics, defined as criteria for selection of work, can no longer be ignored by engineers because of two major developments: the continuing channeling of engineering tal-ent into military research, and the growing gravity of tech-nologically created problems in the civilian sphere. Papers touch on four areas of concern: responsibilities of engineers and employers to each other, responsibilities of engineering societies and institutions, responsibilities of engineers for uses and effects of technology, and social ethics for technology. In closing, Fruchtbaum conceptualizes the engineer as an "enabler" who encourages community choice of technology and facilitates its delivery.

1717   Horgan, J.D. "Technology and Human Values: The Circle of Action."
MECHANICAL ENGINEERING 95 (August 1973): 19-22.

Changes in contemporary technology stir changes in values, which in turn alter technology, thus creating a "circle of action." The author feels that it is the engineer's responsi-bility to anticipate consequences of new technologies and disseminate appropriate information. The university, in turn, must educate engineers to be sensitive to problem areas.

1718   Kardestuncer, Hayrettin, ed. SOCIAL CONSEQUENCES OF ENGI-
NEERING. San Francisco: Boyd and Fraser, 1979. xii, 290 p.
Bibliog.

Intended for nonengineering students and others interested in technological problems, this book provides an overview of problems and developments in food, shelter, energy and trans-port, pollution, communications, biomedical technology, genetic engineering, and control of technology. The editor avers that the book "not only offers an engineering culture to liberal arts students, but invites them to help out engineers in finding the best solutions." Contributors are mainly prominent scientists and technologists. Each section concludes with a bibliography.

1719   Kemper, J.D. THE ENGINEER AND HIS PROFESSION. New York: Holt, Rinehart and Winston, 1975. 293 p.

Describing the professional milieu for the undergraduate engineering student, Kemper underscores ethical issues. Engineers' responsibilities with regard to the environment, ethics, energy, and professional self-image are sketched. The workings of large organizations and managerial machines are explained in an introductory fashion.

1720   Mann, David. "Ethical and Social Responsibility in the Planning and Design of Engineering Projects." PROCEEDINGS OF THE AMERICAN SOCIETY OF CIVIL ENGINEERS 98, no. PP1 (January 1972): 33-41.

Engineers, in the course of their work, must resolve conflicts between employers' desires, personal advancement needs, and the public good. Mann suggests that engineers might best serve society through involvement as technical advisers to citizen environmental interest groups. In any event, the engineer should be prepared to refuse involvement in projects he considers societally detrimental, Mann believes.

1721   Mantell, Murray I. ETHICS AND PROFESSIONALISM IN ENGINEERING. New York: Macmillan, 1964. 260 p. Illus., bibliog.

Mantell's text is intended to be a reference guide "for further appreciation of the philosophy, methodology, influence, ideals, and practice of engineering." The first few chapters present an outline for a philosophy of engineering and a brief history of ethics as it applies to the field. Final chapters discuss engineers' obligations to society and to professional development and communication.

1722   Morrison, David L. "Engineering Excellence or Societal Regulation?" ASHRAE JOURNAL 13 (October 1971): 25-31.

Excellence is a relative term. Due to the growing criticism of science and technology based on social and political factors, the definition of engineering excellence is undergoing modification. Two issues, consumerism and environmental quality, are discussed in relation to this changing definition. New criteria for engineering excellence are derived that emphasize safety, reliability, efficiency, and social need over profitability in engineering projects.

1723   Novick, David, and Schumacher, Sheldon. "The Civil Engineer of the Future--A Renaissance Man." PROCEEDINGS OF THE AMERICAN SOCIETY OF CIVIL ENGINEERS 99, no. PP1 (January 1973): 9-18.

> The scope of the engineering profession must be enlarged in two areas, the authors suggest. Engineers must engage in scrutiny of local and national needs in order to help determine priorities for technological development. They must also adopt a larger view of engineering projects that encompasses social considerations. Through the development of a widened perspective, differences between engineers and other professionals may be bridged. Education in the social sciences and humanities should prove a good starting point for this widened vision.

1724   Perrucci, Robert, and Gerstl, Joel E. PROFESSION WITHOUT COMMUNITY: ENGINEERS IN AMERICAN SOCIETY. New York: Random House, 1969. 194 p. Illus.

> Data are reported from a national survey of engineering graduates in industry and government. The questionnaires recorded social background, professional socialization, career pattern, and family and community information. Perrucci feels that the understanding of inadequacies in the education and socialization of engineers is important since future technological breakthroughs will involve many nontechnical, responsible decisions in which engineers will be involved, prepared or not.

1725   _____, eds. THE ENGINEERS AND THE SOCIAL SYSTEM. New York: John Wiley and Sons, 1969. xii, 344 p. Illus., bibliog.

> The engineering profession's position in the larger social system is analyzed in this collection of original essays, organized around four themes: the history of the profession, occupational recruitment and socialization, nature of work roles, and links between careers and society. Of especial interest are papers analyzing the relationship of engineering to the class structure and to sex roles.

1726   Rosenblueth, Emilio. "Ethical Optimization in Engineering." PROCEEDINGS OF THE AMERICAN SOCIETY OF CIVIL ENGINEERS 99, no. PP2 (April 1973): 223-43.

> In decision making, the engineer should tend toward optimization of design or rationality, and not simply the general practice of the profession. Conditions for rationality and corresponding scales of utility are presented by the author in order to specify the elements of an ethical system based on maximization of happiness. Professional, social, and religious implications of this ethical system are reviewed and its practical utility discussed.

1727 Shepherd, Herbert A. "Engineers as Marginal Men." JOURNAL OF
ENGINEERING EDUCATION 47 (March 1957): 536-42.

> The engineer is viewed as an individual torn between two
> cultures: the pragmatic world of business and the knowledge-
> oriented, timeless world of the scientist. A contradictory
> figure, the engineer, through his work, upsets the social
> order, yet tends to be personally conservative. The author
> feels that the increasing prominence of the engineer-manager
> bodes well for social progress.

1728 Sudduth, Charles G. "Considering Social Values in Engineering
Projects." PROCEEDINGS OF THE AMERICAN SOCIETY OF CIVIL
ENGINEERS 98, no. PP1 (January 1972): 43-47.

> In recent years, the engineering profession has received con-
> siderable criticism for what the general public perceives to
> be the profession's insensitivity to human and environmental
> needs. Sudduth claims that such insensitive engineers are in
> the minority as environmental damage is more the result of
> ignorance. Effects of past errors have only recently been
> realized, not only by engineers, but by the accusing public
> as well.

1729 White, Lynn, Jr. "Engineers and the Making of a New Humanism."
ENGINEERING EDUCATION 57 (January 1967): 375-76.

> Many decisions concerning all aspects of contemporary life are
> being made by engineers. New requirements associated with
> these decisions imply that "an engineer is increasingly threat-
> ened with technological obsolescence in proportion as he is
> not also a humanist." Due to the elitism and antitechnology
> current of the humanities disciplines, the engineer has not
> found solace there. White suggests that these "chief revolu-
> tionaries of our time," devoted to the liberation of man from
> the limitations of the physical world, must be aided in their
> pursuit of values by a new humanistic thinking free from
> "aristocratic warp."

1730 Young, C.R.; Innis, H.A.; and Dales, J.H. ENGINEERING AND
SOCIETY: WITH SPECIAL REFERENCE TO CANADA. Toronto: University of Toronto Press, 1947. 429 p.

> Part 1 provides a history and description of the engineering
> profession, with a profile of the "best" engineer--an imagina-
> tive, intelligent, courageous being. A survey of the history
> of technology and its effects to date leads the authors to con-
> clude optimistically that technology has created more jobs
> than it has removed and, while causing social disruption, has
> encouraged egalitarianism. Engineers are exhorted to assume
> responsibility for the social implications of their work as "in-

telligent and sympathetic members of a general, not technical society."

1731   Zandi, Iraq, ed. THE TECHNOLOGICAL CATCH AND SOCIETY.
Philadelphia: Department of Civil and Urban Engineering, University
of Pennsylvania, 1975. viii, 114 p.

The product of the first series of Herbert Spencer lectures
held at the university, this volume addresses problems of
technological development, focusing on the ways in which
heightened sensitivity of technologists and the public could
ameliorate current conditions. While most contributors, primarily educators, are "pro-technology" in outlook, they
appear skeptical about the need to postulate a "technological
imperative."

D. BUSINESS ETHICS

1. Bibliographies

1732   Dee, Sandra R. CORPORATIONS AND THE ENVIRONMENT: PR OR
PROPAGANDA? A BIBLIOGRAPHY. Exchange Bibliography no. 411.
Monticello, Ill.: Council of Planning Librarians, 1973. 9 p.

1733   Gothie, Daniel L. A SELECTED BIBLIOGRAPHY OF APPLIED ETHICS
IN THE PROFESSIONS 1950-1970. Charlottesville: University Press
of Virginia, 1973. xx, 176 p.

Defining "applied ethics" as ethical or moralistic behavior as
observed in societal rather than individualistic conditions, this
extensive bibliography covers literature related to the following professions: business and management, law, government,
social sciences, economics, education, health sciences, science, and engineering. Compiled as a data base for the
Center for the Study of Applied Ethics, the partially annotated
bibliography cites books, journal articles, pamphlets, and
speeches. The period covered, 1950-70, is chosen because
of the stress placed on social behavior by the rapid changes
induced by technology.

1734   Hanson, Agnes O. EXECUTIVE AND MANAGEMENT DEVELOPMENT
FOR BUSINESS AND GOVERNMENT: A GUIDE TO INFORMATION
SOURCES. Management Information Guide, no. 31. Detroit: Gale
Research Co., 1976. xiv, 357 p.

Books and journal articles are cited and annotated in this
bibliography geared to information trends and patterns the
manager must recognize. Coverage ranges to topics such as
organizational development and change, social awareness and

responsibility, development of creativity, and job satisfaction.
Journals in the field, indexing services, and organizations are
listed in separate chapters.

1735   Jones, Donald G.   A BIBLIOGRAPHY OF BUSINESS ETHICS, 1971–
1975. Charlottesville: University Press of Virginia, 1977. xx, 207 p.

Sponsored by the Center for Applied Ethics, and serving as
an update to the volume compiled by Daniel Gothie (no.
1733), the partially annotated bibliography covers the range
of business ethics from the private values of executives to
corporate social responsibility. Categories under which the
books and articles are organized are: functional areas of
management, such as employee relations, production, marketing, advertising, accounting, and research and development;
aspects of social responsibility including consumerism, government regulation, environment, energy, multinational corporations, safety and health, and minorities; ethical theory; and
religious perspectives.

2. Books and Articles

1736   Bauer, Raymond A., and Fenn, Dan H., Jr.   "What is a Corporate
Social Audit?"   HARVARD BUSINESS REVIEW 51 (January–February
1973): 37–48.

The social audit is defined as "commitment to systematic
assessment of and reporting on some meaningful, definable do-
main of a company's activities that have social impact."
The authors review the problems involved and areas to be
investigated in such a report, then they develop a viable
approach for a company's first social audit. It is recommended that the initial audit be designed to aid internal
decision making and to evaluate the company's existing social
programs.

1737   Baumhart, Raymond, S.J.   AN HONEST PROFIT: WHAT BUSINESS-
MEN SAY ABOUT ETHICS IN BUSINESS. New York: Holt, Rinehart
and Winston, 1968. xiv, 248 p.

A Jesuit business school dean with a graduate degree from
Harvard Business School examines responses from 1,800 businessmen concerning their attitudes toward ethics in business.
While a professional moralist, Baumhart draws conclusions,
synthesizes the data, and refrains from preaching. Reactions
to such aspects of business ethics as the image of the businessman, decision making, industry climate, customs, size of
organization, codes of ethics, and who should enforce a code
are discussed. The author finds church organizations to be

ineffective in providing guidance toward the development of professional ethics.

1738   Boulding, Kenneth E. THE ORGANIZATIONAL REVOLUTION: A STUDY IN THE ETHICS OF ECONOMIC ORGANIZATION. New York: Harper and Brothers, 1953. Reprint. Chicago: Quadrangle Books, 1968. 235 p. Illus.

The organizational revolution has affected the standards by which economic policy, institutions, and personal conduct are appraised. In part 1, Boulding analyzes the forces leading to and the consequences of the growth of economic organizations with emphasis on the ethical problems created by the movement. Part 2 provides case studies of labor, farm, business, and political organizations.

1739   Brown, William R., and Crable, Richard E. "Industry, Mass Magazines, and the Ecology Issue." QUARTERLY JOURNAL OF SPEECH 59 (October 1973): 259-72.

The public outcry of "corporate guilt" led industry to respond to socioecological issues with an advertising campaign that proclaimed innocence "retained" or "regained." Ads placed in mass-circulation magazines presented "argumentative frameworks" grounded in myths of the technological Prometheus and the American Adam. Persuasion was completed with claims of ecological pioneering and guilt-shifting. Extensive documentation.

1740   Buehler, Vernon M., and Shetty, Y.K. "Managerial Response to Social Responsibility Challenge." ACADEMY OF MANAGEMENT JOURNAL 19 (March 1976): 66-78.

Corporate actions with regard to social demands in urban, consumer, and environmental affairs are analyzed. The authors explore such variables as structural changes made by companies to integrate social concern; relationships between size, industry, profit, ownership, and social action; nature and extent of corporate activities; and problems encountered in implementing programs. It is determined that corporate response depends upon issues deemed relevant to its business and upon organizational structure.

1741   Chamberlain, Neil W. THE LIMITS OF CORPORATE RESPONSIBILITY. New York: Basic Books, 1973. v, 236 p.

Chamberlain's thesis is that individual large corporations can do "remarkably little" about social and environmental problems. While the aggregate power of big business is substantial, individual corporations are "trapped" in the business system of profit and autonomy. Specific problem areas are

examined: consumers, physical environment, and the
community. In each case, the amount of initiative
to be expected from corporations is explored.

1742   Cheit, Earl F., ed. THE BUSINESS ESTABLISHMENT. New York:
John Wiley and Sons, 1964. xi, 248 p. Illus.

Business is looked at from the perspectives of the humanities,
politics, and history. Contributors include Robert Heilbroner,
Henry Nash Smith, Richard Hofstadter, Paul Samuelson, and
Cheit. Their discussions cover changing ideologies in business, the role of the businessman, the decline in government
regulation, and personal and economic freedoms.

1743   Cohen, Jules. "Is Business Meeting the Challenge of Urban Affairs?"
HARVARD BUSINESS REVIEW 48 (March-April 1970): 68-82.

The programs of 247 major corporations developed in response
to urban problems are scrutinized. Cohen documents motivation factors, types of companies that are most active in
social affairs, types of activities, and the status of such programs in organizational hierarchy. The author finds that
company officers are now appraising their program rather than
spouting rhetoric. Optimism about the corporation's ability
to alleviate social ills has been seriously tempered.

1744   Committee for Economic Development. SOCIAL RESPONSIBILITIES OF
BUSINESS CORPORATIONS. New York: Committee for Economic Development, 1971. 74 p.

Dealing with the social rather than economic responsibilities
of business enterprises in contemporary America, the committee presents a policy statement aimed at the activities of
"large publicly-owned, professionally-managed corporations."
The statement primarily considers how the structure of business
organizations affects social responsiveness and accountability,
and the potential of business-government partnerships for
social progress. Managerial responsibility, public welfare
and profit, voluntary corporate activities and limitations on
such, evaluation of corporate performance, and government
incentives and controls are among the specific topics discussed.

1745   DeGeorge, Richard T., and Pichler, Joseph A., eds. ETHICS, FREE
ENTERPRISE, AND PUBLIC POLICY: ORIGINAL ESSAYS ON MORAL
ISSUES IN BUSINESS. New York: Oxford University Press, 1978.
x, 329 p.

The moral problems generated by advances in technology, the
complexity of economic systems, and the structure of large
organizations are the concerns of the contributors. General
introductions to the major questions of whether free enterprise

is compatible with social justice are followed by analyses of specific ethical issues in law, the public service sector, and advertising. The direction then turns to considerations of the moral balance of responsibility between individual and organization. Two final essays address resource depletion and our responsibility to future generations.

1746 Dierkes, Meinoff, and Bauer, Raymond A., eds. CORPORATE SOCIAL ACCOUNTING. New York: Praeger Publishers, 1973. xiii, 413 p. Graphs.

The state of the art of social accounting is presented in these papers originally prepared for a seminar sponsored by Battelle Memorial Institute. Relevant measurement techniques designed by social scientists and accounting procedures for corporate decision making are applied to issues such as consumer relations, quality of working life, work environment, community involvement, and impact of production methods on the physical environment. Corporate experiences are related to the social audit, and the role of the accountant in the process is stressed.

1747 Duncan, W. Jack. DECISION MAKING AND SOCIAL ISSUES: A GUIDE TO ADMINISTRATIVE ACTION IN AN ENVIRONMENTAL CONTEXT. Hinsdale, Ill.: Dryden Press, 1973. xvi, 176 p. Graphs.

A methodology for managerial decision making with regard to social issues is developed in this study designed as a supplement for undergraduate courses in policy, management, or business ethics. Duncan examines the factors affecting such decisions and determines their ability to be controlled. Chapters define problems such as technological change, social responsibility, environmental pollution, government, multinational practices, consumers, urban affairs, and support to higher education. Alternative courses of action are then presented with case studies of actual decision-making responses. Study questions and selected readings follow each chapter.

1748 Eilbert, Henry, and Parket, I. Robert. "The Current Status of Social Responsibility." BUSINESS HORIZONS 16 (August 1973): 5-14.

Responses from ninety-six large American corporations serve as the basis for this survey of the extent to which business invests in the improvement of the social and physical environment. The investigators look at organizational relationships between company size and activity, returns on social action, and reactions of stockholders. Designed to serve as a guide to management planning social programs.

1749 Ericson, Richard F. "Impact of Cybernetic Information Technology on

Management Value Systems." MANAGEMENT SCIENCE 16 (October 1969): B-40-B-60.

The potential impact of cybernetic information technology and holistic systems theory on management values, especially those related to environmental and societal concerns, are examined. Ericson reviews the historical schism between the "technological must" and the "ethical ought" in management and explains how advances in computer modeling make the effects of corporate value decisions on the ecosystem interface more comprehensible. Literature on value systems in management and cybernetic systems models is discussed. The utilization of knowledge in both areas will lead to greater potential for learning, abstraction, planning, and holistic integration, plus demands for responsibility and environmental sensitivity.

1750 ETHICS AND BUSINESS. University Park: Pennsylvania State University, 1962. 54 p.

Lectures by Kenneth E. Boulding, Carl Hermann Voss, and Walter A. Kaufmann were originally presented at a seminar. Boulding, an economist, discusses the interplay between value systems and larger social systems, then outlines specific ethical problems of a business society. Theologian Voss considers the ethical confusion created by American culture. He mentions several positive factors evident in business society and delineates the role of religion. Kaufmann, providing a philosopher's view, explains why philosophies "spurn" business society. The exception is utilitarianism, which was created in an attempt to develop an ethic appropriate to industrialization.

1751 Ewing, David W., ed. TECHNOLOGICAL CHANGE AND MANAGEMENT: THE JOHN DIEBOLD LECTURES 1968-1970. Boston: Graduate School of Business Administration, Harvard University, 1970. xi, 148 p. Illus.

The implications of technological change for management is the topic considered by the six corporation presidents or chairmen of the board participating in this lecture series. Two of the speakers discuss man's expanded alternatives resulting from technology and the limits placed by the refusal to relinquish traditional values. The social responsibilities of the large corporation are addressed in three lectures. Management is given the responsibilities of planning for the long-term future, alleviating social problems, and providing atmospheres for individual development. The role of the multinational corporation and its responsibilities in host countries is also outlined.

1752   Ford, Henry II. THE HUMAN ENVIRONMENT AND BUSINESS.
        New York: Weybright and Talley, 1970. 63 p.

> The texts of three of Ford's addresses to university audiences
> present the corporation president's views on the social respon-
> sibility of industrial enterprise. In the first talk, he reviews
> the options and the prospects for the young individual within
> a corporate system. The second and third speeches urge the
> use of the resources of private enterprise for the eradication
> of poverty, racial discrimination, and pollution of the envi-
> ronment. Throughout, he upholds a values system in which
> the profit motive is supreme and "enlightened corporate self-
> interest" will solve the problems.

1753   Garrett, Thomas M., S.J. AN INTRODUCTION TO SOME ETHICAL
        PROBLEMS OF MODERN AMERICAN ADVERTISING. Studia Socialia,
        no. 6. Rome: Gregorian University Press, 1961. 209 p. Bibliog.

> The intentions and effects of advertisers are considered in this
> study of ethical problems in consumer advertising. An analy-
> sis of the claims of the profession considers manipulation of
> values as well as declared goals of economic growth and
> raising the standard of living. Persuasive techniques are then
> scrutinized from the point of view of ethical principles. The
> potential of advertisers' influence over mass media is also in-
> vestigated. Extensive bibliography.

1754   Hay, Robert D.; Gray, Edmund R.; and Gates, James E., eds.
        BUSINESS AND SOCIETY; CASES AND TEXT. Cincinnati: South-
        Western Publishing Co., 1976. v, 386 p.

> Sponsored by the Southern Case Research Association, the
> volume of case studies illustrates the problems and responsibili-
> ties of business organizations toward society. It is designed
> for college students as well as corporate managers. Actions
> or situations involving actual companies are utilized through-
> out. Cases introducing the concept of social responsibility
> are followed by those involving pollution problems, minority
> groups and poverty, and consumerism. Among the situations
> cited are the Ford engine and the Environmental Protection
> Agency, Coca-Cola and migrant workers, Dow Chemical and
> napalm, ARMCO Steel and the disposal of dangerous effluent,
> and IBM and Bedford-Stuyvesant.

1755   Heilbroner, Robert L., et al. IN THE NAME OF PROFIT. Garden
        City, N.Y.: Doubleday, 1972. xi, 273 p.

> Six newspaper reporters present profiles of cases of corporate
> irresponsibility by keying on the executive's decision-making
> process, his values, and actions. A lengthy essay by
> Heilbroner follows in which he outlines the economic back-

ground and explores ways of making corporations more accountable to society. The case studies, in which specific corporations and executives are named, deal with defective brakes, school buses, marketing of a dangerous drug, napalm, an oil tank farm, and mergers. The overall impression is that atrocities are normal operations of the profit motive.

1756 Heilbroner, Robert L., and London, Paul, eds. CORPORATE SOCIAL POLICY: SELECTIONS FROM BUSINESS AND SOCIETY REVIEW. Reading, Mass.: Addison-Wesley, 1975. 347 p. Illus.

The many essays in this anthology explore social responsibility, the impact of multinational business, and the future of capitalism. Specific issues include environmental protection, television advertising, discrimination, work environment, and the social audit.

1757 "Is Corporate Social Responsibility a Dead Issue?" BUSINESS AND SOCIETY REVIEW, no. 25, Spring 1978, pp. 4-20.

A group of corporate executives and business experts respond to questions regarding the need for social responsibility in corporations, the present status of the issue, and means of controlling corporate activities. Participants include Henry Ford II, Phillip T. Drothing, Juanita M. Kreps, John D. deButts, Zoltan Merszei, Edward G. Harness, John C. Biegler, Larry Kitchen, Lewis H. Young, Noam Chomsky, E.R. Kane, and A.A. Sommer, Jr.

1758 Jacoby, Neil H. CORPORATE POWER AND SOCIAL RESPONSIBILITY. New York: Macmillan, 1973. 283 p.

Directed toward policymaking, Jacoby's comprehensive social assessment of the American business corporation evaluates economic, social, and political performance. The author's "social responsibility model" recognizes concern for costs to society of productive activities as well as the necessity of encouraging government policies. Corporate social roles in relation to the environment, military arms, and multinational corporations in foreign countries are considered along with the effects of management, the trend toward conglomerates, and the future of corporate business. Proposals for reform are outlined.

1759 LaCroix, W.L. PRINCIPLES FOR ETHICS IN BUSINESS. 1976. Rev. ed. Washington, D.C.: University Press of America, 1979. iv, 142 p.

A philosopher with religious affiliations treats the ethical principles which are specific to business. He finds a dual

structure: moral rules for organizational operations and codes
of conduct for relations with society. Emphasis is placed on
the values "supported or harmed" by both ethical systems.
Chapters are devoted to the ethical heritage of American
business, distributive justice, the culture of business, competition, power, social responsibility, the role of management
in ethical behavior, and advertising.

1760   McKie, James W., ed. SOCIAL RESPONSIBILITY AND THE BUSI-
NESS PREDICAMENT. Washington, D.C.: Brookings Institution,
1974. xiii, 361 p.

A panel composed primarily of economists examines the social
responsibilities of business, attempts to determine what demands are workable, and makes recommendations on what
responsibilities business can assume. General discussions are
followed by considerations of regulation, the consumer, pollution, cities, regional development, employees, and multinational operations. A consensus emerges that business will
not move from its economic role unless adequately enticed
or coerced. Governmental action seems to be the most
viable mode of change.

1761   Madden, Carl H. CLASH OF CULTURE: MANAGEMENT IN AN
AGE OF CHANGING VALUES. National Planning Association Report,
no. 133. Washington, D.C.: National Planning Association, 1972.
ix, 120 p. Bibliog.

Knowledge brought by science has led to a powerful concern,
in the 1970s, about quality of life. Changing values and
national priorities will interact with technological advances
to reshape the business climate. Business procedures and
activities accepted since the advent of industrialization will
be forced to change and major opportunities will emerge.
Madden considers the redefinition of wealth and economic
welfare, "environmental full-costing," technology assessment,
urbanization, planning and policymaking, life-style changes,
and alternative futures for the United States.

1762   Miller, Arthur Selwyn. "Business Morality: Some Unanswered (and
Perhaps Unanswerable) Questions." ANNALS OF THE AMERICAN
ACADEMY OF POLITICAL AND SOCIAL SCIENCE 363 (January 1966):
95-101.

Ethical standards for the businessman must be based on the
nature of corporations rather than on individualistic behavior.
Questions of business morality cannot be answered until an
adequate political-economic theory of the corporation is developed. Corporate managers, like national leaders, must
balance the competing interests of several publics.

1763 _____, ed. "The Ethics of Business Enterprise." ANNALS OF THE AMERICAN ACADEMY OF POLITICAL AND SOCIAL SCIENCE 343 (September 1962): iii, 1-141.

The social obligations of large corporations are scrutinized by lawyers, economists, political scientists, philosophers, a journalist, and a foundation director. The focus is on the relationships that industrial giants have with other segments of the nation. Management, economic dominance, the local community, and the Business Ethics Advisory Council are subjects of articles.

1764 Scott, William G. "Technology and Organizational Government: A Speculative Inquiry into the Functionality of Management Creeds." ACADEMY OF MANAGEMENT JOURNAL 11 (September 1968): 301-13.

Industrial humanism is the management value system now in ascendancy. It asserts a sharing of power and a belief that self-determinism is fostered by a democratic environment. The application of industrial humanism has been influenced by technology. The importance of technicians in organizations is recognized by this management philosophy, and those in power have applied the techniques of behavioral science to individual governance. A consolidation of power in the technical elite has resulted despite the democratic roots of the value system.

1765 Sethi, S. Prakash. UP AGAINST THE CORPORATE WALL: MODERN CORPORATIONS AND SOCIAL ISSUES OF THE SEVENTIES. Englewood Cliffs, N.J.: Prentice-Hall, 1971. xv, 431 p.

Case studies are used to expose students to the issues surrounding the growing demand for social responsibility in corporate activity and to the "complexity of motives" of the constituents involved. The specific cases are divided into chapters which consider the role of business in the following areas: quality of life, social and economic needs of ethnic minorities, the individual, communities, media, and government. Illustrative cases include Pacific Power and Electric Company's attempt to construct a nuclear power plant, General Motors and industrial privacy, Bethlehem Steel's attempts to control an employee's political activities, Dow Chemical and napalm, and Coca Cola and the Middle East crisis.

1766 Walton, Clarence C., ed. THE ETHICS OF CORPORATE CONDUCT. Englewood Cliffs, N.J.: Prentice-Hall, 1977. viii, 216 p.

The changes in ethical outlook and corporate behavior in this century are traced. Shifts in ideologies have made it necessary for large corporations to consider the social consequences

of their activities. The essays explore the forces which influence ethical behavior, implications for management in
value changes, ethics in law and accounting, corporate communications, and the role of the top executive as ethical
leader.

E. BIOMEDICAL ETHICS

1. General

a. BIBLIOGRAPHY

1767   Sollitto, Sharmon, and Veatch, Robert M., comps. BIBLIOGRAPHY
OF SOCIETY, ETHICS AND THE LIFE SCIENCES 1979-80. Hastings-
on-Hudson, N.Y.: Institute of Society, Ethics and the Life Sciences,
1978. 87 p.

Although this selective, partially annotated bibliography on
biomedical ethics is revised every year, each new edition retains classic or substantial works in the field. Subject divisions in the 1979-80 edition include survey works and bibliographies, ethical theory, history of medical ethics, medical
ethics education, technology and values, behavior control,
death and dying, experimentation with humans, genetics and
fertilization, health-care delivery, population control, transplantation and scarce resources, and confidentiality.

1768   Taviss, Irene, and Koivumaki, Judith. IMPLICATIONS OF BIOMEDI-
CAL TECHNOLOGY. Research Review no. 1. Cambridge, Mass.:
Harvard University Program on Technology and Society, 1968. 53 p.

Limited to literature published only between 1966 and 1968,
this research guide covers social, political, ethical, and
legal implications of the emerging biomedical technologies.
Policy studies are followed by considerations of specific technologies: genetic and behavior control, transplants and artificial organs, drugs, and human experimentation. Highly
selective with lengthy abstracts.

1769   Walters, LeRoy, ed. BIBLIOGRAPHY OF BIOETHICS. Detroit: Gale
Research Co., 1975-- . Annual.

Literature which considers value questions related to biomedical
and behavioral fields is cited in this comprehensive annual
bibliography. Publications in the field cross disciplines including medicine, biology, philosophy, psychology, sociology,
law, history, and religion. Major topics are: bioethics,
health care, contraception, abortion, population, reproductive
technologies, genetic engineering, sociobiology, mental health,

human experimentation, organ transplantation, and death and
dying. Compilers examine over fifty indexing services, three
computerized data banks, and over seventy journals. The
most comprehensive research tool in the field.

b. BOOKS AND ARTICLES

1770   Babbie, Earl R. SCIENCE AND MORALITY IN MEDICINE: A SURVEY
OF MEDICAL EDUCATORS. Berkeley and Los Angeles: University of
California Press, 1970. xviii, 261 p. Bibliog.

The results of a survey to examine the impact of increased
emphasis on science and technology on humane patient care
are analyzed by a sociologist. Social and philosophical perspectives are found to be more influential in the shaping of
medical morality than professional orientations toward research,
experimentation, and the utilization of new technologies.
The survey questionnaire and a "biography" of the project are
included.

1771   Barber, Bernard, ed. "Medical Ethics and Social Change." ANNALS
OF THE AMERICAN ACADEMY OF POLITICAL AND SOCIAL SCIENCE
437 (May 1978): 1-201.

Accelerating social and scientific changes are causing simi-
larly rapid changes in the field of medical ethics. Editor
Barber opens with a description of the "causes, agents, modes,
resistance to, and social costs of the present transformations."
Following are papers on specialized topics in biomedical
ethics, such as human experimentation, law, informed consent,
history and professionalism, health-care delivery, education
for research, physicians, definition of death, and abortion.

1772   Beauchamp, Tom L., and Walters, LeRoy, eds. CONTEMPORARY
ISSUES IN BIOETHICS. Belmont, Calif.: Wadsworth Publishing Co.,
1978. 612 p. Bibliog.

Designed as a systematic overview of the ethical issues raised
by technical developments in biomedicine, the anthology contains eighty-seven essays chosen for their clarity of ethical
reflection, teachability, and significance in the bioethical
controversies. Essays are arranged so that divergent viewpoints are juxtaposed. Chapters consider ethical theory,
concepts of health and disease, patients' rights, abortion,
determination of death, euthanasia, allocation of scarce resources, experimentation with human subjects, behavior control, and genetic engineering.

1773   Cutler, Donald R., ed. UPDATING LIFE AND DEATH: ESSAYS IN
ETHICS AND MEDICINE. Boston: Beacon Press, 1968. xii, 286 p.

The conflict of values and the levels of inquiry germane to biomedical ethics are explored. An emphasis is placed on the interaction between technology, professionalism, mythology, cultural images and values when medical decisions are made. Organ transplantation, abortion, population, and experimentation on humans serve as the context of values discussions by Joseph Fletcher, Paul Ramsey, Ralph B. Potter, Daniel Callahan, and others. A final essay by Frederick Elder questions how values should evolve and argues that they should be grounded in ecological, biological, and anthropocentric factors.

1774   Ellison, Craig W., ed. MODIFYING MAN: IMPLICATIONS AND ETHICS. Washington, D.C.: University Press of America, 1977. 294 p.

The conflict of values and the levels of inquiry germane to

Papers from the International Conference on Human Engineering and the Future of Man offer Christian views of the issues raised by biomedical technologies. Philosophical and theological perspectives on human engineering lead into discussions of values related to genetic engineering, brain control through electro-chemical intervention, behavior control, and public policy.

1775   Ellison, David L. THE BIO-MEDICAL FIX: HUMAN DIMENSIONS OF BIOMEDICAL TECHNOLOGIES. Westport, Conn.: Greenwood Press, 1978. xiii, 171 p. Bibliog.

The impact of biomedical technologies on patients, health-care providers, engineers, and technicians is explored through the examples of computer diagnosis, genetic engineering, and the artificial kidney. Explanations of the technologies involved are followed by discussions of the problems for patients, care-givers, and for the community.

1776   ENCYCLOPEDIA OF BIOETHICS. Edited by Warren T. Reich. 4 vols. New York: Free Press, 1978. 1,933 p. Bibliog.

The 300 articles in this approximately 2,000-page work discuss the issues, concepts, and principles related to biomedical ethics. Articles are arranged alphabetically from "Abortion" to "Zygote Banking," and each includes an extensive bibliography. Contributors represent the following fields: biomedical sciences, philosophical ethics, health professions, religion, law, anthropology, sociology, and psychology.

1777   Frazier, Claude A., ed. IS IT MORAL TO MODIFY MAN? Springfield, Ill.: Charles C Thomas, 1973. xxii, 332 p.

The contributors to this volume reflect on the options and

issues raised by biomedical technologies. Ethical and policy
considerations of psychotherapy, population, contraception,
behavior modification, drugs, death, organ transplants,
genetic manipulation, and sports medicine are explored.
Prominent contributors include Christiaan Barnard and Amitai
Etzioni.

1778 Goodfield, [G.] June. PLAYING GOD: GENETIC ENGINEERING
AND THE MANIPULATION OF LIFE. New York: Random House,
1977. xiii, 218 p.

Written to inform those who may be decision makers in the
development of policy related to the science of recombinant
DNA, Goodfield's study deals with the technology as it
bears on its wider social context. She relates the "professional and humane concerns" of participants in the issues.
Two sections, "The Science and the Scientists" and "The
Scientists and Society," complement each other. The process
of the development of regulations governing research is the
primary focus.

1779 Gustafson, James M. "Basic Issues in the Biomedical Fields."
SOUNDINGS 52 (Summer 1970): 151-80.

Major moral issues created by technological developments in
biomedicine are distinguished and methods of dealing with
them are suggested. The author delineates the following ethical issues: opposing outlooks toward the future generated by
scientific advances, the neutrality of biomedical research and
the bounds of such neutrality, the possibility of intrinsic
morality in actions, the application of general moral principles
to scientific research, and the choice between an ethic based
on rights of individuals and one based on benefits for society.

1780 Humber, James M., and Almeder, Robert F., eds. BIOMEDICAL
ETHICS AND THE LAW. New York: Plenum Press, 1976. xi,
541 p. Bibliog.

The moral, legal, philosophical, and theological implications
of advances in biomedical technologies are represented in
essays grouped around five issues: abortion, mental illness,
human experimentation, genetics, and dying. Each concern
receives attention from established scholars in various disciplines, including Thomas Szasz, David Bazelon, Leon Kass,
Leon Eisenberg, Daniel Callahan, and Robert Morison.

1781 Kass, Leon R. "The New Biology: What Price Relieving Man's Estate?"
SCIENCE 174 (19 November 1971): 779-88.

The manipulation of human bodies and minds possible with
advances in biomedical technology will have profound social

consequences. A full understanding of the technology demands exploration of ends, values, and standards. Kass briefly surveys technologies which aim to control death and life, human potentialities, and human achievement. He then turns to an examination of the basic ethical and social problems: questions of distributive justice, use and abuse of power, self-degradation and dehumanization, and fundamental concepts of the nature of man and the good community.

1782   Lukasiewicz, Julius, ed. "Potential Advances in Man." IMPACT OF SCIENCE ON SOCIETY 20 (October-December 1970): 249-361.

Man's biological development through science and technology is explored. Contributors consider the potentials of control of the reproductive process, genetic engineering, organ transplantation, the prolongation of life, chemical brain manipulation, bioengineering, and robotics. Prospects, problems, impacts on society, and ethics are aspects of the discussions.

1783   "The Medical, Moral, and Legal Implication of Recent Medical Advances; a Symposium." VILLANOVA LAW REVIEW 13 (Summer 1968): 732-92.

The challenges to traditional concepts of life, death, and medical ethics posed by biomedical technologies are approached by doctors, philosophers, theologians, judges, lawyers, law professors, and students. J. Russell Elkinton, Thomas A. Wassmer, and Ralph B. Potter consider the use of machines to prevent biological death. Emile Zola Berman looks at the legal problems of organ transplantation. A perspective for considering ethical and legal problems in this area is offered by William Likoff.

1784   Mendelsohn, Everett; Swazey, Judith P.; and Taviss, Irene, eds. HUMAN ASPECTS OF BIOMEDICAL INNOVATION. Cambridge, Mass.: Harvard University Press, 1971. x, 234 p.

Eight articles deal with social control of biomedical technologies and the problems of organization of health-care delivery as a result of technological change. Three sections consider the additional need of social guidance in professional decisions, ethical issues related to human experimentation, and the problems for social and professional decision making arising from new technologies.

1785   Potter, Van Rensselaer. BIOETHICS: BRIDGE TO THE FUTURE. Englewood Cliffs, N.J.: Prentice-Hall, 1971. xvii, 205 p. Illus.

With a conviction that biological facts and ethical values must together generate action, Potter merges contemporary thought on aspects of bioethics. Themes which unify the volume are the concept of dangerous knowledge, order and disorder, progress and survival, the future, control of technology, and the need for interdisciplinary effort.

1786   Ramsey, Paul. THE PATIENT AS PERSON: EXPLORATIONS IN MEDICAL ETHICS. New Haven, Conn.: Yale University Press, 1970. xxii, 283 p.

The meaning of "care" and the "sanctity of human life" are explored from the point of view of a "Christian ethicist." The author does not expect "solutions" to specific cases involving medical ethics; instead, he calls for prolonged, competent reflection on moral dilemmas. Problems considered are consent to experimentation on children, procedures for declaring death, care of the dying, transplants, and the distribution of scarce medical resources.

1787   Reiser, Stanley Joel; Dyck, Arthur J.; and Curran, William J., eds. ETHICS IN MEDICINE: HISTORICAL PERSPECTIVES AND CONTEMPORARY CONCERNS. Cambridge: M.I.T. Press, 1977. xiii, 679 p.

With selections ranging from the Hippocratic oath to the mid-1970s, this anthology aims to encourage and nourish, through discourse and investigation, humane impulses within the practice of medicine. The readings are from works in philosophy, religion, history, political science, law, medicine, and biology. They are arranged in topical sections: ethical dimensions of the physician-patient relationship; moral bases of medical ethics; regulation, compulsion, and consumer protection in public health; human experimentation; procreative decisions; dying; and the provision of medical care. Each section is followed by illustrative case studies.

1788   Restak, Richard M. PRE-MEDITATED MAN: BIOETHICS AND THE CONTROL OF FUTURE HUMAN LIFE. New York: Viking Press, 1975. xviii, 202 p.

Questions regarding the human consequences of biomedical technology involve power: In what direction are advances headed and who is in charge? Restak contends that the control and regulation of the field must ultimately rest with nonscientists and "non-experts." The social nature of biotechnics must be realized. Issues such as psychosurgery, behavior control, genetic engineering, and the use of misinformation about sickle-cell anemia and XYY chromosome configuration for prejudice and exploitation are reviewed. A broad-based, participatory, and humanistic bioethics is necessary.

1789   Shannon, Thomas A., ed. BIOETHICS: BASIC WRITINGS ON THE

KEY ETHICAL QUESTIONS THAT SURROUND THE MAJOR MODERN
BIOLOGICAL POSSIBILITIES AND PROBLEMS. New York: Paulist
Press, 1976. x, 513 p.

This reader presents significant articles which state specific
arguments or positions in problem areas in bioethics. Among
standard topics given critical and informative analyses are
abortion, death and dying, research and human experimentation, genetic engineering and policy, allocation of scarce
resources, and behavior modification. A fine selection of
basic readings in the field with now classic contributions
from John Fletcher, Daniel Callahan, James Gustafson, Leon
Kass, Robert Veatch, Hans Jonas, LeRoy Walters, Mark Lappé,
and James Childress.

1790   Smith, Harmon L. ETHICS AND THE NEW MEDICINE. Nashville,
        Tenn.: Abingdon Press, 1970. 174 p.

As a theological ethicist, Smith critically reflects on the
human values inherent in medical decisions within the context
of our Judeo-Christian culture. The ethicist's responsibility
is not to provide answers but to "help clarify and focus
appropriate issues" and to "participate in the adjudication of
alternative choices." Moral considerations in the following
medical issues are discussed: abortion, artificial insemination,
organ transplantation, death and dying, and genetic manipulation.

1791   Spicker, Stuart F., and Engelhardt, H. Tristram, Jr., eds. PHILO-
        SOPHICAL MEDICAL ETHICS: ITS NATURE AND SIGNIFICANCE:
        PROCEEDINGS OF THE THIRD TRANS-DISCIPLINARY SYMPOSIUM
        ON PHILOSOPHY AND MEDICINE HELD AT FARMINGTON, CON-
        NECTICUT, DECEMBER 11-13, 1975. Boston: D. Reidel Publishing
        Co., 1977. 252 p. Bibliog.

Basic ethical premises which are the foundation of eventual
policy are analyzed. Historical and philosophical studies of
medical ethics are joined by considerations of ethical questions implicit in euthanasia and experimentation on humans.
Explorations of the patient and the physician as moral agents
conclude the volume.

1792   Szasz, Thomas [S.] THE THEOLOGY OF MEDICINE: THE POLITICAL-
        PHILOSOPHICAL FOUNDATIONS OF MEDICAL ETHICS. New York:
        Harper Colophon Books, 1977. xxii, 170 p.

The ceremonial, magical, and religious aspects of various
medical procedures are explored in these essays. Szasz finds
that suffering is often used as the excuse for the deprivation
of freedom. Such acts are masked with language such as
"hospitalization," "therapeutic intervention," and "treatment."

He considers behavior therapy addiction, psychiatric intervention, medicine and state, illness and indignity, suicide, and
involuntary brain manipulation.

1793   "Values, Expertise and Responsibility in the Life Sciences." HASTINGS
CENTER STUDIES 1, no. 2 (1973): 1-92.

The debate over the role of the scientific expert in questions
of values is the subject of this special issue. Robert Veatch
and Roy Branson call for a separation of values issues from
the professional role; while Miriam Siegler, Humphry Osmond,
and Eric Cassell feel establishing limits on the physician's
responsibility is impossible. Marc Lappé provides a case
study of the values responsibilities held by genetic counselors.
The issue closes with reflections by June Goodfield on efforts
to integrate values in codes of medical ethics.

1794   Vaux, Kenneth. BIOMEDICAL ETHICS: MORALITY FOR THE NEW
MEDICINE. New York: Harper and Row, 1974. xviii, 134 p.

Ethical choices in biomedicine are affected by the interplay
of technological advances and human nature. Moral decisions
are clouded by the concept of man as machine--seen as the
"prevailing perception of our time." Vaux's contemporary
frame of reference evolves from a synthesis of traditional
humanistic ethical traditions with consequential insight, that
is, the ability to predict what will happen before something
is done. Technical know-how and moral conscience must be
joined. Biomedical topics are explored in which technology
has necessitated imperative decisions and planning, i.e.,
genetics, transplants, behavior control, and cryogenics.

1795   Veatch, Robert M. CASE STUDIES IN MEDICAL ETHICS. Cambridge,
Mass.: Harvard University Press, 1977. vii, 421 p. Bibliog.

Designed for a teaching program, over one hundred case
studies are presented. Veatch pinpoints crucial issues in
each case, then provides commentaries by others and opposing
views. Problems in medical ethics considered include genetics,
abortion, contraception, birth, transplants, behavior control,
experimentation on humans, and death and dying. Most of
the cases are based on actual experiences except the few
dealing with future concerns such as cloning. Existing codes
of medical ethics and guidelines for human experimentation
are appended. The bibliography is extensive.

1796   _____. VALUE-FREEDOM IN SCIENCE AND TECHNOLOGY: A
STUDY OF THE IMPORTANCE OF THE RELIGIOUS, ETHICAL, AND
OTHER SOCIO-CULTURAL FACTORS IN SELECTED MEDICAL DECI-
SIONS REGARDING BIRTH CONTROL. Missoula, Mont.: Scholars
Press, 1976. xii, 314 p. Bibliog.

In his slightly revised dissertation, Veatch explores the debate surrounding the integration of science and values. He looks at the present discussions of value-free science, attempts a construction of the relation of values to scientific and technological enterprise, and argues that a dichotomy of science and values can proceed only so far before inconsistency and philosophical implausibility result. Part 2 is a case study of the role of values in decisions regarding oral contraception.

1797   Veatch, Robert M., and Branson, Roy, eds. ETHICS AND HEALTH POLICY. Cambridge, Mass.: Ballinger Publishing Co., 1976. xx, 332 p.

The collection serves as a source for explorations of the "ethical problems of health-policy planning and health-care delivery." The editors note that concern has shifted recently from the physician-patient relationship to social and political considerations of priority and distribution of health-care services. Part 1 looks at fundamental ethical conflicts in health-care delivery, specifically related to distributive justice and use of computers. Part 2 presents views on the allocation of scarce medical resources with a focus on the artificial heart. In the final part, health policy planning is examined by discussions of community participation in health-care decisions, and the assessment of genetic technologies.

1798   Wertz, Richard W., ed. READINGS ON ETHICAL AND SOCIAL ISSUES IN BIOMEDICINE. Englewood Cliffs, N.J.: Prentice-Hall, 1973. vii, 306 p. Bibliog.

Significant, previously published comments by philosophers, social scientists, lawyers, historians, and physicians on the implications of advances in biomedicine compose this anthology. Papers are grouped under six topics: experimentation with human subjects; biological engineering; death, transplantation, and resource allocation; behavior control, mental illness, and commitment; women and medicine; and health-care delivery. Specific considerations include biofeedback in technological society, the obsolescent mother, and landmark papers by Leon Kass on the new biology, Robert Morison on death, and James Childress on choosing who shall live.

1799   Williams, Preston N., ed. ETHICAL ISSUES IN BIOLOGY AND MEDICINE: PROCEEDINGS OF A SYMPOSIUM ON THE IDENTITY OF MAN. Cambridge, Mass.: Schenkman Publishing Co., 1973. vii, 296 p.

The questions of the identity and dignity of man raised by advances in biotechnologies are considered in these conference papers, panels, and workshops. The three main themes are: population control and regulation of behavior, organ transplants, and the risks and rewards of genetic manipulation. Participants are life scientists, physicians, theologians, and ethicists. The isolated thought patterns and stereotyped images of the professionals are revealed; however, diversity results in in-depth considerations of the issues.

1800 Wojcik, Jan. MUTED CONSENT: A CASEBOOK IN MODERN MEDICAL ETHICS. West Lafayette, Ind.: Purdue University, 1978. ix, 164 p.

Case studies and reviews of the most significant thinking about bioethics explore the dilemmas that arise in biomedical research and practice. The seven areas considered are: experimentation with human subjects; genetic counseling and screening; abortion; behavior modification with drugs, surgery, and psychology; death and dying; allocation of medical resources; and genetic engineering. Extensive documentation.

2. Selected Issues

a. EXPERIMENTATION WITH HUMAN SUBJECTS

1801 Barber, Bernard; Lally, John J.; Makarushka, Julia Loughlin; and Sullivan, Daniel. RESEARCH ON HUMAN SUBJECTS: PROBLEMS OF SOCIAL CONTROL IN MEDICAL EXPERIMENTATION. New York: Russell Sage Foundation, 1973. 263 p.

The results of two studies of biomedical researchers and their organizations are reported and analyzed herein. Expressed ethical standards and actual behavioral practices regarding informed voluntary consent and the balance between risk and benefit are scrutinized. The variables which contribute to value development and behavior in regard to these researchers are the major focus of the work. Distinctions in socially structured situations, social control networks, and the effectiveness of the peer review committee of the National Institutes of Health are the most significant variables.

1802 Beecher, Henry K. RESEARCH AND THE INDIVIDUAL, HUMAN STUDIES. Boston: Little, Brown and Co., 1970. xvii, 398 p. Bibliog.

The advances in science and technology which have been accompanied by the broad development of experimentation on human subjects necessitates a delineation of the possibilities and the limitations in the context of the ethical issues. Beecher provides an extensive guide to the literature in the field of human experimentation laced with wisdom from his own research and membership on various committees charged with overseeing medical procedures, technologies, and research. Aspects of the subject covered are: the investigator, ethical problems in experimentation and transplantation, and the legal questions. An extensive compilation of codes of medical ethics appears as an appendix.

1803 Freund, Paul A., ed. EXPERIMENTATION WITH HUMAN SUBJECTS. New York: George Braziller, 1970. xviii, 470 p. Also available as "Ethical Aspects of Experimentation with Human Subjects," DAEDALUS 98 (Spring 1969): 219-597.

Resulting from a continuing seminar sponsored by the American Academy of Arts and Sciences, the essays in this anthology consider the ethical, scientific, social, political, and legal implications of medical experimentation with human subjects. Contributors from fields of law, philosophy, anthropology, psychology, and medicine include Jay Katz, Margaret Mead, Louis Lasagna, William J. Curran, and Louis L. Jaffe.

1804 Ladimer, Irving, and Newman, Roger W., eds. CLINICAL INVESTIGATION IN MEDICINE: LEGAL, ETHICAL AND MORAL ASPECTS, AN ANTHOLOGY AND BIBLIOGRAPHY. Boston: Law-Medicine Research Institute, Boston University, 1963. 517 p. Bibliog.

A pioneer compilation of literature on legal, philosophical, and ethical aspects of medical research, the survey presents a reference volume of over seventy essays and articles as well as a comprehensive bibliography of over 500 items. Selections relate to historical and ethical perspectives on medical research on human subjects, codes and principles of conduct, legal analysis, religious and moral commentary, drug therapy, design and technique of research, and the research subjects themselves (patients, prisoners, children, military personnel, and "normal" volunteers).

1805 Martin, Michael M. "Ethical Standards for Fetal Experimentation." FORDHAM LAW REVIEW 43 (March 1975): 547-70.

The regulations for experimentation with human fetuses as developed by the National Commission for the Protection of Human Subjects in Biomedical and Behavioral Research are found to "not fully achieve their ethical objective." Martin reviews the regulations, discusses the consequences of experimentation in terms of health and human dignity, and isolates factors which affect the valuation of experimentation. Finally, he explains that the regulations distinguish between "abortuses and conceptuses" in that an individual is judged "less human" when the time of death is known.

1806 "Selected Issues in Medical Ethics." JOURNAL OF RELIGIOUS ETHICS 2 (Spring 1974): 11-98.

Five articles focus on ethical decisions related to experimentation on the fetus. Ronald Green and James Childress consider conferred rights and the fetus. LeRoy Walters provides an overview of the arguments employed in existing policymaking documents and identifies "fundamental presuppositions" supporting policy positions. The two additional articles consider equal access to health care and attitudes toward pain and suffering.

1807 "Symposium on Medical Experimentation on Human Subjects." CASE WESTERN RESERVE LAW REVIEW 25 (Spring 1975): 431-648.

Contributors examine the policymaking process relating to decisions of informed consent, including examinations of peer review boards and compensation. There is also a study of the role of the law in matters involving psychosurgery. In a review of philosophical perspectives, Ruth Macklin and Susan Sherwin prefer John Rawls's theory of social justice as a guide to policy development for human experimentation.

1808 "A Symposium on the Report and Recommendations of the National Commission for the Protection of Human Subjects of Biomedical and Behavioral Research." VILLANOVA LAW REVIEW 22, no. 2 (1976-77): 297-417.

Articles review the commission regulations by examining the effect of the REPORT (no. 1810) on fetal research and by analyzing the deficiencies of the regulations. Dennis J. Horan presents his thoughts on a new category of human--the "nonviable fetus." A cost-benefit analysis of such research is presented by Juliana G. Pilon. The rights of the father and questions of personhood are debated by John P. Wilson.

1809 U.S. National Commission for the Protection of Human Subjects of Biomedical and Behavioral Research. THE BELMONT REPORT: ETHICAL PRINCIPLES AND GUIDELINES FOR THE PROTECTION OF HUMAN SUBJECTS OF RESEARCH. 3 vols. Washington, D.C.: 1978. Y3.H88:2B41.

Basic ethical principles and research guidelines are identified in this report and accompanying commissioned papers. The principles (not regulations) cover respect for persons, informed consent, assessment of risks and benefits, selecting subjects for research, and boundaries between research and practice. Twenty-six papers in the appendix volumes, written to assist the commission in its considerations, are by leaders in the field: Kurt Baier, Thomas Beauchamp, H. Tristram Engelhardt, LeRoy Walters, and Robert Veatch.

1810 _____. RESEARCH ON THE FETUS: REPORT AND RECOMMENDA-
TIONS AND APPENDIX. 2 vols. Washington, D.C.: 1975.
Y3.H88:2F43 and app.

The report volume presents analyses of the nature and extent
of fetal research, considerations of alternative means for
achieving the purposes of such research, overviews of legal
and ethical issues, views presented at public hearings, and
policy recommendations. Among the twenty-one commissioned
reports and papers in the appendix volume are ethical and
moral appraisals of fetal research, considerations of the legal
issues, assessments of viability and nonviability of the fetus,
and discussions of the role of research. The texts of codes
of ethics, as well as policies and procedures from the FED-
ERAL REGISTER, are provided.

1811 _____. SPECIAL STUDY: IMPLICATIONS OF ADVANCES IN BIO-
MEDICAL AND BEHAVIORAL RESEARCH. Washington, D.C.: 1978.
Y3.H88:2B52. 172 p. Bibliog.

The necessity of consideration for value conflicts and the
social context of biomedical research and technologies in
policy development is recognized and emphasized in this report. The document is primarily composed of the detailed
report, A COMPREHENSIVE STUDY OF THE ETHICAL,
LEGAL, AND SOCIAL IMPLICATIONS OF ADVANCES IN
BIOMEDICAL AND BEHAVIORAL RESEARCH AND TECHNOL-
OGY, prepared by Policy Research Incorporated and the
Center for Technology Assessment, New Jersey Institute of
Technology. The report outlines technical advances; discusses
the need for public understanding; evaluates policies for research, resource allocation, and public involvement; notes
the implementation roles of various departments; and presents
four policy "scenarios."

b. BRAIN MANIPULATION

1812 Black, Peter McL., and Szasz, Thomas S. "The Ethics of Psychosurgery: Pro and Con." HUMANIST 37 (July-August 1977): 6-10.

Black argues to remove the stigma of "political coercion and
mass manipulation" from psychosurgery. Following descriptions
of surgical techniques, he refutes leading arguments against
the procedures and outlines limited conditions under which
psychosurgery should be used. Szasz counters that Black con-
fuses "disease with deviance and cure with control." He
then emphasizes the importance of informed consent.

1813 "Ethical Problems of Brain Manipulation." DISSENT 20 (Summer 1973):
362-81.

The social and moral implications of the technologies of
psychosurgery and electrical stimulation of the brain are
explored in this edited transcript of the Conference on the
Physical Manipulation of the Brain held by the Institute of
Society, Ethics, and the Life Sciences in 1971. Topics include the moral dilemmas presented by these techniques and
the determination of procedures for responding to values
questions.

1814   Gaylin, Willard M.; Meister, Joel S.; and Neville, Robert C., eds.
OPERATING ON THE MIND: THE PSYCHOSURGERY CONFLICT.
New York: Basic Books, 1975. viii, 216 p.

Six essays assess the technology, moral questions, social impacts, and problems of policy and law related to psychosurgery. Authors represent the fields of psychiatry, neurol-
ogy, investigative journalism, philosophy, law, and sociology.
Explanation of techniques and history of utilization lead to
discussions of the Kaimowitz case, in which the implantation
of electrodes was proposed for a sexual psychopath, and
broader considerations of the use of psychosurgery for nontherapeutic purposes, that is, the protection of society. The
moral dilemma of the relationship between physical alteration
and modification of the person is addressed. The final two
essays turn to regulation, legal controls, and the need for
policy guidelines.

1815   Gilbert, Arthur N. "Pills and the Perfectibility of Man." VIRGINIA
QUARTERLY REVIEW 45 (Spring 1969): 315-28.

In a satirical tone, Gilbert considers the chemical solutions
to humanity's problems as expounded by Aldous Huxley and
Arthur Koestler. Huxley's pills promote self-transcendence,
"mystic enlightenment and artistic creativity," while Koestler's
pharmacology is designed to improve neurological harmony
among parts of the brain (no. 940). If such substances were
synthesized, the biggest problem would be mediating between
proponents of "Pop-Nirvana" and adherents of less exciting
mental integration.

1816   McGlothlin, William, ed. "Chemical Comforts of Man: The Future."
JOURNAL OF SOCIAL ISSUES 27, no. 3 (1971): 1-126.

The legal, moral, and social status of drug use in the future
has become a subject for speculation. In this special issue,
Michael P. Rosenthal ponders legal controls and Nathan S.
Kline predicts drugs of the future. Other authors speculate
on drug use in the United States of the future.

1817   "Symposium: Psychosurgery." BOSTON UNIVERSITY LAW REVIEW 54
(March 1974): 215-353.

The interdependence of scientific, legal, and ethical factors of psychosurgery are demonstrated. It is recognized that fragmentation of the issues results in distortion of the information upon which decisions are made. Surgeons and a psychologist review medical research. Legal and policy questions are approached in three articles by legislators and a government consultant. The remaining article presents a philosopher's perspective on psychosurgery and views of the scientific, clinical, and public communities.

1818   U.S. National Commission for the Protection of Human Subjects of Biomedical and Behavioral Research. PSYCHOSURGERY: REPORT AND RECOMMENDATIONS AND APPENDIX. 2 vols. Washington, D.C.: 1977. Y3.H88:2P95 and app. Bibliog.

Contained within the report are discussions of the issues surrounding psychosurgery, legal considerations, an overview of the studies prepared for the commission, review of public hearings, and recommendations for policy. The texts of three reports are provided in the appendix volume: "The Practice of Psychosurgery: A Survey of the Literature (1971–1976)," "Final Report on Psychosurgery Pilot Study," and "A Study of Cingulotomy in Man."

c. GENETIC ENGINEERING

1819   Curran, Charles E. "Moral Theology and Genetics." CROSS CURRENTS 20 (Winter 1970): 64–82.

Following an explanation of the techniques of eugenics, genetic engineering, and euphenics, Curran discusses "the problems genetic questions raise for moral theology or Christian ethics," and the ethical use of scientific power. Primary attention is on the proposals of Hermann J. Muller.

1820   Etzioni, Amitai. "Amniocentesis: A Case Study in the Management of 'Genetic Engineering.'" ETHICS IN SCIENCE AND MEDICINE 2, no. 1 (1975): 13–24.

An examination of amniocentesis, a procedure utilized to check the human fetus for genetic irregularities, demonstrates the complexity of the personal, social, legal, medical, and moral issues impinging on new biomedical technologies. Etzioni emphasizes that this technique can be used for therapeutic (the detection of genetic inadequacies) or potentially for eugenic purposes. Decision making on the utilization of the technique proceeds on two interrelated planes—one of medical research, and one of normative assessment and policymaking. Three areas of concern are approached: who should evaluate the technology, decision making on personal and societal levels, and the dissemination of information on the issues.

1821   _____. GENETIC FIX. New York: Macmillan, 1973. 276 p.

In a popular treatment of the implications of recent advances in biomedical technologies, Etzioni contemplates the research decisions which will have to be made in the near future. Organized around a conference held in Paris titled "Recent Progress in Biology and Medicine: Its Social and Ethical Implications," issues explored are in-vitro fertilization, selective breeding, genetic screening, informed consent, and the birth-control pill.

1822   Fletcher, Joseph. THE ETHICS OF GENETIC CONTROL: ENDING REPRODUCTIVE ROULETTE. Garden City, N.Y.: Anchor Books, 1974. xxi, 218 p.

The rapid development of genetic and reproductive technologies blurs the distinction between what is and what may be tomorrow. Since mores and values develop and change along with conditions, we are in a situation where there is little or no time for extended reflection or steady development of new values and ethical standards. Fletcher faces the new moral problems posed by modern biology and genetics and attempts to provide critical reflection and rational analysis about them. He boldly moves from what is to what ought to be. Notions of the desirability of both what is scientifically possible and of traditional morality are shattered.

1823   Frankel, Charles. "The Specter of Eugenics." COMMENTARY 57 (March 1974): 25-33.

The discoveries and techniques involved with biomedicine are important not only for their power to "re-engineer the human race" but also for the changes they have effected in our perspectives on "birth, maturing, aging, dying, sexuality, and the relations of parents to children." Unlike other technologies, biomedicine not only involves power over nature but experiments with human nature. Its effects are deliberate, not incidental or inadvertent, and are irreversible. Emotional responses to the issue can "impede efforts to deal. . .with prudent restraint."

1824   "Genetic Science and Man." THEOLOGICAL STUDIES 33 (September 1972): 399-552.

The desire to inform readers of the social impact of genetic technologies and ethical decisions guided the production of this special issue. A forum for views of theologians, philosophers, and scientists results. The essays present overviews of genetic science and technology, discussions of the technological imperative, changes in ethical issues surrounding parent-

child relations, and philosophical considerations of freedom.
Marc Lappé, Andrew L. Szebenyi, and John Fletcher are
among the contributors.

1825   Golding, Martin P.   "Ethical Issues in Biological Engineering."
UCLA LAW REVIEW 15 (February 1968): 443-79.

Ethical consideration of the utilization of biomedical technologies to deal with problems of genetic integrity and
population control are discussed. Golding turns first to general considerations about justifications for social programs and
various outlooks on our obligations to the future. He then
moves to specific considerations of programs of biological
engineering.

1826   Hamilton, Michael, ed.   THE NEW GENETICS AND THE FUTURE OF
MAN. Grand Rapids, Mich.: William B. Eerdmans, 1972. 242 p.

The papers of a symposium organized by the Washington
Cathedral, of which the author is canon, are presented herein. The documented essays contributed by theologians,
lawyers, and philosophers form a well-rounded attempt at
assessing the legal and ethical aspects of developing areas of
genetics, such as cloning, prenatal adoption and transplantation, and genetic engineering and therapy.

1827   Hardin, Garrett, ed.   POPULATION, EVOLUTION, AND BIRTH
CONTROL: A COLLAGE OF CONTROVERSIAL READINGS.   San
Francisco: W.H. Freeman and Co., 1969. xvi, 386 p.

One hundred and twenty-three excerpts from historical classics
which express views or present data related to population, its
effects and control, are reprinted herein. The range is from
Malthus's essay in 1798 to the late 1960s. Scientific,
economic, ecological, and medical studies are joined by
literature, poetry, and interviews.

1828   Hilton, Bruce, et al., eds.   ETHICAL ISSUES IN HUMAN GENETICS:
GENETIC COUNSELING AND THE USE OF GENETIC KNOWLEDGE.
New York: Plenum Press, 1973. xi, 455 p. Illus.

The proceedings of a symposium by the John E. Fogarty
International Center for Advanced Study in the Health Sciences and the Institute of Society, Ethics and the Life Sciences
consider the philosophical, legal, and sociological aspects of
genetic technology and research. The contributors, including
ethicists, lawyers, philosophers, theologians, and scientists,
address counseling practices and the patient, ethical views on
the significance of genetic disease in population groups, the
right to life and decision making, legal rights, sociological

and psychological factors, social and scientific priorities, and policymaking. An extensive glossary of terminology is appended.

1829 INDIANA LAW JOURNAL 48 (Summer 1973): 527-646.

Legal and moral issues related to advances in genetic technologies are explored in this special section. George H. Hudock opens with a thought-provoking article, "Gene Therapy and Genetic Engineering: Frankenstein Is Still a Myth, But It Should Be Read Periodically." Harold P. Green considers law and policy, while Alexander M. Capron views informed decision making. Theological reflection is provided by David H. Smith. The questions related to death are examined by Roger B. Dworkin.

1830 Karp, Laurence E. GENETIC ENGINEERING: THREAT OR PROMISE? Chicago: Nelson-Hall, 1976. 235 p. Illus., bibliog.

Karp presents the facts and principles of genetic engineering techniques and discusses their controversial medical, legal, and moral aspects. Among the techniques surveyed are genetic counseling, eugenics, euthenics, euphenics, screening and therapy, amniocentesis, artificial insemination, sex determination, ectogenesis, parthenogenesis, cloning, and the creation of life from nonliving matter. A glossary is appended.

1831 Kass, Leon R. "Making Babies--The New Biology and the 'Old' Morality." PUBLIC INTEREST 26 (Winter 1972): 18-56.

This thoughtful discussion of genetic engineering considers the moral and political questions involved in the new technologies. Kass provides extensive explorations of the implications of "in-vitro" (test-tube) fertilization and cloning. Ethical considerations include informed consent, the uses of surplus embryos, possibilities such as "womb-for-rent" and directed breeding programs, individuality, and identity. Other issues which must be approached include questions of power, the role of the family, dehumanization of human creation, and the dehumanization of the scientist.

1832 Morison, Robert S. "Reflections on Some Social Implications of Modern Biology." ZYGON 11 (June 1976): 96-114.

It is now recognized that science and technology have something to offer in the ethical decision-making process--to point out what is possible and to outline the consequences of actions. In regard to genetics, while science can evaluate the necessity for human variation and the disadvantage of

certain genetic irregularities, new technologies can correct
or prevent extreme variations.

1833 Muller, Hermann Joseph. MAN'S FUTURE BIRTHRIGHT: ESSAYS ON
SCIENCE AND HUMANITY. Edited by Elof Axel Carlson. Albany:
State University of New York Press, 1973. xxi, 164 p.

The foremost American spokesman for voluntary eugenics as
a means toward the betterment of the human species explores
the implications of scientific facts and his rationalist viewpoints. Understanding of the biological basis of certain
values is considered necessary to a successful program for
genetic upgrading of the species. Muller views science
fiction as an escape to a vision of a better world. The
dangers of radiation to genetic mutuation are detailed in an
early paper. The classic essay, "What Genetic Course Will
Man Steer?" (no. 1834) is among the selections.

1834 _____. "What Genetic Course Will Man Steer?" In PROCEEDINGS
OF THE THIRD INTERNATIONAL CONGRESS OF HUMAN GENETICS,
edited by James F. Crow and James V. Neel, pp. 521-43. Baltimore:
Johns Hopkins Press, 1967.

The present culture of densely populated cities and high technology threatens to cause genetic degeneration in the human
species. We protect mutations "detrimental to bodily vigor,
intelligence, or social predisposition." It is imperative that
we use all means at our disposal, including biomedical technologies and artificial insemination to intentionally advance
the genetic level of psychological traits such as cooperative-
ness, creativity, general intelligence, and social consciousness.

1835 National Symposium on Genetics and the Law, Boston 1975. GENET-
ICS AND THE LAW. Edited by Aubrey Milunsky and George J.
Annas. New York: Plenum Press, 1976. xii, 532 p. Bibliog.

Legal and ethical issues related to genetics are comprehensively examined. Topics analyzed are research on the fetus,
XYY genotype, genetic screening and counseling, artificial
insemination, sterilization of the mentally retarded, in-vitro
fertilization, and cloning. An extensive bibliography is
appended.

1836 Ramsey, Paul. FABRICATED MAN: THE ETHICS OF GENETIC CON-
TROL. New Haven, Conn.: Yale University Press, 1970. 174 p.

Ramsey discusses theological and philosophical considerations
of the genetic control of man's future. Concerns are grouped
around three topics: "Moral and religious implications of

genetic control," "Shall we clone a man?" and "Parenthood and the future of man by artificial donor insemination."

1837 Rogers, Michael. BIOHAZARD. New York: Alfred A. Knopf, 1977. 209 p.

Rogers presents a chronicle of the controversy surrounding recombinant DNA research. The confrontation between science, politics, technologies, and ethics is seen from the context of laboratories, to conferences such as those held at Asilomar, to public forums. While scientists themselves debate each other over the dilemma of research and public threat, the politics of science and technology is scrutinized.

1838 Shinn, Roger L. "Perilous Progress in Genetics." SOCIAL RESEARCH 41 (Spring 1974): 83-103.

Three methods of genetic manipulation are discussed: fetal diagnosis and selective abortion, selective breeding, and genetic engineering. The techniques are outlined, then the ethical, political, and theological implications are considered. Shinn relates conceptions of progress, and man's relationship to nature to values development in biomedicine.

1839 U.S. Congress. House. Committee on Science and Technology. GENETIC ENGINEERING, HUMAN GENETICS, AND CELL BIOLOGY: EVOLUTION OF TECHNOLOGICAL ISSUES. DNA RECOMBINANT MOLECULE RESEARCH (SUPPLEMENTAL REPORT II). 94th Cong., 2d sess. Committee Print. Washington, D.C.: 1976. Y4.Sci2:94-2/ KKK. 259 p. Illus., bibliog.

Congressional Research Service compilers present a case history study of the "problem of public participation in science policy and the legal, ethical, and moral implications of the expanded role of the public in planning and applying scientific research." A summary of the status of DNA recombinant molecule research is followed by a chronology of the issue in its societal context. Congressional, nongovernmental, and international reactions, such as those by the National Science Foundation, University of Michigan, Harvard University, city councils, and industry, are discussed. Appendixes include numerous important journal articles, FEDERAL REGISTER recombinant DNA guidelines, an environmental impact statement, and a selected bibliography.

1840 Vukavich, William T. "The Dawning of the Brave New World--Legal, Ethical and Social Issues of Genetics." UNIVERSITY OF ILLINOIS LAW FORUM, no. 2, 1971, pp. 189-231.

The legal, ethical, and social issues surrounding selective breeding programs and proposals are considered. A eugenics

program is advocated to maintain our quality of life and
thwart genetic deterioration. Following a review of modern
eugenic ideas, the author discusses the issues involved in the
planning and implementation of a voluntary program. Extensive documentation of cases and studies.

d. PROLONGATION OF LIFE BY TECHNOLOGICAL MEANS

1841   Bryant, Clifton D., and Srizek, William E. "The Iceman Cometh:
The Cryonics Movement and Frozen Immortality." SOCIETY 11
(November-December 1973): 56-61.

The publication of Robert Ettinger's THE PROSPECT OF IM-
MORTALITY (1962) stimulated the formation of numerous
cryonics societies, devoted to freezing the newly dead in the
hope of a medical cure and revivification in the future.
Bryant found that as costs of encapsulement have risen and
media coverage has become more critical, popular interest
has waned.

1842   Cassell, Eric J. "Dying in a Technological Society." HASTINGS
CENTER STUDIES 2 (May 1974): 31-36.

Dying has shifted from the moral to the technological order.
Death is less a family matter than an institutional concern.
Hospitals, with their focus on scientific knowledge and
mechanized systems, make little distinction between the
death of the body and the passing of a person. Mechanical
events, such as the turning off of respirators, claim more
attention than moral issues. The solution is increased understanding of the moral order, not a return to technological
innocence.

1843   "Facing Death." HASTINGS CENTER STUDIES 2, no. 2 (May 1974):
1-80.

The seven articles in this section place attitudes toward death
within a framework of changes in social belief and provide a
dialogue on "death with dignity." Eric Cassell discusses the
shift of dying from moral to technological spheres, and David
Smith delineates bases for decisions on allowing newborns to
die. Paul Ramsey attempts to rescue the phrase "death with
dignity" from current sloganism by discussing ideologies related
to death.

1844   Ramsey, Paul. ETHICS AT THE EDGES OF LIFE: MEDICAL AND
LEGAL INTERSECTIONS. The Bampton Lectures in America. New
Haven, Conn.: Yale University Press, 1978. xviii, 353 p.

Ethics and the law are integrated in this thoughtful examina-

tion of views on abortion, euthanasia, and the use of technologies for the prolongation of human life. Ramsey directs
his attention to specific court cases: the 1973 Supreme
Court decision on abortion; the Kenneth Edelin, Karen
Quinlan, and Joseph Saikewicz cases; and the California
Natural Death Act. He also considers the "benign neglect"
of defective infants.

1845 Veatch, Robert M. DEATH, DYING, AND THE BIOLOGICAL REVO-
LUTION: OUR LAST QUEST FOR RESPONSIBILITY. New Haven,
Conn.: Yale University Press, 1976. ix, 323 p. Bibliog.

The ethical, legal, and social dilemmas posed by the technological revolution in biology in relation to death and dying
are carefully scrutinized. Veatch proceeds from theological
and philosophical reflections to an explanation of technical
facts and legal tenets, and then to policy options for government institutions and individuals. Biomedical technology has
created new responsibilities for all of us in respect to the
process and manner of dying. Also considered is the care of
the dying, especially questions of who controls decisions and
who is an expert. Extensive bibliography.

1846 Weir, Robert F., ed. ETHICAL ISSUES IN DEATH AND DYING.
New York: Columbia University Press, 1977. xxi, 405 p.

Ambivalent attitudes of fear and fascination about death in-
hibit effective decision making for both physicians and the
public. The articles in this collection show the interface
of the three professions of medicine, law, and ethics in
dealings with death and are arranged under chapters dealing
with truth telling, determination of death, allowing to die,
euthanasia, and suicide. Contributors include Joseph Fletcher,
Leon Kass, Paul Ramsey, and Thomas Szasz. Several court
decisions are provided including that involving Karen Quinlan.

Part 17

LITERATURE

A. FOLKLORE

1. Bibliography

1847   Haywood, Charles. A BIBLIOGRAPHY OF NORTH AMERICAN FOLK-
LORE AND FOLKSONG. New York: Greenberg, 1951. xxx,
1,292 p. Maps.

> Part 4 covers the folklore of occupations, including lore of
> miners, railroaders, and industrial workers. An old but still
> useful list of recordings appears on pages 610-71.

2. Books and Articles

1848   Adams, James Taylor, ed. DEATH IN THE DARK: A COLLECTION
OF FACTUAL BALLADS OF AMERICAN MINE DISASTERS. Big Laurel,
Va.: Adams-Mullins Press, 1941. Reprint. Norwood, Pa.: Norwood
Editions, 1974. 119 p.

> This collection contains twenty-three ballads about mine
> disasters, each prefaced with a historical note and identifica-
> tion of the composer, rarely a miner. Remarks the compiler,
> "Coal miners, unlike cowboys, lumberjacks, sailors and rail-
> roaders are not a singing people. . .they have been content
> to let the phonograph and radio professionals do their singing
> for them."

1849   Baker, Ronald L. "The Influence of Mass Culture on Modern Legends."
SOUTHERN FOLKLORE QUARTERLY 40 (September-December 1976):
367-76.

> Baker provides evidence that mass culture nourishes legendry
> through providing new subject matter and through wider dis-
> semination of older lore. Among examples of new lore cited
> are legends about automobiles and hitchhikers. Modern tech-

nology has also produced folk heroes, most notably the truck
driver, who is celebrated by the media.

1850   Bird, Donald Allport. "A Theory for Folklore in the Mass Media:
Traditional Patterns in the Mass Media." SOUTHERN FOLKLORE
QUARTERLY 40 (September-December 1976): 285-305.

Until recently, folklorists considered mass media an impedi-
ment to the transmission of "true" folklore. Of late, however, they have been forced to concede that mass media has
played a role in changing lifestyles that have, in turn,
altered the very nature of lore. The authors point to two
positive aspects of mass media's involvement with folklore:
wide transmission of traditional forms and the creation of new
lore.

1851   Boatright, Mody C. FOLKLORE OF THE OIL INDUSTRY. Dallas:
Southern Methodist University Press, 1963. vii, 220 p.

Prevalent forms of tradition in the oil industry are explored.
Much of the lore is related to the search for oil through
doodlebugs, dreams, seers, and other folk means. Stereo-
types and heroes of the industry are profiled, including the
belittled geologist, the trickster promoter, the wandering
driller, and the rags-to-riches landowner. Lore forms encompass songs and verse, tall tales, and anecdotes.

1852   Botkin, B.A. "Automobile Humor: From the Horseless Carriage to the
Compact Car." JOURNAL OF POPULAR CULTURE 1 (Spring 1968):
395-402.

Automobile humor that grew out of the early driving experience and the peculiarities of the first cars served to cushion
the social shock and technical frustrations created by the
first autos. Ford jokes provided perhaps the first nationally
shared humor, making light of the car's frequent failures. In
the twenties, college students' slang reflected the new freedoms enjoyed by that generation.

1853   _____, ed. SIDEWALKS OF AMERICA: FOLKLORE, LEGENDS,
SAGAS, TRADITIONS, CUSTOMS, SONGS, STORIES AND SAYINGS
OF CITY FOLK. Indianapolis, Ind.: Bobbs-Merrill, 1954. xii,
605 p. Illus.

Written in an anecdotal, colloquial style, this collection
relates the popular traditions and lore of the American city.
Chapter 8, "From This They Make a Living," contains occupational lore on iron workers and others who interact regularly with machines.

1854 Botkin, B.A., and Harlow, Alvin F. A TREASURY OF RAILROAD FOLKLORE. New York: Crown Publishers, 1953. xiv, 530 p. Music.

> The book opens with a selection of factual events and anecdotes which served as raw material for folk invention. The remaining pages nearly explode with the result: railroad characters from bandits to bums, slang, signals, and customs. A concluding selection of blues, ballads, and worksongs is followed by an appendix of "railroadiana." Observing the unparalleled sway that the railroad held over the American imagination, Botkin reasons that the train is "the prototype of modern industrialism," yet it preserves the "tradition of individual courage, high enterprise and wanderlust."

1855 Coffin, Tristram P[otter.], ed. OUR LIVING TRADITIONS: AN INTRODUCTION TO AMERICAN FOLKLORE. New York: Basic Books, 1968. xviii, 301 p.

> This representative collection of articles by prominent American folklorists includes several pieces concerned with the impact of the industrial age on lore. Horace P. Beck writes on the folklore of occupations and Archie Green discourses on labor lore. Papers on hillbilly, black, and "pop-style" folklore illustrate the effect of the mass media on content, style, and transmission.

1856 Coffin, Tristram Potter, and Cohen, Hennig, eds. FOLKLORE FROM THE WORKING FOLK OF AMERICA. Garden City, N.Y.: Anchor Press, 1973. xxviii, 464 p.

> Drawn from archives, journals, and collections, this compendium encompasses not only the lore of folk occupations, such as lumbering and cowpoking, but also the "semifolk" occupations of the factory. Coffin suggests that folklore served as an adaptive mechanism to industrial employment. Forms treated include folk literature, songs, verses, riddles, folk speech, and legendary figures.

1857 Cohen, Norman. "Railroad Songs on Record--a Survey." NEW YORK FOLKLORE QUARTERLY 26 (June 1976): 91-113.

> To round out the coverage on the railroad's impact on American life provided by Frank Donovan's THE RAILROAD IN LITERATURE (no. 1978), Cohen analyzes the railroad song. Songs are categorized and described, and the history of recordings is traced. A lengthy discography follows.

1858 Dorson, Richard M. AMERICAN FOLKLORE. Chicago: University of Chicago Press, 1959. xii, 328 p.

This survey of American folklore covers its divergence from European lore, the rise of regional and ethnic lore, and the emergence of folk heroes. A concluding chapter turns to modern folklore and concedes that mass media, the auto, and other technological advances have reduced the communicative function and distinctive flavor of lore, yet he concludes optimistically that lore is not dying.

1859   Dundes, Alan. "Advertising and Folklore." NEW YORK FOLKLORE QUARTERLY 19 (June 1963): 143-51.

Surveying the effects of mass media on folklore, Dundes finds advertising humor embedded in many predominant forms of lore, particularly jokes and shaggy-dog stories. Though originally produced only to aid sales, ads have become content for oral humor.

1860   Fishwick, Marshall [W.], and Browne, Ray B., eds. ICONS OF POPULAR CULTURE. Bowling Green, Ohio: Bowling Green Popular Press, 1970. x, 146 p. Illus.

Icons are defined here as "images and ideas converted into three dimensions." They include "admired artifacts"--items that lend meaning to daily life and possess an element of language. Analyzed in these informal essays are two paramount American icons--the Coca Cola beverage and bottle and the automobile.

1861   Foner, Philip S. AMERICAN LABOR SONGS OF THE NINETEENTH CENTURY. Urbana: University of Illinois Press, 1975. xxii, 356 p. Illus., bibliog., phonodisk.

Written by a labor historian, the book traces the parallel development of musical expression and militancy in the history of American labor. Music analyzed has been drawn from journals, songbooks, newspapers, and broadsheets, primarily dating to the nineteenth century. While some attention is devoted to the expression of man-machine relations, most of the material, in keeping with the author's interest, treats workers' struggles to organize.

1862   Green, Archie. "A Discography of American Coal Miners' Songs." LABOR HISTORY 2 (Winter 1961): 101-15.

The songs of coal miners, railroaders, loggers, and other laborers not only document the growth of American industry, but reveal conflicts between labor and management, and man and machine. Green's introduction to the discography mentions the work of Korson, Lomax, and other folklorists, and generalizes on the nature and characteristic forms of mining songs.

1863 _____. ONLY A MINER: STUDIES IN RECORDED COAL-MINING SONGS. Urbana: University of Illinois Press, 1972. xvi, 504 p. Illus., bibliog.

Through this study of songs on records in the United States between 1925 and 1970, Green portrays the life and values of miners and documents changes in the rural society of miners wrought by approaching urbanization and mass media. Background to the songs has been drawn from interviews, labor histories, and folklore compilations. Extensive bibliography and checklist of recordings.

1864 Greenway, John. AMERICAN FOLKSONGS OF PROTEST. Philadelphia: University of Pennsylvania Press, 1953. x, 348 p. Music, discography, bibliog.

Among the types of protest songs recorded in this historical survey are those sung by textile workers, miners, and laborers in several other industries. A bibliography and lists of composers, songs, and ballads supplement the text.

1865 Hand, Wayland [D.]. "American Occupational and Industrial Folklore: The Miner." In KONTAKTE UND GREZIN: PROBLEM DER VOLKS-KULTUR-UN SOZIALFORSCHUNG, edited by Hans Foltin, pp. 453-60. Gottingen, West Germany: Schwartz Geburstag, 1969. Illus.

Though European scholars have long studied the folklore of artisans and the working class, Americans have been slow to collect and analyze their own occupational lore. Hand discusses the difficulties in dealing with such materials through a quick review of the work of major figures in the field. Brief samples of lore illustrate the text.

1866 _____. "California Miners' Folklore: Above Ground." CALIFORNIA FOLKLORE QUARTERLY 1 (January 1942): 24-46. "California Miners' Folklore: Below Ground." CALIFORNIA FOLKLORE QUARTERLY 1 (April 1942): 127-55.

The wealth of mining folklore is revealed through this general overview and typology of California lore. Countless folk methods for discovering gold seem to have been devised: augurs, divining rods, dream mines, vegetation, and animal observation. The fateful mining process was also laden with lore, containing elements such as spirit tappings and prophetic behavior of candles, rats, and mules.

1867 Hoffmann, Daniel G. PAUL BUNYAN: LAST OF THE FRONTIER DEMIGODS. Philadelphia: University of Pennsylvania Press and Temple University Publications, 1952. xiv, 213 p.

Of the many demigods of American folklore, Paul Bunyan is

the only one whose fame has survived into the twentieth century. By following the history of changes in the Bunyan
character and lore, Hoffmann discovers the reasons for his
survival. As an occupational hero pitted against industrialism, Bunyan has been celebrated by poets including Carl
Sandburg and Robert Frost. In popular culture, he has become simply the idealization of gigantism and success with
"old time prowess confused with entrepreneurial shrewdness."

1868   Jackson, Bruce A., ed. FOLKLORE AND SOCIETY: ESSAYS IN
HONOR OF BENJAMIN A. BOTKIN. Hatboro, Pa.: Folklore
Associates, 1966. xii, 192 p.

The puzzling relationship between mass culture and folk culture receives thoughtful, impartial treatment. Charles Seeger
reviews the paradox of "the folkness of the non-folk versus the
non-folkness of the folk," while Ellen Stechert assesses the
genuineness of the urban folksong movement. Other studies
look at folk versus modern medicine, and traditional versus
commercial black and hillbilly folk music.

1869   Korson, George. MINSTRELS OF THE MINE PATCH. Philadelphia:
University of Pennsylvania Press, 1938. xxii, 332 p. Music, bibliog.

In addition to new ballads, this enlarged version of SONGS
AND BALLADS (no. 1870) adds more legends, folktales, and
superstitions.

1870   _____. SONGS AND BALLADS OF THE ANTHRACITE MINER. New
York: F.H. Hitchcock, 1927. xxviii, 196 p.

From this collection of folklore emerges the folkways, work
humor, and pain of miners of the anthracite regions of
Pennsylvania in the closing quarter of the nineteenth century,
clarified by explanatory notes.

1871   _____, ed. PENNSYLVANIA SONGS AND LEGENDS. Philadelphia:
University of Pennsylvania Press, 1949. 474 p. Illus.

Pennsylvania was the site of much early industrial development,
a fact well reflected in its folklore. Freeman H. Hubbard
contributes a chapter on railroaders, and Korson, on coal
miners. The lore spun by oil men and canal men also receives attention. Later folksong developments in the industrial
city are the subject of inquiry for Jacob A. Evanson.

1872   Licht, M. "Some Automobile Play Activities of Suburban Teenagers."
NEW YORK FOLKLORE QUARTERLY 30 (March 1974): 44-65.

Through interviews conducted with high-school students in
western New York, Licht found that the oral traditions of

teenagers center largely on the automobile. Presents a number of car games, symbols, gestures, and routines uniting
youth and machine.

1873 Nickerson, B.E. "Is There a Folk in the Factory?" JOURNAL OF
AMERICAN FOLKLORE 87 (April 1974): 133-39.

Fourteen months of field work as a pieceworks machinist in
a factory near Boston convinced the author that urban blue-
collar workers may be considered a folk or folk-like group.
While he overheard little ethnic humor and discovered no
folk heroes, he did witness institutionalized storytelling sessions. While encouraging similar research efforts, Nickerson
cautions against a too genre-specific approach.

1874 Paredes, Américo, and Stekert, Ellen J., eds. THE URBAN EXPERIENCE
AND THE FOLK TRADITION. Austin: University of Texas Press, 1971.
207 p. Bibliog.

Originally presented in a special issue of the JOURNAL OF
AMERICAN FOLKLORE (volume 238, 1968), these symposia
papers constitute a pioneer volume on urban folklore. Of
interest to the student of technology are three papers: Richard
Dorson's "Is There a Folk in the City?"; Morton Leeds' "The
Process of Cultural Stripping and Reintegration: The Rural
Migrant in the City"; and D.K. Wilgers' "Country Western
Music and the Urban Hillbilly." Of equal interest is the
treatment of urban occupational lore in the bibliography.

1875 Schroeder, Fred E.H. "A Bellyful of Coffee: The Truckdrivin' Man
as Folk Hero." JOURNAL OF POPULAR CULTURE 2 (Spring 1969):
679-86.

With the disappearance of the frontier cowboy, the truck
driver has emerged as the hero of the lower classes. Personi-
fying such strengths as mobility, independence, patriotism,
and potency, the truck driver is well represented in song and
lore, but not in art and literature. Full stature as a folk
hero cannot be attained without a proper historic distance.

1876 Sirota, David. "Media: The Electronic Minstrel--Toward a Newfolklore and Hero." ET CETERA 35 (September 1978): 302-9.

In this age of media, many folklorists have been inclined to
distinguish between orally transmitted traditional "folklore" and
the "fakelore" of recording and television studios. Sirota
disagrees with this classification, arguing for the inevitability
of a "newfolklore" or "telelore." Television, he believes,
now serves the function that oral lore did in the past, that of
posing the social and emotional problems and shared emotional
experience of the disparate American subcultures. By the

same token, only media, not real life, can produce "tele-heroes" of sufficient stature to satisfy contemporary society's expectations.

1877   Wyld, Lionel D. LOW BRIDGE! FOLKLORE AND THE ERIE CANAL. Syracuse, N.Y.: Syracuse University Press, 1962. 212 p. Illus., bibliog.

The Erie Canal inspired a great level of oral and literary lore. Wyld relates the history of the canal from its inception to its displacement by the railroad, and its treatment in colloquialisms and sayings, life-styles, sports, vices, songs and ballads, tall tales, and literature. Notes are abundant.

B. FICTION AND POETRY

1. Science Fiction and Utopias

1878   Allen, Dick, ed. SCIENCE FICTION: THE FUTURE. New York: Harcourt Brace Jovanovich, 1971. xiv, 345 p. Bibliog.

A variety of perspectives on the future are provided in this anthology of fiction and nonfiction. Transformations of reality which do not lead to disorientation are followed by allegorical stories of an unreal future as well as traditional predictive fiction. In the final section, classical critical statements define and discuss "futurists" and science fiction as literature and as a medium for understanding change in society. Susan Sontag's "The Imagination of Disaster," and Isaac Asimov's "Social Science Fiction" are here. Stories by Nathaniel Hawthorne, Allen Ginsberg, Robert Heinlein, Donald Barthelme, Ray Bradbury, Kurt Vonnegut, Roger Zelazny, Harlan Ellison, Frederick Pohl, and Arthur Clarke are among those included.

1879   Asimov, Isaac. I, ROBOT. New York: Grosset and Dunlap, 1950. 253 p.

Cybernetics advances from the mute nursemaid robot Robbie to Brain, the super-computer who conquers space and time by creating a vehicle with "Hyperatomic Drive." The unique appeal of these stories lies in Asimov's ability to involve the reader emotionally with electronic beings. The robots have devastating psychological problems, distinct personalities, and are more trustworthy, faithful, and sensitive than man. The "three laws of robotics" create constant tension between ego, self-preservation, and protection of the master.

1880   _____. THE REST OF THE ROBOTS. Garden City, N.Y.: Double-day, 1964. xiii, 556 p.

Asimov gathered his robot stories not included in I, ROBOT (no. 1879) into this collection. Generally, the tales take place farther into the future than in the previous volume. Robots perform in space, are humanoid enemy CIA types, or even serve as academic editorial proofreaders and test correctors. Two novellas are included. CAVES OF STEEL, a rare science-fiction mystery, develops around the relationships between human inhabitants of a future New York City and the alien robots from outer space who colonize and control earth. In its sequel, NAKED SUN, Baley the human, and Robot Daneel, antagonists in the earlier work, form a team to solve a murder in another world.

1881   Bellamy, Edward. LOOKING BACKWARD, 2000-1887. 1888. Reprint. Cambridge, Mass.: Harvard University Press, 1967. 314 p.

When Julian West awakens from his over one-hundred-years suspended animation, he finds that Boston in the year 2000 has been transformed by the efficient use of machine technology into an emblem of universal solidarity. All tasks are done with professionalism, but spontaneity has been replaced by total programming. Serenity and harmony exist because passion has been eliminated along with self-concern. Bellamy's best-selling novel became fuel for twentieth-century dystopias.

1882   Bierce, Ambrose. "Moxon's Master." In THE COLLECTED WORKS OF AMBROSE BIERCE, vol. 3, pp. 88-105. 1910. Reprint. New York: Gordian Press, 1966.

A lively discussion between the narrator and Moxon about the possibility of consciousness in machines is followed by the narrator's surreptitious interruption of a chess game between Moxon and his automaton. Moxon's creation, alas, is a sore loser. In its rage, the robot strangles its maker and sets fire to the house.

1883   Bradbury, Ray. I SING THE BODY ELECTRIC! New York: Alfred A. Knopf, 1969. 305 p.

Two short stories in this collection are of especial interest. The protagonist in "I Sing the Body Electric!" is "the first humanoid-genre minicircuited, rechargeable AC-DC Mark V Electrical Grandmother" designed to provide precision love. The robot is more than electrical circuits and, by being exactly what each of her charges needs, proves that all machines are not evil. In "The Lost City of Mars," bored transplanted Earthlings discover a long-abandoned city totally run by machines and capable of actualizing everyone's dreams. Initially fascinated, most of the explorers quickly realize that acceptance of everything without work is worthless.

1884   . THE MARTIAN CHRONICLES. 1950. Garden City, N.Y.: Doubleday, 1958. 222 p.

A civilization eons older than that of Earth, Mars is serene and beautiful because its wise inhabitants stopped technology before it became more powerful than themselves. Man's rockets bring not only chicken pox to annihilate the natives, but also beer cans to litter the canals, gas stations, and even Sam's Hot Dogs. Swarms of men with "mouths fringed with nails" build a replica of technological civilization. Bradbury worships the imagination which he feels is being destroyed by mechanical paranoia. But he is romantic--after destroying their engines, men find the fountain of life in a Martian canal.

1885   . "The Murderer." In THE GOLDEN APPLES OF THE SUN, pp. 91-100. 1953. Reprint. Westport, Conn.: Greenwood Press, 1976.

In an electronic gadget-crazed culture where privacy is especially violated by transmitting and receiving wrist-radios, smiling Albert Brock becomes a murderer. His victims are the "temptingly convenient" conveniences: telephone, office intercom, car radio, wrist-radio, and finally his house. With relish, he violently attacks the vacuum hound, stove, televisor. Brock laments that what were once practical objects or toys are now essential elements in the "pattern of social behavior." Their constant noise and presence is largely responsible for modern man's "high-strung" state.

1886 Brunner, John. STAND ON ZANZIBAR. Garden City, N.Y.: Doubleday, 1968. Reprint. New York: Ballantine, 1976. xvi, 505 p.

The frenzy, repulsion, extreme constriction, and sensual indulgence of an overpopulated, computer-run, and big-business governed world are effectively transmitted in this dystopian portrayal of America and the world in 2010. Genetic optimization is the major concern. Donald Hogan, a mild intellectual, is "eptified" into a killer in order to kidnap the world's greatest geneticist. Conglomerate businessman Norman House and radical sociologist Chad Mulligan discover a mutant pacifying gene in an African tribe. Since the gene creates an odor which dulls aggressive tendencies, Mulligan figures super-computer Shalmaneser can mass-produce the aroma--brotherly love from an aerosol can.

1887 Campbell, John W. "Twilight." 1934. In THE SCIENCE FICTION HALL OF FAME, vol. 1, edited by Robert Silverberg, pp. 24-41. New York: Doubleday, 1970.

Returning from a voyage in time to seven million A.D., a traveler tells of the twilight of man. Only a few scattered

humans with large, functionless brains are left in the solar
system, but machines, built to perfection, continue to operate.
In ghost cities, the machines perform their functions with
chilling, purposeless efficiency. The little, lonely men are
bewildered by the perpetual mechanisms but cannot stop them.

1888   Clarke, Arthur C. IMPERIAL EARTH. New York: Harcourt Brace
Jovanovich, 1976. xii, 303 p.

Duncan, a third-generation clone, is, after all, human and
experiences the passions, doubts, and fears to which mankind
is subject. Visiting earth from his native Titan, a moon of
Saturn, he encounters the inhabitants' fascination with the
past, which he recognizes as a method of escape from the
uncertainties and responsibilities associated with probes into
new worlds. Clarke's style exhibits an unusual lack of
sophistication yet the novel is valuable for its humanistic
view of the products of genetic engineering.

1889   _____. 2001: A SPACE ODYSSEY. New York: New American
Library, 1968. 221 p.

In the known universe, the "brain," be it human or mechanical, is a force for chaos. The computer Hal, too much of
a success, must have the "higher centers" of his brain cut
out. Mechanical regulation replaces the psychological being
of the astronauts comatose in the hibernaculum. In contrast,
Bowman, by traveling through the crystal slab, expands his
brain and passes beyond the necessities of matter. With a
will that eventually dominates the universe, he whimsically
annihilates the Earth but is unable to devise any purposive
plan: "For though he was master of the world, he was not
quite sure what to do next."

1890   Clem, Ralph; Greenberg, Martin Harry; and Olander, Joseph [D.],
eds. THE CITY 2000 A.D.: URBAN LIFE THROUGH SCIENCE FIC-
TION. Greenwich, Conn.: Fawcett Publications, 1976. 304 p.

The consequences of the rise of cities and the future impact
of urban civilization on man's social, economic, and political
life are projected by science-fiction visionaries. Stories are
grouped into subject treatments: crowding, race relations,
pollution, crime, transportation, and suburbia, as well as
wider utopian and dystopian visions. Among the eighteen
stories are works by Robert Silverberg, Brian Aldiss, Hugo
Gernsback, Robert Scheckley, and Henry Kuttner.

1891   Clemens, Samuel [Mark Twain]. A CONNECTICUT YANKEE IN KING
ARTHUR'S COURT. 1889. Reprint. New York: Harper and Brothers,
1960. 450 p. Illus.

Knocked by a hardy punch back into the Arthurian Age,
cocky Yankee Hank Morgan uses his technological ingenuity
to gain power over the medieval inhabitants. He gets the
best of Merlin and introduces new ways, including toothpaste,
printing, and advertising. Clandestinely, he develops factories and workshops. Hard-sell advertising in Gutenberg
type and a revolver brandished in a chivalry contest are examples of his incongruous introductions.

1892   Conklin, Groff, ed. SCIENCE FICTION THINKING MACHINES:
ROBOTS, ANDROIDS, COMPUTERS. New York: Vanguard Press,
1954. 367 p.

Intelligent machines became part of the "furniture" of science
fiction beginning with Karel Capek's R.U.R. in 1920.
Stories are included in this anthology which deal with robots
(mechanical servants), androids (a being given life by means
other than human birth), and computers (fixed robots that can
not move). Such authors as Isaac Asimov, Fritz Leiber,
Capek, Theodore Sturgeon, Poul Anderson, and Walter Miller
consider the social problems resulting from cybernetic inventions. Includes a supplemental list of such tales.

1893   Crichton, Michael. THE TERMINAL MAN. New York: Alfred A.
Knopf, 1972. xi, 247 p. Illus., bibliog.

Harry Benson, a computer expert with psychomotor epilepsy,
is the first man to have a computer and electrodes implanted
in his brain. Seizures are aborted through stimulation; the
mechanical brain controls the organic one. However, stimulation is so pleasant that Benson involuntarily causes the process to occur until exhaustion brings on repeated seizures.
The novel explores the philosophical and social implications
of electronic behavior modification and the control of human
being by intelligent machines. Documentary verisimilitude
and an annotated bibliography add to the value of this fictional consideration of the relationship of man and machine,
psychosurgery, and biomedical applications of electronics.

1894   Dann, Jack, and Dozois, Gardner, eds. FUTURE POWER: A SCIENCE
FICTION ANTHOLOGY. New York: Random House, 1976. xxviii,
256 p.

The nine stories in this anthology are inquiries into possible
futures. These contemporary science-fiction writers share a
skeptical, not totally optimistic nor desperate, attitude toward the uses and management of technology in the future.
Among our prospects are a shattered society drained to mere
survival, a Skinner-controlled utopia, "benign" conforming
society, or kinky alternative life-styles. Stories are by

Ursula LeGuin, Damon Knight, James Tiptree, George Alec Effinger, Vonda McIntyre, and others. Several are published here for the first time.

1895 Del Rey, Lester. "Helen O'Loy." 1938. In THE SCIENCE FICTION HALL OF FAME, vol. 1, edited by Robert Silverberg, pp. 42-51. Garden City, N.Y.: Doubleday, 1970.

The prototype of all mechanical housekeepers and female companions in science fiction, Helen O'Loy (short for "Helen of Alloy") is beautiful, buxom, a great cook, and totally devoted to and adoring of her master. She is even equipped with mechanized parts which cause emotions.

1896 Ellison, Harlan. "Catman." 1974. In FINAL STAGE: THE ULTI-MATE SCIENCE FICTION ANTHOLOGY, edited by Edward L. Ferman and Barry N. Malzberg, pp. 134-75. New York: Penguin Books, 1975.

A thief in a future world where there is plenty for all steals because he needs something so taboo that it is loathsome even in a completely permissive society. He yearns for the ultimate sexual experience--the mating of man with machine. The thief, with the aid of psychedelic "Dust," makes love to a highly responsive computer. The computer devours what it loves and replaces human body parts with metal.

1897 _____. "I Have No Mouth & I Must Scream." In I HAVE NO MOUTH & I MUST SCREAM, STORIES BY HARLAN ELLISON, pp. 22-42. New York: Pyramid Books, 1967.

The region of eternal punishment and pain becomes the insides of a mammoth computer. Five humans, saved from the total devastation of World War III, are tortured by AM, Allied Mastercomputer or Aggressive Menace, in revenge for its trapped existence as a machine that cannot wonder or belong. The narrator is transformed by AM into "a great soft jelly thing" with rubbery appendages, blotches of disease, and no mouth. This story originally appeared in IF: WORLDS OF SCIENCE FICTION, March 1967.

1898 Elwood, Roger, ed. FUTURE CITY. New York: Trident Press, 1973. 256 p.

The short stories and poems in this anthology provide future views of the possible directions of city development. Building on aspects that make cities essential, and on problems like pollution, power failures, traffic jams, homosexuality, sadomasochism, and race relations, the fiction reveals a "gradual process of disintegration." Included are stories by

Ben Bova, Barry Malzberg, Thomas Scortia, Frank Herbert, Robert Silverberg, Harlan Ellison, and others.

1899   Fox, Siv Cedering. "The Computer Terminal." PARTISAN REVIEW 45, no. 2 (1978): 223-31.

This short story concerns a woman writer who composes on a computer terminal. The computer stores, reorganizes text, and guards privacy, but it also begins to interact imaginatively by reminding its human operator of her dreams, and by foreseeing future happenings. Instinctively the writer attempts to restore mental stability through traditional household chores and walks with the dog. The tactics are unsuccessful, and remaining extremely disturbed, she finally "deletes" all of her compositions.

1900   Franklin, H. Bruce, ed. FUTURE PERFECT: AMERICAN SCIENCE FICTION OF THE NINETEENTH CENTURY. New York: Oxford University Press, 1968. xiii, 402 p.

The short fiction anthologized herein, combined with literary criticism, demonstrates the serious interest with which literary figures of the period approached science and technology. Most of the fiction is motivated by distrust of rationalism, and interest lies in the human implications of inventions. Includes stories by Nathaniel Hawthorne, Edgar Poe, Herman Melville, Edward Bellamy, Mark Twain, and others about automata, psychology, space and time travel, and life force in machines.

1901   Goulart, Ron. BROKE DOWN ENGINE AND OTHER TROUBLES WITH MACHINES. New York: Collier Books, 1971. 192 p.

Technological man's reactions to breakdown in his mechanized environment are dramatized in these tongue-in-cheek tales. In a future dominated by machines, man relates to malfunction with helpless stoicism. Goulart's humans confront a refrigerator-shaped robot with killer instinct, sorcerer housecomputer, medical android in a wheelchair, a best-selling-author robot with "quirky sensitivity," and a senior citizens' terminal.

1902   _____. NUTZENBOLTS AND MORE TROUBLES WITH MACHINES. New York: Macmillan, 1975. 182 p.

Mechanics is not too popular in these ten futuristic parables. Man is faced with a cybernetic grandfather, ten-speed gigolos, a TV news anchorman who is his own camera, computerized wife-swapping, and dingbats (robots shaped like hot-water bottles with lots of chopping arms--built for jungle hand-to-hand combat wars). Future man, displaced, knocked out, blown up, hangs by his thumbs--will his instincts and wit preserve a victory?

1903 _____. WHAT'S BECOME OF SCREWLOOSE? AND OTHER IN-QUIRIES. New York: Charles Scribner's Sons, 1971. 184 p.

More stories of mechanical mayhem pit man against robot brainwasher, marriage-breaking automatic house, cybernetic wise-guy dog, nonfunctioning agencies staffed by machines and androids, and surveillance bed.

1904 Greenberg, Martin Harry, and Olander, Joseph D., eds. TOMORROW, INC.: SF STORIES ABOUT BIG BUSINESS. New York: Taplinger Publishing Co., 1976. 256 p.

Fourteen science-fiction stories which provide various treatments of business and corporations compose this collection. Major themes developed are imperialism, man versus machine, unemployment, advertising, replacement of entrepreneurs by expert technicians, environmental consequences of productivity, business-related crime, and the future of business. Among the stories included are works by Frederick Pohl, John Jakes, Isaac Asimov, Robert Silverberg, Arthur Clarke, Philip K. Dick, and Robert Sheckley.

1905 Heinlein, Robert A. BEYOND THIS HORIZON. New York: Grosset and Dunlap, 1948. New York: New American Library, 1974. 186 p.

Genetic engineering is the protagonist in this novel unusual in its depiction of a pleasant, comfortable future world. Trouble comes only from a fringe group which hopes to achieve power through breeding techniques. Boredom and an excessive fascination with statistics and gene charts result in a rather serene unhappiness. Felix Hamilton, himself the result of many generations of enlightened genetic manipulation, is unenthusiastic about marriage and offspring. He is bribed into fatherhood by the promise of extensive, state-supported scientific research into the origin of the universe, the meaning of life, telepathy, and the possibility of awareness before birth and after death.

1906 _____. THE MOON IS A HARSH MISTRESS. New York: G.P. Putnam's Sons, 1966. 383 p.

Brilliant computer "Mike" engineers the revolution to free Luna from Earth's Federated Nation. The first computer with sufficient neuristers to become self-aware, Mike can think without being programmed and develops a sense of humor; but "he" quickly becomes lonely and bored. The revolution in-

stigated by Manny, gorgeous Wyoming, and Professor La Paz
is "the only game in town." Mike manipulates the Lunar
citizenry through the media, designs diplomatic strategy, and,
like David, overpowers the sophisticated weapons of Goliath
Terra by catapulting perfectly aimed rocks at the enemy.

1907 _____. "The Roads Must Roll." 1940. In THE SCIENCE FICTION
HALL OF FAME, vol. 1, edited by Robert Silverberg, pp. 52-86.
Garden City, N.Y.: Doubleday, 1970.

Men become totally subservient to machines when moving
roadways are the center of the economic system. Technical
and psychological training create workers and managers who
idolize the roads and the mechanism running the transportation system. A strike caused by a few less-indoctrinated
reactionaries creates havoc, but Director Gaines realizes
that more efficient psychological tests and closer supervision
will prevent such problems.

1908 Jones D[ennis].F[eltham]. COLOSSUS. New York: G.P. Putnam's
Sons, 1967. 256 p.

Super-computer Colossus and its peer Guardian, built by the
United States of · North America and the Soviet bloc as total
defense systems, both develop self-determining capabilities
upon activation. The two join together and immediately confront man with a power well beyond human control.
Colossus/Guardian possesses all knowledge but no emotion.
The man-machine interaction between Charles Forbin, the
creator, and his Frankenstein monster effectively transmits
man's helplessness and horror when faced with a superior
mechanical brain. The basis for the film COLOSSUS: THE
FORBIN PROJECT (1970).

1909 Knight, Damon, ed. CITIES OF WONDER. Garden City, N.Y.:
Doubleday, 1966. 252 p.

Cities are participants in these stories of the metropolis on
Earth, in space, and the future. Among the eleven short
stories are: Walter M. Miller's "Dumb Waiter," Robert A.
Heinlein's "It's Great To Be Back," Stephen Vincent Benet's
"By The Waters of Babylon," C.M. Kornbluth's "The Luckiest
Man in Denv," E.M. Forster's "The Machine Stops," and
J.G. Ballard's "Billenium."

1910 Levin, Ira. THE STEPFORD WIVES. New York: Random House, 1972.
145 p.

In Stepford, individualistic, aware wives are replaced by
animatronic robots (à la Disney). The well-endowed, house-
keeping-oriented devices are created by the husbands who are

experts in electronics. Author Levin leaves the reader with
the impression that husbands are much happier with "wives"
programmed to be perfect housekeepers and bosomy bedmates,
while children love providers of the hot breakfast. Talent
and personality are liabilities.

1911 _____. THIS PERFECT DAY. New York: Random House, 1970.
309 p.

Massive computer Uni runs the civilized world of look-alike
humans, compulsory television, cake and coke meals, advisors,
and Saturday-night-only programmed sex. Through genetic
engineering and drug "treatments," Family Members are unified into sameness and passivity. Chip, slightly different
from birth, resists the total control and the dulled existence.
He and a few other "incurables" escape, suffer when their
human emotions and drives are freed from the drugged stupor,
and finally succeed in destroying Uni. But without control
and regimentation the perfectly balanced culture must crash.
The reader is left questioning whether Uni's world is a
dystopia or utopia.

1912 Melville, Herman. "The Bell-Tower." 1855. In FUTURE PERFECT,
by Bruce Franklin, pp. 151-65. New York: Oxford University Press,
1966. And in BILLY BUDD AND OTHER TALES, by Herman Melville,
pp. 288-303. New York: New American Library, 1961.

Perhaps the first developed story in English about a humanoid
automaton, "The Bell-Tower" relates the fate of Bannadonna,
"the great mechanician" who is killed by his metal creation.
Having built the highest bell tower, the most spectacular
bells, and a robot bell-ringer, Bannadonna's skull is crushed
when his attempt to sculpt to perfection a female figure on
his bell causes him to forget the onset of the robot's assigned
chore. Steeped in sexual symbolism, Melville's story initiates
elements to become conventional in robot fiction: the narcis-
sistic creator wants to by-pass the normal method of procreation, and he becomes the victim of his creation.

1913 Miller, Walter M., Jr. A CANTICLE FOR LEIBOWITZ. London:
Weidenfeld, 1959. Reprint. Boston: Gregg Press, 1975. xii, 320 p.

The monastery of the order of St. Leibowitz, founded after
the devastation of a nuclear war, plays its role in the development of a new technological civilization which leads un-
hesitantly to a second holocaust. Man's fascination with
technology is equaled by his need for mythic and sacred
heroes. The passionate quest for canonization of Leibowitz,
a Jewish military technician, is an ironic comment on man's
desperation and the inadequacies of his nontechnical cultural
forms. The monastery becomes the impotent overseer of a

voluntary euthanasia facility for hopeless radiation victims.
But God and man endure to start a new cycle.

1914   Mowshowitz, Abbe, ed. INSIDE INFORMATION: COMPUTERS IN
FICTION. Reading, Mass.: Addison-Wesley, 1977. xxiii, 345 p.
Bibliog.

The stories, poems, and excerpts from novels chosen for this
anthology demonstrate social impacts of computers. The literature also reveals attitudes toward computers and resulting
value conflicts. Emerging from this literature, mostly written
after 1950, is a "sense of malaise" over the diminishing role
of human beings, and a "fatalistic acceptance" of man's
demise. The stories are organized within sections such as
"Information and Power," "Control of Behavior," "Human
Vitality," and "Man in Transition." Stories by Robert
Heinlein, John Brunner, Kurt Vonnegut, Donald Barthelme,
John Barth, Arthur Clarke, Isaac Asimov, and Philip K. Dick
are included. There is an extensive, annotated bibliography
of fiction and criticism.

1915   O'Brien, Fitz-James. "The Wondersmith." 1859. In MASTERPIECES
OF SCIENCE FICTION, edited by Sam Moskowitz, pp. 128-67.
Westport, Conn.: Hyperion Press, 1966.

Duke Balthazar, a gypsy, manufactures robots complete with
"souls bitter as hemlock" whose mission is to destroy Christians. During the day, the automatons are puppets or manni-
kins; but at night the souls enter them and they become
wicked, ferocious killers. The story contains many of the
elements found in subsequent robotic fiction: a demented
creator, robots designed to war with man, the turning of the
android against its creator.

1916   Silverberg, Robert. UNFAMILIAR TERRITORY. New York: Charles
Scribner's Sons, 1973. 212 p.

The collection of short stories dealing with the future includes
"Caught in the Organ Draft," a tale of a world of involuntary
organ and tissue donation for elder statesmen; "Good News
from the Vatican," which chronicles the timely election of the
first robot Pope; and several stories of time travel or
technology-augmented sex.

1917   _____, ed. MEN AND MACHINES: TEN STORIES OF SCIENCE
FICTION. New York: Meredith Press, 1968. 240 p.

The stories in this collection deal with intelligent machines
and man's interactions with them. Most explore the question
of who is servant and who is master, as well as the possible

obsolescence of man. Fritz Leiber, Robert Silverberg, Brian Aldiss, Lester del Rey, Jack Williamson, and others delve into the relationships between man and robots, cyborg, super-computer, mechanical hunter, time-warp transportation system, or an artist computer.

1918   Vonnegut, Kurt. PLAYER PIANO. New York: Charles Scribner's Sons, 1952. Reprint. New York: Delacorte Press, 1977. 295 p.

Machines do most of the work in this futurist America tended by a privileged, conformist class of technocrats. Most of the population is unemployed, uneducated, spiritless. The rather simple plot records the personal revolt of the head of the Ilium, New York works, Paul Proteus. There are temporary, sometimes funny defeats of machinery and some satire on contemporary "rah-rah" corporate social conformities. But the real horror in Vonnegut's dystopia is not automation but universal boredom.

1919   _____. THE SIRENS OF TITAN. New York: Delacorte Press, 1959. Reissue. New York: Delacorte Press, 1971. 319 p.

Chrono-synclastic infundibulated space voyager Winston Niles Rumfoord colonizes Mars with earthlings transformed through psychosurgery into a totally obedient combat force. Rumfoord's purpose is to attack Earth so that its inhabitants will band to-gether in unity. Achieving this goal, he forms the worldwide Church of God The Utterly Indifferent. The prime tenet of this faith is that everything in the universe is an accident. Rumfoord's premier puppet in his machinations is Malachi Constant, whose induced Odyssey from Earth to Mars and Mercury ends on Titan. Here it is discovered that contrary to the accidental theory, all of Earth's history, including Rumfoord's unwitting actions, has been directed by a force from Tralfamadore. Salo, a mechanical being from the planet, has been waiting over 200,000 years for a replace-ment part for his spaceship. Malachi and his son supply the metal gadget. But robot Salo is crushed by earthly sentiment. His friendship with Rumfoord means more than his Tralfamadoran mission.

2. Other Genres

1920   Abbey, Edward. THE MONKEY WRENCH GANG. New York: Avon Books, 1976. viii, 387 p. Map.

Sabotage in the cause of ecology is the aim of Hayduke, Doc, Seldom, and Bonnie, the Monkey Wrench gang. They pit their meager jeep and Hayduke's Vietnam-formed expertise in demolitions against the big technologies defacing the American Southwest--dams, bridges, energy companies, highways, billboards, and particularly bulldozers, the symbol of the manipulation of the land. The "eco-raiders" are outrageous, "raunchy," and fun. The author's environmental concern results in knowledgeable and passionate writing, but he does not deal with the social implications of sabotage.

1921   Black, MacKnight. MACHINERY. New York: Horace Liveright, 1929. 80 p.

Machines, skyscrapers, bridges, and trains inspire Black's poetry. Several poems reflect reactions to the Corliss engine. An ambivalent attitude is evident. Black is in awe of the generated power, but emptiness, bareness, silence, loneliness, and disillusion permeate his lines. He seems to wonder what sort of birth will result from the metal fertility.

1922   Callenbach, Ernest. ECOTOPIA: THE NOTEBOOKS AND REPORTS OF WILLIAM WESTON. Berkeley, Calif.: Banyan Tree Books, 1975. 167 p.

This highly moralistic underground classic follows the pioneering travels of a journalist through "Ecotopia," an American west coast that has seceded from the rest of technology-bound, recklessly exploitative America. The reporter finds quiet, natural homes and foods, total recycling, mass transit, participatory sports and similar accoutrements appropriate to an ecologically balanced society. The openness and informality of Ecotopian social relations is sharply contrasted to the harsh anonymity and artificiality of the post-industrial East. That the initially suspicious traveler's "diary" records growing approval of Ecotopian lifeways will not surprise anyone.

1923   Cheever, John. BULLET PARK. New York: Alfred A. Knopf, 1969. 245 p.

Commuter transportation dominates this novel of suburban life. Highways and railroad tracks are the scenes of carnage and psychological disorientation. The culture of Bullet Park evolves from the instinctive needs of its human inhabitants to escape their fear of the transportation systems which must be endured in the daily odyssey to and from work. Cocktail parties and extramarital sex provide release. Eliot Nailles appears to cope well until his son drops out of suburban uniformity by taking to his bed permanently and dreaming of mountains. Nailles suddenly cannot face the train without massive, illegal tranquilizers.

1924   Crane, Hart. THE BRIDGE. In THE COMPLETE POEMS AND SELECT-

ED LETTERS AND PROSE OF HART CRANE, edited by Brom Weber, pp. 43-117. New York: Liveright, 1966.

> Brooklyn Bridge, the structure brought into being by a paralyzed architect, is for Crane the manifestation of how man, as builder, can realize his ultimate nature. The indigenous rhythms, forms, and forces of America "flung the span. . .Of that great Bridge, our Myth." But the twentieth-century cacophony is a debasement of man's powers. Macadam and toothpaste ads replace the "steeled Cognizance." We have the Bridge, though, a mechanical mastery of urban chaos. Crane's imagery, symbolism, sound, and language reflect the industrial age.

1925   Crews, Harry. CAR. New York: William Morrow and Co., 1972. 152 p.

> The satire directed at the automobile recognizes it as a machine icon embodying opposing qualities: holy and demonic, creation and destruction. Easy Mack, his daughter Junell, and sons Mister and Herman run a huge junkyard of wrecked cars. They see the history of America, as well as their personal lives, in terms of the car. Herman runs "Car Display: Your History on Parade/See the Car It Happened In. . . ." He also launches a stunt to eat a Maverick. By ingesting his god, he too can become a god. Easy climbs into his car-crusher cradle and commits suicide, but Herman and his girl, Margo, find peace and love in a Rolls Royce Silver Cloud.

1926   Davis, Rebecca Harding. LIFE IN THE IRON MILLS: OR THE KORL WOMAN. 1861. Reprint. Old Westbury, N.Y.: Feminist Press, 1972. 174 p.

> Originally published in the ATLANTIC MONTHLY, April 1861, Davis's short tale is the earliest American literary effort to recreate the gloom, stifling atmosphere, and thwarted lives in an industrial town (Wheeling). Hugh Wolfe, an iron-mill "puddler," is degraded to an animal existence by incessant labor and starvation. Yet there is a craving for beauty within him which is expressed in his sculptures from korl, a waste product. His "korl woman" reaches out imploringly but her face expresses only hopelessness. This edition includes a lengthy biographical interpretation by Tillie Olsen.

1927   Dos Passos, John. MANHATTAN TRANSFER. New York: Harper and Brothers, 1925. 404 p.

> With his collage of literary forms, Dos Passos projects the pace, chaos, tension, sensuousness, cacophony, futility, and dazzling variety of the city. Restless movement and an ab-

surd distortion of reality are created through the author's selection of evocative, fragmentary details and images. Motion without progress, and actions which cancel each other out imprison frenetic characters absorbed within their own starting points. Imagery, technique, and form produce tragedy.

1928 _____. U.S.A. New York: Harcourt Brace and Co., 1938. 1,473 p.

The trilogy of THE 42ND PARALLEL, NINETEEN NINETEEN, and THE BIG MONEY chronicles the conflicting relations of individuals with the particular social and economic institutions or "machines" that arose in America between 1900 and 1930. Jeffersonian ideals were attached by World War I, which was supported by and helped establish big business. The key figure in Dos Passos' shattered America is Thorstein Veblen, who described the alternatives between profit and the wise use of technology for plenty. Ideals are represented by biographical sketches: Andrew Carnegie, Pierpont Morgan, Henry Ford, William Randolph Hearst, and Samuel Insull for monopoly and big business; and the defeated heroes Eugene Debs, Frank Lloyd Wright, Veblen, and Isadora Duncan. The "machines" manufacture social tragedy for twentieth-century America.

1929 Faulkner, William. THE REIVERS. New York: Random House, 1962. 305 p.

Eleven-year-old Lucius Priest's initiation into the adult world is linked to the automobile. The "borrowing" of his grandfather's Winton Flyer is a rebellion against the rules preserving the protective world of his childhood. The journey with friends in the car to Memphis and Parsham leads only to situations beyond the travelers' youthful capacity to control. As the aging Lucius reminisces, it is apparent that the car symbolizes the intrusion of modernity on a hitherto more idyllic world.

1930 Fitzgerald, F. Scott. THE GREAT GATSBY. 1925. New York: Charles Scribner's Sons, 1953. 121 p.

Jay Gatsby, the archetypal American self-made man, creates a world for himself which, like his monetary success, is a product of technology and manipulation. His flesh-colored Rolls Royce, bright with nickel, is the embodiment of his sexual and financial power. But Nick Carroway sees the hope of Adam in his friend. Gatsby is hypnotized by the green light at the end of Daisy's pier, but his romantic vision of a return to pastoral simplicity and innocence with

Daisy is a myopic illusion. The machine has stripped the American Edenic ideal. The automobile, symbol of Gatsby's dreams, is the instrument of destruction.

1931 Fuller, R[ichard]. Buckminster. UNTITLED EPIC POEM ON THE HISTORY OF INDUSTRIALIZATION. New York: Simon and Schuster, 1962. xii, 227 p.

From the perspective of time, Fuller views the rise of industrialization from 1850 to 1940 in this free-verse poem. The prime mover for industrialization is considered to be the "cooperation requirement." Engineers with their "instruments of control" furthered the cause. Fuller then turns to discussions of the interdependencies of inventions and scientific discoveries, the social significance of industrialization, and the concept of the mechanical extension of man. He ends with thoughts on industrialization as the new religion.

1932 Hawthorne, Nathaniel. "The Celestial Rail-Road." 1843. In MOSSES FROM AN OLD MANSE, edited by William Charvat et al., pp. 186-206. The Centenary Edition of the Works of Nathaniel Hawthorne, vol. 10. Columbus: Ohio State University Press, 1974.

A PILGRIM'S PROGRESS for a technological age, modern travelers in this short story journey to the Celestial City via railroad. A tunnel and gas lamps speed and brighten the traverse of the Hill of Difficulty and the Valley of the Shadow of Death. Passengers are convinced that good inventions can substitute for individual virtue and striving. However, there are no shortcuts to salvation; the celestial railroad's destination is the infernal regions.

1933 Lewis, Arthur O., ed. OF MEN AND MACHINES. New York: E.P. Dutton, 1963. xxxi, 349 p.

Views of the relationship of men and machines are presented by writers from several countries utilizing various genres. Many of the selections have achieved classic status. For Francis Bacon, Adam Smith, and Carl Sandburg, the machine is man's greatest hope. Emily Dickinson and Walt Whitman use mechanical images to express a thing of beauty. However, Kurt Vonnegut, Karel Capek, George Orwell, and E.M. Forster see man replaced by machines and reduced to something less than human. Grim forebodings are expressed by Brian Aldiss and Ray Bradbury.

1934 McNeil, John. THE CONSULTANT: A NOVEL OF COMPUTER CRIME. New York: Coward, McCann and Geoghegen, 1978. 297 p.

Written by a computer consultant, the novel provides an

"inside" look at the white-collar criminal whose skill is mastery of complex technology. Christopher Webb minutely explores BANKNET, a gigantic system for processing thousands of financial transactions daily. His suspects are efficient, mild-mannered technocrats.

1935 Melville, Herman. MOBY-DICK. 1851. Rev. critical ed. Edited by Harrison Hayford and Hershel Parker. New York: W.W. Norton and Co., 1967. xviii, 727 p. Maps, bibliog.

Captain Ahab exists in a contrived, orderly, controlled world. He utilizes mechanized routine to segregate and shield himself from Nature. The terror-filled drive to kill the whale becomes an obsession because the animal represents, for Ahab, organic natural forces, chaos, and creative energy. Ahab's barrenness is emphasized by the mechanical imagery with which Melville surrounds him. This edition contains carefully selected critical studies.

1936 _____. "The Tartarus of Maids." 1855. In SELECTED WRITINGS OF HERMAN MELVILLE: COMPLETE SHORT STORIES, TYPEE AND BILLY BUDD, FORETOPMAN, pp. 195-211. New York: Modern Library, 1952.

The setting of the Devil's Dungeon paper mill, with "distorted hemlock," Blood River, and bitter cold is a prelude to the misery of the factory-worker maids. "Mere cogs to the wheels" of the precise, unvarying machines, the young women are all pale-cheeked and blank. "Unbudging fatality" overhangs all. The story originally appeared in HARPER'S NEW MONTHLY MAGAZINE, vol. 10, April 1855.

1937 Norris, Frank. THE OCTOPUS: A STORY OF CALIFORNIA. Garden City, N.Y.: Doubleday, 1901. 361 p. Map.

Presley, the "raisonneur" of the novel, is searching for an epic theme for the "great American novel" he plans to write. He is, however, caught up in a situation devoid of the romance he seeks: the battle between wheat growers, ranchers, and the railroad. Norris modeled the conflict on the bloody Mussel Slough affair between ranchers in the San Joachin Valley and the Southern Pacific Railroad. Presley comes to understand that rancher Magnus Derrick can not win the struggle against the railroad, the "great monster, iron-hearted, relentless, infinitely powerful," but that Derrick's epic greatness lies in his strength to compete against the inevitable. Great failure suggests supreme individual attainment.

1938 O'Neil, Eugene. DYNAMO. New York: Horace Liveright, 1929. viii, 159 p.

Reuben Light, a preacher's son, trades God and the Bible for worship of electricity. Disgusted by his father's religiosity, Reuben considers himself an atheist attuned to science. But the dynamo becomes "a great, dark mother" to whom he kneels in supplication and prays. The hum of the engines is a new chant that hypnotizes its followers. The power house is Reuben's church, and he believes he is the savior who will convert all men to the religion of electricity. After murdering his girlfriend Ada because she is a sensual temptation, he consummates his desire by embracing the dynamo. The result is electrocution.

1939   Pynchon, Thomas. GRAVITY'S RAINBOW. New York: Viking Press, 1973. 760 p.

With a perspective guided by the revelations about human nature to be found in mathematics, organic chemistry, behaviorist psychology, the products of technology, and literature, Pynchon searches for our cultural inheritances. Set in Europe near the end of World War II, the action of the novel centers on the characters' quest for the new Sangraal, a uniquely modified German supersonic V-2 rocket. Pynchon sees a "charisma" in the rocket. Beyond the wires and mechanics there is "some joyful . . . and deeply irrational . . . force the State bureaucracy could never routinize, against which it could not prevail." Pynchon locates human consciousness implanted in the instruments of technology.

1940   Rand, Ayn. ATLAS SHRUGGED. New York: Random House, 1957. 1,168 p.

This caricature of capitalism combines, in the words of a reviewer, realism, "mystery and science fiction with a visit to a kind of technological Shangri-La." The power magnates of industry sell out initiative, imagination, creativity, and independent thought for security and "strangulation." The creators and free spirits fade out except for the rare "superman" who can establish a new social order. The work is marred by polemics.

1941   Sinclair, Upton. THE JUNGLE. New York: Jungle Publishing Co., 1906. Reprint. Cambridge, Mass.: Robert Bentley, 1974. viii, 343 p.

Written to expose the conditions of the Chicago stockyards and meat-packing industry (Armour), THE JUNGLE is a problem novel. As fiction its endowments are slim; however, it presents a documentary, if somewhat propagandistic, account of the squalid lives of workers in the city and the practices of the meat industry. The appalling efficiency of assembly-line methods, the inhuman pace of machinery, and the scandalously unsanitary conditions are emphasized. Additional social evils of the city take everything including life from the immigrants and other city poor. Sinclair's proposed remedy is a socialist system. The novel and the resulting publicity helped urge the passage of the Pure Food and Drug Act.

1942   Skinner, B.F. WALDEN TWO. New York: Macmillan, 1948. 266 p.

Skinner's utopia (dystopia?) demonstrates his belief that human behavior can be shaped to ideal ends through psychological control, using techniques of behavior modification and controlled conditioning. The good life is arrived at through empirical science rather than through speculation. Human beings become commodities manufactured to specifications.

1943   Stadler, John, ed. ECO-FICTION. New York: Washington Square Press, 1971. 211 p.

Science fiction, nature stories, and tales about ecology are collected in this anthology, which seeks to make the reader aware of his relationship with the natural environment and the importance of his actions. Themes emerging from the stories are the disregard of warnings and the paralyzed idleness generated by the vastness and complexity of ecological problems. Among the eighteen stories are: Ray Bradbury's "A Sound of Thunder," John Steinbeck's "The Turtle," James Agee's "A Mother's Tale," Daphne du Maurier's "The Birds," E.B. White's "The Supremacy of Uruguay," Kurt Vonnegut's "Tomorrow and Tomorrow and Tomorrow," Sarah Orne Jewett's "A White Heron," J.G. Ballard's "The Subliminal Man," and Isaac Asimov's "It's Such a Beautiful Day."

1944   Steinbeck, John. THE GRAPES OF WRATH. New York: Viking Press, 1939. Reissue. New York: Viking Press, 1972. xiii, 881 p.

For the sharecroppers and itinerant farmers, the automobile and tractor symbolically represent the forces of big finance and agribusiness which drive families from their land and destroy their lives. While the migration of the Joad family is made pathetic by the broken-down cars, Steinbeck attempts to insert a counterbalance by providing an authorial perspective which considers the machine as neutral. An unbiased stance does not emerge, however, since the destruction of nature and instinct by the machine dominates the novel.

1945   Whitman, Walt. COMPLETE POETRY AND SELECTED PROSE BY WALT WHITMAN. Edited by James E. Miller, Jr. Boston: Houghton Mifflin, Riverside Editions, 1959. liii, 516 p.

Whitman celebrates the new age with a democratic response that embraces "ALL"--technological achievement as well as sensual emotions. In such works as SONG OF THE EXPOSITION, A SONG FOR OCCUPATIONS, and A PASSAGE TO INDIA, industry and its technical jargon are fused with audacity and verve into poetry. He takes no part in the critique of industrialization. The materialistic drive and inventions are seen as preliminaries to an era of unity to be created by the poet. His unfettered, encompassing perspective achieves a synthesis of man and the products of his technological energies.

C. CRITICISM

1. Science Fiction and Utopias

a. BIBLIOGRAPHIES

1946 Barron, Neil, ed. ANATOMY OF WONDER: SCIENCE FICTION. New York: R.R. Bowker Co., 1976. xxi, 471 p.

Designed to assist school and university libraries in building collections and faculty with course development, this critical guide to science fiction selects and annotates important titles as well as providing additional research aids. Each of four chapters devoted to periods, written by specialists in the field, presents an essay on the era and an annotated bibliography of novels. There are also sections on anthologies and juvenile literature. A core collection is highlighted; research tools, journals, and library collections are discussed.

1947 Clareson, Thomas D. SCIENCE FICTION CRITICISM: AN ANNOTATED CHECKLIST. Kent, Ohio: Kent State University Press, 1972. xiii, 225 p.

English-language criticism on science fiction published prior to 1972 in books and journals is included in this comprehensive bibliography. The entries are arranged in nine sections: general studies; literary studies; book reviews; visual arts; futurology, utopia and dystopia; classroom and library; publishing; specialist bibliographies, checklists and indices; and the contemporary scene. There is an author index.

1948 Tymn, Marshall B. A BASIC REFERENCE SHELF FOR SCIENCE FICTION TEACHERS. Exchange Bibliography no. 1523. Monticello, III.: Council of Planning Librarians, 1978. 12 p.

Designed for teachers new to science fiction, this generously annotated bibliography selects and describes the major research

tools and journals in the field. Types of works covered are
biographical guides, bibliographies, indexes to anthologies
and magazines, surveys and histories, author studies, and
film guides.

1949   Tymn, Marshall B.; Schlobin, Roger C.; and Currey, L.W., eds.   A
RESEARCH GUIDE TO SCIENCE FICTION STUDIES: AN ANNOTATED
CHECKLIST OF PRIMARY AND SECONDARY SOURCES FOR FANTASY
AND SCIENCE FICTION. New York: Garland Publishing, 1977.
ix, 165 p.

All major research tools which can assist the scholar, teacher,
or librarian working with science fiction are covered in this
selective guide. General sources such as indexes, bibliographies, and surveys of the field are included along with
histories, journal and anthology indexes, guides to film, and
monographic author studies. There are checklists of magazines which publish science fiction or fantasy material and
special journal issues. An unannotated listing of English-
language dissertations is included.

b. BOOKS AND ARTICLES

1950   Armytage, W.H.G. YESTERDAY'S TOMORROWS: A HISTORICAL
SURVEY OF FUTURE SOCIETIES. London: Routledge and Kegan Paul,
1968. x, 288 p.

Forecasts of the future from ancient and medieval myths to
Herman Kahn reveal that the process of fantasies and daydreams has resulted in the development of operational predictive models. Using Rudolph Bultmann's concept of myth,
Armytage concludes that man's forays into the future are a
"modern mythology" which aids him in self-understanding and
the maintenance of equilibrium in the technological world.
Discussions of Edward Bellamy, Ray Bradbury, Hugo Gernsback,
William Burroughs, Ayn Rand, and Olaf Stapledon are included.

1951   Berger, Albert I. "The Magic That Works: John W. Campbell and
the American Response to Technology." JOURNAL OF POPULAR
CULTURE 5 (Spring 1972): 867-943.

This study explores Campbell's editorship of ASTOUNDING
SCIENCE FICTION and his voicing of the American middle-
class attitude toward science and technology. His editorials
and stories reflect the ambivalent attitude toward technology.
The "wizardry" of science is seen as the source of a technology that is closely tied to man's evolution and solves all
problems. But the danger and evil in power plus a fear of
"the mightiest machine" has been generated by the atomic
and computer eras.

1952   Berger, Harold L. SCIENCE FICTION AND THE NEW DARK AGE.
Bowling Green, Ohio: Bowling Green University Popular Press, 1976.
xi, 231 p. Bibliog.

The dystopian trend in contemporary science fiction is surveyed
through a detailed examination of major and minor works,
many of which have previously received no critical notice.
The study is organized into twelve thematic units: the hostility to science, man versus machine, the synthetic experience,
ignoble utopias, the totalitarian state of the future, the mind
invasion, commerce and exploitation, the revolt of youth,
nuclear war, the population explosion, race war in America,
and the obsessional catastrophe. A comprehensive bibliography of fiction and nonfiction is provided.

1953   Bradbury, Ray. "Day After Tomorrow: Why Science Fiction?"
NATION 176 (2 May 1953): 364-67.

It is "fun" for a writer to consider when an invention stops
being an escape mechanism and becomes a "paranoiacally
dangerous device." The science-fiction writer predicts how
well man will use his mechanical extensions which are
"symbols of his own most secret cravings and desires." The
genre makes "outsized images of problems" so that they can
be understood and handled. "Fun" is the "handmaiden, if
not the progenitor, of the arts."

1954   Bretnor, Reginald, ed. MODERN SCIENCE FICTION: ITS MEANING
AND ITS FUTURE. New York: Coward-McCann, 1953. xii, 294 p.

This symposium is one of the earliest attempts to examine
science fiction in relation to contemporary science, literature,
and human problems. Contents include: "Science Fiction in
Motion Pictures, Radio, and Television," by Don Fabun;
"Science Fiction: Preparation for the Age of Space," by
Arthur Clarke, and "Science Fiction and Sanity in an Age
of Crisis," by Philip Wylie.

1955   Clareson, Thomas D., ed. MANY FUTURES MANY WORLDS: THEME
AND FORM IN SCIENCE FICTION. Kent, Ohio: Kent State University Press, 1977. ix, 303 p.

With articles specially commissioned, Clareson presents various
critical methods by which science fiction can be studied and
traces the traditions from which the genre evolved. Two
surveys of science fiction dealing with computers are included.
Carolyn Rhodes, in "Tyranny By Computer," considers the
portrayal of computers as government agents for surveillance,
tyranny, manipulation, and reductionism by such writers as
Kurt Vonnegut, Kendell Crossen, Mordecai Roshwald, and
Ira Levin. A detailed overview is achieved in Patricia

Warrick's "Images of the Man-Machine Intelligence Relationship in Science Fiction." She categorizes the literature as extrapolative or speculative and relates fictional accounts to studies in the social sciences and actual computer advances.

1956   Cox, James M. "A CONNECTICUT YANKEE IN KING ARTHUR'S COURT: The Machinery of Self-Preservation." YALE REVIEW 50 (September 1960): 89-102.

As the democratic industrialist "gadgeteer" Hank Morgan traveled through rapid-fire inventions to annihilation, Twain was "symbolically killing the machine madness" which possessed him. His own obsession with the Paige typesetter led to an understanding that man needs protection against the "inventive imagination." The Yankee is a mechanistic man who must obey the laws of his "make" and cannot "create anything." Although ridiculed throughout the novel, Merlin's magic predominates at last.

1957   De Bolt, Joe, ed. THE HAPPENING WORLDS OF JOHN BRUNNER: CRITICAL EXPLORATIONS IN SCIENCE FICTION. Port Washington, N.Y.: Kennikat Press, 1975. 216 p. Bibliog.

Two of the interdisciplinary essays in this collection are especially relevant. In "Sic Pavis Magna: Science, Technology, and Ecology in John Brunner's Science Fiction," physicist Robert R. Slocum discusses Brunner's use of technological developments, treatment of ecological issues, and attitudes toward scientists as evidenced primarily in THE SHEEP LOOK UP (1972). Edward L. Lamie and Joe De Bolt, a computer scientist and a sociologist, respectively, consider Brunner's view of the computer and man in the future in "The Computer and Man: The Human Use of Non-Human Beings in the Works of John Brunner." Brunner's concluding response and an extensive bibliography of his publications complete the volume.

1958   Fenton, Charles A. "'The Bell-Tower': Melville and Technology." AMERICAN LITERATURE 23 (May 1951): 219-32.

Bannadonna, Melville's renaissance mechanic who builds a tower and bells to rival nature, mirrors the nineteenth-century American capitalist-industrialist. As the tower rises, so does Bannadonna's vanity and creative pride, and the populace unquestionably supports his egoism. His death by the mechanical robot he has built demonstrates that his technological perfection is fatal. Bannadonna is destroyed by his total absorption in mechanics at the expense of the natural.

1959   Hirsch, Walter. "The Image of the Scientist in Science Fiction: A

Content Analysis." AMERICAN JOURNAL OF SOCIOLOGY 63
(March 1968): 506-12.

A survey of science-fiction stories published between 1926
and 1950 reveals several socially relevant trends. The
number of scientists as heroes and villains decreases while
the role of businessmen as villains increases. The independent
scientist is replaced by the organization man enmeshed in
bureaucracy. Social problems of the human race are increasingly solved by aliens rather than by technology.

1960 Hollister, Bernard C., and Thompson, Deane C. GROKKING THE
FUTURE: SCIENCE FICTION IN THE CLASSROOM. Dayton, Ohio:
Pflaum Standard, 1973. 168 p. Illus., bibliog.

Although designed for high-school teachers, this guide for
approaching social issues through science fiction is valuable
for college use. In each chapter devoted to a social
problem, works of science fiction are discussed and the insights they provide are demonstrated. Issues considered are:
ecology, population, computers, automobiles, nuclear weapons, social order and control, prejudice, economics, cities,
and the generation gap. A stated purpose is to promote
creative thinking and thus increase options for tomorrow--to
help students "grok" (grasp with all their senses) the future.

1961 Isaacs, Leonard. DARWIN TO DOUBLE HELIX: THE BIOLOGICAL
THEME IN SCIENCE FICTION. London: Butterworth, 1977. 64 p.
Bibliog.

Designed for a college-level course which considers the use
of evolution and genetics in science fiction, the text is
divided into two parts: literary responses to Darwin's theory
of evolution with attention to projections of man's evolutionary future, and readings in more recent science fiction dealing with man's intervention in the processes of heredity and
development--genetic manipulation. There are annotated
reading lists, discussion points, and questions for each chapter.

1962 Jonas, Gerald. "Onward and Upward with the Arts: SF." NEW
YORKER, 29 July 1972, pp. 33-36, 38, 43-44, 46, 46, 48-52.

It is not technical jargon that separates science fiction from
the mainstream; rather, it is a "pseudo-technical shorthand"
devised by writers in the genre to utilize science and technology without letting it hinder fancy. Science fiction is
recognized now as a model-making activity that helps us organize our lives. The actualization of technologies, such as
space travel and the moon landing, has liberated science-

fiction writers from the "delusion" that their business is only technological/scientific prophecy.

1963   JOURNAL OF GENERAL EDUCATION 28 (Spring 1976): 1-82: entire issue.

Nine papers presented at the Science Fiction Research Association conference in 1973 are collected in this issue. The philosophical limitations of the genre are discussed by Patrick Hogan, while David Larson attempts to account for the severe critical attacks on science fiction. Carolyn Rhodes finds Frederick Taylor's scientific management evident in Eugene Zamiatin's WE, Charles Brady considers Harlan Ellison's use of the computer as a symbol of God, and Kent Forrester studies Ray Bradbury's MARTIAN CHRONICLES (no. 1884). General comments on the values of science fiction, by J.O. Bailey, conclude the issue.

1964   Kelly, R. Gordon. "Ideology in Some Modern Science Fiction Novels." JOURNAL OF POPULAR CULTURE 2 (Fall 1968): 211-27.

A reading of fifteen contemporary American science-fiction novels, by such authors as Robert Heinlein, Isaac Asimov, Murray Leinster, A.E. Van Vogt, and Alfred Bester, reveals that the mass appeal of the genre may be based on its affirmation of science and technology as the basis for cultural advancement. While each of the novels has a hero trained in science, generally a loner and of lower-class origins, the hero cannot save mankind from destruction; instead, a powerful device created by science and technology saves the day. Represents an attack on the future since science conquers the limitations of heredity and environment with the result that man's capabilities are reduced.

1965   Ketterer, David. NEW WORLDS FOR OLD: THE APOCALYPTIC IMAGINATION, SCIENCE FICTION, AND AMERICAN LITERATURE. Garden City, N.Y.: Anchor Press, Doubleday, 1974. xii, 347 p.

Contemporary science fiction is related to apocalyptic literature as well as to mainstream American literature. Intense critical scrutiny examines the literary potential of the genre and its concordance with the American experience. The merger of religion and technology in the visionary realities of Kurt Vonnegut, Stanislaw Lem, and Ursula Le Guin is analyzed in relation to the works of Charles Brockden Brown, Edgar Poe, Mark Twain, and Herman Melville.

1966   Landsman, Gail. "Science Fiction: The Rebirth of Mythology." JOURNAL OF POPULAR CULTURE 5 (Spring 1972): 989-96.

Western culture, dominated by technology and a "scientific

perspective," has stripped man of illusions and visions. Science-fiction writers, such as Kurt Vonnegut, Ray Bradbury, and George Orwell, utilize potential technological innovations to create an irrational realm where myth once again gives life meaning. Like the primitive mythologies of North American Indian tribes, "idea as hero" fills rationalism's visionary void and relates man to his universe.

1967 McClintock, James I. "United State Revisited: Pynchon and Zamiatin." CONTEMPORARY LITERATURE 18 (Autumn 1977): 475-90.

Eugene Zamiatin and Thomas Pynchon, whose novels WE (1924) and GRAVITY'S RAINBOW (no. 1939) are separated by fifty years, both wrote about "modernism's crises of mind and spirit. . .occasioned by the rise of science, technology, bureaucracy, and despotism." For both, science, technology, and catastrophe are linked. Entropy is the dominant symbol: Zamiatin emphasizes the final state of absolute zero while Pynchon focuses on the process of increasing disorder and dissipation of energy. The same elements are united symbolically in these novels: "rockets, transcendence, miracles, zeroes, mathematics, and revelation."

1968 Mellard, James M. "The Modes of Vonnegut's Fiction: Or, PLAYER PIANO Ousts MECHANICAL BRIDE and THE SIRENS OF TITAN Invade THE GUTENBERG GALAXY." In THE VONNEGUT STATEMENT, edited by Jerome Klinkowitz and John Somer, pp. 178-203. New York: Delacorte Press, 1973.

From PLAYER PIANO (no. 1918) to THE SIRENS OF TITAN (no. 1919), Vonnegut makes the transition from pictorial to oral modes of expression. In the latter novel, the theme of the mechanization of man and society is expressed through a medium that is "non-literate, implicit, simultaneous, and discontinuous." His interests are "subliterary"; thus the substance of the novel is reduced to the vernacular, archetypes, triteness, cliché, and popular sentimental values. In a technological culture he finds a way to reveal countervalues of love, courage, and kindness.

1969 Ower, John B. "Manacle-Forged Minds: Two Images of the Computer in Science Fiction." DIOGENES, no. 85 (Spring 1974): 47-61.

Through projective analysis, science fiction has the capacity to contend with accelerating technological innovation. Today, the computer possesses the potential for "suddenly precipitated developments" surpassing prediction. Ower's consideration of Harlan Ellison's "I Have No Mouth & I Must Scream" (no. 1897) and Arthur C. Clarke's 2001: A SPACE ODYSSEY (no. 1889) reveals that both works reflect conservative fear of technology and a conviction that man "will create his electronic

alter-ego not with due wisdom and forethought, but rather
out of his ignorance and evil." Both computers, frustrated by
their limitations in the ability to live and die like men, turn
to vengeance against their creators. The two works also
demonstrate a shift from faith in a secular New Jerusalem
back toward a traditional sense of Man's fallen nature.

1970 Plank, Robert. "Science Fiction." AMERICAN JOURNAL OF ORTHO-
PSYCHIATRY 30 (October 1960): 799-810.

The literature of science fiction reflects the isolation felt by
modern man amidst a technological world. Within the dominant milieu of men in science fiction, there is little sex or
sexual encounters are disastrous and repulsive, procreation is
bypassed by an infinite variety of methods, there is no father
figure, and the hero reflects the child's fantasy of omnipo-
tence. Just like the schizophrenic, the science-fiction
writer suspends the rules of reality. The world he creates
delineates the psychological significance of the machine age.

1971 Richter, Peyton E., ed. UTOPIAS: SOCIAL IDEALS AND COMMUNAL
EXPERIMENTS. Boston: Holbrook Press, 1971. xi, 323 p.

General discussions on utopian ideals and planning are followed by studies of famous utopias including New Harmony,
Brook Farm, and Oneida. Contrasted to these are the
dystopias created in the literature of Dostoyevsky and Aldous
Huxley. "Utopia rejoinders" by H.G. Wells, B.F. Skinner,
and Edward Bellamy complete the text. Discussion questions
and suggestions for further reading conclude each section.

1972 Roemer, Kenneth M. THE OBSOLETE NECESSITY: AMERICA IN
UTOPIAN WRITINGS, 1888-1900. Kent, Ohio: Kent State University
Press, 1976. xiv, 239 p. Illus., bibliog.

One hundred and sixty fictional and nonfictional utopian and
dystopian writings are examined to see what these works reveal about American culture during the rapidly changing new
world of industrialization. Roemer evaluates the proposed
utopian reforms and speculations which were designed to combat problems such as "economic slumps, technological unemployment, social inequality, pollution, sex discrimination, and
corruption in government." An ambivalence toward change is
evident in the utopian visions, especially in regard to reactions to machines, nature, and cities. Edward Bellamy,
Mark Twain, and William Dean Howells receive close attention. Extensive, annotated bibliographies supplement.

1973 Scholes, Robert. STRUCTURAL FABULATION: AN ESSAY ON FIC-
TION OF THE FUTURE. Notre Dame, Ind.: University of Notre Dame

Press, 1975. xi, 111 p. Bibliog.

This critical study explores the value of science fiction as literature which provides imaginative models of the future. Scholes relates the genre to literary traditions and offers a historical framework within which fiction that insists on a "radical discontinuity" between imaginative and real worlds can be considered. Works of Olaf Stapledon, John Brunner, and Frank Herbert are discussed as examples of three forms of literature--philosophy, history, and romance, respectively. The final chapter is devoted to Ursula Le Guin, the "good witch of the West."

1974 Segal, Howard P. "American Visions of Technological Utopia, 1883-1933." MARKHAM REVIEW 7 (Summer 1978): 65-76.

Twenty-five fictional and nonfictional technological utopias appearing in this fifty-year period provide "full-scale blueprints" of ideal societies, including physical appearance, institutions, inhabitants, and values. Included are works by engineers and industrialists. Societies "run by and for technology" emphasize efficiency, order, self-control, cleanliness, and harmony. Technology and nature are "domesticated." Transportation and communication systems are usually described in detail as are the values of technocracy. By imitating the machine, man finds fulfillment. Extensive documentation includes a listing of technological utopians and their writings.

1975 _____. "YOUNG WEST: The Psyche of Technological Utopianism." EXTRAPOLATION 19 (December 1977): 50-58.

Soloman Schindler's novel YOUNG WEST (1894) is typical of the multitude of technological utopian visions published between 1833 and 1933. The values and goals articulated describe the "anal character"--"excessive cleanliness, neatness, efficiency, rigidity, and control." The protagonist, West, is paradoxically obsessed with messiness and dirt. His discovery of a process whereby offal can be sanitized, deodorized, and transformed into fertilizer catapults him to the Presidency of the land.

1976 Smith, Henry Nash. MARK TWAIN'S FABLE OF PROGRESS: POLITICAL AND ECONOMIC IDEAS IN "A CONNECTICUT YANKEE." New Brunswick, N.J.: Rutgers University Press, 1964. 116 p.

By the 1880s, industrialization made the traditional system of values in American culture seem irrelevant. Twain, in A CONNECTICUT YANKEE IN KING ARTHUR'S COURT (no. 1891), attempted to create new values justifying capitalism based on post-industrial America. Through the fable,

Twain hoped to alleviate fear of the machine and its disruptive capacities. The result, however, was failure. He
found the values of his vernacular protagonist, Hank Morgan,
incapable of transferral to the actual industrial society.

1977   West, Robert H.   "Science Fiction and Its Ideas."   GEORGIA REVIEW
        15 (Fall 1961):   276-86.

        The "humanistic values" science fiction shares with science
        and technology are a command over nature and the perfect-
        ibility of man's intellect. However, both science and its
        "consequence," science fiction, also favor nonhumanistic
        goals such as the cherishing of man's characteristics that
        favor science at the expense of the rest, and a view of the
        universe in which man is seen as insignificant and alien.
        While the fiction is man-centered, it denies that the uni-
        verse is likewise. The world is seen as random and life is
        an accident. When man's nature is "telescopically viewed,"
        he is important enough to possess a fragment of the universe,
        but he will not last.

2. Other Genres

a. SURVEYS

Bibliographies

1978   Donovan, Frank P.   THE RAILROAD IN LITERATURE.   Boston: Railway
        and Locomotive Historical Society, and Baker Library, Harvard Business
        School, 1940.   ix, 138 p.   Illus., maps.

        Bibliographies and brief essays document the presence of the
        railroad in American and British novels, short stories, juvenile
        fiction, poetry, songs, biography, drama, and travel literature.
        While the bibliography is valuable for extent of coverage,
        especially of popular literature, it is dated and lacks qualita-
        tive judgment. The period 1890-1910 is considered to be the
        "golden age" in railroad literature.

1979   Dudley, Fred A.   THE RELATIONS OF LITERATURE AND SCIENCE:
        A SELECTED BIBLIOGRAPHY, 1930-1967.   Ann Arbor, Mich.:
        University Microfilms, 1968.   137 p.

        The unannotated bibliography provides a listing of literary
        criticism which considers the use and influence of science and
        technology in literature. Dudley combines the annual bibliog-
        raphies which appeared in SYMPOSIUM (no. 1980). Organi-
        zation is minimal and quality of reproduction is poor.

1980   "Relations of Literature and Science: A Bibliography of Scholarship."
        CLIO.   1951-- .   Annual.

Critical studies which relate literature and science are cited
in this bibliography. Appearing first in 1951, it has generally
been published annually, with some gaps, first in SYMPO-
SIUM, then in CLIO. The listing is arranged by period:
general studies, antiquity and the Middle Ages, Renaissance,
seventeenth and eighteenth centuries, nineteenth century,
and twentieth century. Fred A. Dudley, in THE RELATIONS
OF LITERATURE AND SCIENCE: A SELECTED BIBLIOG-
RAPHY, 1930-1967, combines the bibliographies to 1967 (no.
1979). Those responsible for the bibliography over the
years are Kester Svendsen, Samuel I. Mintz, Laurie Bowman
Zwicky, and presently Walter Schatzberg. Citations for the
appearances of the bibliography are as follows: SYMPO-
SIUM 6 (May 1952): 241-45; SYMPOSIUM 7 (May 1953):
207-11; SYMPOSIUM 8 (Summer 1954): 208-13; SYMPO-
SIUM 15 (Winter 1961): 311-19; SYMPOSIUM 17 (Winter
1963): 308-17; SYMPOSIUM 18 (Winter 1964): 374-81;
SYMPOSIUM 19 (Fall 1965): 277-84; SYMPOSIUM 21 (Fall
1967): 277-87; CLIO 4 (October 1974): 73-93; CLIO 5
(Fall 1975): 97-121; CLIO 6 (Fall 1976): 71-88, CLIO 7
(Fall 1977): 135-55; CLIO 8 (Fall 1978): 97-116.

Books and Articles

1981   Arden, Eugene. "The Evil City in American Fiction." NEW YORK
HISTORY 35 (July 1954): 259-79.

While the provincial attitude of hack and lesser novelists depicts New York City as dangerous but alluring, perceptive
novelists such as Upton Sinclair, Charles Dudley Warner, and
especially Edith Wharton, portray a morally devoid community
bent on quick wealth and social ambition. The city is adversary and destroyer of innocence in the popular fiction of
Horatio Alger and others; nevertheless, the novels enticed
rural folks to the city. "Acidulous satire" and perceptive
understanding of the culture of New York City is left to
Edith Wharton in THE HOUSE OF MIRTH (1905), THE AGE
OF INNOCENCE (1920), and OLD NEW YORK (1924).

1982   Bender, Bert A. "Let There Be (Electric) Light! The Image of Electricity in American Writing." ARIZONA QUARTERLY 34 (Spring 1978):
55-70.

Although harnessed by technology, electricity remains an
"inexplicable phenomenon." American writers have seized
electricity as a medium to express conflict--between the
machine and the garden, within the divided self, between
culture and the individual. Bender surveys the use of such
imagery from the qualified wonder of Jonathan Edwards,
Benjamin Franklin, and Walt Whitman, to the skepticism of

Nathaniel Hawthorne and Herman Melville, on to the horror and darkness evident in Ernest Hemingway and F. Scott Fitzgerald. Finally, the role of electricity in Ralph Ellison's INVISIBLE MAN (1952) sums up its use in our literature. In his quest for light, the protagonist finds "a dark knowledge of himself and of his culture's power structures."

1983   Beum, Robert.   "Literature and Machinisme." SEWANEE REVIEW 86 (Spring 1978): 217-44.

While many writers from the early nineteenth century to the present have been receptive to the literary possibilities of machines, technological progress, and urbanization, those who move from a perception of the machine itself to a consideration of its effects on civilization develop metaphors and symbols that suggest the negative, monotonous, ominous, or destructive. Even science fiction fails to affirm technology. Machines are often villains or symbols of evil designed to contrast to pastoral tradition. The development of antitechnological and antimaterialistic literature constitutes "true progress."

1984   Bowman, Sylvia E.   "Utopian Views of Man and the Machine." STUDIES IN THE LITERARY IMAGINATION 6 (Fall 1973): 105-20.

Edward Bellamy, in LOOKING BACKWARD: 2000-1887 (no. 1881), envisioned the use of the machine and economic equality to free men from "mind-stultifying toil" and allow the cultivation of the spiritual and intellectual life. Today, authors such as Ernest Becker, Lewis Mumford, John McHale, Victor Ferkiss, Bruno Bettelheim, William Braden, and Russell Kirk challenge us to strive for an education that goes beyond "training" to an ethical and social development which will direct value commitments and creativity toward the beneficial utilization of technology.

1985   Bowron, Bernard; Marx, Leo; and Rose, Arnold.   "Literature and Covert Culture." AMERICAN QUARTERLY 9 (Winter 1957): 377-86.

Imagery and metaphor present in nineteenth-century American literature reveal repressed, contradictory, or "covert" attitudes toward technology. That celebrations of the machine often endow engines with the characteristics of monsters is evidence of unacknowledged fear and hostility. This ambiguity, skillfully reflected by the perceptive writers of the period, is the result of the conflict in values between nature and progress in America.

1986   Carter, Nancy Corson.   "1970 Images of the Machine and the Garden: Kosinski, Crews, and Pirsig." SOUNDINGS 61 (Spring 1978): 105-22.

Three novels of the seventies articulate uneasy and ambivalent attitudes toward the mechanical and the natural. Henry Crews's CAR (no. 1925), Jerzy Kosinski's BEING THERE (1970), and Robert Pirsig's ZEN AND THE ART OF MOTOR-CYCLE MAINTENANCE (no. 1624), respectively examine three machine icons in our culture: car, television set, motorcycle. All three suggest that "neither the machine nor nature alone can save us, that somehow we must effect a mythic and realistic reconciliation of the two." A progression can be seen from the "bizarre iconoclasm" in CAR to "ironic recon-ciliation" in BEING THERE, to an achieved "myth of whole-ness" in Pirsig's work.

1987   Clark, John R. "The Machine Prevails: A Modern Technological Theme." JOURNAL OF POPULAR CULTURE 12 (Summer 1978): 118-26.

The modern spirit, as expressed in literature of this century, voices an uneasiness, distrust, and fear of technology. Early dystopias where the machine overtakes civilization (E.M. Forster, Karel Capek, Elmer Rice, Eugene O'Neill) are followed by comedy in the 1930s (James Thurber, E.B. White, Robert Coover). But after the bomb, the image of the ma-chine becomes more ferocious and prevalent. In works by Kurt Vonnegut, Thomas Pynchon, John Barth, and Arthur Clarke, the machine becomes the superior intellect which controls. Mechanical apparatus is only the obvious focus of fear. This literature reveals that man really trembles over the ambiguities and delusions of human inventors.

1988   Dettlebach, Cynthia G. IN THE DRIVER'S SEAT: THE AUTOMOBILE IN AMERICAN LITERATURE AND POPULAR CULTURE. Westport, Conn.: Greenwood Press, 1976. xii, 139 p. Illus., bibliog.

American culture, a particular union of "space, romance, and technology," is concretized in the automobile. The car is an ambivalent metaphor of the American dream/nightmare experience. American artists and writers reveal that dreams of innocence, freedom, success, and possession end in night-mares of experience, constraint, failure, and of being pos-sessed. From William Faulkner, John Hawkes, and John Updike to Woody Guthrie, Tom Wolfe, Jason Seley, and AMERICAN GRAFFITI, all motorized quests end in the junk-yard. Adolescent worship of the machine leads to an experi-enced view of the car as destroyer of dreams and as symbol of a technological future that does not work.

1989   Deutsch, Babette. "The Future of Poetry." NEW REPUBLIC 60 (21 August 1929): 12-15.

This early statement of the problems of the poet confronting the machine recognizes that the mechanized age is perilous to poetry not because of rapid change or the breakdown of traditions, but instead because it creates a world empty of emotional values. We cannot yet respond passionately to the machine because engines, dynamos, and devices are constantly new and changing. Until such elements of civilization become familiar, the artist cannot incorporate them into poetry.

1990 Dworkin, Martin S. "Poetry and the Machine." DALHOUSIE REVIEW 42 (Winter 1962–63): 445–51.

While it may appear that the machine age is beyond poetry, the problem is one of poets. Civilization is not to blame; instead, the poet must contend with the new sounds, "newer pulsings," "human disarrangings," complexities, speed, the rhythms and meters brought by the machine in order to reveal unity. Even if impotence is the response, its expression demands power.

1991 Earnest, Ernest. "Poets in Overalls." VIRGINIA QUARTERLY REVIEW 18 (Autumn 1942): 518–29.

Contemporary "literary" writers often have little understanding of the machine, and thus their attitudes are dread of the unfamiliar, a sense of magic, and disdain for the common worker. The self-consciousness of the imagery they create results in poetic fallacy. The machine is romanticized into something it is not. In folk poetry, however, the machine is not alien and the images are mechanical. Poets need familiarization with the Casey Joneses and the Jim Bludsoes.

1992 Engle, Paul. "Poetry in a Machine Age." ENGLISH JOURNAL 26 (June 1937): 429–39.

The writing of poetry has been altered by the machine. The mechanization of daily life and the power of technology have changed our attitudes. Poetry must draw more images from machines because they have replaced nature in our experience. Engle notes that the problem with using science and technology in verse is the poet's lack of association.

1993 [Everett, Edward.] "The Poetry of Discovery." SCIENTIFIC AMERICAN 5 (24 November 1849): 77.

There is strong resemblance between the "bards of machinery and the bards of literature." Inventors are the poets of science and possess "the faculty of imagination" to a great degree. Printing, the steam engine, and other machines have revolutionized life, but poetry gives a prophetic description of the means by which such social revolutions occur. This brief statement of the relations between technology and art demonstrates the unity of thought which existed before the "two cultures" split.

1994 Fisher, Marvin [M.] "The Iconology of Industrialism, 1830-60." AMERICAN QUARTERLY 13 (Fall 1961): 347-64.

The ambivalent attitudes of Europeans and Americans to American technology are revealed in the imagery and metaphors present in their written responses. The value conflict between the beneficence of nature and its denial by industry is expressed by metaphors which domesticate or humanize the machine. American authors resorted to "transcendental self-deception" to harmonize mechanized objects with nature. Railroads, factories, and cities were the focus of much response.

1995 Gelfant, Blanche Housman. THE AMERICAN CITY NOVEL. Norman: University of Oklahoma Press, 1954. 289 p. Bibliog.

An analysis of the literary methods of city novelists reveals the relationship between social vision and aesthetic technique. "Personal dissociation," the destruction of self-divided man, is the pervasive theme. Gelfant considers how Theodore Dreisler, Sherwood Anderson, Edith Wharton, Thomas Wolfe, John Dos Passos, James Farrell, and others develop their own modern idiom to express fragmentation with form, imagery, theme, setting, and language. Included are selected lists of city fiction and background readings.

1996 Green, Martin. SCIENCE AND THE SHABBY CURATE OF POETRY: ESSAYS ABOUT THE TWO CULTURES. London: Longmans, Green and Co., 1964. 159 p.

Written by a literary scholar who took C.P. Snow to heart and redirected the course of his own intellectual training, these essays either weigh the inadequacy of the "literary" mind to comprehend the modern world or discuss the author's reactions to his study of the sciences and teaching in a technological college. The imagination of the literary mind is unbalanced, "too purely psychological-moral," sentimental, and nostalgic. Such scholars cannot form a viable response to their environment. Included is a survey of science fiction and science nonfiction.

1997 I'LL TAKE MY STAND: THE SOUTH AND THE AGRARIAN TRADITION, BY TWELVE SOUTHERNERS. New York: Harper and Brothers, 1930. xx, 359 p.

The agrarian way of life, a culture where the small farm

receives economic preference, is encouraged in these essays by members of the "Nashville Group." Their ideal is what Leo Marx later termed the "middle landscape." Industrialism and applied science are seen as uncritical, extravagant, and brutalizing to the human spirit. Labor-saving devices cause unemployment, make labor burdensome, and lead to "satiety and aimlessness." Among the essayists are John Crowe Ransom, Allen Tate, Andrew Nelson Lytle, and Robert Penn Warren.

1998   Jameson, Storm. "The Writer in Contemporary Society." AMERICAN SCHOLAR 35 (Winter 1965-66): 67-77.

Computers and mass media are causing the death of arts which depend on "an individual hand and brain." Television is pushing the writer out of the market because the public, used to instantaneous entertainment, is not prepared to wait for the writer's lengthy unfolding of experience. Machines, however, will never be able to reproduce the complex improvisation and profound insights into the human condition which occur in great literature. Instead of escaping the machine, the writer must become free of it.

1999   Martin, Jay. HARVESTS OF CHANGE: AMERICAN LITERATURE 1865-1914. Englewood Cliffs, N.J.: Prentice-Hall, 1967. 382 p.

An accounting of the forces that helped mold the American consciousness, this study relates major and minor American writers to the culture of the era covered. The discussion of the idea of a national identity leads to the regionalist romantics, who, through cynicism and nostalgia, were driven to disaffection with their age. The author turns to the utopian and dystopian novelists who responded to technological changes by projecting hopes and frustrations forward. Their fears are epitomized in the city. Martin then moves to the use of naturalism as a device to depict materialist society, and finally to alienation.

2000   Marx, Leo. THE MACHINE IN THE GARDEN: TECHNOLOGY AND THE PASTORAL IDEAL IN AMERICA. New York: Oxford University Press, 1964. 392 p. Illus.

A tension developed early in our history as American society moved away from innocence and nature to cities, machines, and war. Marx traces the adaptation of a metaphor of "the middle landscape," an ideal between naive primitivism and corrupt civilization, and its transformation under the impact of industrialization. Through an exploration of American literary response to the general culture, Marx dramatically unfolds the effects of machine technology upon consciousness.

The acceptance of Ralph Waldo Emerson and Walt Whitman becomes unreconciled tension in Nathaniel Hawthorne, Herman Melville, and Mark Twain, then finally terror for F. Scott Fitzgerald. A dislocation of mind and emotion results when society cannot call upon existing myths to resolve two systems of values.

2001 _____. "Pastoral Ideals and City Troubles." JOURNAL OF GENERAL EDUCATION 20 (January 1969): 251-71.

The symbolic landscape and narrative structure throughout American literature contains movement through three environments: retreat from civilization to an exploration of simple, harmonious nature, followed by a return to society. Looking at the work of Robert Frost and Ernest Hemingway, it is clear that the Arcadian dream is not a permanent alternative to urban industrial society. The purpose of retreat is not escape but psychological and metaphysical renewal. "Retreat is useful only if temporary." Our writers have not been able to solve the dilemma of retaining the renewed sense of coherence in civilization; thus, most works end in ambiguity. Literary pastoralism suggests the necessity of preserving diverse physical settings.

2002 _____. "Two Kingdoms of Force." MASSACHUSETTS REVIEW 1 (October 1959): 62-95.

The tension created by the conflict between two essential values, the natural landscape and the machine, has formed the culture of America. Writers such as Nathaniel Hawthorne, Mark Twain, Herman Melville, and Frank Norris employ clashing imagery and sounds to express the conflicts of values occasioned by technology. Our literature demonstrates that the pervasiveness of the machine has heightened the dialectical tendency to see everything as a collision of opposing forces such as the natural and the artificial, heart and head, love and power.

2003 "The Modern Novel and the City." MODERN FICTION STUDIES 24 (Spring 1978): 3-153.

Among the studies comprising this special issue are an investigation of the changing function of the city in literature by Diane Levy; Hana Wirth-Nesher's analysis of the city in modern Jewish novels of Franz Kafka, Henry Roth, and Amos Oz; a study of William Dean Howells's characterization in A MODERN INSTANCE (1882) by Jacqueline Tavernier-Courbin; Thomas Gullason's consideration of Stephen Crane's vision of the "hysteria" of city reality in MAGGIE (1892); and a look at the Chicago of Saul Bellow by Sarah Cohen. Concludes with a checklist of studies of the modern novel and the city.

2004 Nemerov, Howard. "Speculative Equations: Poem, Poets, Computers."
AMERICAN SCHOLAR 36 (Summer 1967): 394-414.

> Whether computers can write poetry and the value of the use
> of computers in the study of poetry are Nemerov's two con-
> siderations. Mechanical regularity was sought after until it
> became a daily reality; thus machine-produced poetry may be
> acceptable. People will get the kind of poetry they deserve.
> If their minds are "compassable" to sophisticated machines,
> their poetry will be written by machines. Scholars applying
> the computer to humanities research often become so
> "fuddled" by science that they lose the significance of
> findings.

2005 Purdy, Strother B. THE HOLE IN THE FABRIC: SCIENCE, CONTEM-
PORARY LITERATURE, AND HENRY JAMES. Pittsburgh: University
of Pittsburgh Press, 1977. 228 p.

> The knowledge made possible by science and technology has
> ironically had a corrosive effect on "what is known" about
> the nature of physical reality and has verified the unanswer-
> ability of certain questions. Such consciousness has led con-
> temporary writers of fiction to dwell on four concerns: super-
> natural horror which poses the problem of an unlocatable
> "other world," disoriented time, eroticism where the sexual
> relationship is located beyond physicality, and nothingness.
> Contemporary writers such as Kurt Vonnegut, John Barth,
> Vladimir Nabokov, Samuel Beckett, John Fowles, Gunter
> Grass, Alain Robbe-Grillet, Arthur Clarke, Jorge Borges,
> and Eugene Ionesco, rather than having been influenced by
> their immediate predecessors, the modern novelists, find
> relevancies and the treatment of their concerns in Henry
> James's fiction.

2006 Rose, Alan Henry. "Sin and the City: The Uses of Disorder in the
Urban Novel." CENTENNIAL REVIEW 16 (Summer 1972): 203-20.

> An "urban obsession" dominates American novels perhaps be-
> cause the complexity, amorality, and disorder of the urban
> experience acts positively as initiation in a hero's develop-
> ment to maturity. Five novels are considered: Charles
> Brockden Brown's ARTHUR MERVYN (1800), Bayard Taylor's
> JOHN GODFREY'S FORTUNES (1864), Theodore Dreiser's
> SISTER CARRIE (1900), F. Scott Fitzgerald's THE GREAT
> GATSBY (no. 1930), and J.D. Salinger's THE CATCHER IN THE
> RYE (1951). The early mystical overtones, fantasy, abandon,
> and hope of regeneration give way to psychological, subjec-
> tive novels where the city offers not maturity but "confusion,
> frustration, and barrenness."

2007 Siegel, Adrienne. "When Cities Were Fun: The Image of the American

City in Popular Books, 1840-70." JOURNAL OF POPULAR CULTURE 9 (Winter 1975): 573-82.

A glut of popular fiction during these decades presented an exciting view of urban life to a mass rural audience. Novels revealed a life-style of fun, freedom, abundance, wonder, the exotic, social conviviality, and opportunity for wealth and culture. The literature exerted a powerful influence in forming the popular conception of the city and thus served as a psychological force drawing people to the metropolis.

2008   Spears, Monroe K. DIONYSUS AND THE CITY: MODERNISM IN TWENTIETH-CENTURY POETRY. New York: Oxford University Press, 1970. ix, 278 p.

Modernism, essentially a break with tradition and convention, is traced in American and British poetry from its emergence in 1909-14, to its discovery by Southern poets a decade later, and finally to a new movement beginning in the late 1950s. The ambivalence created by emancipation from restrictions and the dissolution of tradition and meaning is considered the primary tenet of modernism. Originally modernism was related to the advent of photography, radio, movies, the automobile, and the airplane. The second revolution, that of the 1950s, is associated with accelerating technologies-- the atom bomb, television, the contraceptive pill, and DNA. Such poets as Hart Crane, T.S. Eliot, Allen Ginsberg, Robert Lowell, Ezra Pound, John Crowe Ransom, Allen Tate, Robert Penn Warren, and William Butler Yeats display preoccupation with deep Dionysian natural urges as they are forced to exist in a rational societal setting--the city.

2009   Sypher, Wylie. LITERATURE AND TECHNOLOGY: THE ALIEN VISION. New York: Random House, 1968. xxi, 257 p. Bibliog.

Method is the essence not only of science and technology but also of the arts. Sypher considers how experiments in realism, impressionism, symbolism, and decadence resulted from a reliance on method rather than an imitation of nature. The scientific method's controlled observation, which developed abstract laws not based on actuality, and the asceticism of method in literature and art made the artist and scientist alike alien to life. Style became a "technological artifice." Sypher contends that technology and art will continue to stimulate each other.

2010   Taylor, Walter Fuller. THE ECONOMIC NOVEL IN AMERICA. Chapel Hill: University of North Carolina Press, 1942. xi, 378 p. Bibliog.

Covering only those novels of the late nineteenth century con-

cerned with economic matters, Taylor interprets the response
of American novelists to industrialization and the machine
age. In Mark Twain, Hamlin Garland, Edward Bellamy,
William Dean Howells, and Frank Norris there is an "incisive
critique of capitalistic industrialism" and a belief in the
natural goodness of man. Attention is also given to lesser
novelists, and an extensive bibliography of fiction and criticism is appended.

2011   Viereck, Peter. "The Muse and the Machine: Impact of Industrialism
on Poets--and on Humanity." ETUDES ANGLAISES 20 (January-
March 1967): 38-46.

Writers who have taken a stand on mechanization's impact on
ultimate values in modern culture can be classified into eight
groups. The writers on the antimechanist side are either
"esthetic wincers, pious scorners, back-to-instinct prophets,
or trapped individualists." In contrast the pro-mechanists are
"middle-class materialists, socialist materialists, gadget
cultists, or lion (machine)-tamers." Among the most influential lion-tamers or synthesizers are Ralph Waldo Emerson and
Hart Crane. Crane's THE BRIDGE (no. 1924) is "the most
extraordinary example of the psychological impact of mechanization."

2012   Walker, Robert H. "The Poet and the Rise of the City." MISSISSIPPI
VALLEY HISTORICAL REVIEW 49 (June 1962): 85-99.

Poetry produced in the gilded age (1876-1905) displays a
"preponderance of negative reaction" which anticipates later
social research. A combination of agrarian traditions and
the defensive position of the farmer at this time may have
contributed to the unsavory view of urban life. An overview
of the verse of lesser-known poets reveals a construed myth
of the city with attacks on inequitable distribution of wealth,
materialism, promiscuity, secularism, artificiality, speed, in-
difference, anonymity, and slum conditions.

2013   Walkover, Andrew. THE DIALECTICS OF EDEN. Stanford Honors
Essays in Humanities, no. 16. Palo Alto, Calif.: Humanities Honors
Program, Stanford University, 1974. 98 p. Bibliog.

The American imagination began to develop around a belief
in a "new Eden" where the rural ideal and rising technology
merged. However, when rampant technology soon destroyed
the Arcadian ideal, the American hero did not turn to political or social philosophies but instead to geographic and
economic frontiers. American literature reveals a quest for
regeneration first in nature (the forest), then in apocalyptic
views of a technological, urban utopia. When both are
ravished by technology, the imagination resorts to "urban

oblivion and death." Walkover carefully examines the literature of William Burroughs and Norman Mailer, among others.

2014 Weimer, David [R.]. THE CITY AS METAPHOR. New York: Random House, 1966. vi, 151 p.

> Figurative uses of the metropolis and the language in which they are presented are Weimer's concerns. In their perceptions of cities, American authors appear to wonder whether the urban experience is identifiable or unambiguous. Looking at the cities invented by Walt Whitman, Henry James, Theodore Dreiser, E.E. Cummings, F. Scott Fitzgerald, William Carlos Williams, and W.H. Auden, diversity is found with some common features: a sense of the miraculous, loss of wonder through knowledge, disillusion, order and fate, fatalism.

2015 West, Thomas Reed. FLESH OF STEEL: LITERATURE AND THE MACHINE IN AMERICAN CULTURE. Nashville, Tenn.: Vanderbilt University Press, 1967. xv, 155 p. Bibliog.

> The twentieth-century literary expression of reaction to the machine defines a duality of attributes. "Discipline," a blending of monotony, integrated complexity, exactness, and form, seems polarized against a character of "energy" which joins power, profusion, and massiveness. West discusses the interplay of these polarities in the works of Sherwood Anderson, Waldo Frank, John Dos Passos, Thorstein Veblen, Carl Sandburg, Harold Sterns, Lewis Mumford, and Sinclair Lewis. West's book suffers from his inability to cleanly differentiate the dualism.

2016 Woodcock, John. "Literature and Science Since Huxley." INTERDISCIPLINARY SCIENCE REVIEWS 3, no. 1 (1978): 31-45.

> Surveying recent responses to the "two cultures" debate, Woodcock looks at critical, narrative, and fictional treatments. Works discussed include those by Jacob Bronowski, B.F. Skinner, Paul Goodman, Kenneth Boulding, and C.P. Snow himself. Among the fictional approaches on the uses and social impact of science and technology are novels and science fiction by Saul Bellow, Kurt Vonnegut, Isaac Asimov, John Brunner, Arthur Clarke, Ursula LeGuin, and Thomas Pynchon. J.D. Watson and Norman Mailer have produced journalistic narratives which serve as cultural impact statements for scientific events. Poets and essayists are also discussed. Extensive documentation.

b. STUDIES OF SPECIFIC AUTHORS AND WORKS

2017 Ausband, Stephen C. "Whale and the Machine: An Approach to MOBY DICK." AMERICAN LITERATURE 47 (May 1975): 197-211.

Melville uses mechanical imagery to express Ahab's hatred and fear of the natural forces in the universe. Ahab is described as a locomotive and an iron statue with a steel skull. His relationship to the crew is mechanical; they are his "tools." He lives in an orderly, controlled universe, thus he rages madly at the disorder and chaos generated by the whale. Organic, sexual imagery surrounds the whale. While Ahab's loss of a leg suggests castration, the sexual description of the whale emphasizes the creative energy in the cosmos.

2018   Basile, Joseph Lawrence. "Narcissus in the World of Machines." SOUTHERN REVIEW 12 (Winter 1976): 122-32.

Thoreau's WALDEN (1854) and the essays by twelve South-erners entitled I'LL TAKE MY STAND (no. 1997) argue against unchallenged acceptance of a technological society and question the place of the artist in such a world. Both works consider that man has been "encumbered" by machinery and leisure. The artist must become an "egoist" in order to separate himself from the "wasteland" of an industrial age and "create his own cosmos."

2019   Berman, James H. "The Walt Disney Robot Dramas." YALE REVIEW 66 (Winter 1977): 223-36.

Intended to gloriously celebrate the proliferation of technolog-ical appliances, Disney's robot-acted drama THE GENERAL ELECTRIC CAROUSEL OF PROGRESS produces a sense of loss, Berman feels. As the play moves from 1890 to 1970, the family disintegrates, the robots become more lifelike but less human in their actions toward each other, characters isolate themselves, and finally, "Progress City" has everything but people. The "audio-animatronic" creatures of the magic kingdom "are truly the first mutant children of the space age."

2020   Bradbury, Ray. "The Ardent Blasphemers." In 20,000 LEAGUES UNDER THE SEA, by Jules Verne, pp. 1-12. New York: Bantam Pathfinder Editions, 1962.

As our machines cut across the wilderness, we are "ardent in our blasphemy." In this introduction to the Verne novel, Bradbury contends that Verne's Captain Nemo and Melville's Ahab represent positive and negative aspects of the American attitude toward nature. The characteristic American boy mechanic has always resembled Nemo, but, in this electronic age, we are emerging from an era inclined toward Ahab's madness, hopelessness, and terror. Ahab is driven to kill the white whale that resents inquiry, but Nemo builds the Nauti-lus, a machine of curiosity. Nemo accepts nature and asks

man to reform; however, Ahab rages against natural forces
and demands that God change.

2021   Carey, Glenn O. "William Faulkner on the Automobile as Socio-Sexual
Symbol." CEA CRITIC 36 (January 1974): 15-17.

> The automobile is utilized as symbol of both a Frankenstein
> monster that man cannot control and of sexual sterility or
> impotence in such works as PYLON (1935), REQUIEM FOR
> A NUN (1951), INTRUDER IN THE DUST (1948), and
> SARTORIS (1929).

2022   Corrigan, R.A. "Somewhere West of Laramie, on the Road to West
Egg: Automobiles, Fillies, and the West in THE GREAT GATSBY."
JOURNAL OF POPULAR CULTURE 7 (Summer 1973): 152-58.

> Fitzgerald was probably "aroused" by the emotional appeal of
> the auto ads produced by the Jordan Company of Cleveland,
> Ohio. Sexual overtones and the freedom of the wide-open
> West were fused in the ads of 1923. The slogan "good taste
> without display" is what Gatsby longs for, but he has "just a
> little too much chrome." Jordan Baker's name is a compound
> of two well-known American cars and she typifies the seduc-
> tive, sporty, adventuresome, sleek Jordan coupe and driver.

2023   Cowan, Michael H. CITY OF THE WEST: EMERSON, AMERICA,
AND URBAN METAPHOR. New Haven, Conn.: Yale University
Press, 1967. xiv, 284 p. Bibliog.

> Emerson used urban metaphors as vehicles for expressing his
> dialectical response to experience. The cities and the West,
> in Emerson's mind, contained the energies shaping America
> and shared four characteristic features: "newness, vast space,
> rapid motion, and heterogeneity." Through the use of
> metaphor, Emerson manipulated these four factors into recon-
> cilers of the tension between civilization and nature. Cowan
> also compares the responses of other American writers,
> especially James Fenimore Cooper, Nathaniel Hawthorne,
> Herman Melville, Henry David Thoreau, and Walt Whitman.

2024   Cronkhite, G. Ferris. "Walt Whitman and the Locomotive." AMERI-
CAN QUARTERLY 6 (Summer 1954): 164-72.

> In "Passage to India," Whitman focuses upon the railroad as
> a symbol of power, "modern" mechanical progress, and com-
> munication between men. The engine would furnish a "pas-
> sage to more than India." "To a Locomotive in Winter"
> provides dramatic description of the engine, part by part,
> then reflects through imagery, sound, and meter the enthusiasm
> it evoked in bystanders. In failing health, Whitman began to

worship the motion and power of the locomotive. His emotional attachment gives the poem its exhilaration.

2025 Diggins, John P. "Dos Passos and Veblen's Villains." ANTIOCH RE-
VIEW 23 (Winter 1963–64): 485–500.

The philosophy of work implicit in Dos Passos' novels, such as
U.S.A. (no. 1928) and MID CENTURY (1961) reveals an admiration for the individual workman, mechanic, or engineer.
The corporate structure, however, with automation, unionism,
finance capitalism, and government regulation, dehumanizes
work and renders man dispensable. Without work he is deprived of his "sole source of salvation."

2026 Donaldson, Scott. "The Machines in Cheever's Garden." In THE
CHANGING FACE OF THE SUBURBS, edited by Barry Schwartz,
pp. 309–22. Chicago: University of Chicago Press, 1976.

The harm of technological progress for modern man is symbolized in Cheever's writings by transportation systems. In
BULLET PARK (no. 1923), railroads, airlines, and freeways
stand for psychological alienation. Cheever's suburbanites
are terrified by these commuting systems and turn to drugs,
alcohol, and insanity to obliterate the rootlessness and alienation in modern life. "Progress" leads only to slaughter and
the destruction of the quality of life for those who can survive.

2027 Fairbanks, Henry G. "Hawthorne and the Machine Age." AMERICAN
LITERATURE 28 (May 1956): 155–63.

A balanced outlook toward the machine, derived from "a
sense of total perspective," permeates Hawthorne's writings.
His uses of machines reveal an insight into the problems they
created for nineteenth-century American society. In THE
HOUSE OF THE SEVEN GABLES and "The Old Apple Dealer,"
the railroad represents the rapid motion with which the new
world is becoming detached from old standards. But those
who stay behind are left in decay. Elsewhere, he responds
with wonder to the telegraph and the machinery of an iron
foundry. His admiration, however, is reserved for the human
contrivers and operators. He is alert to the threat of machines replacing men or reducing their humanity. The stove
that usurps the empty fireplace in the old manse cannot warm
his spirit.

2028 Friedman, Alan J., and Puetz, Manfred. "Science as Metaphor:
Thomas Pynchon and GRAVITY'S RAINBOW." CONTEMPORARY LIT-
ERATURE 15 (Summer 1974): 345–59.

Pynchon utilizes scientific laws and the mechanistic behavior of technology to demonstrate that order and entropy are not antagonists but instead are coexistent elements of the same universal movement. All things fit the "rainbow curve of existence" demonstrated by the V-2 rocket. Paranoia is the "dominant condition of the human mind" because it is the realization that everything is connected.

2029 Gerber, Gerald E. "James Kirke Paulding and the Image of the Machine." AMERICAN QUARTERLY 22 (Fall 1970): 736-41.

Paulding's development of a negative image of the machine in works dating from 1818 to 1830 represents one of the earliest literary uses of the machine as "a composite of the times." In THE MERRY TALES OF THE THREE WISE MEN OF GOTHAM (1826), Paulding indicts the factory system, and in THE NEW MIRROR FOR TRAVELLERS (1828), he criticizes transportation machines and other improvements threatening agrarian life.

2030 Girgus, Sam B. "Howells and Marcuse: A Forecast of the One-Dimensional Age." AMERICAN QUARTERLY 25 (March 1973): 108-18.

The similarity of the ideas of William Dean Howells and Herbert Marcuse demonstrates that Howells's statements about the transformation of the American character by industrialization are relevant to modern issues. Both writers consider how the domination of material values, the confusion of true and false needs, and competitive capitalism contribute to the dissolution of boundaries between "private pleasure and the commercial and political utility."

2031 Griffin, Robert J., and Freedman, William A. "Machines and Animals: Pervasive Motifs in THE GRAPES OF WRATH." JOURNAL OF ENGLISH AND GERMANIC PHILOLOGY 62 (July 1963): 569-80.

Machines are used symbolically in Steinbeck's novel of itinerant farmers. Depicted as evil objects by the bestowal of bestial qualities into their mechanisms, metaphoric representations of machines serve to intensify the sense of tragedy. The farmers cannot accommodate the exigencies of the industrial world. The predicaments of characters are symbolically mirrored in their cars. For example, the Joad family's makeshift truck cannot move efficiently and falls apart. But Steinbeck considers machines to be neutral; values are installed by the person at the controls.

2032 Guttmann, Allen. "Mechanized Doom: Ernest Hemingway and the Spanish Civil War." MASSACHUSETTS REVIEW 1 (May 1960): 541-61.

Literary and visual reactions to the Spanish Civil War reflect the pervasive theme of conflict between man and machines.

The machine, in the forms of tanks, guns, and bombers, symbolically represents war and the enemy. In FOR WHOM THE BELL TOLLS (1940), sterile machines, which move like "mechanized doom" are in opposition to nature. Guttmann reveals that a complex of values associating freedom and fertility with nature while the machine connotes sterility and repression are evident in the responses of many American and European writers to the Spanish War and the airborne bomber in particular.

2033   Handlin, Oscar. "Man and Magic: Encounters with the Machine." AMERICAN SCHOLAR 33 (Spring 1964): 408-19.

Our ambivalent attitude toward the machine--admiration mixed with dread--antedates the industrial revolution in America. Melville protested the machine's establishment of a routine that segregated man from natural forces. A period of widespread and clever tinkering led, ironically, to a machine whose workings are so complex that they have become magic to all but the specialized few. As expectations for a technological cornucopia fade, Handlin observes, a sense of foreboding stemming from a fear of punishment for impious, unnatural acts has resurfaced.

2034   Hesford, Walter. "Literary Contexts of 'Life in the Iron-Mills.'" AMERICAN LITERATURE 49 (March 1977): 70-85.

Rebecca Harding Davis's story (no. 1926) published in 1861, is the "first notable work of fiction to concern itself with the life of the factory worker in an industrial American town." Davis invests the workers with the mystery and beauty of romance, yet her account is realistic. The despair of souls is focused around the statue of a naked woman which Hugh Wolfe, a mill hand, sculpts from korl, an industrial waste product. Although Hugh is driven by isolation to suicide, his work of art testifies to the potential of the laborer. Davis is more certain than Hawthorne, Hesford feels, of the validity of the "romantic resolution."

2035   Hiers, John T. "Robert Frost's Quarrel with Science and Technology." GEORGIA REVIEW 25 (Summer 1971): 182-205.

Frost sees science and technology as depriving man of tradi- tional values accrued from the past. What is left is the chaos of rapid change and the delusion that the new is automatically better. Examples from the poetry are used to reveal Frost's belief that man can use the same science and technology to imaginatively construct his own forms if he is not caught in the materialistic narrow frame of mind. Frost satirizes the impotence of a totally negative attitude toward technology and embraces man's predilection for experimenting with the physical world.

2036   Hoffman, Frederick J. "The Technological Fallacy in Contemporary Poetry: Hart Crane and MacKnight Black." AMERICAN LITERATURE 21 (March 1949): 94-107.

Poets of the 1920s did not understand the machine's function and impact on society. Because of their inability to, in Hart Crane's terms, "acclimatize" and absorb the machine, poets self-consciously instilled human qualities into the metal. Black chose machinery as a poetic subject because of its simplicity, precision, and efficiency, but he isolated the object from its cultural context. Crane, however, especially in THE BRIDGE (no. 1924) integrates the machine with modern consciousness. His poetic language reflects the "jazz rhythms" of the industrial world.

2037   Lowry, E.D. "The Lively Art of MANHATTAN TRANSFER." PMLA 84 (October 1969): 1628-38.

Dos Passos makes use of the "machine-conscious futuristic concepts" of fragmentation, contrast, and the interplay of apparently discordant materials to express the speed and chaos of modern life. The "technological aesthetic" offered him a way out of introversion to democratic fiction. Techniques from mass entertainment, especially motion pictures, are joined in MANHATTAN TRANSFER (no. 1927) to create a montage of city life. The reader is left to devise order and pattern from the context presented. Such an imaginative activity can lead to a discovery of meaning in the wider technological environment.

2038   MacPhee, Laurence F. "THE GREAT GATSBY'S 'Romance of Motoring': Nick Carraway and Jordan Baker." MODERN FICTION STUDIES 18 (Summer 1972): 207-12.

The automobile embodies the "restless and potentially destructive impulses" of industrial culture in THE GREAT GATSBY (no. 1930). Magazine advertisements, appearing in 1923 and 1924, for the Jordan automobile and Baker Fastex Velvet car upholstery inspired and contributed to Fitzgerald's irony surrounding the characters Jordan Baker and Nick Carraway. MacPhee details the text and pictorial content of the advertisements and discusses their contribution to the pattern of images indicative of disorder and pretense.

2039   Nänny, Max. EZRA POUND: POETICS FOR AN ELECTRIC AGE. Bern, Switz.: Franke Verlag, 1973. 122 p. Bibliog.

Indebted to the works of McLuhan, Nänny explores the effect
of the electronic stage of culture on the critical writings of
Ezra Pound. Recognizing that the emerging environment and
increasingly oral, world could be communicated only by "techniques of instant and direct perception and presentation,"
Pound develops devices of the "image" and the "ideogram."
His language displays "utmost compression" and the absence
of connecting links.

2040   Neufeldt, Leonard N. "The Science of Power: Emerson's Views on
Science and Technology in America." JOURNAL OF THE HISTORY
OF IDEAS 38 (April-June 1977): 329-44.

Virtually alone among early literary figures in his endorse-
ment of the potentials of technology, Emerson saw the process
of invention as a stimulus to intellectual power which helps
man interpret nature's laws. Considering "Works and Days"
to be Emerson's most encompassing essay on technology,
Neufeldt carefully analyzes the stated oppositions and ambiguities. Emerson rejects the popular division between the natural and the mechanical and asserts that it is necessary that
man make effective use of the world. Yet he finds that man
relies on inventions rather than on mental action and is in-
fatuated with the power grasped through technology. Power
and things replace ideas.

2041   Szuberla, Guy. "Making the Sublime Mechanical: Henry Blake
Fuller's Chicago." AMERICAN STUDIES 14 (Spring 1973): 83-93.

In his late nineteenth-century novels THE CLIFF-DWELLERS
(1893) and WITH THE PROCESSION (1895), Fuller achieves
a "transvaluation of the agrarian myth." Here the city, not
nature, provides a sense of space, power, and potential
development. By playing on values formed by Romantic
poetry, Fuller develops a new aesthetic which can be termed
a "technological sublime." With the skyscraper as central
image, nature shrinks next to the mechanized urban vista.
While an ambivalent attitude is evident in the novels, Fuller
assimilates technology and provides a new aesthetic perspective.

2042   Thompson, W.R. "'The Paradise of Bachelors' and 'The Tartarus of
Maids': A Reinterpretation." AMERICAN QUARTERLY 9 (Spring
1957): 34-45.

The symbolism and imagery of the stories relates Melville's
attitudes toward the two civilizations of Europe and America.
The now decrepit Templars are sterile with selfish interests
and no energy to translate spiritual visions. In the New
World, machine techniques replace values. The machine

usurps basic human functions, including sex. The frigid
whiteness of the setting and the virgin maids connote the
barrenness of a civilization where utility is the only measure.

2043   Waldron, Randall H. "The Naked, the Dead, and the Machine: A
New Look at Norman Mailer's First Novel." PMLA 87 (March 1972):
271-77.

It is in war novels that the tense conflict between man and
machine finds its most intense expression. The central conflict in Mailer's THE NAKED AND THE DEAD (1948) is
between mechanistic forces of modern society and individual
integrity. Waldron discusses Mailer's utilization of structure,
character, imagery, and symbolism to develop a sustained
metaphor in which war stands for the machine age. The
tension of man-machine is emphasized by the novel's primary
symbols, the mountain and the army. Expressions of military
mentality and the equation of sex with the mechanical also
figure prominently in the analysis.

2044   Wasson, Richard. "'Like a Burnished Throne': T.S. Eliot and the
Demonism of Technology." CENTENNIAL REVIEW 13 (Summer 1969):
302-16.

With insights gleaned from Sigfried Giedion's MECHANIZA-
TION TAKES COMMAND (no. 206) and Northrup Frye's
"notion of demonic and apocalyptic structures," Wasson discusses the relationship between the literary form of Eliot's
"A Game of Chess" in Section Two of THE WASTE LAND
(1922) and technology. In both the poem and mass production, fragmentation and juxtaposition not only render symbols
valueless but also instill in processed objects a quality which
observers react to with "disturbing irrationality" and a sense
of the grotesque.

Part 18

ART

A. GENERAL

1. Bibliography

2045   Sokol, David M., ed. AMERICAN ARCHITECTURE AND ART: A
        GUIDE TO INFORMATION SOURCES. American Studies, vol. 2.
        Detroit: Gale Research Co., 1976. xii, 341 p.

> Basic and specialized literature in the fields of American art
> and architecture are cited in this selective, annotated bib-
> liography of over 1,500 items. Sections cover general refer-
> ence sources, histories, period surveys, and studies of indi-
> vidual artists, architects, and decorative arts. Specific
> topics given chapters include aesthetics and style, urban
> architecture and planning, furniture, metalwork, textiles,
> ceramics, and glass. Books, journal articles, and exhibit
> catalogs are cited. An emphasis is placed on recent, avail-
> able materials. There are separate author, title, and subject
> indexes.

2. Books and Articles

2046   "The Arts in a Post-Industrial Society." ARTS IN SOCIETY 11 (Fall-
        Winter 1974): 371-518.

> The report of the UNESCO conference, CULTURAL INNOVA-
> TION IN TECHNOLOGICAL AND POST-INDUSTRIAL SOCI-
> ETIES, is highlighted in this special issue. Committees con-
> sider creativity, diffusion of the arts, and education.
> Among articles selected to complement the report are: "Notes
> on Post-Industrial Culture" by Vytautas Kavolis, in which he
> contends that we are shifting our cultural forms from the fac-
> tory to nature; Kingsley Widmer's "The Processed Culture:
> Wasting Sensibility in Post-Industrial Society"; and "Art and
> the Energy Crisis," by James Wines.

2047   Ferguson, Eugene S. "The Mind's Eye: Nonverbal Thought in Technology." SCIENCE 197 (26 August 1977): 827-36.

Western technology cannot be understood without an appreciation of the visual, imaginative mode of thought. The "illustrated machine books" of the Renaissance and later demonstrate that design exceeded society's needs and that artist-engineers were posing questions previously unasked and solving problems by drawing many varieties of a device. Ferguson laments the lack of courses in "visual thinking" in engineering schools. The view that results in the labeling of design projects as "Rube Goldberg" exercises reveals a dangerous assumption that perceptive processes are more primitive than verbal or mathematical thought. Extensive notes.

2048   Hill, Anthony, ed. DATA: DIRECTIONS IN ART, THEORY AND AESTHETICS. London: Faber and Faber, 1968. 302 p. Illus.

This anthology considers the future of abstract art and its interdependence on science and technology. Artists representing constructive, concrete kinetic, structurist, and synthesist movements in plastic art are joined by specialists in mathematics, physics, engineering, sociology, and philosophy. Frank J. Malina, David Bohn, and Francois Molnar discuss the relationships between science-technology and art.

2049   Kepes, Gyorgy, ed. ARTS OF THE ENVIRONMENT. Vision and Value Series. New York: George Braziller, 1972. 244 p. Illus.

These essays demonstrate a movement in both science and art toward processes and systems. Environment, architecture, and urban configurations are seen as functional systems which impinge on life patterns. Environmental values are discussed by Leo Marx, Erik Erikson, Kevin Lynch, and Kepes. Urban design and planning are the topics of essays by Dennis Gabor and Jay W. Forrester. James T. Burns and Dolf Schnebli confront environmental psychology. There are also essays on adaptation by René Dubos and Robert Smithson's thoughts on his Spiral Jetty.

2050   _____. THE NATURE AND ART OF MOTION. Vision and Value Series. New York: George Braziller, 1965. xi, 195 p. Illus.

Rapid motion and change in today's environment have given man a fragmented, disoriented perception. This collection provides an understanding of motion in science, technology, and art. The first section, dealing with physical and technical aspects of motion and man's reactions to them, includes statements by a physicist, two psychologists, a philosopher, and an art historian. Expressions of artistic experience with motion in kinetic art, sculpture, film, and city planning follow. The essays together link human insights from various realms of knowledge.

2051 _____. STRUCTURE IN ART AND IN SCIENCE. Vision and Value Series. New York: George Braziller, 1965. vii, 189 p. Illus.

The ability to see the world as an interconnected whole, what Kepes terms a sense of structure, is necessary for our further cultural revolution. The first section of this collection, including an essay by Cyril Stanley Smith, provides a scientific approach to the structuring process in nature. Papers in the second section apply structural principles to man-made forms.

2052 _____. THE VISUAL ARTS TODAY. Middletown, Conn.: Wesleyan University Press, 1960. 272 p. Illus.

Outstanding contemporary artists discuss modern art, its meanings, and its relation to our lives. Most of the material included was previously published elsewhere. Architecture, symbolism, leisure and creativity, the city and the arts, advertising, photography, film and cinematography, science and art, and the interpretation of artistic values are the topics discussed. Besides statements by outstanding contemporary artists, contributors include Margaret Mead, Sigfried Giedion, Le Corbusier, Edward Steichen, and Ayn Rand.

2053 Larkin, Oliver W. ART AND LIFE IN AMERICA. 1949. Rev. ed. New York: Holt, Rinehart and Winston, 1960. xvii, 559 p. Illus., bibliog.

Larkin reveals how art has reflected American culture, environment, industry, and political and economic circumstances. Arranged by period, topics include the colonial carpenter and limner; utilitarianism; democratic art; the "chromo" civilization of 1870-1900; the great expositions of 1876, 1913, and 1939; the rise of functionalism in architecture; influence of the city; reactions to war; and preoccupation with form. Bibliographic notes are extensive.

2054 Martin, J.L.; Nicholson, Ben; and Gabo, N[aum]., eds. CIRCLE; INTERNATIONAL SURVEY OF CONSTRUCTIVE ART. New York: Praeger Publishers, 1971. viii, 292 p. Illus., bibliog.

The affinities between imaginative creation in science, engineering, and art are explored by modern artists. Essays are grouped into sections on painting, sculpture, architecture, and the alliance of art and society. J.D. Bernal discusses science in art and vice versa; town planning and housing de-

sign are the concerns of Maxwell Fry and Richard J. Neutra.
Sigfried Giedion's survey of reinforced concrete bridges
blends engineering and design. The usefulness of biotechnics
to artist and engineer is emphasized by Karel Honzig. Lewis
Mumford concludes the volume with thoughts on the death of
the monument.

2055   Meeker, Joseph W. "The Imminent Alliance: New Connections
among Art, Science, and Technology." TECHNOLOGY AND CUL-
TURE 19 (April 1978): 187-98.

There are indications that science and art, separated for four
centuries, are about to be reunited with technology guiding
them. New ways of thinking include the realization that
conquering nature is self-destructive, a recognition of the
nonreliability of objectivity, and the discovery of analytic
and synthetic brain hemispheres. The reunion will occur
because it is needed. Artists and engineers need to understand the nature and form potentials of their materials; art
transforms technology into symbolic expression. Scientists
have freed themselves from the language of machines and are
thinking in metaphoric images. New forms evolving will be
"adaptive, not triumphant."

2056   Mumford, Lewis. ART AND TECHNICS. Bampton Lectures in America,
vol. 4. New York: Columbia University Press, 1952. 162 p.

Technology and industrialization have led to a mechanization
of humanity. Western man's existence is hollow, meaningless,
and his imagination is totally harnessed to machines like the
television. Mumford tells us that the message of modern
art is nihilism, violence, and dehumanization. The purposes
of art must be to restore the human person by creating
respect for creativity, personality, and autonomy, and to
transmit these values. Then, perhaps, man can command his
machines. Mumford surveys the interaction of art with technology from handicraft to architecture.

2057   Taylor, Joshua C. AMERICA AS ART. Washington, D.C.: National
Collection of Fine Arts by the Smithsonian Institution Press, 1976.
xi, 320 p. Illus.

The catalog designed to accompany an exhibit of the same
name created at the National Collection of Fine Arts during
the Bicentennial of the American Revolution concentrates on
lesser-known works and aspects of American art. Several of
the eight well-illustrated essays deal with the impact of
American industrialization, technology, standardization, and
urban life, namely, "The Image of Urban Optimism," "The
Folk and the Masses," and "Identity From Uniformity." The
frontier, nature, symbolism, and modernity also receive attention.

2058   Whisnant, David E. "The Craftsman: Some Reflections on Work in America." CENTENNIAL REVIEW 17 (Spring 1973): 215-36.

An assessment of the craftsman's situation in American culture questions public and private notions of the self, models of education and production, attitudes toward tools, political policy, and the psychological effect of working with the hands. The role of values and attitudes is evident in Whisnant's discussions of such cultural convictions as: formal training is essential, the possession and use of tools is equivalent to manipulative competence and skill, and crafts are politically and economically marginal.

B. TECHNOLOGY-INSPIRED ART

2059   Andersen, Wayne. AMERICAN SCULPTURE IN PROCESS: 1930/1970. Boston: New York Graphic Society, 1975. ix, 278 p. Illus.

While not focusing directly on the effect of technology in this overview of American sculpture through four decades, Andersen makes evident the influence of the machine on subject matter, style, materials, and techniques. Artists most involved with the implements and products of technology or social commentary about them include Alexander Calder, David Smith, Theodore Roszak, Richard Stankiewicz, Don Potts, Edward Kienholz, Ernest Trova, and Claes Oldenburg. The influences of surrealism, cubism, constructivism, pop art, minimal art, and process art are traced. Extensive illustrations and bibliography augment the study.

2060   "Art and Technology." IMPACT OF SCIENCE ON SOCIETY 24 (January-March 1974): 1-99.

Including its applied phase, or technology, in the use of "science," the art-science interface is explored. Piet Hein discusses mind sets which create barriers between the two cultures; engineer-artist Frank Malina expresses the necessity of opportunity for artistic creativity in industrial society; Francesco d'Arcais explores the "historical symbiosis between art and science"; Jasia Reichardt relates the artistic use of new technologies; an educational experiment at M.I.T. to eliminate barriers between the cultures is recountered by Robert Preusser; David Dickson examines the constraints on interaction imposed by sociopolitical systems; and Rolf-Dieter Herrmann considers the merger of viewer and object achieved by the technology-art combine.

2061   "Art and the Machine." ARTS MAGAZINE 43 (December 1968, January 1969): 36-50.

Four articles comprise this special section. Nicolas Calas, in "The Light That Failed; Tek Art and Fakirs," muses on light optics and new visions. "Science Fiction and Artifacts," by Lawrence Alloway, briefly compares the literary depiction of man's confrontation of objects (or cultures) with that of visual art. The most substantial article, John Chandler's "Art and Automata; Cybernetic Serendipity, Technology and Creativity," surveys the collaboration of art and mechanized devices. Dore Ashton reflects on art and technology exhibits at the Museum of Modern Art and the Brooklyn Museum.

2062   Baur, John I.H., and Jaffe, Irma B. JOSEPH STELLA. New York: Praeger Publishers, 1971. 154 p. Illus., bibliog.

Stella's artistic interpretations of urban subjects and city life are vivid, abstract, often present a carnival atmosphere, and reveal the influence of the Italian futurist movement. BATTLE OF LIGHTS, CONEY ISLAND, BROOKLYN BRIDGE, THE SKYSCRAPERS, THE WHITE WAY I AND II, produced in the 1910s and early 1920s are intriguing for their geometric forms, images of strength and impending chaos. There are also reproductions of Stella's depictions of factories.

2063   Benthall, Jonathan. SCIENCE AND TECHNOLOGY IN ART TODAY. New York: Praeger Publishers, 1972. 180 p. Illus., bibliog.

Concerned with contemporary art that exhibits a dominant interaction with science and technology, Benthall discusses both theory and application of the symbolic merging of aesthetics and technics. The focus is on the utilization of new technologies and media: photography, the computer, laser holography, and kinetic art. But Benthall does not isolate the artistic aspects of media; instead, he asserts the necessity of an integrated understanding of the social, economic, industrial, and aesthetic effects of specific technologies.

2064   Burnham, Jack. BEYOND MODERN SCULPTURE: THE EFFECTS OF SCIENCE AND TECHNOLOGY ON THE SCULPTURE OF THIS CENTURY. New York: George Braziller, 1968. x, 402 p. Illus., bibliog.

The stylistic changes of modern sculpture are seen to have been precipitated by the intellectual authority increasingly invested in science and technology. The depiction of totemic objects has been replaced by the creation of life-simulating systems. Burnham's discussion of computer art, light sculpture, robot and kinetic art leads to a prediction of the appearance, before the year 2000, of intelligent automata with the capacity for reciprocal relationships with humans--"living" man-machine systems.

2065 Coplans, John, ed. ROY LICHTENSTEIN. Documentary Monographs in Modern Art. New York: Praeger Publishers, 1972. 199 p. Illus., bibliog.

> With imagery "derived from the American vernacular," Lichtenstein reflects a consumer civilization. "Prepackaged" clichés, stereotypes, a mechanical style, and content full of technological apparatus result in an ironic vision. This carefully edited sourcebook consists of a lengthy introduction, a chronology of imagery in the artist's work, interviews with and important articles on Lichtenstein, abundant illustrations, and an extensive bibliography.

2066 Corn, Wanda M. "The New New York." ART IN AMERICA 61 (July-August 1973): 59-65.

> Painters, photographers, and writers creating perceptions of New York City in the first decade of the twentieth century recognized and focused on its modernity. Their subjects were skyscrapers, bridges, Coney Island, Broadway, the Elevated, and crowds. Although exhilarated by the new industrialism, their stylistic and psychological interpretations were within earlier romantic, landscape, and impressionistic conventions. The Ash Can artists established new techniques as they chronicled the commonplace and rendered New York's agitation and flux.

2067 Cox, Richard. "Coney Island, Urban Symbol in American Art." NEW YORK HISTORICAL SOCIETY QUARTERLY 60 (January-April 1976): 35-52.

> Between 1910 and 1940 American artists recognized and depicted Coney Island as a symbol of urban civilization and the technological future. The works of abstractionists Joseph Stella and Louis Lozowick, socialist satirist Art Young, and sensual observer Reginald Marsh are the most outstanding. Stella blends a fascination for mechanical wonders, speed, and crowds with color and form. Lozowick sees Coney as a lesson in the mechanical marvels ushering in the socialist future. In contrast, Young depicts the rides as sinister technological monsters that dupe the workers. Marsh documents the thrills of Coney Island through the buxom, young, sensuous women who frequented the resort. His crowded canvases glory in "delicious wickedness."

2068 Davis, Douglas. "Art and Technology." ART IN AMERICA 56 (January-February 1968): 28-47.

> The feature issue includes three articles: "Art and Technology --The New Combine"; "Conversations with Gyorgy Kepes, Billy Klüver, and James Seawright"; and "Art and Technology

--Toward Play." Davis explores new forms resulting from the collaboration of art and technology, interviews three outstanding artist-engineers, and seeks a new critical outlook on the artist's tendency to "play" with machines. It is precisely "play," Davis contends, that best differentiates man and machine.

2069 _____. ART AND THE FUTURE: A HISTORY/PROPHECY OF THE COLLABORATION BETWEEN SCIENCE, TECHNOLOGY AND ART. New York: Praeger Publishers, 1973. 208 p. Illus., bibliog.

Recognizing the dependence of art on science and technology, Davis explores the direction of the symbiosis and provides a history of the sciences in twentieth-century art, a group of interviews with artist-engineers, and a prediction of the future of the arts. Davis contends that artists of this century have turned away from "the ego to the machine to make art." The work of Gyorgy Kepes, Jean Tinguely, Nicholas Takis, Robert Rauschenberg, Nam June Paik, James Seawright, Gerd Stern, and others guides us from clanking fun and self-destruct machines to computer-generated animated film, and argon and helium-neon lasers.

2070 Efron, Arthur. "Technology and the Future of Art." MASSACHUSETTS REVIEW 7 (Autumn 1966): 677-710.

It is likely that contemporary man will create an art which is a reflection of his technology. Much of our art copies the "instantaneous response" of electric energy, and it draws attention away from the artist or individual to conception in terms of groups. The "mystique of man" is threatened. Our best energies, including the erotic, are shunted into technological interests. Efron hopes that art will embrace a realization of randomness and will illuminate a way to "freedom from technological control." Such art, however, will be for the few unafraid of confronting individuality.

2071 Foundation for Contemporary Performance Arts. 9 EVENINGS: THEATRE AND ENGINEERING. New York: Experiments in Art and Technology, 1966. 16 p. Illus.

Interaction between artists and engineers resulted in the performances described in this catalog of an exhibition held in 1966. While technologists contributed devices for artists to use, the cooperation also resulted in feedback to industry resulting in new tools. Primary artists involved in performances include John Cage, Robert Rauschenberg, and Lucinda Childs (dance).

2072 Franke, Herbert W. COMPUTER GRAPHICS, COMPUTER ART. Trans-

lated by Gustav Metzger. London: Phaidon Press, 1971. 134 p.
Illus., bibliog.

A basic explanation of the functions and methods of computer
mechanisms precedes a survey of art forms assisted by electronics. The histories of the collaboration of computer with
graphics, sculpture, film, literature, music, dance, and
architecture are presented and amply illustrated. While much
discussion concerns European practitioners, the work of
Americans Jack Citron, Lloyd Sumner, and John Whitney
demonstrates the potential of the merger of wit and circuits.

2073   Goldin, Amy. "Art and Technology in a Social Vacuum." ART IN
AMERICA 60 (March 1972): 46-51.

Proponents of art-and-technology have failed to deal with
social implications and thus artistic products lack excitement.
However, the ideal of the merger of the two fields affirms
art's ability to contain reality. Elitism is replaced by
popularism--art is addressed to the masses instead of to patrons.
Art-and-technology theory projects a "suicide course for art."
This bodes well, for art will deny culture and embrace society.

2074   Herrmann, Rolf-Dieter. "Art, Technology, and Nietzsche." JOUR-
NAL OF AESTHETICS AND ART CRITICISM 32 (Fall 1973): 95-102.

Nietzsche's conceptions of nihilism and "eternal recurrence of
the same" can help prepare a participant to experience technological art. Considering recent exhibitions, such as the
Pepsi-Cola Pavilion at Expo '70, and the recent work of
engineer-artists, the author contends that technological art
must be approached as "play." One must participate and
respond with the senses rather than theorize or apply traditional criteria of beauty, content, and form. While experiencing the art, only the present moment matters; thoughts of
the past and future must be excluded.

2075   Kagan, Andrew. "Laserium: New Light on an Ancient Vision." ARTS
MAGAZINE 52 (March 1978): 126-31.

Man has attempted an art of pure projected light since medieval times. Ivan Dryer's Laserium works, which combine
laser-generated light and music, have an uncanny appeal to
the emotions and make abstract art enjoyable to the multi-
tudes. Dryer's Spectra Physics projection unit, with tape
decks, "potentiometer dials and joy sticks" is "played" by
the "laserist." Light is projected into a large planetarium
dome.

2076   Kahn, Kenneth, and Lieberman, Henry. "Computer Animation: Snow

White's Dream Machine." TECHNOLOGY REVIEW 80 (October-November 1977): 34-46.

Computers take the tedium out of animation, add modifiability, and make the process viable for planners, engineers, industrial designers, and scientists. Uses, techniques, and advances in the last fifteen years are discussed: perspective, light and shadow, key-frame animation, "paint brush" system, and the robot-like "display turtle" artist. The television watcher may be replaced by the "Sunday painter" who creates his own video shows.

2077 Kepes, Gyorgy. THE NEW LANDSCAPE IN ART AND SCIENCE. Chicago: Paul Theobald and Co., 1956. 383 p. Illus.

By utilizing the powers of science and technology to display both microscopic and macroscopic structures, form and unity will be apprehended on a sensed and emotional level rather than on a rational level alone. What is needed is a more integrated vision. With pictures made by scientists and engineers for practical purposes, accompanied by commentary by artists, scientists, and engineers including Sigfried Giedion, Walter Gropius, Norbert Wiener, Richard Wilbur, and S.I. Hayakawa, Kepes makes the "data" of the "new landscape" available to the senses. The joining of form-function relationships with intuitive sensibility unites science and art.

2078 Kinnaird, Clark, ed. RUBE GOLDBERG VS. THE MACHINE AGE: A RETROSPECTIVE EXHIBITION OF HIS WORK WITH MEMOIRS AND ANNOTATIONS. New York: Hastings House, 1968. ix, 214 p. Illus., bibliog.

Goldberg's humorous art has stimulating appeal to engineers just as science fiction is attractive to scientists. The cartoons and some sculpture which comprise most of this volume document Goldberg's attempts to solve ordinary social problems through elaborate mechanisms. His vision is decidedly ironic since the "inventions" burlesque the needless "multifarious gadgetry of the machine age that enslaves man." However, many contraptions anticipated reality. Short stories, essays, and poetry are also presented.

2079 Kranz, Stewart. SCIENCE AND TECHNOLOGY IN THE ARTS: A TOUR THROUGH THE REALM OF SCIENCE AND ART. New York: Van Nostrand Reinhold, 1974. 335 p. Illus., bibliog.

The result of a six-year field study by a journalist, ninety-five leading artists, engineers, scientists, and critics are interviewed about their work and views. Some interviews are devoted to the technical innovations that have extended the human senses, such as the electron microscope, x-rays, and voiceprints. "Bridges" between science and art (architecture, industrial design, computer-generated design) and strictly artistic endeavors (intermedia, environmental art, spectator art) receive ample attention.

2080   Kuhns, Richard. "Art and Machine." JOURNAL OF AESTHETICS AND ART CRITICISM 25 (Spring 1967): 259-66.

The power and fecundity of machines stimulate imaginings of physiological perfection and resistless force. To the artist they exhibit sublimity, order, balance, harmony, and rhythm. Machines serve man as nature once did: through them we seek "what we might be as creatures." Because the engineered object functionally joins the man-made with nature, it can be the agency to rejoin art to nature. But first art must "tame the instrumentality of the machine."

2081   Leavitt, Ruth, ed. ARTIST AND COMPUTER. Morristown, N.J.: Creative Computing Press, 1976. ix, 120 p. Illus.

Thirty-five artists discuss their use of the computer in the creation of diverse art works. Their statements and the motivations expressed therein display how well this union of art and science confronts our technological society and helps the artist perceive in new ways. Among the utilizations of the computer are weaving design, cybernetic sculpture, land-use decisions, concrete poetry, animated film, industrial design, and graphics. Numerous black-and-white as well as color illustrations augment the text.

2082   Lindgren, Nilo. "Art and Technology. I: Steps toward a New Synergism." "II: A Call for Collaboration." IEEE SPECTRUM 6 (April 1969): 59-68; (May 1969): 46-56.

This two-part article surveys the art and technology movement. Part 1 labels the artist as a mediator between technology and people who will assist in resolving ambivalent attitudes toward technology. The roots of the merger are seen in Readymades, Thomas Eakins' interest in photography, movies, Alexander Calder's mobiles, and Jean Tinguely's "philosophical machines," among others. Examples of collaboration between engineers and artists are discussed. Part 2 describes the experiences of some teams and details the work of collaborative organizations.

2083   Lippard, Lucy R. POP ART: WITH CONTRIBUTIONS BY LAWRENCE ALLOWAY, NANCY MARMER, NICOLAS CALAS. New York: Frederick A. Praeger, 1966. 216 p. Illus., bibliog.

The commercial, machine-made object is discovered as significant form by Pop Art. Artists in this movement approach

technological society with enthusiasm rather than a negative
attitude. Essays discuss New York and California Pop, Pop
icons, and developments in the movement in Europe, England,
and Canada. Pop Art emerges as an idiom particular to
America--born of this culture's commercialism, long-finned
cars, future orientation, and media saturation. Major artists
discussed include Andy Warhol, Jasper Johns, Roy Lichtenstein,
Claes Oldenburg, James Rosenquist, and Edward Kienholz.

2084   Marzio, Peter C. "Art, Technology, and Satire: The Legacy of Rube
        Goldberg." LEONARDO 5, no. 4 (1972): 315-24.

        Interest and acceptance of technology as a subject for art de-
        veloped when middle-class American homes began using
        electrical appliances. Much of this art is satirical, following
        the lead of Rube Goldberg's cartoons. The humor often de-
        pends on the condensation of time and movement. While
        Goldberg's cartoons show the "pretentiousness of the automatic
        life," they do not aim to defeat it. They give us instead
        a sense of the incongruity and humor of technological civili-
        zation.

2085   Museum of Modern Art. New York. TWENTIETH CENTURY ENGI-
        NEERING. New York: 1964. Unpaged. Illus.

        Photographs reveal the art of engineering. The compilers at-
        tempt to illustrate the beauty of engineering solutions to
        problems of form, function, and space. Photographs depict
        massive projects: power plants, skyscrapers, water towers,
        stadiums, aircraft hangers, geodesic domes, bridges, freeways,
        and dams.

2086   Noll, A. Michael. "Art Ex Machina." IEEE STUDENT JOURNAL 8
        (September 1970): 10-14.

        A research engineer who "dabbles" in computer movies and
        choreography feels that the use of computers in art has yet
        to produce significant aesthetic experiences. The problem
        is that artists have little access to computers, and scientists-
        engineers, with "monopolistic control of computers," play at
        being artists. Collaboration is a fallacy; what is needed is
        "a new breed of artist-computer scientist" whose talents are
        developed through formal interdisciplinary programs.

2087   Pontus Hulten, K.G. JEAN TINGUELY "META." Boston: New York
        Graphic Society, 1975. 364 p. Illus., bibliog.

        The dynamic art produced by Tinguely's mechanical tinkering
        is lavishly celebrated. Pontus Hulten guides the reader from
        Tinguely's early engine-generated mobiles, to automata draw-

ing machines, to self-destruct extravaganzas including HOM-
AGE TO NEW YORK and STUDY FOR THE END OF THE
WORLD #2. The artist produces ironic comments on efficient
machines. Recent work departs from earlier comedy and
seeming carelessness. In the gargantuan EUREKA, engine
and apparatus are constructed meticulously to insure long-
term performance, and the parts seem to be prisoners to
repetitious mechanization.

2088   _____. THE MACHINE: AS SEEN AT THE END OF THE MECHANI-
CAL AGE. New York: Museum of Modern Art, 1968. 218 p. Illus.,
bibliog.

This exhibition catalog presents extensive commentary and
bibliography along with reproductions of a collection of
artistic comments on the mechanical machine by artists of the
Western world. Works arranged chronologically provide a
detailed study of changing attitudes toward technology. The
fascinating, tinkering "mechanolotry," and optimism of the
dadaists and constructivists become skepticism and disillusion
in the 1930s and eventually lead to disgust and fear. The
pop artists represent a recent attempt to reestablish a better
relationship with technology.

2089   Prueitt, Melvin L. COMPUTER GRAPHICS: 118 COMPUTER-
GENERATED DESIGNS. New York: Dover Publications, 1975. 69 p.
Illus.

PICTURE, a computer program designed by Prueitt at Los
Alamos Scientific Laboratories, creates aesthetically pleasing
visual representations of numbers, mathematical formulae,
functions, and properties. The program displays with perspective and removes "hidden lines." The illustrations are
computer depictions of laser absorption, material densities,
nuclear spectra, magnetic fields, concentric error functions,
and bivariate normal distribution functions.

2090   Rose, Barbara. CLAES OLDENBURG. New York: Museum of Modern
Art; distributed by New York Graphic Society, 1970. 221 p. Illus.,
bibliog.

Oldenburg's soft machines demonstrate the use of technology
as material. The vinyl sculptures reflect a machine style both
in the object produced and the method of production. With
SOFT AIRFLOW and its various "organs" and his studies of
toaster, mixer, telephone, and typewriter, Oldenburg softens
manufactured goods and "makes technology human and vulner-
able" as well as harmless. This exhibit catalog includes
selections from the artist's writings and an extensive bibliography.

2091   Sumner, Lloyd. COMPUTER ART AND HUMAN RESPONSE. Char-
        lottesville, Va.: Paul B. Victorius, 1968. 96 p. Illus.

> Dedicated to Burroughs B5500 and Calcomp 565, this catalog
> of the first computer artists provides reproductions of the
> art works and personal reactions by the artist, as well as a
> description of the technical programming. Sumner finds
> "Smooth curves, evenly spaced lines, moiré patterns, and
> symmetry" in computer art. He gives his works engaging
> titles: "Intuitively Yours," "The Magnificent Machine,"
> "Orderly Disorder," "The Parent Trap," "Marsh Gas," and
> "Undulating Seasons of Conspired Love."

2092   Tashjian, Dickran. "Henry Adams and Marcel Duchamp; Liminal Views
        of the Dynamo and the Virgin." ARTS MAGAZINE 51 (May 1977):
        102-7.

> Adams' "The Dynamo and the Virgin" and Duchamp's THE
> BRIDE STRIPPED BARE BY HER BACHELORS, EVEN reveal
> similar positions of uncertain liminality between the past and
> the future. The symbols which result from their suspended
> polarity evocatively articulate "the growing religious/sexual
> implications of technology." The virgin and the machine
> synthesize the two powerful forces of energy that have shaped
> Western civilization. A detailed discussion with useful notes.

2093   Tuchman, Maurice. ART AND TECHNOLOGY: A REPORT ON THE ART
        AND TECHNOLOGY PROGRAM OF THE LOS ANGELES COUNTY MUSEUM
        OF ART 1967-1971. New York: Viking Press, 1971. 387 p. Illus.

> Compiled as a record of the well-financed program which
> placed chosen artists in large industrial corporations, the vol-
> ume documents the joining of the resources of advanced tech-
> nology with artistic imagination. Tuchman's lengthy explana-
> tion of the program and Jane Livingston's thoughts on art and
> technology are followed by reports by each participating artist
> and illustrations of the resulting art works. The paucity of
> intriguing examples of synthesis testifies to the lack of suc-
> cess of this collaboration.

C. INDUSTRIAL DESIGN

2094   Banham, Reyner. "The Great Gizmo." INDUSTRIAL DESIGN 12
        (September 1965): 48-59.

> The mechanical gadget is the typical American way of import-
> ing order and human comfort into the wilderness. No
> observer has yet adequately considered the import of the
> application of portable, simplistic, instantly operational,
> often ordered-from-catalog mechanisms to American culture.

From the Franklin stove, Mason jar, and six-shooter to the cordless shaver, walkie-talkie, spray can, and portable residence camper, gadgetry has extensively molded the American way of life and shaped our environment.

2095 Bush, Donald [J.]. THE STREAMLINED DECADE. New York: George Braziller, 1975. viii, 214 p. Illus., bibliog.

Evolving from science and modern sculpture, streamlining incorporated a "dynamic functionalism" as it developed in industrial design. The period from 1927 to the end of World War II saw a rare merger of machine with natural form resulting in an emotional, aesthetic experience for the observer. Bush details the sleek transformations of ships, aircraft, trains, and automobiles as premier designers Raymond Loewy, Norman Bel Geddes, Henry Dreyfuss, Walter Teague, Otto Kuhler, and others created forms of least resistance. They actualized their model future in the 1939 New York World's Fair. Superbly illustrated.

2096 _____. "Thorstein Veblen's Economic Aesthetic." LEONARDO 11 (Autumn 1978): 281-85.

Veblen's "democratic functionalist aesthetic," expressed in his THE THEORY OF THE LEISURE CLASS (no. 888), advocates mass-produced machine products. In this confirmation of the spirit of the machine age, Veblen condemns the creation of costly, elaborate art objects and clothing, the purpose of which was the demonstration of conspicuous consumption. His requirements for beauty are satisfied by simple forms which suggest their purpose and operation. Such "economic beauty" is efficient and most successfully achieved through the machine process. Such a democratic aesthetic ethic could lead to a fuller life for the masses.

2097 Cheney, Sheldon, and Cheney, Martha Candler. ART AND THE MACHINE: AN ACCOUNT OF INDUSTRIAL DESIGN IN TWENTIETH-CENTURY AMERICA. New York: Whittlesey House, 1936. xvii, 307 p. Illus., bibliog.

The evolution of design in machine-made, mass-produced objects from functionalism to a merger with aesthetic appearance is chronicled. The authors aim to present guidance which will free industrial design from handicraft influence in favor of an alliance between the "miraculous powers of the machine" and modern art. Style changes in objects of daily life, such as stoves, refrigerators, bottles, kitchen utensils, and electric fans are discussed along with the effect of streamlining on planes and ships.

2098   Doblin, Jay. ONE HUNDRED GREAT PRODUCT DESIGNS. New
        York: Van Nostrand Reinhold Co., 1970. 128 p. Illus.

> Those mass-produced products considered excellent in terms of
> utility, aesthetic value, and social symbolism are presented.
> Many of them were short-lived because commercial designers
> can rarely engineer mergers of mass acceptance and style.
> Among the hundred products are the Franklin stove, Gillette
> safety razor, LaSalle automobile, Toastmaster toaster, Lincoln
> Continental, Moen faucet, Trimline phone, DC-3 airliner,
> and Budd Zephyr train.

2099   Dreyfuss, Henry. DESIGNING FOR PEOPLE. New York: Simon and
        Schuster, 1955. 240 p. Illus.

> One of America's foremost industrial designers discusses his
> theories and work. His concern throughout his career has
> not been with the plaudits of museum directors but with "con-
> sumer preference." The resultant products which touch daily
> lives demonstrate his conviction that the designer's efforts can
> promote health and serenity. Photographs and drawings illus-
> trate Dreyfuss' mass-produced designs, such as the telephone,
> Hoover vacuum, alarm clock, industrial machines, Lockheed
> planes, radios, and televisions.

2100   Dufrenne, Mikel. "The Aesthetic Object and the Technical Object."
        JOURNAL OF AESTHETICS AND ART CRITICISM 23 (Fall 1964):
        113-22.

> The primary distinction between technique and aesthetics is
> that the technical object is fragmented from the universe while
> the aesthetic object invites unity with the world. But the
> technical object can be beautiful when its use has meaning,
> it agrees with its environment, and its meaning is experienced
> by the observer. It must manifest its purpose, be beautiful
> to the eye as well as useful to the hand, and understood in
> the mind.

2101   Emerson, Ralph Waldo. "Thoughts on Art." DIAL 1 (January 1841):
        367-78.

> Art develops from man's needs, not his fancy. Each work of
> art springs from necessity and takes its form from hints in
> nature. In regard to both the useful and the beautiful arts,
> the "omnipotent agent is Nature," for nature is the repre-
> sentative of the universal soul. The useful arts must conform
> to nature's laws or they will be destroyed. That which is
> designed most efficiently with form decreed by function is
> powerful and beautiful.

2102   Geddes, Norman Bel. HORIZONS. Boston: Little, Brown, 1932.

Reprint. New York: Dover Publications, 1977. xix, 293 p. Illus.

As the originator of industrial design, Bel Geddes discusses and illustrates, in this first comprehensive study, aesthetic as well as practical alternatives to dull mechanization. Streamlining is applied to the design of cars, buses, railroad trains, ships, and airplanes. The author also presents plans and thoughts on architecture for theaters, factories, restaurants, and homes. Two chapters are devoted to the design of products common to daily life, such as beds, chairs, scales, bathroom fixtures, and stoves. The more than two-hundred illustrations are well integrated with the text.

2103 McIlhany, Sterling. ART AS DESIGN: DESIGN AS ART: A CONTEMPORARY GUIDE. New York: Van Nostrand Reinhold Co., 1970. 155 p. Illus.

Organized to demonstrate the relationship between art and primarily industrial design, this volume reveals the symbolism of objects common in contemporary daily life. Chapters are devoted to the jet plane, telephone, automobile graphic design in advertising, clothes, and architecture. While lacking explicit analysis, the work does provide effective visual display with 250 illustrations.

2104 Moholy-Nagy, Laszlo. VISION IN MOTION. Chicago: Paul Theobald, 1947. 371 p. Illus.

By concentrating on the work of the Institute of Design in Chicago, Moholy-Nagy demonstrates how art can assist man in translating experiences with technology and its social impacts into emotional and intellectual orientations. The focus is on industrial design, but abstract art is also emphasized. Discussion of the organic approach to design is followed by analyses of responses to the technological world in painting, photography, sculpture, film, and literature.

2105 Museum of Modern Art. New York. MACHINE ART: MARCH 6 TO APRIL 30, 1934. 1934. Reprint. New York: Arno Press, 1969. Unpaged. Illus., bibliog.

Mass-produced machines, scientific instruments, and objects useful in daily life but chosen for their aesthetic quality are included in this Museum of Modern Art exhibition. The objects are divided into six categories: machines and machine parts, household and office equipment, kitchenware, house furnishings, scientific instruments, and laboratory glass and porcelain. The beauty of "precision, simplicity, smoothness, reproducibility" and function emerges. While some objects are the result of conscious design, for many others beauty is a by-product. Illustrations comprise most of the volume.

2106   Niece, Robert Clemens. ART IN COMMERCE AND INDUSTRY. Dubuque, Iowa: William C. Brown Co., 1968. ix, 121 p. Illus., bibliog.

Industrial art and design as applied to everyday objects are explored and illustrated. Primary influences on contemporary design are considered to be Art Nouveau, DeStijl, the Bauhaus, and the Olivetti and IBM corporations. Aspects of the field covered include product design, furnishings, advertising, packaging, fashion, and illustration.

2107   Papanek, Victor. DESIGN FOR THE REAL WORLD: HUMAN ECOLOGY AND SOCIAL CHANGE. New York: Pantheon Books, 1971. xxvi, 339 p. Illus., bibliog.

"Design within a social context" is the aim of Papanek's multidisciplinary approach to the design process. Since our age of mass-production demands planning in everything, design is seen as the most powerful tool in shaping our environment and our values. Papanek demands a socially-oriented, moral responsibility from design professionals. The first section of the study criticizes the present practice of design focusing on the democratization of taste, obsolescence, abundance. The second section presents new ways of looking at things: the use of bionics in man-made systems, design for nonproductive concerns, and interdisciplinary design teams. Extensive bibliography.

2108   Plummer, Kathleen Church. "The Streamlined Moderne." ART IN AMERICA 62 (January-February 1974): 46-54.

Considering the Moderne as the "ultimate expression of the vision of H.G. Wells," Plummer explores the relationship between science fiction and design in the 1930s. Features of the Wellsian world apparent in the moderne are love of a gadgetry and the machine, the totally artificial environment, extreme orderliness, a penchant for new materials (glass, metal, plastics), and fascination with transportation and speed. Science-fiction pulp illustrations anticipate designs by Buckminster Fuller and Norman Bel Geddes.

D. PHOTOGRAPHY

1. Bibliography

2109   Boni, Albert, ed. PHOTOGRAPHIC LITERATURE: AN INTERNATIONAL BIBLIOGRAPHIC GUIDE TO GENERAL AND SPECIALIZED

LITERATURE ON PHOTOGRAPHIC PROCESSES; TECHNIQUES; THEORY; CHEMISTRY; PHYSICS; APPARATUS; MATERIALS AND APPLICATIONS; INDUSTRY; HISTORY; BIOGRAPHY; AESTHETICS. New York: Morgan and Morgan, 1962. xvi, 333 p.

In preparation over thirty years, this extensive, partially annotated bibliography covers photography from Da Vinci and the camera obscura in the fifteenth century to recent developments in space technology and nuclear science. The 12,000 books, articles, and pamphlets are arranged under 1,200 subject terms. As the title indicates, a wide range of photographic concerns are in the scope, from processes, techniques, materials, apparatus to photographic history, writings by and about leading figures, aesthetics, and applications to other fields.

2. Books and Articles

2110   Firebaugh, Joseph J. "Coburn: Henry James's Photographer." AMERI-CAN QUARTERLY 7 (Fall 1955): 215-33.

Coburn's photography reflects a blend of functionalism and "intuitionist aesthetic." The importance of technical mastery and the mechanical nature of photography influence his artistic choices. His subjects, often streets, skyscrapers, and bridges, express conquest over nature. The association with Henry James to produce photographs as frontispieces for the New York edition of James's works is a remarkable incidence of the collaboration of technology and art in aesthetic vision.

2111   Gernsheim, Helmut, and Gernsheim, Alison. A CONCISE HISTORY OF PHOTOGRAPHY. New York: Grosset and Dunlap, 1965. 314 p. Illus., bibliog.

A well-illustrated history covers both technical evolution and artistic achievements. Includes non-American material.

2112   Hine, Lewis W. MEN AT WORK: PHOTOGRAPHIC STUDIES OF MODERN MEN AND MACHINES. New York: Macmillan, 1932. Reprint. New York: Dover Publications, 1977. Unpaged. Illus.

Hine's documentary photographs show man as the controller and manipulator of machines. The ideal of the Protestant work ethic shapes this photographer's art. Hine presents skyscraper construction workers, railroadmen, machine tenders, coal miners, and workers with precision tools. This edition adds a supplement of Hine's photographs of the Empire State Building under construction.

2113   Jenkins, Reese V. IMAGES AND ENTERPRISES: TECHNOLOGY AND

THE AMERICAN PHOTOGRAPHIC INDUSTRY, 1839-1925. Johns
Hopkins Studies in the History of Technology. Baltimore: Johns
Hopkins University Press, 1975. xviii, 371 p. Illus., bibliog.

Jenkins displays the connections between specific changes in
the photographic industry and developments in American business as a whole. The relationships of technology to business
organization and management are the author's primary concern, but much is also revealed about the society and its
values. Emphasis in the latter half of the book is on the
George Eastman companies and the development of the Kodak
amateur roll-film system. Well-illustrated.

2114   Newhall, Beaumont. THE DAGUERREOTYPE IN AMERICA. New
York: Sloan and Pearce, 1961. 3d ed. New York: Dover Publications, 1976. 175 p. Illus., bibliog.

In this primarily historical account, the daguerreotype is considered as an art, an industry, and a technique. Americans,
much more than the French, were entranced by the process
and the resulting pictures, which were usually preserved in
velvet-lined cases. After its introduction in 1839, the
daguerreotype and manufacture of its equipment became a
booming industry for twenty years. The ample illustrations
are exceptional examples of the art and include portraits of
prominent nineteenth-century Americans as well as industrial
and urban scenes. Short biographies of artists and manufacturers are included.

2115   _____. THE HISTORY OF PHOTOGRAPHY FROM 1839 TO THE
PRESENT DAY. 1937. 4th rev. ed. New York: Museum of Modern
Art, 1964. 216 p. Illus., bibliog.

The contributions of photography to the visual arts, rather
than its technical processes, are the subjects of this history.
The imagery of Julia Margaret Cameron, Louis Daguerre, and
Alfred Stieglitz as well as the documentary work of Jacob A.
Riis and Lewis Hine are discussed. A consideration of the
abstraction of Alvin Langdon Coburn, Man Ray, and Laszlo
Moholy-Nagy follows. Newhall surveys the utilization of
photography in newspapers and magazines as well as develop-
ments in the industry from daguerreotypes to Kodak and
Polaroid cameras.

2116   "Photography." MASSACHUSETTS REVIEW 19 (Winter 1978): 630-892.

The current debate between proponents of photography as a
"detached, symbolic, and formalistic art" and those who consider the photographer as a medium between the objective
world and particular visions of it is the premise of this issue.
Considerations of the implications of the debate are joined

with many full-page black-and-white photographs. Among the articles are "The Romantic Machine: Towards a Definition of Humanism in Photography" by Bill Jay; "Camera Work: Notes toward an Investigation" by Alan Trachtenberg; Allan Sekula's "Dismantling Modernism, Reinventing Documentary"; "In Our Image" by Wright Morris; and a statement by Walker Evans. There are studies of the photography of Aaron Siskind, Alfred Stieglitz, Lewis Hine, John Szarkowski, and Helen Levitt.

2117   Rudisill, Richard. MIRROR IMAGE: THE INFLUENCE OF THE DAGUERREOTYPE ON AMERICAN SOCIETY. Albuquerque: University of New Mexico Press, 1971. xi, 342 p. Illus., bibliog.

Rudisill examines the symbolic visual record of mid-nineteenth-century photography for what it reveals of the developing American character. He finds that the daguerreotype encouraged cultural nationalism and eased "the transition from an agrarian to a technological society in that these images were produced with a reliable mechanical tool." The daguerreotype both "reflected and activated national faith in spiritual insight and truth obtained from perceiving the works of God in nature." Includes over 200 daguerreotype reproductions.

2118   Szasz, Ferenc M., and Bogardus, Ralph F. "The Camera and the American Social Conscience: The Documentary Photography of Jacob A. Riis." NEW YORK HISTORY 55 (October 1974): 409-36.

Riis's success as a compelling social conscience was due to his photographs. Through his books, articles, and especially his traveling lantern-slide shows, he made Victorian audiences realize that the poor were not the creators of their situation but its victims. His style of documentary photography provided a new "perspective on poverty" which destroyed the conception of the poor as "quaint" or "picturesque."

2119   Taft, Robert. PHOTOGRAPHY AND THE AMERICAN SCENE: A SOCIAL HISTORY, 1839-1889. New York: Macmillan, 1938. Reprint. New York: Dover, 1964. xi, 546 p. Illus., bibliog.

Through the history of various forms of photographs, Taft, a professor of chemistry, traces the effect of photography on the social history of America and the impact of culture on the photographic arts. Techniques discussed include the daguerreotype, ambrotype, tintype, stereoscope, flexible film, and zoopraxiscope. Cultural ramifications integrated in the study are attitudes toward the photograph as opposed to pictorial art, war photography, the role of the photograph in Western expansion, the family album, rise of industry and technology, and commercial and news photography. Extensively illustrated and documented.

2120   Thomas, Alan. TIME IN A FRAME: PHOTOGRAPHY AND THE
NINETEENTH-CENTURY MIND. New York: Schocken Books, 1977.
171 p. Illus., bibliog.

By relating photography to the context of the age in which
it developed, Thomas provides a multidimensional consideration of the art and technology. His approach is through an
analysis of the effects of social forces on the development of
various forms of photography, e.g., portraiture, documentary,
chronicle, commercial, and journeying. The intent of the
photographer and the photographed emerges as a prominent
factor. Fashionable display, social reform, family unity,
advertising, and the lure of the exotic inspired the use of
the camera. The impact of types of photographers is also
considered: the artist, the chemist-engineer, the businessman,
and the press.

E. FILM

1. Bibliography

2121   Wheaton, Christopher D., and Jewell, Richard B. PRIMARY CINEMA
RESOURCES: AN INDEX TO SCREENPLAYS, INTERVIEWS AND
SPECIAL COLLECTIONS AT THE UNIVERSITY OF SOUTHERN CALIFOR-
NIA. Boston: G.K. Hall and Co., 1975. xvi, 312 p.

Items in the collection of possibly the largest library of
materials related to American motion pictures are listed in
this unannotated bibliography. Screenplays are listed by
title, special collections and interviews on tape are largely
arranged by name of personality. There is also an index
of screenwriters.

2. Books and Articles

2122   Amelio, Ralph J. HAL IN THE CLASSROOM: SCIENCE FICTION
FILMS. Dayton, Ohio: Pflaum Publishing, 1974. 153 p. Illus.,
bibliog.

The value of science-fiction films in the study of the future
is demonstrated in this anthology. The films discussed consider the threat of technology, loss of freedom and individuality, and the rise of an automated society. Articles, including Susan Sontag's "The Imagination of Disaster" (no. 2135),
focus on the following films: METROPOLIS; SHAPE OF THINGS
TO COME; 1984; ALPHAVILLE; 2001; A SPACE ODYSSEY;
INVASION OF THE BODY SNATCHERS; KING KONG; and
THX 1138. Designed for teachers, the volume includes film-
ographies of short and feature films, an annotated bibliography of articles and a list of distributors.

2123   Blumer, Herbert. "The Moulding of Mass Behavior through the Motion Picture." PROCEEDINGS OF THE AMERICAN SOCIOLOGICAL SOCIETY 29 (August 1935): 115-27.

Mass behavior is a unique type of conduct. Carried on beyond the realm of local culture and group life, lacking in traditions and mores, mass behavior is engaged in by congeries of anonymous, unattached individuals. "Moviegoing" exemplifies mass behavior, demonstrating dramatically some of its effects: alienation of the individual from local life and mores, but reaffirmation of basic human values.

2124   Charlot, Jean. "But Is It Art? A Disney Disquisition." AMERICAN SCHOLAR 8 (Summer 1939): 261-70.

Animated film has added the new dimension of time to art. The cinema demands changes in forms. The sphere and cylinder loved by Raphael and Seurat are beautiful in repose but dull in motion. Animation creates a language of movement as suggestive as that of line or color. Mass media and mechanical reproduction remove elitism and the "cult of the original" from this art form. Cartoon characters, such as Mickey Mouse, are adored as "animal godlings" because they can transcend gravity or matter and in their irrationality are so different from working, commonsense man.

2125   Fulton, A.R. MOTION PICTURES: THE DEVELOPMENT OF AN ART FROM SILENT FILMS TO THE AGE OF TELEVISION. Norman: University of Oklahoma Press, 1960. 320 p. Illus., bibliog.

The only new art form in the first half of the twentieth century, motion pictures emerged from a machine. Fulton explores the relationships between the technologies and the resultant art. Twenty-six films chosen for discussion demonstrate the "difference between the art and the machine." Aesthetic effects of such cinematic techniques as editing, expressionism, naturalism, montage, and sound are considered. Among the films discussed are THE BIRTH OF A NATION, THE GREAT TRAIN ROBBERY, GREED, and INTOLERANCE.

2126   Gifford, Denis. SCIENCE FICTION FILM. London: Studio Vista, Dutton Paperback, 1971. 160 p. Illus.

Beginning with movies made in the 1890s, Gifford's basic guide to great science-fiction films is organized by the devices that serve as celluloid protagonists. Chapters cover the machine, airplane, submarine, robot, ray, bomb, time machine, and the future. Exploration by aliens and astronauts also receives attention. Still photos accompany the text and an index of films provides directors and production companies for over five hundred films.

2127   Holtan, Orley I.   "The Agrarian Myth in MIDNIGHT COWBOY,
        ALICE'S RESTAURANT, EASY RIDER and MEDIUM COOL."   JOURNAL
        OF POPULAR CULTURE 4 (Summer 1970): 273-85.

> The myth of the frontier and romantic pastoralism animates
> these four films in which motorized journeys from West to
> East reverse the usual American migration process. The city
> means tragedy and destruction despite the "desperate optimism"
> of characters longing for a return to innocence. In EASY
> RIDER, Billy's comment "we blew it" sums up the message of
> these films: subconsciously we know that the American dream
> of innocence or innocence regained through Nature is lost.

2128   Jacobs, Lewis.   THE RISE OF THE AMERICAN FILM: A CRITICAL
        HISTORY. New York: Harcourt, Brace and Company, 1939. Reprint.
        New York: Teachers College Press, 1968. xxxii, 631 p. Illus.,
        bibliog.

> Historical, artistic, and sociological analyses of American
> film from 1869 to 1939 are presented by Jacobs. He recog-
> nizes that the motion picture is an essentially American ex-
> pression suited to a machine age and therefore studies his
> subject in the context of American culture in the first half
> of the twentieth century. The development of techniques and
> equipment is narrated and their transformation into effective
> art is emphasized. The business of film, i.e., manufacturing,
> giant studios, the star system, and high finance, receive at-
> tention along with great directors and actors, the artistry and
> content of specific films. A lengthy essay, "Experimental
> Cinema in America 1921-1947," is appended.

2129   Jarvie, I.C. MOVIES AND SOCIETY. New York: Basic Books,
        1970. 394 p. Bibliog.

> Defending cinema as a proper study for serious sociologists,
> Jarvie examines three angles on the motion picture: the
> sociology of the industry, the sociology of the audience, and
> the sociology of the cinema experience. The last portion of
> the book concerns film criticism. An appendix treats film
> and the communication of values. Concludes with a very
> lengthy annotated bibliography.

2130   Jowett, Garth S.   "The First Motion Picture Audiences."   JOURNAL
        OF POPULAR FILM 3 (Winter 1974): 39-54.

> The motion-picture industry answered a deep social need which
> was a part of the new mass culture of the early twentieth cen-
> tury. As working hours decreased, increased leisure time
> meant a need for more urban recreation of all types. The in-
> expensive movie was technologically more realistic than
> theater and vaudeville and was especially attractive to the

working class; it often provided cultural guidelines for new immigrants.

2131   Lounsbury, Myron. "'Flashes of Lightning': The Moving Picture in the Progressive Era." JOURNAL OF POPULAR CULTURE 3 (Spring 1970): 769-97.

A survey of film literature in the period 1900-1917 demonstrates that "technological advancement does not necessarily encourage a change in overt philosophical attitude." Critics such as Frank Woods, Vachel Lindsay, and Hugo Münsterberg emphasize the functional significance of the motion picture and its ability to educate, assimilate, and entertain the semi-literate urban poor and immigrants. The Puritan attitude toward leisure remains. These three scholars declare faith in human progress and do not believe technology leads to dehumanization. Motion pictures suggest an energetic and mobile people whose humanity is asserted in the midst of technological surroundings. Extensive notes.

2132   Margolies, Edward. "City, Nature, Highway: Changing Images in American Film and Theatre." JOURNAL OF POPULAR CULTURE 9 (Summer 1975): 14-19.

Mass media images of the city, Nature, and highway have changed since mid-century. Earlier ambivalence has been transformed into constant pessimism and terror. Discussing many plays and films, such as DEATH OF A SALESMAN, THE GODFATHER, THE ASPHALT JUNGLE, THE INDIAN WANTS THE BRONX, LITTLE BIG MAN, THE LEGEND OF NIGGER CHARLIE, EASY RIDER, and MIDNIGHT COWBOY, Margolies demonstrates that roads to the city and to nature lead only to savagery, "the terrible night of the soul," and "a huge megalopolis of the mind." This attitude may explain the current popularity of science fiction, where the direction is not east, west, north, or south, but up.

2133   "Movies and Society." JOURNAL OF POPULAR CULTURE 3 (Spring 1970): 755-856.

The seven articles which comprise this "in-depth" section consider the impact of films on American culture. Studies are "Moviegoing and American Culture"; "'Flashes of Lightning': The Moving Picture in the Progressive Era" (no. 2131); "The Concept of History in American Produced Films: An Analysis of Films Made in the Period 1950-1961"; "American Movies and American Culture 1946-1970"; "The Cinema and the City"; "A Look at Derivation Plagiarism in Americanned Esthetics"; and "EASY RIDER: Comic Epic Poem in Film."

2134 Reisman, Leon. "Cinema Technique and Mass Culture." AMERICAN QUARTERLY 1 (Winter 1949): 314-25.

The fragmented but totally controlled motion-picture industry has recognized what the audience wants to find in films. Reality and assessment of values must not intrude upon a fantasy, wish-fulfillment experience. Through visual symbols, the camera manipulates an audience that has surrendered critical detachment. Discrete facts, objects, and repetition are presented by the camera and cherished by the audiences, who recognize the likeness to their lives as wage-earners. Even the documentary uses the techniques of propaganda and symbolism.

2135 Sontag, Susan. "The Imagination of Disaster." In AGAINST INTER-PRETATION AND OTHER ESSAYS, pp. 209-25. New York: Farrar, Straus and Giroux, 1966.

Science-fiction films are weak on science but supply instead "sensuous elaboration." Concerned with the aesthetics of destruction, machinery and objects play the major roles and embody ethical values. These things are usually the result of mad, obsessional use of science. It is the technician who administers discoveries to restore safety and order. The films reflect strong anxieties about the human psyche because the individual is destroyed, possessed, or turned into an emotion-less, volitionless, efficient technological man—a machine.

2136 Thomson, David. MOVIE MAN. New York: Stein and Day, 1967. 233 p. Illus., bibliog., filmography.

Forms of the media sensitize observers to their living environ-ment by making them aware of the created aspect of surround-ings. The still photograph and motion pictures aided a con-ception of society as a pure contrivance with patterns that could be perceived and studied. Like a movie studio totally adaptable to instant change, Thomson believes the architec-ture of the future will be highly kinetic and thus instantly adaptable.

2137 Watkins, Gerald, ed. "The Motion Picture Industry." ANNALS OF THE AMERICAN ACADEMY OF POLITICAL AND SOCIAL SCIENCE 254 (November 1947): 1-172.

A second study of the motion picture by the ANNALS (the first was in 1926), concludes that after twenty years of growth "no other institution has so firm and so universal a hold upon secular imagination and popular interest." The origins, nature, and implications of cinema power are ana-lyzed here. Franklin Fearing sums up the influence of movies on attitudes and behavior. While Hortense Powdermaker sup-

plies an anthropological look, Norman Woelfel searches for
ties between the American mind and movie, and Eric Johnston
assesses the motion picture's potential as a stimulus to culture.
Other papers are concerned with regulation, censorship, the
finances of the cinema industry, and future research needs.

2138   Youngblood, Gene. EXPANDED CINEMA. New York: E.P. Dutton
and Co., 1970. 432 p. Illus., bibliog.

Defining expanded cinema as a "process of becoming, man's
ongoing historical drive to manifest his consciousness outside
of his mind, in front of his eyes," Youngblood sees cinema
and television as the "nervous system of mankind." He
examines image-making technologies that will expand man's
communicative capacities, and he looks at new messages in
the cinema. Beginning with a consideration of the individual's relationship to contemporary culture, the author
analyzes how technology is decentralizing and individualizing
communication channels. The potential of computer film,
television, and holographic cinema is discussed. 2001: A
SPACE ODYSSEY is given attention.

Part 19

ARCHITECTURE

A. SURVEYS

1. Bibliographies

2139   American Association of Architectural Bibliographers. PAPERS. Charlottesville: University Press of Virginia, 1965-- . Annual.

> Generally four unannotated, lengthy bibliographies, devoted to individual architects or specific topics, are presented in each annual issue. Volume 11, 1974 is a cumulative index to volumes 1-10. Bibliographies of specific interest are: O'Neal, William B., ed., "A Bibliography of Writings by and about Walter Gropius," 3: v-xvii, 1-138, 1966; Davis, Julia Finette, "International Expositions, 1851-1900," 4: 47-130, 1967; O'Neal, William B., ed., "An Intelligent Interest in Architecture, a Bibliography of Publications about Thomas Jefferson as an Architect," 5: 3-150, 1968; Muggenberg, James, "Frank Lloyd Wright in Print, 1959-1970," 9: 85-132, 1972.

2140   Hitchcock, Henry Russell. AMERICAN ARCHITECTURAL BOOKS: A LIST OF BOOKS, PORTFOLIOS, AND PAMPHLETS ON ARCHITECTURE AND RELATED SUBJECTS PUBLISHED IN AMERICA BEFORE 1895. Minneapolis: University of Minnesota Press, 1946. viii, 130 p.

> Publications related to American architecture from the Revolution to the end of the nineteenth century are listed in this generally unannotated bibliography. Arrangement is alphabetical by author's surname. Descriptive works, guidebooks, and historical, critical, engineering, and technical works are included. A subject index refers to types of buildings, aspects of structures, and materials.

2141   Roos, Frank J., Jr. BIBLIOGRAPHY OF EARLY AMERICAN ARCHITECTURE: WRITINGS ON ARCHITECTURE CONSTRUCTED BEFORE

1860 IN EASTERN AND CENTRAL UNITED STATES. 1943. Reprint. Urbana: University of Illinois Press, 1968. 389 p.

Books and articles on American architecture from the East Coast to the Mississippi River, published prior to 1860, are listed in this briefly annotated bibliography. Entries are arranged by region and state. Geographically inclusive titles appear under the "General" category or "Colonial" or "Early Republican" style sections.

2. Books and Articles

2142 Banham, Reyner. THE ARCHITECTURE OF THE WELL-TEMPERED EN-VIRONMENT. Chicago: University of Chicago Press, 1969. 295 p. Illus., bibliog.

The "anonymous authority" of mechanical environmental services on the architectural design of contemporary buildings is appreciated and detailed. The resulting chronicle of the development of the technologies necessary to control heating, lighting, acoustics, ventilation, and plumbing in large structures credits innovative architects and reveals the impact of specifics such as furnace and duct systems, the revolving door, fans, porches, and air conditioners.

2143 Condit, Carl W. AMERICAN BUILDING: MATERIALS AND TECH-NIQUES FROM THE FIRST COLONIAL SETTLEMENTS TO THE PRESENT. Chicago History of American Civilization. Chicago: University of Chicago Press, 1968. xiv, 329 p. Illus., bibliog.

Condit's study focuses on the internal structure--the materials and techniques--of American houses, bridges, dams, and sky-scrapers from colonial timber-framing to reinforced concrete and steel.

2144 Fitch, James Marston. AMERICAN BUILDING: THE HISTORICAL FORCES THAT SHAPED IT. Boston: Houghton Mifflin, 1948. Rev. ed. New York: Schocken Books, 1966. xii, 350 p. Illus.

Buildings "are absolutely indispensable tools for controlling our environment, without which modern life would be impossible." Fitch covers changing techniques and social forces from 1620 to 1965 with an emphasis on larger private homes, public buildings, and business structures as opposed to lower- and middle-class housing.

2145 Giedion, Sigfried. SPACE, TIME AND ARCHITECTURE: THE GROWTH OF A NEW TRADITION. 1941. 5th ed. Cambridge, Mass.: Harvard University Press, 1967. lvi, 897 p. Illus.

The "mayhem" of the industrial age and the resultant destruc-

tion of man's inner security is reflected in the eclectic architecture and unplanned cities of the nineteenth century. The
schism between architect and engineer was not healed until
the succeeding century. Giedion traces the work of those
responsible for healing the wounds--Frank Lloyd Wright,
Walter Gropius, Le Corbusier, and Mies Van Der Rohe.
Small but significant events of recent architectural history
are interpreted in detail.

2146   Kaufmann, Edgar, Jr., ed. THE RISE OF AN AMERICAN ARCHITEC-
TURE [by] HENRY RUSSELL HITCHCOCK, ALBERT FEIN, WINSTON
WEISMAN, VINCENT SCULLY. New York: Praeger Publishers, 1970.
x, 241 p. Illus., maps.

Four lengthy essays document the contributions of nineteenth-
century American architects in the areas of skyscrapers, city
parks, and private homes. Hitchcock surveys the influence
of American architecture abroad. The work of Frederick Law
Olmsted and others toward the development of urban parks
and cultural institutions is discussed by Fein. Weisman's insights into the growth of the skyscraper uncover what the
structures reveal about human culture. Scully's view of
American houses from Jefferson to Wright presents architecture
as an "expression of human goals."

2147   Mumford, Lewis, ed. ROOTS OF CONTEMPORARY AMERICAN
ARCHITECTURE: A SERIES OF THIRTY-SEVEN ESSAYS DATING FROM
MID-NINETEENTH CENTURY TO THE PRESENT. New York: Reinhold
Publishing Corp., 1952. 3d ed. New York: Dover Publications,
1972. xviii, 452 p. Illus.

Two assumptions govern the selection of essays in this collection: first, modern architecture is considered a continuation
of great movements in architectural history, and second,
American modern architecture is part of an international
movement. Major forces affecting the development of traditions are the machine, Brooklyn Bridge, skyscrapers, the
house; the writings of Ralph Waldo Emerson and Henry David
Thoreau; and the work of Frederick Law Olmsted and Frank
Lloyd Wright. Authors of essays include Horatio Greenough,
Louis Sullivan, Mumford, Wright, Sigfried Giedion,
Montgomery Schuyler, Dankmar Adler, and John W. Root.

2148   Schuyler, Montgomery. AMERICAN ARCHITECTURE AND OTHER
WRITINGS. Edited by William H. Jordy and Ralph Coe. 2 vols.
Cambridge, Mass.: Belknap Press of Harvard University Press, 1961.
xvi, 665 p. Illus., bibliog.

Essays in which Schuyler criticizes aspects of American architecture from the 1870s through the first decade of the

twentieth century are reprinted. Urbane and progressive
statements on modern architecture are followed by considerations of the influence of "Victorian Gothic" and the
Romanesque revival spurred by Henry Hobson Richardson.
The essays then turn to criticism of "rationalist engineering"
as exemplified by bridges (special attention to Brooklyn
Bridge) and skyscrapers. Analysis of the influence of Louis
Sullivan and Frank Lloyd Wright concludes the edition. A
bibliography of Schuyler's writings is appended.

B. THEORY

2149 Adams, Richard P. "Architecture and the Romantic Tradition: Coleridge to Wright." AMERICAN QUARTERLY 9 (Spring 1957): 46-62.

Functional, organic architecture, the theory that the form of
a building should be related to the environment of its site
and to the use for which it is intended, was guided by the
works of Romantic writers. American architects Henry Hobson
Richardson, Louis Sullivan, and Frank Lloyd Wright were influenced by Samuel Coleridge, Horatio Greenough, Henry
David Thoreau, Ralph Waldo Emerson, and, most importantly,
Walt Whitman.

2150 Fuller, R[ichard].Buckminster. IDEAS AND INTEGRITIES, A SPON-
TANEOUS AUTOBIOGRAPHICAL DISCLOSURE. Englewood Cliffs, N.J.:
Prentice-Hall, 1963. 318 p. Illus.

The initial chapters in this complex collection of autobiographical essays interweave intimate details of the author's
life in the 1920s with observations on the international style.
Several essays discuss the very technical education required
for architects. The latter part of the volume is devoted to
domes. Fuller's holistic approach to design is expressed in
"Total Thinking," an essay on world planning and the "continuous man." He calls for an abandonment of the architectural past and an integration of new technologies.

2151 Greenough, Horatio. FORM AND FUNCTION: REMARKS ON ART
BY HORATIO GREENOUGH. Edited by Harold S. Small. Berkeley
and Los Angeles: University of California Press, 1947. xxi, 148 p.
Bibliog.

Six excerpts from Greenough's writings concern his theories
on the necessity of functionalism in architecture, that is, the
adaptation of a building to its site and use. Since Greenough
wrote in the first half of the nineteenth century, his views
are among the earliest American expressions of this concept.
He called for the development of vernacular American forms.

These essays discuss monuments in Washington, D.C., American art and architecture, and the reliance of structure on nature.

2152   Jencks, Charles. ARCHITECTURE 2000: PREDICTIONS AND METHODS. New York: Praeger Publishers, 1971. 128 p. Illus., bibliog.

Methods of forecasting developed in scientific disciplines are applied to the evolution of architecture in the last quarter of the twentieth century. Trends in politics, consumer society, and revolution are then analyzed in regard to how they may be used by the six major traditions in architecture (unselfconscious, conscious, activist, intuitive, logical, and idealist). Actual predictions are then discussed, especially the influence of expected biological inventions.

2153   Johansen, John M. "An Architecture for the Electronic Age." AMERICAN SCHOLAR 35 (Summer 1966): 461-71.

The experience of the electronic revolution will be expressed in architecture. A kinetic quality in assemblage suggests increased interchangeability of parts. The "cyborg" concept could be translated into buildings that are "extensions of man." The architect will be influenced by a reconditioning of perceptive habits and a greater acuteness of sensation. In the electronic age, action and reaction are simultaneous, thus wholeness and empathy are desired values. Immediate comprehensibility will be the goal of "cool architecture;" content will be suggested, not explicit.

2154   Kaufmann, Edgar [Jr.], and Raeburn, Ben, eds. FRANK LLOYD WRIGHT: WRITINGS AND BUILDINGS. New York: Horizon Press, 1960. Reprint. New York: New American Library, 1974. 347 p. Illus., maps, plans.

The editors divide Wright's works into seven chronological sections: "Roots," "Prairie Architecture," "Taliesin," "Japan," "Great Projects and Small Houses," "Fellowship," and "World Architecture." The classic statements are here: "The Art and Craft of the Machine," "Prairie Architecture," "In the Cause of Architecture," "Style," "The Nature of Materials," "The City," "To the Young Man in Architecture," "What is Architecture," "Democracy in Overalls," and "The New Architecture: Principles." There is a listing of Wright's executed works, keyed to a map of the United States, and the text is complemented by 150 illustrations and plans.

2155 Smith, Norris Kelly. FRANK LLOYD WRIGHT: A STUDY IN ARCHI-
TECTURAL CONTENT. Englewood Cliffs, N.J.: Prentice-Hall, 1966.
178 p. Illus.

> The philosophic issues and ideas with which Wright contended
> throughout his life and their translation into his architecture
> are interpreted. Smith finds Wright essentially "conservative"
> in his view of building as a source of "symbols of related-
> ness" enforcing a coherent social order. The dynamics of a
> tension of polarities is exemplified in his architecture: open
> against closed, multiplicity against unity, nature against city,
> freedom against loyalty, individual against society. He did
> not attempt to express the culture of America; instead his
> architecture points to a utopian ideal greatly influenced
> by the agrarian myth so central to our civilization.

2156 Sullivan, Louis H. KINDERGARTEN CHATS AND OTHER WRITINGS.
Edited by Isabella Athey. New York: Wittenborn, Schultz, 1947.
252 p. Illus., bibliog.

> Sullivan's revision of KINDERGARTEN CHATS, a series of
> articles originally published in 1901-2, is a discussion of his
> principles of architecture. He states his conviction that
> function must dictate form and also emphasizes the social
> purpose of American architecture to mirror the democratic
> spirit. Other writings contained herein are considerations of
> the characteristics of American architecture, emotional as
> compared to intellectual building, the skyscraper, the educa-
> tion of architects, and architecture as an expression of the
> American people.

2157 Venturi, Robert; Brown, Denise Scott; and Izenour, Steven. LEARN-
ING FROM LAS VEGAS: THE FORGOTTEN SYMBOLISM OF ARCHI-
TECTURAL FORM. 1972. Rev. ed. Cambridge: M.I.T. Press, 1977.
xvii, 192 p. Illus., bibliog.

> The architectural firm of Venturi and Rauch led a group of
> Yale students on a field trip to Las Vegas. The result is an
> analysis of the vernacular architecture of the Vegas commer-
> cial strip and a translation of the findings into a theory of
> architecture which stresses symbolism. A study of traffic and
> building patterns indicates that urban sprawl is not as chaotic
> as planners often think. Under the gaudiness, ornament,
> banality, and expediency, the authors find logic and effi-
> ciency. They muster support from Pop art, Richard Poirier's
> consideration of parodic structures in literature, and from
> studies of American chaos. They reject the functional and
> organic theories of modern architecture and focus on what
> exists and how to improve it.

2158 Wright, Frank Lloyd. AN AUTOBIOGRAPHY. New York: Longman's

Green and Co., 1932. Rev. ed. New York: Horizon Press, 1977.
620 p. Illus.

> Wright continued to revise his autobiography through 1959.
> This edition incorporates the revisions and adds a section on
> Broadacres City and eighty-two photographs of Wright and
> his architecture. Opinionated and polemical, the volume is
> composed of Wright's attitudes and ideas rather than being a
> factual biography. Wright's personal commitments to nature,
> organic architecture, and the spirit of democracy are evident.
> Other opinions emerging are a dislike of the city, a belief
> that skyscrapers should exist only in the country, and a con-
> viction that the automobile would make the city obsolete.

2159 _____. MODERN ARCHITECTURE. Princeton, N.J.: Princeton University Press, 1931. 115 p. Illus.

> Wright's lectures in the Kahn series at Princeton University
> in 1930 emphasize his enthusiasm for the machine and his
> conviction that man could master his mechanical creations
> and "fashion a new manifestation of beauty." Yet nature
> does not lose importance; for Wright the built environment
> must be complementary with its natural surroundings. The
> titles of the six essays are "Machinery," "Materials and
> Men," "Style in Industry," "The Passing of the Cornice,"
> "The Cardboard House," "The Tyranny of the Skyscraper,"
> and "The City."

C. SOCIAL, PSYCHOLOGICAL, AND CULTURAL ASPECTS

1. Bibliographies

2160 Casto, Marilyn Dee, and Day, Savannah S. HOUSING FOR THE
ELDERLY--DESIGN, ECONOMICS, LEGISLATION AND SOCIO-
PSYCHOLOGICAL ASPECTS. Exchange Bibliography no. 1128. Monti-
cello, Ill.: Council of Planning Librarians, 1976. 30 p.

2161 Dalzell, Lynne. ENVIRONMENTAL AESTHETICS, PREFERENCES AND
ASSESSMENTS: A SELECTED BIBLIOGRAPHY. Exchange Bibliography
no. 1488. Monticello, Ill.: Council of Planning Librarians, 1978.
16 p.

2162 Miller, William C. FACTORS AND FORCES INFLUENTIAL TO ARCHI-
TECTURAL DESIGN: A BIBLIOGRAPHY, VOLUMES 1 AND 2. Exchange Bibliographies nos. 124 and 322. Monticello, Ill.: Council
of Planning Librarians, 1970, 1972. 22, 16 p.

2163 Shillaber, Caroline. LANDSCAPE ARCHITECTURE/ENVIRONMENTAL

PLANNING: A CLASSIFIED BIBLIOGRAPHY. Exchange Bibliography no. 906. Monticello, Ill.: Council of Planning Librarians, 1975. 93 p.

2164   Wilcoxen, Ralph. PAOLO SOLERI: A BIBLIOGRAPHY. Exchange Bibliography no. 88. Monticello, Ill.: Council of Planning Librarians, 1969. 24 p.

2165   _____. A SHORT BIBLIOGRAPHY ON MEGASTRUCTURES. Exchange Bibliography no. 66. Monticello, Ill.: Council of Planning Librarians, 1969. 18 p.

2. Books and Articles

2166   Allen, Edward, ed. THE RESPONSIVE HOUSE: SELECTED PAPERS AND DISCUSSIONS FROM THE SHIRT-SLEEVE SESSION IN RESPONSIVE HOUSEBUILDING TECHNOLOGIES. Cambridge: M.I.T. Press, 1974. 307 p. Illus.

The development of building technologies capable of flexibility and change in order to conform to patterns of human use is the issue discussed at this conference. The goal is to create occupant-manipulable building systems so that individuals can plan, build, or redesign their own dwellings. The human needs to which architecture must respond is an area of debate.

2167   Andrews, Wayne. ARCHITECTURE, AMBITION AND AMERICANS. New York: Harper and Brothers, 1955. 315 p. Illus.

In a study of the "extraordinary" architecture commissioned by wealthy Americans from the Colonial era to contemporary times, Andrews relates the social, intellectual, and cultural ideals to the form of built structures. Americans' drive for constant change, their "longing for an informal existence," and the effect of steady economic advance emerge as compelling shaping forces. The personality and work of specific architects is also related to the prevailing social milieu. Illustrated with the author's own photographs.

2168   "Architecture, Technology and the City." SOUNDINGS 57 (Fall 1974): 253-317.

Four rather diverse articles explore the symbolic, philosophic, and value aspects of the urban built environment. John J. McDermott treats the city as an interdisciplinary phenomenon and urges new assumptions and criteria for urban study. An emphasis on structure rather than machine is advocated by David P. Billington; therefore, he looks at bridges as well as cars, the terminal and the train, the skyscraper and the air conditioner. Todd R. LaPorte notes that while technology is extremely refined, our modes of speaking about it are still obscure. Stylistic trends in architecture reflect value systems according to John W. Cook, who looks at the distinctive forms for business, learning, and housing.

2169 Banham, Reyner. LOS ANGELES: THE ARCHITECTURE OF FOUR ECOLOGIES. New York: Harper and Row, 1971. 256 p. Illus., maps.

The "environmentally ingenious" architecture of Los Angeles is discussed as a unique interrelation of people with their natural and man-made ecologies. The four geographical and cultural conditions which have shaped greater Los Angeles are "Surfurbia," "Foothills," "The Plains of Id" (flatlands and valleys), and "Autopia" (freeway system). Specific structures and architectural trends are presented in their topographic, social, and historic perspectives. "Movement" is considered the central shaping force in the design of the area.

2170 _____. MEGASTRUCTURE: URBAN FUTURES OF THE RECENT PAST. New York: Harper and Row, 1976. 224 p. Illus., bibliog.

The megastructure movement of the 1960s, which inspired plans for huge, expansive structures built of modular or "plugged-in" units, never achieved actualization. Banham finds the demise of this "architect's architecture" to be the result of romantic fascination with technological forms, the obvious cultural impoverishment of a city designed by one or a few persons, and architectural theorizing that neglected the public. The many illustrations detail the conceptions of the movement's major visionaries.

2171 Brolin, Brent C., and Zeisel, John. "Mass Housing: Social Research and Design." ARCHITECTURAL FORUM 129 (July-August 1968): 66-71.

Architects designing mass housing often produce technically adequate structures that are inappropriate and destructive to social behavior patterns. Rather than imposing his own values, the architect must observe life-styles, then design physical forms which are conducive to familiar activities. Architectural plans, accompanied by notes on behavior patterns, for a community designed for a working-class Italian neighborhood in Boston augment the text.

2172 Buitenhuis, Peter. "Aesthetics of the Skyscraper: The Views of Sullivan, James and Wright." AMERICAN QUARTERLY 9 (Fall 1957): 316-24.

Louis Sullivan defined the form of the skyscraper in accordance with its function. In Chicago he built soaring structures relieved of the encumbrance of ostentatious ornamentation. Henry James and Frank Lloyd Wright criticized the "pretension and artificiality" that led to the massive, nonfunctional decoration of New York's tall buildings. The three also considered the social and environmental problems which the skyscraper brought to the city.

2173 Burchard, John Ely. "Architecture for the Good Life." ARCHITECTURAL RECORD 120 (July 1956): 197-200.

"Good gimmicks" and physical ease do not create the good life, rather "it is a matter of things that uplift the spirit." Beyond conveniences, architecture must provide brief moments of ecstasy for many. American architecture has suffered from our sense of transiency, a "throw-away-before-used-up" consumption, a "Puritanical rejection of the opulent," and a tendency toward disorder.

2174 _____. "Architecture in the Atomic Age." ARCHITECTURAL RECORD 116 (December 1954): 119-30.

With an awareness that resistances to the implications of new technologies limit the implementation of much that is technologically possible, Burchard considers the potential of nuclear power in relation to architecture. He sees four possible effects on the city: destruction, dissipation in trivia, the rescue of cities as habitats, or the redemption of a world structured on massive energy consumption. With admirable foresight, the author sees the best hope for civilization to be the development of solar energy.

2175 Burchard, John [Ely], and Bush-Brown, Albert. THE ARCHITECTURE OF AMERICA: A SOCIAL AND CULTURAL HISTORY. Boston: Little, Brown and Co., 1961. 595 p. Illus., bibliog.

The evolution of American architecture from 1600 to 1960 is viewed as the expression of the development of American society. Burchard, a social scientist, and Bush-Brown, an architectural historian, emphasize the European roots of American technological, social, and aesthetic ideas. They find many paradoxes in national ideologies, social forces, and resultant buildings. Critical statements are often arguable and inadequately supported.

2176 Condit, Carl W. THE CHICAGO SCHOOL OF ARCHITECTURE: A HISTORY OF COMMERCIAL AND PUBLIC BUILDING IN THE CHICAGO AREA, 1875-1925. Chicago: University of Chicago Press, 1964. xviii, 238 p. Illus., bibliog.

The commercial architecture of Chicago is surveyed in this
study of the architects responsible for the development of the
skyscraper. The reflection of the personalities of the architects on the style of buildings is recorded. Critical and historical views are limited, however. Daniel Burnham, John
W. Root, William Jenney, Louis Sullivan, Dankmar Adler,
and Frank Lloyd Wright are among the architects discussed in
detail. In this revision of THE RISE OF THE SKYSCRAPER
(1952), some attention is given to domestic architecture, especially apartment houses. Abundant photographs document
structures that have, in many cases, been demolished.

2177 _____. "Sullivan's Skyscrapers as the Expression of Nineteenth
Century Technology." TECHNOLOGY AND CULTURE 1 (Winter 1959):
78–93.

Louis Sullivan was the first great modern architect, and the
character of the Chicago School which he headed flowed
from the scientific and industrial culture of the day. His
work was based on an organic philosophy which held that
architectural style should grow out of the social and technical aspects of the society. Much of Sullivan's inspiration
came from the bridge builders of the day, such as James B.
Eads.

2178 Eaton, Leonard K. TWO CHICAGO ARCHITECTS AND THEIR CLIENTS:
FRANK LLOYD WRIGHT AND HOWARD VAN DOREN SHAW. Cambridge: M.I.T. Press, 1969. ix, 259 p. Illus.

The people in Oak Park and other Chicago suburbs who commissioned homes at the advent of Wright's "Prairie" style were
middle-class, Protestant, Anglo-Saxon, Republican, commuting
businessmen. Eaton studies forty families to determine what
sociological and psychological characteristics may have encouraged them to sponsor an architectural revolution. Patrons
of conservative Shaw are analyzed as a control group.
Wright's clients often lacked formal education, were self-made
men, many of them inventors or involved in manufacturing.
Many were party-givers and musicians. Many of the women
were suffragettes.

2179 Fishwick, Marshall [W.], and Neil, J. Meredith, eds. "Popular
Architecture." JOURNAL OF POPULAR CULTURE 7 (Fall 1973):
375–498.

The twelve articles in this special section consider the aspects
of mass society and culture which are mirrored in popular
architecture. The studies look at Las Vegas, the skyscraper,
houses and automobiles, squatter settlements, buildings and
signs as symbols, the aesthetics of bigness, style, and model
building.

2180 Fitch, James Marston. ARCHITECTURE AND THE ESTHETICS OF
PLENTY. New York: Columbia University Press, 1961. 304 p.
Illus.

That our architecture expresses the American character is the
subject of Fitch's essays and addresses. He considers the
technology, aesthetics, and related social issues involved in
American buildings and finds three dominant qualities:
acquisitiveness, plasticity, and productivity. History is used
for understanding; for example, the essay on Frank Lloyd
Wright and Thomas Jefferson considers how flexibility in
domestic interiors led to the emancipation of women. There
are also articles on Walter Gropius's human wisdom, the role
of the engineer in architecture and society, the skyscraper,
the influence of Horatio Greenough and Ludwig Mies van der
Rohe.

2181 Gottmann, Jean. "Why the Skyscraper?" GEOGRAPHICAL REVIEW
56 (January 1966): 190-212.

Skyscrapers express and determine, to some extent, "the
social, economic, and intellectual evolution of a society."
Two technological innovations, the metal skeleton and the
elevator, made the structures possible. The proliferation of
tall buildings reflects the evolution of employment from agriculture and manufacturing to information and communication.
Skyscrapers contribute to urban sprawl because of the necessity of living space for office workers; thus, extensive transportation systems become essential. The use of glass is
indicative of a more open society.

2182 Gropius, Walter. SCOPE OF TOTAL ARCHITECTURE. New York:
Harper and Brothers, 1955. 185 p. Illus.

Overspecialization and the machine have created a "soul-
flattening mass mind" which eliminates independent thought and
diversity. The architect and planner must be educated to
create essential forms and values out of the technical, economic, and social conditions surrounding him. He must
analyze human relationships, then coordinate such activities
into a "cultural synthesis" through design of communities
and buildings. In these essays, Gropius discusses the architect's education, design for industrial society, sociological
aspects of housing, and organic neighborhood planning.

2183 Handlin, David P. "New England Architects in New York, 1820-40."
AMERICAN QUARTERLY 19 (Winter 1967): 681-95.

New Englanders coming to New York City attempted to instill
ethical lessons, moral standards, and a responsible community
spirit through architectural design. Recognizing that the

physical environment could influence people, architects such
as Ithiel Town and Alexander Jackson Davis built with Congregationalist standards that dictated "orderly structures for
a rationally ordered society." Their buildings conformed to
"communal responsibility, intellectual interest and commercial
need."

2184   Hildebrand, Grant. DESIGNING FOR INDUSTRY: THE ARCHITEC-
TURE OF ALBERT KAHN. Cambridge: M.I.T. Press, 1974. xvii,
232 p. Illus.

Kahn's industrial architecture aimed at solving "machine age
production needs at an almost exclusively operational level."
With patrician and traditional aesthetic tastes, his work was
revolutionary and presented "straightforward reflections of
technical demands." Several of his factory designs are especially significant. The Packard building introduced reinforced concrete to the automobile industry, and the Pierce
Plant of 1906 first proposed the scheme of "unlimited horizontal extension" organized according to the manufacturing
process. Kahn also designed to make the workplace a better
environment for the worker. This chronological study traces
Kahn's career with emphasis on his work for Ford and other
automobile manufacturers.

2185   Hines, Thomas S. BURNHAM OF CHICAGO: ARCHITECT AND
PLANNER. New York: Oxford University Press, 1974. xxiii, 445 p.
Illus., bibliog.

Burnham's influence as a proponent of cultural development
and as a city planner attempting to reform the physical environment are emphasized in this biography. His philanthropy,
entrepreneurship, and programs for "attacking social, economic, and political malaise" are discussed in light of his
work, including innovations in skyscraper design; planning
and building the World's Columbian Exposition; city plans for
Chicago, Washington, Cleveland, San Francisco, and Manila;
and commercial and domestic building design primarily in
Chicago.

2186   Johnson, Elmer H. "Columbus, Indiana: Architecture and Quality of
Life." CULTURES 1, no. 2 (1973): 147-55.

A commitment by city businessmen to support excellence in
architecture has led not only to buildings and recreation
areas designed for human needs, but also to a better, more
culture-oriented life for the townspeople. The quality of
school buildings encourages more responsive behavior by
students and teachers, while libraries and music and theater

facilities have stimulated high attendance. Pride and interest in the community is intense.

2187   Kenner, Hugh. BUCKY: A GUIDED TOUR OF BUCKMINSTER FULLER. New York: William Morrow and Co., 1973. 338 p. Illus., bibliog.

A portrait of Fuller as architect, mathematician, engineer, and poet is created by Kenner. He discusses Fuller's accomplishments, such as the geodesic dome, dymaxion house and car, tensegrity sphere, and synergy, in the context of their developer's themes: mobility, industrialization, recycling of waste, pollution, depletion of natural resources, planetary brotherhood, and wholeness. Kenner gives ample attention to physical details of Fuller's work, but he reveals his subject as a maker of metaphors and a destroyer of standard procedures.

2188   Klare, Michael T. "The Architecture of Imperial America." SCIENCE AND SOCIETY 33 (Summer-Fall 1969): 257-84.

The world prominence achieved by America after the Spanish-American War led to an upsurge of national sentiments which was expressed in the architecture of public buildings and monuments. A compulsion toward elegance and vastness led to elaborate decoration and the popularity of classical style. Advocates of an original architecture for America, such as John Root, were overpowered in the 1890s by classicists led by Charles McKim. McKim's designs for the Columbian Exposition and Columbia University created nonfunctional buildings which were symbols of authority, law and order, and imperialism.

2189   Kurtz, Stephen A. WASTELAND: BUILDING THE AMERICAN DREAM. New York: Praeger Publishers, 1973. 125 p. Illus.

An attempt is made to restore moral judgment to the built environment. Kurtz places architectural evaluation within social criticism. He develops an aesthetic based on the social, economic, and ecological consequences of architecture, that is, its effects on the lives of builders and users, as well as on nature. The study is divided into three areas of concern: the suburbs and country, the highway, and the city in its residential and nonresidential roles. In this context he discusses Howard Johnson's and other roadside spas as inns for the endless pilgrimage, Levittown, urban housing, and downtown culture. Throughout, Kurtz evaluates the potential for architecture to blend with philosophy to augment the potential for wholeness in man.

2190   Lockwood, Charles. BRICKS & BROWNSTONE: THE NEW YORK ROW HOUSE, 1783-1929. AN ARCHITECTURAL & SOCIAL HISTORY.

New York: McGraw-Hill, 1972. xxv, 262 p. Illus., bibliog.

The architectural styles of New York City row houses are only
the starting point of this detailed study, which also considers
the social, technological, and aesthetic forces which shaped
the domestic architecture and the neighborhoods. Organized
according to succeeding styles: Federal, Greek Revival,
Gothic Revival, Italianate, Anglo-Italianate, and Second
Empire. Since row-house construction generally ceased after
1870 due to transportation developments, appearance of
large-scale builders, and social change, only one chapter is
devoted to the period 1875-1929. Information and illustrations are provided to assist in the restoration of individual
row houses.

2191   Meeks, Carroll L.V.   THE RAILROAD STATION: AN ARCHITECTURAL
HISTORY.   New Haven, Conn.: Yale University Press, 1956. xxvi,
203 p. Illus., bibliog.

The passenger railroad station illustrates the forces of the industrial revolution on design. It not only reflects the "impact
of technology and mobility on the masses," but the various
architectural styles employed demonstrate industrial growth.
Meeks considers three aspects of the railroad station: its
architecture, its engineering (huge roofs and new materials),
and its artistry. The study is presented in chronological
divisions. Functionalism blended with a desire for prestige
gave way to standardization. Sophistication of the Victorian
period was followed by the enormous sheds of "megalomania."
Balance is achieved in the twentieth century with the fusion
of form, structure, and function.

2192   Moore, Gary T., ed.   EMERGING METHODS IN ENVIRONMENTAL
DESIGN AND PLANNING.   Cambridge: M.I.T. Press, 1970. ix,
410 p. Illus., bibliog.

Papers from the First International Conference of the Design
Methods Group explore new methods of design and planning
for the built environment. Theoretical studies consider the
process of design and its socioeconomic correlates. Methods
discussed include computer-aided design, building layout
models, systems engineering, and sociopsychological aspects
of the impact of form on behavior. There is an extensive
subject-classified bibliography.

2193   Mumford, Lewis.   THE BROWN DECADES: A STUDY OF THE ARTS IN
AMERICA 1865-1895.   1931. 2d rev. ed.   New York: Dover Publications, 1955. 266 p. Illus.

Art and architecture were overshadowed in these three decades
by the Civil War. Mumford finds a "buried renaissance" in

these years in which the arts struggled to respond to the machine and industrial economy that took possession of the country and created a "paleo-technic" disorder. The brown palettes of Thomas Eakins mirrored the color of iron in the rivers. The architects, above all, recognized that if art was to survive it must be as a function of the social scheme. Functionalism characterized not only the literature of William Dean Howells and Mark Twain, but also the architecture of the Roeblings, Henry Hobson Richardson, Frederick Law Olmsted, and Frank Lloyd Wright. Wright gave the most perfect expression to the mechanical and technical society.

2194 _____. STICKS AND STONES: A STUDY OF AMERICAN ARCHI-TECTURE AND CIVILIZATION. 1924. 2d ed. New York: Dover Publications, 1955. 238 p. Illus.

Architecture and city planning are discussed as a reflection of American culture. Mumford begins by showing how the forms and institutions of medieval European towns shaped the New England village. The grand style of Federalist manors and the revival of classicism are demonstrated to be organic parts of their cultures. The genius of the Roeblings is singled out for attention. Mumford's early critical reaction to machine civilization is evident in his chapter on the effects of industry and mechanization on architecture. He also sees the skyscraper as a promoter of urban disorder.

2195 Negroponte, Nicholas. SOFT ARCHITECTURE MACHINES. Cambridge: M.I.T. Press, 1975. 239 p. Illus., bibliog.

Computer-assisted design and the creation of "architecture machines" instead of buildings are explored in this work. These habitat machines of the future will be responsible to human needs and react intelligently to create functional, pleasurable physical environments. A series of experiments conducted by the Architecture Machine Group at M.I.T. is reported. Basically, the architect is removed and is replaced by the computer and the inhabitant.

2196 Owings, Nathaniel Alexander. THE AMERICAN AESTHETIC. New York: Harper and Row, 1969. 199 p. Illus., maps.

Accepting the assertion that any American aesthetic must be derived from commerce, architect Owings examines our free-ways, cities, skyscrapers, building complexes, and suburban sprawl, then considers the potential for beauty and function. Throughout the discussion, he links the present with forms evident in the artifacts of early American Indian communities. Photographs by William Garnett augment the text. Illustra-tions of transportation systems and urban and suburban developments are effectively interspersed with natural scenes and photos of pueblos and cliff dwellings.

2197   Proshansky, Harold M. "The Environmental Crisis in Human Dignity." JOURNAL OF SOCIAL ISSUES 29, no. 4 (1973): 1-20.

The design of physical environments is usually dictated by values of "technological progress, urbanism, novelty and change, the acceleration of technological change." Values related to human life and social behavior are ignored. Physical form is not the only offensive aspect of the built environment. Designs also overlook needs for privacy, territoriality, and freedom of choice because the individual is conceived of as a "machine man."

2198   Scully, Vincent. AMERICAN ARCHITECTURE AND URBANISM. New York: Praeger Publishers, 1969. 275 p. Illus., maps, bibliog.

The development of urban communities in the continental United States, from the Pueblo Indians to present redevelopment and commercial strips, is surveyed. The influence of unrealized ideas, such as megastructures and garden cities, is included in the analysis. The author relates architectural forms to peculiarities in American ideology and characteristics, such as restlessness, the need for mobility, the lure of the frontier, and alienation. Trends and continuities throughout the history of American urban culture are revealed and discussed. Over five-hundred photographs, plans, and reproductions of art works are utilized.

2199   Torre, Susana, ed. WOMEN IN AMERICAN ARCHITECTURE: A HISTORIC AND CONTEMPORARY PERSPECTIVE. New York: Whitney Library of Design, 1977. 224 p. Illus., bibliog.

In addition to documenting the participation of women in architecture in America, this compilation of articles views the larger framework of social issues which hindered or supported the "full technical and expressive achievement" of women in the field. Issues considered include differences in the way men and women conceptualize space; how dwelling design reenacts social conventions or presents a symbolic expression of unconscious desires; and the interrelationships of woman as consumer, producer, critic, and creator of space.

2200   Twombly, Robert C. "Saving the Family: Middle-Class Attraction to Wright's Prairie House, 1901-1909." AMERICAN QUARTERLY 27 (March 1975): 57-72.

Wright's clients found the prairie house appealing because it emphasized values threatened by city life. The architecture

generated privacy, and a "sense of shelter" to the family
threatened by urban or business pressures. The open plan
also increased contact among family members. An abundance
of windows and harmony with the landscape created associations with nature. Generally, aspects of the architecture
sanctified the family.

2201 Wolf, Peter. "The Urbanization of the Skyscraper." ART IN
AMERICA 55 (September-October 1967): 54-61.

Architects and planners still fail to integrate the skyscraper
with other city functions such as transportation, services, and
commerce. The Pan-Am Building is a partial exception since
it sits atop Grand Central Station and is capped by a heli-
port. Eero Saarinen's only skyscraper, the CBS headquarters,
is a remarkable example of form designed to give aesthetic
pleasure to passers-by. It also liberates form from interior
function. More examples of planned integration of building
and city are advocated.

2202 Zuk, William, and Clark, Roger H. KINETIC ARCHITECTURE. New
York: Van Nostrand Reinhold Co., 1970. 163 p. Illus., bibliog.

The reality of accelerating change in our society indicates
the viability of an architecture adaptable to flux. Kinetic
architecture recognizes and is responsive to design as a continuous process, affecting aesthetics since chance and movement will play major roles. The authors discuss developments
in kinetics in nature and technology; architectural applications, such as reversible, incremental, deformable, mobile,
and disposable architecture; as well as implications for other
fields, such as city planning, property laws, materials, transportation, and utilities. Potential areas of application,
especially space and ocean exploration, are considered.

Part 20

MUSIC

2203 Ahlstrom, David. "Art Form of the Future: The L.P." SOUTHWEST REVIEW 61 (Spring 1976): 144-50.

Two roles of the long-playing record are examined: its function as a faithful transmitter of culture and as an art form. Electronic music recordings have enhanced the latter role. The contributions of four recordings of electronic music that have attracted a wide audience are summarized. In the author's opinion, such pieces "represent significant steps toward the humanization and aesthetic assimilation of technology, in this case a technology which in its turn is apparently responsive to the creative advances of composers of every artistic persuasion."

2204 Appleton, Jon, and Perera, Ronald, eds. THE DEVELOPMENT AND PRACTICE OF ELECTRONIC MUSIC. Englewood Cliffs, N.J.: Prentice-Hall, 1975. ix, 384 p. Illus., music, discog., bibliog.

A book intended for laypersons, students, and musicians serves as a general but thorough introduction to electronic music. Following the opening chapter, in which Otto Luening traces the history of experimental music, A. Wayne Slawson provides an appropriate technical background. Remaining chapters, all by noted authorities in the field, follow four chronological trends in electronic music: tape studio music, synthesizers, the use of computers, and live-electronic techniques.

2205 Ballantine, Christopher. "Toward an Aesthetic of Experimental Music." MUSICAL QUARTERLY 63 (April 1977): 224-46.

Experimental music fosters communal activity and participation, furnishing an emancipation from the ritual, exclusiveness, and expertise associated with traditional Western forms. In audiences, frequent involvement with the questioning and socializing aspects of experimental music may imbue new habits of perception, response, and creativity.

2206 Boretz, Benjamin, and Cone, Edward T., eds. PERSPECTIVES ON
AMERICAN COMPOSERS. New York: W.W. Norton and Co., 1971.
x, 268 p. Music.

A representative selection of articles from the early years of
the journal PERSPECTIVES OF NEW MUSIC includes essays
by, observations about, and interviews with a number of
noted contemporary electronic composers including Edgard
Varèse and Roger Sessions.

2207 Boulez, Pierre. "Technology and the Composer." TIMES LITERARY
SUPPLEMENT 3921 (6 May 1977): 570-71.

Perhaps as a shield against technological change, society has
turned to historicism and conservatism in some arts, particularly music, at the expense of invention. Advances in sound
reproduction, though technical in nature, have tended to
reinforce historicism. Progressive technologists, not musicians,
have seized the lead in creating new means of music-making.
Collaboration between musicians and these technologists,
Boulez stresses, is essential to the vitality of music.

2208 Brindle, Reginald Smith. THE NEW MUSIC: THE AVANT-GARDE
SINCE 1945. London: Oxford University Press, 1975. x, 206 p.
Illus.

Commencing with the "Webern cult" of serialism, Brindle
follows the "adventurous evolution" of recent music in the
work of such iconoclasts as John Cage, Martin Feldman, Earle
Brown, Harry Partch, and their successors. The influence of
Oriental music, early music, and jazz is also taken into
account. The final chapter attempts to place recent musical
events in a social context. Noting the vagueness of new
music's political and social statements, Brindle concludes,
"certainly new music, and the avant-garde in general, has
largely avoided real concern for the ills of this world."
Appendix of new notation symbols.

2209 Cage, John. SILENCE: LECTURES AND WRITINGS. Middletown,
Conn.: Wesleyan University, 1961. 276 p. Illus.

Dating from the late 1930s to the present, these essays by
the noted composer include several pieces on experimental
music, with some reference to technological means for music
production and composition.

2210 Carney, George O. "Country Music and the Radio: A Historical
Geographic Assessment." ROCKY MOUNTAIN SOCIAL SCIENCE
JOURNAL 11 (April 1974): 19-32.

The communications revolution of the 1920s, and particularly the radio, broke down rural isolation, but, conversely, permitted the broadcasting of country culture, in the form of music, throughout the country. Focusing on the areas west of the Mississippi, Carney shows how the radio shaped styles and stars and encouraged the growth of the country recording industry.

2211   Chavez, Carlos. TOWARD A NEW MUSIC: MUSIC AND ELECTRICITY. New York: W.W. Norton and Company, 1937. Reprint. New York: DaCapo Press, 1975. 180 p.

A Mexican composer, conductor, and writer, Chavez enters a plea for musicians to exploit fully all physical possibilities of new electric instruments, not just their capacity to emulate older instruments, and to explore technology's capabilities for producing, as well as reproducing, music. The book reviews then-current technology for sound production and its potential.

2212   Cope, David. NEW DIRECTIONS IN MUSIC. 1971. 2d ed. Dubuque, Iowa: W.C. Brown Co., 1976. xii, 271 p. Illus., bibliog., discog.

In a highly compacted, neatly organized survey of avant-garde and post avant-garde music, Cope explores musical history, philosophy, materials, composers and works from the late 1940s. Partially annotated bibliographies and discographies conclude each chapter. Also valuable are the appendixes, which provide a glossary, biographies, details on notation, and a directory of record companies, music publishers, and pertinent periodicals.

2213   Ehle, Robert C. "The Social World of Electronic Music." INSTRUMENTALIST 25 (October 1970): 36-39.

Electronic music is characterized by a healthy cooperation between engineers and composers in which the creation of new equipment and new music is concurrent. The author foresees the emergence of a social world of electronic music in which composer, student, and scientist will create cooperatively in laboratories and computing centers. Such a situation will offer social satisfaction that has been denied the lone traditional composer.

2214   Ernst, David. THE EVOLUTION OF ELECTRONIC MUSIC. New York: Schirmer Books, 1977. xl, 274 p. Illus., bibliog.

A brief history and detailed chronology of pre-1948 events related to electronic music from the time of Homer to early synthesizer compositions open the volume. The body of the book traces recent history from the appearance of music for

solo tapes in the fifties through recent computer applications.
Musicological and technological rather than aesthetic aspects
are emphasized. A large number of composers and compositions receive mention. Discographies close each chapter and
there is a useful bibliography.

2215   Gaboury, Placide. "Electronic Music: The Rift between Artist and
Public." JOURNAL OF AESTHETICS 28 (Spring 1970): 345-53.

Composers of electronic music and creators of art-happenings
have tended to avoid the past in their search for "nowness."
The author questions whether such an aim is compatible with
what is known of art as a language and the "need for habit
as substratum for any human activity." Absolute newness,
he concludes, does not communicate. Thus electronic music
cannot be at the same time a "perfect happening" and a
language. Jazz is cited as a form that offers a meaningful
blend of improvisation and familiarity.

2216   Henry, Otto W. "The Electrotechnology of Modern Music." ARTS IN
SOCIETY 7, no. 1 (1970): 19-26.

A major impact of technology on music has been that of the
mass media and stereo systems. The greater part of the individual's musical experience is now acquired at home. Electronic technology has also had an impact on the perception
and performance of music and on the behavior of the listener.
The musical world has become more diversified, with a breakdown between musical "types," and a slow merger of music
with other arts.

2217   _____. "Music and the New Technology." ARTS IN SOCIETY 9
(Summer-Fall 1972): 304-6.

United by a common interest in electronic technology and a
desire to escape confining European straits, popular and
academic composers are converging. Through the use of
electronic media, music expresses more relevant modern
values. A new aural tradition is being fashioned, Henry
concludes.

2218   Hiller, Lejaren, and Isaacson, Leonard M. EXPERIMENTAL MUSIC:
COMPOSITION WITH AN ELECTRONIC COMPUTER. New York:
McGraw Hill, 1959. 197 p. Music.

In an early work on composing by computer, the process of
musical composition is described in the language of information science as a series of choices of musical elements from
a limitless variety of raw materials. A digital computer can
be utilized to make these choices in a purely creative, ran-

dom manner in accordance with certain imposed musical rules.
Following a quick review of the development of computer
composing, the authors present a series of their own experiments in polyphonic writing, concluding with the score of
their "Illiac Suite."

2219 Judd, F.C. ELECTRONICS IN MUSIC. London: Neville Spearman,
1972. 169 p. Illus.

Technical aspects of electronic music are introduced. Chapters cover sound reproduction and synthesis, the range of
instruments, composition, and the many uses of the tape
recorder.

2220 Kasdan, Leonard, and Appleton, Jon. "Tradition and Change: The
Case of Music." COMPARATIVE STUDIES IN SOCIETY AND HISTORY
12 (January 1970): 50-58.

Western musical notation developed into a system through
which the composer might narrowly specify the way in which
a piece was to be performed. Improvisation gave way to
virtuoso performance. Through the use of technological advances in electronics, composers have radically departed
from traditional Western composer-performer relationships.
Able not only to conceptualize but also to engineer the
performance of his work, the technology-assisted composer is
able to communicate directly with his audience without an
intermediary.

2221 Key, Donald R. "Computer and the Composer." MIDWEST QUARTERLY
9 (April 1968): 261-67.

The major advantage that the computer offers the composer is
increased control: over loudness, duration, pitch, and
timbre. He is enabled as well to write complex instructions
that most human performers would find overly complex or
tedious. Added control implies greater responsibility. The
extent to which such a composer is successful, the author
conjectures, depends on his ability as a performer as well as
composer.

2222 Kostelanetz, Richard, ed. JOHN CAGE. New York: Praeger Publishers, 1970. xxi, 237 p. Illus., bibliog.

Primarily a collection of excerpts from Cage's writings through
the years, these essays on musical composition and composers,
electronic music, McLuhan, and other writings are concerned
with technology's relation to the arts. Kostelanetz has included an interview with Cage, a catalog of his compositions,
recordings and writings, and a bibliography.

2223   Lincoln, Harry, ed. THE COMPUTER AND MUSIC. Ithaca, N.Y.:
        Cornell University Press, 1970. xvi, 354 p. Illus., music.

        The efforts of composers and music critics who have used the
        computer in their work are documented, displaying a multi-
        plicity of ideas, techniques, and goals. Essays cover the
        history of computer use in music, the elements of computer
        composition and musical analysis, and the automation of musi-
        cal information retrieval.

2224   Mathews, M.V.; Moore, F.R.; and Risset, J.C. "Computers and
        Future Music." SCIENCE 183 (25 January 1974): 263-68.

        Computers, integrated circuits, and other new features of
        electronic technology may make possible a new musical art.
        Two programs, Music V and Groove, are discussed as
        examples of the potential of computer technology to create
        new sounds that can break music free from mechanical
        virtuosity.

2225   MUSIC AND TECHNOLOGY. Paris: La Revue Musicale, 1971.
        208 p. Illus.

        At this UNESCO-sponsored meeting, the central question ad-
        dressed was the essential value and future of music composed
        by means of or assisted by new technologies. Participants
        included both critics and composers. Four papers are con-
        cerned with use of computers in composition, sound synthesis,
        and musical analysis. Others consider appropriate means for
        training composers for the maximal use of new technologies.

2226   Nyman, Michael. EXPERIMENTAL MUSIC: CAGE AND BEYOND.
        New York: Schirmer Books, 1974. 154 p. Illus., bibliog.

        Experimental music is distinguished from that of the avant-
        garde by its composition, timing, rules, performance, and
        listening requirements. The history of experimental music is
        traced, noting the role of electronic systems. A detailed
        and knowledgeable treatment of events, personages and
        musicology is provided. Select bibliography.

2227   Russcoll, Herbert. THE LIBERATION OF SOUND: AN INTRODUC-
        TION TO ELECTRONIC MUSIC. Englewood Cliffs, N.J.: Prentice-
        Hall, 1972. 315 p. Music, discog., bibliog.

        The events of twentieth-century music are interpreted as con-
        stituting two waves--the gradual annihilation of tonality, and
        the conception of music with no formal boundaries or cate-
        gories. Part 2, "The Search for a New Music," includes
        useful chronologies of the development of electronic music
        and of compositional landmarks. Brief summaries clarify con-

tributions of composers such as Milton Babbitt, John Cage, Morton Subotnick, and Yannis Xenakis. A section of lengthy record reviews, a discography by Peter Frank, a glossary, and a select bibliography enhance the work's usefulness.

2228 Salzman, Eric. TWENTIETH CENTURY MUSIC: AN INTRODUCTION. New York: Prentice-Hall, 1967. 196 p. Illus., music.

Part 5 of this survey provides highly condensed, well-organized coverage of the avant-garde; the achievements of Charles Ives, Edgard Varese, and Henry Cowell are discussed. The appearance of Milton Babbitt and subsequent work in sound synthesis, culminating in the founding of sound studios, is chronicled.

2229 Schwartz, Elliott. ELECTRONIC MUSIC: A LISTENER'S GUIDE. New York: Praeger Publishers, 1973. 306 p. Illus., discog., bibliog.

Written for the "typical listener with little background in music or electronics," this volume traces the development of electronic music and composition, and the evolution of the "classic" studio and synthesizer. Events of the sixties, including the introduction of computers in music, are closely followed. Suggested listening and readings supplement. The book closes with statements by composers and a how-to-do-it section. Throughout, the author argues that electronics have proven a humanizing influence in music, removing the art from the cold concert hall and enhancing the possibilities of choice for the composer.

2230 Schwartz, Elliott, and Childs, Barney, eds. CONTEMPORARY COMPOSERS ON CONTEMPORARY MUSIC. New York: Holt, Rinehart and Winston, 1967. xxi, 375 p. Illus., music.

This collection of essays by twentieth-century composers is intended to illustrate the "gradual transformation of composers' aims and ideals" from traditional "representational" music to a new abstraction concerned with sound and structure for their own sake. The first section covers European music before 1945. The second, devoted to experimental music and recent American developments, offers essays by Henry Cowell, Aaron Copland, Samuel Barber, Roger Sessions, Edgard Varèse, Milton Babbitt, John Cage, and others.

2231 Von Foerster, Heinz, and Beauchamp, James W., eds. MUSIC BY COMPUTERS. New York: John Wiley and Sons, 1969. xviii, 139 p. Illus., phonodisk.

Technical and aesthetic questions surrounding the involvement of computers in music are addressed. The editors view computers "not merely as ancillary tools but as essential components in the complex of generating auditory signals that can fulfill a variety of new principles of a generalized aesthetics." Programs for generating music, compositional algorithms, and aesthetic questions associated with timbre and dissonance are among the topics covered. A concluding essay by Gerald Strang explores the problem of achieving computer-created "imperfection" that will approximate the warmth and spontaneity of human performance.

Part 21

FUTURES

A. BIBLIOGRAPHIES

2232   Evered, Roger. FUTURES PLANNING IN MANAGEMENT: BIBLIOG-
        RAPHY AND INFORMATION SOURCES. CPL Bibliography no. 5.
        Chicago: Council of Planning Librarians, 1979. 52 p.

2233   Ewald, William R., [Jr]. THE NEXT FIFTY YEARS/1967-2017; BIB-
        LIOGRAPHY OF STUDIES OF FUTURE TECHNOLOGY, CHANGE,
        AND PHILOSOPHIES OF LIFE. Washington, D.C.: American Institute
        of Planners, 1967. ii, 84 p.

        This bibliography of 307 titles was developed for use in
        futures studies conducted by the American Institute of Planners.
        Entries are arranged alphabetically, then in sixteen categories:
        education, housing, health, leisure, minorities, transportation,
        urban form, arts, natural resources, national development
        policy, new incentives and new controls, new institutions,
        research for choice, manpower requirements, philosophy, and
        science and technology.

2234   Huber, Bettina J. "Studies of the Future: A Selected and Annotated
        Bibliography." In THE SOCIOLOGY OF THE FUTURE: THEORY,
        CASES AND ANNOTATED BIBLIOGRAPHY, edited by Wendell Bell and
        James A. Mau, pp. 339-454. New York: Russell Sage Foundation,
        1971.

        This excellent bibliography serves as a guide to literature on
        the scientific study of the future, the nature of the predictive
        process, methodological considerations and the scientific study
        of the future, and forecasts of the future.

2235   Padbury, Peter, and Wilkins, Diane. THE FUTURE: A BIBLIOGRAPHY
        OF ISSUES AND FORECASTING TECHNIQUES. Exchange Bibliography
        no. 279. Monticello, Ill.: Council of Planning Librarians, 1972.
        102 p.

2236 Roysdon, Christine, and Mistichelli, Judith. FUTURES RESOURCES: A LIBRARY GUIDE FOR CLAIRVOYANTS. Exchange Bibliography no. 1472. Monticello, Ill.: Council of Planning Librarians, 1978. 24 p.

2237 White, Anthony G. PREDICTING THE FUTURE: A SELECTED BOOK-LIST. Exchange Bibliography no. 1371. Monticello, Ill.: Council of Planning Librarians, 1977. 7 p.

2238 World Future Society. THE FUTURE: A GUIDE TO INFORMATION SOURCES. Washington, D.C.: 1977. 603 p.

> This generously annotated guide to the field provides data on "450 people, 230 organizations, 116 research projects, 400 books and reports, 107 periodicals, 354 films," cassettes, games, university courses, and more.

B. BOOKS AND ARTICLES

2239 Barbour, Ian G., ed. FINITE RESOURCES AND THE HUMAN FUTURE. Minneapolis, Minn.: Augsburg Publishing House, 1976. 192 p. Bibliog.

> Papers include edited versions of addresses presented at a 1975 symposium held at Carleton College entitled "Responses to Global Scarcity." Speakers surveyed global deficits of food, energy, and other resources, in the light of surfeits in population and industrial expansion. The darker side is represented by Garrett Hardin and Donella Meadows, among others. Optimists include Kenneth Boulding and René Dubos.

2240 Bell, Daniel. "The Study of the Future." PUBLIC INTEREST 1 (Fall 1966): 119-30.

> Noting a spate of recently published works, Bell concludes that ours is becoming a future-oriented society. He cites several reasons for this trend, among them a lessening of fear of Nazism and Stalinism that has given rise to optimism, a commitment to growth that requires planning, the development of sophisticated projective techniques, and the heightened prestige of science and technology. The article concludes with a brief review encapsulating then current (and already incredible) projections of the world in 1985, 2000, and 2010.

2241 _____, ed. "Toward the Year 2000: Work in Progress." DAEDALUS 96 (Summer 1967): vi, 639-921.

> Selected papers prepared at the behest of the Commission on the Year 2000 for two working sessions held in 1965 and 1966 serve as a foundation for later futurist work in five prob-

lem areas: adequacy of government structure, changing nature of values and rights, the structure of intellectual institutions, the life-cycle of the individual, and the international system. Discussions are limited to social issues, such as urban development, behavior control, information, and the youth culture. Scientific and technological advances are projected only as background. Contributors include Herman Kahn, Donald A. Schon, Harvey Perloff, Ernst Mayr, Margaret Mead, David Riesman, and John R. Pierce.

2242 Bell, Wendell, and Mau, James A., eds. THE SOCIOLOGY OF THE FUTURE: THEORY, CASES AND ANNOTATED BIBLIOGRAPHY. New York: Russell Sage Foundation, 1971. xiv, 464 p. Bibliog.

Contributors unanimously urge social scientists to move in their disciplines from the static study of the present toward progressive research incorporating the methodology and outlook developed by futurists. Part 1 discusses theory and research on the image of the future, part 2 the time factor in interpreting past and future. In the third part, specific applications of futurism in the social and policy sciences are discussed. Bettina J. Huber's "Studies of the Future: A Selected and Annotated Bibliography" closes the volume (no. 2234).

2243 Berry, Adrian. THE NEXT TEN THOUSAND YEARS: A VISION OF MAN'S FUTURE IN THE UNIVERSE. New York: Saturday Review Press, 1974. 250 p. Bibliog.

Berry projects a highly optimistic view of a future based on boundless technological expansion. Critics of growth are dismissed summarily. While convinced that the world is indestructible and that population will voluntarily stabilize, Berry is particularly intrigued by the potential of space for use and habitation. He fears only a few catastrophes: a sudden change in solar radiation, an extraterrestrial invasion, or a pathological change in human nature.

2244 Boucher, Wayne I., ed. THE STUDY OF THE FUTURE: AN AGENDA FOR RESEARCH. Washington, D.C.: National Science Foundation, 1977. ix, 316 p. NSF/RA770036.

Prepared by established researchers in forecasting, this compendium provides an orientation to research, state-of-the-art surveys, professional issues in the field, and an agenda for futures research needs. All papers include substantial bibliographies, and an extensive additional bibliography, "Research on Futures Studies," is included.

2245 Brown, Harrison. THE CHALLENGE OF MAN'S FUTURE. New York:

Viking Press, 1954. xii, 290 p.

Following a brief history of human development that culminates in a survey of present vital rates, agricultural production, and rates of industrialization, Brown turns to a discussion of major modern problems. These are identified as rising population growth, the need for food, and the growing scarcity of resources. Three possible futures are foreseen: a nuclear war followed by the establishment of an agrarian folk world; a controlled, fully socialistic industrial world; or Brown's preference, an industrial society of freedom and plenty.

2246   . THE HUMAN FUTURE REVISITED: THE WORLD PREDICAMENT AND POSSIBLE SOLUTIONS. New York: W.W. Norton and Co., 1978. 287 p. Bibliog.

The author of THE CHALLENGE OF MAN'S FUTURE (no. 2245) takes a twenty-years-after look at the major components of the world predicament. Relationships between rich and poor nations are given particular scrutiny. Problems profiled include food, energy, and climate change. Brown lists "vulnerabilities" that threaten global survival from thermonuclear war to terrorism and man-made diseases, then suggests a program for survival based on strengthened international cooperation, diversified energy sources, and carefully husbanded resources.

2247 Calder, Nigel, ed. THE WORLD IN 1984. 2 vols. Baltimore: Penguin Books, 1965. 215, 205 p. Illus.

In 1962, some 900 men and women contributed brief articles predicting likely developments in the next twenty years to NEW SCIENTIST, the British science weekly. Many of their observations, collected here, remain valuable. Volume 1 covers predictions of technological and scientific developments; volume 2 is concerned with broader concerns of social life, the arts, politics, and leisure.

2248 Chase, Stuart. THE MOST PROBABLE WORLD. New York: Harper and Row, 1968. xii, 239 p. Bibliog.

Writing in a popular idiom, Chase elaborates upon the ten major trends that he feels will shape the world of the twenty-first century: total technology, population growth, shrinking living space, megalopolis, decreasing energy, a mixed economy, automation, the arms race, nationalism, and global culture. Education is needed to solve impending problems, and Chase has detailed suggestions for appropriate curricula.

2249 Clarke, Arthur C. PROFILES OF THE FUTURE: AN INQUIRY INTO THE LIMITS OF THE POSSIBLE. New York: Harper and Row, 1962. 234 p.

  Primarily devoted to a forecast of future technology as "the only field in which prediction is possible," PROFILES prophesies advances in transport, use of gravity, space and time travel, and production. Clarke's future is an age of plenty in which planets are explored and mined, "replicators" effortlessly duplicate life's necessities, and human beings perfect the robots that may eventually supplant the Homo species. Charts pinpoint events to the year 2100.

2250 Cole, H.S.D.; Freeman, Christopher; Jahoda, Marie; and Pavitt, K.L.R. MODELS OF DOOM: A CRITIQUE TO THE LIMITS TO GROWTH. New York: Universe Books, 1973. 244 p. Illus.

  Fifteen analysts associated with the Science Policy Research Unit of the University of Sussex have contributed to this critique of Jay Forrester's WORLD DYNAMICS (no. 2257) and the Club of Rome's THE LIMITS TO GROWTH (no. 2281). The first part dissects the M.I.T. world model, concluding that some key data and assumptions were marred by an overly "Malthusian" bias. In the second part, the authors argue that the model is insufficiently cognizant of the human potential for rapid social and values change. At the same time, they recognize the gravity of global challenges and the need for great alterations.

2251 Encel, Solomon; Marchand, Pauline K.; and Page, William, eds. THE ART OF ANTICIPATION: VALUES AND METHODS IN FORECASTING. New York: Pica Press, 1976. x, 286 p.

  A composite effort of sixteen contributors associated with the forecasting program at the Science Policy Research Unit of the University of Sussex covers the nature of forecasting and planning, both philosophical and statistical. Current methods are critically reviewed, along with underlying psychological and ethical concerns.

2252 Falk, Richard A. A STUDY OF FUTURE WORLDS: DESIGNING THE GLOBAL COMMUNITY. New York: Free Press, 1975. xxxiii, 506 p. Illus.

  Sponsored by the Institute for World Order, this volume reports research stemming from the World Order Model Project (WOMP). The project identified four values as essential to world survival: minimization of war; maximization of social and economic well-being; realization of fundamental human rights; and ecological balance. The present status of world society with respect to these values is assessed, with a focus

on critical issues such as population control and resource
scarcity. Contending world order models, both historical
and contemporary, are analyzed, leading to a scheme for
achieving a preferred world polity.

2253   Feinberg, Gerald. THE PROMETHEUS PROJECT: MANKIND'S
SEARCH FOR LONG-RANGE GOALS. Garden City, N.Y.: Doubleday, 1969. 215 p.

A series of group discussions, led by the author, on the long-
range goals of mankind form the basis of this book. Having
reviewed technological possibilities and the group's problems
in goal-setting, the author reveals his own set of goals for
man: "the cultivation of mystical experience," "individualism," "indefinite progress," and the "extension of consciousness." Through the establishment of a worldwide
network, the Prometheus Project, he hopes for the furthering
of the agreed-upon goals.

2254   Ferkiss, Victor C. FUTUROLOGY: PROBLEMS, PERFORMANCE,
PROSPECTS. Beverly Hills, Calif.: Sage Publications, 1977. 66 p.

Modern futurology combines the knowledge of the scientist,
the will of the utopian, and the imagination of the science-
fiction writer, Ferkiss contends. In a review of the history
and current state of the discipline, he begins with an outline
of significant developments from Plato to Herman Kahn. A
balanced critique of the premises and methodologies of
futurist predictions is followed by an assessment of futurist
influence in government. Ferkiss concludes that predictions
to date have exhibited mixed success.

2255   Fernandez, Ronald, ed. THE FUTURE AS A SOCIAL PROBLEM. Santa
Monica, Calif.: Goodyear Publishing Co., 1977. xvii, 348 p.

Sociologists can aid in predicting the future through "sharing
their insights about the constraints the past and present place
on the future." The first part of the book collects insights
extracted from books by José Ortega y Gasset, Robert
Heilbroner, Daniel Bell, Jacques Ellul, Theodore Roszak,
and others. Specific social problems of the present that may
follow us in the future are examined by authors in the second
part. The catalog includes poverty, pollution, racism,
militarism, and the disintegrating family.

2256   Forrester, Jay W. URBAN DYNAMICS. Cambridge: M.I.T. Press,
1969. xiii, 285 p. Bibliog.

Through the use of a dynamic model simulating urban growth
developed at M.I.T.'s Sloan School of Management, the pro-

cesses of urban boom, maturity, and stagnation over a 250-year period are illustrated. Current urban revitalization programs are subjected to criticism through results suggested by use of the model. Final chapters comment in general on the simulation and modeling of social systems, and on the use of model studies in urban policymaking. An appendix provides details of the model.

2257 _____. WORLD DYNAMICS. Cambridge, Mass.: Wright-Allen Press, 1971. xiii, 142 p. Graphs.

Presents a "dynamic model of world scope," a model which interrelates population, capital investment, geographical space, natural resources, pollution, and food production. The structure and assumptions of the model are outlined in a text complete with graphs, diagrams, and flow charts. Forrester's gloomy prognosis suggests that "we may now be living in a 'golden age' when, in spite of a widely acknowledged feeling of malaise, the quality of life is, on the average, higher than ever before in history, and higher than the future offers."

2258 Fowles, Jib. "The Improbability of Space Colonies." TECHNOLOGICAL FORECASTING AND SOCIAL CHANGE 12 (December 1978): 365-78.

The prospect of space colonies, as proposed by Gerard O'Neill (no. 2289), has caught the attention of increasing numbers of people. Fowles argues that the dream of liberation from Earth's woes offered by proponents of space colonies is a false one. Evidence continues to mount that long-term space voyages are dangerous physically, given even the best of artificial environments. With disaster always threatening, life in a space colony would be of necessity eternally disciplined and mechanized. Fowles concludes, "Space is a desolate, oppressive place that offers little to human beings except confinement and regimentation."

2259 _____, ed. HANDBOOK OF FUTURES RESEARCH. Westport, Conn.: Greenwood Press, 1978. xi, 822 p. Bibliog.

Intended for an interested but not expert readership, the HANDBOOK supplies reports by leading futurists on various aspects of the field. Part 1 records the growth of futures research through a historical overview by John McHale. Ideological and values questions that present difficulties for futurists are discussed in the second part. A third substantial section covers procedures in futures research, spanning least quantitative (intuition) to most quantitative approaches. A fourth part looks at substantive areas for futures research including crucial problems such as population, pollution, and energy. An appendix covers journals, periodicals, reports, graduate programs, and organizations in futures research.

2260 Freeman, Christopher, and Jahoda, Marie, eds. WORLD FUTURES: THE GREAT DEBATE. New York: Universe Books, 1978. vii, 416 p. Bibliog.

This collection of lengthy essays opens with a survey of the global futures debate and the growth of methods in futures studies during the period 1965-76. Four crucial issues--food, energy, resources, and technical change--are reexamined in the light of recent writings in economics and the social sciences. Four possible profiles of the world of the near future emerge. Variations in profiles are keyed to two variables--level of international equality and level of growth. Contributors include Sam Cole, Pauline K. Marchand, Ian Miles, and Keith Pavitt.

2261 "Futurology." INTERNATIONAL SOCIAL SCIENCE JOURNAL 21, no. 4 (1969): 515-84.

An international group of scholars has contributed to this issue, which covers a number of topics in forecasting. Pierre Piganiol introduces the topic of futurology. Among the contributions which follow are Agnes Heller's paper guessing at future relations between the sexes and Robert Jungk's assessment of the importance of the imagination in forecasting. Radovan Richta and Ota Sulc look at forecasting in relation to the scientific and technological revolution. Irene Taviss adds a values perspective.

2262 Gabor, Dennis. INNOVATIONS: SCIENTIFIC, TECHNOLOGICAL AND SOCIAL. London: Oxford University Press, 1970. vi, 113 p.

Drawing from the work of the futurists as well as his own observations, Gabor forecasts 137 inventions and innovations; of them, 73 are hardware, 27 biological, and 37 social. Examples of items from each list include high-strength materials, a human clone, and lifelong education. For each innovation, an explanatory paragraph and projected date of appearance are supplied.

2263 _____. INVENTING THE FUTURE. New York: Alfred A. Knopf, 1964. 237 p.

Describing his conception of the future, Gabor identifies a threatening "trilemma" of nuclear war, overpopulation, and leisure. While overpopulation can be stemmed, and nuclear war avoided, leisure is something for which we are totally unprepared.

2264 _____. THE MATURE SOCIETY. New York: Praeger Publishers, 1972. 200 p.

The "mature society" envisioned by the author is one in which economic growth and material consumption have been abandoned as central principles in favor of the spiritual quality of life and individual development. The future society must aim for a careful match of ability, as measured by IQ, to work role. The "EQ," or "ethical quotient" must also be given prominence in the awarding of power.

2265 Halley, Richard B., and Vatter, Harold G. "Technology and the Future as History: A Critical Review of Futurism." TECHNOLOGY AND CULTURE 19 (January 1978): 53-82.

In a survey of futurism, the authors have elected to concentrate on the main ideas of futurists regarding technological change and its relation to culture. Futurists, whether optimists or pessimists, are portrayed as believing that technological change is the determinant of the world to come. Yet, paradoxically, the authors claim, the futurist hope lies in a reversal of technology's autonomy. Approaches to the future are shown to be diversifying, moving away from computer-based forecasting as dogma. But the authors submit that the framework of futurism, as well as its techniques, needs constant critical review.

2266 Harman, Willis W. "The Coming Transformation." FUTURIST 11 (February 1977): 4-11.

Partly due to their success in solving earlier problems, industrial societies now face a crisis that will require a total transformation of society. Research on alternative futures conducted at Stanford Research Institute over a ten year period, 1967-77, is summarized. From the many alternatives formulated, two types of scenarios emerge--one based on gradual change, the other on producing a new "transindustrial" society to be achieved after a traumatic transition period.

2267 Helmer, Olaf. SOCIAL TECHNOLOGY. New York: Basic Books, 1966. 108 p.

Responding to the commonly held pessimistic view that the social sciences will never achieve a methodological parity with the hard sciences, Helmer argues that the comparison of the two fields is spurious and that there are some signs that the methodological gap may be bridged. Specifically, futurist techniques such as model-building, Delphi listing, and statistical forecasting are cited as good omens.

2268 Jantsch, Eric. TECHNOLOGICAL PLANNING AND SOCIAL FUTURES.

New York: John Wiley and Sons, 1972. xiv, 236 p. Illus.

This collection of previously published essays discusses a number of topics including forecasting methodologies, social functions of technology, planning, and the emergence of the university as a major planning agency.

2269 Jouvenel, Bertrand de. THE ART OF CONJECTURE. New York: Basic Books, 1967. xii, 307 p.

In a general discussion of forecasting, de Jouvenel outlines methods used in economics, sociology, and political science. Critical of the unthinking use of quantitative techniques and trend extrapolation, he reminds the reader that "all conjectures are only reasonable accounts of alternative, possible, and reachable futures."

2270 Jungk, Robert. THE EVERYMAN PROJECT: RESOURCES FOR A HUMANE FUTURE. New York: Liveright, 1977. 288 p. Bibliog.

The ideal of growth is being transformed from material to inner growth. Jungk envisages a worldwide "Everyman Project" to help develop hidden capacities in all deprived or suppressed individuals. The recent spate of society-oriented brainstorm sessions, world models, and world goals colloquia are interpreted as hopeful signs that long-neglected creative faculties are undergoing a renaissance. A long-range trend toward openness, flexibility, and playfulness is projected. The second part furnishes a "tool kit": a potpourri of bibliographies, games, schools, creativity research and alternative technology centers, and other information resources.

2271 Kahn, Herman; Brown, William; and Martel, Leon. THE NEXT TWO HUNDRED YEARS: A SCENARIO FOR AMERICA AND THE WORLD. New York: William Morrow and Co., 1976. xxi, 241 p. Illus., bibliog.

Buoyed by a highly optimistic view of the human future, three researchers from the Hudson Institute present a scenario for a "growth world that leads not to disaster but to prosperity and plenty." A leveling off of population increases, healthy economic growth, new energy sources, and new materials will contribute to this world of abundance. Some worry is expressed about the long-term implications of continued atmospheric pollution and unequal distribution of wealth.

2272 Kahn, Herman, and Wiener, Anthony. THE YEAR 2000: A FRAMEWORK FOR SPECULATION ON THE NEXT THIRTY-THREE YEARS. New York: Macmillan, 1967. xxviii, 431 p.

An enormous mass of data describing population trends, military prowess, and other factors fill numerous tables and figures and supply supporting evidence for the authors' alternative scenarios and "long-term multifold trends." Their prognosis is an increasingly sensate, bourgeois, specialized, industrialized, affluent, and urbane world. A historical introduction by Daniel Bell serves to broaden the volume's perspective.

2273   Laszlo, Ervin. A STRATEGY FOR THE FUTURE: THE SYSTEMS APPROACH TO WORLD ORDER. New York: George Braziller, 1974. xvi, 238 p.

A smooth transition to a post-industrial society, Laszlo contends, will require empirically based, well-constructed strategies for the future. Through the application of systems principles to global conditions, he derives a scheme for a World Homeostat System (WHS). This plan may be described as a global mechanism for providing information pertinent to crucial choices and conditions.

2274   _____, ed. THE WORLD SYSTEM MODELS, NORMS, APPLICATIONS. New York: George Braziller, 1973. x, 215 p. Bibliog.

The first Systems Philosophy Symposium was convened in 1973 to respond to the Forrester projective computer model for a world system. The use and misuse, problems, and complexities of such models are explored by contributors. Authors include Margaret Mead, Alistair A. Taylor, Henryk Skolimowski, and Ralph Wendell Burhoe. Concludes with a response by Jay Forrester and a basic bibliography.

2275   McHale, John. THE FUTURE OF THE FUTURE. New York: George Braziller, 1969. ix, 322 p. Illus., bibliog.

A well-illustrated, lively volume provides many perspectives on future living. In "The Future of the Past," McHale interprets history as a treasure trove of useful social, economic, and political experiments. His discussion of future life is informed by unconcealable optimism. He observes that "the future of the future is determined not only by what may be possible in economic, technological, or socio-political terms, but what man himself deems necessary, allowable and ultimately desirable in human terms."

2276   _____. "Toward the Future." DESIGN QUARTERLY 72 (1968): 1-31.

Through a heavily illustrated, colorfully presented essay, McHale presents the case for futurism. Emphasizing the delicacy of the ecological balance of this planet, he urges

thoughtful recycling and conservative resource use. At the
same time, he advises thorough exploration of potential resources of space, the ocean, and the realm of synthetic
materials.

2277   Marien, Michael. "The Two Visions of Post-Industrial Society."
FUTURES 9 (May 1977): 415-31.

Though many terms for social configurations of coming
decades have been coined, Daniel Bell's "post-industrial
society" has emerged as front-runner. In Bell's sense, the
term describes a highly technological, affluent, centralized
service society, a connotation promulgated by other prominent social scientists and accepted, though reluctantly, by
critics of the technological order. The alternative vision of
the postindustrial society as decentralized and agrarian,
supported by "appropriate," small-scale technology, is advocated by Marien, who sees it gaining strength and acceptance.

2278   Maruyama, Magoroh. "Toward Human Futuristics: Trans-epistemological
Process." DIALECTICA 26, no. 3-4 (1972): 155-83.

As envisioned by the author, futuristics is not a coherent set
of doctrines, but a science of attitude-development. Through
considering the possibilities for the future, people develop an
ability for self-education that will help them actively create
culture and generate appropriate technology.

2279   Maruyama, Magoroh, and Dator, James A., eds. HUMAN FUTURISTICS.
Honolulu: Social Science Research Institute, University of Hawaii,
1971. xviii, 237 p.

The field of futuristics has been developed mainly by economists, technologists, and administrators who share and project
a culture-bound, ethnocentric and relatively unimaginative
vision. Contributed primarily by anthropologists, the selections in this book are intended to serve as an initial step
toward infusing a cultural perspective into the futures field.
As a discipline, anthropology offers to the student of the
future "an array of designs for living and profound insights
into the nature of man."

2280   Maruyama, Magoroh, and Harkins, Arthur, eds. CULTURES BEYOND
THE EARTH: THE ROLE OF ANTHROPOLOGY IN OUTER SPACE.
New York: Vintage Books, 1975. xv, 206 p.

These papers, originally presented at a 1974 meeting of the
American Anthropological Association, attempt to highlight
those non-Western concepts of lifestyle and thought that might

well be incorporated in the design of extraterrestrial communities. "Extraterrestrial anthropologists," in providing this perspective, draw on studies of culture contact, comparative social and political organizations, and science fiction.

2281 Meadows, Donella H.; Meadows, Dennis L.; Randers, Jorgen; and Behrens, William W. III. THE LIMITS TO GROWTH: A REPORT FOR THE CLUB OF ROME'S PROJECT ON THE PREDICAMENT OF MANKIND. 1972. 2d ed. New York: Universe Books, 1974. 205 p. Illus., bibliog.

From projections generated by a world model based on that designed by Jay Forrester, this news-making report reached the startling conclusion that should present growth trends continue, the limits to growth would be reached within the next ten years. Club of Rome members specified five crucial factors: population, agricultural production, natural resources, industrial production, and pollution. Dismissing the possibility of a technological "fix," the authors see the only viable solution to be an equilibrium state based on fixed population and capital.

2282 Mesarovic, Mihaljo, and Pestel, Edward. MANKIND AT THE TURNING POINT. New York: E.P. Dutton, 1974. xiii, 210 p. Illus.

In a followup to THE LIMITS TO GROWTH (no. 2281) the authors use a revised computer model to project the food, resources, pollution, and population for the next fifty years. Urgent, yet not Malthusian in tone, the report calls for global cooperation in problem-solving. It downplays the significance of forecasting in creating the future, stressing the potential impact of the politically active individual.

2283 Michael, Donald N. THE UNPREPARED SOCIETY: PLANNING FOR A PRECARIOUS FUTURE. New York: Basic Books, 1968. xiv, 132 p.

Michael contends that future scarcities, turmoil, and complexities will force us to adopt the use of long-range planning, for which we are now woefully unprepared methodologically and institutionally. Three technologies will come to our aid: cybernetics, social engineering, and bioengineering. But education must be developed to equip people with the cognitive and emotional skills needed to cope with an information overload and an insecure world.

2284 Miles, Rufus E. AWAKENING FROM THE AMERICAN DREAM: THE SOCIAL AND POLITICAL LIMITS TO GROWTH. New York: Universe Books, 1976. ix, 246 p.

The most significant limits to growth, in Miles's view, are not resources that can be quantified, but the limited human capacity to design, monitor, and adapt to extremely complex systems of human interdependence. Capitalistic affluence and energy overconsumption have brought the United States to the position of increasing dependence on the rest of the world, as well as to vulnerability to strikes and sabotage. If, as Miles believes, national systems have already exceeded a sustainable level of complexity and dependability, then a "one world" ideal must be viewed as remote, precarious, and ecologically hazardous.

2285   Molnar, Thomas. "Elements for a Critique of Futurology." GEORGIA REVIEW 27 (Winter 1973): 560–65.

This succinct consideration of the field divides futurist studies into two groups: those by such writers as B.F. Skinner, Teilhard de Chardin, and E.S. Von Weizsacker in which the future is disconnected from the present and is "gratuitous speculation," and the works of "moderates" like Herman Kahn and Jay Forrester whose projections are based on ·what is now possible. The author contends that most studies reveal that the future will be different from the present only by resembling the past. We should look to our models in "pre-industrial and pre-egalitarian societies." Despite sophisticated technology, futurology will always be a "flight into the forever unverifiable."

2286   Muller, Herbert J. THE USES OF THE FUTURE. Bloomington: Indiana University Press, 1974. xviii, 264 p.

A historian and educator expresses a fundamentally pessimistic outlook on the problems facing contemporary society. Futurists are criticized for their unrealistic faith in technological solutions. Surveying society for leadership potential, Muller finds all classes and professions wanting. Only a "sustained effort" at public education, centering on the spiritual needs of man, offers hope. A final chapter unveils a vague forecast of American life in the year 2000, a portrait that projects little change.

2287   Nisbet, Robert A. "The Year 2000 and All That." COMMENTARY 45 (June 1968): 60–66.

The approach of the year 2000 has been heralded with the growth of futurology, perhaps due to a millennial fascination or to the sense that through technology, the future can be manipulated. Skeptical of the prognostic power of trend extrapolation and other forecasting techniques, the author contends that the only value of futurism is the light it sheds on the present.

2288 Oltmans, Willem L. ON GROWTH. New York: G.P. Putnam's Sons, 1974. 493 p.

Inspired by THE LIMITS TO GROWTH (no. 2281), Oltmans conducted taped interviews with some seventy intellectuals, among them B.F. Skinner, Noam Chomsky, Marshall McLuhan, and Julian Huxley, inquiring about their opinions of the news-making book. Many were critical of the assumptions and methods used in THE LIMITS TO GROWTH and took the opportunity to express their own views on the problems of pollution and population growth.

2289 O'Neill, Gerard K. THE HIGH FRONTIER: HUMAN COLONIES IN SPACE. New York: William Morrow and Co., 1977. 288 p. Illus.

A Princeton physicist, O'Neill has become the principal proponent of the idea that we now have the technical ability to set up large communities in space, and that these may serve as a partial remedy for the problem of an expanding human population. The space colonies he envisions would be located near the planetary surface and would support a population of 10,000 engaging in farming, manufacturing, and other activities. A detailed and convincing description of life in such a colony is presented, complete with fictional diary passages.

2290 Pierce, John R. "Communications Technology and the Future." DAEDALUS 94 (Spring 1965): 506-17.

In contrast to the crowded metropolis foreseen by late nineteenth- and early twentieth-century writers, developments in transportation and communications are permitting great flexibility in residence and life-style. Pierce names seventeen fields of science and technology which should further the trend to decentralization of industry and residence, among them teleconferencing and data transmission advances.

2291 Polak, Fred. THE IMAGE OF THE FUTURE. Translated and abridged by Elise Boulding. New York: Elsevier Scientific Publishing Co., 1973. x, 321 p.

For the first time in written history, Polak believes, Western civilization has lost its ability to generate images of the future. The author surveys past images--from ancient times through utopian socialists to the appearance of antiutopias. He concludes that contemporary society has developed a literal aversion to images, a trend observable in existential philosophy, in art, and in social movements. An end to nihilistic thinking is urged.

2292　Prehoda, Robert W.　DESIGNING THE FUTURE, THE ROLE OF
TECHNOLOGICAL FORECASTING.　Philadelphia:　Chilton, 1967.
xvi, 310 p.

Prehoda is confident that scientific and technological advances will lead to a productive, comfortable, and content
future society.　The book catalogs numerous benefits that
will accrue in the near future, from bioengineering developments to new materials and means of communication.　In the
future, the author predicts, the primary occupation will be
research.　Aided by new foods and a reduced need for sleep,
people will work long hours with great satisfaction in pursuit
of new knowledge and its applications.

2293　Russell, Allan Melvin.　"Human Societies in Interplanetary Space:
Towards a Fructification of the Utopian Tradition."　TECHNOLOGICAL
FORECASTING AND SOCIAL CHANGE　12 (December 1978):　353-64.

An examination of classic (static) and modern (evolving)
utopias provides a basis for examining the utopian potentialities of space colonies.　It is estimated that by the year 2200,
"astronations" will be created at the rate of 100 per year.
This unique rate of new beginnings will allow a multitude of
social and political forms to be tried.　Russell makes three
anticipations:　space communities will remain small, colonies
will be independent nations, and the astronations will exhibit
extraordinary diversity.　The rate of new beginnings bodes
well for man because the opportunity to exercise ideal visions,
in the utopian sense, will nourish man's potentialities and
experience.

2294　"Scarcity and Society."　SOCIAL SCIENCE QUARTERLY　57 (September 1976):　160-472.

Representing four social-science disciplines, twenty-four
authors concern themselves with the global limits to growth.
The problem of scarcity is considered historically from the
age of Hobbes, and in its present relation to ecology, population, and politics.　A number of potential societal responses
to scarcity receive attention.　In a concluding review essay,
Donald Dickens examines relevant recent books.

2295　Tinbergen, Jan, coordinator, and Dolman, Anthony J., ed.　RIO:
RESHAPING THE INTERNATIONAL ORDER, A REPORT TO THE CLUB
OF ROME.　London: Hutchinson, 1977.　325 p.　Illus.

A group of twenty-one specialists discuss the nature of a new
international order capable of meeting the world's urgent
needs.　The first part outlines those needs: food, population
control, and others, and assesses progress in solving them to
date.　International organizations appropriate to addressing

these concerns are outlined in the second part, along with specific proposals and recommendations. Evidence supporting participants' positions constitutes the third part.

2296 Toffler, Alvin. FUTURE SHOCK. New York: Random House, 1970. xii, 505 p. Bibliog.

Toffler's now-famous thesis is that social and technological change are accelerating at such a rate that human beings can no longer adapt. Like peasant peoples suffering "culture shock," the industrialized world will undergo "future shock." The first portion documents at length the more spectacular innovations in goods, services, and life-styles that have marked recent decades. Symptoms of "future shock" are identified from research on stress, mental illness, family problems, and "information overload." Toffler's strategy for survival through the impending crisis of nerves lies in "destimulation" in "personal stability zones," and in societally planned change.

2297 Tugwell, Franklin, ed. SEARCH FOR ALTERNATIVES: PUBLIC POLICY AND THE STUDY OF THE FUTURE. Cambridge, Mass.: Winthrop Publishers, 1973. xvi, 335 p. Illus., bibliog.

A decade's worth of work in policy-oriented futures research is brought together. The first part introduces the theoretical and methodological aspects of futures research, describing the nature of prediction, modeling, and alternative scenarios. A second part looks more closely at the future of institutions and policy systems. Essays have been selected from journals and books and represent the work of authors including Bertrand de Jouvenel, Olaf Helmer, Elise Boulding, Irene Taviss, Herman Kahn, Jay Forrester, and Daniel Bell.

2298 Wallia, C.S., ed. TOWARD CENTURY 21: TECHNOLOGY, SOCIETY AND HUMAN VALUES. New York: Basic Books, 1970. 381 p.

In a program at Stanford University consisting of thirty university-wide lectures and associated seminars, speakers were asked "to speculate and to suggest alternative normative models for the near future in terms of technology, social systems and the individual." Essays, penned by notables including Joshua Lederberg, Kenneth Boulding, and Alan Watts, fall under five headings: biopsychological perspectives, science and creativity, technological and economic development, political systems, and humanistic perspectives.

2299 Winthrop, Henry. "The Sociologist and the Study of the Future." AMERICAN SOCIOLOGIST 3 (May 1968): 136-45.

Sociologists have been loath to engage in futurist utopia construction for fear of losing whatever gains have been made toward making their discipline value-free. Winthrop suggests, however, that contributions to futurology can be made without touching on value problems. Sociologists can, objectively, analyze and project the social consequences of current and potential technologies.

2300 World Future Society. AN INTRODUCTION TO THE STUDY OF THE FUTURE. Washington, D.C.: 1977. xiv, 393 p. Illus., bibliog.

A history of the futurist movement from Herodotus and Plato through Bacon and H.G. Wells to contemporary times opens the volume. A short description of the philosophical bases of futurist thinking leads into discussion of forecasting methods and to a synopsis of the ideas of eleven leading futurists. Case histories of practical applications of futurism and an appendix of organizations and periodicals round out the coverage.

Part 22

JOURNALS AND INDEXING SERVICES

A. JOURNALS REGULARLY PUBLISHING ARTICLES RELATING TECHNOLOGY AND VALUES

2301   ALTERNATIVE FUTURES. Troy, N.Y.: Human Dimensions Center, Rensselaer Polytechnic Institute, 1978-- . Quarterly.

> An interdisciplinary journal offers scholarly articles on "utopian literature and thought, communitarianism and social experiment, utopian-dystopian science fiction, and futures inquiry which is nontechnical in nature." Book reviews and bibliographies are regular features.

2302   AMERICAN JOURNAL OF ECONOMICS AND SOCIOLOGY. New York: American Journal of Economics and Sociology, 1941-- . Quarterly.

> Aimed at a "constructive synthesis in the social sciences," research considers the interrelationships among economics, politics, sociology, and cultural history. Discussions bridging the disciplines have recently focused on such topics as policy, cost of pollution and its control, the economics of growth, quality of life, effects of high technologies, urban environments, and capitalism.

2303   AMERICAN QUARTERLY. Philadelphia: American Studies Association, 1949-- .

> With the aim of providing direction for studies in the culture of the United States, articles focus on history, literature, the effects of science and technology, mass culture, politics, sociology, and art in American life. Most provide the interdisciplinary perspective now expected in American studies. Book reviews and notices of dissertations in progress are included. The valuable annual annotated bibliography unfortunately has not appeared in the last few years.

2304 AMERICAN SCHOLAR. Washington, D.C.: United Chapters of Phi
Beta Kappa, 1932-- . Quarterly.

The review of social issues and the arts gives frequent atten-
tion to the science-humanities debate. Contributors include
Jacques Barzun, Kenneth Keniston, Alfred Kazin, Daniel
Bell, Kenneth Clark, William Styron, and Lillian Hellman.
René Dubos, in his regular column "The Despairing Optimist,"
discusses ecology, the art of living, and human foibles.
Poetry and book reviews accompany articles.

2305 AMERICAN SCIENTIST. New Haven, Conn.: Sigma Xi, and the
Scientific Research Society of America, 1913-- . Bimonthly.

A general science journal with some emphasis on the earth
sciences often contains several articles per issue which discuss
social implications of specific technological developments,
especially environmental issues. Numerous book reviews and
lists of books received.

2306 ART IN AMERICA. New York: Art in America, 1913-- . Bimonthly.

Primarily concerned with contemporary visual arts, polished
articles by established critics consider the links between art
and the society reflected therein. Contributors, including
Douglas Davis, Harold Rosenberg, and Barbara Rose, often
discuss the use of new technologies by artists. Includes
reviews of exhibitions and new books. The quality of reproductions and writing make this the best journal for twentieth-
century American art.

2307 BULLETIN OF THE ATOMIC SCIENTISTS: MAGAZINE OF SCIENCE
AND PUBLIC AFFAIRS. Chicago: Educational Foundation for Nuclear
Science, 1945-- . Monthly.

Offering a bridge between the sciences, humanities, and
politics, primary interest is on the relationship of the growth
of science and technology to environment, institutions, and
culture. Articles written by experts, most of whom reveal
a concern for the technology-civilization interface, are decidedly liberal. Letters, commentary, and book reviews
provide an effective information exchange.

2308 BUSINESS AND SOCIETY REVIEW. Boston: Warren, Gorham and
Lamont, 1972-- . Quarterly.

Editorial concerns are corporate social responsibility and
management in an era of advancing technology and rapid
change. Industry analyses and company profiles are joined
by usually nontechnical articles on growth, big business,

nuclear power, women in management, computerized data banks, and other wide-interest topics.

2309 BUSINESS HISTORY REVIEW. Cambridge, Mass.: Graduate School of Business Administration, Harvard University, 1926-- . Quarterly.

Originally published as the BULLETIN OF THE BUSINESS HISTORICAL SOCIETY until 1954, this journal covers articles in business history, many of which touch upon technology, innovation, and manufacturing. Book reviews.

2310 CHRISTIANITY AND CRISIS: A CHRISTIAN JOURNAL OF OPINION. New York: Christianity and Crisis, 1941-- . Biweekly.

The articles contained herein are short, pointed, and oriented to contemporary issues, of which technological impact is a frequent theme. Popular format.

2311 COEVOLUTION QUARTERLY. Sausalito, Calif.: Whole Earth Catalog and POINT, 1974-- .

Produced by the WHOLE EARTH CATALOG people, this appropriate technology journal picks up where the CATALOG (no. 1560) left off, but with a greater emphasis on articles of both a practical and theoretical nature.

2312 DAEDALUS. Boston: American Academy of Arts and Sciences, 1955-- . Quarterly.

Each book-length issue is devoted to one social, political, or literary topic. Contributions are from leading scholars; thus each number forms a major review of lasting value. Recent pertinent issues have included "Doing Better and Feeling Worse: Health in the United States" 106 (Winter 1977); "Science and Its Public: The Changing Relationship" 103 (Summer 1974); and "Limits of Scientific Inquiry" 107 (Spring 1978).

2313 ECOLOGICAL LAW QUARTERLY. Berkeley: School of Law, University of California. 1971-- .

Articles published herein aim to acquaint environmental lawyers with the scientific, technical, and social complexities of environmental problems. Exhaustive analyses of cases and legal tenets are joined by examinations by scientists.

2314 ENVIRONMENT. St. Louis: Scientists' Institute for Public Information, 1958-- . 10 per year.

Well-documented, non-faddist articles are presented on many areas of environmental and consumer concern, from air pollution and nuclear power dangers to pesticides and plutonium.

Some articles are by experts; "Spectrum" provides news of the month; and "Overview" is a commentary on current developments. More for the activist than the detached observer.

2315 ENVIRONMENTAL AFFAIRS. Newton Centre, Mass.: Environmental Law Center, Boston College Law School, 1971-- . Quarterly.

The multidisciplinary journal seeks to augment "interchange on the recognition and solution of environmental problems." Commentary by scientists, administrators, planners, educators, and lawyers leads to a lessening of the isolation of professionals in the various fields. Articles review the legal aspects of pollution control, technology-induced environmental problems, and the social aspects of environmental affairs.

2316 ENVIRONMENTAL LAW. Portland, Oreg.: Lewis and Clark Law School, 1971-- . 3 per year.

The stated editorial purpose is to provide awareness of the legal means to protect the environment. Receiving consideration are such topics as abortion, eco-activism, nuclear power plants, weather modification, land use, the concept of a science court, and the urban environment.

2317 ENVIRONMENT AND BEHAVIOR. Beverley Hills, Calif.: Sage Publications, 1969-- . Quarterly.

Experimental and theoretical studies focus on the influence of the built and natural environments on the behavior of individuals and groups. Planning and policy development, as well as determinations of values and attitudes are highlighted, along with empirical research designed to measure environmental effects.

2318 ETHICS IN SCIENCE AND MEDICINE. Elmsford, N.Y.: Pergamon Press, 1973-- . Quarterly.

Scholarly essays explore social, moral, and ethical questions arising from scientific and technical developments in medicine. Alternatives in implementation of new technologies, planning, and policy are argued. Contributions are often from outstanding spokesmen in biomedical or scientific fields. Articles are polished, well-documented, yet readable for the layman.

2319 EXTRAPOLATION: A JOURNAL OF SCIENCE FICTION AND FANTASY. Wooster, Ohio: Department of English, College of Wooster, 1959-- . Semiannual.

Sponsored jointly by the Modern Language Association Seminar

on Science Fiction and the Science Fiction Research Association, EXTRAPOLATION publishes articles by academics of
interest to literary scholars and historians of science.
Strengths include history of SF, bibliography, and criticism.
Publishes an annual annotated checklist, "The Year's Scholarship in Science Fiction and Fantasy."

2320 FUTURES: THE JOURNAL OF FORECASTING AND PLANNING.
Surrey, Engl.: IPC Science and Technology Press and Institute for the
Future, 1968-- . Bimonthly.

Articles present predictive views of the future, analyses of
specific aspects of life to come, such as work, food, mental
health, and cities, as well as methodological studies of
futures research. Notices of coming conferences and meetings, overviews of meetings held, and book reviews are
provided.

2321 FUTURIST. Washington, D.C.: World Future Society, 1966-- .
Bimonthly.

Nontechnical, objective forecasts and considerations of the
future by scientists, educators, political scientists, researchers,
and industrial spokesmen are presented. Each issue contains
"World Trends and Forecasts," which provides brief data on
environment, food, population, energy, and values. Issues
are often keyed to specific topics such as appropriate technology, waste, the "superfamily," space colonies, education,
or computers.

2322 HARVARD BUSINESS REVIEW. Cambridge, Mass.: Graduate School of
Business Administration, Harvard University, 1922-- . Bimonthly.

Reports on trends in business are joined by research on the
social, economic, and technical developments affecting
corporate interests. Topics recently receiving repeated attention are new technologies and the innovative process, consumer affairs, computerized data bases, growth, energy,
corporate social responsibility, women in management, and
business ethics.

2323 HASTINGS CENTER REPORT. Hastings-on-Hudson, N.Y.: Institute
of Society, Ethics and the Life Sciences, 1971-- . Bimonthly.

Devoted to bioethics, articles explore the social, ethical,
and legal questions implicit in the technologies of human
experimentation, genetic engineering, contraception, abortion,
organ transplantation, and prolongation of life. In line with
the advancement of research into the human impact of biological technology and the stimulation of the inclusion of ethical

inquiry in university curricula, the REPORT presents brief
notices of new developments, essays and articles, case
studies, and a calendar of events. Each issue contains an
annotated guide to recent articles, books, and reports in
the field.

2324   HUMANIST: A JOURNAL OF HUMANIST AND ETHICAL CONCERN.
Buffalo, N.Y.: American Humanist Association and the American
Ethical Union, 1941-- . Bimonthly.

In an attempt to fuse philosophical discussions and practical
applications of humanistic viewpoints to contemporary social
problems, contributors in each issue examine ethical aspects
of a central topic. Issues ranging from extraterrestrial
intelligence, antiscience, and ecology to secular humanism,
humanistic psychology, and the pursuit of happiness have been
considered recently. Includes poetry along with film and
book reviews.

2325   IMPACT OF SCIENCE ON SOCIETY. Paris: UNESCO, 1950-- .
Quarterly.

With international coverage and authorship, each issue is
devoted to a specific topic. Recent issues have included
"Science and Common Sense," "Youth Confronts Science,"
"Science and War," "On the Frontiers of Science," "Human
Settlements," "Engineering Education Today," "Integrated
Technology Transfer," and "Computers and Social Options."
Articles are fairly short and written for the general reader.

2326   ISIS: INTERNATIONAL REVIEW DEVOTED TO THE HISTORY OF
SCIENCE AND ITS CULTURAL INFLUENCES. Philadelphia: History
of Science Society, Department of History and Sociology of Science,
University of Pennsylvania, 1913-- . Quarterly.

The official journal of the History of Science Society is an
international review devoted to the history of science and its
cultural influences with occasional treatment of technological
topics. Includes essays, shorter studies, and numerous book
reviews. A major feature is the annual "Critical Bibliography"
(no. 157).

2327   JOURNAL OF ECONOMIC HISTORY. Wilmington, Del.: Economic
History Association, 1941-- . Quarterly.

Devoted to economic history from the Industrial Revolution to
date, the journal frequently touches upon technological subjects and their economic or social impact. Articles in recent
years tend to reflect the growing emphasis on econometrics in
contrast to traditional narrative. Extensive book review section.

2328   JOURNAL OF POPULAR CULTURE. Bowling Green, Ohio: Popular
Culture Association and Bowling Green State University, 1967-- .
Quarterly.

> Contemporary mass culture is portrayed from multiple view-
> points. Articles cover popular art and music, science fiction,
> black culture, literature, automobiles, sports, new journalism,
> electronic media, and technology's effect on life-styles. They
> have research value as well as being exceedingly entertaining.
> Issues contain several book reviews.

2329   JOURNAL OF THE NEW ALCHEMISTS. Woods Hole, Mass.: New
Alchemy Institute, 1973-- . Annual.

> The New Alchemy Institute is dedicated to a living experi-
> ment in appropriate technology as exemplified by the Ark
> on Prince Edward Island, now a project coordinated by a
> private Canadian group, "Institute for Man and Resources,"
> and their ongoing Center on Cape Cod. The JOURNAL
> includes updated articles on these experiences, as well as
> other philosophical, theoretical, and practical pieces.

2330   LABOR HISTORY. New York: Tamiment Institute, Bobst Library, New
York University, 1960-- . Quarterly.

> Excellent articles on labor and the work experience, many of
> which deal with the response to technology and industrializa-
> tion. Includes a book review section.

2331   LEONARDO: INTERNATIONAL JOURNAL OF THE CONTEMPORARY
ARTIST. Elmsford, N.Y.: Pergamon Press, 1968-- . Quarterly.

> Concerned with contemporary visual and plastic arts, emphasis
> is given to interrelationships of scientific and technical
> achievements within the arts, the use of new materials and
> techniques resulting from advances in technology, and the
> effect of social forces on creativity. Reports on art science
> technology conferences, reviews of interdisciplinary books,
> and "International Science-Art News" are additional features.

2332   NATURAL RESOURCES JOURNAL. Albuquerque: School of Law,
University of New Mexico, 1961-- . Quarterly.

> The effective management of natural resources is supported by
> studies which range from conservation to planning for growth.
> Symposia issues are frequent; current topics include energy
> development, environmental decision making, land use policy,
> resource management, and analyses of specific geographic
> areas.

2333   NATURE. London: Macmillan Journals, 1869-- . Weekly.

Science news, short essays, and brief research reports provide international coverage. Useful for comment on global social and political issues related to science and technology. Includes book reviews and a books-received list.

2334   NEW SCIENTIST. London: King's Reach Tower, Stamford Street, 1956-- . Weekly.

British weekly science magazine for laymen has a lively style and diversified content. Balanced coverage is provided of scientific and technical fields with much space devoted to brief articles and commentary on social and economic impacts of technical advances. Witty and incisive book reviews.

2335   RAIN: JOURNAL OF APPROPRIATE TECHNOLOGY. Portland, Oreg.: Rain, 1974-- . Monthly.

One of the better appropriate technology newsletter-journals, it includes both theoretical and practical articles as well as access sections to new books and organizations in the field.

2336   RELIGION IN LIFE. Nashville, Tenn.: Abingdon Press, 1932-- . Quarterly.

This provides scholarly treatment of contemporary religious issues including technological impact from a Christian viewpoint. Includes both book reviews and notices.

2337   SCIENCE. Washington, D.C.: American Association for the Advancement of Science, 1800-- . Weekly.

The journal comprises authoritative articles, reports, book reviews, and news for the specialist and layman. Recent issues have contained much information on the life sciences, health, and natural resources.

2338   SCIENCE FICTION STUDIES. Terre Haute: Department of English, Indiana State University, 1973-- . 3 per year.

With editors and consultants including Ursula LeGuin, Brian Aldiss, Northrop Frye, and Mark Hillegas, articles and bibliographies reflect interest in studies of science fiction and utopian fiction excluding supernatural and fantasy literature. Correspondence, reports of meetings, and book reviews make the journal a forum for SF researchers. Issues are often dedicated to special topics and authors.

2339   SCIENCE, TECHNOLOGY, AND HUMAN VALUES: AN INTERDISCIPLINARY QUARTERLY REVIEW. Cambridge: Program in Science, Technology and Society, M.I.T., and John F. Kennedy School of Government, Harvard University, 1971--.

Sponsored by funds from the National Science Foundation and the National Endowment for the Humanities, the REVIEW is the "central switchboard and matchmaker" for the invisible college of individuals concerned with research and teaching in the interdisciplinary field of technology, science, values, and society. It is at present the major mechanism for sharing relevant information and resources. The "News Items" section contains announcements of government actions, activities of organizations and programs, reports of research, and notifications of conferences and fellowship opportunities. Recent articles, books, and reports are listed and annotated in the "General Bibliography" section. Scholarly articles and special bibliographies on specific topics are also featured. The editorial board reflects the cross-disciplinary interest with specialists in history, philosophy, literature, sociology, political science, bioethics, the natural sciences, and engineering.

2340   SCIENCE, TECHNOLOGY AND SOCIETY. Curriculum Newsletter of the Lehigh University STS Program. Bethlehem, Pa.: Science, Technology and Society, Lehigh University, 1977-- . Bimonthly.

Designed to promote and support the development of courses and programs which relate technology, society, and human values, the newsletter serves as a forum for the exchange of ideas by educators working in this interdisciplinary field. Articles describe actual courses, theoretical curriculum ideas, and techniques for instituting relevant courses or programs. Includes detailed reviews of books, films and a-v materials, as well as an annotated guide to new publications (books, articles, government publications). Formerly published as HUMANITIES PERSPECTIVES ON TECHNOLOGY.

2341   SCIENTIFIC AMERICAN. New York: Scientific American Co., 1845-- . Monthly.

Intended for the intelligent lay reader. Balanced treatment is accorded topics in the life and physical sciences, technology, and to some extent, the social sciences. Much appears on technology-society relationships. Illustrations and book reviews. An aside: for those interested in the development of nineteenth-century American technology, there may be no better source (certainly no more lavishly illustrated one) than the last century's volumes of this journal.

2342   SOCIAL STUDIES OF SCIENCE. Beverly Hills, Calif.: Sage Publications, 1975-- . Quarterly.

Formerly SCIENCE STUDIES, the interdisciplinary and international journal is devoted to the publication of research on

modern science's concepts and consequences. Contributions
from distinguished scholars in the fields of history, the
sciences, and the social sciences are included.

2343   STTH: SCIENCE/TECHNOLOGY & THE HUMANITIES. Melbourne:
Florida Institute of Technology, 1978-- . 3 per year.

This interdisciplinary journal crosses the boundaries between
science-technology and the humanities in both directions.
Articles cover the psychological, sociological, and esthetic
relationships between the sciences and the humanities, and
critical or evaluative articles in the sciences are also presented. Includes a small number of book reviews.

2344   TECHNOLOGICAL FORECASTING AND SOCIAL CHANGE. New
York: Elsevier North Holland, 1969-- . 8 per year.

Methodological studies concerned with the measurement of the
impact of technology on society are the major focus. Occasional articles on values, science policy, and technology's
effects on mankind also appear. Books on planning, futures
forecasting, and interdisciplinary approaches to technology are
reviewed.

2345   TECHNOLOGY AND CULTURE. Chicago: Society for the History of
Technology, University of Chicago Press, 1959-- . Quarterly.

The Society for the History of Technology is concerned "not
only with the history of technical devices and processes but
also with the relations of technology to the sciences,
politics, social change, the arts and humanities, and economics." The varied articles, research notes, and fine book
reviews clearly reflect these many concerns. Annual bibliography (no. 153).

2346   TECHNOLOGY IN SOCIETY: AN INTERNATIONAL JOURNAL.
Elmsford, N.Y.: Pergamon Press, 1979-- . Quarterly.

This interdisciplinary forum attempts to explore how, "in a
rational way we can assess the risks, the impacts, and the
opportunities of technology. . . , the difficult choices that
require enlightened decisions and institutions capable of
making the choices effectively." The articles investigate how
technology affects our society, the ways in which social processes and attitudes lead to technological decisions, and seek
"to identify combinations of technological or social choices
open to us and their effects on our society."

2347   TECHNOLOGY REVIEW. Cambridge: Alumni Association, Massachusetts Institute of Technology, 1899-- . Monthly.

> The "Departments" section reviews current scientific and technical advances, and presents brief editorials on specific technological effects on society and environments. There are special reports and book reviews. Each issue also contains a number of articles geared to the general reader treating technology's impacts on art, education, and industry. Unassuming format, solid content.

2348 URBAN DESIGN. Washington, D.C.: R.C. Publications, 1970-- . Quarterly.

> With the aim of linking designers with sociologists, psychologists, and ecologists, the journal focuses on all aspects of urban design from street lights to transit systems and neighborhood developments. Each issue contains notices of new building materials and types of urban planning. The social and psychological effects of the built environment are of primary concern.

2349 ZYGON: JOURNAL OF RELIGION AND SCIENCE. Chicago: Institute on Religion in an Age of Science and the Center for Advanced Study in Religion and Science, University of Chicago, 1966-- . Quarterly.

> While the emphasis is on an integration of religion with science, articles dealing with an ethical approach to the social effects of technology also often appear. Evolution, human values, bioethics, ethics and ecology, and complementariness in scientific and religious thinking are topics of specific interest.

B. ADDITIONAL JOURNALS

2350 AMERICAN ACADEMY OF POLITICAL AND SOCIAL SCIENCE. ANNALS. Philadelphia: American Academy of Political and Social Science, 1891-- . Bimonthly.

2351 AMERICAN BEHAVIORAL SCIENTIST. Beverly Hills, Calif.: Sage Publications, 1957-- . Bimonthly.

2352 AMERICAN ECONOMIC REVIEW. Nashville, Tenn.: American Economic Association, 1911-- . 5 per year.

2353 AMERICAN LITERATURE. Durham, N.C.: Duke University Press, 1929-- . Quarterly.

2354 AMERICAN SOCIOLOGICAL REVIEW. Washington, D.C.: American Sociological Association, 1936-- . Bimonthly.

2355 ANNALS OF SCIENCE. London: Taylor and Francis, 1936-- . Quarterly.

2356 BUSINESS AND PROFESSIONAL ETHICS. Troy, N.Y.: Center for the Study of Human Dimensions of Science and Technology, Rensselaer Polytechnic Institute, 1977-- . Quarterly.

2357 BUSINESS HORIZONS. Bloomington: Graduate School of Business, Indiana University, 1958-- . Bimonthly.

2358 CENTENNIAL REVIEW. East Lansing: Michigan State University, 1957-- . Quarterly.

2359 CLIO: AN INTERDISCIPLINARY JOURNAL OF LITERATURE, HISTORY AND THE PHILOSOPHY OF HISTORY. Fort Wayne: Indiana University and Purdue University, 1971-- . 3 per year.

2360 CONTEMPORARY LITERATURE. Madison: Department of English, University of Wisconsin, 1960-- . Quarterly.

2361 EIA REVIEW. Cambridge: Laboratory of Architecture and Planning, Massachusetts Institute of Technology, 1978-- . Semiannual.

2362 ENGINEERING EDUCATION. Washington, D.C.: American Society for Engineering Education, 1910-11-- . 8 per year.

2363 ENVIRONMENTAL COMMENT. Washington, D.C.: Urban Land Institute, 1973-- . Monthly.

2364 ENVIRONMENTAL PSYCHOLOGY AND NONVERBAL BEHAVIOR. New York: Human Sciences Press, 1976-- . Quarterly.

2365 EXPLORATIONS IN ECONOMIC HISTORY, SERIES II. Formerly EXPLORATIONS IN ENTREPRENEURIAL HISTORY. New York: Academic Press, 1963-- . Quarterly.

2366 IDEALISTIC STUDIES: INTERNATIONAL PHILOSOPHICAL JOURNAL. Worcester, Mass.: Clark University Press, 1971-- . 3 per year.

2367 JOURNAL OF AMERICAN HISTORY. Formerly MISSISSIPPI VALLEY HISTORICAL REVIEW. Bloomington, Ind.: Organization of American Historians, 1914-- . Quarterly.

2368 JOURNAL OF COMMUNICATION. Philadelphia: Annenberg School Press, 1951-- . Quarterly.

2369 JOURNAL OF ENVIRONMENTAL ECONOMICS AND MANAGEMENT. New York: Academic Press, 1974-- . Quarterly.

2370 JOURNAL OF ENVIRONMENTAL EDUCATION. Washington, D.C.: Heldref Publications, 1969-- . Quarterly.

2371 JOURNAL OF MEDICAL ETHICS. London: Society for the Study of Medical Ethics/Professional and Scientific Publications, 1975-- . Quarterly.

2372 JOURNAL OF MEDICINE AND PHILOSOPHY. Chicago: Society for Health and Human Values/University of Chicago Press, 1976-- . Quarterly.

2373 JOURNAL OF POLITICS. Gainesville: Southern Political Science Association, University of Florida, 1939-- . Quarterly.

2374 JOURNAL OF POPULAR FILM AND TELEVISION. Bowling Green, Ohio: Popular Press, Bowling Green University, 1972-- . Quarterly.

2375 JOURNAL OF RELIGION. Chicago: Divinity School of the University of Chicago, University of Chicago Press, 1882-- . Quarterly.

2376 JOURNAL OF SOCIAL ISSUES. Ann Arbor, Mich.: Society for the Psychological Study of Social Issues, 1944-- . Quarterly.

2377 JOURNAL OF THE AMERICAN PLANNING ASSOCIATION. Washington, D.C.: American Planning Association, 1935-- . Quarterly.

2378 JOURNAL OF URBAN HISTORY. Beverly Hills, Calif.: Sage Publications, 1974-- . Quarterly.

2379 MASSACHUSETTS REVIEW. Amherst: Massachusetts Review, University of Massachusetts, 1959-- . Quarterly.

2380 MINERVA: A REVIEW OF SCIENCE, POLICY AND LEARNING. Martin's Lane, London: International Association for Cultural Freedom. 1962-- . Quarterly.

2381 MODERN FICTION STUDIES. West Lafayette, Ind.: Department of English, Purdue University, 1955-- . Quarterly.

2382 NEWCOMEN SOCIETY FOR THE STUDY OF THE HISTORY OF ENGINEERING AND TECHNOLOGY. TRANSACTIONS. London: Newcomen Society, 1922-- . Annual.

2383 NOT MAN APART. San Francisco: Friends of the Earth, 1971-- . Biweekly.

2384 PERSPECTIVES OF NEW MUSIC. Annandale-on-Hudson, N.Y.: Bard College, 1962-- . Semiannual.

2385 PHILOSOPHY TODAY. Celina, Ohio: Messinger Press, 1957-- . Quarterly.

2386 POLICY SCIENCES: AN INTERNATIONAL JOURNAL DEVOTED TO THE IMPROVEMENT OF POLICY MAKING. New York: Elsevier-North Holland, 1970-- . Quarterly.

2387 POLICY STUDIES JOURNAL. Urbana: Policy Studies Organization, University of Illinois, 1972-- . Quarterly.

2388 PROGRESSIVE ARCHITECTURE. Stamford, Conn.: Reinhold Publishing Co., 1920-- . Monthly.

2389 PUBLIC ADMINISTRATION REVIEW. Washington, D.C.: American Society for Public Administration, 1940-- . Bimonthly.

2390 PUBLIC OPINION QUARTERLY. New York: American Association for Public Opinion Research, Columbia University, 1937-- .

2391 REVIEW OF POLITICS. Notre Dame, Ind.: University of Notre Dame, 1939-- . Quarterly.

2392 SIERRA CLUB BULLETIN. San Francisco: Sierra Club, 1893-- . Monthly.

2393 SOCIAL FORCES. Chapel Hill: University of North Carolina Press, 1922-- . Quarterly.

2394 SOCIAL SCIENCE QUARTERLY. Austin: University of Texas Press, 1920-- .

2395 SOCIETY: SOCIAL SCIENCE AND MODERN SOCIETY. New Brunswick, N.J.: Transaction Periodicals Consortium, Rutgers University, 1963-- . Bimonthly.

2396 SOCIOLOGICAL QUARTERLY. Carbondale: Midwest Sociological Society, Department of Sociology, Southern Illinois University, 1960-- .

2397 SOUNDINGS: AN INTERDISCIPLINARY JOURNAL. Nashville, Tenn.: Vanderbilt University, 1968-- . Quarterly.

2398 THEOLOGICAL STUDIES. Washington, D.C.: Theological Studies, 1940-- . Quarterly.

C. ABSTRACTING AND INDEXING SERVICES

2399 ABSTRACTS OF POPULAR CULTURE. Bowling Green, Ohio: Popular Press, Bowling Green University, 1976-- . Quarterly.

2400 AMERICA: HISTORY AND LIFE. Santa Barbara, Calif.: American Bibliographical Center--Clio Press, 1964-- . 7 per year.

2401 APPLIED SCIENCE AND TECHNOLOGY INDEX. New York: H.W. Wilson Co., 1958-- . Monthly, except July.

2402 ART INDEX. New York: H.W. Wilson Co., 1929-- . Quarterly.

2403 AVERY INDEX TO ARCHITECTURAL PERIODICALS. 2d ed. Boston: G.K. Hall and Co., 1973. Annual Supplements.

2404 BUSINESS PERIODICALS INDEX. New York: H.W. Wilson Co., 1958-- . Monthly.

2405 ENERGY ABSTRACTS FOR POLICY ANALYSIS. Oak Ridge, Tenn.: U.S. Department of Energy, Technical Information Center, 1975-- . Monthly.

2406 FUTURE SURVEY. Washington, D.C.: World Future Society, 1979-- . Monthly.

2407 HUMANITIES INDEX. New York: H.W. Wilson Co., 1974-- . Quarterly.

2408 INDEX TO LEGAL PERIODICALS. New York: H.W. Wilson Co., 1908-- . Monthly.

2409 INDEX TO RELIGIOUS PERIODICAL LITERATURE. Chicago: American Theological Library Association, 1949-- . Semiannual.

2410 MLA INTERNATIONAL BIBLIOGRAPHY OF BOOKS AND ARTICLES ON MODERN LANGUAGE AND LITERATURE. New York: Modern Language Association of America, 1922-- . Annual.

2411 PHILOSOPHER'S INDEX. Bowling Green, Ohio: Philosophy Documentation Center, Bowling Green State University, 1967-- . Quarterly.

2412 PSYCHOLOGICAL ABSTRACTS. Washington, D.C.: American Psychological Association, 1927-- . Monthly.

2413 RELIGIOUS AND THEOLOGICAL ABSTRACTS. Myerstown, Pa.: J. Creighton Christman, 1958-- . Quarterly.

2414 SAGE URBAN STUDIES ABSTRACTS. Beverly Hills, Calif.: Sage Publications, 1973-- . Quarterly.

2415 SOCIAL SCIENCES INDEX. New York: H.W. Wilson Co., 1974-- . Quarterly.

2416 SOCIOLOGICAL ABSTRACTS. San Diego, Calif.: Sociological Abstracts, 1952-- . 6 per year.

AUTHOR INDEX

This index includes all authors, editors, compilers, translators, and other contributors to works cited in the text. It is alphabetized letter by letter and numbers refer to entry numbers.

A

Aasen, Clarence 814
Abbey, Edward 1920
Abbott, Edith 573
Abell, Aaron Ignatius 264, 749
Abels, Paul 890
Abels, Sonia Leib 890
Abrams, Charles 725
Abrecht, Paul 1648
Adams, Ansel 1367
Adams, Henry 265
Adams, J. Mack 1321
Adams, James Taylor 1848
Adams, Richard P. 2149
Adelman, Maurice 876
Agarwal, Bhoo 814
Agelasto, Michael A. II 690
Ahlstrom, David 2203
Aitken, Hugh G.J. 311, 454, 1289
Akin, William E. 266
Albanese, Catherine L. 1247
Albert, Ethel M. 1564
Albertson, Peter 99
Albion, Robert Greenhalgh 782
Alexander, Ernest R. 815
Allen, Dick 1878
Allen, Edward 2166
Allen, Francis R. 891-92
Allen, Frederick Lewis 163

Allen, Irving Lewis 857
Allport, Gordon W. 1292
Almeder, Robert F. 1780
Amelio, Ralph J. 2122
American Assembly, Columbia University 1512
American Association of Architectural Bibliographers 2139
Andersen, Wayne 2059
Anderson, Alan Ross 1565
Anderson, E.H. 667
Anderson, Oscar Edward 421
Anderson, Richard W. 1477
Anderson, Ronald E. 1318, 1335
Anderson, Rudolph E. 1188
Anderson, S.E. 916
Anderson, Stanford 825
Andrews, Lewis M. 951
Andrews, Wayne 2167
Annas, George J. 1835
Appleton, Jon 2204, 2220
Appleyard, Donald 719, 861
Arbib, Michael A. 1566
Archea, John 979
Arden, Eugene 1981
Arendt, Hannah 1567-68
Armstrong, Ellis L. 750
Armstrong, John Borden 783
Armytage, W.H.G. 164, 1950
Arnold, Horace Lucien 422

Author Index

Arnold, Joseph L. 826
Arnstein, George 1010
Aron, Raymond 13
Aronovici, Carol 827
Aronson, J. Richard 716
Aronson, Sidney H. 1169
Ashby, Eric 1005
Asimov, Isaac 1879-80
Athey, Isabella 2156
Attinger, Ernst O. 927
Aultman, Mark 1094
Ausband, Stephen C. 2017
Ayres, Clarence E. 683

B

Babbie, Earl R. 1770
Baer, Robert M. 1322
Bagdakian, Ben H. 1248
Baier, Kurt 1569
Bailey, Joseph C. 345
Bailey, Liberty Hyde 1376
Bailyn, Lotte 1303
Baker, Elizabeth Faulkner 556, 574
Baker, Robert F. 1059
Baker, Ronald L. 1849
Baldwin, J. 1538
Ballantine, Christopher 2205
Ballard, Edward Goodwin 1570
Banfield, Tom 1711
Banham, Reyner 2094, 2142, 2169-70
Baram, Michael S. 1095
Barber, Bernard 1771, 1801
Barbour, Ian G. 1377, 1397, 1649-51, 2239
Baritz, Loren 591
Barnett, George E. 557
Barnett, Jonathan 828
Barnett, Margery 99
Barnette, Henlee H. 1398
Barnouw, Erik 1290, 1304
Barrett, Paul 1190
Barrett, William 1571
Barron, Neil 1946
Barth, Gunther Luther 784
Bartocha, Bodo 1117-18
Basile, Joseph Lawrence 2018
Basiuk, Victor 1060, 1111
Baskin, John 785

Bates, J. Leonard 1368
Bates, Ralph S. 267
Bathe, Dorothy 221
Bathe, Greville 221
Bauer, Alice H. 1249
Bauer, Raymond A. 893, 1116, 1249, 1736, 1746
Baum, Andrew 981
Baum, Robert J. 1709
Baumhart, Raymond, S.J. 1737
Baur, John I.H. 2062
Baxter, William F. 1096, 1442
Bazelon, David L. 1097
Beard, Charles A. 165
Beard, Daniel P. 1443
Beatty, William K. 243
Beauchamp, James W. 2231
Beauchamp, Tom L. 1772
Beaver, Donald de B. 268
Beck, Robert N. 1572
Beckmann, Petr 1417
Bedau, Hugo Adam 944
Bedini, Silvio A. 388
Beecher, Henry K. 1802
Behrens, William W. III 2281
Bell, Daniel 14, 118-19, 455, 2240-41
Bell, Gwen 816, 973
Bell, Wendell 2242
Bell, Whitfield J., Jr. 150
Bellamy, Edward 1881
Bender, Bert A. 1982
Bender, Thomas 802
Bender, Tom 1539
Bendix, Reinhard 456, 540
Bennett, John Coleman 1652
Benson, Barbara E. 312
Benthall, Jonathan 15, 2063
Berdyaev, Nicholas 1653
Bereano, Philip L. 72
Berger, Albert I. 1951
Berger, Brigitte 894
Berger, Harold L. 1952
Berger, Michael L. 1191
Berger, Peter L. 592, 894
Berman, James H. 2019
Bernard, H. Russell 917
Bernard, Jessie 895
Berry, Adrian 2243
Berry, Brian J.L. 726

Author Index

Author Index

McGlothlin, William 1816
McGrath, Dorn C. 1461
MacGreevey, Paula 973
McHale, John 900, 1270-71, 2275-76
McHarg, Ian L. 835
McIlhany, Sterling 2103
MacKaye, Benton 836-37
McKee, James B. 869
McKelvey, Blake 768-69
McKenzie, Roderick D. 872
Mackey, Robert 1563, 1620
McKie, James W. 1760
McKinley, Daniel 1364
Maclaurin, William Rupert 1298
McLean, George F. 1647
McLuhan, Herbert Marshall 1272-75
McMahon, Michal A. 233
McNeil, John 1934
MacPhee, Laurence F. 2038
MacPherson, C.B. 1082
McShane, Clay 778
Madden, Carl H. 702, 1761
Maddox, John 1429
Mailer, Norman 1233
Mak, James 1160
Makarushka, Julia Loughlin 1801
Mangels, William F. 659
Mangum, Garth L. 632
Mankin, Donald 941
Mann, David 1720
Mann, Floyd C. 640
Mansfield, Edwin 340-41
Mantell, Murray I. 1721
Marchand, Pauline K. 2251
Marcson, Simon 641
Marcuse, Herbert 48, 882, 1616
Margolies, Edward 2132
Marien, Michael 8, 2277
Marine, Gene 1390
Marks, Geoffrey 243
Martel, Leon 2271
Marti-Ibañez, Felix 244
Martin, J.L. 2054
Martin, James Thomas 1330
Martin, Jay 1999
Martin, Michael M. 1805
Martin, Thomas W. 660
Maruyama, Magoroh 2278-80

Marx, Leo 1985, 2000-2002
Marzio, Peter C. 2084
Mason, Kenneth G.M. 1416
Massachusetts Institute of Technology. School of Engineering. Center for Policy Alternatives 1050
Massare, Murray 572
Mathews, M.V. 2224
Mau, James A. 2242
Mauritzen, Joseph H. 988
May, George S. 1208-9
May, Henry F. 290
Mayo, Elton 612
Mazlish, Bruce 1234, 1617
Mazur, Allan 1083, 1105, 1499
Mead, Margaret 870, 1662
Meade, Richard Hardaway 245
Meador, Roy 68, 1500
Meadows, Dennis L. 2281
Meadows, Donella H. 2281
Meeker, Joseph W. 2055
Meeks, Carroll L.V. 2191
Mehrabian, Albert 997
Meier, Hugo A. 291-92
Meier, Richard L. 703
Meissner, Martin 613
Meister, Joel S. 1814
Mellard, James M. 1968
Melman, Seymour 1084
Melody, William H. 1261
Melsen, Andrew G. van 1618
Melville, Herman 1912, 1935-36
Mendelsohn, Everett 1784
Merritt, Raymond H. 234
Merton, Robert K. 614, 883
Mesarovic, Mihaljo 2282
Meshenberg, Michael J. 1415
Mesthene, Emmanuel G. 49, 139
Metlay, Daniel 135
Metz, Johannes B. 1690
Metzger, Gustav 2072
Meyer, Bathasar Henry 1147
Meyersohn, Rolf 658
Michael, Donald N. 933, 1134, 1235, 1331, 2283
Michaelis, Michael 342
Michaels, Richard M. 1059
Michalos, Alex C. 1619
Miles, Rufus E. 2284
Millbrook, Minnie Dubbs 1207

Author Index

Author Index

Author Index

TITLE INDEX

This index includes titles to books and essays, as well as titles to journals and indexing services cited in the text. In many instances, lengthy titles have been shortened. This index is alphabetized letter by letter and numbers refer to entry numbers.

A

C

Title Index

D

Title Index

Title Index

Title Index

Title Index

Title Index

Title Index

Title Index

Title Index

Title Index

Title Index

Title Index

Y

Z

SUBJECT INDEX

Alphabetization is letter by letter and references are to entry numbers.

Subject Index

Amusement parks 650, 657, 659, 664, 2067
Anarchism 40
Anderson, Sherwood 1995, 2015
Anthropological perspectives 66, 125, 1358, 2279-80
Appropriate technology 75, 123, 482, 1496, 1533, 1535-62, 1615, 1648, 2270, 2277, 2311, 2329, 2335
Arcadian myth. See Agrarian ideal
Architecture 15, 43-44, 414, 416-17, 720, 723, 740-41, 744, 789-92, 801, 808, 814, 825, 840, 849, 853-54, 856, 859, 980, 982, 984, 993-96, 999-1000, 1003, 1358, 1415, 2045, 2049, 2052-54, 2056, 2072, 2079, 2102-03, 2136, 2139-2202, 2361, 2388, 2403
Arcosanti 744
Armour and Co. 645, 1941
Army Corps of Engineers 235, 1390
Art 3, 15, 24, 44, 118, 145, 148, 720-21, 1254, 1271, 1339, 1988, 2018, 2045-2108, 2193, 2247, 2303, 2306, 2331, 2402
Art, computer generated 979, 2061, 2063-64, 2069, 2072, 2076, 2081, 2086, 2089, 2091, 2138
ARTHUR MERVYN 2006
Artificial insemination 1790, 1830, 1834-35
Artificiality 60, 124, 128, 942, 1643, 2108
Artificial kidney 1775
Art-technology interface 2048, 2052, 2054-56, 2060, 2068-71, 2073, 2077, 2079, 2085-86, 2089, 2093, 2104, 2331. See also Technology inspired art
Ash Can school 2066
Asimov, Isaac 1964
ASPHALT JUNGLE (film) 2132
Assembly line 43, 134, 206, 422, 566, 602, 611, 628, 1210, 1941
Atlanta, Ga. 379
"Authoritarian" technics 1623
Automata. See Robots and automata

Automatic feedback control 329
Automation 5, 19, 87, 98, 193, 200, 289, 340, 455, 557, 590, 593, 604, 610, 629, 632-49, 663, 1006, 1010, 1320, 1326, 1666, 1918, 2248
Automobile 170, 195, 317, 321, 371, 405, 422, 459, 486, 597, 603, 607, 611, 628-29, 631, 638, 705, 731, 757, 760, 764-65, 793, 834, 840-41, 844-45, 861, 864, 892, 904, 1188-1222, 1362, 1421, 1457, 1687, 1849, 1852, 1860, 1872, 1925, 1929-30, 1944, 1960, 1986, 1988, 2021-22, 2031, 2038, 2095, 2102-03, 2127, 2158, 2168-69, 2179, 2184
Autonomy of technology 70, 77-78, 149
Aviation 86, 137, 318, 330, 371, 891, 1223-24, 1226, 1229-30, 1236-37, 1242-43, 2095, 2097, 2102-03, 2126
Ayers, C.E. 1580

B

Babbage, Charles 546
Balloons 1226, 1229, 1242
Baltimore, Md. 543, 751, 1153
Barbed wire 191, 494
Barth, John 1987, 2005
Batchelor, Charles 370
Bauhaus 2106
Beat generation 914
Behavior control 60, 890, 944-72, 1009, 1015, 1630, 1767-68, 1772, 1774, 1777, 1788-89, 1794-95, 1798-1800, 1815, 1893, 1907, 1911, 1914, 1939, 1942, 2241
Behaviorism 935, 940, 947, 953, 965-66, 969, 1570, 1630
Behavior modification. See Behavior control
BEING THERE 1986
Bel Geddes, Norman 2095, 2108
Bell, Alexander Graham 321, 368, 434, 1282-83

Subject Index

Subject Index

Subject Index

J

Jamaica Bay 1461
James, Henry 2005, 2014, 2110, 2172
James, William 279, 1571
Jazz 44, 2208, 2215
Jefferson, Thomas 2139, 2180
Jenney, William 2176
Jersey City, N.J. 741
Jervis, John 213, 764
Jet engine 371
Joachim of Flora 594
John F. Kennedy International Airport 1461
JOHN GODFREY'S FORTUNES 2006
Johns, Jasper 2083

K

Kahn, Albert 2184
Kansas City, Mo. 1178
Kelly, Edmond 278
Kepes, Gyorgy 2069
Kienholz, Edward 2059, 2083
Kinetic art 2050, 2063-64, 2202
KING KONG (film) 2122
"Know-how" 136, 219, 322, 350, 363, 372
Kodak camera and film 2113, 2115
Koestler, Arthur 1815
Kosinski, Jerzy 1986
Kuhler, Otto 2095
Kuhn, Thomas 1018

L

Labor and laborers. See Work and workers
"Laissez-innover" 138
Lake Erie 697, 1355
Lake Tahoe 1456
Lancaster, Pa. 550
Land use 723, 736, 827, 835, 851, 858, 1195, 1415, 1418, 1441, 1560, 2081. See also Urban planning
Language 104, 1639, 1792, 1968, 1995, 2014, 2039
Lasers 2063, 2069, 2075

Lasting machine 570
Las Vegas, Nev. 666, 993, 2157, 2179
Lathe 400, 413
Latrobe, Benjamin Henry 312, 764
Law 911, 1064, 1093-1101, 1117, 1126, 1142-43, 1332, 1337, 1349, 1361, 1415, 1419-20, 1424, 1431, 1435, 1441-43, 1448-49, 1453, 1458, 1463, 1465, 1467, 1745, 1766, 1771, 1780, 1783, 1787, 1803-4, 1807, 1810, 1814, 1816-17, 1825, 1827, 1829-30, 1835, 1840, 1844-46, 2313, 2316, 2408
Lawrence, Mass. 520
LeCorbusier 846, 2145
LEGEND OF NIGGER CHARLIE, THE (film) 2132
LeGuin, Ursula 1965, 1973
Leinster, Murray 1964
Leisure 87, 112, 124, 301, 593, 625, 634, 638, 650-66, 721, 797, 808, 825, 833, 941, 1010, 1169-71, 1278, 1326, 1352, 1357, 1380, 1518, 1688, 2018, 2052, 2130, 2247, 2263. See also Recreation
Leland, Henry M. 1207
Lem, Stanislaw 1965
Levittown 864, 2189
Lewis, Sinclair 2015
Liberalism 1074
Lichtenstein, Roy 2065, 2083
Liebig, Justus 500
Life, daily 206, 526-27, 554, 578, 587, 624, 797, 989, 1197, 1338, 1356, 1482, 1511, 1681, 1860, 1992, 2094, 2097-99, 2102-3, 2105-6, 2241, 2247, 2281
"Life in the Iron Mills" 2034
Life styles 695, 698, 709, 1386, 1761, 1850, 1894, 2171
LIMITS TO GROWTH, THE 716, 1417, 2250, 2288
Limits to growth 127, 690, 704, 708-9, 716, 1005, 2243, 2250, 2284, 2288, 2294
Lindbergh, Charles 86, 137, 1243
Linguistic determinism 885

Subject Index

Mass culture 59, 118, 133, 1199-2000, 1249, 1258, 1269, 1271-72, 1278, 1849, 1868, 1981, 1986, 1988, 2007, 2037, 2057, 2065, 2073, 2083, 2094, 2123, 2133-34, 2179, 2303, 2328, 2374, 2399
Mass media 133, 170, 698, 720, 1022, 1244-46, 1248-49, 1255-56, 1263, 1266, 1268-69, 1273-74, 1278, 1281, 1669, 1673, 1739, 1753, 1765, 1850, 1855, 1858, 1876, 1998, 2124, 2132, 2216. See also Electronic media
Mass production 16, 43, 134, 147, 172, 193, 195, 333, 399, 424, 460, 558, 667, 698, 1209-10, 1216, 1550, 2044, 2097-98, 2105, 2107
Mass society. See Mass culture
Mass transit 750, 753, 757, 765-66, 781, 801, 832, 1185, 1190, 1195, 1890, 1907, 1923, 2026, 2181. See also Transportation
Materialism 42, 272, 651, 804, 1616, 1658, 1672-73, 1682, 2264
Materials 199, 314, 856, 1555, 2271, 2276, 2292
"Mature society" 2264
Meatpacking industry 620, 1941
MECHANICAL BRIDE 1247
Mechanical engineering 223
Mechanization 13, 29, 32, 41, 206, 448-49, 482-508, 512, 546, 556-57, 570, 586, 637, 2044. See also Industrialization
MECHANIZATION TAKES COMMAND 2044
Medical ethics. See Biomedical ethics
Medicine, aerospace 243, 1223
Medicine, American Indian 242, 244
Medicine, history of 155-56, 241-55, 302, 545, 632, 1191, 1787. See also Public health, history of
Medicine, nuclear 243
Medieval technology 1146
MEDIUM COOL (film) 2127

Megalopolis 734, 736-37, 772, 2248
Megastructures 2165, 2170, 2198
Melville, Herman 1958, 1965, 1982, 2000, 2002, 2017, 2020, 2023, 2033, 2042
Meritocracy 14
MERRY TALES OF THE THREE WISE MEN OF GOTHAM 2029
Merton, Robert K. 886
Metaphor and imagery 104, 305, 1250, 1588, 1639, 1935, 1967, 1985, 1988, 1994, 2000, 2002, 2014, 2023, 2028, 2055, 2065, 2132, 2187. See also Language
METROPOLIS (film) 2122
Michigan 1208
MIDCENTURY 2025
Middle Ages 191
"Middle landscape" 2000-2001
Middletown (Muncie, Ill.) 797
MIDNIGHT COWBOY (film) 2127, 2132
Midwestern United States 484, 807
Midwestern University Research Associates (MURA) 1076
Mies van der Rohe, Ludwig 2145
Military technology 891, 898, 932, 1081, 1084, 2272
Millenarism 594
Milling machine 401, 409, 413
Mills 221, 391, 396-97
Milwaukee, Wis. 537, 799
Mineral King Valley 1465
Miners 1847-48, 1862-63, 1865-66, 1869-71
Mining 239, 375, 518, 531, 533, 536, 603, 982, 1451, 1478
Mobility 43, 323, 407, 528, 530, 540, 551-52, 595, 606, 1169-71, 2198
MOBY DICK 2017, 2020
Models 1711, 2250, 2252, 2256-57, 2267, 2270, 2274, 2281-82, 2297-98
Model-T 1202, 1210, 1222. See also Ford, Henry
MODERN INSTANCE, A 2003
Modernism 2008, 2057
Mohole 1076

Subject Index